PLANET
SIMPSON

This edition published by Ebury Press, 2005
First published by Random House of Canada, 2004
First published in America by Da Capo Press, 2004
First published in Great Britain by Ebury Press, 2004

3 5 7 9 10 8 6 4 2

First published by Ebury Press
Random House, 20 Vauxhall Bridge Road, London SW1V 2SA

Random House Australia (Pty) Limited
20 Alfred Street, Milsons Point, Sydney, New South Wales 2061, Australia

Random House New Zealand Limited
18 Poland Road, Glenfield, Auckland 10, New Zealand

Random House South Africa (Pty) Limited
Isle of Houghton, Corner Boundary Road & Carse O'Gowrie, Houghton, 2198, South Africa

The Random House Group Limited Reg. No. 954009

www.randomhouse.co.uk

A CIP catalogue record for this book is available from the British Library.

ISBN 009190336X

Designed and typeset by Textype, Cambridge
Cover design by Dave Breen
Printed and bound in Great Britain by Bookmarque Ltd, Croydon, Surrey

Papers used by Ebury Press are natural, recyclable products made from wood grown
in sustainable forests.

For Ashley – I choo-choo-choose you

ACKNOWLEDGEMENTS

More people assisted with the writing of this book than I could possibly thank, beginning with the countless people who've generously traded favourite *Simpsons* lines, quotes and theories with me over the years. My greatest debt of gratitude, though, is owed to my brilliant wife, Ashley Bristowe, who in addition to tolerating years of my Simpsonian babble is also my first, most compassionate and most exacting editor, not to mention the uncredited co-author of pretty much all of my best ideas.

I also owe an enormous debt to Anne Collins, my fantastic editor. Without her patience, wisdom and occasional (and much-deserved) cries of *enough!* in the margins, this would be a much weaker book. Whatever excesses and errors remain are mine alone, and survive despite her valiant efforts. Thanks also to Hannah MacDonald and Claire Kingston at Ebury Press for their editorial input, their hard work, and especially their patience.

I also have to thank a great many people for their assistance earlier in this book's and/or this writer's evolution: Iain Deans and A.G. Pasquella, my brothers-in-literary-arms, who were instrumental in convincing a deluded business student to embrace the writer's life; Geoffrey S. Smith at Queen's University, who taught me how to see the bigger picture buried in the trivialities of pop culture; Douglas Bell, my friend and reluctant mentor; Neil Morton, my daring editor (and great friend) at *Shift*, who conceived and assigned the essay that got this whole project started; Sam Hiyate, who helped turn that essay into a viable book proposal; David Lavin, my steadfast agent, who helped sell the thing and continues to advocate tirelessly on its behalf; and finally my parents, John and Margo Turner, who bit their tongues and opened their wallets for years to keep this fledgling writer alive.

I'd also like to thank Ian Connacher, Martha Sharpe, Andrew Heintzman, Carolyn Smart, Lynn Cunningham, David Hayes, George Russell, Laas Turnbull, Felix Vikhman, Greig Dymond, Barnaby Marshall, the McConnell and Bristowe clans, and anyone else I may have forgotten who has provided guidance, editorial support or financial assistance for this book.

In closing, gentle reader, I'd like to thank you. "What's that?" you say? Me thanking you? No, it's not a misprint. For you see, I enjoyed writing this book as much as you enjoyed reading it.

PLANET SIMPSON

Chris Turner

EBURY
PRESS

CONTENTS

FOREWORD

by Douglas Coupland

SEVEN SHORT PARAGRAPHS ABOUT PLANET SIMPSON

A few times in my life I've met people whom I call pop cultural blanks. They look just like you and me, except their parents were missionaries or hippies and they spent that formative and most important part of their lives – years when they ought to have been undergoing thousands of hours of unmonitored TV viewing – doing something else instead, like whittling or staring at clouds or exercising. [*Insert a brisk shudder here.*] I mention this because the common trait these people share is that if they could have added one pop culture event to their formative years, they wish they could have watched *The Simpsons*. Always. To paraphrase their common snivelling: 'Who the hell is Troy McClure?'

It's hard for me to imagine life without *The Simpsons* – it would be, if nothing else, a drab place indeed. Imagine a life without . . .

- Apu's affair with the Squishee Lady
- Beloved cigarette spokesmascot, Menthol Moose
- Patty and Selma wondering why Maggie hasn't touched her Manwich
- Malibu Stacy's lunar rover
- Mr Burns's loafers ('Former gophers')
- Ralph Wiggum accidentally viewing porn ('Everybody's hugging.')
- Anything to do with Cletus the Slack-Jawed Yokel
- Lard Lad
- The Monorail

- Mr Sparkle
- Marge's gambling addiction
- Bart saying that actually knowing the answers on a test 'was like a whole different kind of cheating'.

Chris Turner writes about *Simpsons* parties in Kingston, Ontario, in the early 1990s. I used to go to the same kind of parties in the Bay Area and they were loads of fun. Traffic on the 280 from Palo Alto into San Francisco on Thursday nights was always a bit heavier, and the feeling of reuniting with your pack at one's bar of choice felt to me much like what a cocker spaniel must feel after being removed from a transport cage and being reunited with the family after a ten-hour flight in the luggage hold. In the early 1990s, irony had yet to conquer and devour Western culture. Trailblazers had to find pale comfort amid tiny cliques of the converted who simply knew which way the wind was blowing – as well as the location of Springfield's perpetual tyre fire. But, as with most avant-garde cliques, early Simpsons fans found comfort in beer, powerless gatherings in basement suites and Moe's Tavern-like pubs, and through their collective, sometimes pot-induced, irony-free identification with Lenny and Carl's wonderment of just what, exactly, made the donut rack rotate in the Springfield nuclear power plant's cafeteria.

The Simpsons have, of course, evolved into a shorthand for several generations in need of collapsing baffling modern-day situations into powerful folkloric parallels. Said Milhouse's father to Homer after separating from Milhouse's mother: 'One day, your wife is making you your favourite meal. The next day, you're thawing a hot dog in a gas station sink.' Or how about Bart's admonishment to Lisa, squeamishly covering her eyes at the gory bits of a *Space Mutant* flick: 'If you don't watch the violence, you'll never get desensitised to it.' Or finally, Marge Simpson's astonishment that news broadcaster Kent Brockman is playing tennis on the Simpson family's new tennis court: 'I can't believe that Kent Brockman is playing tennis with us on our own tennis court!'

In 1990-something I had lunch with a friend who was a former *Simpsons* writer. Her office was in a building known as the '*Simpsons* Compound' on the Fox lot in Los Angeles. The building resembled, if anything, the third-best two-storey motel in a place without motels, like Dar es Salaam or Volgograd. My friend told me that the building was accorded a special 'let them do their own thing' privilege by Fox. Non-*Simpsons* staff on their bikes and golf carts stayed way clear. Back before reality TV and Google, people still didn't quite get the show's sensibility. It had to come from some alien place where the inhabitants possessed either uncanny clairvoyance or time-travelling abilities.

Of course the current challenge now facing the *Simpsons* creative team is whether they can keep pace with contemporary society's ability to out-ironicise itself – but then this has always been the show's challenge. People are always saying, '*The Simpsons* has really lost it', or, '*The Simpsons* is really good again', but that's all hogwash. If the *Simpsons* creative team hasn't fumbled the ball in fourteen years, it's hardly likely to fumble it now – but don't let this lull them into a sense of false safety. (Hey writers, *The Family Guy* is biting at your ass.)

If this book were to have an alternative title, it would most likely be, *How to Cook for Forty Humans.* If that makes no sense to you, chances are you probably haven't read this far anyway. If it does make sense, you'll understand the treat that's coming your way just a few pages from here. Mmmmmm . . . grease. Smithers, release the hounds.

INTRODUCTION

The Birth of the Simpsonian Institution

I wish it was the sixties
I wish I could be happy
I wish, I wish, I wish that something would happen
Radiohead, 'The Bends'

Once in a great while, we are privileged to experience a television event so extraordinary, it becomes part of our shared heritage. *1969*: Man walks on the moon. *1971*: Man walks on the moon . . . again. Then for a long time nothing happened. Until tonight.
Krusty the Clown, Episode 4F12
('The Itchy & Scratchy & Poochie Show')

ON THURSDAY, 21 JANUARY 1993, around 8.20 p.m. (Eastern Standard Time), I was standing on the edge of a dance floor at a campus pub called Alfie's with a glass of cheap draught beer in my hand. The dance floor before me was packed with people, all of them waiting – as I was – for the next mind-blowing riff from the in-house entertainment.

There was no band up on the stage at Alfie's on this night, though, and no dancers gyrating sweatily out on the dance floor, either. Instead, all the pub's chairs and tables were jumbled into a kind of auditorium arrangement, covering the stage and half of the dance floor and every other inch of available space. Every seat in the joint was taken, and all eyes were fixed on a big-screen TV set up in the middle of the dance floor itself, where the third and final act of Episode 9F11 of *The Simpsons* ('Selma's Choice') was about to begin.

Now, 9F11 had already had some crowd-pleasing moments. The premise of the episode is that one of Marge's aunts, Gladys, has died a bitter spinster, setting a panicked Selma (one of Marge's ghoulish twin sisters) on a quest to have a child before her biological clock runs out. The episode opens with a TV commercial for Duff Gardens – a theme park inspired by Springfield's favourite brew – that shows the Duff 'Beer-quarium', an enormous mug of beer full of 'the happiest fish in the world'. (This joke played especially well with the Alfie's crowd, with hooting and cheering accompanying the image of one fish, cross-eyed and smiling, bumping repeatedly into the glass.)

As Selma sets about the doomed task of finding a father for her child – via video personals, random passes at assorted minor characters and a visit to the sperm bank – 9F11 fills in with the usual grab bag of great gags: Selma shows her sexy side by tying a lit cigarette in a knot using only her mouth; while on a date with the blind, shrivelled midget Hans Moleman, she imagines a rec room full of sightless children bumping cluelessly into each other; the Sweathog whose sperm is available for purchase turns out, to everyone's disappointment, not to be Horshack; and, in a stellar example of *The Simpsons'* ability to condense note-perfect parody into a few short seconds, another TV commercial for Duff Gardens features a brief snippet of the teen variety act Hooray! for Everything singing a saccharine bastardi-sation of Lou Reed's 'Walk on the Wild Side', in a wonderfully silly send-up of Up with People. All in all, it had been a solid episode so far, and certainly no one nursing their beers through the second commercial break that night had any reason to be disappointed.

By the dawn of 1993, however, the crowds that gathered around North America to watch *The Simpsons* had come to expect each episode to be not just *solid* but full-on *transcendent*. By this time, *The Simpsons* was what network executives call an 'appointment show' – that rare breed of TV programme you schedule your evenings around, the kind you want to share with your peers. In the consummate college town of Kingston, Ontario, where I kept my *Simpsons* appointments each Thursday at 8.00, observance of the show verged on a religious rite: practically every pub in town broadcast *The Simpsons* live every week because otherwise nobody would show up for cocktails until 8.30 at the earliest. Which is to say that for many of us watching that Thursday night – at Alfie's and elsewhere – the critical bar had been set vertiginously high, and this new episode had only one act left to meet this lofty standard.

The show came back on, and the crowd at the pub went quiet. Because Homer is sick (he's been picking away at a rotting ten-foot hoagie for weeks) it has fallen to Selma to take Bart and Lisa to Duff Gardens. Chuckles from the crowd as Bart and Lisa point out four of the beer-bottle-costumed Seven Duffs: Tipsy, Queasy, Surly and Remorseful. Somewhat scattered – but deeper – laughter as they enter the Hall of Presidents to watch tacky animatronic former statesmen (including Abraham Lincoln recast as 'Rappin' A.B.') sing the praises of Duff Beer. Cut to the Simpsons' living room, where Marge and Homer are settling in to watch *Yentl*. Cut back to Duff Gardens, where Bart, Lisa and Selma are poking around a souvenir stand. Bart approaches a display of clunky sunglasses. He reads the label: 'BEER GOGGLES – See the world through the eyes of a drunk!'

All at once, the pub shook with a single great roaring laugh. It was like a force of nature, this laugh, spontaneous and open-mouthed and *enormous*. It was as if a train were suddenly there in the room, its horn blaring. It nearly drowned out the next line: Bart puts on the beer goggles and turns to Selma, who has morphed fuzzily into a voluptuous babe, striking a seductive pose. 'You're charming the pants off of me,' she says in a sultry voice. The laughter seemed to expand exponentially. People were doubled over, had tears streaming down their faces, were pounding tables with fists. I'm not kidding – the gag just *destroyed* the crowd. It was as if that single gag was written for precisely this audience, an act of clairvoyance in which some TV-writer wizard had invaded the brains of everyone in the bar, rooted around for just the right common reference and then brought it flawlessly to life.

The last few minutes of the show played out to continued laughter, especially after Lisa drinks the water that carries the boats through the 'Little Land of Duff' ride, which causes her to hallucinate like an acidhead on a bad trip and proclaim herself 'the lizard queen'. In the end, Selma realises she wants not a child but a little version of herself, and the episode closes with her singing Aretha Franklin's 'Natural Woman' to her iguana, Jub-Jub. As the credits rolled, the exhausted Alfie's crowd fell to aftershock giggles and happy recountings of newly minted favourite lines. The feeling was much like that moment when the house lights come up after a brilliant musical performance and the audience members blink incredulously at each other, all of them united in the certainty that they have just witnessed something huge – something, maybe, that's never been seen before.

By the standards of *The Simpsons*' Golden Age – roughly, early 1992 to mid-1997 – this was not an extraordinary episode. This was par for the course. This was the minimum payoff that could be expected *every week*. In Alfie's and a thousand other campus pubs, in dormitory common rooms and rec rooms and living rooms, in local taverns and sports bars – in all of these and more – we gathered by the millions to watch a TV broadcast that was delivering, in half-hour instalments, a landmark event akin to The Beatles taking the stage on *The Ed Sullivan Show*. Or, in another, more accurate way, something like the band's whole career: each week was a new hit single that could delight or enlighten or transform, or do all three at the same time.

This was especially true by the time Episode 9F11 slayed the crowd at Alfie's in January 1993. After two seasons or so as a clever cartoon – a smart, irreverent and innovative TV show – *The Simpsons* had vaulted onto a higher plane of satiric expression. To belabour The Beatles analogy just a little more, *The Simpsons* had, midway through its third season, pulled off a transformation much like the Fab Four's move from the lovely but featherweight pop of 'I Want to Hold Your Hand' to the paradigm-shifting complexities of *Revolver* and *Sgt. Pepper*.

In autumn 1992 alone, nearly every new episode of *The Simpsons* that aired had been an instant classic. 9F02 ('Lisa the Beauty Queen')[1] offered a vicious but ultimately touching take on beauty pageants, combined with a scathing indictment of cigarette advertising. 8F18 ('A Streetcar Named Marge') seamlessly – not to mention hilariously – lampooned Broadway musicals, the philosophy of Ayn Rand, and *The Great Escape*. There had also been a genuinely thoughtful meditation on the nature of God (9F01, 'Homer the Heretic'); an elaborate self-satirising spoof of movies based on TV shows (9F03, 'Itchy & Scratchy: The Movie'); a re-imagining of *Lord of the Flies* that mercilessly satirised the merchandising machine of the modern entertainment industry (8F24, 'Kamp Krusty'); and a handful of warp-speed romps through gags and references so dense they almost defied cataloguing. Episode 9F07 ('Mr Plow'), for example, took well-aimed satirical shots at infomercials, pretentious Calvin Klein ads, commercials in which middle-aged white men attempt to rap, America's car dependency and the environmental damage wrought by same, and the celebrity-laden, circus-themed variety shows of the 1980s. It featured guest-voice performances by Linda Ronstadt, Adam 'Batman' West and voice-acting genius Phil Hartman, and worked in smart, funny references to Nazi Germany, President George Bush Sr., former Reagan aide and Ross Perot running mate James Stockdale, *Leave It to Beaver*, the board game Hungry Hungry Hippos, third-rate Fox Network 'current affairs' programmes, and *Citizen Kane* – all in 23 seamless minutes.

In subsequent weeks and years, *The Simpsons* brewed a mix of killer one-off gags, laser-guided social satire, robust character development and pure comedic joy into a potion so intoxicating that it became by far the most important cultural institution of its time: the equal of any single body of work to emerge from our pop-cultural stew in the last century in *any* medium. It was The Beatles *and* the Stones. It was Elvis *and* Chuck Berry. It was that big, that unprecedented, and that important. And it also grew so monumental – so fixed on the cultural map – that it now seems impossible to imagine contemporary pop culture without it.

But the rock & roll metaphor is not quite right. Rock & roll hit with the singular force of an atomic bomb – and was indeed a perfect cultural expression of the massive shift in consciousness rent by the splitting of the atom. *The Simpsons* was more like climate change: it built incrementally, week by week, episode by episode, weaving itself into the cultural landscape slowly but surely until it became a permanent feature, a constant reminder that just beneath the luxurious surface of this prosperous time lurked much uglier truths. Pop music, as the force that more or less invented youth culture – and the force that most clearly defined its first couple of generations – has an inimitable pride of place. There can never again be an explosion to equal Elvis's first shimmies of hip or The Beatles' first tosses of moptop. This, indeed, was a key component of the evident malaise that afflicted pop culture in the early 1990s. 'The question of the death of rock comes up because rock & roll – as a cultural force rather than as a catchphrase – no longer seems to mean anything,' decreed the rock critic Greil Marcus in the August 1992 issue of *Esquire*.

It no longer seems to speak in unknown tongues that turn into new and common languages, to say anything that is not instantly translated back into the dominant discourse of our day: the discourse of corporatism, selfishness, crime, racism, sexism, homophobia, government propaganda, scapegoating and happy endings.

Rock & roll had given several generations in the West its blueprint for change and its idiom for criticising the mainstream, but now it *was* the mainstream, a reinforcement of the status quo. It once provided a 'myth of wholeness' (Marcus's phrase), but now it spoke mainly of fragmentation – across genres and subcultures, across age groups and ethnicities, across demographic clusters and product lines.

And if rock was dead, was the counterculture laid to rest alongside it? Was it the end of (pop) history?

Don't have a cow, man.

With the emergence of *The Simpsons*, the myth of wholeness was reborn, no longer codified in three-minute pop songs but in half-hour cartoons. Western culture has in recent years become an almost irredeemably fragmented thing, counted in webpage hits and record sales, endlessly quantified and analysed and synthesised and then co-opted and thus corrupted by advertisers, focus groups, test audiences, pollsters, pundits and on down the line, all the while changing so quickly and in so many directions that it has never really been nailed down. (Maybe no cultural moment ever really is.) But when they watched *The Simpsons*, all those scattered, slivered *I*s became *we*s, if only for thirty minutes each week (more often after the show went into syndication). We were being defined by the show. Shaped by it. Even united by it, or as close to that state as we came, anyway.

There's a tendency, when attempting to discuss the broad strokes of a cultural era, to lapse into a royal *we* – to invent a mass phenomenon out of one's own passion for the subject. With respect to *The Simpsons*, though, I'll embrace the *we*, because here it is accurate. If there was a single cultural signpost announcing the emergence of a generation/era/movement/whatever, a monument to a widespread yearning for progress, truth, honesty, integrity, joy, a final rejoinder to every vacuous corporate press release and cloying commercial script and prevaricating political sound bite – it was *The Simpsons*.

Greil Marcus and other rock historians speak of a secret language created by rock & roll, of its role as the passport into a new and all-encompassing worldview. It was not just music: it was a gateway. Inside the club there were new constitutions, new laws and freedoms, a radical reconfiguration of democracy. The key was the secret language of the music – and if you didn't get it, you were forever locked outside. 'Because something is happening here / But you don't know what it is,' Bob Dylan teases the hapless square Mr Jones on 'Ballad of a Thin Man', in one of rock & roll's most direct acknowledgements of its exclusivity. But pop music, as Marcus admits, had lost its status as gatekeeper by the early 1990s. It was no longer the mystic rune of the culture, and decoding its riddles no longer necessarily revealed the true spirit of the age. Better, in the 1990s, to look to *The Simpsons*.

Come back with me to my bucolic university campus – Queen's University in Kingston, Ontario – for a clear picture of this shift in pop-cultural equilibrium. Step inside Clark Hall Pub, the preferred watering hole for devotees of the so-called 'alternative' culture of the early 1990s. This was where I usually watched new episodes of *The Simpsons*, because it had the best music, cheapest draught, and most casual overall vibe of any bar in town. It also better suited my angry-young-man attitude: it was the best place in town to find the long-haired and flannel-shirted, the dyed-haired and multiply pierced. The stereo blared Smashing Pumpkins and Nirvana and slightly more exotic fare like Public Enemy and Ministry and the Butthole Surfers, and in the brief intervals of fade-out semi-silence between songs, you might catch a snippet of conversation about the latest Coen Brothers film or the merits of Charles Bukowski. It was, in short, a typical den of alternative culture, and I have no doubt there was a similar joint or three in every college town and big city in the English-speaking world.

I was a DJ at Clark for the last two and a half years of my undergraduate studies, and the view from the DJ booth gave me a pretty clear picture of the various forces of unity and division among the pub's patrons. Pop music was the unifying attraction – students came to Clark because its DJs played stuff no other pub in town would – but it was also a divisive force: there were people there who adored the heavy riff rock coming out of Seattle, others who were fanatically devoted to the Britpop of Oasis and Blur and a dozen lesser bands, others still who only really got down to the molten industrial roar of Nine Inch Nails et al.

Even when the whole gang came together as one on the dance floor, the music often subverted its own presumption of rebellion. Case in point: 'Killing in the Name', a ferocious rant against conformity by the agitprop rap-rock band Rage Against the Machine. The song had been adopted as a kind of theme song by one of the freshman classes, so as soon as its opening riff boomed out of the pub's speakers, the small dance floor would quickly fill with aspiring engineers. Dressed in identical gold school jackets, some sporting the remnants of punk-style mohawks that had become the official Frosh Week haircut of the engineering school, the future employees of DuPont and Procter & Gamble would leap up and down in unison, bashing into each other in the tight knot of a mosh pit. By the time the song reached its howling final chorus, fists would be raised, the entire floor rising and falling as one, every voice screaming along: 'Fuck you, I won't do what you tell me.' Here were engineering students at an exclusive university, clad in a mix of countercultural fashions old and new, bouncing together with an almost military precision in an ironic homage to punk's nihilistic anti-dance. And screaming: *Fuck you, I won't do what you tell me.*

Nirvana lead singer Kurt Cobain despaired when his alienated punk was used as a soundtrack for football highlights, when the front row at his concerts came to be filled with the same kind of jocks who used to beat him up in high school. Rock & roll, even at its most abrasive or ostensibly anti-authoritarian, was far too much a part of the mainstream by this point to retain the subversive power it once had, and too fragmented to speak to (or for) the entirety of the mass culture it had joined.

And into this cultural vacuum came *The Simpsons*.

Consider another of Clark Hall Pub's traditions: a Friday-afternoon piss-up that was known as 'Ritual'. Every Friday at noon, the pub would open its doors for six hours of debauchery, hosting engineering students tossing back a few pints to make their upcoming classes less dreary, first-year students making their first foray into serious collegiate binge-drinking, and a rotating cast of regulars. One of the most popular features of Ritual was the early-afternoon re-broadcast of the previous night's episode of *The Simpsons*. (Or the previous Sunday's episode, once the show moved to Sunday nights in autumn 1994.) Most of those in attendance had already watched the new episode earlier that week, quite possibly right there on Clark's giant pull-down screen. They were watching this time to *absorb* it, to pick up the gags they'd missed and commit to memory the ones they'd delighted in the first time. Once the show went into syndication in 1994 – with repeat episodes available to most North American viewers at least twice and as many as six or seven times every weekday – this absorption ritual became a much broader phenomenon.

The Simpsons thus became not just a show you watched but a language you spoke, a worldview you adopted. It indeed became the primary metaphor I would use in conversations with most of my close friends and colleagues. I'm not alone in this. A lengthy feature article in the *Los Angeles Times* in February 2003 profiled a cross-section of Americans, from high-school students to university professors, who use *Simpsons* references to illustrate everything from their day-to-day foibles to Nietzschean philosophy. 'Aren't you sick of the way so many people use a moment from *The Simpsons* as a metaphor for real life?' the writer Bob Baker lamented. 'Isn't it like living in a society that adopted Esperanto without letting you vote? Have we lost so many vestiges of mass culture that a TV show – a cartoon! – has to be the glue that holds postmodern society together?' Well, yes – but I'm not sick of it. *Something is happening here, but you don't know what it is – do you, Mr Baker?*

Because the thing is, *The Simpsons* isn't Esperanto, but it *is* a language – a language heavily tilted towards insubordination. It's a stealthy, subversive smart bomb sitting in the middle of primetime. Disguised as an inconsequential children's confection – a mere cartoon – *The Simpsons* erupts each week in a series of spectacular satirical detonations, expressing a deeper contempt for authority than anything else on primetime and as sustained a critique of mainstream society as anything else in the pop culture of the day. Several of the show's creators are on record – repeatedly – as saying that the main goal of *The Simpsons*, beyond making its fans laugh, is to inculcate them with a strong distrust of authority.

And largely because of its cartoon disguise, *The Simpsons* has been permitted a degree of freedom unparalleled in mainstream entertainment. The only real controversy it has raised centred on the idea that Bart was a bad role model for kids. The show has otherwise felt free to comment, as sharply and derisively as it likes, on every controversial issue of its time, from religion to sexual orientation to drug use, from political hypocrisy to corporate crime. Countless other live-action sitcoms – not to mention hip-hop artists and shock-rockers and videogame makers – find themselves mired in scandal any time they even nudge issues *The Simpsons* has addressed head-on and at length.

The Simpsons has formulated mainstream culture's most widely spoken critical vernacular, its most prominent dissenting opinion, its surest way to indicate whether the person you were speaking with was Dylanesque hip or Mr Jones square. If, say, you are at a party, and someone blurts out one of Homer's patented *D'oh!*s – well, everyone knows about *D'oh!* I mean, it's in the damn dictionary. *The Simpsons* is not about catchphrases – it spent a whole episode mocking catchphrases. But if you were – I don't know – talking to someone about the environmental record of the local DuPont plant, and you lapsed into a Burns-like hiss and said, 'All those bald children are arousing suspicion', and the person you were talking to started laughing – or, better yet, replied in his own Burnsian rasp, 'I'll take that statue of Justice too' – *then* you knew you were talking to a kindred spirit, a fellow traveller, a true Simpsonian.

The Simpsons is in some respects a more powerful cultural force than rock & roll, particularly because it crosses more boundaries (especially those of age) than rock did even in its world-shaking first phase. Admittedly, there does seem to be an age barrier roughly coincident with the invention of Saturday-morning cartoons as a block of programming expressly for children in the early 1970s. If you'd hit puberty by then, you were probably never conditioned to watch cartoons regularly, and what's more you might well have come to think of them as silly kids' stuff, and so perhaps you haven't been able to take *The Simpsons* seriously. But even that border is at least semi-porous. Fans of *The Simpsons* range from the former American poet laureate Robert Pinsky to the Archbishop of Canterbury, from British Prime Minister Tony Blair to anti-corporate activist Ralph Nader. It's as big in Western Europe as it is in America, and it's got rabid fans from Argentina to Thailand and from Australia to Russia. I've seen an excerpt of the show used to illustrate a point in a fortysomething mountain guide's avalanche-safety lecture, and I've heard my mother repeat many times the story of my then-four-year-old nephew marching into her kitchen to tell her that he knew 'that God-man in the sky' wasn't real because Homer Simpson told him so. I've spent entire evenings speaking to close friends almost exclusively in *Simpsons* references. I can only imagine its stature among the generation of kids like my nephew who are being raised on it. All of which is to say that it's a far easier club to join than the one described in 'Ballad of a Thin Man'. The only real price of entry is a love of humour and/or of cartoons, plus (for more serious viewers) a strong sense that the world as it's described by the mainstream – in political speeches, on the news, in ads for breakfast cereal and in the sermons of the local preacher – is fundamentally false. The show's enormous popularity is indeed the clearest example going of just how widespread such scepticism has become.

This has always been the tricky thing about the underworld described in 'Ballad of a Thin Man', about the world delineated by the twentieth century's landmark cultural events: many of the truly pivotal moments were shared by only a very few. We all wish we'd been at the Cavern in Liverpool in 1962, or at Woodstock in 1969, or at the Hacienda in Manchester in 1986. We wish we'd been invited to have a drink at the Algonquin Hotel in New York circa 1926 or to share a toke at a North Beach coffee house in San Francisco circa 1955. Certain Paris cafés sound like they were pure cultural heaven in the 1920s and again in the 1950s. The same goes for certain districts of London and New York in the mid-1960s and again in the mid-1970s. I would have loved to have seen Charlie Parker live in Montreal in 1953 or Jimi Hendrix at Monterey in 1967 or The Clash in London in 1978. Even as I embraced Nirvana's *Nevermind* in late 1991, I could pick up a magazine and learn that the real explosion had happened a year earlier – or maybe three – in Seattle. I went to Kathmandu in 1999 and wished I'd been there in 1968. There's often an immediacy to pop culture that leads to instant obsolescence, a sense that most of what we're experiencing is a second-rate retread or a watered-down version of the seminal moment we all wish we'd been a part of. And so, as consolation, we feed on the fallout of these events. We buy the album, see the movie, read the book.

But what if the seminal event was a mass broadcast, *a weekly TV show*, something that practically the whole world could witness unadulterated and undiminished? There'd be limits to its impact, certainly – attending a concert or chatting boozily in a bohemian café are often much more visceral experiences than watching TV – but there'd also be a liberating power to it, a strength drawn from its near-universal accessibility. This, for starters, is why *The Simpsons* matters. It's the big cultural tent of its time, and even if there are so many different subcultural booths underneath that it's a stretch to say there's a single common currency passing hands at all of them, this diminishes the show's significance not at all. If there *is* a common cultural currency, it's got Homer Simpson's picture on it.

The importance of *The Simpsons*, though, stretches beyond its enormous global popularity. In addition to being the touchstone of its age, the show is also its foremost pop chronicle. There are few trends or issues or world events since the show's debut that have not been worked into the sprawling tapestry of *The Simpsons*. The show provides a lens of unprecedented scope through which to view the shifting cultural landscape of the last 15 years. In the pages that follow, I'll examine both how the show defined the pop culture of its time and especially how it documented it. And if the show's documentary role sometimes dominates the discussion, this is because it is the more tangible function. It's difficult to say with any conviction, for example, how many people in the world identify with Homer, have worked his *D'oh!* into their own lexicon, are in some way *explained* by their habit of watching his antics on TV. What's far more certain is that Homer and the rest of the Simpsons – and the dozens of other characters who inhabit their hometown of Springfield, USA, and the adventures they all have there – have created a detailed satirical reflection of the world we live in.

To understand the nature of mainstream America, its hopes and dreams and insatiable appetites, look to Homer Simpson (Chapter 2). For an explanation of how the style and ethos of punk rock became a massive mainstream phenomenon in Western culture in the 1990s, watch Bart closely (Chapter 3). For a picture of the re-emergence of progressive activism in the West over the same period, study Lisa (Chapter 5). Marge, meanwhile, can help explain what happens to a society whose traditional authorities have lost their credibility and whose religious institutions have lost much of their resonance (Chapter 6). The diabolical Mr Burns shows us why those author-ities are no longer trusted in the first place (Chapter 4). The Simpsons' travels across America and around the world offer a vivid illustration of the way the United States acts in world affairs, and the way the rest of the world responds to America – and *The Simpsons* (Chapter 8). And their adventures in cyberspace, both on the show and on the Internet itself, document the birth and evolution of a powerful new medium of communication (Chapter 7). The show's celebrity visitors – and its own place in the showbiz world – chart the massive and fast-growing influence of the culture of celebrity on society at large (Chapter 9). And the show's extraordinary penchant (and talent) for self-reference, pop-cultural allusion and media criticism offers an elaborate picture of postmodernism, in all its glory *and* its shame, and of the hypermediated society that created it (Chapter 10).

But before we get to all that, a caveat: this is, in the end, *my* version of *The Simpsons.* The show's canvas is far too broad, and the culture it reflects far too diverse and fragmented, for me or anyone else to be able to offer a completely comprehensive or definitive analysis. Instead, I offer an account of *The Simpsons* and its time that is idiosyncratic and sometimes quite personal. I discuss details about the show that I've found compelling and those fragments of Western culture where I've noticed a connection with the show, an intersection or resonance with its themes and characters.

And now, like it says on the Krusty the Clown posters at Springfield Elementary School, 'Give a hoot . . . Read a book!' This one, I mean.

NOTES & MARGINALIA

1. **A brief note on production codes:** Every episode of *The Simpsons* is assigned a production code and a title. In this case, the production code is 9F02, the title 'Lisa the Beauty Queen'. The production code indicates the batch in which it was produced (9F here) and the position in that batch (02). Alas, the codes don't really say anything clearly. Season 1 was 7G, Season 2 was 7F, next came 8F and 9F, then back to 1F and on up to 5F, at which point the sequence changed to AABF, BABF, CABF, etc. As well, the codes indicate episodes that were *produced* in the same season, even if they aired in separate ones. From Season 2 onward, the show has generally been produced in batches of 22–25 episodes, but a couple of episodes from each batch have usually not been broadcast until the following season. The first two episodes broadcast in Season 4, for example, were from the 8F batch, while the remaining 20 were from 9F (and two further 9F episodes aired in Season 5). And – yet more confusion – the final two numbers refer to the order in which the episodes were *produced*, not the order of broadcast. Episode 9F17, for example, was aired a week before 9F16.

All of that said, I will generally use both production code and title on first citation and the production code only on shorthand reference. This is partly a tip of the cap to *The Simpsons'* hard-core fans, who have long used production codes as a kind of insider's shorthand, and partly a question of simple practicality. Trucking out, for example, Episode 3F19's full official title – 'Raging Abe Simpson and his Grumbling Grandson in "The Curse of the Flying Hellfish"' – every time I refer to it would quickly grow tiresome, as would a clumsy phrase such as 'The One Where Homer's Dad Tries To Recover the Art His Old Army Unit Stole from the Nazis'.

CHAPTER 1

The Life and Times of The Simpsons

The truth is what is, not what should be. What should be is a dirty lie.

Lenny Bruce

Yes, the Simpsons have come a long way since an old drunk made humans out of his rabbit characters to pay off his gambling debts. Who knows what adventures they'll have between now and the time the show becomes unprofitable?

Troy McClure, Episode 3F31 ('The Simpsons 138th Episode Spectacular')

THE CREATION MYTH

ACCORDING TO LEGEND, ACCORDING TO the press, according (more or less) to the word of its creator, *The Simpsons* was born in a single fevered moment.

They say it happened like this. It was early 1987. Matt Groening, a 33-year-old underground cartoonist, was sitting outside the office of James L. Brooks, an acclaimed Hollywood producer. Brooks had been a titan of network television in the 1970s (executive producer of *The Mary Tyler Moore Show*, *Lou Grant* and *Taxi*, among others), and more recently was the celebrated creator of the feature film *Terms of Endearment*, for which he won three Oscars (as producer, director and writer). At the moment, he was the executive producer of a quirky variety show called *The Tracey Ullman Show*, set to air soon on the infant Fox Network. Brooks had called Groening in for a meeting, which was to start in fifteen minutes. They were to discuss turning Groening's acclaimed comic strip, *Life in Hell*, into a series of animated vignettes to fill space between the *Ullman Show*'s live skits.

Groening and Brooks had met once before, a year earlier, at the urging of Brooks's producing partner, Polly Platt, who was a fan of *Life in Hell*. That time, they'd talked about turning the comic strip into a full-blown feature film. Nothing had come of it. But here Groening was, back again in the antechamber of big-time Hollywood, being offered another chance to bring his work to TV.

Maybe Groening was thinking, as he waited, about the years of menial labour that had marked his decade-long tenure in Los Angeles to that point: work as a chauffeur, as a clerk at a punk record store, as a circulation manager for the *L.A. Weekly*, schlepping stacks of newspapers around the city in a beat-up Dodge Dart. Perhaps he was thinking about the characters that populated his *Life in Hell* strip: a misanthropic one-eared bunny named Binky, a dysfunctional duo in matching fezzes called Akbar and Jeff. The strip rarely had much in the way of set-ups or punchlines. It had no sight gags and didn't even have much movement – sometimes nothing more than the heads of Akbar and Jeff in identical poses in panel after panel. Instead it was long on wordplay and social commentary, chock full of marketing parodies and philosophical musings. How could this world possibly be brought to 24-frames-per-second life? The strip had seen some success by this point – a book called *Love Is Hell* had sold 20,000 copies in the Christmas rush of 1984, and the strip had been syndicated nationally to several dozen alternative newspapers – but this was network TV, the marketing muscle of a giant media conglomerate, an audience of millions. Another realm entirely. How could Groening persuade Brooks that these static, simple, black-and-white drawings were the blueprint for a cartoon?

And then, so the story goes, Groening came to a sudden and disturbing realisation: if he walked through the door of Brooks's office and pitched his *Life in Hell* cartoon and – *Woo-hoo!* – Brooks bought it, he'd lose the rights to all the characters he'd created and spent years drawing. They'd become the property of Fox, of some mammoth multinational corporate entity called News Corp. So Groening, a graduate of free-spirited Evergreen State College in deeply countercultural Olympia, Washington, a ten-year veteran of the anti-corporate alternative press, decided in an instant to save his creative soul. He wouldn't offer *Life in Hell* to Fox. He would come up with something else right then and there.

In the minutes remaining until his meeting, Groening dashed off the rough sketches of a new idea: a series of shorts about a hideously dysfunctional family, a sort of anti-sitcom starring an oafish father, a harried mom, three bratty kids. Racing against the clock, he gave them a good old generic American surname – Simpson – and then assigned them first names stolen from his own family. The father was Homer, after Groening's own dad. The mother was Marge, from his mom's Margaret. The daughters – like his own sisters – were Lisa (a second-grader) and Maggie (a pacifier-chomping infant). The nastiest kid of all would be ten-year-old Bart (an anagram of 'brat').

Brooks bought it.

On 19 April 1987, right after the first skit in the third episode of *The Tracey Ullman Show*, North America's TV screens – the relatively few in those days that were tuned to Fox, anyway – filled with the world's first glimpse of *The Simpsons*. In that opening segment, Homer enters Bart's bedroom to tuck him in. Bart asks a philosophical question, and Homer replies with a glib dismissal. It's a 24-second scene. Later in the show, another 15 seconds: Marge tucks in Lisa, who's seized by dread at her mother's mention of bedbugs. Then there are 33 seconds of Marge singing the timeless lullaby 'Rock-a-Bye Baby' to Maggie. And then 33 seconds more, as all three Simpson kids – each of them accidentally freaked out by their parents' bedtime talk of bedbugs and falling cradles – come storming into their parents' room and pile into Homer and Marge's bed. Elapsed time: one minute, 45 seconds. This was Episode MG01 ('Good Night'). This was how *The Simpsons* introduced itself to the world.

The drawing and animation were blatantly crude, thick-lined and primary-coloured – at best, the rough draft of a big-time network cartoon.[1]

It was so primitively drawn it might as well have been lifted directly from the rough sketches Groening had scribbled to show to Brooks. The characters were as two-dimensional as the drawings, the vignettes far too short for anything as sophisticated as 'character development'. The central gag – *kids find ironic horror in bedtime platitudes* – was as simplistic as the animation. All of which is to say that it's extremely likely that no one watching, from the folks at home to Groening and Brooks themselves, knew they'd witnessed the debut of the longest-running cartoon in the history of American television, the first baby steps of an institution that would become one of the most-watched TV shows on earth and the most influential cultural enterprise of its time.

The embryonic *Simpsons* chugged along unassumingly for the next two years. Every week, *The Tracey Ullman Show* would be interspersed with four quick snapshots of this vulgar family, each of them 20 or 30 seconds in length, together comprising a simple story arc: four-part mini-fables, animated analogues to the four-panelled comic strips that had populated newspapers around the world for a century. They had a premise, a set-up, a payoff – and not much else. The Simpson kids engage in a burping contest, only to be upstaged by their gluttonous father. Bart and his dad play catch in the backyard, precipitating a series of violent accidents. The whole family visits the zoo, where they're revealed to bear numerous similarities to the monkeys.

In *Ullman*'s third season, these glimpses stretched into a sustained scene of a minute or so, but the animation remained extremely lo-fi and the gags continued to clang in a series of single notes. In one third-season short, Bart and Lisa join the studio audience of their favourite TV show – a banal kids' series starring an ill-tempered clown named Krusty – and Bart picks a fight with its star. In another, the whole family enrols in group therapy and quickly finds a remedy for its chronic dysfunction as it unites in its hatred of the therapist. And so on.

Overall, the *Ullman Show* aired 48 of these short cartoons. Forty-eight slices of Simpson family life, 48 mild variations on a somewhat unorthodox but ultimately rudimentary theme. Namely: that the American family in the late twentieth century was loutish and vulgar, a slow-burn nightmare. Groening's TV debut attracted profiles by mainstream newspapers like *The Washington Post* and *Newsday* – although it should be noted that both gave *Life in Hell* higher billing than his odd little Ullman shorts. Indeed, so insignificant did these silly cartoons seem that when the BBC brought *The Tracey Ullman Show* to British television, it edited the *Simpsons* cartoons out.

Yet something exceptional was happening here. It was a time when North American TV screens were dominated by saccharine family sitcoms like *The Cosby Show* and *Family Ties* or nostalgic one-liner fests like *Cheers*. Movie screens were filled with big-budget studio dreck, and pop charts were dominated by bands better known for their skilled use of hairspray and makeup than for their music. 'Rough' and 'crude' could seem, in this context, like reasonable facsimiles of 'bracing' and 'honest'. At the very least, the *Simpsons* shorts offered a quick peek into a nasty world where stories didn't inevitably have morals and Father emphatically did not Know Best.

Clearly, someone at the Fox Network saw some potential. The third season of *The Tracey Ullman Show* (1988–89) featured the longest *Simpsons* shorts yet, upgraded from bumpers to full-blown features on equal footing with the live-action skits. There was even a two-parter called 'Maggie in Peril' that clocked in at more than two minutes and sprawled in its miniature way over two episodes of *Ullman*. There was talk of a half-hour Christmas special, further talk of turning these Simpson characters into the stars of a full-blown series.

The Simpsons as we know it was about to emerge from the womb.

EPISODE 1: EXPLODING OUT OF THE GATE

The first full episode of *The Simpsons* was a Christmas special that premiered on Sunday, 17 December 1989. 'Simpsons Roasting on an Open Fire' was a great leap forward. If the show didn't quite emerge from the *Ullman* womb fully grown, it appeared at the very least to be an extremely precocious toddler – a half-hour parodic romp through the standard tropes of the typical Christmas cartoon, with echoes of *A Christmas Carol* and *Miracle on 34th Street* as well. The premise: Homer doesn't get his Christmas bonus down at the power plant, and the family's savings jar has been emptied to remove Bart's new tattoo. Homer tries to rescue Christmas with a part-time job as a shopping-mall Santa Claus and an ill-advised bet at the dog track, to no avail. But just when it looks like Christmas is ruined, he adopts the losing greyhound – a lovable pooch named Santa's Little Helper – and Christmas is saved.

In 'Roasting', we see the first glimmering hints of the show's razor-sharp satire. We also encounter several key minor characters for the first time, from the irritatingly perfect neighbour Ned to drunken Barney and gruff Moe down at Moe's Tavern. As well, we're introduced to Homer's callous boss Mr Burns and his sycophantic sidekick Smithers, and to the notion that Homer is a downtrodden Everyman caught in the gears of a brutally Darwinian economy. Lisa, meanwhile, delivers a short academic lecture on the psychological weight of the relationship between father and daughter, hinting at the analytical genius her character will develop – she's no longer merely a complement to bratty Bart.

Even more portentously, there's a brief glimpse of the dizzying spiral of self-referential metahumour to come, as Bart urges his father to place the bet at the dog track. 'Aw, come on, Dad,' Bart pleads, 'this can be the miracle that saves the Simpsons' Christmas. If TV has taught me anything, it's that miracles always happen to poor kids at Christmas. It happened to Tiny Tim, it happened to Charlie Brown, it happened to the Smurfs, and it's going to happen to us!' No wonder the special was a surprise ratings champ, carrying Fox to the highest Sunday-night ratings it had ever received. 'Roasting' came first in viewership in its timeslot that night among adults aged 18 to 49, despite the fact that 12 per cent of American homes still didn't receive Fox.

The first season of *The Simpsons* – only 12 more episodes, barely half as many as the standard American network TV show – debuted in January 1990. It soon became the biggest hit in Fox's history, the first Fox series to win its timeslot outright, at least through February and March that year. In less than six months, *The Simpsons* was transformed from a clever curiosity on a marginally popular but critically respected show – a cult hit within a cult hit – to the biggest pop-cultural phenomenon of 1990. A mere two or three years later, *The Simpsons* was a full-blown institution – the smartest and most resonant pop icon of its time – a status it preserved for well over a decade.

Before we get to all of that, though, let's take a step back to look at how *The Simpsons* was transformed from a crude vignette to an expansive satirical masterpiece in the first place.

SEASON 1: A FLAILING NETWORK & A CREATIVE JUGGERNAUT

It's worth recalling the Fox Network's acute desperation back in 1989. At the time, Fox was still unavailable in many markets – 'a coat-hanger network', scoffed NBC entertainment kingpin Brandon Tartikoff, referring to the home-made antenna attachment presumably needed to tune it in from its spot on the upper reaches of the UHF broadcast band. Fox had only just introduced original primetime programming (in 1987) and had barely enough of it to fill two evenings a week. It had no hits. Its schedule had until recently included a sitcom entitled *Women in Prison*.[2] Fox was, in short, a laughing stock. So even the small amount of buzz around the animated segments on *Ullman* made the *Simpsons* a bona-fide hot property.

Still, Fox *was* a TV network, and selling it on an irreverent, unconventional cartoon series, at a time when no other primetime network series was a cartoon, took considerable effort. 'The people who make decisions about what goes on television, in my experience, their eyes don't light up when you say "innovative",' Matt Groening later told a newspaper reporter. 'They want to be able to compare to something else that's already been on. We had to sell them on the family angle, as a *Flintstones* for the nineties.' But even this tidy pitch didn't clinch it. Groening said it was only a pre-arranged deal to have the show's star, Bart Simpson, appear in commercials for Butterfinger candy bars that sold Fox on *The Simpsons.* At any rate, the new series got a wary green light from the Fox suits. It had half a season to prove itself.

Groening and his co-creators – Brooks and veteran sitcom writer Sam Simon (*Taxi, Cheers*) – weren't so thankful for the opportunity that they gave themselves over completely to the corporate thinking of their Fox patrons. Instead, they insisted on – and received – complete creative control. There would be no notes from network executives, no focus-group reports, no mid-season retooling hiatuses. The show's creators would be the final arbiters on all things Simpsonian. They could even ignore some of the more ludicrous directives from Fox's censors (a posture they'd maintain through the years).[3] Such a level of creative control is an extraordinarily rare and sacred thing in network television, and it's unlikely they would have received it from any other network. It has proven to be a vital factor in the show's originality, permitting everything from its left-field references to its unorthodox humour to the sharpness of its satire – all the clever/quirky/eggheaded stuff that usually gets smoothed out by the corporate production process. *The Simpsons* was to become like nothing else on TV in part because it was allowed to be produced like nothing else on TV. It was allowed to express the true, undiluted vision of its creators.

And what about that vision? Well, for starters, Groening was clear about what he didn't want to make: a sitcom. 'Sitcoms,' he told an *Los Angeles Times* reporter just before the debut of the Christmas special, 'are about people who live together and say vicious, witty things to each other, which ends up sounding unlike any real character in life. On *The Simpsons*, we want to have some of that, but we found it doesn't work if the characters anticipate their own cruelty. If they know in advance that they're going to do something mean or mean-spirited, it's no longer funny. But if they're out of control and a victim of their own impulses – so Homer impulsively strangles Bart – it becomes funny. In general, the characters are emotional powder kegs, and they can explode in a second.'

In the same interview, Groening explained that Brooks shared his commitment to this slightly skewed realism: 'Back at the very beginning of the series, James L. Brooks talked about an ambition for the show, which was to go for moments of non-cartoony emotional reality that would make people forget they were watching a cartoon. The way to do that is to place a far greater emphasis on writing and acting than has been the case with virtually every other animated TV series.'

And so *The Simpsons* assembled its creative team carefully. It already had actors for the main roles – the same ones who'd been doing the Simpson family's voices for the *Ullman* shorts. They were Dan Castellaneta as Homer, Julie Kavner as Marge, Nancy Cartwright as Bart, and Yeardley Smith as Lisa. Only one of them – Nancy Cartwright – was a voice actor by training. To round out the cast, the show's creators went looking for versatile actors with as little cartoon experience as possible, people who hadn't spent their whole careers doing broad cartoon caricatures. Thus, auspiciously, they found Hank Azaria and Harry Shearer, both veterans of live-action comedy. In time, Azaria and Shearer would add dozens of key supporting characters to *The Simpsons*, who would populate the Simpsons' hometown of Springfield with the same twisted realism that governed the lives of the family members themselves.

Even more important, though, would be the new show's writers. *The Simpsons* was to become the most writer-driven cartoon in the history of animation, if not the most writer-driven series that television has ever seen. This was very much by design. Assembling a team of great writers was a far higher priority for Groening and company than finding a top-notch animation studio. It would be the writers who would set the show's tone, develop its characters and map out its plot lines – who would, in short, define the show. Here, the creators stumbled on a bit of serendipity without which *The Simpsons* as we know it quite simply wouldn't exist.

It all began with a zine – a handmade, self-published mini-magazine called *Army Man*, put together by a comedy writer named George Meyer, a veteran of the early, anarchic days of *Late Night with David Letterman* and the mid-1980s morass of *Saturday Night Live*. After Meyer's tour of duty on the stagnant *SNL*, he lost interest in the TV-comedy game. He quit the show in 1987, moved to Boulder, Colorado, and picked away at a screenplay for Letterman's production company. And there, as a lark, he put together a little zine. Called it *Army Man: America's Only Magazine*. Got some comedy-writer friends of his to contribute a gag or two. Produced three issues in total.

Meyer sent his zine to a select list of a couple of hundred friends – which, given his former career, included a number of people working in TV comedy. Thus did it come into the hands of *Simpsons* executive producer Sam Simon. And Simon, like almost every other person who has seen *Army Man*, thought it was one of the funniest things he'd ever read – a gift from a Divine Satirist who had decided to bestow upon him a guarantee that *The Simpsons* would be not just good but brilliant. Simon needed writing talent – fast – but now he wouldn't have to rely on whichever old sitcom hands didn't have work just then on *The Cosby Show*. Not at all: *Army Man* had provided him with a hand-photocopied calling card from writers who were made to order. Post-haste, Simon hired Meyer and a number of other *Army Man* contributors, including John Swartzwelder and Jon Vitti, and all of them became irreplaceable members of the show's staff.

Meyer, Swartzwelder and Vitti have written or co-written more than 90 *Simpsons* scripts over the years, but that only begins to hint at the importance of Simon's providential discovery of *Army Man*. The *Army Man* cohort is the cell from which *The Simpsons*' humour metastasised, and is as responsible for the show's genius as Groening or anyone else. Swartzwelder is a legendarily reclusive former advertising copywriter; very little is known about him beyond the fact that he is the most prolific writer in the show's history – the author of more than 50 episodes – and that he is widely regarded as one of its best. 'Write this down,' *Simpsons* writer Dan Greaney ordered a *New York Times* reporter in 2001. 'John Swartzwelder is the best writer in the world today in any medium.' Greaney is certainly entitled to his opinion, but many in the *Simpsons* writing room believe that title actually belongs to George Meyer.

The key to Meyer's importance in the *Simpsons* cosmology lies in how the show is produced. Every episode begins not as a drawing or an actor's character sketch but as a script. And each script – which usually bears the single byline of its original author – is only a blueprint. The real alchemy, as David Owen noted in a 2000 *New Yorker* profile of his old college pal George Meyer (which stands as probably the most detailed description of the show's creative process extant), takes place in a conference room at Fox Studios known as the 'rewrite room' – or, more reverentially, The Room.

In The Room, a script will go through as many as a half-dozen rewrites before the voice actors even see it. It'll be subjected to a couple more after the actors have given it a read-through, and even more as the animation goes from rough sketch to polished product. The production of any given episode of *The Simpsons* takes as many as nine months from first draft to finished cartoon, and any given script is open to rewriting the whole time. 'A good *Simpsons* script is when you change 75 per cent and everyone goes, "Good script", staff writer Matt Selman told *The New York Times*. 'A bad script is when you change 85 per cent and everybody goes, "Bad script". Either way, the final draft is at least as much a product of The Room as it is of the writer whose name comes after 'Written by' in the opening credits. And for most of *The Simpsons*' existence, the undisputed lord and master of The Room has been George Meyer.

Jon Vitti told *The New Yorker* an anecdote that vividly illustrates Meyer's influence on the show. *The Simpsons* had been the subject of a fawning profile in *Entertainment Weekly* that heaped special praise on an episode Vitti had written. It cited five incidental gags as the episode's highlights – and all five had been added to Vitti's script in The Room by George Meyer. 'That kind of thing happens to all the show's writers all the time,' said Vitti. 'A show that you have the writer's credit for will run, and the next day people will come up to you and tell you how great it was. Then they'll mention their two favourite lines, and both of them will be George's.'

In his profile, David Owen contends that Meyer's sensibility reverberates through episode after episode of *The Simpsons*. For example, Meyer is deeply fascinated by blatantly dishonest advertising – the butter-substitute Country Crock, for example, captivates him because it manages to tell two big lies ('it's not from the country; there is no crock') in only two words. Ad parodies, cloying infomercials and crass billboards are similarly ubiquitous in Springfield. Meyer is also one of the primary guardians of *The Simpsons*' strong social conscience, along with the stridently anti-authoritarian Matt Groening. Furthermore, Meyer is a voracious viewer of documentaries – a passion that dovetails neatly with the show's commitment to realism.

The clearest evidence of Meyer's comedic sensibility, however – beyond *The Simpsons* itself, that is – is *Army Man*. Its closest mass-market cousin is probably the 'Deep Thoughts' vignettes that appeared on *Saturday Night Live* in the early 1990s. (Jack Handey, the author of 'Deep Thoughts', once shared an office with Meyer.) *Army Man*'s humour, according to the *Los Angeles Times*, 'lingers in a sort of netherworld of what its crafters call "meta-humour," a humour so involuted, so intertwining the absurd, the stupid and the clever that it walks a line invisible to most of the world'. Here's an example from the front page of *Army Man* No. 1 (the 'Astonishingly Primitive Debut Issue!'):

The Employment Counselor

Don't expect to just waltz in on your first day and be accepted by the other employees of the tanning parlor. Tradition demands an initiation period. The important thing is not to 'break' under all the hazing. Let's say someone whacks your thermos with a tanning wrench, shattering the delicate liner. You may be shocked to find your iced tea full of broken glass, but brother, you'd better just drink it all down. Otherwise, they'll leave you alone, but they'll never respect you.

And another:

A Plea for Sanity

In all the furor about salad spinners, has anyone thought to check with the lettuce?

These are classic jokes so refracted through a cracked mirror they're almost Cubist. This is what Meyer and his *Army Man* cohort brought *The Simpsons*: brilliant one-off gags and tangents, surprising inversions of expectation, elaborate re-imaginings of classic comedic forms. The style, in short, of *The Simpsons'* unique comedic art.

So let's quickly map *The Simpsons'* creative nucleus. From Matt Groening came the foundation: the form, the structure, the main characters. Groening established the show's satirical values: a deep distrust of authority and a permanent commitment to subverting it. He also brought a solid understanding of how cartoons work – he once said his favourite *Simpsons* gag ever was an elaborate homage to Wile E. Coyote in Episode 7F06 ('Bart the Daredevil'), in which Homer fails to leap Springfield Gorge on a skateboard, tumbles to the bottom of the gorge, is loaded onto a gurney and airlifted by helicopter into a waiting ambulance. The ambulance then roars off and ploughs into a nearby tree, sending Homer's gurney rolling out the back door and once again tumbling into the gorge.

James L. Brooks was the showbiz heavyweight, the guy with enough clout in Hollywood to get *The Simpsons* on the air and to secure vital creative control. But he also brought a unique sensibility to the adventure, honed on the un-ironic, even downright moralistic fare he'd delivered in *Terms of Endearment* and *Taxi*. He more than anyone understood that *The Simpsons* would only endure if it had strong, sympathetic characters.

Sam Simon, meanwhile, assembled the show's massively talented writing staff and in the early years guided the writing itself. Simon was the first 'show runner' – the executive producer who guides the freeform comedy of The Room like a conductor and then collates it along with the original scripts into actual half-hour narratives. He was the first to recognise that animation permitted the show to go anywhere and do anything, to cram Springfield with as many nooks and crannies and colourful characters as it wanted. (By the third or fourth season, other writers took over the 'show-runner' job.)

Upon this bedrock was laid Meyer and company, whose fractured take on modern life injected a strong dose of anarchic energy and jazzy comedic rhythm into the show. Rounding out the writing staff were several veterans of unconventional 1980s comedy programmes such as *It's Garry Shandling's Show*, *Not Necessarily the News* and *Sledge Hammer!* – among them the long-serving *Simpsons* writer-producer duos of Al Jean & Mike Reiss and Jay Kogen & Wallace Wolodarsky.

There were also some fateful early decisions on the production side. Right out of the gate, Brooks decided to hire a tiny, obscure animation studio called Klasky/Csupo to elaborate on Matt Groening's rough black-and-white sketches. The world-famous visages of the show's characters, the bold primary colours used to colour them and their world, the way Bart's eyes bulge when Homer strangles him – all of these key details were contributed by two animators employed by Klasky/Csupo, David Silverman and Wes Archer. In particular, their decision to use a palette of only two hundred colours (the average cartoon employs more than one thousand) brought to *The Simpsons* a highly distinctive look that has become as much its signature as Homer's bleated *D'ohs*.

What's more, Klasky/Csupo was instrumental in the fight with Fox to keep *The Simpsons* unpolished. Here's how founding partner Gabor Csupo explained it to *Newsday* in 1995: 'We said, okay, we're gonna keep the crudeness, because we like that raw, street style, almost punkish and very two-dimensional, purposely primitive animation. But we wanted to make shocking colors, like the bright yellow faces and the blue hair on Marge. When they saw it [at the network], they screamed, they didn't wanna do it. And we said, 'Why? These are the craziest characters, why do you want normal color?' We just fought and fought, and finally they gave in.'

Klasky/Csupo's stripped-down work on the first few seasons is not likely to win any lifetime achievement awards – indeed the studio was replaced by Film Roman in the show's fourth season, at which point *The Simpsons* took on the smoother, more iconic look it's sported ever since – but the studio did play a significant role in attracting attention to the show in the first place. Amid the glossy fare that dominated network TV at the time, the choppy animation and Day-Glo hues of *The Simpsons* broadcast the show's rebelliousness even more vividly than Bart's potty mouth and Homer's boorish belches. A bored channel surfer who landed on *The Simpsons* might well have thought some pirate underground cartoonist had hijacked the airwaves. Which, in a way, was exactly what had happened.

And all of it – not just the crude drawings but the crass characters, the writing that veered anarchically between erudition and profanity, the whole chaotic package – was as bracing in 1990 as the 'race records' that crackled out of cheap transistor radios had been to music 35 years before. As bracing, and also as compelling, as calamitous, as relentless and flat-out noisy. Whatever other merits the first season of *The Simpsons* possessed, it certainly made an unholy racket. It was a pop explosion.

BARTMANIA!

Was there a bigger pop-cultural phenomenon in 1990 than *The Simpsons*? Not by a long shot.

It wasn't the ratings – or the fact that Fox quickly turned it into a mammoth merchandising machine, selling officially licensed T-shirts and dolls and mugs and a hundred other novelties to the tune of $750 million by the end of 1990 – that put it at the top. A whole list of TV shows actually beat *The Simpsons* in the ratings for the 1989–90 season (among them such long-forgotten series as *Chicken Soup*, *Grand* and *Dear John*). And two merchandising juggernauts outsold *The Simpsons* that year: the hit children's cartoon *Teenage Mutant Ninja Turtles* and the kiddie-pop band New Kids on the Block.

No, the truly rare cultural force that *The Simpsons* tapped during its first 13-episode run was *resonance*. Pop-cultural resonance is what distinguishes the millions of records sold by The Beatles from the millions sold by Pat Boone, the $108 million in box-office receipts collected by *Pulp Fiction* in 1994 from the $145 million taken in by *The Santa Clause*. When a pop hit has resonance, it isn't merely consumed. The audience connects with the resonant cultural object, identifies itself with it, *absorbs* it. The relationship itself is largely intangible, but it does throw off discernable phenomena. In the case of *The Simpsons* in the summer of 1990, you could see its resonance on the millions of North American torsos covered by Bart Simpson's likeness and a word balloon broadcasting one of his catchphrases – DON'T HAVE A COW, MAN! or AY, CARUMBA! or UNDERACHIEVER AND PROUD OF IT.

At first, though, real resonance looks no different than hula-hoop hype. A case in point is The Beatles, who in 1963 seemed destined for the dustbin of disposable-teen-idol history. And so did *The Simpsons* circa 1990.

The entire Simpson family, seated on their living-room couch, adorned the cover of the 17 March 1990 issue of *TV Guide* beneath a headline proclaiming them 'TV's hot new primetime family' – as accurate a moment as any to mark the start of Simpsonmania, which would roll on for the rest of the year (disguised, often as not, as Bartmania). In the due and inevitable course of a pop tidal wave, the show's characters – especially Bart – were splashed across the covers of *Time* and *Newsweek*, *Rolling Stone* and *Mad* magazine, even *Mother Jones*. In 1990 practically every newspaper and TV news broadcast in the English-speaking world took a stab at explaining the show's sudden and stupefying popularity: it was a return to family values or a wholesale rejection of same, the post-Reagan rebirth of liberalism or the dawn of a harder and more cynical time, the salvation or else the downfall of Western civilisation. All pundits agreed, though, that *The Simpsons* was the hottest thing since whatever had got its picture on the cover of the *Rolling Stone* six months earlier.

Soon, there were racks of T-shirts in every store (the American department-store chain J.C. Penney even had full-blown *Simpsons* boutiques in many of its outlets), along with sporadic calls from schools across the US to ban those self-same subversive T-shirts for corrupting young minds. America's humourless drug czar, the ever-moralising William Bennett, made headlines by publicly berating the residents of a drug-rehab centre for watching the show.[4] Before the year was out, Bart had become a balloon in the Macy's Thanksgiving Day parade in New York, had been declared one of the year's 'most intriguing people' by *People* magazine, and had made the New Year's Eve cover of *Time* ('The Best of '90 – Yes, Bart, even you made the list'). *The Simpsons* had cracked the Nielsen Top Ten (a columnist for New York's *Newsday* even speculated that if it were on 'a real network', it would be 'far and away' the number one show in the nation). According to one study, a mere 14 per cent of Americans recognised the Simpson family during the *Ullman* days; by November 1990, 85 per cent could tell Bart from Homer, and the show had jumped the pond to Britain's fledgling Sky TV.

Pop fads, though, are as susceptible as apples to the discoveries of Sir Isaac Newton, and the law of pop gravity soon went to work on Bartmania. As early as June 1990, Burger King couldn't find enough buyers for the *Simpsons* figurines it was hawking. (The surplus dolls eventually ended up as prizes in games of chance at seedy carnivals across America and, more surreally, as tchotchkes in Eastern European bazaars.) In January 1991, even as the cash-grabbing album *Simpsons Sing the Blues* was perched at No. 4 on the *Billboard* chart, *USA Today* observed that the show's halcyon days were behind it. '*The Simpsons* is still hot,' decreed the tabloid barometer of mainstream America, 'though not as hot as last summer.' Although it remained far and away Fox's most popular programme, the show would never again see ratings like those it had in the spring of 1990.

As Bart T-shirts got stuffed into boxes already overflowing with Rubik's Cubes and sequined Michael Jackson gloves in attics and basements across North America, it could well have come to pass that *The Simpsons* itself would fade quickly into oblivion. Pop culture has the short-term memory of a goldfish, and any number of hot new trends loomed enticingly on the horizon.[5] Up to this point, the show itself was more promise than payoff. Many of the episodes in the first and second seasons were no more elaborate, really, than any other half-hour yukfest on the idiot box – it was just an animated sitcom with a smart mouth and a bad attitude. And the animation came across as merely crude after the raw punk thrill of it wore off.

Sam Simon had been anticipating the possibility of a fast fade from the very start. 'His motto,' Matt Groening told *The New York Times* many years later, 'was "thirteen and out" – the network's initial order was for 13 episodes, and he thought the whole thing was going to be a failure.' (In his defence, Simon claimed he thought the motto would be taken as a licence to experiment, not as a fatalistic acceptance of failure.)

Two things saved *The Simpsons* from this fate. First, the show hadn't just supernovaed across the mainstream radar screen, it had struck a certain segment of its mass audience as something potentially worthy of its hype. Emphasis on *potentially*: it looked and felt like nothing else on TV or anywhere else, but what would it do to keep resonating now that the first wave had crested?

The second important thing is what the show's writers did as Bartmania started to fade. Instead of lamenting the dimming of the spotlight, they introduced The Riff.

THE RIFF

The Riff began its lexical life as a noun that describes the short musical phrase upon which a jazz song is built – the repeated section that holds down the musical fort while the soloists bop off on elaborate flights of innovative fancy. As a verb, 'riff' was for a long time intransitive (and still is, as far as the *Oxford English Dictionary* is concerned): 'to riff' was simply to play a riff.

More recently, though, and more to the point, the verb has gone transitive. To riff on something is to begin from a basic premise – from the riff – and to build it out and up through wild new tangents into something unique and compelling. To riff on something is to do the opposite of what a jazz riff does. It's not about holding down the fort but about adding ornate new wings to the joint.

The late, great stand-up comedian Lenny Bruce was one of the first non-musicians to both employ and embody this meaning of The Riff. He referred to his elliptical comedic rants as riffs, and he developed them by riffing on a news item, an anecdote, a comedic premise. It was by way of such riffing that Bruce transformed stand-up comedy from 'Guy walks into a bar' into an hour-long monologue about the nature of obscenity, peppered with tangents on the semiotics of the word 'fuck' and readings from the proceedings of his own obscenity trials (for example).

Thanks in large part to Bruce, along with a few other bebop-era comedians such as Mort Sahl and (later) George Carlin, The Riff has come to be one of the dominant modes of pop discourse, emerging in everything from comedy to the layered musical digressions of rave DJs to the footnote-laden fiction of David Foster Wallace to the tangential dialogues about esoterica in the films of Quentin Tarantino. One of the main differences between contemporary pop culture and that of previous generations is The Riff. And, when it's done right, it's also one of the main things that makes pop culture great. For instance, sampling a few seconds from another song can be simply piggybacking on a more gifted predecessor, but sampling at its best is the gateway to an entirely new form of musical composition. Similarly, the digressions and allusions in Tarantino's movies are neither incidental details nor pandering attempts to hiply 'connect' with an audience – they're evidence of some of his greatest and most innovative talents as a screenwriter and filmmaker. And it was The Riff that saved *The Simpsons* from post-mania stagnation.

Let me explain.

The basic premise of *The Simpsons* is right out of sitcom-land: it's a series about family life in a typical American town. As in many sitcoms, the town is an idealised, somewhat nostalgic American burg from a time that never existed, with just enough contemporary window-dressing to make it resonant. *The Simpsons* focuses, like many sitcoms, on the day-to-day trials and tribulations of a cohesive nuclear family, with each episode introducing a new element that throws the family's staid life into disequilibrium and then following the resulting attempt to return to stasis. There's a blue-collar working dad, a nurturing stay-at-home mom, 2.3 kids, a dog and a cat. In a nod to modernity, Dad works at a nuclear power plant, but his life is otherwise superficially identical to that of the grey-suited head of household on *Father Knows Best* – a paragon of idealised 1950s family life that was, just like *The Simpsons*, set in an Anytown USA called Springfield. (The reference, Matt Groening has admitted, was intentional.) Mom makes big hearty meals of stuff like pork chops and meatloaf every night, the son's got a slingshot he borrowed from the 1950s tucked into his back pocket, the family car is a station wagon of 1970s vintage, the TV set's got a pair of old-school rabbit ears on top, and the town is populated by nosy neighbours and reverends who know all their (dutiful) parishioners by name and small businesses run by locals who know all their (loyal) customers by name. *The Simpsons*, in fact, is set not in the nostalgic hometown of Matt Groening's own childhood but in the amalgamated Everyhometown depicted in the sitcoms of his childhood – and those of the rest of the show's creators too. The show's subject, then, is not even a soup can; it's a *picture* of a soup can.

And yet, from this second-generation photocopy, the show's writers have painted a series of sprawling satirical portraits worthy of Hieronymus Bosch. The Simpson family has expanded to include paternal grandparents (a senile old grandfather and an absentee grandmother who was once a hippie saboteur), two ghoulish aunts on the maternal side, friends and enemies for each of the family members (even infant Maggie has that baby with the one eyebrow). And a major or minor plot in any given episode might tighten its focus on any given one of these characters. The same goes for the balance of Springfield's population, which grows with each new episode: there are crooked cops and shifty lawyers, emasculated school principals and immigrant convenience-store clerks, a never-ending parade of celebrities (real-world stars as well as Springfield natives) – a great phalanx of minor characters who can appear as mere faces in an angry mob or else suddenly morph into pseudo-protagonists. And no Springfieldianite[6] is so incidental or strange that he or she can't become a key cast member. The town's populace includes, for example, a scurvy old sea dog named Captain McCallister (complete with squinty eye, corncob pipe and grunted *Arrr*s) and a delusional hipster named Disco Stu, a dude decked out in a sequined jumpsuit, platform shoes and white-boy Afro who thinks it's still 1976. Both Stu and the sea captain have been transformed from one-off gags to recurring characters.

The town itself has also been ceaselessly transformed and expanded, becoming a hyper-developed piece of land containing: movie and animation studios; a dozen museums; an army base; a steel mill; factories making boxes, Spirograph toys and fake vomit; an ethnically diverse Lower East Side and a decrepit Skid Row; a tar pit; an oceanfront; a gorge; and a mountain range. Any given inch of this real estate might be filled with tacky billboards or odd storefronts or a cacophony of wacky radio broadcasts or mindless TV shows or trailers for moronic movies. The New York of the average TV sitcom is a quiet, sparsely populated and rather monotonous place in comparison to the Springfield of *The Simpsons*. This is the lush setting produced by several hundred riffs.

Though animation allowed Springfield to expand elastically, the cartoon medium could also have been seen as a limitation by the show's creators. By the late 1980s, cartoons – along with closely allied art forms such as comic books and daily comic strips – had been relegated to the ghetto of children's novelties. Mass-market animation trafficked in cutie-pie morality tales (such as *The Smurfs* or *The Care Bears* or especially Disney) and formulaic superhero adventures (from classics like *Superman* and *Spiderman* on down to *Teenage Mutant Ninja Turtles*) and thinly veiled merchandising ploys (for boys' toys such as GI Joe and the Transformers and for girls' toys such as the truly outrageous Jem and My Little Pony). But there was a large and growing number of people in North America who, though no longer little kids, had spent their entire television-watching lives glued to cartoon shows, since cartoons were practically the *only* programmes on TV – not counting educational fare like *Sesame Street* – created solely for them, rather than their Baby Boomer parents. There was, then, a brief window of opportunity to capture this audience before it completely abandoned the form out of disgust for kiddie-themed, product-shilling crap. But how to catch their attention? How to overcome the prejudice that an animated show was juvenile by association? *The Simpsons*' creators wisely decided to strike a deft balance between realism and the visual pyrotechnics permitted by the medium.

From its earliest days, the world of *The Simpsons* has mostly obeyed our physical laws. Though they might be four-fingered, though their skin is the yellow of a ripe banana, the Simpsons and their associates usually act and move like real, live, 3-D people. Their eyes do not bug out of their heads on five-foot-long stalks like the characters in Chuck Jones's Warner Bros. shorts, and they don't fly like Superman. There are no talking animals or anthropo-morphic tea kettles. Instead, *Simpsons* characters display more nuanced cartoon touches – slight exaggerations of facial expression (Homer's wide-eyed, tongue-wagging screams of *Wauggghhh!*, for example) or a single cartoonish feature in an otherwise semi-realistic body (most notably Marge's towering blue exclamation point of a hairdo). This delicate balance between the realistic and the cartoonily absurd is perhaps best illustrated by the way the characters – Homer especially – respond to physical violence. Homer frequently endures trauma of Wile E. Coyote proportions – he has bashed his head against pretty much every solid object in Springfield, for example, and has tumbled down most of its steepest slopes. Although there's a Wile-E.-ness in his ability to withstand such blows, Homer doesn't collapse into an accordion upon impact and slink away wheezing out musical notes as his body expands and contracts squeezeboxily. Instead he suffers bruises and oozes blood and breaks limbs, seeks medical attention, winds up in traction. He falls like a cartoon, but he lands like a real person.

When it comes to its animation style, as opposed to its plotting, the show is anti-riff, differentiating itself from the great masses of cartoons by being conservative and subtle, by forgoing broad gestures and visual flourishes – by making a Day-Glo-hued world of four-fingered blobs with overbites seem in some ways more *real* than the live-action programmes on the other channels.

Still, as if to demonstrate their mastery of the cartoon form, the show's creators have concocted three recurring motifs that allow them to go to town on the animation and assemble a few visual riffs every now and then to rival the written ones. The first of these is the Halloween show. There has been one of these 'Treehouse of Horror' episodes every season since the second, and each Treehouse is subdivided into three ghost stories – three chances to abandon Springfield's usual realism for cartoon physics. The Halloween episodes have provided a platform for spoofs of *King Kong*, *Dracula* and zombie movies, and presented us with images of Lisa as a giant snail and Bart as a mutant hybrid of human and housefly. Season 7's Halloween instalment, Episode 3F04 ('Treehouse of Horror VI'), opened the door for the show's only foray into 3-D computer-graphics animation. And the Treehouses have spawned their own recurring characters: two tentacled green space cyclops named Kang and Kodos. The Halloween shows, in short, guarantee that one episode per season will be given over to full-on cartoon-style whimsy.

The anarchic-animation genie also pops out of the bottle in the show's many dream sequences. When an overworked Homer falls asleep at the wheel of his car in Episode 8F06 ('Lisa's Pony'), for example, his mind's eye takes us on a cartoony ride to Slumberland, a Disneyesque fantasia in which his car turns into an inviting four-poster bed carried high into the sky by winged angels and plunked down upon a pillowy cloud, thence to drift serenely past an anthropomorphic moon that smiles down beatifically upon sleeping Homer. (This sequence will frequently pop into my head as I settle into bed after a particularly exhausting day.) Another time, Homer meets with the German industrialists who have bought Springfield's nuclear plant, and when they tell him they come from 'the land of chocolate', he drifts off into a whimsically animated chocolate vision. And so it frequently goes on *The Simpsons*, with the careful realism of day-to-day life punctuated by bursts of giddy fantasy.[7]

By far the most gleeful visual riffing on *The Simpsons*, though, occurs in 'The Itchy & Scratchy Show', the cartoon-within-a-cartoon that Bart and Lisa watch religiously. It's a hyperbolic extended parody of classic cartoons, particularly violent cat-and-mouse duels and even more particularly Hanna-Barbera's *The Tom & Jerry Show*. It's pretty much impossible to do justice in words to the ultraviolet eye candy of 'Itchy & Scratchy'. (Which dance is it that Itchy the mouse does, post-decapitation, around the spewing fountain of Scratchy the cat's carotid artery? Is it the Mexican hat dance?) Suffice to say that each snippet of 'Itchy & Scratchy' packs as much frenetically paced action, sight-gaggery and physical humour into its half-minute of screen time as a half-dozen Road Runner cartoons and a dozen *Tom & Jerry*s. But the fun doesn't stop there: 'Itchy & Scratchy' is a stream-of-cartoon-consciousness forum, a visual free-riffing zone. Here are anthropomorphic animals and zany warp-speed pacing, too-elastic limbs and bulging eyes. Here is Scratchy, done up as the Sorcerer's Apprentice *à la* Mickey Mouse in *Fantasia*, dicing up an army of marching Itchys with an axe, only to have them invade his bloodstream as vapour and consume him from within. Here is Scratchy in a barber's chair (echoes of Bugs Bunny in the classic short 'Rabbit of Seville'), shampooed with flesh-eating ants, his bare skull then ratcheting up through the roof into a television set in the apartment above, where a jumpsuited Elvis Presley passes judgement. 'Ahh, this show ain't no good,' he says of the cat skull contained by his TV, and blasts it with a revolver. Here is a kind of condensed version of the history of animation, doled out in dense morsels.

The 'Itchy & Scratchy' shorts, and the rest of *The Simpsons*' sporadic adventures in classically cartoony animation, reveal an avant-garde master's offhand ostentation – as if Picasso were asked to do a landscape and churned it out with parodic perfection. *Yes, sure – we* could *be doing this. Look, here it is in all its glory. But this has been done, and we are busy with something else entirely.*

'Itchy & Scratchy' notwithstanding, the show's finest riffs are in the writing, not the pictures. And it's in those riffs that you can most clearly see the evolution of the show from its humble Early Days through its jaw-slackeningly inventive Golden Age and into its faded-but-still-very-good Long Plateau.

And so, kids, here in brief is an anatomy of how the show ramped itself up to the Golden Age, courtesy – *hyuh-yuh-yuh-yuh* – of Krusty the Clown.

We first met Krusty way back on the *Ullman* show. Bart and Lisa, already big fans, attend a taping; they had believed *The Krusty the Clown Show* was giving them a window on a whole zany world, but they find out it is merely a tawdry stage set. A disillusioned Bart unmasks Krusty for the audience, telling them, 'Kids in TV land – you're being duped.' The short ends with Krusty strangling bratty Bart as Homer so often does. Like many great *Simpsons* riffs, Krusty begins with a simple, clichéd premise – there's this TV clown, see, and he's far less lovable in person than on camera[8] – a one-note gag about how TV is, you know, artificial.

When we meet Krusty again, there's a bit more to him. During Season 1, it becomes clear that his entertainment empire looms large over Springfield, even extending to Bart's breakfast cereal and lunch box, both of which bear Krusty's grinning visage. And then, with Episode 7G12 ('Krusty Gets Busted') late in Season 1, the real riffing begins. Krusty's TV sidekick frames him for armed robbery, and Homer emerges as a key witness to the crime. The plot is one-dimensional, a single level of arrow-straight narrative with only the slightest diversions from sitcom orthodoxy. Krusty is still a cantankerous TV clown, though he's given a bit of a back story (delivered in news reports about his arrest for robbery), and we're introduced to several new elements of his show, including cheesy product plugs, merchandising tie-ins and (most portentously) the existence of that nasty sidekick, an erudite gentleman named Sideshow Bob.

And so it goes through the Early Days – big steps forward that fall short of revolutionary. In Season 2, we get an episode-long look at the inner workings of the animation studio that produces 'Itchy & Scratchy', which also introduces two new characters to Krusty's cavalcade: Sideshow Mel (replacing the incarcerated Sideshow Bob) and a camouflaged brute named Corporal Punishment. Another episode opens with Krusty shamelessly shilling for a local amusement park called Mount Splashmore and subsequently defending the park to venomous reporters, touching upon the wages of fame.

By the middle of Season 3, Krusty has become a character with enough depth to carry a whole episode – 8F05 ('Like Father, Like Clown') – exploring his troubled relationship with his rabbi father. The moment the cameras stop rolling on *The Krusty the Clown Show* in this episode, we're quickly ushered backstage to see a depressed, depraved Krusty calling phone-sex lines and then reluctantly trudging off to have dinner with the Simpsons (to thank them for helping him clear his name after his arrest back in Season 1). Maybe some magical alchemy occurs the moment Krusty crosses the threshold of the Simpson home; at any rate, the rest of 8F05 uses flashback scenes of Krusty's orthodox-Jewish childhood to explore the history of Jewish involvement in American entertainment, and then examines the nature of faith and forgiveness in a secular age. It is a pivotal episode – the first truly brilliant riff on the life and times of Krusty the Clown. The Krusty we see on *The Simpsons* hereafter is a Krusty who has left the Early Days behind and come into the Golden Age.

When he appears front-and-centre in the Season 4 finale a little over a year later – 9F19 ('Krusty Gets Kancelled') – the Golden Age is in full swing. The animation is crisper and smoother and iconically *whole*, the pace and density of the writing have increased exponentially, the plots are now looping and multi-levelled. And good ole *hyuh-yuh-yukk*ing Krusty the Clown is now the stepping-off point for examinations of the nature of modern celebrity culture, the machinations of the mass media, and the history of television.

The premise of 9F19 is that Krusty's been driven off the air by a hip new kids' show hosted by a wise-assed ventriloquist's dummy named Gabbo, and is bound for the fallen-idol gutter. So the Simpson children decide to resurrect his career by rounding up a handful of his ultra-famous friends for a comeback special. First, there's a quick little riff on what's happened to poor Sideshow Mel since Krusty got kancelled: he's serving up fast food at the Gulp 'n' Blow. Krusty shows up to recruit him for the special, but – in a nifty little reversal of expectation – it turns out that Mel prefers hawking tacos in an environment where his boss, one Mr Johansson, respects his work. This incidental scene takes quick satirical jabs at labour relations in both the entertainment and service industries, and milks a gag or two out of the anachronistically protective nature of Mr Johansson and the clumsy incompetence of the Pimple-Faced Kid, who works alongside Mel. Later in the episode, Sideshow Mel breaks down and becomes a surprise guest on the comeback special, joining Krusty in a tearful rendition of 'Send in the Clowns', which broadly parodies the schmaltzy on-screen reunions of bickering showbiz greats throughout history.

But Mel's merely the *minor* riff on the Sideshow gag. It turns out that among Krusty's famous pals is his 'worthless half-brother', the actor Luke Perry, who when 9F19 was first broadcast in 1993 was at the peak of his stardom as the brooding bad boy on *Beverly Hills, 90210*. He's supposed to appear on the comeback special as 'Sideshow Luke Perry', complete with the grass skirt and giant bone through his hair made famous by Sideshow Mel. But at rehearsal he upstages Krusty, fashioning an antique carousel from a balloon when Krusty had only made a crude horsey. Krusty is ready to toss him off the show, but Perry pleads for some kind of role 'for Mom's sake'. Dissolve to a quick dream-sequence riff, with Krusty envisioning a skit in which he fires Sideshow Luke Perry out of a cannon into a brick wall, then flashing to a copy of *Peephole* magazine with a massively disfigured Perry on the cover. So Sideshow Luke Perry makes it onto the special, where a cannon is wheeled out and he is loaded into its muzzle. Krusty fires away, but he's set the trajectory too high, and Perry is launched like a baby-faced rocket right out of the studio. First, he sails through the window of the nearby Museum of Sandpaper, passing through its full abrasive length and out the other side. Then it's straight through the window of the Kwik-E-Mart, where it just so happens that Apu, the store's proprietor, is setting up a display of giant jars of acid, which Perry ploughs through ('My face! My valuable face!' he wails). His momentum carries him out the window, and then – blessedly, he thinks – into a pillow factory. He sighs in relief. There is a one-beat pause. We see a hard-hatted man in the foreground, squatting over a detonator. A roaring explosion, and the pillow factory collapses. We cut back to the Krusty special still in progress. And *that*, kids, is a Golden Age riff. *Hyuh-yuh-yuh-yuh!* [9]

Thanks for the heads-up, Krusty. And now, with a bit more background detail and a lot less Krusty, let's look at the anatomy of the three ages of *The Simpsons*.

THE THREE AGES OF THE SIMPSONS

'It always amazes me,' Matt Groening told a reporter on the eve of the show's full-length debut in 1989, 'how few cartoonists in print or animation go after the bigger issues, the kinds of things that keep you lying awake in the middle of the night. Questions about death and love and sex and work and relationships. And that's what I try to do, inject the stuff that people really care about into my [*Life in Hell*] cartoons. With *The Simpsons* we're trying to do that, too.' This was no empty boast. *The Simpsons* of the Early Days (1987–91) was still learning how to hone its satirical edge into a mighty samurai sword, but it did show signs of the fierce comedic warrior it would become. It's amazing that it made this transition in the face of the kind of sudden fame and instant money that usually turn devil-may-care radicals into ultra-cautious conservatives. And it's doubly amazing that it succeeded despite a potentially catastrophic decision by Fox's brains trust.

That decision: at the start of Season 2, Fox moved *The Simpsons* from its Sunday night timeslot to 8.00 on Thursday evenings, placing it in direct competition with NBC's *The Cosby Show*, which for five straight years had been the most popular show on American television.

At first, *The Simpsons* held its ground against the mighty Cos: on 11 October 1990, the first night the two programmes aired head-to-head, *Cosby* edged *The Simpsons* by one-tenth of a ratings point, a statistical blip in national-TV terms; about 100,000 more Americans had watched Bill and his squeaky-clean family than had watched slovenly Homer and his brood of foul-mouthed, underachieving brats.

This was a moral victory for *The Simpsons*. The show hadn't simply taken on *Cosby*, it had confronted it with an episode that was a direct rebuke to the moralising culture of the *Cosby* era. To the teachers who'd banned Bart's 'Underachiever and proud of it' T-shirts, to the humourless drug czars who'd decried it as a burden on society, to the millions who'd been living for years in a world in which Bill Cosby's impeccable family had been held up as both the ideal and the reality – to all of these people, *The Simpsons*' season premiere, Episode 7F03 ('Bart Gets an F'), was a big fat booming invitation to eat Bart's shorts.

It went like this: Homer and Marge have been called into Springfield Elementary to meet with the school psychiatrist to discuss Bart's bad grades and chronic misbehaviour. 'I think what we have on our hands here,' lectures the shrink, 'is a classic case of what laymen refer to as fear of failure. As a result, Bart is an underachiever, and yet he seems to be – how shall I put this? – proud of it.' Cut to Homer's perspective, just as he's zoning out on the doctor's blather. 'One of his problems may be his short attention span, which can lead to blah blah blah blah . . .' And so on, through blah after scolding blah, in a scene that both mocks the doctor's uptight moralising and lays whatever blame there is for Bart's behaviour squarely at his father's feet.[10]

A few episodes later, in 7F09 ('Itchy & Scratchy & Marge'), the argument against *Cosby*-style family values is made even more strongly as Marge leads a moral crusade against 'Itchy & Scratchy' that in its self-righteous hypocrisy directly mimics the one against *The Simpsons*. Never mind the drop in the ratings (it fell out of the Top 30, while *The Cosby show* fell to fifth): Season 2 of *The Simpsons* was the show's first bold stride in reformulating the tone of pop culture for the 1990s. The long gauzy daydream of the Reagan/Thatcher/ Mulroney era was *over*, man. If *The Simpsons* had its way, there would be no more easy moralistic fantasies, no more glossy corporate-pop confections, no more mortgaging the future to pay for today's deficit-ridden bacchanal.

There would be, at least for half an hour each Thursday, no more lies. What's more, even during the first few months of its duel with *Cosby*, the critical raves started to trickle in. *The Boston Globe*, for example, called it 'the most intelligent adult comedy on television', while *USA Today* named *The Simpsons* the 'most deserving hit' of 1990. By April 1992 *The Cosby Show* was off the air. *The Simpsons*, meanwhile, was the top-rated show in its time slot for Americans aged zero to 34 and an emerging international phenomenon that was amassing large and growing audiences throughout the English-speaking world.

And this was the point at which the show began its quick transition from its fans' favourite TV show to their central metaphorical framework for understanding modern life. This was the birth of a mass cult.

The dawn of the Simpsonian Golden Age (1992–7) didn't happen all at once, but rather in fits and starts throughout the first half of Season 3. In the season's second episode – 8F01 ('Mr. Lisa Goes to Washington') – the show hit a level of political satire far more angry and forceful than ever before. A couple of episodes later, Bart gets a job as an errand boy for the Springfield Mafia, inspiring an extra-rapid succession of especially inspired left-field gags (the mobsters inexplicably adore Manhattan cocktails; the psychic hired to find one of their victims can only spout predictions about celebrity relationships; Troy McClure hosts a marvellously absurd educational film about the origins of chocolate). In another episode, Marge's need for a break from the stresses of being a full-time homemaker inspires riffs in several directions about the impact of her absence: while Marge's vacation takes us inside the Troy McClure-hosted paradise of the Rancho Relaxo spa, Bart and Lisa explore the horrors of living with their gruesome aunts, and Homer sets off on a desperate hunt for runaway Maggie.

Slowly but surely throughout Season 3, the key elements gather: the pace speeds up; gags become more pointed and elaborate; premises no longer spawn single straight lines of plot but instead split into multiple vectors and layers. And then, on or about Episode 8F13 ('Homer at the Bat') – which tells the tale of Mr Burns's efforts to win the local softball championship by hiring nine Major League superstars as ringers – it all comes together in an episode of relentless madcap humour in the service of a fully developed plot, with dozens of great jokes that produce huge laughs even as they reveal deeper layers of characterisation, and a platoon of guest stars seamlessly integrated. With 8F13, the Golden Age had arrived.

We'll come shortly to a more detailed discussion of the myriad comic tools and techniques employed by *The Simpsons* to scale these heights and to stay there for five extraordinary seasons. For now, suffice it to say that the ever-more-hyperbolic critical raves and awards the show received, its eventual institutionalisation and deification, the gathering of a quasi-religious cult following that dedicated itself to cataloguing each episode's nuances and references obsessively, the very existence of this book you're reading right now – all of this is a direct result of the sustained virtuosity of the Golden Age.

Season 4, for example, is flawless. It is 22 episodes – a total running time equal to about four full-length movies – of the best comedy in the history of television. I would put Season 4 of *The Simpsons* up against any four films hand-picked from the careers of Woody Allen or Charlie Chaplin. I'd take it over any four Shakespeare comedies or any four Philip Roth novels. Taken as a whole, the Golden Age as I've defined it – Seasons 4 through 8, give or take an episode or two – is more than *44 hours* of near-perfect satire. During this five-year run, *The Simpsons* was wicked smart but never pedantic, bellyache-inducingly funny but never pandering. And this was not the product of a single fevered mind, but of dozens of producers and writers (not to mention hundreds of animators). The Beatles, in comparison, were but four men, and their peak creative period was five years long only by the most generous of estimates. You'd indeed be hard-pressed to find *any* other collaborative creative enterprise that has put together a stretch of sustained brilliance as long as that of *The Simpsons*.

It was, in short, some kinda run.

Simpsons fans soon began to realise that their favourite show had not only become a good deal better, it had also become a treasure trove of obscure references and incidental details – the very sort of things, in fact, that were becoming prime commodities on the Internet, which by momentous coincidence had just begun to emerge as a mass medium. The show's unparalleled density meant that it rewarded its fans each week for deepening their obsession, offering up a wealth of allusions and asides and in-jokes to trade and catalogue. And so *The Simpsons'* online fan base – centred around the alt.tv.simpsons newsgroup, among the most heavily trafficked news-groups of the early 1990s – soon became one of the most populous and robust communities on the Internet.

When *The Simpsons* entered syndication in autumn 1994, quickly becoming a five-times-a-week fixture on North American TV, the barrage of humour contained in each episode was now available to a mass audience, not just to the hard core fans who had the foresight to tape it each week. I'd indeed hazard a guess that the transformation of *The Simpsons* from popular

TV show to beloved, quasi-religious institution began right around the time it hit syndication. It was only with such daily visits to the temple that the show's faithful saw just how rich their new theology truly was.

Typically, the mainstream press took quite a bit longer to grasp *The Simpsons*' import (indeed, there remain large sectors of the mass media that still haven't got a handle on it). Except for routine annual review/preview articles that invariably noted that the show remained one of the smartest and funniest on TV and the odd feature on the sudden abundance of animation on the prime-time schedule, the mass media didn't really start to treat the show like the work of genius it had become until about four years into its five-year Golden Age.

Two unrelated events appear to have awakened the press to the enormity of the show's achievement. The first came in February 1997, when Fox aired the 167th episode of *The Simpsons*, marking the point at which the series surpassed *The Flintstones* as the longest running primetime cartoon in American history. The second event came just a few months later: *The Simpsons* won a Peabody Award, a laurel usually given to investigative journalists and documentary filmmakers. (The Peabody folks lauded *The Simpsons* 'for providing exceptional animation and stinging social satire, both commodities which are in extremely short supply in television today'.) Whether it was the Peabody or the *Flintstones* milestone, or neither, there commenced a flurry of superlative-laced reviews and institutional plaudits that continues to this day.

The Simpsons, it was now widely understood, was not just a TV show but an institution.

And it's a funny thing about institutions: just as *The Simpsons* was being recognised as a permanent and unique feature on the cultural landscape, it started to slip. It didn't slip that much, mind you, but after such a stretch of near-flawlessness, even tiny errors stood out like graffiti on a Monet. The show took a quick tumble off its dizzying peak, followed by a long and relatively stable existence on what I'm calling the Long Plateau.

The broadcast that marked that abrupt plunge remains to this day among the weakest episodes in *Simpsons* history: 4F23 ('The Principal and the Pauper'), the second instalment of Season 9. In it, Principal Skinner – a main supporting character since the first season – is suddenly and inexplicably revealed to be an impostor. He's actually a former juvenile delinquent named Armin Tamzarian who stole the identity of Seymour Skinner, the head of his platoon in Vietnam, after the latter went missing in action. The real Skinner (voiced by Martin Sheen) returns to Springfield after five years in a

Vietnamese POW camp and twenty more as a slave labourer in China, and Tamzarian flees town to restart his seedy life in Capital City. A blatant, continuity-scrambling plot twist of this sort might've been forgivable if the result had been as funny or as sharply satirical as the classics of the Golden Age, but alas it's emphatically not. It was a sudden and disturbing new low for the show.

This hard truth was no secret at all down *Simpsons* way. In an interview a few years later, Harry Shearer – the voice of Principal Skinner, among dozens of other classic characters – said 4F23 was one of the weakest *Simpsons* scripts he'd ever seen, a concern he expressed to the show's writing staff at the first read-through. Regardless, the Tamzarian episode went ahead. In its final minutes, however, the people of Springfield decide they prefer the impostor Skinner to the real one, so they run the real Skinner out of town and convince Tamzarian to return. Down at the Springfield train station, as the real Skinner – tied to a railcar – disappears into the distance, there follows this self-referential *deus ex machina*:

Tamzarian:	Well, this is a lovely gesture, but we still have to face the fact that I'm not really Seymour Skinner.
Homer:	Oh, no we don't. Judge Snyder?
Judge:	By authority of the City of Springfield, I hereby confer upon you the name of Seymour Skinner, as well as his past, present, future, and mother.
Skinner:	Okay.
Judge:	And I further decree that everything will be just like it was before all this happened. And no one will ever mention it again . . . under penalty of torture.
	[*The crowd cheers.*]

It's some compensation, perhaps, that the show issues so overt a *mea culpa* – and indeed that this *mea culpa* is among the cleverest scenes in the whole episode. It also warrants mention that 4F23, as craptacular as it is, still sports a couple of virtuoso gags. In the episode's opening sequence, for example, the ever-irritable Superintendent Chalmers arrives at Springfield Elementary for a party in Skinner's honour. As he enters the teachers' lounge, Mrs Krabappel asks him hospitably, 'Can I offer you a cup of coffee-flavoured Beverine?' Chalmers offhandedly replies, 'Yeah – I take it grey with Cremium.' The trouble, though, is that it's one of the only inspired moments in the whole episode.

For season after season of *The Simpsons* during the age of the Long Plateau (1997–), loyal viewers have sustained themselves with such moments of ingenious riffing, stranded between the merely good and the occasional visitations by hideous beasts like Armin Tamzarian. Still, the average Long Plateau episode is a wonderful thing compared with the overwhelming majority of the comedies that have polluted the TV and movie screens of the West over the last several decades. There's no more persuasive testimony to the continued quality of *The Simpsons* than its good standing at one of the most vicious of online institutions: Jump The Shark (www.jumptheshark.com), a website dedicated to pinpointing and cataloguing the moments when various TV series have 'jumped the shark'. The phrase refers to an infamous episode of *Happy Days* in which a waterskiing Fonzie literally jumps over a shark, and is defined on the site thusly:

> It's a moment. A defining moment when you know that your favorite television programme has reached its peak. That instant that you know from now on . . . it's all downhill. Some call it the climax. We call it 'Jumping the Shark.' From that moment on, the programme will simply never be the same.

At the site, long lists of possible shark-jumping moments for any given series are suggested and voted on by the general public.

Soon after the website's launch in December 1997, 'jumping the shark' moved into mainstream usage in North America. Indeed, *The Simpsons* has twice made direct references to it: Homer jumps a shark as part of a montage during the closing credits of a Season 13 episode, and the opening credits of the Season 14 premiere feature a couch gag in which Homer, his family perched on his back, waterskis into the Simpson living room and onto the couch, finally taking a seat with a shark dangling from each leg. These self-accusations notwithstanding, as of May 2004 *The Simpsons* is the only current TV series on Jump The Shark's exclusive list of shows that have 'Never Jumped' – 61 per cent of voters believe it has never completely lost its edge.

The Golden Age *is* over, though. And in general, it's the triumph of wacky premise and kinetic plot over rock-solid character and gleefully satiric writing that seems to have dragged *The Simpsons* down to the less rarefied altitudes of the Long Plateau. You can see the decline most clearly in the episodes that have focused on supporting characters, which feel all too palpably as if they began from a late-night-brainstormed *What if . . . ?* As in: *What if Moe the bartender got a facelift and became a soap-opera star?* Answer: Episode BABF12 ('Pygmoelian'). And: *What if Apu and his wife had octuplets and what if they wound up as an attraction at the Springfield Zoo?* BABF03 ('Eight Misbehavin").

This *What if . . . ?* device is so hackneyed it's been parodied by *The Simpsons* itself – in Episode DABF12 ('Gump Roast'), an episode from Season 13 in which a Friars-style roasting of Homer is used as a pretext for a string of clips from old episodes. Over the closing credits, a song plays to the tune of Billy Joel's 'We Didn't Start the Fire'. The first few verses are a rapid-fire summary of the many crazy adventures *The Simpsons* has presented to date, and it concludes with a reassurance that the show's writers still have plenty of ideas:

> They'll never stop *The Simpsons*
> Have no fears
> We've got stories for years
>
> Like Marge becomes a robot
> Maybe Moe gets a cell phone
> Has Bart ever owned a bear?
>
> Or how 'bout a crazy wedding
> Where something happens
> And do-do-do-do-do

The Simpsons, self-aware to a fault, knows it's no longer perfect. It can even be quite funny as it admits that it's no longer perfect. Doesn't that at least partially excuse it?

If awards and rave reviews are any measure, the answer appears to be yes. Even as *The Simpsons* was descending from the Golden-Age heights down to the Long Plateau, it rapidly skipped past institutionalisation into full-blown canonisation in the estimation of the guardians of mainstream culture. By mid-2003, the show had won 20 Emmy Awards, including eight for outstanding animated programme.[11] *The Simpsons* got a star on Hollywood's Walk of Fame in 2000. It won the Peabody in 1997 and received its first-ever Golden Globe nomination for best comedy series in 2003 (the first time a cartoon had ever been nominated). And in the six-year gap between these last two laurels, critical praise for *The Simpsons* went from mere acknowledgement that it was a very good TV show to increasing recognition that it was a cultural institution, a unique body of work that had transcended its medium and defined its time. It has been called 'TV's answer to the Great American Novel' and the primetime-TV equivalent of Manet's *Olympia*. *Time* named it the best TV show of the twentieth century; the *Seattle Times* declared it one of the '52 Works That Changed the Millennium'. It has gone on like this.

In early 2003, after several years of constant praise from seemingly every corner of mainstream Western society, Matt Groening told a reporter, 'We were going to bring down America in 1990. We had people very, very upset about the show. And now either our critics and enemies have come around, or given up. I think that's the nature of pop culture. Today's outrage is tomorrow's beloved classic.'[12]

And now let's move on to the question of where that beloved classic came from.

ANCESTORS OF THE SIMPSONS (I): ANTHROPOMORPHIC ANIMALS, LATE-NIGHT TALK SHOWS & SUCH-AND-SUCH

Appropriately enough for a show that's an animated parody of the classic sitcom, many of *The Simpsons*' most obvious antecedents are cartoons and old sitcoms. But in marked similarity to humanity's place on the food chain in the diagram that Troy McClure shows little Jimmy in the Meat Council educational filmstrip *Meat and You: Partners in Freedom*, *The Simpsons* is an omnivorous consumer of comedy. It's not so much the end of a sequential progression as the central node of a multivalent ecosystem, feeding as it pleases on a wide range of comedic forms – old cartoons and sitcoms, yes, but also late-night talk shows and sketch-comedy troupes.

Herewith, a *Meat-and-You*-style schema of the show's televisual influences:

Ancestors of *The Simpsons* (I)

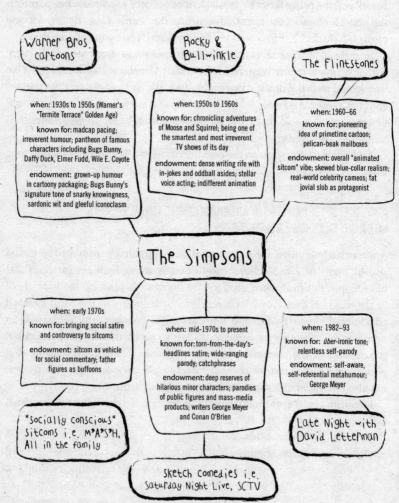

Warner Bros. cartoons

when: 1930s to 1950s (Warner's "Termite Terrace" Golden Age)

known for: madcap pacing; irreverent humour; pantheon of famous characters including Bugs Bunny, Daffy Duck, Elmer Fudd, Wile E. Coyote

endowment: grown-up humour in cartoony packaging; Bugs Bunny's signature tone of snarky knowingness, sardonic wit and gleeful iconoclasm

Rocky & Bullwinkle

when: 1950s to 1960s

known for: chronicling adventures of Moose and Squirrel; being one of the smartest and most irreverent TV shows of its day

endowment: dense writing rife with in-jokes and oddball asides; stellar voice acting; indifferent animation

The Flintstones

when: 1960–66

known for: pioneering idea of primetime cartoon; pelican-beak mailboxes

endowment: overall "animated sitcom" vibe; skewed blue-collar realism; real-world celebrity cameos; fat jovial slob as protagonist

The Simpsons

when: early 1970s

known for: bringing social satire and controversy to sitcoms

endowment: sitcom as vehicle for social commentary; father figures as buffoons

when: mid-1970s to present

known for: torn-from-the-day's-headlines satire; wide-ranging parody; catchphrases

endowment: deep reserves of hilarious minor characters; parodies of public figures and mass-media products; writers George Meyer and Conan O'Brien

when: 1982–93

known for: *über*-ironic tone; relentless self-parody

endowment: self-aware, self-referential metahumour; George Meyer

"Socially conscious" sitcoms i.e. M*A*S*H, All in the family

Late Night with David Letterman

Sketch comedies i.e. Saturday Night Live, SCTV

From these varied sources, *The Simpsons* built its exoskeleton: a solid, resonant foundation drawn from sitcoms and classic cartoons, a funhouse built on top of this foundation using blueprints from late-night TV and sketch comedy. The result: the vast warren of media outlets and storefronts packed full of minor characters that has made Springfield such a lush satirical environment.

And then, to fill this warren with crazy schemes and witty rejoinders – with great comedy *writing* – *The Simpsons* drew upon the definitive comedic lineage of postwar America: Boomer humour.

ANCESTORS OF *THE SIMPSONS* (II): BOOMER HUMOUR BEGETS EGGHEAD HUMOUR

The term 'Boomer humour' comes from Tony Hendra's excellent and expansive history of the phenomenon, *Going Too Far*. It refers to a revolution in comedy that began with the edgy stand-ups who worked nightclubs and coffee houses in the 1950s and ran in a fairly direct line all the way through to *The Simpsons*' own writing staff. Boomer humour, Hendra explains, was best characterised by the adjective 'sick' – meaning it seemed like the product of a sick, deranged mind. Boomer humour went too far, confronting and disturbing its audience at least as much as it entertained and amused. By the late 1970s, Hendra argues,

> Boomer humour had overtaken rock and roll as the strongest surviving expression of the [Baby Boom] generation's ideas, attitudes, debates, and priorities. Furthermore, it was a far more comprehensive representation, since willy-nilly it dealt directly with those ideas, attitudes, debates and priorities and with those who opposed them. In the struggle for the hearts and minds of the largest generation in history, therefore, humour was a principal contender.

Boomer humour, in other words, was the last remaining mainstream repository of a strongly oppositional counterculture. And in time it moved from Boomer counterculture to Simpsonian mainstream, earning an extraordinary number of degrees from Harvard University along the way and becoming an over-educated PhD thesis on the nature of comedy that's best described as 'egghead humour'.

Here's how it passed from *outré* nightclubs to *The Simpsons*' rewrite room:

Ancestors of *The Simpsons (II)*

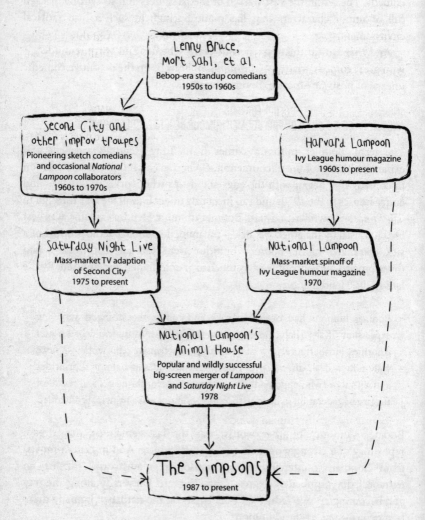

Lenny Bruce, Mort Sahl, et al.
Bebop-era standup comedians
1950s to 1960s

Second City and other improv troupes
Pioneering sketch comedians and occasional *National Lampoon* collaborators
1960s to 1970s

Harvard Lampoon
Ivy League humour magazine
1960s to present

Saturday Night Live
Mass-market TV adaption of Second City
1975 to present

National Lampoon
Mass-market spinoff of Ivy League humour magazine
1970

National Lampoon's Animal House
Popular and wildly successful big-screen merger of *Lampoon* and *Saturday Night Live*
1978

The Simpsons
1987 to present

It's this egghead layer[13] of Simpsonian comedy that often elevates the show to a kind of highbrow pop art and pretty much always gives it more social and political heft than all but the most eggheaded of North America's other media outlets. *The Simpsons* is smarter than TV news, more insightful than most major newspapers, more thoughtful than *Time* or *Newsweek* and at least as sophisticated as *The New Yorker* or *The Economist*. And this is thanks largely to the work of its brainiac Harvard alumni and the equally intellectual non-Ivy Leaguers who round out the staff.

ANCESTORS OF THE SIMPSONS (III): FOR IRONIC DETACHMENT, BLAME CANADA

Now, speaking of those non-Ivy Leaguers on *The Simpsons*' creative team, it's no coincidence that, for most of the show's run, at least a couple of them have been Canadians. Since the early days of Boomer humour in the late 1960s, any A-list comedy-writing team in the American entertainment industry has included a Canuck or two. This phenomenon – that Canadians have long been disproportionately represented in the upper echelons of American comedy – is often noted in Canada but is unknown almost everywhere else. Indeed, ringing off the list of Canadian comedians who've achieved international fame via Hollywood is something of a national pastime in Canada. (There's Dan Aykroyd, Eugene Levy, John Candy, Martin Short, Catherine O'Hara, Mike Myers, Phil Hartman, Jim Carrey . . .) One of Boomer humour's most sacred institutions – *Saturday Night Live* – was created by a Canadian (Lorne Michaels) and has steadily employed Canadian writers and comedians since its first season. Probably the most innovative sketch comedy troupe of the 1980s, *The Kids in the Hall*, was entirely Canadian. And so on down the line to current *Simpsons* staffers Tim Long and Joel Cohen. Canadians, that is, have always been key players in Boomer humour and the Simpsonian comedy it inspired.

Other than providing Canadians with a fun hobby, what does this phenomenon mean? That's a tricky question to answer and a very difficult thing to quantify. Still, if we grant that Canadian humorists have been central to the development of American satire since the Second World War and that Canadians are in certain respects fundamentally different from Americans – in their overall worldview, their fondness for irony and self-deprecation, their reflexive discomfort with arrogance and self-aggrandisement – then we can begin to see a uniquely Canadian tone at work in that satire, a tone that has lodged itself deep within *The Simpsons*' comedic style.

I'm just going to plough on here, and you can correct for my native bias. First, in an uncharacteristically brash generalisation, I have to say that Canadians tend to be a good deal more introspective and self-effacing than Americans, much slower than their southern neighbours to celebrate their triumphs and much quicker to expose their flaws. This is a disposition, note, that is ripe for the development of satire. Another fundamental difference is that many Americans believe – are in fact raised to believe – that everyone else in the world lives like they do, or else *wants* to live like they do, and that the American way of life is compelling to practically everyone. Whereas Canadians are raised with the absolute certainty that not even their closest neighbours live like they do, nor want to, and that their way of life is not even particularly compelling to those neighbours. What's more, America's enormous global influence – politically and economically as well as culturally – and Canada's comparative invisibility confirm these beliefs to some degree. America sees itself everywhere, Canada almost nowhere. The former thus develops a highly insular and inwardly focused culture, the latter an obsessively outward-looking culture. And the place Canadians most often gaze out upon is their big, brash next-door neighbour. This has provided Canada with a point of view utterly unique in the world: Canadians are by nature and circumstance experts in American studies, nearly as well versed as Americans themselves in the society and culture of the United States, able to identify every cultural referent, able indeed to pass for Americans – to produce pop culture that an American audience frequently mistakes for its own. Canadians almost instinctively *get* American culture, but at the same time they are profoundly aware that they are not entirely *of* it. And this allows Canadians to be critical of it with a degree of detachment impossible for an American, even as their privileged point of view ensures that their criticisms ring true.

This, then, is the Canadian influence on American satire, from Boomer humour on down to *The Simpsons*: ironic detachment, an ability to criticise America more deeply and satirise it more sharply than native-born Americans. Canadians have a natural predisposition towards going further and deeper with their satire than an American might be inclined to – towards 'going too far', as Hendra puts it – and this is born of a Canadian's much smaller investment in America's sacred myths. And it's an influence that's a good deal greater than the simple fact that there are always a few Canadian citizens on *The Simpsons'* writing staff.

Perhaps the best indication of the show's awareness of its Canadian influence is that it has frequently and consistently paid homage to Canada the best way it knows how: by dropping Canadian references into the show itself. Canada is largely invisible in the majority of American pop culture, a nonentity as little known and as unexamined as the vast, featureless blob that squats on the top part of your average map of the United States. On *The Simpsons*, though, Canada pops up seemingly every time there's an incidental detail to be filled in. Homer picks up his newspaper to avoid a heavy talk with Marge and announces, 'Oooh – "Canada to Hold Referendum". Sorry, Marge, can't talk now.' Bart drives down to Knoxville, Tennessee, on spring break, passing an enraged father on the highway who bellows that he's taking the family back to Winnipeg.[14] And as these brief moments mount over the years, the show seems to tell its viewers that, in stark contrast to much of American pop culture, Canada matters on *The Simpsons*.

DESCENDANTS OF *THE SIMPSONS*

If some of the connections between *The Simpsons* and its antecedents seem a little vague, there was no missing the animation boom the show inspired. After *The Simpsons*' epochal debut, primetime TV grew more littered with Simpsonian progeny with each passing year. The Bartmania of 1990 naturally spawned a wave of half-assed imitations as every network hurriedly churned out a clever cartoon of its own to try to exploit the hype. In time, though, a far more lasting – and more interesting – phalanx of grown-up cartoons (and a few cartoon-like live-action shows) took to the airwaves, amounting to something of an animation renaissance.

Here's an overview of the two most significant ancestral lines *The Simpsons* has spawned:

Descendants of *The Simpsons*

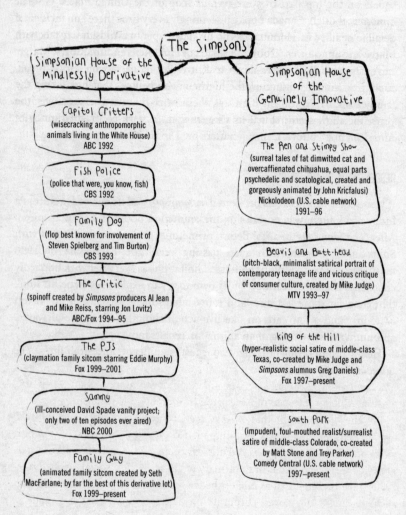

The Simpsons

Simpsonian House of the Mindlessly Derivative

Capitol Critters
(wisecracking anthropomorphic animals living in the White House)
ABC 1992

Fish Police
(police that were, you know, fish)
CBS 1992

Family Dog
(flop best known for involvement of Steven Spielberg and Tim Burton)
CBS 1993

The Critic
(spinoff created by *Simpsons* producers Al Jean and Mike Reiss, starring Jon Lovitz)
ABC/Fox 1994–95

The PJs
(claymation family sitcom starring Eddie Murphy)
Fox 1999–2001

Sammy
(ill-conceived David Spade vanity project; only two of ten episodes ever aired)
NBC 2000

Family Guy
(animated family sitcom created by Seth MacFarlane; by far the best of this derivative lot)
Fox 1999–present

Simpsonian House of the Genuinely Innovative

The Ren and Stimpy Show
(surreal tales of fat dimwitted cat and overcaffeinated chihuahua, equal parts psychedelic and scatological, created and gorgeously animated by John Kricfalusi)
Nickelodeon (U.S. cable network)
1991–96

Beavis and Butt-head
(pitch-black, minimalist satirical portrait of contemporary teenage life and vicious critique of consumer culture, created by Mike Judge)
MTV 1993–97

King of the Hill
(hyper-realistic social satire of middle-class Texas, co-created by Mike Judge and *Simpsons* alumnus Greg Daniels)
Fox 1997–present

South Park
(impudent, foul-mouthed realist/surrealist satire of middle-class Colorado, co-created by Matt Stone and Trey Parker)
Comedy Central (U.S. cable network)
1997–present

Of this raucous brood, two shows in particular illustrate the way *The Simpsons'* innovations have been extended by its descendants: *South Park* and *King of the Hill*.

South Park, for its part, takes a revolutionary leap past *The Simpsons* in the irreverence department,[15] featuring as it does a gang of misbehaving prepubescents whose fondness for expletives and racial slurs make Bart Simpson look like a choirboy, a school-cafeteria cook who frequently breaks into lusty, double entendre-laced song, and plot lines in which a character might find himself with an elaborate alien satellite dish implanted in his ass or a pet who winds up on Big Gay Al's Big Gay Boat Cruise. And let's not forget, either, that its first trademark recurring gag was the brutal murder of one of its main characters every episode (OH MY GOD, THEY KILLED KENNY! the commemorative T-shirts exclaimed). *South Park* is also revolutionary in its visual style, meticulously animated to look like it has been rendered in construction paper using crude stop-motion. (Check out the show's flawless synching of mouth movements with voiceovers if you're inclined to think of *South Park*'s animation as *genuinely* crude.)

As for *King of the Hill*, it's the brainchild of Mike Judge (who also created *Beavis and Butt-head*) and former *Simpsons* writer Greg Daniels, but its debt to Homer and company stretches beyond Daniels's résumé. If *South Park* is the logical next step beyond *The Simpsons* in terms of anarchic subversion, then *King of the Hill* – a carefully crafted, character-driven satire of middle-class Texan life – stands as an inspired elaboration of *The Simpsons'* celebrated realism. *King of the Hill* is not just more lifelike than *The Simpsons*, it's damn near as realistic as anything else – police dramas, reality TV, the news, *anything* – currently on TV. And it accomplishes this even though, like *The Simpsons*, it's quite cartoonishly drawn. The secret, again, is in the writing, which in the case of *King of the Hill* verges on naturalism.

But the greatest debt that *King of the Hill* and *South Park* and the rest owe to *The Simpsons* has nothing to do with the specifics of plot or writing. What *The Simpsons* did for cartoons was simply to carve out a space for them as pop culture's primary engines of sharp social satire. In the 1990s, cartoons emerged as one of the few safe havens for real subversion in an increasingly kid-gloved corporate mediascape. *South Park* has made a career out of dropping its cardboard cut-out shorts and dumping all over social taboos. *Beavis and Butt-head* brought to TV an unprecedented level of unredeemed nihilism. *King of the Hill* has had to become one of the most acute social critics on television in order to achieve its stunning realism. And they've all found the leeway to explore controversial subject matter and depict modern society's ugliest truths because they are cartoons.

To cite one example of the extra leeway given to cartoons: *That '70s Show* – broadcast, like *The Simpsons*, on Fox – features a recurring gag in which the show's teenage protagonists sit in a circle in a smoky basement trading non sequiturs. Although it's painfully obvious that they're stoned to the bejesus, the show has never once depicted any of the kids toking on a joint. By comparison, in Episode DABF11 ('Weekend at Burnsie's') of *The Simpsons*, Homer spends practically the entire episode in the attic passing joints and trading bong hits with Otto the bus driver. This expanded satirical licence has on rare occasions been extended to live-action TV – Fox's *Malcolm in the Middle*, a chaotic portrait of a hyper-dysfunctional American family, is essentially a live-action adaptation of *The Simpsons* – but for the most part it has remained the exclusive playpen of animated series.

The Simpsons has also had a pervasive influence on the broader culture, particularly in setting the default tone of its discourse. This is something that's perhaps best glimpsed anecdotally. You can see it, for example, in the enormous popularity of *The Onion*, 'America's Finest News Source', an online newspaper that trades exclusively in made-up news. And you see it also in the meteoric rise of *The Daily Show with Jon Stewart*, a nightly satirical-news show that started out on the fringes of American cable and has become an influential forum for A-list American politicians hoping to reach sceptical young voters. (Excerpts from *The Daily Show* are regularly aired on CNN International.) In the first days of 2004, Canada's staid new prime minister, Paul Martin, hired Scott Feschuk – *The National Post*'s sardonic TV critic and author of a smart-assed book entitled *Searching for Michael Jackson's Nose and Other Preoccupations of Our Celebrity-Mad Culture* – as his speechwriter. And the Simpsonian tone is all over the Internet, where discussion forums on almost any topic often dissolve into one-liner competitions, where absurdities (dancing hamsters, lustful and linguistically challenged Turkish men, outdated and linguistically challenged Japanese videogames) are as likely as anything else online to become international sensations, and where hackers frequently slap up parody websites to announce their successful infiltrations of the august online homes of *The New York Times* and CNN. In the age of *The Simpsons*, winking irony and smirking parody are increasingly the default communication tools for everything from political discourse to the nightly news.

Here's an even more direct example of *The Simpsons*' influence. As the United States began its march to war in Iraq in 2002 and early 2003, and as opposition began to emerge most stridently from France, news outlets throughout the English-speaking world took to using the epithet 'cheese-eating surrender monkeys' as a shorthand dismissal of the French. There it all was – the long-standing stereotype of the French as snobbish cowards, the glib arrogance of the American (and, to a lesser extent, the British) government in the face of French criticism, the perennially prickly alliance between France and the US and Britain – summed up in a single zippy phrase. Few of the reporters who employed it, though, bothered to note its provenance: Groundskeeper Willie, the cantankerous Scottish janitor at Springfield Elementary School, who barks the line in Episode 2F32 ("Round Springfield'), after budget cuts force the school to use him as its French teacher. '*Bonjourrrr*, you cheese-eating surrender monkeys!' Willie trills to the class in his thick Scottish brogue.

The sudden ubiquity of the phrase illustrates with striking clarity the seamlessness with which Simpsonian dialogue can merge with serious public discourse. It didn't need attribution because it seemed like exactly the sort of line that could have emerged naturally from the culture at large. Was it an Australian headline-writer's invention? A one-liner from an English comedian? One of Donald Rumsfeld's snarky press-conference rebukes? An inspired moment from an online wit, a throwaway remark from some Internet discussion group that then got bounced anonymously from inbox to inbox around the world? It could have come from any of them, because to some degree all of them now speak a satirical language they learned from *The Simpsons*.

The Simpsons has become the new repository of the West's common metaphors, the wellspring of its most resonant quotes, the progenitor of its default tone. In generations past, writers or politicians looking for rhetorical inspiration – a line or anecdote that a broad audience would easily recognise and immediately understand – might have looked to the Bible, or to Greek mythology, or to Shakespeare, or more recently to rock & roll. In the years to come, I'd wager, they'll tend more and more to cite *The Simpsons*. Simpsonian is well on its way to becoming the global village's most widely spoken pop-cultural lingua franca – the parlance of our times.

REALITY TV: THE SATIRICAL UNIVERSE OF THE SIMPSONS

There's an excellent definition of satire in Tony Hendra's *Going Too Far*. He is careful to differentiate satire from lesser forms of humour such as parody and irony – not to mention comedic raw materials like sight gags and wordplay and hyperbole. 'Satire,' Hendra writes, 'is defined as intellectual judo, in which the writer or performer takes on the ideas and character of his target and then takes both to absurd lengths to destroy them.' Satire only works, then, insofar as its subject matter is familiar, comprehensible, known. Realistic.

The Simpsons has created a whole satirical universe, a place as vast and varied as mass culture has ever seen (indeed possibly as expansive as any fictive universe in the history of storytelling). And this dense world has provided *The Simpsons* with the firm foundation of realism necessary for its satirical work. On *The Simpsons*, the main characters, the setting, even the basic premise of the series are satirical. The show builds from the notion that the Simpson family is an average American household living in a typical American town. The rich characterisation of the family members and the lushness of their surroundings all enhance the notion – and it's a deeply subversive notion – that this mess of a family and its degraded hometown are 'realistic'. I'll examine the Simpsons themselves in much greater depth in later chapters, but one detail about Homer will suffice to illustrate the seditiousness buried in this supposed realism: he's a low-level technician at the local nuclear power plant.

'Television touches on an issue then dances away from it and never comes back to it,' Groening explained to a British reporter. 'So it has the illusion of having a strong point of view, but the real point of view of television is that nothing matters, because it's going to be replaced in the next millisecond by something different, and then replaced again and again. That's one reason why, in conceiving the show, I made sure that Homer worked in a nuclear power plant, because then we can keep returning to that and making a point about the environment.' *The Simpsons*' continuing satirical examination of the rapaciousness of big business and its contempt for the health of the planet stem from the careful selection of the show's realistic touches.

A quick survey of Springfield reveals myriad other ways in which realism has been put to work in the service of satire. The mayor is 'Diamond Joe' Quimby, a Kennedy soundalike and a terminally corrupt womaniser who invariably treats his constituents with contempt. The town's commerce is controlled by an ancient billionaire tyrant, Mr Burns, a creature of pure malevolence whose nuclear power plant has turned the fish in the local river into three-eyed mutants. The local cop, Chief Wiggum, is clueless, incompetent, occasionally abusive, and on the take. One local film hero, Troy McClure, is a talentless phony ravaged by substance-abuse problems and sexual deviance; another, Rainier Wolfcastle, is a misanthrope with a

Schwarzenegger accent and close ties to the Republican Party. Celebrities from our world – from Leonard Nimoy to Ron Howard, from Tony Blair to George H.W. Bush – are invariably portrayed as contemptible in one way or another. The proprietor of the Kwik-E-Mart, the Indian immigrant Apu Nahasapeemapetilon, loves his adopted country because he is free 'to say and to think and to *charge*' whatever he wants. The holyrolling Reverend Lovejoy cares little about the spiritual concerns of his flock but revels in leading empty-headed moral crusades. Springfield is a place in which no authority is legitimate and no leader uncorrupted. The parents are all bumbling, the teachers indifferent, the politicians guided by naked self-interest.

And Springfield has proven to be totally recognisable around the world because it rings true. When we laugh along, we're admitting on some level that we *do* live in a world of corrupt authorities, clueless leaders and rapacious businessmen. We are presented in every episode of *The Simpsons* with hard truths about the hideous mess of our own world, and we laugh along because we see ourselves in those nasty yellow faces. And to face up to this sort of unvarnished, unpleasant reality is a powerfully subversive thing.

Which brings us to the point of *The Simpsons*, and to the intent of its creators, several of whom, thankfully, have been quite blunt on the issue. 'Is there a purpose to *The Simpsons*?' a reporter from ABC's *20/20* asked George Meyer in 2002. Meyer, the show's most influential writer-producer, replied: 'If there is, it's to get people to re-examine their world, and specifically, the authority figures in their world.'

Matt Groening, meanwhile, has reiterated time and again that the point of his work is to entertain and subvert. It's a phrase he has in fact repeated, almost word for word, in almost every interview: 'Entertain and subvert – that's my motto.' He said it to an Australian reporter in 2000. Essentially the same quote appeared in a *Toronto Star* feature from 1994, in a *Washington Post* story from 1990. Here's Groening, then – a man who, as *The Simpsons* attests, has a deep understanding of how the mass media functions – repeating that same phrase over and over. Knowing, surely, that the only way to guarantee that a line will make it into a news story is to make it quick and punchy, knowing too that the only way for the line to outlive a twenty-four-hour news cycle and become a genuine motto is to repeat it every chance he gets. 'Entertain and subvert.' Which is to say: *This is all deliberate, kids. We want you to laugh, sure, but we also want you to think. To think and question and perhaps, yes, to reject this stinking pile of self-interested hypocrisy that is the established order.*

The show's creators have wilfully set out to illustrate the gap between What Is and What Should Be. And perhaps, in so doing, to subvert it, to shrink it, to erase it.

SATIRICAL ANATOMY (I): WHAT IS & WHAT SHOULD BE

This needs a little elaboration.

It begins, as so much modern satire does, with Lenny Bruce. In April 1964, Bruce had a two-week engagement at the Café au Go-Go in New York. Tony Hendra was part of the opening act, and in *Going Too Far* he writes about the monologue on the Kennedy assassination that got Bruce busted for obscenity:

> There was a new routine that very few audiences responded to. Bruce was clearly obsessed by the interpretation *Life* magazine had put on clips from the Zapruder film showing the presidential car immediately after the firing of the shot – or shots. Jackie Kennedy was sprawled on the trunk as if trying to get out of the backseat. *Life*'s version was that she had been going for help. Since the limousine had already speeded up and a Secret Service agent had seconds later rushed to cover her with his body, that seemed like a somewhat unlikely motivation. The official line seemed to be that the President's wife would never do anything so unsaintly as try to save herself from further gunfire. Nonetheless the clips gave the lie to that pious assumption. Or, as Bruce put it, she appeared to be 'hauling ass to save ass.' He added, quite justifiably, who wouldn't? The fatuity lay in *Life*'s trying to persuade the public that what their eyes told them had happened had not happened at all, and that what they were seeing was something that fit into the prevailing hagiography.

The pictures showed What Is in no uncertain terms, but *Life* insisted on telling the tall tale of What Should Be. It was an anecdote that remained in Bruce's act until he died two and a half years later, and he drove home the moral of the story – of so many of his stories – in his autobiography, *How to Talk Dirty and Influence People*: 'There is only what *is*. The what-*should*-be never did exist, but people keep trying to live up to it. There is only what *is*.'

The whole point of satire is to broadcast in blazing hundred-foot-high neon the gap between What Is and What Should Be. 'Satire,' Hendra writes, 'functions on the gap between reality and fantasy; its dynamic is to reduce pretension and presumption to the tangible and recognizable.' Satire makes the lie manifest, and by so doing exposes it, weakens it, destroys it – or at least *attempts* to destroy it. This, according to scholars – or at least according to *a* scholar – is a key function of all American humour. That scholar is Louis D. Rubin Jr., who in his 1973 essay, 'The Great American Joke', notes that 'a central motif of American humor [is] the contrast, the incongruity between the ideal and the real'. And though this motif is present in all kinds of humour, Rubin argues that it's particularly common – and powerful – in American humour, because America's ideals are so central to its society and so celebrated in its history and culture. The Great American Joke, Rubin writes, 'arises out of the gap between the cultural ideal and the everyday fact, with the ideal shown to be somewhat hollow and hypocritical, and the fact crude and disgusting'.

Demonstrating and exploiting the existence of this gap is an American satirical tradition that dates at least to Mark Twain's Huckleberry Finn, whose jaunt down the mighty Mississippi is a satirical journey through the overblown ideals and nasty realities of nineteenth-century America. In Huck's parroting of the pervasive racism of his day, for example, we see the official version of What Should Be. In his growing friendship with the runaway slave Jim, in his commonsense discovery of Jim's essential humanity, Huck learns to accept What Is. And so it has gone for The Great American Joke, from Mark Twain to H.L. Mencken to Lenny Bruce to *National Lampoon*. If you look closely at a recent map of the United States of America and find the chasm where The Great American Joke lives – scenic, satirical Hypocritical Gap – there you'll find Springfield, USA.

It's in Hypocritical Gap that you'll find Homer Simpson's bumbling parenting and Bart's brattiness and Mr Burns's insatiable greed and the rest of the satirical stuff that has made *The Simpsons* meaningful. By portraying a cartoonishly overstated but still familiar portrait of What Is, the show has waged a relentless assault on the pompous ramparts of What Should Be. *The Simpsons* has used the Great American Joke to reveal and dismantle Western society's Big Lies. This is the nature of the subversion Groening has talked so much about.

As for the entertainment part of Groening's motto – well, the way *The Simpsons* goes about subverting is just funny as all hell.

SATIRICAL ANATOMY (II): A PARTIAL TAXONOMY OF SIMPSONIAN HUMOUR

'Funny' is an extremely broad and highly subjective term. It can encompass anything from slip-on-a-banana-peel sight gags, scatological humour and *Three Stooges* horseplay to the dark satire of Stanley Kubrick's *Dr Strangelove*, the politicised rants of George Carlin and P.J. O'Rourke, and the bizarre comedy-as-performance-art of Andy Kaufman and Tom Green (not to mention the tradition of literary comedy that dates back to Chaucer and Shakespeare). The monumental genius of *The Simpsons* is that it manages, at its best, to deploy seemingly every weapon at its disposal – the whole humour-industrial complex, if you will.

Now, a *full* taxonomy of Simpsonian humour would take an even thicker tome than this one, and it would surely be tiresome. That said, it's worth a closer look at a few of the most potent weapons in *The Simpsons*' arsenal.

1. Surface gags

Much like the classic Warner Bros. cartoons, *The Simpsons* is able to appeal to both adults *and* tykes – and to appeal across geographic, ethnic and political divisions – because it never lets its brains completely overwhelm its gut. At its most base, this means sight gags a' plenty. As with almost all Simpsonian humour, though, the simple sight gag is rarely as straightforward as a mere vaudevillian pratfall or Stoogeian eye gouge. Consider, for example, Homer's efforts to dispose of a troublesome trampoline of his recent acquisition in Episode 1F05 ('Bart's Inner Child'), which gives rise to one of the show's most overt and inspired tributes to the Warner cartoons. There are several gags in the sequence, but the most impressive has Homer taking the trampoline to the edge of a cliff and simply tossing it into the deep crevice below. We watch it plummet into a decidedly Wile-E.-esque desertscape, where it impales itself on a rocky spike and then springs Warnerly back the way it came. Homer, meanwhile, gloats over a job well done, even as the trampoline's shadow falls over him. It slams down upon him and bounces up and down on his head, hammering him into the ground. Homer remains there, stuck in the outcropping, his feet dangling precariously out the bottom. This, already, is an impressively elaborate homage. Then comes the apparent punchline: 'If this were a cartoon,' Homer announces, 'the cliff would break off now.' Dissolve to night-time, and Homer's still trapped. 'I'm thirsty,' he whines. All at once, the outcropping *does* break off, finally sending him tumbling to the canyon floor.

This is what *The Simpsons* often does with a surface gag: it twists, it escalates, it toys anarchically with the form. Or perhaps it will take the riff in the other direction, as for example in Episode 9F22 ('Cape Feare'), in which Krusty's diabolical former sidekick Sideshow Bob steps on the business end of a yard rake, causing its handle to spring up and thwack him in the face in a gag right out of a Three Stooges routine. Then Bob takes another step, hits another rake head, receives another thwack in the face. Another step, another thwack. Again and again and again. The sequence continues for a full half-minute, nine rake thwacks in all, in a daring demonstration of the inherent comedy in repetition. The first thwack, you might chuckle a bit at such a shopworn gag. Same goes for the second and third. By the fourth or fifth, you're perhaps finding the gag a little tedious. By the seventh or eighth thwack, though, the humour of the scene re-emerges, amplified exponentially.[16] A simple, clichéd joke has been dramatically, hilariously subverted by not subverting it at all.

Another of comedy's most common superficial hooks is the catchphrase. As *Saturday Night Live* has been demonstrating for several years now, the catchphrase can easily become a comedic crutch, drained of any real humour through overuse. Still, there is no shortage of catchphrases on *The Simpsons*: Homer has his *D'oh*s, Bart his *Ay, carumba*s and *Don't have a cow*s, Marge her worried *Hmmm*s, Mr Burns his hissed *Excellent*s. Even baby Maggie's got her pacifier slurps. But on *The Simpsons*, this tired trick has been employed carefully, sparingly, as a punctuation mark or character trait, never as an excuse for lazy writing. In fact, a full episode (1F11, 'Bart Gets Famous') mocked the very idea of catchphrase-based humour. In the episode, Bart rises to stardom – and falls just as fast – as a catchphrase-spouting drone on *The Krusty the Clown Show*. His trademark line, 'I didn't do it', ignites a pop craze, complete with talk-show appearances, merchandise tie-ins, a mindless rap song, and the addition of the 'I Didn't Do It' Dancers to Krusty's show. The episode ends with Bart back in the familiar confines of the Simpson living room, forgotten and discarded by the trend-mongering public. 'And now,' Lisa tells him, 'you can go back to just being you, instead of a one-dimensional character with a silly catchphrase.' On cue, Homer clumsily smashes a lamp. 'D'oh!' he exclaims. Bart immediately pipes up: 'Ay, carumba!' Suddenly, the room is crowded with a half-dozen other characters who spout their own catchphrases one after the other.

On *The Simpsons*, there is no shortage of standard tropes, but they inspire elaborate send-ups like this one, not formulaic overuse. Elsewhere, such tried-and-true humour might be employed to resuscitate a fossilised schtick or used as a vehicle for one of the show's patented obscure references. Or both. Consider the often-lifeless comic technique of massive hyperbole. On *The Simpsons*, for example, Homer's boss, Mr Burns, is ludicrously elderly, setting up countless jokes about just how unbelievably old he is. This could easily veer into the dreary territory of a by-the-numbers talk-show monologue, but for the inventive arcana brought in to demonstrate Burns's advanced age. One of the finest of these moments occurs in Episode 3F14 ('Homer the Smithers'), in which Burns's sycophantic assistant Smithers takes a vacation, leaving Burns to fend for himself. We soon find Burns at his desk, answering his phone for the first time in a very, *very* long time. 'Ahoy-hoy?' he says, upon picking up the receiver. This greeting, as historians of communications technology might know and diligent viewers of *The Simpsons* would figure out, was telephone inventor Alexander Graham Bell's suggestion for the standard greeting to be intoned upon answering a call on his new device.[17] Thomas Edison's neologism – *Hello* – would eventually win the day, however, and Bell's choice would gather a century of dust until Mr Burns came along to revive it. And to demonstrate just how far *The Simpsons* is willing to go to revive a tired gag.

More than anything, though, it's the show's density that saves it from ever letting its surface humour become one-note. If a catchphrase is intoned or a head slammed into an overhanging beam, it will likely as not be part of a larger series or an elaborate parody or a broader episode-length satire, or else it will be followed by another joke of another kind altogether. There's simply never any downtime for jokes to get tired in. This points to one of the show's finest bits of recurring surface humour: the one-off gag. This is often a background detail or non sequitur, a quick tangent flawlessly integrated into the show to keep the comedic energy high. A representative example: midway through Episode 9F06 ('New Kid on the Block'), we find Bart and Lisa's new babysitter – a hip, tomboyish girl named Laura – on the phone to Springfield's underappreciated Afghani restaurant, ordering exotic takeout food for their dinner. Cut to an empty restaurant with a sign reading TWO GUYS FROM KABUL, where two brooding Afghani men glare at each other over a desk. There is a perfect pregnant pause, and then one barks at the other, 'Sometimes I think you *want* to fail!' Then the phone rings, and the two guys from Kabul wrestle over it as the episode continues along its merry way. In tone, in timing, in realistic detail – across the board – this is a perfect comedic vignette.

Sometimes golden one-offs like this are used merely as background detail, as additional density for the hardcore fans to ferret out during repeat viewings. (This is, in fact, a key reason why *The Simpsons* has been such a mammoth success in syndication: each viewing is a revelation.) Again, a single telling example of a common Simpsonian phenomenon: in Episode 8F04 ('Homer Defined'), we find the Simpsons at their breakfast table. Homer is reading a newspaper called *US of A Today* – a set-up for a quick gag about the dumbed-down and relentlessly boosterish American national newspaper *USA Today*. Lisa voices a criticism of the paper, and Homer replies: 'This is the only paper in America that's not afraid to tell the truth – that everything is just fine.' This is something of a one-off in itself, but the remarkable bit of densifying detail is the headline of the paper he's holding, which is a perfect take on *USA Today*'s brand of chirpy non-news. 'America's Favorite Pencil', the headline reads. '#2 Is #1.'

The surface-level one-off gag is also an ongoing testament to *The Simpsons*' mastery of the humorous non sequitur. Indeed one of the show's most beloved minor characters – Ralph Wiggum, Springfield Elementary's seven-year-old non-sequitur-generating machine – sends the show off at an oblique angle or two every time he opens his mouth. Dim little Ralph is always ready with an oddball line, something like 'Me fail English? That's unpossible!' or 'Oh, boy – sleep! That's where I'm a Viking!' But Ralph's penchant for nonsensical utterances has also produced inspired one-offs, such as the time in Episode 1F18 ('Sweet Seymour Skinner's Baadasssss Song') that he notices Bart Simpson's dog (brought to school for show and tell) crawling by in the classroom's heating vent. 'Um, Miss Hoover?' Ralph pipes up. 'There's a dog in the vent.' Miss Hoover, wearily: 'Ralph, remember the time you said Snagglepuss was outside?' Ralph, in his trademark matter-of-fact tone: 'He was going to the bathroom.' (For the uninitiated, Snagglepuss was an anthropomorphic pink lion in bow tie and French cuffs who starred in the Hanna-Barbera cartoons of the 1960s and was best known for the catchphrase 'Heavens to Murgatroid!')

It's not just Ralph, either. In the service of an absurdist one-off, Homer's father, Abe, might fall into a dream in which he's Queen of the Old West, with the makeup and garters to prove it. Or a fight might break out down at Moe's Tavern over who was the best prime minister in British history (Barney the drunk says Lord Palmerston, baseball legend Wade Boggs votes for Pitt the Elder). Or Homer might come into Burns's office while Burns is stoned to the bejesus on ether and ask him to sponsor his (Homer's) bowling team, and Burns might mistake Homer for Poppin' Fresh, the spokesblob for Pillsbury-brand frozen pastries, whose 'tubes of triple-bleached goo' gave Burns his robust physique, and Burns might then write Homer a cheque, and later, sober, Burns might discover it and wonder why he'd written a cheque for bowling, and then Burns's bootlick Smithers might notice that the memo on the cheque reads 'To my pal Poppin' Fresh', and Smithers might then run the data through a computer to see which employees of the power plant could possibly have passed for Poppin' Fresh, and before the computer settles on Homer Simpson, it might first find a partial match with the greatest one-off *Simpsons* character of all time, one Pops Freshenmeyer,[18] whose file photo reveals him to be a cartoonish Germanic janitor with a push-broom moustache. Yes, something like that might happen in the service of a tangential *Simpsons* gag.

2. Referential humour

It is a truism of contemporary pop culture that it is highly derivative, preternaturally self-aware, hyper-allusive. Postmodern, to employ an oft-muddied term properly. Some of it can indeed appear to be nothing more than a scattershot collage of references to other things: bits of pop-cultural esoterica, bygone moments in time, big ideas and long-abandoned theories so deeply embedded in our culture that we might not even know where they originally came from. It follows, then, that *The Simpsons* – as an astute and realistic documentarian of its age – overflows with allusion and reference and name-checking of phenomena both recent and archaic. In fact, the show is a sprawling study in postmodernist self-reference and a ground-breaking, pace-setting practitioner of the unique brand of comedy – let's call it 'referential humour' – produced by postmodern culture. Such referential humour is so central to *The Simpsons* that it deserves its own chapter. (Good thing, then, that I've included one: Chapter 10.)

For now, it should be sufficient to note that referential humour is a core tool in the show's comedy and a key component of its satire. And, quickly, to take a look at a couple of prime examples of the phenomenon – one a blink-and-you'll-miss-it incidental gag, the other an extended, multipronged parody.

First, the incidental gag. It's nothing more than some set-dressing for Episode 9F11 ('Selma's Choice'), a background detail as the Simpsons stop for a quick bite to eat on their way to the funeral of Marge's Aunt Gladys. As they pull up to the restaurant, we catch a glimpse of a sign that reads: THE BUZZING SIGN DINER. The lettering is in neon; the sign is buzzing. The gag is built on the hoary cliché of old-time Hollywood that every grimy diner has a run-down, buzzing neon sign out front. The sign's message refers to its own condition, and that condition refers to a phenomenon that's a stereotypical element of old movies. It's a deconstruction of a deconstruction of a cliché. This single incidental detail serves as a concise, workable summary of what's meant by the term 'postmodern'.

The extended parody occurs in Episode 8F18 ('A Streetcar Named Marge'). In the episode, Marge lands a part in a community theatre production of a play called *Oh! Streetcar!* – a musical adaptation of Tennessee

Williams's *A Streetcar Named Desire* – and she has to enrol Maggie in daycare so she can attend rehearsals. Maggie winds up at the Ayn Rand School for Tots, a daycare centre built on the austere, hyper-individualistic philosophical principles of Ayn Rand (best known for her novels *The Fountainhead* and *Atlas Shrugged*). Signs on the walls of the daycare centre read A IS A and HELPING IS FUTILE, misbehaviour is sternly punished by solitary confinement, and parental substitutes – especially pacifiers – are strictly forbidden. All of this is consistent with the extreme self-reliance advocated by Rand (and more fanatically by her latter-day disciples). The confiscation of the pacifiers, meanwhile, sets up the second layer of the parody: an extended homage to *The Great Escape* in which pacifier-dependent Maggie and her fellow tots rig up an elaborate, marvellously inventive scheme to sneak Maggie into the school director's office to retrieve their pacifiers, which plays out to *The Great Escape*'s famous theme music. Post-liberation, Maggie tosses the pacifiers to her co-conspirators like candy at a VE Day parade, and the floor of the vast main hall of the Ayn Rand School for Tots is soon filled with babies contentedly munching on their pacifiers, setting up the final parody inspired by this subplot. When Homer arrives to pick up Maggie, he's confronted with a preternaturally quiet room full of tots, their eyes following him carefully, the slurping sounds of their pacifier-sucking echoing eerily in the large room. Homer tiptoes through the maze of babies, retrieves Maggie and backs out cautiously – finishing this absurd, babies-as-predatory-birds allusion to the climactic scene in Alfred Hitchcock's *The Birds*.

So there you have it: in a minor subplot about Maggie's adventures in daycare, we're given a wicked parody of Ayn Rand's philosophy and hilarious, note-perfect homages to Steve McQueen and Hitchcock.

And that, for now, is all you really need to know about just how expertly *The Simpsons* employs referential humour.

3. The good joke, better joke principle

One of the most widely held theories used to answer the simple but enigmatic question of why humans laugh is called 'incongruity theory'. As Tad Friend explains in a 2002 *New Yorker* article, the theory traces its roots to seventeenth-century philosopher Blaise Pascal, who observed, 'Nothing produces laughter more than a surprising disproportion between that which one expects and that which one sees.'

According to incongruity theory, [Friend writes] in the joke 'I went to my doctor for shingles – he sold me aluminum siding,' our (tiny) pleasure arises in two stages: surprise and then coherence. The seeming story line of the joke (the doctor will treat shingles, the disease) collapses, but we instantly realise that the anomaly can be explained by another story line (the doctor sells shingles, the product).

But there is, Friend notes, a more recent theory, put forward by an Austrian psychologist named Willibald Ruch, that argues for the existence of a third stage. Here's Friend, paraphrasing Ruch:

> In this new wrinkle on incongruity theory, the third stage is 'detecting that actually what makes sense . . . is pleasant nonsense,' that 'the ability to "make sense," to solve problems, has been "misused" – and this feeling is generally associated with pleasure.' This third-stage realisation, Ruch says, is what makes us laugh.

Or, more precisely, while the second stage of the process might make us titter, the third stage is what makes us *really* bust a gut. It's only a theory, of course, but *The Simpsons* is in many ways a long-form proof of it, inasmuch as there's probably never been another comedic enterprise that's milked as much humour from incongruity as *The Simpsons* has.

Ironic juxtaposition, the inversion of expectation, the twisting and bending of long-standing cultural forms into clever new shapes – these are as central to *The Simpsons*' humour as Homer's stupidity. In Episode 1F13 ('Deep Space Homer'), for example, an inversion of a common conversational tic's expected implication gives rise to one of the finest single comic lines in the show's history. The line comes at the end of a gruelling competition between Homer and Barney to see which one NASA will select as the token blue-collar slob on its next manned mission to space. 'Gentlemen,' a NASA official tells them, 'you've both worked very hard, and in a way, you're both winners. But in another, more accurate way, Barney's the winner.'

At their full-bore riffing best, these sorts of gags are responsible for a Simpsonian phenomenon I'll call the 'Good Joke, Better Joke Gag' – that is, a gag sequence in which the first (more obvious, more expected) good joke is spun into another or even several more (unexpected, incongruous) better jokes. A bit of absurdist wordplay, for example, might set up a quick, expectation-inverting tangent – as it does in Episode 1F07 ('The Last Temptation of Homer') when Homer becomes smitten with a sexy new co-worker. He heads down to Moe's Tavern for some discreet, bartenderly advice about his romantic quandary. 'See,' Homer says to Moe, 'I've got this friend named . . . ' He pauses, obviously hunting for a plausible pseudonym. 'Joey Jo-Jo . . . Junior . . . Shabadoo . . . ' Moe, not buying the ruse, cuts him off: 'That's the worst name I ever heard.' A man sitting at the bar jumps to his feet, bursts into tears and flees in shame. Barney calls sympathetically after him, 'Hey! Joey Jo-Jo!'

More elaborate are the show's many sequences in which a single gag is reiterated several different ways, reaching higher peaks each time. Each new peak is a surprise, and the impact is cumulative: the final gag in a Good Joke, Better Joke sequence is much funnier than it would be on its own, and exponentially funnier than the first in the series. A case study: in Episode 1F07, there's a sequence of events that demonstrates Mr Burns's disdain for the safety of his workers and the lawfulness of his power plant. It begins after a particularly flagrant abuse of safety regulations draws the attention of the Department of Labor, which sends a gaggle of agents to descend into the plant on ropes to accost Burns. (A subtle Good Joke, playing on the drab image of government bureaucrats.) 'This man is an illegal alien!' declares one of the agents, pointing to the swarthy-looking drone next to Burns. 'That's preposterous!' Burns fumes. 'Zutroy here is as American as apple pie.' Zutroy then bleats out a few syllables in some odd, utterly unintelligible accent. (Better Joke.) Another agent points out that they found a missing Brazilian soccer team working in the plant's reactor core. 'That plane crashed on *my* property!' Burns rages. (Better Joke squared.) Finally, the officials demand to see changes – a female employee, for starters. 'All right,' Burns reluctantly concedes. 'I'll bring in a woman. But I still stand by my hiring policies.' The moment Burns finishes this declaration, a duck waddles by, clad in a hard hat and dragging a wagon. The duck quacks plaintively. 'Get back to work, Stuart!' Burns barks. (Better Joke cubed.)

In a Good Joke, Better Joke sequence like this one, a momentum is built, a harmonious combination of comedic elements that come together into something that's almost symphonic. Almost.

4. Symphonic humour

If Burns's sketchy-hiring-practices sequence is merely a skilful quartet, rest assured that Simpsonian humour, at its best, is the comedic equivalent of a full symphony. Especially during the Golden Age, *Simpsons* gags sometimes display a perfection of pitch and cadence, a gemlike exquisiteness of form and a mastery of execution. These are moments of true aesthetic genius. This is symphonic humour.

These moments, though, need not be drawn out to an operetta's length, nor do they necessarily need full brass and woodwind sections. Sometimes, indeed, they are blinkingly brief. I'm thinking here of a background detail in Episode 3F21 ('Homerpalooza'), an extended parody of the alternative-rock phenomenon in early-1990s pop music in which Homer is recruited to tour as a sideshow freak with the Hullabalooza Festival, a Lollapalooza-like rock festival. Homer's recruitment occurs when he takes Bart and Lisa to check out the Springfield stop on the tour. In the first excited flush of arrival, Homer and his kids wander through a maze of merchandise stalls and non-musical attractions. As they explore, they wander past an elaborate attraction fronted by a banner that reads BUNGEE JUMP AGAINST RACISM. In four words, in the background of a scene, The Simpsons has summarised, deflated and laid to rest the uniquely vapid brand of political activism so common in the early 1990s and its intersection with faux-rebellious lifestyle trends. In four words.

On other occasions, The Simpsons can reach symphonic pitch in a one-off gag that riffs on a deeply engrained pop-cultural trope or an established sequence of Simpsonian gags – or both. A paramount example: over the years, events on the show have made it clear that Seymour Skinner, the principal of Springfield Elementary School, is a deeply scarred Vietnam veteran. In a Season 3 episode, for example, he mentions in passing that he saw 'some awful things in 'Nam' as he contemplates the defacement of the statue of the school's mascot. By Season 4, he's having full-fledged flashbacks, on one occasion breaking down over the school's public address system as he recalls the Valentine's Day massacre of his old platoon mate Johnny. This sets the stage for Skinner's extraordinary monologue in Episode 3F10 ('Team Homer'), which comes about when Bart arrives at school in a T-shirt emblazoned with the slogan DOWN WITH HOMEWORK. When Bart displays the shirt for his classmates, it inspires a full-blown riot, and he winds up in Skinner's office. 'So,' Skinner says solemnly, eyeing the T-shirt. 'We meet again, Mad magazine.' Bart asks him how he knows where it came from. Skinner walks to his office window. And there, stage-lit by the Venetian blinds, he delivers a soliloquy:

The year was 1968. We were on recon in a steaming Mekong delta. An overheated private removed his flak jacket, revealing a T-shirt with an iron-on sporting the Mad slogan UP WITH MINI-SKIRTS. Well, we all had a good laugh, even though I didn't quite understand it. But our momentary lapse of concentration allowed Charlie to get the drop on us. I spent the next three years in a POW camp, forced to subsist on a thin stew made of fish, vegetables, prawns, coconut milk – and four kinds of rice. [With angry passion] I came close to madness trying to find it here in the States, but they *just can't get the spices right* . . .

This is a fantastic goof on the long-standing argument that the anti-authoritarian *Mad* magazine of the 1950s was a significant contributor to the social revolt of the 1960s in America. And there's a fine bit of characterisation in there: *of course* ultra-bland, ruler-straight Skinner didn't get even the crudest of 'subversive' gags. The timing, too, is superlative: the brief pause before the kicker – '*four* kinds of rice' – as Skinner explains his subsistence meal, the sudden anger as he bemoans his inability to duplicate it back home. But more than any of that, this is simply a masterful use of inverted expectation, a revelatory twist on the pop stereotype of the haunted Vietnam vet with his tales of brutal torture. For how, after all, do an increasing number of us in the West most commonly interact with Vietnam but by dining on its delicious food? How many of us – especially those of us too young to have experienced the war firsthand – now find it impossible to dehumanise the people of Vietnam and to accept their portrayal in so many movies about the war as faceless, torture-happy thugs because (at the very least) we regularly gain firsthand experience of the Vietnamese people and their culture directly at the myriad Vietnamese restaurants that dot our cityscapes? Every reference the show made to Skinner's tour of duty in Vietnam to this point was a massive set-up for this spectacular reversal. This is the sort of gag you reference in lieu of expanding your own arguments in conversation with your peers.

At their very best, *The Simpsons'* symphonic sequences find a level of looping, multilayered humour that functions so densely and on so many fronts that they achieve a kind of transcendence. There is, for example, a sequence in Episode 1F13 ('Deep Space Homer') that's quite simply among the finest comedic moments in the history of television. It utilises sight gags and ironic juxtapositions and comic allusions. It's got a satirical layer, some parody, several unexpected incongruities. It begins with 'average-naut' Homer in outer space, tearing open a bag of Ruffles potato chips. The chips float off in all directions in the zero-gravity cabin. Race Banyon, one of Homer's fellow astronauts, notes anxiously that they could clog the instruments. The other – Buzz Aldrin – has a bigger worry. 'Careful!' he exclaims in horror. 'They're ruffled!' Homer springs into action, releasing his safety belt and floating gracefully around the capsule to devour the bobbing chips, his elegant journey an homage to the spacecraft ballet in Stanley Kubrick's *2001: A Space Odyssey*. It looks like Homer's saved the day, but then he accidentally smashes into the capsule's experimental ant colony, sending ants and shards of glass careening throughout the cabin (and possibly ruining forever NASA's chances of determining whether ants can be taught to sort tiny screws in space). Cut to mission control down on terra firma, where a NASA official informs the astronauts that the musician James Taylor is going to play them some of his own brand of laidback adult-contemporary music. And so the chaotic scene inside the capsule is set to the serene strains of Taylor's 'Fire and Rain'.

Then cut to Kent Brockman with continuing coverage of the space mission. After a quick intro, Brockman goes live to the space capsule – just as one of the free-floating ants bobs by inches in front of the camera lens, filling the screen. Brockman wastes no time in jumping to conclusions. In grave tones, he sums up the scene:

> Ladies and gentlemen, uh, we've just lost the picture, but, uh, what we've seen speaks for itself. The Corvair spacecraft has apparently been taken over – 'conquered,' if you will – by a master race of giant space ants. It's difficult to tell from this vantage point whether they will consume the captive Earthmen or merely enslave them. One thing is for certain: there is no stopping them – the ants will soon be here. [*Turns to second camera, then somewhat jovially*] And I, for one, welcome our new insect overlords. I'd like to remind them that as a trusted TV personality I can be helpful in rounding up others to toil in their underground sugar caves.

It's worth noting that towards the end of Brockman's treasonous commentary, an artist's depiction of his sci-fi scenario appears over his shoulder. It should be noted, too, that this whole sequence transpires in less than three minutes, and that the episode continues along at this breakneck pace and further elaborates some of the gags. (When we return to Brockman's anchor desk a few scenes later, for example, there's a hand-lettered sign taped up on the wall behind him that reads HAIL ANTS.)

There's a lot more that could be noted about this sequence, and about this episode. Here's one last thing: it's certainly one of the strongest episodes of *The Simpsons*, no doubt about it. Definitely in the Top Five. But it's not the best episode ever.

SATIRICAL ANATOMY (III): BEST. EPISODE. EVER.

Drum roll please. (Actually, before we get down to it, I should mention that I was firm in the following judgement well before *Entertainment Weekly* went and made the same pick for best-ever *Simpsons* episode. I can produce witnesses.) Ahem. Drum roll please. The best episode of *The Simpsons* ever made – the one that most deftly combines all the many elements of its expansive setting and skewed realism and enduring characterisation and stinging satire – is Episode 9F15 ('Last Exit to Springfield').[19]

And in light of this honour, let's examine 9F15 in its entirety, shall we?

TV Guide summarised the plot thusly: 'Homer's brain serves him well in negotiations with Burns over the union dental plan, which is of great importance to the braces-bound Lisa. Dr Joyce Brothers has a cameo.' The episode tells the tale of Homer's short-lived job as union president during a heated labour dispute at the Springfield Nuclear Power Plant. It is sometimes called 'the strike episode'.

Note first that the title of this episode – 'Last Exit to Springfield' – is a play on *Last Exit to Brooklyn*, Hubert Selby's scathing literary portrait of twentieth-century labour relations. In addition to being funny practically from first frame to last, the episode is a veritable primer in twentieth-century labour history. It references Depression-era folk songs, Jimmy Hoffa-era thuggery, and modern-day corruption and decay. The episode mocks the American health-care system and British oral-hygiene habits. There are references to *Citizen Kane*, *Batman*, the Three Stooges, The Beatles and Dr Seuss. Episode 9F15 of *The Simpsons* should be taught in schools. In history, economics, social studies, literature *and* art classes. It's flawless.

The only thing about 9F15 that's less than full-blown genius is its opening credits. As with every other episode of *The Simpsons*, 9F15's credits feature a 'chalkboard gag' (the line Bart's writing on the chalkboard as the credit sequence begins) and a 'couch gag' (a twist of events that befalls the Simpson family at the end of every credit sequence as they converge on their living-room couch to watch TV). This episode's chalkboard gag is surprisingly flat: MUD IS NOT ONE OF THE 4 FOOD GROUPS. This in a space that's featured everything from far cleverer kiddie humour (THERE WAS NO ROMAN GOD NAMED 'FARTACUS') to political punditry (FIVE DAYS IS NOT TOO LONG TO WAIT FOR A GUN) to arch self-reference (I AM NOT A 32-YEAR-OLD WOMAN). Its couch gag, meanwhile, is fun if unspectacular: the couch transforms into a tentacled brown monster that swallows the Simpsons up as they settle into it. (By way of example of an inspired couch gag, one of them has the family entering the living room and running to the couch on different planes, as if moving through an M.C. Escher painting.)

As soon as 9F15 gets underway, however, all vestiges of mediocrity are quickly eradicated. It opens with a broad satire of ultraviolent, under-intelligent action movies – some formulaic clunker in which a mustachioed arch-villain named Mendoza is holding a lavish dinner party to introduce his 'most diabolical creation, Swank – ten times more addictive than marijuana'. (A clever shot in passing at American war-on-drugs rhetoric, marijuana having been proven non-addictive in countless scientific studies.) The moment after Mendoza raises a toast to human misery, however, muscled action hero McBain suddenly explodes out of the ice sculpture on the banquet table and immediately utters a Teutonically accented line of stereotypical dry cool wit: '*Ice* to see you.' McBain then opens fire with an Uzi, annihilating everyone in the room, including the cellist who was playing the dinner music, and leaving only Mendoza unharmed. Alas, our hero is felled by a poisoned salmon puff, collapsing to the floor as Mendoza bursts into maniacal laughter.

Cut to the Simpson living room, where Homer tells Bart that no one in real life could possibly be that evil. Then cut to the office of nuclear-plant titan C. Montgomery Burns, who's midway through a maniacal laugh identical to Mendoza's as he watches a labourer dangling from a scaffolding outside his enormous office window. It turns out Burns is waiting for a representative from the union that defends the nuclear plant's workers. The rep is late. 'He hasn't been seen,' Burns's lackey Smithers notes, 'since he promised to clean up the union.' Cut quickly to a football game, where a player trips over a pile of raised earth in the shape of a human body – an allusion to the long-standing rumour that postwar Teamsters boss Jimmy Hoffa was killed by the Mafia and buried under a football stadium that was then under construction in New Jersey. Cut back to the power plant, where Burns is going over the new union contract. Outraged at its myriad benefits and perks, he's sent into a reverie about how much better it was in the old days.

And so cut to a magnificent flashback, a dense thirty-second précis of labour relations during the industrial revolution in America. It's Springfield in 1909, and a curly haired, lollipop-licking Burns is accompanying his grandfather to his atom-smashing factory. Burns the elder finds a few stray atoms in a departing worker's pocket lint and has him carried off by his goons. As the kid is dragged away, he calls back in the squeaky voice used for generic service-industry drones in modern-day Springfield: 'You can't treat the working man this way. One day we'll form a union and get the fair and equitable treatment we deserve! Then we'll go too far, and get corrupt and shiftless, and the Japanese will eat us alive!'

'The Japanese?' Burns the elder retorts xenophobically. 'Those sandal-wearing goldfish tenders? Bosh! Flimshaw!' Burns, back in present day, tells

Smithers ruefully, 'We should have listened to that boy, instead of walling him up in the abandoned coke oven.'

In a series of short, snappy scenes, it transpires that Burns has arbitrarily cut the dental plan from his plant's union contract and Lisa Simpson has learned that she needs braces. Along the way, poor Ralph Wiggum has been made to look through *The Big Book of British Smiles* (a series of headshots of smiling Britons with crooked, chipped and rotten teeth), and Bart has briefly lapsed into the diction of a turn-of-the-century carny.

It has presumably become apparent by now that, even by the lofty standards of *The Simpsons*, Episode 9F15 is black-hole dense with plot, characterisation and gaggery. That's one of the things that separates it from garden-variety Simpsonian genius: not only is the episode an almost-uninterrupted string of great jokes, but every shot in this comedic barrage serves to further the plot, or at least keep it moving along at warp speed.

Next up is a meeting of Local 643 of the International Brotherhood of Jazz Dancers, Pastry Chefs and Nuclear Technicians. After everyone laughs heartily at the notion that their absentee union rep is anything other than six feet under, the assembled membership quickly agrees to trade its dental plan for a free keg of beer at every meeting. As Homer waits in line for his complimentary Duff, however, a realisation slowly dawns on him. Slowly, slowly, *slowly* dawns on him: again and again, Homer hears Lenny's voice calling out, 'Dental plan', then Marge's voice saying, 'Lisa needs braces.' Homer stands, his face a blank slate, as these two phrases rattle around for eight full repetitions. (Like Sideshow Bob's encounter with numerous rakes, it only starts to get funny by around number five, but by the eighth one, it's just hilarious.) Finally, Homer realises that losing the dental plan will mean he'll have to pay for Lisa's braces, and he springs into action to rally his union brothers against the deal. This sets up an absurd one-off in which Homer asks one of his co-workers, Gummy Joe, where he'd be without the dental plan. Gummy Joe turns out to be a grizzled old man in knee breeches, undershirt and floppy hat – a nineteenth-century gold prospector who nonetheless apparently works at Springfield Nuclear Power Plant – and he calls back to Homer, 'Well, I wouldn't have old Chomper here, that's for sure.' Then he uses old Chomper, his one remaining tooth, to poke open a can of pop. In a remarkable feat of comedic balance, Gummy Joe somehow doesn't derail the satirical realism – we seamlessly return to the vote on the union contract. It is summarily rejected, Homer is elected union president, and two beer mugs clink together to bring the first act of 9F15 to a close.

Act Two opens with the Simpsons at the breakfast table, talking over the news of Homer's rise in the ranks of organised labour – and his opportunity to make lifelong connections to the world of organised crime. 'Mmmm,' says Homer. 'Organised crime.' He then drifts into a fantasy, a send-up of *The Godfather, Part II* in which 'Don Homer', in white suit and hat, saunters through a typical street scene from New York in the 1920s, accepting special doughnuts as gifts from pushcart vendors and peasant women.

Back in real life, things roll along through a few quick cuts to Lisa's dental surgery. She's gassed for the procedure, which sets up another flawlessly executed parody, this time of The Beatles film *Yellow Submarine*. Lisa's nitrous oxide-induced trip sees her floating through a gleefully animated Day-Glo dreamscape – an excellent example of *The Simpsons'* ability, when it's warranted, to be straight-up cartoony – that ends with her drifting over a submarine-load of Beatles just before they plough into a campy drawing of Queen Victoria. ('Look, fellas,' Ringo calls as Lisa sails by, 'it's Lisa in the sky.' 'No diamonds, though,' Paul replies.) Lisa then comes to in the dentist's chair and calls maniacally – as per Jack Nicholson's Joker in *Batman* – for a mirror to see the hideous results of being fitted with braces from a time before stainless steel.

Cut now to Burns Manor, where Homer has been dragged by Burns's hired goons to talk over their contract dispute. (This scene opens, incidentally, with Burns in a lavish aviary feeding a vulture in a blink-and-miss-it allusion to *Citizen Kane*.) Burns starts off the proceedings by giving Homer a tour of his enormous mansion, precipitating one of the greatest one-off gags in *Simpsons* history: Burns shows Homer a special room in which a thousand harried, chain-smoking, overworked-writer monkeys are furiously pecking away at a thousand typewriters. Burns tears a sheet from one of the typewriters. '"It was the best of times, it was the *blurst* of times"?' Burns reads. 'You stupid monkey!' Burns crumples the paper and hurls it at the monkey, who has missed the opening sentence of Charles Dickens's *A Tale of Two Cities* by three letters. During the negotiations, Homer's pressing need to urinate leads Burns to think he's too tough to crack. So Burns flies Homer back to the Simpson home by helicopter, promises to crush him like a bug, falls out of said helicopter, gets airlifted off on a gurney (again threatening to crush Homer like a bug), and only abandons his diabolical laughter when his gurney rams into the chimney of a nearby house. There follows a union meeting and a vote to strike, and finally Act Two is over.

The final act opens at the plant gate, where Lisa strums a guitar and sings a 1930s-style pro-union folk song. Burns looks down on the scene from his Eva Perón-style balcony, and orders Smithers to bring him some Depression-style strikebreakers. He gets what he asked for: an office full of tired senior citizens, including Homer's father, Abe, who launches into a meandering monologue that's probably his finest comedic turn ever:

> We can't bust heads like we used to, but we have our ways. One of them is to tell 'em stories that don't go anywhere. Like the time I caught the ferry to Shelbyville? I needed a new heel for m'shoe. So I decided to go to Morganville, which is what we called Shelbyville in those days. So I tied an onion to my belt – which was the style at the time. Now, to take the ferry cost a nickel. And in those days, nickels had pictures of bumblebees on them. 'Gimme five bees for a quarter,' you'd say. Now where were we? Oh yeah. The important thing is that I had an onion tied to my belt – which was the style at the time. They didn't have white onions because of the war. All you could get was those big yellow ones . . .

Exhausted by this monologue, Burns tries another tack – he sets upon the mob with a firehose, setting up a sight gag in which the force of the water sends him flying into the air. Meanwhile, Lisa reprises her protest song and does a quick run-through of 'Classical Gas' for Lenny.

Cut now to a gaily animated sequence of Burns and Smithers running the plant themselves, set to a jovial soundtrack out of a 1940s comedy. And then cut to an episode of Kent Brockman's award-winning current affairs programme *Smartline*, where the night's topic is 'The Power Plant Strike: Argle-Bargle or Fooforah?' After being advised not to talk to union kingpin Homer Simpson, Brockman hands the programme over to Burns for his requested opening tirade. Burns threatens to wreak a terrible vengeance on Springfield, from which no one will be spared. 'A chilling vision of things to come,' Brockman cheerfully summarises. And so cut to the power plant, and to a magnificent escalating-irony gag in which Burns and Smithers pass through a series of locked doors and secret passages (lifted from the opening sequence of the 1960s sitcom *Get Smart*) to get to the room containing the plant's master switch, only to find that the room's rickety screen door is unlocked, half off its hinges and open to the outside world, and that a stray dog is squatting there. Undaunted, Burns quotes *Moby Dick* – 'from hell's heart I stab at thee' – and then shuts off the power to the whole town. In downtown Springfield, rioting and looting commence immediately, and a crowd of townsfolk gathers around a fully lit, scrolling LED sign displaying the message TOTAL BLACKOUT IN SPRINGFIELD in bright electric lights. (Do note the molasses-thick irony.[20])

Okay. Take a deep breath. We've reached the climax, the big finish, the splendiferously brilliant referential gag that's going to top off this extraordinary episode. Here it comes: plunged into darkness, the protesters pause; then Lisa starts strumming her guitar, and they launch once again into song. The sound of their singing fades into the background as we pan up to Burns's balcony, where he steps to the edge and cocks an ear. His malevolent smile is just a bit over-wide, his eyes a touch droopier than usual, turning him into a dead ringer for one of the greatest cartoon villains of all time: the Grinch, from Dr Seuss's *How the Grinch Stole Christmas*. Hearing the voices of the protesters, Burns out-Seusses Seuss: 'Look at them all, through the darkness I'm bringing. They're not sad at all – they're actually *singing*!' He pulls Smithers's face to his with a tug of his bootlick's tie. 'They sing without juicers.' (Pause, push away, consider, tug again on the tie.) 'They sing without blenders.' (Pause, push, consider, tug, deliver perfect final line.) 'They sing without flunjers, capdabblers and smendlers!'

Burns is now ready to deal, so he meets in a boardroom with Homer and gives the union back its dental plan in exchange for Homer stepping down as its head. Homer falls to the floor, whoop-whoop-whoop-whooping like Curly the Stooge as he spins in a circle. Burns notes that Homer's not the brilliant tactician he thought he was. Around Springfield, the lights come back on; the neon signs of the nudie clubs flash luridly once again; the spout down at Fake Vomit Inc. resumes splatting out puddles of imitation puke. And Lisa, wearing fancy new braces, is joined in the dentist's office by her whole family. 'Oh, honey,' Marge notes happily, 'you can hardly see your new braces.' Lisa, button-cute: 'And that's the tooth!'

All of them laugh heartily at the pun, in a broad parody of the way 1970s sitcoms would end with the whole cast gathered and giggling over the crazy adventure they'd just had. Pause for a beat. The dentist speaks up: 'Oops – I left the gas on.' Everyone laughs heartily once again. Fade to credits.

And that, folks, is about the finest, funniest half-hour in TV history.

And that's the tooth.

(Wait a beat.)

(Tumbleweed blows by.)

Well, fine, then – you think up a wittier ending for *your* big sprawling semi-exhaustive overview of the life and times of *The Simpsons*.

Ach. Ingrates.

NOTES & MARGINALIA

1. **Homer's voice change:** Throughout the *Ullman* shorts and on into the first season of *The Simpsons*, Homer's voice had a markedly different timbre from the signature sound that has come to characterise him since. Voice actor Dan Castellaneta – Homer's voice since day one – originally modelled Homer on the perennially crusty Hollywood actor Walter Matthau. Homer debuted with a somewhat thin, sort of jovially world-weary dum-dee-do tone in unagitated moments, and a gruff, menacing growl for his frequent rages. Over the first few seasons of the show, Homer's voice morphed into its now-famous tone – broader and suggesting naïveté and simple cluelessness instead of beaten-down exhaustion, with his agitated voice just a touch less growling. The overall effect of the voice change? Homer comes across more like a duped victim than an enraged antagonist.

2. **Something ribald, no doubt:** The many missteps that characterised the Fox Network's early years are the stuff of bad-TV legend. Some classic Fox flops:

- *Second Chance:* A family sitcom about a dead man sent back to earth to help his younger self make better choices. Starred future *Friend* Matthew Perry as the younger self. Lasted nine episodes in autumn 1987.
- *The New Adventures of Beans Baxter:* An action-packed hour-long drama that followed the (new) adventures of an average kid from Kansas named Beans Baxter as he tried to free his international-man-of-mystery father from the clutches of the Underground Government Liberation Intergroup (U.G.L.I.), led by the dastardly Mr Sue. Not to be confused with *The Original Adventures of Beans Baxter,* which doesn't exist. Lasted 15 episodes in the fall of 1987.
- *Mr. President:* A sitcom about life in the White House, starring George C. Scott as a bumbling Mr President. Made a 1999 *New York Post* list of the 20 worst TV shows of all time. Barely limped through the summer of 1987 before being cancelled.
- *Werewolf:* An hour-long drama tracking the misadventures of a collegiate American werewolf. Lasted a full season – 1987–88. Those were the days.

3. **A case study in eternal vigilance:** As part of an onstage appearance at the National Film Theatre in London, England, in 2000, Matt Groening read some of his favourite directives from Fox's censors, noting that 'in almost every case' *The Simpsons'* producers have been victorious in their efforts to reject said directives. Some of the Fox censors' greatest hits:

- 'To discourage imitation by young and foolish viewers, when Homer begins to pour the hot wax in his mouth, please have him scream in pain so kids will understand that doing this would actually burn their mouths.'
- 'Although it is only a dream, please do not show Homer holding a sign that reads KILL MY BOY.'
- 'After Marge turns off the light, please substitute a line that's more general, such as 'get away from me' or 'stop that,' instead of 'get off me.'
- 'In Act Three, when Marge worries that Bart may become jealous of newborn Lisa, Homer's previously unscripted line 'Bart can kiss my hairy yellow butt' is not acceptable; we believe this crude phrase plays as especially coarse since it is directed at a two-year-old child.'
- 'Bart's line 'Sod off!' and Willie's rejoinder 'I'll give you something to sod off about!' are not acceptable. This phrase refers to sodomy in spite of your set-up about resodding the lawn.'
- 'It will not be acceptable for Itchy to stab Scratchy in the guts and yank his intestine out and use it as a bungee cord.'

4. **Drug czar has cow, man:** On 16 May 1990, William Bennett toured a drug-treatment centre in Pittsburgh, Pennsylvania. Noticing a poster of Bart Simpson on the wall, Bennett turned to the assembled drug addicts and said, 'You guys aren't watching *The Simpsons*, are you? That's not going to help you any.' Of course not. What they needed – as Bennett himself would demonstrate by example later in the decade – was an $8-million gambling habit.

5. **Everybody's doing it:** The ever-changing and oft-vapid lifestyle trends that so dominate contemporary Western culture have on several occasions come in for vicious parody on *The Simpsons* itself. Possibly the finest of these moments: In Episode 9F02 ('Lisa the Beauty

Queen'), Lisa watches the local news, ruefully waiting for a story about the girl who defeated her in the Little Miss Springfield beauty pageant. A voice-over intones : 'Coming up next, a new fad that's sweeping the nation – wasting food!' A clip then shows a man poised above a garbage can in an alleyway, proudly holding aloft a whole roast turkey on a platter. He dumps the bird gleefully into the garbage can, then produces a full carton of milk and proceeds to pour it into the can on top of the turkey. End teaser clip.

6. **A lexical note:** On numerous occasions in *Simpsons* history, the residents of Springfield have been referred to as 'Springfieldians'. In Episode 2F11 ('Bart's Comet'), however, Marge reads aloud the following news item from the *Springfield Shopper*: 'A young Springfieldianite has discovered a new comet, to be known as the "Bart Simpson Comet".' Given that the *Shopper* is most certainly the journal of record in Springfield, and given also that *Springfieldianite* is way funnier than the milquetoast *Springfieldian*, from here on out when referring to the town's residents, I'll use *Springfieldianite*.

7. **Three more fine specimens of the Simpsonian dream sequence:**

(a) In Episode 1F08 ('$pringfield (Or, How I Learned To Stop Worrying and Love Legalized Gambling)'), Homer berates Marge for her opposition to legalised gambling at a recent town meeting. When Marge insists that she spoke in favour of gambling at the meeting, Homer won't back down, noting that he has a 'photographic memory'. In the snapshot of said photographic memory that follows, Homer's recollection of the audience at the meeting includes a man with a penguin perched atop his head, a woman whose head bobs to and fro on a spring like a jack-in-the-box, and an alligator decked out in a burgundy suit.

(b) In Episode 9F05 ('Marge Gets a Job'), Lisa compares her parents working alongside each other at the power plant to Marie and Pierre Curie toiling together to discover radium. The scene dissolves into Bart's version of the life of the Curies, in which the radium they discovered has transformed them into towering monsters with deadly laser beams shooting from their eyes who terrorise downtown Tokyo Godzilla-style.

(c) In Episode 2F05 ('Lisa on Ice'), Lisa frets over what will become of her if the public learns of her failing grade in gym class. Dissolve to her nightmare: she's being sworn in as president of the United States, but the F in gym is discovered, and she's banished to the aptly named Monster Island, where she's pursued by a gaggle of giant fire-breathing beasts. (The sequence's best gag actually isn't visual: as an official condemns Lisa to her fate, he tells her not to worry, that Monster Island is 'just a name'. As Lisa flees the pursuing monsters, she exclaims, 'He said it was just a name!' A man fleeing alongside her replies, 'What he meant is that Monster Island is actually a peninsula.')

8. **The real Krusty the Clown:** The inspiration for Krusty the Clown was a TV clown named Rusty Nails who had a kids' show in Portland, Oregon, when Matt Groening was a kid. Rusty was a Christian clown who hosted a variety show that (among other things) aired old *Three Stooges* shorts. In a 2003 radio interview, Groening noted that it was more the name than the personality of Rusty Nails that inspired hard-living Krusty: 'He [Rusty Nails] was very nice, a very nice guy and a very sweet clown. But he had that name, Rusty Nails, which I found incredibly disturbing as a child because, you know, you're supposed to avoid rusty nails.'

9. **Best sideshow ever:** Though sideshows Bob and Mel get all the screen time, the most inspired sideshow gag might well be a one-off in Episode 9F13 ('I Love Lisa'). It occurs as part of the gala special broadcast to commemorate the 29th anniversary of Krusty's show, featuring clips of great moments in the past. At one point, Krusty introduces an old clip thus: 'I've worked with marvellous second bananas over the years, but none more memorable than Sideshow Raheem.' Cut to an episode of Krusty's show from (apparently) the early 1970s, in which we see Krusty standing onstage next to a towering African-American in sunglasses, caftan and afro. 'Uh, the script says I'm supposed to bonk you with this,' Krusty says nervously, holding up a giant mallet. Sideshow Raheem, in a flat and mildly menacing tone, says, 'I wouldn't.' Krusty makes a peace sign and responds, 'Right on.' Then an anguished groan from Krusty, and then we're back to Krusty in the present day, commenting on the clip: 'Angry, *angry* young man.'

10. **Take *that*, Cosby:** The triumph of Simpsonian realism over Cosby-style idealism was given symbolic finality in a pair of Season 3 episodes: 8F07 ('Saturdays of Thunder') and 8F17 ('Dog of Death'). In 8F07, Homer realises he knows next to nothing about the hopes and passions of his son, so he tries his best to become a dutiful Cosby by attending the National Fatherhood Institute. At the institute, Homer is given a complimentary copy of Bill Cosby's best-selling 1986 book *Fatherhood*. Soon after, he's decked out in the signature geometric-patterned sweaters of *Cosby Show* patriarch Cliff Huxtable. Putting *Fatherhood*'s advice into practice, he helps Bart build a soapbox racer. 'Thank you, Bill Cosby!' Homer exclaims as he and Bart share this bonding moment. 'You've saved the Simpsons!' But of course the racer they build together sucks, and Bart soon rejects his dad's help. So ends Homer's attempt at Cosby-fication. In 8F17 later that season, the point is made again in a background detail: after growing frustrated with a book on home canine surgery, Homer tosses it into the fireplace, where several other books – among them Bill Cosby's *Fatherhood* – are already ablaze.

11. **The biggest farce:** Over the years, *The Simpsons* has won eight Emmy Awards for Outstanding Animated Program, ten Emmys for Outstanding Voice-Over Performance, and two Emmys for Outstanding Music and Lyrics. It has never once even been nominated, however, in the category of Outstanding Comedy Series, nor in any of the other comedy categories in which American TV sitcoms compete. This is owing to the ridiculous conservatism of the Emmys' governing body – the Academy of Television Arts & Sciences – which refuses to consider *The Simpsons* a comedy because it's animated. Thus, in the fifteen years to date that *The Simpsons* has been on the air, the Academy has determined that the following (among others) are better comedy series than *The Simpsons* has ever been: *Murphy Brown, Frasier, Ally McBeal, Sex and the City* and even *Everybody Loves Raymond*.

In the best Simpsonian fashion, the Outstanding Comedy Series of the last fifteen years has had its revenge where it matters – on the show itself. The most pointed swipe at the Emmys: in Episode 8F23 ('Brother, Can You Spare Two Dimes?'). The set-up: because working at the power plant has made Homer Simpson sterile, Mr Burns cooks up a phony award to give him to buy him off. The award, presented at a glitzy gala ceremony, is called the First Annual Montgomery Burns Award for Outstanding Achievement in the Field of Excellence. Homer's kids, attending the ceremony, take note of its speciousness. 'This award show is the biggest farce I ever saw!' says Lisa. Bart: 'What about the Emmys?' Lisa: 'I stand corrected.'

12. **Second-hand news:** So beloved is *The Simpsons*, so voluminous and varied the critical and scholarly interest, that it has overwhelmed the show's ability to respond. This, anyway, might be the reason why this quote from Groening and all other quotes from the show's creators in this book are culled from other media sources. I attempted to contact Groening and many other of the show's principal writers and producers through numerous channels – official and unofficial – to talk to them for this book, all to no avail. In every case, I was referred to a Fox official, and the Fox official's commitment to a recently introduced policy of non-cooperation with writers of books about *The Simpsons* was utterly unwavering (though friendly). There's a part of me that suspects this is a classic case of Fox overzealously guarding its intellectual property – somewhere down the line, perhaps, the behind-the-scenes story of *The Simpsons* will be told in a book published by HarperCollins (which, like Fox, is the property of Rupert Murdoch's News Corp.). For now, though, let's be generous and assume instead that the *Simpsons* team has decided simply to let the work speak for itself.

13. **Three fine examples of Simpsonian egghead humour:**
(a) The highbrow literary reference: In Episode 9F03 ('Itchy & Scratchy: The Movie'), misbehaving Bart is forbidden to see the blockbuster-hit film version of 'Itchy & Scratchy'. Desperate to experience this generation-defining event, Bart resorts to curling up with *Itchy & Scratchy: The Movie: The Novel* by Norman Mailer. He soon gives up on the book, noting that it just isn't the same thing, and drops it in a nearby trash can – where the phonebook-thick tome compacts the bin's contents in an instant. Now, to be in on this joke, you need to know that Norman Mailer has long been known for writing books that exhaustively examine the work of other prominent public figures, among them *Marilyn* (a biography of Marilyn Monroe), *Oswald's Tale* (a biography of Lee Harvey Oswald), *The Gospel According to the Son*

(a fictionalised first-person retelling of the life story of Jesus Christ), *Huckleberry Finn*, *Alive at 100* (an appreciation of Mark Twain's seminal satirical novel) and several books about Pablo Picasso. You'd also need to know that Mailer's works tend to be on the long side.

(b) The high-flown cinematic reference: In Episode 2F08 ('Fear of Flying'), Marge undergoes psychotherapy to find the origins of her fear of flying. In time, a montage of horrific aviation-related memories comes flooding back to her, including one in which she and her mother are visiting an idyllic cornfield when a biplane suddenly swoops down and opens fire on them with its machine guns. The camera angle and composition of the scene – the two characters, the cornfield, the biplane (though not the machine-gun fire) – all create a precise homage to a scene in Alfred Hitchcock's *North by Northwest*.

(c) The apparent non sequitur that actually refers to a previous episode: In Episode 9F10 ('Marge vs. the Monorail'), Homer is watching TV when a trailer comes on for a new movie: *Truckosaurus: The Movie*, starring Marlon Brando as the voice of John Truckosaurus. We see a clip that includes a very good facsimile of Brando's signature hushed delivery. A giant robotic dinosaur holds a car in its claws. 'You crazy car!' says the robotic dinosaur. 'I don't know whether to eat you or kiss you.' Long-time *Simpsons* fans will, of course, recognise the giant robotic dinosaur – Truckosaurus – as the star attraction of a monster-truck rally that the Simpsons attend in Episode 7F06 ('Bart the Daredevil').

14. **Five more beauty references to Canada that were made on *The Simpsons*:**
(a) In Episode 8F01 ('Mr. Lisa Goes to Washington'), Lisa is beaten in the national finals of *Reading Digest*'s patriotic essay contest by an adorable immigrant boy named Truong Van Dinh. The (apparently) full text of Truong's winning essay, 'USA A-OK', is as follows: 'When my family arrived in this country four months ago, we spoke no English and had no money in our pockets. Today, we own a nationwide chain of wheel-balancing centers. Where else but in America, or possibly Canada, could our family find such opportunity? That's why, whenever I see the Stars and Stripes, I will always be reminded of that wonderful word: flag!'
(b) In Episode 3F23 ('You Only Move Twice'), the Simpsons move to a posh high-tech enclave called Cypress Creek. Bart is put into a remedial class at his new school, where he's 'surrounded by arsonists and kids with mittens pinned to their jackets all year round'. Among these misfits is a boy named Gordie. Bart asks the kid why he's in the remedial class. 'I moved here from Canada, and they think I'm slow, eh?' says Gordie, in what might well be the broadest parody of a Canadian accent in the history of American pop culture.
(c) In Episode AABF03 ('Lisa Gets an "A"'), Lisa is uncharacteristically negligent in her schoolwork after becoming addicted to a videogame, and winds up having to cheat on a test. Her perfect grade earns Springfield Elementary a government grant, but at the ceremony at which the grant is bestowed, Lisa insists on announcing that she cheated. The assembled students start to boo Lisa for losing the school its grant, but State Comptroller Atkins (who later turns out to be Otto the bus driver in disguise) cuts them off and defends Lisa. 'What she just did took courage,' says Atkins. 'And where I come from – Canada – we reward courage.'
(d) In Episode DABF06 ('The Bart Wants What It Wants'), Bart embarks on a tumultuous romantic relationship with Greta, the daughter of action hero Rainier Wolfcastle. In the episode's final act, Bart and the rest of the Simpsons travel to Toronto, where Wolfcastle is shooting a movie, and where, obviously, Canadian references abound.
(e) In Episode EABF16 ('The Bart of War'), Bart and Milhouse wind up in separate troops of two rival Boy Scout-like organisations, whose fierce competition comes to a head when Bart's scouts botch a version of the American national anthem and incite a riot at a Springfield Isotopes baseball game. To staunch the flow of bad blood, Sideshow Mel makes a suggestion: 'Let us end this mindless violence and join our hands in song.' Captain McCallister – Springfield's beloved crusty sea captain – immediately agrees. 'Aye,' he says. 'Not a hymn to war, like our national anthem, but a sweet, soothing hymn, like the national anthem of Canada.' The assembled throng promptly joins hands to form the shape of a maple leaf and sings a rousing rendition of 'O Canada'.

15. **The *Simpsons*–*South Park* Mutual Admiration Society:** Midway through its sixth season, *South Park* acknowledged its debt with a full episode dedicated to singing the praises of *The*

Simpsons' enduring quality. Originally aired in June 2002, the episode ('Simpsons Already Did It') features a subplot in which an acquaintance of the *South Park* gang – a weird kid named Butters – adopts the guise of his super-villain alter ego, Professor Chaos, in order to 'wreak havoc', as he puts it, on the world that shunned him. Trouble is, as his faithful sidekick General Disarray repeatedly points out, every scheme he dreams up has already been used on *The Simpsons*. Professor Chaos plans to block out the sun. 'They did that on *The Simpsons*,' retorts General Disarray. Professor Chaos decapitates the head of a local statue, and the TV newscast reporting the incident notes that it's reminiscent of an episode of *The Simpsons*. '*The Simpsons* is a great show,' the newscaster says, 'and we all need reminders like this to keep watching.' Professor Chaos brainstorms a half-dozen other schemes, and after each one, General Disarray pipes up, '*Simpsons* did it.' By the end of the episode, everything Professor Chaos sees starts to seem Simpsonian: General Disarray starts to look like Bart, the town of South Park starts to resemble Springfield, and so on. It's only in the final scene that Professor Chaos/Butters calms down after hearing some wise words from Cartman. 'Dude,' Cartman tells him, '*The Simpsons*'ve done everything already. Who cares?'

A year later, *The Simpsons* would return the compliment in Episode EABF16 ('The Bart of War'), which opens with Bart and Milhouse avidly viewing an episode of *South Park*. Bart wonders aloud 'how they keep it so fresh after 43 episodes' – a huge underestimation of the number of *South Park*s produced to that point (about a hundred), and an echo of a line in 'Simpsons Already Did It' in which Professor Chaos claims he's watched 'all 132 episodes of *The Simpsons*, twice' (the show was approaching its 300th episode at the time). Watching a *South Park* scene rife with violence and flatulence incites Bart and Milhouse to chant 'Cartoon violence! Cartoon violence!' and spurs Marge to change the channel to something more life-affirming. It's about the highest praise *The Simpsons* could offer – the last cartoon that provoked Marge's moralistic ire was the show's very own 'Itchy & Scratchy'.

16. **Syndication cuts make Baby Jesus cry:** This is as good a place as any for a rant-cum-public-service-announcement about the scourge of godless, consumerist syndication cuts that infect reruns of *The Simpsons* like some horrible five-nights-a-week plague. The short version is this: if you've only ever seen a particular episode of *The Simpsons* in syndication, then you haven't really seen it at all. This is because the overwhelming majority of *Simpsons* episodes are edited for syndication to create room for an extra commercial or two. And this amounts to a grotesque mutilation, on a par with removing every twentieth page from a copy of *Hamlet* to insert a coupon for five cents off wax paper.

Here's why: the cuts are made in several tiny spots rather than one big one – perhaps a half-dozen snips per episode, mostly of incidental details that aren't essential to the plot. There are two common results of this practice, both of them deeply scarring. The first is that it screws up the pacing of the episode. Timing is absolutely essential to great humour – it might indeed be the single most important element, the thing that turns good material into comedic genius – and these sporadic cuts ruin *The Simpsons*' brilliant timing. In the case of Sideshow Bob's series of rake-thwacks, for example, the final two thwacks – the ones where the joke goes from laboured to absolutely hilarious – are cut in syndication.

The second consequence of syndication cuts is they are inevitably made to several of a given episode's finest moments – its funniest non sequiturs, its most brilliant one-off gags, all the great incidental-to-the-plot stuff that makes *The Simpsons* so relentlessly funny. Here's one of many egregious examples: in Episode 2F15 ('Lisa's Wedding'), the action flashes forward to Springfield in 2010 – including a glimpse of Springfield Elementary. As Principal Skinner ponders Lisa Simpson's impending nuptials, he pays a visit to her old classroom, where the desks are stacked three storeys high and a TV set at the front of the classroom is the teacher. On the TV set, actor Troy McClure poses a math question: 'Now turn to the next problem. If you have three Pepsis and drink one, how much more refreshed are you? You, the redhead in the Chicago school system?' The little girl appears in an onscreen window. She chirpily answers, 'Pepsi?' McClure, enthusiastically: 'Partial credit!' Then Skinner and Miss Hoover start discussing Lisa's wedding. In syndication, the action moves immediately from the establishing shot of the classroom to Skinner and Hoover's conversation; the Pepsi-sponsored math class – a beer-spewing-out-your-nose-funny satire of corporate encroach-ment on the American education system – has been cut.

It's just barbaric, this practice of syndication cuts. It must be stopped (the glacially slow release of unedited *Simpsons* episodes on DVD is a step in the right direction), and everyone who has colluded in it – the executives at Fox and at the stations that bought the syndication rights, the media buyers at the companies whose ads use the extra time, all of them – should be made to spend eternity listening to their favourite song with every tenth measure removed.

17. Whence Ahoy-hoy? Monty Burns's preferred greeting – *Ahoy-hoy* – was most likely derived from the greeting 'Ahoy!' used in nautical communications. An alternate theory, however, argues that it was derived from a Gaelic greeting used in Alexander Graham Bell's native Scotland.

18. Autobiographical note: As of this writing, there are no two words yet extant in the annals of human communications that are as likely to send me into a fit of hysterical giggling as these two words: 'Pops Freshenmeyer'. Such is the extraordinary power of a great one-off gag on *The Simpsons*.

19. First among equals: When you're talking about a show as good as *The Simpsons*, any of its five – or ten, or twenty – best episodes rank among the finest moments in TV history, and certainly any of the Top Five is as worthy as any other of the coveted title of 'Best. Episode. Ever.' So, then, in order of original air date, here are my picks for the five best *Simpsons* episodes of all time:

- Episode 9F10 ('Marge vs. the Monorail'): It's got a great opening sequence (Mr Burns personally stuffs drums of toxic waste into tree trunks and then buys the statue of Justice at his trial). It's got one of the finest song-and-dance numbers in *Simpsons* history – the rousing 'Monorail!' song a professional con man uses to sell Springfield on same. Throw in brilliant voice work from Phil Hartman as the monorail-hawking huckster Lyle Lanley, a merciless self-lampoon by celebrity guest star Leonard Nimoy, Homer as a monorail conductor, and a town-charter gag, and you've got a classic on your hands.
- Episode 9F15 ('Last Exit to Springfield'): Discussed at length here.
- Episode 1F01 ('Rosebud'): An extended homage to *Citizen Kane*, with C. Montgomery Burns standing in for Charles Foster Kane. Plus Homer having nightmares about *Sheriff Lobo* and staying up all night to eat 64 slices of American cheese, The Ramones giving possibly the finest guest musical performance ever (a punked-up 'Happy Birthday' for Burns), a historical montage featuring Charles Lindbergh and Adolf Hitler, and a snippet from the beloved TV dance show *Soul Mass Transit System*. Genius.
- Episode 1F13 ('Deep Space Homer'): In addition to the aforementioned space-ants sequence, this warp-speed-paced episode's got super-intelligent chimps, savage five-second parodies of *Married . . . with Children* and *Home Improvement*, Homer making angry phone calls to NASA and the White House, Homer lapsing delusionally into a scene from *Planet of the Apes*, Homer relating a tragic anecdote about how he missed out on meeting Mr T at the mall, and Homer humming the jingle for Golden Grahams cereal in the face of impending doom. Plus Buzz Aldrin announcing, 'Second comes right after first!' 1F13's second to none.
- Episode 3F24 ('El Viaje Misterioso de Nuestro Jomer'): The obligatory controversial choice. Yes, it does get overly sentimental at the end, and the reference to John Gray's *Men Are from Mars, Women Are from Venus* is cringe-worthy. But the chili cook-off's a hoot, the psychedelic journey Homer sets off on after eating a Guatemalan insanity pepper is the high-water mark for Simpsonian animation, and Homer's hunt for his soulmate inspires classic gags involving gay black males, furniture salesmen, Batman and short shorts. And Johnny Cash as Homer's spirit-guiding coyote? Best. Celebrity casting. Ever. Johnny Cash trumps John Gray, and the dreamscape of Homer's antacid trip seals it.

20. A case study in ironic background detailing: In Episode 7F07 ('Bart vs. Thanksgiving'), Bart joins his father in the living room to watch the Macy's Thanksgiving Day Parade, a New York holiday tradition whose chief attractions have long included numerous giant balloons in the shape of cartoon characters. As Bullwinkle and Underdog go floating by on the Simpsons'

TV screen, Bart points out that he's never seen any of these characters before, and suggests that characters from 'cartoons made in the last fifty years' should be added. Homer replies, 'Son, this is a tradition. If they start building a balloon for every flash-in-the-pan cartoon character, you'll turn the parade into a *farce*.' Midway through Homer's lecture, the TV screen – unnoticed by him and his son – fills with a giant balloon of Bart Simpson.

CHAPTER 2

Homer's Odyssey

Do I contradict myself?
Very well then I contradict myself,
(I am large, I contain multitudes.)
Walt Whitman, 'Song of Myself'

Damn you, Walt Whitman!
I! Hate! You! Walt! Freaking! Whitman!
'Leaves of Grass,' my ass!
Homer Simpson, kicking Walt Whitman's
gravestone for punctuation,
Episode 3F06 ('Mother Simpson')

A FEW THINGS YOU SHOULD know about Homer Jay Simpson: He is 36 years old (39 in one inconsistent instance), married to Marge and a father of three. Namesake either of Matt Groening's real-life father or of a character in Nathanael West's novel *The Day of the Locust*, or possibly both.[1] Born and raised in Springfield, USA. Safety inspector at the Springfield Nuclear Power Plant. One-time astronaut. One-time mascot for the Springfield Isotopes baseball team. One-time bootlegger. Erstwhile 'Chosen One' – the godhead of a secret society called the Stonecutters. Former food critic for the *Springfield Shopper*. Lead singer and songwriter for the barbershop quartet the Be Sharps (huge in 1985 and then immediately and completely forgotten). Honorary citizen of the city of Winnipeg, Manitoba.[2] Number 22 in a 1995 *Chicago Tribune* ranking and number 10 in a 2002 *TV Guide* ranking of the greatest TV characters of all time (neither of which give Homer anywhere near enough credit). Number 6 on British newspaper *The Independent*'s list of the greatest accidental heroes of the twentieth century (which almost does). Undisputed primary protagonist and unlikely hero of *The Simpsons* since at least its third season.

Homer J. Simpson: America's latest, greatest Everyman. 'Three centuries from now, English professors are going to be regarding Homer Simpson as one of the greatest creations in human storytelling' – so decrees Robert Thompson, the director of Syracuse University's Center for the Study of Popular Television and past president of the International Popular Culture Association. Now we're getting somewhere. But enough of your borax, Poindexter. Let's move on to some of mine. Let's talk about Homer.

Homer is best known as a doughnut-munching, beer-swilling, TV-ogling slob whose most famous utterance – added to the august *Oxford English Dictionary* in June 2001 – is an 'annoyed grunt' that goes like this: '*D'oh!*'[3] His simple-mindedness, his stupidity, his sometimes absolute subservience to his basest desires – these have been consistent hallmarks of his character since *The Simpsons*' first crudely drawn vignettes on *The Tracey Ullman Show*, and they remain an enormous part of his appeal. But how did this indifferent, even callous husband, this big dumb oaf, become the most beloved character on the show? How did Homer come to embody so fully The Meaning of America?

It's worth emphasising right off the top a point that may seem obvious but that often gets lost in broad discussions of The Meaning of America. Namely, that the United States is not as singular and simple a place as it's sometimes portrayed. While it's not exclusively the moral City on the Hill of its Puritan founders or of their latter-day revivalists (your Reagans and G.W. Bushes, your Falwells and Ashcrofts), neither is it the one-dimensional, debased, decayed, dumbed-down wasteland depicted by some of its critics. Any honest accounting of American values must include the nation's considerable lust for pornography (America is home to the world's largest such industry), as well as its foundations in Protestant evangelism (ditto). The easy rhetorical points to be scored from cataloguing the rankest detritus of America's lush pop-cultural jungle – the scoffing denunciations of bling-bling-obsessed gangsta rap or fall-of-Roman reality TV – are easily counterbalanced by pointing out the jaw-dropping inventiveness of Eminem's rhyme schemes or (but of course) the genius of *The Simpsons*. Did the United States of the Simpson age bring the world Crystal Pepsi and the luxury sport-utility vehicle? Well, yes. But it also whipped up the Internet. *Temptation Island*? Again yes. But also the sublime *Sopranos* and the existential hilarity of *Seinfeld*.

This is all critical to keep in mind when you're thinking about Homer, because he is the most American of Simpsons, with all the crassness, confusion, complexity and contradiction that this implies. It's not hard to imagine a British Bart – after all, he frequently lapses into a Cockney accent or a line or two from *A Clockwork Orange*, and the punk aesthetic that spawned him is as much a British as an American phenomenon. It's even easier to envision a doting Indian or Italian mother along the lines of Marge, or a self-righteous crusader from Canada or the Czech Republic who could fill in for Lisa. Homer, though, is pure American: loud, brash and boorish, quick to anger and even quicker to act, as sure of himself as he is certain that nothing's really his fault, but endlessly fascinating and ultimately well-meaning and often even lovable all the same.

The great failing of previous American-TV Everydads was their flatness, their relentless one-dimensionality. Ralph Kramden was a grouchy working-class slob, as was his progeny Fred Flintstone; Archie Bunker was a cranky bigot; bumbling saint Cliff Huxtable and haemorrhaging-heart liberal Stephen Keaton of *Family Ties* were saccharine family *über*-men. Even Homer's own live-action doppelgänger, *Married . . . with Children*'s Al Bundy, did little more than try to out-oaf Homer himself. None of these men could possibly be Everymen unless you accept the fallacy that there's a singular American character and a single version of the American Dream.

Homer certainly traces some of his pedigree to the Kramdens and Flintstones and Bunkers who filled the idiot box before him. In fact, direct references have been made in the show to the latter two characters, in the form of separate re-enactments of the opening credits of *The Flintstones* and *All in the Family*.[4] But the boneheaded dads of sitcoms past tell only half the story. To get a full picture of Homer's brand of oafishness, you have to toss in a healthy dose of another archetype, this one from the ensemble comedies of American cinema: the anarchic ringleader. The zenith (and possibly also the origin) of this species is Bluto Blutarsky, the hyper-charged, incessantly soused perpetual undergrad who orchestrates the mayhem (and steals the show) in *National Lampoon's Animal House*. Bluto – the greatest invention of the late, great comedic actor John Belushi – is a character demarcated by his childlike chaotic energy. Tony Hendra's precise portrait of the Bluto/Belushi archetype in *Going Too Far* reads like a partial summary of Homer:

> Bluto's grossness is delicious and unthreatening . . . Bluto is all instinct, but his fulfillment of his urges harms no one; his satisfaction never involves someone else's loss. . . . Belushi is eternal youth, steamrolling convention, reinventing life, busting with sap, disrupting his surroundings by merely being alive, unsentimental, unambitious, unreflective.

In short, he is almost pure id, the unruly, inventive yin to the responsible, moralising yang of the sober patriarchs of American television. Put the two together in a large canvas sack and watch them churn themselves into a red-white-and-blue froth, a raging, contradictory mass of genius and stupidity, rebellion and conformity, family-valuing responsibility and utter chaos. This is something far closer to the true American character.

This is Homer Simpson.

A SHORT, FRANK DISCUSSION (ACTUALLY MORE LIKE A LONGISH RAMBLING EXAMINATION) OF HOMER'S EXTRAORDINARY ID

It's the base passions you probably notice first. Here is a man who replies to the question 'Would you rather have beer, or complete and utter contentment?' with the simple query 'What kind of beer?' Here, too, is a man who stays up an entire night to work his way methodically through 64 slices of American cheese. A man who knowingly scarfs down expired ham and month-old rotting hoagies, and who installs a children's lightbulb oven in his car for muffins on the go. A man for whom the notion of being a 'Renaissance man' means eating eight different kinds of meat in one afternoon.

If '*D'oh!*' is Homer's claim to ageless, *OED*-level fame, the runner-up might well be '*Mmmm . . .*' *Mmmm . . . donuts. Mmmm . . . beer. Mmmm . . . crumbled-up cookie things.* In one noteworthy instance, Homer eagerly devours pepper spray ('Mmmm . . . incapacitating'). In Episode 2F33 ('Another Simpsons Clip Show'), Marge, trying to make a case for the glory of love, instructs her family, 'Ask your heart what its fondest desire is', sending Homer into a long reverie about foodstuffs he's lusted after: chocolate, invisible cola, snouts, free goo. 'Mmmm . . . something', he concludes, in one of the most succinct summations anywhere of the insatiable desire lodged in the sclerotic aorta of the consumer ethos. And Homer's appetite is as deep as it is wide, a fact made abundantly clear in Episode 9F06 ('New Kid on the Block'). Spurred by a TV commercial, Homer takes Marge for dinner at a new all-you-can-eat seafood restaurant, only to be expelled before he's had his fill. He enlists talentless attorney Lionel Hutz to sue the joint for false advertising, and poor Marge is called to the stand to testify to the shameful truth about the rest of the Simpsons' evening.

Hutz: Mrs Simpson, what did you and your husband do after you were ejected from the restaurant?

Marge: We pretty much went straight home.

Hutz: Mrs Simpson, you're under oath.

Marge: We drove around until 3 a.m. looking for another 'All You Can Eat' fish restaurant.

Hutz: And when you couldn't find one?

Marge: We went fishing. [*Marge breaks down into tears*]

Hutz: [*to jury*] Do these sound like the actions of a man who had '*all* he could eat'?

Of course not: Homer has never had all he could eat. The devil himself once tried to stuff Homer so full of doughnuts that he'd cry for mercy. This took place in hell's 'Ironic Punishments Division' after Homer sold his eternal soul for a single doughnut. He puffed up like a beachball but kept calling for more, exhausting the resolve of the demon in charge of the punishment. There is simply no limit to Homer's appetite, nor is there any shame – or, at least, any self-reflection – in his attempts to satisfy it.

Augmenting Homer's reputation for brain-dead oafitude is his abiding love for the television set, his many years spent in a blissful staring match with its unblinking eye. Homer has been known to sit on his couch excitedly clutching a pennant reading MID-SEASON as he waits to drink in such craptacular Fox-TV mid-season-replacement fare as *America's Funniest Tornadoes*, *All in the Family 1999* and *Admiral Baby*. When Marge suggests that Bart stop watching TV and get some exercise, Homer replies, 'Marge, TV gives so much and asks so little. It's a boy's best friend.' In another episode, Marge gets a job at the nuclear plant, and Homer considers pursuing one of his constantly changing lifelong dreams: living in the woods and keeping a journal of his thoughts, *à la* Thoreau.[5] 'March 15. I wish I brought a TV. Oh, God, how I miss TV!' goes the first imagined entry, as Homer envisions himself sitting ruefully beneath a tree in a bucolic glade. Even when the idiot box turns on him – in Episode 2F06 ('Homer Badman'), when a sleazy tabloid show trumps up a sexual harassment allegation against him – Homer's love abides. After the scandal has been resolved, the episode closes with Homer wrapping his TV in a warm embrace, cooing, 'Let's never fight again.'

What really makes Homer happy, though, is combining his passions. His football-watching regimen is an especially stunning display of the American Everyman at leisure: flanked on his couch by bags of Salt Doodles, Krunchy Korn, chips and pork rinds, he shovels in the snacks with both hands, dunking into two separate bowls of dip, with several cans of ice-cold Duff beer nearby to wash it all down.

The extent to which Homer is a (happy) slave to his various appetites is perhaps most evident in the opening sequence of Episode 9F01 ('Homer the Heretic'). The episode begins with Homer dreaming of his prenatal self enjoying 'a beautiful day in the womb'. Awakening to a freezing cold Sunday morning, Homer decides to skip church, precipitating what he later pronounces the greatest day of his life. Homer's perfect day: he sleeps in; urinates with the door open; takes a warm shower; cranks his thermostat to 100°F, making it possible for him to dance around the house in his underwear to the novelty hit 'Short Shorts' by the Royal Teens; gorges himself on a platter of his patented Space-Age Out-of-This-World Moon Waffles (main ingredients: butter, caramel, liquid smoke); wins a radio trivia contest; watches a Three Stooges movie; watches a public-affairs programme just long enough for it to be interrupted by a football game; eats a bag of chips watching the game; and finds a penny on the floor. This heavenly experience inspires Homer to start his own religion of one. For Homer, consumption is a kind of worship; he feels closest to God – or, if you prefer, to transcendence – when he is ingesting, watching, indulging basic whims. 'He follows his passions 100 percent,' Matt Groening once told a reporter. 'It gets him into a lot of trouble, but there's a part of us that wishes we had the guts to be like Homer and really savor that donut.'

If Homer's doughnut is understood as symbolic – a stand-in for any product, any desire, any random hunger demanding to be sated, a kind of consumer-age widget – then in fact there are quite a lot of us with the guts to be like Homer. This is an age of super-sized fast-food feasts and gargantuan gas-guzzling SUVs, of brain-dead Hollywood epics with nation-sized budgets, of a stock market sent soaring on the speculations of ill-informed day traders, of cities overflowing with bloated exurban sprawl in a macrocosmic version of Homer's blubbery waistline, mammoth big-box stores and overblown McMansions gobbling up countryside like our hero at a buffet. The average size of the American home grew by 17 per cent between 1987 and 1999 alone, and the rate of credit card debt grew even faster. The economic boom that blasted most of the West into ridiculous affluence through the latter part of the 1990s gave rise to an orgy of democratised consumption that, taken as a whole, dwarfed the excesses of the imperial Roman elite. A few big shots in togas puking their dinners into a marble receptacle? Well, check *this* out, Caligula: the United States alone has gobbled up more resources since 1950 than the entire population of the planet managed to consume through all of human history before 1950. But more on all of that later. Let's dive back into the gaping maw of Homer Simpson's tremendous id.

To be sure, there sometimes appears to be little to Homer *but* id. His unwavering stupidity, for example – a core character trait almost as prominent as his appetite for doughnuts and Duff – actively repels the potential wisdom contained in the many and varied experiences of his rich life. Mere moments after being framed and then cleared of sexual harassment charges by the tabloid TV show *Rock Bottom* in Episode 2F06 ('Homer Badman'), Homer finds himself believing the worst about Groundskeeper Willie, as a result of sensationalistic footage and wild accusations by the very same show. 'Hasn't your experience taught you that you can't believe everything you hear?' Marge asks. 'Marge, my friend, I haven't learned a thing,' Homer replies contentedly.

Not an episode of *The Simpsons* goes by without a dense or gullible or flat-out dumb Homer moment. At work, Homer's incompetence, clumsiness and/ or stupidity causes major meltdowns and other disasters with such frequency that the emergency workers in the bright yellow contamination suits call him by name as they pass. On one occasion, a crude Homer dummy (with a bucket for a head, tree branches with gloves on them for arms, and a cassette player blasting Homer's rendition of Donna Summer's 'She Works Hard for the Money' to create an industrious vibe) earns the promotion that has long eluded Homer himself. At home, Bart regularly succeeds in tricking or conning his father – trading him a 'delicious doorstop' for his morning Danish, for example – while Lisa often gives sensible advice to her bumbling dad.

It's usually the same story no matter what situation Homer finds himself in. There's even a certain expression that comes across Homer's face in some episodes – the eyes just a bit wider and blanker somehow, the mouth pouched out a little, the top lip drooping down – that serves to indicate that a particularly dense version of Homer is on the scene. It's a testament to the minimalist art of *The Simpsons'* animation that these few minutely exaggerated details can so convincingly convey the notion of abject stupidity on a visage already so closely associated with dumbness. One of the most drawn-out of these extra-stupid moments occurs in Episode 9F22 ('Cape Feare'), as FBI agents attempt to explain to Homer that his new name will be Homer Thompson now that he's entered the federal Witness Relocation Program. (This transpires, incidentally, because Sideshow Bob is trying to kill Bart; Homer appears later in the same episode sporting a new baseball cap and T-shirt labelled WITNESS RELOCATION PROGRAM.) The goal is for Homer to engage successfully in a short dialogue as 'Mr Thompson'. One of the agents will say, 'Hello, Mr Thompson', and Homer is to reply promptly, 'Hi.' It goes on for some time, Homer responding to each 'Hello, Mr Thompson' with no more than his wide-eyed, pooch-mouthed stare. Finally, the agent tells him, 'When I say "Hello, Mr Thompson," and press down on your foot, you smile and nod.' The agent does so, and after a long blank stare, Homer turns to the other agent and stage-whispers, 'I think he's talking to *you.*' S-M-R-T – I mean, S-M-A-R-T – Homer is not.[6]

This general lack of smarts combines explosively with several other key Homer traits: his laziness, his shamelessness, his total lack of impulse control, his resolute unwillingness to take responsibility for his actions. It is this rich stew of weaknesses and faults that produces much of the anarchic energy that propels the show. Crazy money-making schemes, ill-conceived career changes, poorly planned parenting and self-improvement initiatives – all begin with Homer's rampaging id.

Homer is never more than a microsecond away from sheer panic or total outrage. At the interview that eventually lands him his job at the nuclear power plant, Homer flees the room in a blind panic when presented with the mere scenario of a problem with the reactor. When Bart uses a transmitter to broadcast details of a phoney Martian invasion over the Simpson family's radio, Homer has his shotgun loaded and at the ready before taking the briefest moment to question whether it's a hoax. Another time, more or less unprovoked, he picks a fight with the garbage collectors, and they retaliate by cancelling his service. Lisa asks whether this is one of those situations that could be solved with a simple apology. Homer responds, 'I never apologise, Lisa. I'm sorry, but that's just the way I am.' Later in the same episode, Homer runs for garbage commissioner under the slogan 'Can't Someone Else Do It?' And wins. And spends the entire year's sanitation budget in a month, which he was helpless to prevent, he explains, because he was permitted to sign cheques with a stamp. 'I don't think anything I've ever done is wrong,' he explains after Marge expresses a moment of hesitation at their new-found fondness for exhibitionist sex. After accidentally taking a cannonball in the gut at a rock festival (Episode 3F21: 'Homerpalooza'), Homer is invited to join the tour as a star in the festival's freak show (aka 'the pageant of the transmundane'). That night, he discusses his new vocation with Marge:

Marge: So you want to go on tour with a traveling freak show.

Homer: I don't think I have a choice, Marge.

Marge: Of course you have a choice.

Homer: How do you figure?

Marge: You don't have to join a freak show just because the opportunity came along.

Homer: You know, Marge, in some ways you and I are very different people.

Homer could no sooner refuse an adventure than pass up a purple-flavoured, sprinkle-covered doughnut. He is, as he himself acknowledges, 'a doer – someone who'll act without considering the consequences.' (This, incidentally, was the rallying cry that earned Homer the leadership of a vigilante mob.) Homer knows no restraint, and he weathers the consequences with a surprisingly resilient mix of blind acceptance and deep denial. Consider his strategy for passing the final exam in Nuclear Physics 101 (a course he was forced to take because he is, he admits, 'dangerously unqualified' for the job he's held for years): 'During the exam, I'll hide under some coats and hope that somehow everything will work out.' Amazingly, it usually does for Homer. He is the existential hero rewritten as a highly suggestible, ultra-impulsive force of pure dumb action. If nothing is real, then everything is possible, and if everything is possible, then just do it.

It's worth noting here that in the very first scene of the first Simpsons short on *The Tracey Ullman Show*, Homer answers Bart's existential query ('What is the mind? Is it just a system of impulses? Or is it something tangible?') with a dismissive riddle: 'What is mind? No matter. What is matter? Never mind!' And then he giggles. This hints at the way Homer's impulsive energy has morphed over the years from mere ignorance into trippy stream-of-unconsciousness and finally into a kind of blissful blankness: Homer as Zen-master savant. And it also starts us on the road towards explaining why Homer is more than mere Id Incarnate – and far more sympathetic.

First, though, the trippiness, which began in the first few seasons of *The Simpsons* with the odd rant or, more noticeably, with Homer's occasional lapses into reverie – a journey through the Land of Chocolate, say, or a daydream about a life of organised crime. ('Mmmm . . . organised crime.') As well, the Homer of the first few seasons would sometimes find his lusts leading him into brief flashes of total immersion in the moment – a Homeric variation on the in-the-now thinking that is the goal of many meditation practices. Seeing a piece of pie laid out in the middle of the kitchen floor, he gives not a thought to how or why it found itself there. (It was placed there by Bart as the bait in a Homer-catching leg trap, Homer would soon learn.) In the moment of discovery, though, Homer merely announces, 'Oooh . . . floor pie', and lurches for the prize. In another instance, he chases the last peanut under his couch, emerging instead with a 20-dollar bill. 'Aw, twenty dollars,' he whines. 'I wanted a peanut.' There follows a moment of blank dejection before Homer's brain pipes up, 'Twenty dollars can buy many peanuts.' 'Explain how,' Homer demands. Homer's brain promptly replies, 'Money can be exchanged for goods and services.' 'Woo-hoo!' Homer exclaims, celebrating this newfound wisdom. These first traces of Zen Homer, though, were as easily explained by his sheer thickness as by any kind of liberated mind.

But 'round about Season 6, Homer's dense dreaminess has become an almost psychedelic stream-of-stunned-consciousness. Consider, for example, the last episode of that season (1F20, 'Secrets of a Successful Marriage'), in which Homer becomes the teacher of a night-school course on building a healthy marriage. The class quickly becomes a forum for Homer's juicy gossip about his own marriage. When Marge finds out her deepest secrets have become public knowledge, she urges Homer to figure out a way to teach the class while respecting her privacy. Here's Homer's reply to that simple request:

Look, Marge, you don't know what it's like. *I'm* the one out there every day putting his ass on the line. And I'm not out of order. *You're* out of order. The whole freaking *system* is out of order! You want the truth? You want the truth?! *You can't handle the truth!'* Cause when you reach over and put your hand into a pile of goo that was your best friend's face, you'll know what to do! Forget it, Marge, it's Chinatown!

The confused dolt who took a few seconds to figure out how to turn 20 dollars into a coveted peanut has become a non sequitur-generating machine. Not to mention a pop-cultural sponge: this particular rant chains together famous rejoinders from the classic films (in order of appearance) *And Justice for All*, *A Few Good Men*, *Patton* and *Chinatown*. Combine this trippy quality with the desire-driven, in-the-moment Homer who lusts after floor pie, and you get incomparable scenes like this one from Season 7 (Episode 2F04: 'Bart's Girlfriend'):

> *Homer and Marge are sitting quietly at the kitchen table. Bart, who has been covered in glue as the result of a skateboarding mishap, walks by the kitchen table with the family cat stuck to his back.*
>
> Marge: Have you noticed any change in Bart?
> Homer: [*distantly*] New glasses?
> Marge: No . . . He looks like something might be disturbing him.
> Homer: Probably misses his old glasses.
> Marge: I guess we could get more involved in Bart's activities, but then
>   I'd be afraid of smothering him.
> Homer: [*resigned*] Yeah. And then we'd get the chair.
> Marge: That's not what I meant.
> Homer: It was, Marge, admit it.

The character in this exchange is still recognisably Homer – witness the mix of indifference and hostility towards his son, the dim-witted, sporadically focused mind that plucks a false notion out of thin air ('new glasses') and then treats it as established fact a moment later – but there is a dreamlike, almost meditative quality to his personality now. If it's not an oxymoron, this Homer possesses a complex stupidity, a lack of S-M-R-T smarts that Fred Flintstone never dreamed of. Homer is not merely dense in this scene; his stupidity has a depth to it, a kind of considered dumbness, as if he has focused considerable intellectual resources (and perhaps emotional and economic and technical ones too) on developing his stupidity into something nuanced and elaborate and ultimately sort of monumental.

This quality is sometimes evident in less surreal moments. In particular, Homer will occasionally and quite unexpectedly demonstrate genuine rationality and surprising attention to detail. In the vast majority of these instances, his sudden display of reason is in pursuit of some basic desire. A representative case: in Episode 4F08 ('The Twisted World of Marge Simpson'), Marge has been tossed from her investment club due to her unwillingness to take risks. As she relates to her family the tale of her ouster – which took place at the Municipal House of Pancakes – she mentions that her former investment partners promised to send pancakes to her later by mail. Homer, usually bored by other people's stories, is on the edge of his seat. 'Wait, wait, wait, wait, wait,' he tells his wife, probing. 'Back up a bit now.' A thoughtful pause. 'When are the pancakes coming in the mail?' Building from the single notes of Homer's initial character – this guy, Homer, he's not too bright, and he likes to eat a lot – *The Simpsons* writers have riffed on it like jazz musicians, creating a baroque stupidity that offers not only far richer comedic possibilities but also far greater potential for symbolism and social commentary.

Homer's moments of clarity often give rise, paradoxically, to his greatest insights, his most astute observations on real life in the waning years of the American Century. Sometimes, Homer himself knows he is handing down the common wisdom of age, as when he comforts Bart and Lisa with this over-honest neo-aphorism: 'Kids, you tried your best, and you failed miserably. The lesson is: Never try.' Some hypocrite like Cliff Huxtable might have something to say about how things should be, but Homer is far more likely to tell you how things actually are. An even more trenchant bit of insight springs up in Episode 9F18 ('Whacking Day'), when Lisa expresses her disgust for Whacking Day, the grotesque Springfield tradition in which the whole town celebrates its founding father, Jebediah Springfield, by pounding snakes with clubs:

Lisa:	Dad, everybody likes Whacking Day, but I hate it. Is there something wrong with me?
Homer:	Yes, honey.
Lisa:	Then what should I do?
Homer:	Just squeeze your rage into a bitter little ball, and release it at an appropriate time. Like that day I hit the referee with the whisky bottle. Remember that?
Lisa:	[*resigned*] Yeah.
Homer:	Your daddy hit the referee?
Lisa:	[*further resigned*] Yeah . . .

Homer's not really aware how unconstructive his advice is – he's just telling the truth as he knows it. And, in the process, he makes a far more accurate statement about the way middle America maintains its veneer of contentment and happiness than any other TV father ever has.

It's in character details like these that Homer transcends himself and his oafish archetype, becoming not just the latest and greatest version of a conventional figure in American drama – the dumb dad – but a powerful symbol of consumer-age America itself. This is a point delineated with blunt clarity in Episode 1F12 ('Lisa vs. Malibu Stacy'). Lisa has taken great offence to the sexist tripe that spills out of the mouth of her new talking Malibu Stacy doll ('Don't ask me – I'm just a girl!'), but she has failed to convince the company that manufactures the doll to make any changes. Meanwhile, Homer's father, Abe, has come to the realisation that he's thought of as a useless old crank, and he's at a loss as to how to make himself productive again. He and Lisa sit at the kitchen table in identical states of dejection.

'It's awful being a kid,' Lisa sighs. 'No one listens to you.'

'It's rotten being old,' Abe commiserates. 'No one listens to you.'

Homer walks into the kitchen, bound for the cabinet behind them. 'I'm a white male aged 18 to 49,' he announces contentedly. 'Everyone listens to me – no matter how dumb my suggestions are.' And he pulls from the cabinet a box labelled NUTS AND GUM – TOGETHER AT LAST!

Not only is Homer dumb, he's *influential*. And, as such, he's a perfect stand-in for the average self-absorbed, self-important Baby Boomer. As the most coddled subgroup (white males) of what might well be the most coddled generation in human history, Homer and his peers have had their every whim catered to since birth by a society geared almost exclusively to their priorities alone and a culture finely engineered to capture their attention – and their seemingly bottomless reserves of disposable income. And as a product of the very end of the Baby Boom, Homer's been particularly coddled. He was too young to be scarred by Vietnam; he bumbled through his teens listening not to thought-provoking protest music but to the lunk-headed riffs of 1970s arena rock and the vacuous melodies of 1970s novelty pop (adolescent Homer has been portrayed as a devotee of, among others, Grand Funk Railroad, Queen and the Starland Vocal Band of fleeting 'Afternoon Delight' fame); he walked into a career right out of high school with no previous experience. Every aspect of Homer's comfortable life has simply fallen into his fat lap.

Homer's studied, self-absorbed stupidity is not merely a comedic device (as it was for Ralph Kramden or the Three Stooges), but a satirical one. In a society where coffee must come in cups that read CAUTION: COFFEE IS HOT and car commercials with superimposed disclaimers instructing viewers not to attempt the high-speed stunts they depict, where the premieres of new instalments in Hollywood film franchises are treated as epochal news and the content of the movies (and of TV shows and car commercials and political campaigns) is tested first with focus groups to ensure no one could possibly be offended or confused by it – in this society, Homer is not an anomaly. He's the end product, the natural result. He's the dumbed-down avatar of What Is.

It's not that the America of the Simpson age is irredeemably dumb (although aspects of it certainly are), but that it's so self-absorbed that it might as well be. Think of that other famous Simpson of the 1990s: O.J., a football star from the time of Homer's youth. Take the accumulated media of his murder trial – every newspaper op-ed and lawyer's tell-all memoir and videotape of the white Ford Bronco – and imagine all of it fed into the intake of a great chugging factory, an efficient state-of-the-art facility in which it's churned into bite-sized chunks, packaged into boxes, marketed and sold by a mighty consumer machine without rival in the known universe. See the finished product rolling down the factory's conveyor belt: a lifetime supply of Nuts and Gum.

Homer's base passions set the agenda for his family, for his country, for much of the world. When he's hungry, another acre of rainforest is ploughed under to graze cattle. When he's angry and vengeful, a thousand missiles rain down on the caves of Afghanistan, a thousand more on the desert of Iraq. There's not necessarily any ill intent here: Homer has simply known since the day of his birth that he can have anything he wants. That he *deserves* anything he wants.

And this constant indulgence of Homer's insatiable id leaves the other Simpsons – his wife, his son, his daughters, his father – and everyone else in Springfield and beyond fighting an uphill battle with Homer and with society in general to get any attention paid to their lives at all.

THE EVOLUTION OF A FAMILY MAN

For the most part, the other Simpsons are fully aware that Homer's passions are higher priorities than their own needs. In fact, in the first few years of *The Simpsons'* run, this was the source of one of the show's central tensions: the rest of the family's increasing irritation with what a crappy father and husband Homer was. This early-period Homer – most evident in the *Ullman* shorts and in the first season, but still discernible on occasion as late as the sixth or seventh seasons – was a far cruder, far meaner character, and a far lousier father and husband. In one *Ullman* short, Homer is downright menacing to his wife as he orders her to go silence the kids. (Marge reacts with considerable anger of her own.) As well, those first years established the recurring 'Why, you little …' scenario, in which Homer reacts to Bart's misbehaviour by strangling him mercilessly.[7] An entire episode in Season 2 (7F20, 'The War of the Simpsons') revolves around Homer's deficiencies as a husband, as he and Marge travel to a couples retreat to try and repair their marriage. As the retreat weekend nears its end, the counsellor, Reverend Lovejoy, tells Marge, 'This is the first instance where I've ever told one partner that they were 100 per cent right. It's all his fault. I'm willing to put that on a certificate you can frame.'

The following season, several episodes centred on Homer's deep failings as a father. In one, Lisa is so angry at Homer's inability to bring her a new reed for her saxophone in time for a recital that she only warms up to her father after he buys her a pony. In another, Lisa's ability to predict the winners of football games leads to deep father–daughter bonding – but when Lisa learns that their newfound 'Daddy–Daughter Day' tradition will end with the football season, she finds herself fundamentally questioning her love for him. Another third-season episode opens with Homer submitting to a magazine quiz that tests his knowledge of Bart's interests to determine his 'fatherhood quotient' – and failing thoroughly. 'I don't know jack about my boy,' Homer is forced to admit. And as for his infant daughter, Maggie, the abysmal state of Homer's relationship with her has become a running gag: Homer often can't remember her name, or else how to spell it (her birthday cake reads MAGAGGIE, and Homer asks, 'It's not Magaggie's birthday?'); the first time she's left alone with him, she almost immediately runs away to find Marge; he forgets the very fact of her existence, almost sitting on her on the couch. And so on. This first incarnation of Homer was frequently portrayed as a callous husband and an indifferent father, in many ways the very antithesis of the Cosby-style *über*-dad. And yet …

And yet, even in those early episodes, Homer would often redeem himself in the show's final act. Though exasperated by Lisa's moral convictions, he eventually decides he can no longer enjoy the stolen cable she's been protesting against. Though Lisa will never idolise her dad the way she does her beloved substitute teacher, Mr Bergstrom (an enthusiastic, idealistic intellectual voiced by Dustin Hoffman[8]), by the end of that episode she's giggling along to Homer's self-mocking gorilla impersonation. And even after their disastrous couples retreat, Marge is willing to reconcile with

Homer after he tosses back the biggest fish he's ever caught to demonstrate his selflessness and love for her.

This redemptive side of Homer's personality – his innocence, his kind-heartedness, his deep (if only sporadically evident) love for his family – became much more central to his character in the show's middle-period Golden Age. The Homer of this period is still a lousy husband and father – Bart is still strangled on occasion, Lisa is still misunderstood and under-appreciated, Maggie is still forgotten, Marge is still taken for granted – but Homer now tries much harder, and he almost always means well.

These aspects of his relationship with Marge are explored in Episode 8F18 ('A Streetcar Named Marge'). Finding her homemaking life a little one-dimensional, Marge decides to try out for a part in a local play. As she explains her plans to Homer, his eyes never leave the TV set, and he fills in the pauses in her explanation with a mock-enthusiastic 'Sounds interesting!' The play turns out to be *Oh! Streetcar!* – a musical version of Tennessee Williams's *A Streetcar Named Desire* – and Marge wins the coveted role of Blanche DuBois. At rehearsal, she questions her character's reactions: 'I just don't see why Blanche should shove a broken bottle in Stanley's face. Couldn't she just take his abuse with gentle good humor?' But when a insensitive, horn-honking Homer arrives to pick her up, Marge finally finds Blanche's rage.

That night in bed, the Simpsons' discussion of the play offers a vivid portrait of the rather tenuous equilibrium of their marriage. Faced with Homer's indifference towards her acting, Marge asks, 'Why can't you be more supportive?'

'Because I don't care,' Homer replies. 'I can't fake an interest in this, and I'm an expert at faking an interest in your kooky projects.'

Marge asks why Homer has never mentioned his lack of enthusiasm before.

'You know I would never do anything to hurt your feelings,' he replies.

By the end of the play's premiere, Marge's 'gentle good humor' is long gone. She's nearing a state of total contempt for her husband – until he comes backstage genuinely moved by the show, wishing that Stanley had shown Blanche some respect, and even seeing aspects of himself in the character. This is enough for Marge to reacquaint herself with her husband's essential decency, and she kisses him warmly as the episode ends.

Homer's commitment to fatherhood has improved greatly by this point in the series as well, although his skill level remains extremely low. After Bart is caught shoplifting a videogame, for example, Homer forgoes the usual strangling act and instead attempts to instruct his son in basic morality, though his own trippy, rambling nature eventually takes over:

> How *could* you? Haven't you learned anything from that guy who gives the sermons at church? Captain What's-his-name? We live in a society of laws. Why do you think I took you to all those *Police Academy* movies? For fun? Well, I didn't hear anybody laughing! Did you? Except at that guy who made sound effects. [*Homer imitates the guy and chuckles to himself, then refocuses.*] Where was I? Oh, yeah – stay out of my booze.

On another occasion, Homer has a fight with *his* father that leads him to re-evaluate his own shortcomings as a parent. With unprecedented intensity, Homer tries to transform himself into a model father, lavishing attention on all three of his kids. Bart, though, doesn't need the bike-riding lessons – he already knows how – and Lisa doesn't much enjoy spending time in her new tyre swing because the tyre is filthy and the steel belts jab her skin. 'No offence, Homer,' Bart explains, 'but your half-assed under-parenting was a lot more fun than your half-assed over-parenting.' Lisa concurs, and a dejected Homer walks off, saying, 'I've got to go somewhere and do some serious thinking.' Once he's gone, Bart turns to Lisa. 'I'm sure he meant "serious drinking",' he says. 'That's what I assumed,' Lisa replies.

Note the resigned acceptance here. The volatile, uncaring, irritating Homer of the early seasons is long gone. In its place is an ineffectual yet somehow lovable buffoon – a man whose virtue emerges from the trump card of Baby Boomer values: he means well. Intentions, not results, are what's important, and Homer's sporadic bouts of good intention are enough to outweigh his longer spells of neglect and his enduring incompetence. What's more, the Simpson kids are not only well aware of their father's limitations, they no longer resent them. Meaning well is enough. In this respect, Homer and his children stand in perfect allegorical symmetry with Bill 'I feel your pain' Clinton and the American public (and to a lesser degree the entire relationship between 'Third Way' neo-liberalism and the citizens of the West's democracies). Under Clinton, the weak virtue of meaning well was divorced from results and turned into a kind of all-encompassing, one-size-fits-all public policy. Never mind that the government's economic policies are just as unbalanced and polarising as those of the tightest-fisted conservative; never mind that the drug laws are just as draconian and the environmental safeguards just as lax; never mind most of all that the current government is no less a tool of corporate interests than any other. Focus on the intent, the tone, the deep empathy in the eyes and voice. Do not, above all, hold leaders of any sort – whether in politics, business, entertainment or elsewhere – accountable for their actions (or inactions) *so long as they mean well.*

Much as Homer's kids understand that he cares about them despite his habitual indifference and that he means to be a good parent despite his incompetence, so we in the Western democracies accept (often with scant evidence) that our leaders *mean* to improve the lot of the homeless at home and the destitute abroad, *mean* to do a better job of protecting the planet, *mean* to do all sorts of things to make our lives as wonderful, as they've long promised they will – but there are re-elections to be won, compromises to be negotiated, special interests to be placated. And our corporate leaders *mean* to be socially responsible, but this darn profitability thing keeps getting in the way. And certainly the entertainment industry would love to make meaningful movies and records and TV shows, but there are callow advertisers and simple-minded focus groups to be catered to. Everyone means well, yes, but everyone's hands are tied. Taking responsibility – taking *action* – would be great and all, but at least they mean well.

In the most recent years of *The Simpsons*, the family's tolerance of Homer's best-intentioned bumbling has grown into complete acceptance and a gentle, good-humoured love. The dark spin on this would be to suggest that the Simpsons – like the enslaved citizens in Aldous Huxley's *Brave New World* who crave elaborate amusements, like the hordes of us in the real world who wait in line to spend fifteen bucks on summer blockbusters we know will insult our intelligence – are so deeply to habituated abuse and dysfunction that they've learned to crave it. Or, more optimistically, perhaps they recognise that Homer brings enough fun and excitement into their lives to outweigh (or at least counterbalance) his more destructive qualities. Either way, there is very little resentment – and considerable affection – in Homer's relationship with his family.

The last serious suggestion that Homer and Marge's marriage could be anything other than enduring was in Episode 5F01 ('The Cartridge Family'), which aired early in Season 9. Much earlier in the series, there had been real threats to their union: Marge almost had an affair with a bowling instructor after Homer selfishly gave her a bowling ball for her birthday; the impending divorce of family friends the Van Houtens sent Homer into a panic that led to half-assed over-husbanding, a quickie divorce and a second marriage; and Marge went on a *Thelma & Louise*-style road trip with a new (and newly divorced) neighbour after Homer broke his promise to take her to the ballet. In 5F01, though, Homer nearly goes too far, becoming a gun owner (and card-carrying member of the National Rifle Association) over Marge's repeated objections. After the gun discharges several times on the Simpsons' kitchen table, she makes her final plea. 'Homer,' she says, 'I think you'd agree that I've put up with a lot in our marriage . . .' Homer opens his mouth to protest, but both Bart and Lisa shake their heads no, and he stays silent. 'But this,' Marge continues, 'is the first time since we've been married that I've actually feared for our lives.' Homer seems to acquiesce to her request to get rid of the gun, but merely hides it in the vegetable crisper, where Bart accidentally stumbles upon it. He and Milhouse are about to re-enact the William Tell legend in the Simpson kitchen when Marge walks in. She promptly moves out, taking the kids with her. Finally, Homer admits he's powerless to get rid of the gun himself, and Marge takes it away and agrees to come home. Since this crisis, though, the problems with their marriage have been eminently manageable (a need to spice up their sex life, for example), and the notion that Homer might be undeserving of his wife's love has largely vanished.

Homer's kids have also grown much closer to their father in the show's later years. Bart, in particular, has become Homer's default partner-in-crime, a frequent participant in Homer's various schemes – and an enthusiastic one at that. In one episode in Season 13, for example, Homer gets into a dispute with the phone company over some strange calls listed on his bill, which of course results in service being cut off. The entire family gathers in the Simpson living room to consider the problem. 'Homer,' Marge asks, 'what are you going to do?' Bart kneels on the floor, fingers crossed, praying quietly: 'Crazy scheme, crazy scheme, crazy scheme . . .' 'Get me tools and beer!' Homer announces, and Bart celebrates victory. Lisa, meanwhile, might be less enthusiastic about her father's excesses, but she's no less accepting. For example, when Homer abandons the family car's steering wheel to turn and lavish attention on Bart, Lisa reaches over from the back seat – casually, a little peeved, in an almost reflexive response – to grab the wheel, muttering, 'I got it.' The kids are under no illusions about who their father is, nor about his few strengths and his many weaknesses. They've adjusted accordingly.

Think of Bart and Lisa in these moments as stand-ins for the apathetic citizens of the prosperous West, whose day-to-day lives are cushy and entertaining enough that they merely shrug – *of course* – when they learn of a politician who has stretched the truth or a corporation that has broken the rules. Far more outrageous, far more difficult to comprehend, would be news of a leader who wasn't a liar or a cheat. The Simpson kids are surprised only when their father manages to do something wise. How could such a thing possibly happen?

It happens because it must. And it must because Homer is carrying the full symbolic weight of twentieth-century America on his plump shoulders, and no garden-variety doofus could manage that task. And so, quite despite himself, Homer is an organism of considerable complexity. Nowhere is this more apparent than in Episode 2F14 ('Homer vs. Patty and Selma'), when Homer gambles away his family's entire life savings on pumpkin futures. Disregarding his broker's advice, Homer hangs on to his futures until after Halloween, counting on a January peak. (He even takes to lighting cigars with dollar bills down at Moe's in anticipation of his impending wealth.) Naturally, he soon finds himself faced with the prospect of explaining to Marge that the Simpsons are broke. The night he learns he's lost it all, Homer arrives home to a house clouded with smoke from the omnipresent cigarettes of his loathsome sisters-in-law, Patty and Selma. Barely able to tolerate their presence at the best of times, he insists that they leave.

On the porch, Marge attempts to apologise to her sisters. 'Homer doesn't mean to be rude,' she tells them. 'He's just a very complicated man.'

Suddenly, Homer's head pops out of the bedroom window above, his eyes wide and crazed. He smashes a dinner plate over his head. 'Wrong!' he exclaims.

This is, to be sure, a revelatory moment. For one thing, it illustrates with ludicrous clarity several of the best-known aspects of Homer's character: his impulsiveness, his inherent silliness, his evident, even physical stupidity. It's a great Homer moment – one of my favourites – and I'd like to say it's the *defining* Homer moment, but that would do a grave injustice to the extraordinary dramatic achievement that is Homer J. Simpson. He's a mere moron like Moby Dick is a good-sized fish. A brazen display of dimwit-tedness such as this can't possibly tell the whole story.

Towards the end of the episode, Homer acts out the near-polar opposite of his plate-smashing impulsiveness. Having exhausted several other options for getting back the money he lost in rotted pumpkins without Marge finding out, he takes out a loan from Patty and Selma. But Marge finds out anyway, and Homer has to obtain a chauffeur's licence to keep the second job he's taken to earn the money back. But Patty and Selma – Department of Motor Vehicles employees – deny him a passing grade on his test. With orgasmic joy, they stamp 'Fail' on his written exam, then fire up cigarettes to celebrate, only to be caught by their supervisor, who threatens to take away their recent promotions. Homer is briefly elated, but then he notices the pained expression on Marge's face. He quickly snatches the cigarettes and drags on both simultaneously.

'Those are yours, sir?' the supervisor asks sceptically.

'Yes,' Homer answers. 'I am in flavour country.'

'*Both* of them?'

'It's a big country.'

The sisters' promotions are saved.

'That's a wonderful thing you did for my sisters,' Marge tells Homer.

'I didn't do it for them,' Homer answers. 'I did it for *you*, Marge.'

And, in so doing, he dramatically demonstrates that there is more to his character than his bulbous, bumbling figure might suggest. For every moment of overt stupidity or appalling childishness (or at least for every other one), there is a display of tenderness, of selflessness, of profound love. In Episode 2F14, Homer proves himself to be a loving and compassionate husband, a man capable of great sacrifice as well as selfish indulgence. Indeed, it's his many, many contradictions – concerned *and* negligent father, loving *and* inconsiderate husband, incompetent *and* accomplished worker (he is, after all, a nuclear technician, and he's been to outer space) – that make him so all-encompassing a representative of contemporary America. Homer is, despite his insistence to the contrary, a very complicated man.

As a result, he's a very endearing character, in large part because it's easier to identify with a deeply flawed figure than with a saint. Homer is one of us – an average idiot struggling to succeed in a bewildering world – and so when he's redeemed despite his flaws, his triumph is ours. Even more endearingly, Homer is often fully aware of his many faults. It's much harder to resent a guy for his shortcomings if he's willing to tell you all about them. And, moreover, to perform elaborate acts of contrition: in one instance, Homer apologises to Marge, over a megaphone, for 'the whole marriage up to this point'.

But it's in Episode BABF22 ('HOM Я') from Season 12 that Homer has several of his most self-aware – and most revealing – moments. All of these are precipitated by the discovery that Homer's lifelong stupidity, and the impulsiveness and callousness and general boorishness that have accompanied it, has been caused by a crayon that has been lodged in his brain since he was a toddler. The offending crayon is removed, and Homer's IQ immediately shoots up 50 points. Suddenly, he is a competent, poised, intelligent adult – which leads, of course, to disaster. Homer accidentally proves that God doesn't exist while working on a flat-tax proposal, much to his hyper-religious neighbour's disappointment. Far more catastrophically, Homer becomes a high-achieving employee at the nuclear plant. When he sends his thorough safety report directly to the Nuclear Regulatory Commission, the plant has to be shut down to be brought into compliance.

Homer and most of his close friends are laid off, and he's no longer welcome at his beloved Moe's Tavern. He commiserates with Lisa about the sadness that's apparently inherent in being intelligent, and then heads off to the movies to get his mind off it all. And that's when his newfound smarts become unbearable: not only is Homer unable to see the humour in the film (a romantic comedy starring Julia Roberts and Richard Gere entitled *Love Is Nice*), but he blurts out the ending in advance, spoiling it for everyone else. So it's off to Moe's to get the debilitating crayon reinserted. He returns home with his fists stuffed with lottery tickets, making it clear to the whole Simpson clan that the old, dim Homer is back. 'Dad, how could you?' asks a wounded Lisa. 'We were connecting in such a meaningful way.' The re-crayoned Homer has no reply to this, but then he discovers a note addressed to Lisa that he wrote before he reverted to his old self. 'Lisa,' it reads, 'I'm taking the coward's way out. But before I do, I just want you to know: being smart made me appreciate how amazing you really are.' Given the choice, Homer opts for a return to the blissful ignorance that has made his life so rich and rewarding, for the easier unexamined life – and it's sufficient consolation for Lisa to know that her father understood, for a fleeting moment, that his is the easier path.

There are two nasty truths buried in Episode BABF22. The first is that Homer's life is so successful *because* he's so dumb. Anyone with too much smarts, too great a sense of responsibility, too great a propensity for asking difficult questions, will be hopelessly frustrated by modern American life. It's the dimwitted dolts who live happy and fulfilling lives. A similar argument lies at the heart of the hit film *Forrest Gump* (the Academy's choice for Best Picture of 1994), in which Tom Hanks's mentally challenged Forrest becomes a national hero, while his childhood friend Jenny asks the tough questions and finds only depravity, addiction and fatal disease as her reward. And this point would be hammered home even more dramatically a few years later, with the rise of a smirking frat boy, failed oilman, bumbling baseball-team owner, wannabe baseball commissioner and resolutely anti-introspective non-thinker named George W. Bush to the presidency of the United States.

The other argument implicit in Homer's decision to return to stupidity is more subtle but ultimately far more damning. The key detail here is this: Homer's choice is portrayed as perfectly rational. Obvious, even. Why, after all, would anyone choose a lifetime of disappointment and inner turmoil when successful, contented bliss is only a brain haemorrhage away? The America of Episode BABF22 not only encourages and rewards stupidity, it treats it as the preferable mental state. There is no progressive, enlightened society just around the corner in which probing intelligence will be the desired norm. *Homer* is the desired norm. He is the Everyman. The hero. Agree with Lisa's social critiques all you want, but admit it: Homer is the one you love.

EVERYBODY LOVES HOMER (WITH ONE NOTABLE EXCEPTION WORTH EXAMINING IN SOME DEPTH)

It's still possible to see Homer as an essentially malevolent character – as a 'cowardly, incompetent, deluded, greedy consumer of the American Dream', as the *New Statesman* TV critic, Andrew Billen, once put it. Even as late as Season 12, an episode centres on Homer's attempt to turn his house into a daycare centre, providing an especially pointed illustration of his neglect of his own children. But to see him this way is to miss the point: Homer is the *hero* of *The Simpsons*. He is far and away the most beloved character. And this deep and genuine affection for Homer is felt not only by the other characters in the show but by the vast majority of the audience. In a 2003 poll conducted by BBC Online (tied to a special report entitled 'What the World Thinks of America'), Homer was voted 'the greatest American'. Ever. By a landslide. He took in 47.17 per cent of the vote, with Abe Lincoln a distant second (9.67 per cent) and the bronze going to Martin Luther King, Jr. (8.54 per cent). Now, this was an *online* poll, and I certainly wouldn't want to put too much stock in an online poll (Mr T was chosen the fourth-greatest American in this one), but it does provide fairly dramatic evidence that Homer is the heart and soul of *The Simpsons*. He's not only the show's driving force, he's the main reason millions tune in. And, more importantly, I'd argue that those millions are tuning in not to watch Homer make an ass of himself but to *relate to* Homer as he makes an ass of himself. Not to laugh *at* Homer, but to laugh *with* him. This is a critical distinction. I'll say it again: Homer is the *hero*. Centuries of dramatic convention dictate that we cheer for him. That we are on his side. That, therefore, when critics and fans alike talk about how 'realistic' *The Simpsons* is, they are implying that Homer is plausible as the embodiment of the hopes and dreams and values of his age.

The tacit ridiculousness of this notion – and the fact that it contravenes damn near every single value the society that produced Homer Simpson claims to hold dear – is the subject of one of the most revelatory episodes in the show's history: Episode 4F19 ('Homer's Enemy'). The point, Matt Groening has explained, was to 'explore what it would be like to actually work alongside Homer Simpson'. (This was in a 2000 *Entertainment Weekly* story in which Groening chose 4F19 as his sixth-favourite episode of all time.) The episode was written by John Swartzwelder, quite likely the person with the most intimate understanding of the show's characters – especially Homer. The episode's premise: an *actual* American hero, a man named Frank Grimes, becomes Homer Simpson's co-worker, and immediately and intensely and most of all *necessarily* comes to hate Homer.

Grimes is a hard worker, the kind of Horatio Alger character that America has long claimed as the pinnacle example of its unique virtue. And he is palpably unable to exist in a universe that treats Homer as a decent human being, much less a hero. This is the central conceit at work in Episode 4F19 – that the show's vaunted 'realism' tumbles over like a particleboard Hollywood façade in the face of a light tap from a genuine American.

'Homer's Enemy' is unlike any other *Simpsons* episode – including the many episodes that have featured other real-world figures – for the simple reason that Frank Grimes does not play ball. Unlike Hollywood celebrities and former US presidents and even Fox Network owner Rupert Murdoch, whose appearances bear traces of their real-world selves but are ultimately at the mercy of the show's physics and logic and especially its *values*, Grimes is not immersed in the show's reality. Quite the contrary: he fights like a cornered wolverine against it. What's more, the episode makes the argument that *you* would too.

Grimes is introduced through a TV news segment called 'Kent's People', dedicated to heartwarming slice-of-life stories. Slick Channel 6 anchorman Kent Brockman introduces Grimes – a brush-cutted, bespectacled, white-shirt-and-tied middle-management type with a pinched visage reeking of victimhood – as a man 'who has earned everything the hard way but never let adversity get him down'. Grimes's story is a ludicrously pathetic litany of tragedy and oppression: abandoned by his parents at age four; victim of a silo explosion at age 18; years spent recovering from the accident and studying science via correspondence courses in rare leisure moments; finally, a diploma in nuclear physics. Mr Burns, watching the TV profile from his office at the nuclear plant, is so moved by Grimes's story that he orders his lackey Smithers to recruit Grimes as his new executive vice-president. When Grimes arrives the next day, though, Burns has again been moved by the subject of 'Kent's People' – a heroic dog – and so Grimes is shunted off 'somewhere out of the way' instead. (The dog reappears several scenes later, with a blanket draped over his body reading EXECUTIVE VICE-PRESIDENT.) In this ignoble fashion, Frank Grimes is assigned to the workstation next to Sector 7G's resident incompetent hero, Homer Simpson.

Homer tries to be chummy with Grimes, even sharing one of his best loafing tips, but it's no use. In short order, Homer's standard mix of stupidity, carelessness and incompetence – eating Grimey's lunch, dumping water on the control panel of his workstation to deal with an emergency, calling him 'Grimey' – has totally alienated his hard-working colleague. The final straw comes when Grimes saves an oblivious Homer from taking a swig from a beaker of acid, knocking it from his hands to smash against a nearby wall, only to be reprimanded for damaging the wall and given a pay cut. A short time later, Grimes storms into Homer's work area. 'Hi, Grimey, old buddy,' Homer says. 'I'm not your buddy, Simpson,' Grimes fumes. 'I don't like you. In fact, I hate you. Stay the hell away from me! Because from now on . . . we're enemies.'

This is unprecedented. The only real adversaries Homer has had to this point are his hyper-religious neighbour Ned Flanders (who usually treats Homer with syrupy Christian cheeriness despite Homer's open contempt for him), his horrid sisters-in-law, and former US president George H.W. Bush. Grimey's hatred upsets Homer deeply – after all, Homer is, as he tells Moe the bartender, 'the most beloved man in Springfield'. (This is a big wink at the audience: Homer's only *somewhat* beloved by his fellow Springfieldianites, any number of whom have been burned in his schemes or outraged by his buffoonery, but he is very much the audience's favourite Springfield resident.)

At any rate, Homer feels compelled to win Grimey over. He manufactures a work-related reason for Grimes to come by the Simpson residence, where he hopes to charm his colleague with a lobster dinner and an evening with his lovely family. The plan backfires. A wrung-out, rumpled Grimey arrives, frustrated that he's already late for his night job, only to be completely overwhelmed by the elaborate dimensions of Homer's life. How, Grimey exclaims, can Homer afford his 'palace' of a house when all he can afford is 'a single room above a bowling alley – and below another bowling alley'? Homer points out framed photos of himself with Gerald Ford, on tour with the Smashing Pumpkins, and in outer space. 'Would you like to see my Grammy Award?' Homer asks hospitably. Grimey emphatically would not. Instead, he explodes into a rage, unable to fathom how Homer's 'lifetime of sloth and ignorance' has resulted in a dream house, two cars, a happy family and lobster for dinner. 'And do you deserve any of it?' Grimey rants. 'No!'

'What are you saying?' Homer asks, wounded.

'I'm saying you're what's wrong with America, Simpson,' Grimes replies. 'You coast through life, you do as little as possible, and you leech off of decent, hardworking people like me.' He coughs out a nasty laugh. 'If you lived in any other country in the world, you'd have starved to death long ago.'

If the writers winked at us in earlier scenes, they are by this point jamming their sharp elbows repeatedly into our ribs. It's almost as if Swartzwelder and company wanted to be absolutely goddamn *certain* we got the point: this Everyman of ours, this working-class hero we all adore, this man is *nothing* like what we claim to admire.

Grimey, on behalf of genuine working stiffs everywhere, dedicates the rest of the episode to proving 'that Homer Simpson has the intelligence of a six-year-old'. To that end, he tricks Homer into entering a children's contest to build a model of a nuclear power plant.[9] But Homer, far from being humiliated, wins first prize, and the raucous cheers of the audience quickly drown out Grimey's jeering. They also send poor Grimey over the edge: he lurches around the plant pretending to be Homer – scarfing doughnuts, showing his ass crack, pissing on the toilet seat – and finishes his tirade by seizing a mass of wires labelled EXTREMELY HIGH VOLTAGE. Cut to Grimes's funeral, where Reverend Lovejoy refers to him by the hated nickname 'Grimey' and eulogises blandly until a dozing Homer rouses slightly and bellows, 'Change the channel, Marge!' The assembled mourners laugh heartily, and Lenny announces, 'That's our Homer!'

The final image of Episode 4F19 is of Frank Grimes's casket descending into the earth. This blunt but scathing self-critique closes, then, with *The Simpsons* writers laying to rest the producer-culture values of traditional America – the hard work and sacrifice and rugged individualism on which the nation was founded, and to which its leaders still frequently pay lip service. These empty platitudes aside, modern America is driven by a culture of consumption. Consumption has become the primary focus of the American project and the lead architect of America's value system. This is increasingly true of most of the other affluent democracies, but it's a shift whose impact has been most dramatic in the United States, where those original producer-oriented values were most deeply held and most widely celebrated. It started, of course, long before Homer Simpson started capturing American hearts and minds in the 1990s. In the American historian Warren I. Susman's 1984 study of this massive transformation, *Culture as History: The Transformation of American Society in the Twentieth Century*, he traces the producer-consumer shift back to the beginning of the century.

'Simply put,' Susman summarises, 'one of the fundamental conflicts of twentieth-century America is between two cultures – an older culture, often loosely labelled Puritan-republican, producer-capitalist culture, and a newly emerging culture of abundance.' Homer's destruction of Frank Grimes, however bumblingly unintentional, represents a victory – quite possibly the final victory – of that 'culture of abundance'. It's not just that Homer is rewarded within the context of the show, but that he is such a beloved icon to the show's viewers. Consumer values have clearly eclipsed their older opponent in this conflict.

The eclipse, though, is far from total, and the lingering ambiguities of this struggle are evident not just in Homer's own character but in the audience's understanding of his 'heroism'. As I've already pointed out, Homer is not strictly a consumer. Certain of the core producer values – particularly the importance of family – remain central to his character. And Homer's frequent schemes, doomed to failure as they may be, illustrate the survival of a certain traditional American inventiveness and entrepreneurship. This is, after all, a man who has tried his hand at yeoman farming (he invented a highly addictive tomato-tobacco hybrid called 'tomacco'), who has attempted to corner the markets on sugar and recycled grease, who has run a highly successful bootlegging business. Consumption might be the first thing on Homer's mind, but it's not always the only thing.

And our love for Homer doesn't flow exclusively from the ways in which he embodies our ideal consumer selves. Yes, we love him because he tells us that everything's okay, that it's just fine to be self-indulgent, to drive a gas guzzler and eat junk food and obsess over the minutiae of our favourite celebrities. But this isn't the whole equation. There is also the anti-hero side of Homer, the Belushi-esque subversiveness – as when Homer tosses away the entire apparatus of organised religion after a single joyous morning without church. Far more subversive, though, is the mere fact that he is beloved, that so many viewers identify with him and even in some sense revere him. This is the point so starkly illustrated by his encounter with Frank Grimes: if Homer is the good guy, then the society he lives in is much more deeply flawed – more superficial, more irresponsible, more immoral (or at least amoral) – than most of its inhabitants and practically all of its leaders admit.

To this day, the muscled alpha males of Hollywood cinema continue to reinforce the grand American producer-culture myth of the rugged individual, imbued with an unshakeable moral compass, ready to take the law into his own hands – but only in the face of corrupt authority or, increasingly, in response to a foreign assault. Professional athletes and captains of industry continue to bathe in the holy glow of whitewashed biographies in which hard work and gumption – as opposed to, say, ruthlessness and nepotism – pave the road to success. The heroes on the court or in the boardroom who are revealed to be compulsive gamblers or sexual predators or flat-out cheats, meanwhile, are treated as grotesque exceptions to the otherwise flawless rule. This archetype remains the standard mould for American heroes.

But if Homer is the new Horatio Alger icon[10] – the man who succeeds despite or even because of idiocy and laziness, who lucks into the good life by birth or circumstance, whose good fortune has nothing at all to do with strength of character – then the rules and strictures pushed by pretty much every authority figure going, from teachers and parents all the way up to presidents, are either ludicrously out of date or dangerously deluded wishful thinking. Or they are flat-out lies. This is the most powerful and subversive symbolic point made by Homer's ersatz heroism: to idolise Homer, even a little, is to embrace the deeply flawed truth of What Is over the fairytale version of What Should Be you've long been fed by the powers that be. If we all truly felt the way those voices of authority claim we do (or should), then we'd all agree with Frank Grimes that Homer is a stellar exemplar of what's wrong with America. But we don't. We're glad Grimes is gone. We're cheering for Homer.

Those cheers might not always be unqualified. Another of Homer's strengths as a symbol is that he is complex and conflicted enough that *Simpsons* viewers have as paradoxical a relationship with him as they do with the United States itself. We see evidence of this ambiguity in Lenny and Carl's behaviour in the Frank Grimes episode. Lenny and Carl are by no means blind to Homer's faults, nor do they necessarily excuse or correct them. In fact, the notion that they *could* excuse or correct, that they could intervene in any way at all to somehow steer this powerful force in their lives, seems very distant. Their acceptance of Homer is akin to 'accepting' the weather. Homer is a force of nature – and a ferocious one at that – and Lenny and Carl have had to resign themselves to the fact of him. They've had to acknowledge his existence, his enormous presence, his significant impact (for good or ill) on their lives. This is remarkably similar to the way most of the world feels about America. Love or hate, mild annoyance or smug bemusement, anger or hope – these are somewhere further down on the list of responses. First, there's the need to accept that America will affect your life – significantly – no matter how you feel about it.

In the end, Lenny and Carl side with Homer. As Frank Grimes rants about Homer's many faults, they first offer rote defences – 'Everyone makes mistakes'; 'Give him a break' – and then they just stop listening. After a long pregnant pause at the end of Grimey's rant, Lenny turns to Carl and says, 'So, how *you* doin'?' This reaction is an excellent illustration of the necessary contradictions in any relationship with a force as powerful as America. We can talk about its merits and faults, we can carry with us simultaneous feelings of deep love and intense loathing for various aspects of it, but beyond a certain point there is only redundancy or the hair-tearing frustration that leads Grimey to his inadvertent suicide. Better, then, simply to live with the contradictions. This is as necessary a non-reckoning for Americans themselves as for the billions around the world touched by America's power. Even the most jingoistic American patriots hold a deep and abiding hatred for some aspect of their homeland – those cowardly, amoral hippies, say, or all the immigrants who can barely speak English, or Bill Clinton. And even the shrillest self-critics surely maintain a fierce love for the Bill of Rights, or for a handful of American punk bands, or for Bill Clinton. But few American icons have been able to encapsulate the full measure of this ambivalence. You can find traces of it – in the reluctant but deadly violence of James Dean's rebel without a cause, or in Franklin D. Roosevelt's crippled body and towering statesmanship. But the majority of heroes actively repel ambivalence (FDR disguised his disability, after all) which is what makes them such limited symbols. And, by contrast, what makes Homer such a comprehensive one.

Of course, some lumps of Homer's symbolic weight sit more heavily than others. Emphasis here on *lump*. And *weight*. And *heavily*.

SPRINGFIELD: A CITY ON THE GROW

Insatiable, impulsive, inconsistent Homer is no aberration – he's merely the most dramatic example of an entire social order. When you zoom out from Homer to include the world that spawned him – the media-saturated consumer paradise of Springfield, USA – the enormous and relentless force of the symbolism only grows. Springfield is a town overflowing with frivolous consumer items, wildly unnecessary consumer outlets and hordes of overeager consumers. The downtown streets and the local mall overflow with stores like The Horseradishery, the International House of Answering Machines, and Miscellaneous, Et Cetera. The local Monstro Mart ('Where Shopping Is a Baffling Ordeal') offers an unbeatable bargain on 12 pounds of nutmeg. The Springfield Museum sings its own merits thusly: 'Truth, Knowledge, Gift Shop'. A TV infomercial hawks the Mr Sugar Cube home sugar-cube maker and Spiffy-brand tombstone cleaner, while local TV icon Krusty the Clown lends his name and dubious Seal of Approval to third-rate merchandise ranging from Chocolate Frosted Frosty Krusty Flakes to the Krusty Home Pregnancy Test ('May cause birth defects'). There's a cartoon show called *Action Figure Man* (the how-to-buy-Action-Figure-Man episode was nominated for a Cartoon Award for best writing). Down at the Kwik-E-Mart, the magazine rack includes *Fabergé Egg Owner* and *Ballpoint Pen Digest*. The Simpsons, meanwhile, pass the odd moments when they're not watching TV or buying and consuming things by singing such traditional family folk tunes as the Armour hot dog and Oscar Mayer wiener theme songs – sometimes tossing in the 'I feel like Chicken Tonight!' jingle to make a medley of it. Springfield may have a factory or two, and many locals earn their wages, as Homer does, down at the power plant, but Springfield's raison d'être is quite clearly consumption of the crassest kind: useless trinkets, celebrity-endorsed junk, synthetic simulacra of old staples.

Though a lot of this stuff serves merely as realistic set dressing, there are moments in which the hyper-consumer culture of Springfield moves front and centre – in Episode 4F13 ('My Sister, My Sitter'), for example, when Homer and Marge attend the grand opening of Springfield's brand-new South Street Squidport. At moments like these, the 'satirical' setting seems almost documentary. The Squidport is a local revitalisation project, recasting an historic industrial area as a pedestrian mall. Marge is 'honoured that Springfield has been chosen to host all these upscale chain stores', while the local press listen in amazement as action hero Rainier Wolfcastle confirms that every item on the menu at Planet Hype was personally approved by his secretary. The only anachronistic note comes when a yuppie tourist follows a tunnel from Moe's Tavern's Squidport storefront to its actual downtown location. ('This isn't *faux* dive,' the disgusted yuppie notes. 'This is a dive.') Otherwise, the verisimilitude's pretty much flawless. Here, for instance, is a list of stores and restaurants you can find either at Springfield's Squidport or at the Shops of Mission Viejo in Orange County, California: Just Rainsticks, Everything But Water, My First Tattoo, Piercing Pagoda, The Itchy & Scratchy Store, The Discovery Channel Store, It's a Wonderful Knife, Bag 'n' Baggage, Much Ado About Muffins, The Cheesecake Factory, Crypto Barn: A Place for Codes, Pottery Barn Kids. (Shrewd consumers will perhaps discern that this list alternates between first Squidport and then Orange County outlets.)

The thing is, our own consumer culture more or less defies satirisation. It mocks itself so effectively it can't be mocked, and it vaults into self-parody far too regularly and effectively really to need outside help. In one *Simpsons* episode, a depressed Homer wanders into the Kwik-E-Mart in search of something to lift his spirits. 'Got any of that beer that has candy floating in it?' he asks Apu. 'You know – Skittle Bräu?' Apu informs him there is no such product, so Homer buys a six-pack and a few packages of Skittles. A few years later, the online retailer Cafépress.com could be found hawking everything from T-shirts and baseball caps to coffee mugs and mouse pads emblazoned with the Skittle Bräu logo. The product itself was too silly even for Springfield's overheated consumer culture, but the commodification of the show in the real world has become so extensive and relentless that Skittle Bräu gave birth to a whole line of saleable merchandise.

By way of personal example, I can say that I had occasion, circa 1998, to drink a bottle of juice that went by the name of 'Aunty Goethe's Peachy-Mango Love Pain'. (This was from a line of juices called Uvo, which was competing with or else elaborately parodying the Fruitopia line of pseudo-psychedelic fruit drinks.) A couple of years before that, I inadvertently bought a bunch of *Space Jam* bananas – which is to say, each of the bananas I bought had a tiny ad for the Michael Jordan film *Space Jam* on its label sticker. I can recall, too, how one of the most noteworthy developments to come from the Art Gallery of Ontario's Edvard Munch exhibition in the spring of 1997 was the enormous popularity of *The Scream* paraphernalia (mugs, pillowcases, inflatable dolls) on sale in the gift shop.

Anyone who has lived through these years of dumb affluence and constant acquisition no doubt has their own set of similar touchstones. Statistical glimpses of the society-wide scope of this phenomenon are thick on the ground: the obesity rate increasing from one in eight to one in five Americans from 1991 to 1998; $30 billion spent annually in the United States on lawn care; the total square footage of England's shopping centres clearing four million. Americans spend more money annually on jewellery, watches and shoes ($80 billion) than on higher education ($65 billion), and more time per week shopping (six hours on average) than playing with their kids (40 minutes).

These last two statistical pairings come from a 1997 PBS documentary called *Affluenza*, which gave a name and a pathology to the West's obsession with over-consumption. A subsequent book – *Affluenza: The All-Consuming Epidemic*, by John de Graaf, David Wann and Thomas H. Naylor – defined the illness as 'a painful, contagious, virally transmitted condition of overload, debt, anxiety and waste resulting from the dogged pursuit of more'. The authors argued that this disease was not only rampant among individuals but endemic to the entire hyper-capitalist Western economic system, spawned by 'the obsessive, almost religious quest for economic expansion' that treats a fast-growing gross domestic product as the 'supreme measure of national progress'.

The PBS programme spawned a sequel, *Escape from Affluenza* – a sort of how-to guide for downgrading your definition of affluence and reducing your consumption levels. PBS perhaps needn't have bothered, because the dissatisfaction with hyper-consumption inevitably created its own consumer trend: voluntary simplicity. Hard-core adherents may have taken to shopping in second-hand stores and growing their own vegetables, but the message was purely consumerist by the time it hit mainstream America's newsstands in April 2000 as a grammatically challenged Time Inc. magazine called *Real Simple*, which advocated on behalf of a 'simple' life that included $300 T-shirts and ads for Revlon and Ralph Lauren. Devotees of this consumer trend can presumably also be found at Pottery Barn shopping for ersatz handicrafts and at Restoration Hardware buying fake antiques. Which, come to think of it, are the kinds of stores that hawk their wares at North America's real-world Squidports.

There's an argument that, far from being symptoms of some sociologist's fantasy of a disease, these pseudo-traditional chain stores are in fact emblems of a grand new consensus. In particular, there's social critic David Brooks's 2000 book *Bobos in Paradise: The New Upper Class and How They Got There*. To hear Brooks tell it, America's Squidports, as well as its rapidly growing exurban enclaves and prosperous 'Latte Towns,' are the stomping grounds of a new 'educated gentry' – the 'Bobos' (short for bourgeois-bohemians) – that represents a final happy reconciliation between the bourgeois and bohemian camps that have long stood as the opposing poles in America's culture wars. This reconciliation of 'the antiestablishment style' and 'the corporate imperative' reveals itself in the revolution-rock soundtracks of ad campaigns and in the back-to-basics products on the shelves of Restoration Hardware. In the pages of *The Weekly Standard* (where he is a senior editor), Brooks has also sung the praises of 'Patio Man', who lives in a big-boxed, McMansioned 'Sprinkler City' with a 'Realtor Mom' wife and kids named Haley (a 'Travel Team Girl') and Cody (a 'Buzz Cut Boy'). Patio Man's pride and joy – his personal exurban Arc de Triomphe – is his 'multi-leveled patio/outdoor recreation area', where we can find this triumphal American consumer at perfect peaceful consumptive leisure.

It perhaps goes without saying that a Brooksian take on Homer Simpson would likely depict him as a kind of all-in-one Patio-Bobo-Everyman. And he might well see Springfield as the Latte Sprinkler CityTowne of every middle American's dreams. And to be fair, Brooks's eye for social detail is no less precise than that of *The Simpsons*' writers. It's just that Brooks sees a glorious finish line in the pursuit of happiness in most of the same spots where *The Simpsons* version finds deep cultural rot. The show's writers have taken great care to make Homer lovable enough to carry a long-running primetime series, but they portray Springfield as a sort of grotesque mirror image of America in which smug consumption and empty-headed cultural plenty mask – only thinly – a desperation that verges on total panic.

A panic, I should mention, that finds its shorthand in the recurring mass hysteria and mob rule of the people of Springfield.

THE *WAUGGGHHH!/WOO-HOO!* CYCLE, THE HYSTERICAL MASSES OF SPRINGFIELD & THE SILLY, SILLY CASE OF Y2K

When Homer Simpson screams in terror, it's a hard, throaty sound. His mouth falls agape, his widening eyes show panic. His tongue sometimes emerges, rippling like a sea in a vicious storm. And then the sound explodes, short and quick and reedy or long and wide and growling as the problem dictates. It's the sound you sometimes hear in the show's opening credits as he scrambles to get out of the way of Marge's car in the family garage. It's a big step up from the mild annoyance of *D'oh!* It indicates more serious trouble. It goes: *Wauggghhh!* And then there's its inverse: a high-pitched, celebratory noise delivered through pursed lips after winning a contest to become an astronaut or discovering that ham is on sale. It's always quick and ejaculatory, accompanied on occasion by a raised fist. It goes: *Woo-hoo!*

Much of Homer's life is lived in this constant cycle between horrified panic and exuberant celebration. Mr Burns shows up at his house to watch the big boxing match: *Wauggghhh!* Homer finds Henry Kissinger's glasses in the nuclear plant's toilet: *Woo-hoo!* Former US president Jimmy Carter challenges him to a duel: *Wauggghhh!* A hot-dog vendor appears at a funeral Homer is attending: *Woo-hoo!*

Though these reflexive moments are usually unconnected and quite spread out temporally, there have been occasions when the cycle has been whiplash-inducingly tight. In Episode 9F15 ('Last Exit to Springfield'), for example, Homer the reluctant union leader is required to appear alongside Mr Burns (and, inexplicably, Dr Joyce Brothers) on Kent Brockman's *Smartline* to defend the strike he's leading at the power plant. 'Homer, organised labour has been described as a lumbering dinosaur,' Brockman begins. Homer promptly replies, 'Waugggghhh!' A moment's pause, and then

Brockman continues: 'My director is telling me not to talk to you any-more . . .' Homer: 'Woo-hoo!'

These lurches between extremes are by no means limited to Homer himself. In fact, they're an exaggerated shorthand for the behaviour of the assembled populace of Springfield, who can gather into an angry mob in mere moments and reverse into revelry or else merely disperse just as quickly. The *Wauggghhh!/Woo-hoo!* cycle indeed seems to govern the entire town, particularly when it gathers in large numbers – which it most often tends to do, not incidentally, either to unite behind Homer or to chastise him for one of his excesses. A textbook case: In Episode 3F20 ('Much Apu About Nothing'), a wild bear comes wandering through the Simpsons' neighbour-hood, inciting Homer to lead an angry mob of his fellow citizens to the door of Mayor Quimby's office – twice. The first time is a protest against the 'constant bear attacks' in Springfield (there had been exactly one, con-stituting 'a freakin' country-bear jambaroo' in Homer's reckoning), and the second is a protest against the tax imposed to pay for the new Bear Patrol.

The citizens of Springfield are no less one-minded and malleable in other mass assemblies. The easy answers peddled by self-help guru Brad Goodman, for example, turn the entire town into a pack of self-indulgent overgrown children, and a town meeting to decide the fate of a $3-million municipal windfall is easily won over to the impractical notion of a monorail by the fast-talking pitch and catchy song of slimy huckster Lyle Lanley. Indeed the huddled masses of Springfield can be counted on, pretty much without exception, to behave as a single-minded, over-emotional horde in the face of any new crisis or trend. Homer's sporadic *Wauggghhh!*s and *Woo-hoo!*s can sometimes seem positively cautious by comparison.

Some critics – particularly British ones, for some reason – have long disparaged (or is it praised?) *The Simpsons* for being a deeply cynical show, which has always struck me as a serious misreading. Not all satire is cynical, after all. In fact, most satire builds from a deeply idealistic rage at the hypocrisies of its targets, and *The Simpsons* even gives its stinging satire a fine sugar-coating of sentimental family values. (On which I'll say quite a bit more in Chapter 6.) But if there's one place where the cynic label sticks, it's probably in the series' repeated depictions of the unwashed masses of its America-in-microcosm as brain-dead automatons. In some instances, this portrayal is so broad and blunt that lemmings would seem free-spirited by comparison. Take the extreme case of Episode 4F17 ('The Old Man and the Lisa'), in which Lisa helps a suddenly destitute Mr Burns rebuild his industrial empire on the foundations of an eco-friendly recycling concern.

Burns, malevolent to the core, decides the most profitable way to expand his new business is to knit plastic six-pack rings together into the 'Burns Omni-net', which sweeps the sea floor clean of all living things and processes them into a pink slurry that can be used as insulation, farm feed and engine coolant. Lisa, realising the horrors she has caused, runs out into the Springfield streets, begging her fellow citizens to stop recycling. She comes across a random man and woman. (Notably, neither is part of the show's massive cast of recurring bit characters; they are instead two hyper-generic drones created for this sequence.) Lisa implores them to drop their recycling boxes. 'But you told us to recycle,' the woman answers in a robotic monotone. 'You convinced us it was good,' the man adds just as mechanically. Surely modern America – indeed the modern West generally – is not this easily led, this effortlessly duped. Whatever its faults, it's a touch shrewder as a whole than Homer's *Wauggghhh!/Woo-hoo!* cycle and the panicky Springfield throng let on. Isn't it?

I mean, it's not like you could fool the entire democratic world with one of those dim-witted infomercials hosted by hack actor Troy McClure that convince Homer to buy juice looseners and the rest of the town to attend self-help seminars. Could you?

Fade in. Hack actor Troy McClure sits at a computer, desperately pounding the keyboard with his fist. 'Control-alt-delete does nothing! *Nothing!*' he screams. He turns to the camera, suddenly calm, and flashes a broad Hollywood grin. 'Oh, hi! I'm Troy McClure! You might remember me from such mass panics as "The Metric System: Prelude to Communist Conquest" and "The Africanised Killer Bee Holocaust". But today, I'm here to tell you about the most dangerous force ever to be unleashed on civilisation: the Y2K bug!' McClure rises from his desk and walks stage left; as the camera pans, it becomes evident that the 'workstation' at which McClure was seated was set up on the edge of a large, infomercial-esque stage. 'Now let's meet the one man who can save all of humanity from certain destruction,' McClure continues chirpily. 'Gary North!'

A wild-eyed survivalist (portrayed, perhaps, by Herman, the proprietor of Springfield's military antiques store) walks on stage. McClure introduces him as a 'history professor' and the 'leader of the Y2K-preparedness movement'. 'Now why don't you tell us a little about the horrors that are in store for us,' McClure finishes.

North launches into a lengthy tirade about the apocalypse to be wrought by the fact that the world's computer chips will not be able to cope with the changeover from 1999 to 2000. Banks, public utilities, military communications, financial markets, even railroads will collapse, all because their computer systems recognise only the last two digits of the date and will assume that '2000' is actually '1900'.

'Surely not the railroads,' McClure prods sceptically.

'It's true, Troy,' North continues. In fact, he says, 'it's a disaster greater than anything the world has experienced since the bubonic plague of the four-teenth century.'

McClure turns to the camera in a hokily exaggerated pantomime of horror.

I'm kidding, of course. Gary North never appeared on *The Simpsons*. He never had an infomercial, and he didn't even do press interviews. And it wasn't Troy McClure who called North a professor and Y2K-preparedness leader, it was *The Orange County Register* and the *Ottawa Citizen*, respec-tively. To be fair, other media outlets pointed out that, PhD notwithstanding, North was a committed Reconstructionist – a firm believer that a governing system built on a close reading of the Bible was the only hope for humanity's salvation – and that he had been predicting apocalypse by various means since the early 1980s. Still, North was front and centre in many of the first accounts of the Y2K survivalist movement, the pied piper whose increasingly popular website and newsletter inspired many of the first people to quite literally head for the hills (or at least start planning for it) in 1997 and 1998 to avoid the coming disaster.

Before long, North would find himself in increasingly prestigious company. Ed Yardeni, the chief economist at Deutsche Bank Securities in New York, was by late 1998 predicting a 70 per cent chance of global recession on *his* Y2K-preparedness website. Chain bookstores began filling with books with titles like *Time Bomb 2000* and *Building Your Ark*. When a lengthy feature on the problem appeared in July 1999 in the *Washington Post*, its language was almost indistinguishable from North's own: 'There is nothing that quite compares with the so-called "Millennium Bug". It is potentially planetary in scope. It is potentially catastrophic in consequence.'

Throughout 1998 and 1999, governments and institutions dived full bore into the Y2K problem, spending what was almost certainly too many billions of dollars fixing those glitches that did exist in the computer systems of the world. The Y2K debugging employed 500,000 in the United States alone, while the British government's three-year Y2K programme boasted a £20-billion price tag and included 'What To Do' pamphlets for every household in the UK. And so on, around the globe, with the World Bank, for example, handing US$29 million to Sri Lanka for 'Y2K remediation'.

But at least the overreactions of major institutions had their foundations in real problems. All of that was nothing compared to the collective *Wauggghhh!* of the citizenry of the enlightened West. The panic was most acute in the US, where countless true believers quit their jobs and bunkered down in rural fortresses throughout 1999, but there were few corners of the industrialised world that weren't touched by the fear.

Full disclosure here: I was working at a tech-oriented magazine in Toronto in August 1998 when a long feature in another tech-oriented magazine – *Wired* – about how the Y2K debuggers had themselves gone survivalist made the rounds of the magazine's office, sending me and several colleagues into a mild fever of speculation as to where to hide out come New Year's Eve 1999. It lasted about a week. I never gave it much thought after that, and for entirely non-bug-related reasons I spent New Year's Eve 1999 bobbing on the deck of a large houseboat on Ha Long Bay in Vietnam. Moments after midnight, I bellowed across to another bobbing boat on the bay to enquire whether they were having difficulty with their computers. Oh, how we all laughed. But I digress.

Myself notwithstanding, the less hard-core survivalists were still large enough in number to produce panic-buying sprees across North America on everything from generators and batteries to groceries and medicine. In Canada, grocery stores reported a 3.7 per cent decline in sales in January 2000 as the recently terrified worked through their stockpiles. The US Federal Reserve, meanwhile, dumped $50 billion in banknotes into the national money supply to allow for hoarding, and governments from Canada to Japan kept troops on standby in case of New Year's rioting. All this even though news reports had, by autumn 1999, shifted their focus to sceptical commentary on the overreaction to the Y2K bug.

In the event, the sky didn't fall, the stock market didn't crash, the lights stayed on, and not even Russia could manage a nuclear disaster. In the United States – the heartland of the panic – there were, admittedly, a few cases of calamity: a guy in Albany, New York, for example, got slapped with a $91,000 late charge for returning a movie one hundred years late. For the most part, though, prosperous Westerners awoke groggily to a New Year's Day no more nor less troubled than any other. And for the rest of the year, in myriad ways, they raised their fists and contentedly bleated: *Woo-hoo!*

Do you remember just how smug and complacent and frivolous was the fabled year 2000? It's easy to forget, because Y2K was frivolous in just the right sorts of ways, the kind that burn bright and ubiquitous for fleeting moments and are quickly gone, and because events of such gravity have come to dominate the popular consciousness in the intervening years.

It started in late January, at least in North America, with the Super Bowl, the annual football game and advertising showcase. One of the big stars of the year's ads was a smooth-talking sock puppet who shilled for Pets.com (an online retailer of pet food). After his big break at the Super Bowl, the Pets.com Sock Puppet rode high across the American airwaves for most of February. He sang 'Three Times a Lady' to Diane Sawyer on ABC's *Good Morning America*[11] and 'I Got You, Babe' to Kathie Lee Gifford on *LIVE with Regis and Kathie Lee*, and was asked to comment on *Nightline* about *Peanuts* cartoonist Charles M. Schulz's retirement.

The Pets.com Sock Puppet, though, was exactly the kind of mindless Y2K *Woo-hoo!* phenomenon you could easily have missed, because the real breakaway stars of the 2000 Super Bowl were the Whassup Guys. You might well remember them – the actors who became famous for screeching 'Whassup?' at each other in a Budweiser beer commercial? Anyway, they went well beyond the odd morning-talk-show appearance (though they did those too). They went on tour. They travelled the US, Canada and even the UK, did the Whassup Guys. (The preceding, incidentally, is the trademarked spelling of the term.) They threw out the first pitch at a Texas Rangers baseball game, and made appearances at the NBA all-star game and the NCAA Final Four basketball tournament.

But these, of course, were just overlong Super Bowl spinoffs – preludes to the main event. And the main event of 2000 in most of the English-speaking world was reality TV. There is a perfect, Springfield-mob-like symmetry to the fact that the sustained international pop-cultural craze that immediately followed the Y2K panic involved watching average folks doing nothing of any real consequence in highly contrived environments. The crisis was averted, after all, so why not float through the first celebratory year of the new millennium on the ridiculously fluffy clouds of *Survivor* (in North America) and *Big Brother* (in the UK) and *Who Wants to Be a Millionaire?* (hit versions on both sides of the pond). By August, the weekly vote to see who got tossed from the island on *Survivor* was watched far more closely and debated far more heatedly than the upcoming vote that would decide the American presidency.

And why not? What did an election matter, anyway? In the summer of 2000, the economies of most of the West were on high-speed cruise control. As Francis Fukuyama had argued a decade earlier in his essay 'The End of History', there were no challenges left to the supremacy of Western liberal democracy. If the odd tech stock had taken a dive (as they had begun to), or if there were troubles with the national health care system (as there had been in Britain in early 2000), or if there were political leaders to be picked (as there were in both the US and Canada that year) – well, so what? A cornerstone of the loose consensus of the era was the idea that governments were finally moving towards a richly deserved powerlessness, because the only thing governments knew how to do well was screw up and reward themselves for doing so. And the interests of right-thinking people throughout the free world were wisely fixed elsewhere: on high finance, on the Internet. On *Survivor*. *Woo-hoo!*

I had a unique window on the West's Y2K daydream, I think, because I arrived right in the middle of it. I landed in Toronto in early July 2000 after a year spent living in India. Cultural re-immersion is often a surreal and intense process under any circumstances, as you find yourself confronting the assumptions and prejudices of your native culture as if for the first time. You examine them a little more closely, perhaps, and you can draw fresh conclusions about them you might not have reached if you'd come to the current moment in an unbroken line.

Anyway, *Survivor*-mania felt to me not like cute, lightweight fun but instead like a deeply perverse thing. It felt *wrong*. And wrong not just in the usual ways the highbrow commentators were trucking out on the cable-news shows. It was not because it debased its participants or because it debased its viewers or because it debased society in general. It was not because it claimed to be real when in fact it was extremely artificial. The ugliness of it ran deeper. It suggested, somehow, that something was wrong at the core. That the priorities of the society I'd returned to were so wildly skewed by its extraordinary wealth and power and contentment that *Survivor*, far from being an aberration, an overly gaudy dress at the grand post-millennial ball, was in fact an *accurate* manifestation of the true nature of the society.

I kept running into other dark portents in those first few weeks in Toronto after I returned from India. Down on King Street West one day, walking towards my workplace through Toronto's theatre district, I passed a camera crew from a local TV station. They were filming two young black men as they stopped random passersby to ask if they (the passersby) knew who they (the black men) were. Then one or the other of them or both would screech, 'Whaaahhh-suhhhhhh!' and a sudden, intense, joyful look of recognition would invariably come over the passerby's face. It was the Whassup Guys, still on tour. Another time, walking along Bloor Street West in the Annex in the early evening, amidst the prosperous shoppers and cosy cafés and New Age stores, I came upon a man covered head to toe in teal-and-blue spandex, superhero-style. He accosted me as I passed – which, in my culture-shocked state, scared the shit out of me. I realised he was simply handing me a free product sample, so I took one and hurried off. It was a Listerine Pocket Pak: a tiny plastic case filled with little strips the size and texture of a single piece of Scotch tape. When I put one in my mouth, it dissolved instantly in a burst of mouthwash-flavoured syrup – which also scared the shit out of me.

But I came upon the paramount example of this diseased frivolity in the course of some research I was doing for a magazine story on the vigorous trade in *Ultima Online* characters that had emerged on eBay. Let me explain: *Ultima Online* is a Tolkienesque videogame, the playing of which takes place online in an enormous virtual world called Britannia populated by wizards and elves and such. Apparently, building a powerful character takes tremendous time and effort, and so some experienced players had taken to selling their well-developed characters online for real-world money. I soon discovered that you could also buy gold pieces on eBay – that is, you could buy an amount of the coinage of this virtual world in exchange for legitimate currency, and the gold would then be transferred to your character inside the virtual world. And this was how I discovered that, in the late summer of 2000, *Ultima Online* gold pieces were trading against the US dollar at about the same rate as the Vietnamese dong.

This could easily be one of those slice-of-life stories that TV newscasts slap on at the end of the bad craziness of the rest of the news so that the anchorperson can turn to the camera and smile and chuckle in a what'll-they-think-of-next? sort of way that tells everyone watching that life is really pretty grand and lighthearted after all. It could be that kind of story, but I think it's a particularly ugly kind of lie to treat it as such. Because what this fact means – what it means that the Vietnamese dong and Ultima Online gold pieces were worth about the same in US dollars in the summer of 2000 – is that the triumphant liberal West had by then reached a point where in some real way it saw the nation of Vietnam and the virtual world of Britannia as roughly equal. Both might be interesting places to visit; visitors to both would require currency. That one is an actual place filled with real people and the other a fantasy world created for the amusement of affluent people with tremendous amounts of leisure time – this is still understood, yes, but not as clearly as it once was. And it attests to the existence of a dangerously corrosive self-absorption in the culture, the same corrosion hinted at by the celebration of a lazy, hyper-impulsive ultra-consumer like Homer Simpson as a hero. It's not that there's no soul left to the culture – the darker shades of Homer's character don't negate the goodness in him – but the corrosion is there, and it appears to be spreading.

Western society never looked more Homer-like than it did in the year 2000. Never more id-driven, never more consumption-obsessed, never more interested in the simplest solutions. Never more interested in doing nothing. There were undercurrents of serious problems: a dot-com stock-market bubble showing its first serious signs of structural weakness, for example, and a series of mass protests worldwide against a sketchily defined force called 'globalisation'. And there was a definite but ephemeral sense among growing numbers of the citizens of the most affluent societies the world has ever known that things might be far worse than they appeared on their slick, expensive surfaces. It was a discomfort that had been building for years, an inchoate fear just under the contented façades. This was the free-floating energy that latched on to the Y2K bug and gave it the power to create widespread panic. And, once the emergency had passed, to create such ridiculous frivolity. And this fear would soon meet with genuine cataclysm on a scale that even most Y2K survivalists couldn't have imagined, setting off a great collective *Wauggghhh!* in the West whose reverberations are still being felt today. Four years on, the millennial ball of the year 2000 now looks like quite a desperate party, a buoyant dance of overindulgence before the fear closed back in.

In Episode 2F11 ('Bart's Comet'), Springfield narrowly averts total annihilation. A comet has been hurtling towards it, and the suggested survival strategies of the town's best minds all fail. After abandoning a final attempt to avoid the catastrophe in Ned Flanders's bomb shelter, the entire population of Springfield gathers on the hilltop to wait for the comet's impact, joining together to sing 'Che Sarà Sarà' as cold comfort against the impending doom. But the comet burns itself out before it hits the town, touching down as a rock no bigger than a chihuahua's head. (There is in fact a chihuahua among the assembled townspeople to illustrate graphically the rock's size as it rolls powerlessly to a stop in front of them.) Some of the assembled crowd disperses, joining Moe in his plan to burn down the observatory to ensure that such a crisis never occurs again. The Simpson kids, though, simply marvel at the result – and at the one man who predicted it.

'What's really amazing,' says Bart, 'is that this is *exactly* what Dad said would happen.'

'Yeah,' Lisa adds incredulously. 'Dad was right.'

'I know, kids,' Homer whimpers, gathering his children in his arms. 'I'm scared too.'

NOTES & MARGINALIA

1. Homer's other namesake: *The Day of the Locust* is a relentlessly bleak satirical novel about 1930s Hollywood that portrays Tinseltown as a 'dream dump' rife with decay and misery. Homer Simpson is a pathetic transplanted Midwesterner 'without hope' whose 'anguish is basic and permanent', and whose only brief moments of joy in the novel come from caring for a cold, manipulative wannabe actress. Matt Groening claimed in several interviews at the peak of *Simpsons*-mania in 1990 that the novel was the source of Homer's name (if precious little of his character, except perhaps the basic stupidity thing). 'It's sort of using that character's name to remind me of some of the holes I could possibly fall into, moving to Hollywood,' Groening told a wire-service reporter. Elsewhere and at other times, Groening claimed that Homer was named after his father.

2. Homer J. Simpson, Winnipegger: No joke – on 30 May 2003, the Winnipeg City Council formally granted honorary citizenship to Homer Simpson in a ceremony attended by more than three hundred fellow citizens, several local officials and representatives from Global TV (*The Simpsons*' Canadian broadcaster). It started with an off-the-cuff remark Matt Groening made at the Just for Laughs comedy festival in Montreal in 2002. Noting that Homer was patterned – *very* loosely – after his father (Homer Groening), who was born in Canada, Groening the younger speculated haphazardly about the exact location. 'Uh, if you went straight north from Kansas, where would that be? Winnipeg? Yes, Winnipeg!' A *Regina Leader Post* reporter later ferreted out conclusive evidence that Homer Groening was in fact born in Main Centre, Saskatchewan, a small Mennonite community near Regina.

3. Three fun facts about 'D'oh!':

(a) The origins of '*D'oh!*': An *Ullman*-era *Simpsons* script called for Homer to respond to an unfortunate turn of events thusly: *(annoyed grunt)*. Dan Castellaneta, the voice actor who plays Homer, improvised the exclamation '*D'oh!*' It stuck.

(b) The godfather of '*D'oh!*': Castellaneta freely admits that he lifted Homer's famous catchphrase from James Finlayson, a Scottish actor who played a bald, cross-eyed villain in a number of Laurel and Hardy films in the 1930s. Finlayson's annoyed grunt was a more drawn-out groan – *Dooooohhh!* Castellaneta sped it up to create Homer's trademark yelp.

(c) The *OED* definition of '*D'oh!*': 'Expressing frustration at the realisation that things have turned out badly or not as planned, or that one has just said or done something foolish.'

4. Homer Flintstone, Homer Bunker: *The Flintstones* parody: Episode 9F10 ('Marge vs. the Monorail') opens with a blast of the Springfield Nuclear Power Plant's whistle. Homer races to the parking lot, crashes through the glass window of his car and zooms off down the road, singing his own lyrics to the tune of *The Flintstones* theme: 'Simpson! Homer Simpson! / He's the greatest guy in history / From the town of Springfield / He's about to hit a chestnut tree!' The sequence ends with Homer dutifully ploughing his car into said chestnut tree.

The *All in the Family* parody: Episode 3G02 ('Lisa's Sax') opens with Marge and a cigar-chomping Homer seated at the family piano. They run through three verses of a Simpsonised version of the *All in the Family* theme, the third of which starts with Homer: '"Disco Duck" and Fleetwood Mac', Marge, her voice cracking Edith-Bunkerly: 'Coming out of my eight-track.' Homer and Marge in unison: 'Michael Jackson still was black / Those! Were! The! Days!' There follows a reminder about how *The Simpsons* is filmed before a live studio audience and a brief exchange between Homer and Bart ('Hey dere, Meathead, whaddaya watchin'?') before the parody is abandoned.

5. Ambitious Homer: Over the years, many grand plans have been put forward as Homer's 'boyhood' and/or 'lifelong' dreams. Among them:

- managing a beautiful country singer
- eating the world's biggest hoagie
- running out onto the field during a baseball game
- becoming a monorail conductor
- becoming a contestant on *The Gong Show*

- becoming a blackjack dealer
- owning the Dallas Cowboys

6. Epic stupidity: According to Matt Groening, the *Simpsons* writers have an ongoing competition to see who can write a line 'that represents Homer at his singularly most stupid'. The current behind-the-scenes consensus? The time Homer forgot the name of Jesus. In Episode BABF11 ('Missionary: Impossible') from Season 11, Homer finds himself on a cargo plane bound for missionary work in the South Pacific. 'Save me, Jebus!' he calls as the plane flies into the sunset. Several websites – most prominently Jebus-Is-Lord.com and BabyJebus.com – have since emerged online to spread the Word.

7. The lighter side of domestic violence: In Episode BABF19 ('Behind the Laughter'), the nastiness of *The Simpsons*' early years would come in for some pointed self-mockery. In the episode – a parody of the American cable-music channel VH1's overwrought *Behind the Music* documentaries – a 'real-life' Homer strangles Bart off-screen for criticising the script. 'That horrible act of child abuse became one of our most beloved running gags,' the 'real' Homer notes with ironic pride.

8. Simpsonian pseudonyms: For undisclosed 'contractual reasons', the voice of Mr Bergstrom was listed in the episode's credits as 'Sam Etic'. Only well after the episode's original air date was it finally acknowledged that Dustin Hoffman had provided the teacher's voice, though the episode itself did make several winking references to *The Graduate*. ('Mrs Krabappel, you're trying to seduce me.')

This, though, marks only the second-weirdest pseudonymous appearance on *The Simpsons*. First prize, as in so many weirdness contests, goes to Michael Jackson, who was credited as 'John Jay Smith' when he appeared in Episode 7F24 ('Stark Raving Dad'). Jackson was the voice of Leon Kompowsky, an overweight, bald, white bricklayer from Paterson, New Jersey, whom Homer meets in a mental institution. Kompowsky believes he's the pop star Michael Jackson – so much so that later in the episode he helps Bart write a birthday song for Lisa, and he and Bart sing it as a duet. In addition to insisting on the pseudonym, Jackson lent his voice only to his character's speaking parts, not to the song his character sang with Bart – which Jackson himself had written.

More Jacko-related trivia: Michael Jackson was also the author of 'Do the Bartman', the number-one hit single off 1990's *The Simpsons Sing the Blues*.

9. The future of nuclear energy: In Episode 4F19, three bold visions of the next-generation Springfield Nuclear Power Plant vie for the prize Homer eventually claims. Here they are:

- Ralph Wiggum re-imagines the plant as a Malibu Stacy Dream House relabelled 'power plant'. Smithers likes it, but Burns can't abide the bordello-like frivolity of a hot tub and media room.
- Martin Prince, the resident genius of Bart's class at Springfield Elementary, presents a sleek model that actually works – it even provides the juice to light the auditorium where the contest is held – but Burns dismisses it as too cold and sterile.
- Homer's winning entry is an exact replica of the existing plant, except that fins and a racing stripe have been added to each of the cooling towers.

10. Leaves of grass, his ass? Might Homer Simpson's provenance lie even deeper in American history than Horatio Alger's industrial-age fables? Might he indeed be the modern-day reincarnation of the idealised American common man delineated in Walt Whitman's epic ode to individualism, 'Song of Myself'? A close (and admittedly selective) reading of the poem reveals that Whitman saw Homer coming, and lo, it was good. A shortlist of Whitman's most overtly Homeric passages:

> I loafe and invite my soul,
> I lean and loafe at my ease observing a spear of summer grass.
>
> . . .
>
> What is commonest, cheapest, nearest, easiest, is Me
>
> . . .
>
> I am of old and young, of the foolish as much as the wise
>
> . . .

I accept reality and dare not question it,
Materialism first and last imbuing.

. . .

I dote on myself, there is that lot of me and all so luscious,
Each moment and whatever happens thrills me with joy

. . .

I too am not a bit tamed, I too am untranslatable,
I sound my barbaric yawp over the roofs of the world.

. . .

Woo-hoo!

(*Author's note*: This last-cited passage – *Woo-hoo!* – was the closing line in Whitman's original draft. It was removed at the urging of his publisher, who thought it 'too modern'. Here, for the first time in print, it is restored to its rightful place.)

11. **Great moments in journalism**: The highlight of the Pets.com Sock Puppet's appearance on *Good Morning America*, to my mind, was an exchange with Sawyer's co-host, Charles Gibson, about the puppet's collar that has such an extraordinary Beckett-on-Quaaludes quality to it that it's worth quoting at some length:

Gibson:	I've noticed ever since I first saw you that you wear that . . . you wear that watch around your neck.
Sock Puppet:	Yeah, it's kind of like my collar.
Gibson:	Yeah. Can you show me how you actually read the watch and tell time?
Sock Puppet:	Well, I never said I could tell time. I just sort of wear the watch.
Gibson:	Oh, I see. You can't actually get your head around and see what time it is?
Sock Puppet:	No, but, you know, there's a lot of clocks around, Charlie.
Gibson:	I see. So the watch – the watch is just purely decorative?
Sock Puppet:	Yeah, it's decorative, but it's also pretty sturdy. You know, it's a Timex, so, you know, if I need to I can do this. It keeps on ticking.

CHAPTER THREE

Bart Simpson, Punk Icon

I'm a street-walkin' cheetah with a heart full of napalm
I'm a runaway son of the nuclear A-bomb
I am a world's forgotten boy
The one who searches and destroys

The Stooges, 'Search and Destroy'

Oh, please. This is senseless destruction, with none of
my usual social commentary.

Bart Simpson, Episode 2F18
('Two Dozen and One Greyhounds')

BART SIMPSON, PUNK ICON?

AN AUTOBIOGRAPHICAL NOTE: I WENT to high school in North Bay, Ontario, in the late 1980s and early 1990s. North Bay is only a few hours north of cosmopolitan Toronto, and it's a bit too big for the term 'small town'. Nonetheless, it was a bland suburban hinterland. We were quite out of the loop. Or at least I was. My high-school years were set to a soundtrack of Led Zeppelin and Guns N' Roses and the occasional rumour of something more dangerous – something along the lines of a bootleg tape of N.W.A.'s 'Fuck tha Police' or 'Too Drunk to Fuck' by the Dead Kennedys. (We liked it when they said 'fuck'. That was cool. *Huh-huh. Huh-huh-huh.*) My friends and I wore untucked logoed Polo button-downs and disintegrating deck shoes (which was the style at the time), and we drank too much and then went to the McDonald's parking lot to hang out, watch the fights and try to avoid getting dragged into any. In my final year, I applied to business school. (Got in too, and did a year and a half before I snapped out of it, for reasons I'll get into just a little later.) I thought I might like to be a lawyer one day. Own a BMW. Come back to North Bay – just to visit – and drive it down Lakeshore Drive, past the McDonald's parking lot, show those Neanderthals what *real* power looked like. It was that kind of time, at least in North Bay.

Also: we didn't get Fox. *The Simpsons* was mostly a rumour to me for the first year or two of its existence, and that rumour was mostly Bart. How outrageous he was, how irreverent. How subversive. Bart was dangerous. Some said Bart had to be stopped. The Bart rumour had the same vibe as those murky fourth-generation recordings of N.W.A. and the Dead Kennedys – a vague intimation of *real* rebellion. I wanted to know more about this Bart Simpson.

The first time I met him was on a T-shirt. It was in the summer of 1990 – the Summer of Bart – when *Simpsons* T-shirts were selling at the astounding rate of more than a million *per day* in North America. I believe Bart was riding a skateboard, and I'm pretty sure he was saying DON'T HAVE A COW, MAN. It could've just as easily been I'M BART SIMPSON – WHO THE HELL ARE YOU? or UNDERACHIEVER AND PROUD OF IT or simply AY, CARUMBA! Anyway, there he was: a primary yellow, spike-haired Johnny Rotten, Jr. An untamed punk rocker in primetime. If you were too young to have felt punk's liberating nihilism the first time around or not hip enough to have tracked its reverberations underground during the conformist 1980s – or if, like me, you were both – then Bart was quite possibly your first full taste of punk. And if, as Greil Marcus has suggested, it was 'almost transcendentally odd' to discover the slogans of the revolutionary French underground of 1968 being spat into the pop charts of 1976 by the Sex Pistols,[1] then it was doubly so to find the same phenomenon riding a full-blown mainstream hype wave in 1990. Bart's anarchic visage was genuinely powerful, both because it introduced *The Simpsons* to the masses as an inherently subversive force and because it introduced a subversive force to the mainstream at all. Even if Bart might have seemed like a sanitised version of the real thing to anyone who'd seen the Pistols themselves in 1976 or the Dead Kennedys in 1984, for the rest of us he had some genuine edge to him. After a decade of life in toothless Cosbyland, Bart brought some real bite to the mainstream, even if he was chewing with baby teeth.

More precisely, *The Simpsons* hit bland TV-land with the propulsive, sarcastic force of a Pistols record. Not just Bart but the entire show felt as irreverent and seditious and scruffy as the fuck-you heroes of punk. The pop world had apparently gone so long without even the vaguest whiff of dissidence that a ten-year-old boy who carried a slingshot and mouthed off to his parents and teachers – 'rebellious' acts that were surely routine occurrences in every elementary school in the land – stormed the culture like a pint-sized Che Guevara.

And so it was Bart who found himself at the centre of the maelstrom of controversy stirred up by the show's early success. Bart T-shirts, for example, particularly the UNDERACHIEVER AND PROUD OF IT versions, were repeatedly held up by America's moral watchdogs as conclusive evidence that the show was hauling all of Western civilisation to hell on a skateboard. This kid – who by his own admission was little more than 'this century's Dennis the Menace', and who his creator, Matt Groening, acknowledged was based on no more dangerous a figure than legendary 1950s ass-kisser Eddie Haskell of *Leave It to Beaver* – this seemingly harmless, seemingly standard-issue class clown of a kid surely struck some deep chords in his subversion-starved audience.

Bart was, it turned out, a punk for all seasons. He didn't excite only those of us stuck in the cultural tundra of northern Ontario. Surfer dudes professed their love for Bart, and so did pious Jewish kids in Bart Simpson yarmulkes. Bootleg Bart T-shirts abounded, everything from Rasta Bart to Bart Sanchez (a streetwise Latino) to Nazi Bart.[2] Of particular note – and particular fascination to the media – was the 'Black Bart' phenomenon. Throughout the summer and autumn of 1990, a dark-skinned, soul-brother Bart was an unauthorised African-American icon, a staple image on the T-shirts hawked by inner-city street vendors nationwide. Bart was depicted as Malcolm X or Michael Jordan; or he appeared arm in arm with Nelson

Mandela, denouncing apartheid; or he copped a ghetto attitude, proclaiming in a word balloon, YOU WOULDN'T UNDERSTAND – IT'S A BLACK THING. A bratty middle-class white kid had become a highly flexible hero to poor urban blacks – a stunning reversal of the regular flow of cool, one with few precedents in the annals of pop culture. While commentators were divided on the question of *why* black youth had adopted Bart as an icon – did they identify with his outsider status, or were there not enough legitimate black icons in the mass media, or was this just another trivialisation of black America's struggle? – no one could deny that black kids had accepted Bart as one of their own.

Punk wasn't dead, as another T-shirt of the era asserted. In fact, it was beaming right into every living room in the land. And it was finding an audience every week far greater in number, and far more diverse in ethnic background, than any punk band had cumulatively played to over its entire career.

Alright then: this Bart dude's a punk. But what kind of punk is he? Is he a misanthrope like Johnny Rotten? A bored hipster like Joey Ramone? Does he have the ferocious antiauthoritarian streak of American hard core heroes like Black Flag and Minor Threat? Or the immutable social conscience of The Clash? The answer is a little of each of these, but not too much of any one in particular. Which is what makes Bart such an all-encompassing (if incomplete) emblem of the multivalent forces of the first wave of punk – a harbinger of the boiled-down version of the punk ethos that was the foundation for the self-reliant indie movements that breathed new life into pop music, feature film and the fledgling Internet in the first half of the 1990s. Divorced from the unique socioeconomic factors that had ushered in its messy birth (the impoverished and rapidly decaying English and American cities of the 1970s), punk became something far more accessible than it ever was as a style of music and dress. Some of the bands that made innovative music and some of the directors who reinvigorated movie-making and damn near all of the pioneers of online content may not have looked or sounded particularly punk. But the overwhelming majority of them were inspired by and (to varying degrees) dedicated to its core values: strident, even nihilistic opposition to all authority; a preference for authenticity over virtuosity; a bias towards extreme subject matter; and, most importantly, a deep faith in the liberating power of the DIY (do-it-yourself) approach – that is, the belief that anyone with a guitar or camera or computer, a strong will and a bright idea could create culture (and the bright idea was optional, actually).

After incubating for more than a decade on the fringe, punk invaded the mainstream wholesale in the 1990s, and conquered it, and was eventually subsumed into it, not just in music but in all media. It became a chart-topping, blockbusting phenomenon. It landed on the covers of mass-circulation magazines and the pages of major newspapers. It provided the soundtrack and tone for snack-product commercials. And before long, it was entirely *inside*, another costume hanging on the racks of the great department store of consumer identities, a torn, safety-pinned T-shirt tucked neatly between the hippie's beads and buckskin vests and the disco diva's sequined blouses.

Of course, punk was – and is – much, much more than this. It was the over-amped crash cart that restarted rock & roll's bloated heart. It was, as Greil Marcus reckoned, 'not a musical genre' but 'a moment in time . . . a chance to create ephemeral events that would serve as judgments on whatever came next'. It remains pop culture's most strident and enduring rejection of the version of 'progress' articulated by the avatars of triumphal capitalism. It *was* a musical genre – also a tone, an attitude, a fashion statement, a worldview. It was – and remains – malleable. It encompasses the heavy garage pop of its UK founders, the fuzzed-up, sped-up, straight-ahead rock & roll of The Ramones, the fractal pop of Talking Heads, the noise compositions of the Velvet Underground and Sonic Youth, the sloppy bar-band rock of The Replacements, the funkified folk of Ani DiFranco. It doesn't really apply to Blink 182 (who sound like a punk band), but it likely does apply to Wilco (who only infrequently sound like one). It applies to a genre of science-fiction writing (cyberpunk) and of British literary fiction (the Irvine Welsh-led 'Scottish Beats'). It almost fits as a catch-all for the wave of independent filmmakers (Quentin Tarantino, Richard Linklater, Kevin Smith, Robert Rodriguez, the Boyle/Hodge/Macdonald team, etc.) who rejuvenated a flatlined Hollywood in the early 1990s. And it seems at least half-accurate as a shorthand for the anything-goes spirit of freedom, innovation and entrepreneurship that catapulted the Internet from the obscurity of academic research into the fat centre of mainstream culture. Not only is punk not dead, but for a good portion of the 1990s it was far too ubiquitous and multifaceted to be captured in the visage of one ten-year-old prankster.

But reduce punk to a single cohesive message blipped momentarily into the collective consciousness, and it can look a lot like a smirking neon-yellow cartoon face on the cover of *Rolling Stone*, especially if it's juxtaposed against a handful of the other pop icons who filled the same space in 1990: Janet

Jackson, Tom Cruise, Billy Joel. In such a brief glance it becomes iconic: a dismissal, a categorical rejection – a *de-NYE-ul!*, a *de-NYE-ul!*, a *de-NYE-ul!*, as Kurt Cobain howled over the final crashing chords of 'Smells Like Teen Spirit'. So yes: a denial, a raised fist, a middle-fingered salute, a queen with blacked-out eyes, a safety pin or sneering mouth.

Or a catchphrase: *Eat my shorts.*

BART SIMPSON: LI'L NIHILIST

Like any good punk rocker, Bart had the nihilism thing down from the very beginning. Though not so much pissed off as extremely undisciplined, the Bart Simpson of the *Ullman* shorts is either fighting with his sister, inciting his father to murderous levels of rage, executing dangerous stunts that end in cartoonish levels of disaster, or simply spitting snarky one-liners at whatever authority figure crosses his path. This appetite for destruction continued to be the defining feature of the smart-assed kid who dominated many episodes of the first few seasons of *The Simpsons* – the version that spawned Bartmania – though his methods and motivations show considerably more nuance than the nasty white-trash brat of the *Ullman* era.

The Bart Simpson who took the first full-length episodes of *The Simpsons* by storm is a corrosive force, bad to the bone and dangerous to know. This is a kid whose mother routinely frisks him for weapons before they leave for church, a kid whose parent–teacher interviews require eyewitnesses to recount his 'atrocities' using dolls as props. This, too, is a kid whose instinct for disorder is so deeply bred that as a foetus he took advantage of the attention lavished on him by a sonogram to moon the doctor. In fact, the only non-celebrity adult Bart respects is Otto, the perpetually stoned bus driver, because Otto lets the kids throw stuff at cars and tries to tip the bus on sharp turns. When the disembodied voice of a haunted house urges Bart to kill his entire family, Bart simply asks, 'Are you my conscience?' And you can tell he suspects that it is. Another time, it's Bart himself who notes his skill at being 'a bit underhanded, a bit devious, a bit – as the French say – *Bartesque*'. No wonder, then, that Mr Burns sees in Bart a kindred spirit, 'a creature of pure malevolence'. Think of Bart's mischievous cackle in anticipation of some act of senseless destruction as a training-wheels version of Johnny Rotten's gleefully malevolent laughter over the opening strains of 'Anarchy in the U.K.'

Episode 7F07 ('Bart vs. Thanksgiving') is a representative example from Season 2 of the way Bart's constant misbehaviour drives many early episodes of *The Simpsons*. It opens with Bart and Lisa in a meaningless squabble over glue, instigated of course by Bart. He then mocks the Thanksgiving Day parade his father is watching and attempts to 'help' his mother with Thanksgiving dinner – a half-assed effort at something constructive that proves more irritating than helpful. And he finishes off Act One by destroying Lisa's painstakingly constructed centrepiece with his carelessness. Sent to his room without any dinner as punishment, Bart sneaks out and has a grand old time on the wrong side of Springfield's tracks, unrepentant, dining on free turkey at a soup kitchen. Only as the meal ends does he admit to himself that he misses his family. But when he returns home, momentarily grateful, he pauses at the door to consider how he'll be greeted. In a fantasy sequence, Bart imagines himself surrounded by his whole family, who mock him with dark laughter and point accusing fingers even as he tries to apologise, blaming him for all the trouble in their lives. It ends with Uncle Sam himself declaring, 'It's your fault America has lost its way!' Even when Bart allows himself to care about his world, it would seem, the reflexive derision of the whole society pushes him back to rejection, destruction, nullification.

This last, of course – nullification, the embrace of nothingness – is at the core of nihilism as a philosophy, and is generally a bit beyond young Bart's ken. On occasion, though, he does manage to embody not just the style but the substance of nihilism. A case in point is Episode 7F08 ('Dead Putting Society'), in which Lisa attempts to mould Bart into a master mini-golfer by introducing him to the riddles of the Zen masters. 'Embrace nothingness,' she instructs. 'You got it,' he replies, faking it, mocking the very idea of the exercise. When Lisa asks, 'What is the sound of one hand clapping?' Bart smugly replies, 'Piece of cake,' displays a single hand, slaps fingers against palm. Never mind the metaphysics, Bart's got that silly ancient riddle solved.

Bart's far too clever to be taken in by dusty myths; he's only interested in tearing them apart. At times, there's seemingly nothing worthy of exemption from his wrecking ball, as in Episode 3F02 ('Bart Sells His Soul') – which centres, as it says in the title, on Bart's sale to the first interested bidder of that part of himself that is purportedly most sacred. Dismissing the soul as a meaningless fairy tale 'made up to scare kids, like the bogeyman or Michael Jackson', Bart peddles his own to Milhouse for five dollars. When he tells Lisa about the sale – the proceeds of which went to buy cheap sponges in the shape of dinosaurs – a second chapter is added to Bart's *Dialectics*:

Lisa:	[*incredulous*] What? How could you *do* that? Your soul is the most valuable part of you.
Bart:	You believe in that junk?
Lisa:	Well, whether or not the soul is physically real, Bart, it's the symbol of everything that is fine inside us.
Bart:	[*condescendingly*] Poor, gullible Lisa. I'll keep my crappy sponges, thanks.
Lisa:	Bart, your soul is the only part of you that lasts forever. For five dollars, Milhouse could own you for a zillion years!
Bart:	Well, if you think he got such a good deal, I'll sell you my conscience for four-fifty.
	[*Lisa walks off*]
Bart:	[*calling after her*] I'll throw in my sense of decency too. It's a Bart sales event! Everything about me must go!

Here Bart is the epitome of the world-weary hipster, using the degraded language of modern marketing to sell off the most sacred parts of himself because he knows that some cheap sponge is more real, hence more valuable, than even the loftiest of abstract principles. Soul, conscience, decency – rubbish. Saccharine fantasies for the deluded masses, who are too unsophisticated to see that they hold no more true consequence than the pitches of a used-car salesman. Imagine him transformed for these dialogues, as in one of the T-shirts he inspired: Poseur Bart, complete with black turtleneck and shades, dismissing the superstitions of the pre-modern age with a blast of bile as quick and easy as the catchphrases that made him famous. *Eat my shorts, Thomas Aquinas! Don't have a cow, Descartes!*

But Bart isn't actually this cynical, and he can't hold the pose for long. The Thanksgiving episode ends with reconciliation and heartfelt emotion. 'The only reason to apologise,' Lisa tells him, 'is if you look deep down inside yourself, and you find a spot, something you wish wasn't there because you feel bad you hurt your sister's feelings.' He looks, and soon finds it, and proffers possibly his first genuine apology in the series' history. The same deal with his Zen training: Bart sees right through the one-hand-clapping bit, but when Lisa forces him to ponder the notion of a tree falling in the forest with no one there to hear it, Bart finds his Buddha-nature right quick. And the loss of his soul soon has Bart dashing around town in a panic, desperate to get it back. In one of the show's most intense displays of spiritual anguish, Bart is reduced to tears, repenting, beseeching God Himself to return his soul. (In the end, Lisa buys it back for him.) Bart may be an incorrigible brat, but underneath his destructive façade he's also a believer.

BART SIMPSON: MEDIA JUNKIE

Bart's world-weariness is not entirely a pose – he, more than any other Simpson, is an exemplary product of our media-saturated, celebrity-obsessed age, with the paradoxical mix of cynicism and adoration that it so often spawns. The cultural vanguard of the 1990s was populated by jaded hipsters sporting similar mixes of obsession and derision. Withering contempt for the most populist segments of mainstream culture (e.g. Oprah's aphorisms, the saccharine romanticism of Meg Ryan films, the bland, bloated pop of chart-toppers like Mariah Carey and Hootie & the Blowfish) was of course *de rigueur*. But it was usually accompanied by religious devotion to certain other segments of the culture – and not just underground phenomena (the lush pop of Guided by Voices or Belle and Sebastian, say) but also icons of bygone eras (maybe swing music or the beautiful-loser romanticism of the Beat writers) and even certain mainstream stuff like *The Simpsons* itself.

Much like these pop-obsessed anti-popsters, Bart has a raging love/hate affair with his culture. First the hate: it is born of mass culture's relentless repetitiveness, its cloyingly sweet bromides, the fact that it has clearly never met a formula or cliché that it didn't love (and couldn't beat into the ground). By its sheer ubiquity, the mass media is guaranteed to spew out something or other to irritate everyone. And so we find Bart driven into a rage when he's forced to watch Lisa's beloved *Happy Little Elves Meet the Curious Bear Cub* video. 'Oh, man, I can't take it anymore,' he exclaims. 'But I want to see what happens,' Lisa protests. 'You *know* what happens,' her brother moans. 'They find Captain Quick's treasure. All the elves dance around like little green idiots. I puke. The end.' Or there's the time that Marge, tucking her son in, quotes Forrest Gump's legendary needlepoint-samplerism about life being like a box of chocolates. Bart erupts in protest, popping a pail over his head and pounding on it to avoid hearing the part about never knowing what you're gonna get. It is of course an implicit and ongoing irony in *The Simpsons* that Bart is irritated by media-generated cliché, given that he himself has released more catchphrases into the pop-cultural ether than any other character on the show[3] and was the centre of its most enormous and simplistic wave of hype.

But if Bart finds much to hate in pop culture, he finds plenty more to love.

Indeed he finds most of his life's meaning – its dominant metaphors, its heroes and villains, its wisdom, its very sense of its own importance – in that same pop culture he loathes. Bart is, after all, a kid who sometimes dreams in Warner Bros cartoons, who suddenly finds a work ethic in pursuit of a rare *Radioactive Man* comic book, who realises his purpose in life is to witness a particular episode of 'Itchy & Scratchy' in which Scratchy (the oft-tortured cat) finally gets even with Itchy (the sadistic mouse). And who, note, sleeps contentedly under Krusty the Clown bedsheets.

It's this last relationship – Bart's deep, multifaceted, abiding love for Krusty – that is the most meaningful. (It might well be the most meaningful relationship Bart has outside of his immediate family.) And Bart's depth of feeling for Krusty is not entirely unreciprocated – in fact, he gets considerably more face time with his hero than most of us ever will with ours. Indeed Bart often intervenes directly in Krusty's life and work. With his sister's help, Bart has resuscitated Krusty's career after a rival drove him off the airwaves and has reunited him with his estranged father. Bart has been a guest star on *The Krusty the Clown Show*, and he recruited Jay Leno to help turn Krusty into an observational comic. In a neat bit of cartoon metaphysics, though, Bart's personal relationship with Krusty never interferes with his starstruck idol worship. His room remains a paraphernalia-stuffed shrine to his favourite entertainer, and he watches the show religiously, without an insider's jaded eye. And in a writer's wink at the illogic of all of this, Krusty doesn't even remember who Bart is when they meet again after another career resuscitation. Thus Bart's relationship with Krusty remains governed for the most part by a standard pop-cultural dynamic: Krusty produces TV shows of varying quality and tons of merchandise of almost universally poor quality, and Bart eagerly laps it all up.

In Episode 8F24 ('Kamp Krusty'), Bart displays the impressive depth of his commitment to Krusty after the clown's abysmal, abusive summer camp finally exhausts his patience. When Krusty fails to show up for a scheduled personal appearance at the camp and is replaced by a weaving-drunk Barney Gumble in poorly applied clown nose and makeup, Bart rises in protest. 'I've been scorched by Krusty before,' he rants. 'I got a rapid heartbeat from his Krusty-brand vitamins, my Krusty Kalculator didn't have a seven or an eight, and Krusty's autobiography was self-serving, with many glaring omissions. But this time, he's gone too far!' Ultimately, Bart is appeased (after leading a full-scale campers' revolt rife with allusions to *Lord of the Flies*) when Krusty finally arrives and takes the whole gang to Tijuana ('the happiest place on earth!').

What's most worth noting, though, is the staggering breadth of Bart's encyclopaedic knowledge of his favourite celebrity and his willingness to maintain (or at least renew) his devotion through the kind of disappointments that would cause lesser acolytes to lose their faith entirely. Weary though Bart may be of certain preachers and amulets and holy sites, he is ultimately a die-hard, tithe-paying member of the church of pop.

Bart's faith in Krusty has on several occasions very nearly cost him his life at the hands of Krusty's criminal sidekick, Sideshow Bob. A full-blown psychopath, Bob repeatedly attempts (usually via murder most foul) to have his revenge on Bart. In symbolic terms, Bob's hatred for Bart seems to suggest that the show is making two somewhat related points about the costs and benefits of avid worship at the altar of pop culture. The first is that undue adulation of a marginally talented celebrity (i.e. Krusty) might show a weakness of character that warrants – or at least invites – homicide. The second is that Bart is caught in the crossfire of the war between highbrow and lowbrow culture. After all, Sideshow Bob is far and away the most classically 'cultured' figure in the entire *Simpsons* universe. Forget his origins as a big-footed, red-afroed TV sidekick: Robert Underdunk Terwilliger is a one-man temple of the fine arts. First, of course, there's the voice, rendered as a feast of mid-Atlantic anglophilia by *Frasier* star Kelsey Grammer, all rolled *r*s and erudition. Bob's a Yale grad, a gourmet given to sipping wine in his dressing room and bemoaning the lack of 'a decent local marmalade' in Springfield, a regular reader of *The Springfield Review of Books* (which he notes can be enjoyed for its 'amusing caricatures of Susan Sontag and Gore Vidal' as well as its text). He once built a model of Westminster Abbey in a bottle. He can quickly shift from advancing on Bart with a huge knife to sending the boy to heaven with an accomplished performance of the entire score of *H.M.S. Pinafore*.

Sideshow Bob's first televised words – spoken as he takes over Krusty's show after framing him for robbery – testify to his superior breeding: he announces that he is finally free from 'the crude glissandos of this primitive wind instrument' (the slide whistle he 'spoke' through on Krusty's version of the show). And it turns out that his betrayal of Krusty is for the most altruistic of reasons: to transform his crude clown show into a high-minded 'Cavalcade of Whimsy', bringing readings from *The Man in the Iron Mask* and thoughtful lessons about 'nutrition, self-esteem, etiquette, and all the lively arts' to children's television. In a later scheme, Bob tries to eliminate the 'chattering cyclops' of television altogether. Bob is, in short, a snob, a firm believer in the superiority of classical music, old books and all the other refinements of the pre-pop age.

He's also a raging, arch-conservative Republican, a perfect stand-in for the critics of *The Simpsons* – and of pop culture's rough-edged output in general – who stand firm in their belief that America's children (if not all Americans) need desperately to be saved from themselves. If only the unruly kids were made to take their bitter canonical cultural medicine, they'd surely learn to behave like proper nineteenth-century citizens.

The Simpsons' writers respond by whacking Bob in the face with a rake, and then another, and again another – nine times in all. Highbrow culture can eat their shorts and then rot away in jail. That particular cultural battle is over, and the fun lowbrow stuff won by a landslide. Punk rock – crude, expletive-laced punk – has had far greater impact on our culture than anything any symphony orchestra on the planet has produced since 1977. It even has far greater artistic merit, if art is understood to be a creative enterprise rather than a finely honed imitative craft, and if it's also understood to be good art only insofar as it can reveal something new about the nature of existence to its audience. Same goes for *The Simpsons*, of course – with 'new' being one operative word and 'audience' the other. The show packs more originality and *new* insight into a single episode than a dozen hundred-year-old classics on *Masterpiece Theatre*, and any given episode informs the worldview of a group of people exponentially larger than the total readership of John Updike's entire oeuvre.

The either/or structure of this debate is, of course, artificial and increasingly irrelevant. 'Highbrow' and 'lowbrow' were the inventions of a now-eclipsed order that attempted, unsuccessfully, to barricade older cultural forms behind a hierarchy. This point is John Seabrook's, from his 2000 book *Nobrow: The Culture of Marketing – The Marketing of Culture*, in which he argues that this old classification system has been replaced by a new hierarchy called 'Nobrow'. 'In Nobrow,' Seabrook explains, 'subculture was the new high culture, and high culture had become just another subculture.' *The Simpsons* is pure Nobrow, able to slide as effortlessly as Bob himself from slide-whistling slapstick to talk of Susan Sontag, and ultimately oblivious to any prejudicial classifications. It's not so much that lowbrow bludgeoned highbrow to death with a dozen rakes; it's that both of them have been subsumed into the one-stop-shopping megamall of pop.

At any rate, Bart is fully on the side of pop. In addition to his dedication to Krusty, he's a lover of action-movie spectacle and the goriest of videogame violence. When the Simpsons steal cable, Bart's first instinct is to start up an underground porn theatre for his schoolyard chums. He's an avid comic-book collector, a skateboarder, a budding graffiti artist (infamous across

Springfield for his 'El Barto' tag). He devours Krusty burgers and the biggest sundaes on the menu at Phineas Q. Butterfat's 5600 Flavors Ice-Cream Parlor. He's a sugar junkie, addicted to the ultra-sweet squishees at the Kwik-E-Mart and the Broadway-style-show-tune-singing benders they can induce.

Lisa says it best when she makes the case that Bart is a pure product of the culture's basest elements. This comes in Episode 5F15 ('Girly Edition'), when Lisa and Bart become co-anchors of a lightweight children's news programme called *Kidz Newz*. After Bart's shameless pandering to the lowest common denominator nearly gets him killed, Lisa supplies him with an infotainment-style justification. 'In a way,' she editorialises, 'isn't he everyone's son? For you see, that little hellraiser is the spawn of every shrieking commercial, every brain-rotting soda pop, every teacher who cares less about young minds than about cashing their big, fat paychecks. No, Bart's not to blame. You can't create a monster and then whine when he stomps on a few buildings.' The pseudo-educational news show is soon cancelled, replaced by *The Mattel and Mars Bar Quick Energy Chocobot Hour*. True to form, Bart is immediately hooked on this new pop confection.

BART SIMPSON: IDEALIST (SORT OF)

It's a safe bet that Bart truly doesn't give a damn about what any stuffy old windbag has to say about the distinctions between high and low culture and the rest of it, anyway. We come now to a key point about the punk essence of Bart: that his primary motivation is rarely simple destruction but rather a deep-seated opposition to all authority. What makes Sideshow Bob unique is not that he's Bart's enemy, but that he's the only enemy Bart hasn't wilfully chosen. The remainder of the long list of his foes are people that Bart has openly antagonised, all but daring them to take him on.

Bart's pranks, schemes and general disruptiveness[4] are of course well known to the assorted authorities in his life, none of whom has ever successfully broken Bart's rebellious will. His father, whose inability to discipline Bart is a running joke, falls victim to a prank involving a can of Duff beer over-agitated in a paint mixer that blows the roof off the house and puts Homer in a wheelchair. Mrs Krabappel (Bart's teacher) and Principal Skinner have tried everything from expulsion to locking Bart in the basement to get him to behave, all to no avail. (Mrs Krabappel finds dim consolation in mocking Bart openly whenever he fails.) During his brief stint as the Simpsons' neighbour, President George H.W. Bush feels compelled to spank Bart 'for the good of the nation'; Bart's response is to enlist Homer to help him plague the ex-president with locusts and other nuisances. Even Mr Burns – a man capable of effortlessly bending judges and federal regulatory officials to his will – can't force Bart to submit to his authority. When Burns rejects Bart as a candidate to become his heir, the boy immediately sets to hurling rocks through every window of the old tycoon's house. And when Burns fails to shower the Simpsons with riches after Bart donates blood to save his life, it's Bart, not Homer, who maintains his righteous anger long enough to mail the nasty letter to Burns that he and Homer compose together. No question: Bart obeys no authority but his own, and snaps back instinctively against any and all others.

Less evident, though, is what motivates Bart to rage against the machine. Is it simply a lack of discipline? Garden-variety juvenile delinquency? An evil heart? Or might Bart's rejection of authority grow from a profound sense of alienation from the society that it represents? It just might. In Episode 3G02 ('Lisa's Sax'), for example, we learn that mainstream success has been closed to Bart since the moment he entered institutional society on his fateful first day of school. 'School will be fun!' young Bart enthuses as he hurries for the bus. A short while later, still keen to fit in, Bart sits in a circle with his classmates, playing a hand-clapping game. 'B-I-(clap)-(clap)-O!' Bart chants. 'B-I-(clap)-(clap)-O! B-I-(clap)-(clap)-(clap)! And Bingo was his name-o!' A teacher, clipboard in hand, looks on. 'Added extra clap – not college material,' she notes, shutting Bart out of the corridors of mainstream acceptance mere hours after he first enters them. The rest of his first week at school is filled with similar misfortunes, and it's only when he makes other kids laugh in the schoolyard that he begins to feel like he belongs. Principal Skinner catches him in his 'potty talk' and orders him to stop. 'You listen to me, son,' Skinner tells five-year-old Bart. 'You've just started school, and the path you choose now may be the one you follow for the rest of your life. Now, what do you say?' A long pause as Bart considers. And then – speaking slowly, deliberately – he replies: 'Eat my shorts.' Bart's fate is sealed.

Perhaps this explains why, a few years later, once Bart has a few more years of class-clowning and authority-tweaking under his belt, one of the only adults whose logic makes sense to him is Fat Tony, the Mafia boss who gives Bart his first part-time job. This occurs in Episode 8F03 ('Bart the Murderer'), after Bart takes a tumble off his skateboard through the door of Fat Tony's Legitimate Businessman's Social Club, and turns out to have a natural knack for picking horses and fixing Manhattans.[5] After a few days spent doing menial chores at the social club, Bart is promoted to a more important job – storing stolen cigarettes in his bedroom – which is what first raises his suspicion that his bosses are less than legitimate. The following life lesson ensues:

Bart: Say, are you guys crooks?

Fat Tony: Bart, um . . . is it wrong to steal a loaf of bread to feed your starving family?

Bart: No.

Fat Tony: Suppose you got a large starving family. Is it wrong to steal a truckload of bread to feed them?

Bart: Uh-uh.

Fat Tony: And what if your family don't like bread, they like cigarettes?

Bart: I guess that's okay.

Fat Tony: Now, what if instead of giving them away, you sold them at a price that was practically giving them away? Would that be a crime, Bart?

Bart: Hell, no!

Thus endeth the lesson. And Bart, fully convinced, takes to wearing 'soopoib' tailored suits around the house, singing 'Witchcraft' and asking for 'three fingers of milk.' But when Fat Tony and his cronies pin the blame for a local murder on 'Don Bartholomew' – Bart, that is – even this authority proves unworthy of Bart's respect. He turns his back on the mob. Bart has learned that *no* authority can be trusted.

On a few other occasions, Bart flirts with joining the Establishment – including a brief, appealing taste of fascism when he's made a hall monitor, mirroring the ease with which punk has found itself co-opted by neo-Nazis. In general, though, Bart's an outsider and he knows it, defining his entire persona by Springfield's disapproval.

Bart finds out just how much he craves censure in Episode 1F05 ('Bart's Inner Child'), in which self-help guru Brad Goodman holds Bart up as a shining example of the 'inner child' that the assembled masses of Springfield should be emulating. Goodman asks Bart to explain why he has disrupted the seminar with his smart-ass remarks. 'I do what I feel like,' Bart answers. This is adopted as the guiding philosophy of Springfield, and Bart becomes a hero to the whole town. In short order, Bart finds his attempts to crack jokes in class drowned out by the Bart-like one-liners of numerous fellow students, and he can't indulge in his patented spitting off the overpass because it's already jam-packed with a mob of gleeful spitters. Bart takes his predicament to Lisa: 'Lis, everyone in town is acting like me. So why does it suck?' Lisa, as always, has an insightful answer at the ready: 'It's simple, Bart. You've defined yourself as a rebel. And in the absence of a repressive milieu, your societal niche has been co-opted.'

Fortunately, Springfield's love affair with self-help quickly leads to mass catastrophe: the town's inaugural 'Do What You Feel Festival' goes down like a pop-psychological Altamont, replete with un-double-bolted collapsing bandstands, runaway Ferris wheels, and a zoo-animal stampede (perhaps suggesting that even as a role model, Bart can't help but destroy). And soon Bart can return to his natural place, defying authority figures instead of being one.

That there are traces of an embryonic idealism at work in Bart's chronic transgressions is confirmed by his relationship with his loving mother. Marge knows full well her boy is no angel, but she remains steadfast in her love and support. In an early episode, she lays out her understanding of her son to Milhouse's mother, who has forbidden her son to spend time with Bart. 'I know Bart can be a handful,' Marge explains, 'but I also know what he's like inside. He's got a spark. It's not a bad thing.' She pauses. 'Of course,' she admits, 'it makes him *do* bad things . . .'

If Bart's not quite a crusading idealist, he does at least have a creative impulse, something worth nurturing. And so Marge thinks of him as her 'special little guy' – a misunderstood, marginalised kid with real potential and a kind heart. It's a faith that's rewarded by Bart's repeated redemptions, his last-minute discoveries of a morally sound core in himself. When he violates his mother's ban on spending time with Nelson the class bully, he winds up accidentally killing a mother bird with Nelson's BB gun, and then, guilt-ridden, becomes a doting mother hen to the eggs left behind. In Episode 2F04 ('Bart's Girlfriend'), Principal Skinner executes an elaborate sting to catch Bart misbehaving, using as bait Groundskeeper Willie in full Highland Scots regalia – including kilt sans underwear – in a public display for the sham holiday 'Scotchtoberfest'. Bart falls for the sting, fitting balloons to Willie's kilt to reveal his, um, willie to the assembled crowd. But later in the same episode, Bart refuses to participate with Reverend Lovejoy's borderline sociopathic daughter, Jessica, in a heist of the collection plate money, despite having a high-grade crush on her. 'Stealing from the collection plate is really wrong!' Bart tells her. 'Even *I* know that.' There's no apparent limit to the lengths Bart will go to emasculate an authority figure, but he's not given to crime for its own sake. For Bart, there needs to be a reason. If he stops short of full-out idealism, well, that's Lisa's job.

Bart's fuzzy politics are quite a bit like punk's own: the music loud, abrasive, unpolished – maybe even awful to some ears, seemingly devoid of redeeming qualities – the lyrics sometimes crude and profane, advocating sacrilege or riot or even murder. And yet beneath that clamour is a fiercely angry, relentlessly idealistic heart. An idea perhaps as simple and reflexive as this: to tear something down is to yearn to see something else – something better – in its place.

BACKHANDED IDEALISM (I): ROCKIN' IN THE NEW WORLD

The atomic bomb on Nirvana's *Nevermind* – the song that would almost single-handedly obliterate the hair-metallic, candy-popping, brain-dead '80s aesthetic in pop music and usher in several years of angry rock sludge – was the first track. 'Smells Like Teen Spirit' opens with a melodic, hiccupping jangle of clean classic riff rock. It bounces along like that for a full bar . . . starts to repeat itself . . . and then, just when you start tapping your foot along to this pretty little confection, right at the midpoint of its second run, the bomb drops: four thundering explosions from the drums, three dense beats each, clearing the way for a ferocious roar from the rest of the band. And incinerating nearly two decades of middle-of-the-road Top Forty pap for good measure.

I remember the first time I heard 'Teen Spirit' – and here we take a jaunt back to the pop-cultural hinterland of northern Ontario. It was in a basement rec room during a big booze-soaked Christmas house party in 1991, my last year of high school. The way it lives in my memory (with an asterisk of admission that I was blearily, blurrily drunk), I'd got tired of the Super Sounds of the '70s in the main room upstairs – I think it was either the second full-volume blaring of The Eagles' 'Hotel California' or the third of John Cougar's 'Jack and Diane' that got me moving – and I wandered downstairs, where a small knot of classmates and a handful of collegiate boyfriends of classmates were gathered around a stereo in extremely low light, reverently listening to . . . something else entirely. Listening to an *extraordinary* noise. Listening over and over and over again. Hooked by the fuzzy, ferocious guitars, I took a seat, and by the second run-through of 'Teen Spirit' I too was grooving along, bouncing my legs, rocking my head. Transported. The legendarily indistinct lyrics were even hazier after a dozen of whatever I was drinking that night, but on each listen another snippet would spring out, hold in my mind's eye, and then detonate: a couplet about how fun it was to lose and pretend, an oxymoronic assertion that the singer was bad at the things he was best at. The lines that really stuck, though – that would continue to rattle around my mind for days afterwards, with new shockwaves set off each of the thousand times I listened to the song in the coming months, smashing through long-standing barriers in my teenage mind – the real crux of it was found in the howling chorus, in which Cobain bawled about his own contagious stupidity and his jaded desire for mindless entertainment. Cryptic? Not one fucking bit. It seemed obvious and enormous and unassailably true: it was an arch-ironic consumerist pose of Homeresque indolence, a complete condemnation of bored overstimulated teenagehood, a vivid declaration that mindless passivity was the worst place you could possibly be. It was, as Cobain roared in the final line, a denial. Of what? Of potentially anything. The song gave voice to a rage I didn't know I had, turned the world upside down, brought all prior assumptions into question. A denial? Hell, yes.

Possibly the most famous line in 'Teen Spirit', though, is the last mumbled lyric of the final verse. 'Oh well, whatever, nevermind,' Kurt Cobain drones, seeming to negate the snarling rebuke of the chorus. The music that would fill the bomb crater left by 'Teen Spirit' – which would reluctantly adopt the moniker 'grunge' – was unwaveringly gloomy, lending credence to the notion that the youth of the early 1990s were terminally pissed off, disaffected beyond salvation, cynical to the core. The balance of *Nevermind* brims over with further rejections: of youthful hipness, of romantic love, of the band's own fans, of Cobain himself. To say the whole album is bile-soaked only begins to describe the disgust Cobain dispenses. And because this rage was so vague and sometimes contradictory, *Nevermind* seemed to be all but begging to be dismissed.

It wasn't, of course. *Nevermind* rocketed to the top of the charts, Nirvana's home base of Seattle became 'the next Liverpool' (so enthused the cover of *Rolling Stone*), and the loathsome mainstream swallowed Cobain and his indie-rock revolutionaries whole, commodified them and churned them out to the masses, first as 'grunge' and later as the more expansive 'alternative rock'. The consequences were, at first, quite positive, even refreshing. For one thing, bands like Pearl Jam, Soundgarden and Smashing Pumpkins (to name only the trio most frequently associated with the grunge phenomenon) were far superior to the hairsprayed metal bands, teenie pop and fake country they dislodged from the pop charts. As well, numerous artists who'd long toiled in obscurity (three more or less random examples: Sonic Youth, The Pixies, Dinosaur Jr) finally saw their first real mainstream success. What's more, the alternative rock 'genre' was loose enough – both as a recording industry and as a fan base – that it embraced hip-hop artists (Cypress Hill, Public Enemy, Beastie Boys), industrial-metal bands (Ministry, Nine Inch Nails) and even its own aging forefathers (Neil Young, Johnny Cash).

But as the media frenzy built and record sales climbed, things got uglier. Trendspotting journalists and major-label publicity departments discovered 'the next Seattle' in more places than any sane person would bother to keep track of. Flannel shirts quite famously appeared for a time on fashion-show runways. Fans of this alternative music, meanwhile – in fact the youth of the 1990s generally – were soon labelled 'slackers': disaffected, lazy, apolitical, lost. Some mention might be made in all of this hype about economic decline or moral decay or rising divorce rates. But the possibility that a deeper and more fundamental critique of society was at work, suggestions that the music's popularity might indicate a degree of free-floating alienation of alarming proportions – these were largely left out of the mass media's understanding of the alt-rock explosion. To be fair, a significant portion of the audience was into it simply because it was hip. And to be even fairer, and to quote Bart Simpson, 'making teenagers depressed is like shooting fish in a barrel'. But what if there was more to it than garden-variety teen angst? What if alternative rock had something in common with, just for example, a contemporary TV cartoon that boasted its own intense social critique?

On the surface, the alt-rock world might seem to have little in common with *The Simpsons*. The most glaring difference: *The Simpsons* is extremely funny, which can be said about precious few alternative albums. But if the *songs* weren't always funny,[6] the *musicians* often were, especially in their almost invariably mocking interactions with the mainstream media. Many alternative rockers were irreverent, iconoclastic, smart-assed. They professed to hate dogma and detest pretence. They mocked artifice. Ask them a straight question, and they'd answer in the sardonic tones of *The Simpsons*.

This was most certainly true of Nirvana. Cobain and bassist Krist Novoselic even invented a running gag they used during the *Nevermind* media circus to suss out the intelligence of the interviewer. It consisted of a fake back-story for the band claiming they had met at art college when Cobain expressed an interest in Novoselic's sculpture. Journalists who fell for the story would continue to be baited for the remainder of the interview.

And then there was the band's 'live' performance of 'Smells Like Teen Spirit' on the long-running BBC programme *Top of the Pops*, which is simply one of the finest piss-takes in the history of televised rock & roll. Performers on *Top of the Pops* are expected to mime along to a recording of their hit, but at the time Nirvana recorded its appearance, the show's guests were provided with a live microphone which set up the knockout punch in a hilariously inept performance that laid out the artifice of the show for all to see. As the opening riff of 'Teen Spirit' played, Cobain gently strummed his guitar, nowhere near in time. Novoselic hopped around the stage like a speed-addled bunny, tossing his bass around in total indifference to the fact of the song, and drummer Dave Grohl simply bashed at his kit randomly and eventually knocked significant parts of it over. But the real gem was Cobain's live vocal: he crooned his way through the song in a deep, throaty monotone, smiling smarmily as he turned the band's hit single into the worst lounge-act standard of all time. The deconstruction was total. The band, the song, the programme, musical performance on television, TV itself – all were torn apart, laid out in pieces, stripped of their power. It was a masterful piece of satire.

The most Simpsonesque incident in the great alternative-rock explosion, though, was undoubtedly the Lexicon Hoax. This was the moment that Seattle's alt-rock scene, as if directly channelling Matt Groening and company, struck a satirical chord identical to that of *The Simpsons*. It arose from a vain attempt by *The New York Times* to codify the youthquake emanating from the Pacific Northwest. America's venerable journal of record decided it needed some subcultural detail to round out a feature on the grunge phenomenon. So a *Times* reporter called the offices of Sub Pop Records, Nirvana's former label and the indie epicentre of the Seattle music scene, to dig up some colour. The reporter reached Megan Jasper, the label's publicist, and asked for some samples of grunge slang. Jasper fed the reporter a long list of 'grunge speak,' which the *Times* printed verbatim on 15 November 1992, in a sidebar entitled 'Lexicon of Grunge: Breaking the Code'.[7] 'Wack slacks', the *Times* explained, were old ripped jeans; a loser was called a 'cob nobbler'; and the age-old teen pastime of hanging out was referred to by grungesters as 'swingin' on the flippity-flop.' A fine bit of pop-cultural reportage. Except that Jasper had made up every word of it, more or less off the top of her head. As a high-profile testament to the gullibility of the mainstream media in full hype mode, it was a success beyond measure – a prank so perfect it seemed scripted. Not even *The Simpsons* could have done it better.

The show did, however, leave its own satirical mark on the alt-rock explosion – in Episode 3F21 ('Homerpalooza'). The episode opens with Homer slowly coming to the realisation that he's no longer hip in the eyes of his kids. In a desperate bid to regain his cool, he takes Bart and Lisa to 'Hullabalooza', a corporate-sponsored alt-rock festival that's a mirror image of the Lollapalooza festivals that criss-crossed North America every summer through most of the 1990s. Hullabalooza even features several artists who played at Lollapalooza (and who provided the voices for the Simpsonised versions of themselves): Smashing Pumpkins, Sonic Youth and Cypress Hill.

In the episode, Homer is soon invited to join the Hullabalooza tour, sharing the stage with the giants of alternative music as he takes cannonballs to the belly as part of the festival's freak show. There's a remarkably natural fit to this crossover. You can see it when Pumpkins front man Billy Corgan approaches Homer backstage to tell him he likes his act. 'I'm Billy Corgan, Smashing Pumpkins,' says Corgan. 'I'm Homer Simpson, smiling politely,' Homer answers. There's a sense not of discrete universes colliding (as can sometimes be the case with *Simpsons* celebrity appearances) but rather of the icons of the same universe finally meeting.

There's also a knowingness to the show's portrayal of the alt-rock scene that suggests at the very least that *The Simpsons*' writers were far better versed in the music and its accompanying culture than were the overwhelming majority of mainstream journalists. No false grunge lexicons here – even the minor details have the show's usual pinpoint accuracy. REGISTER NOT TO VOTE reads a sign on a Hullabalooza booth, nailing perfectly the alternative scene's paradoxical mix of activism and apathy. The most tragicomically precise snippet of satire, though, occurs as Homer takes the stage for his act. Cut to two slouching teens in the audience done up in grunge flannel, their faces perfect masks of boredom. 'Oh, here comes that cannonball guy,' the first one says, his voice thick with the laconic derision that was alt-rock's default tone. 'He's cool.' The second one, in a similar drawl: 'Are you being sarcastic, dude?' 'I don't even know anymore,' the first one replies, the irony in his voice replaced with real, anguished confusion.

This is the danger of dedicating yourself to denial: it can numb you to everything. It can even erase you completely. No one demonstrated this more profoundly than Kurt Cobain. There was genuine, passionate idealism in his work and in his life, but most viscerally there was a strain of nihilism so virulent and inward-looking that it was ultimately indistinguishable from total self-negation. 'Don't know what I want, but I know how to get it / I wanna destroy the passerby' – this self-confident desire to tear it all down summarised the Sex Pistols' brand of nihilism. By Nirvana's time, however, Cobain's loathing had become a far more specific and insular thing, his destructive rage aimed primarily at personal targets: his critics, the celebrity machine generally – and himself. *In Utero* – the band's follow-up to *Nevermind* – was a darker, heavier album. If *Nevermind* was a single cathartic explosion, then its sequel, packed with scratching and wailing guitars, pummelling drums and soul-sick moans, sounded like the aftermath, an impotent fit amid the rubble, doomed to end in self-destruction. And throughout the album, Cobain yearns for this nullification: he begs to be raped and hated, to be tossed in a fire, to be washed over with blame. In the end, exhausted, he apologises for anything and everything.

There are many myths about Kurt Cobain, too many myths. Too many lessons tacked on to his suicide. He is an object lesson in the ravages of drug abuse. He was a martyr on the altar of fame, a victim torn apart by the great grinding gears of modern celebrity. He was a helpless man-child, destroyed by an evil seductress. Or he was a poet doomed to self-destruct, a fragile symbol of a dying world. There might be shreds of truth in any or all of these. What is certain, though, is that his work demonstrates an obsession with the connected themes of alienation, destruction and self-negation. In his journals and in interviews he talked frequently about an incurable pain in his stomach, and just as frequently about the tremendous burden of guilt he carried – for being male, for being white, for being heterosexual, for being American. For being born into immense comfort, for scaling the heights of success to a place of ultimate privilege and for finding all of it completely lacking in solace. His suicide, like any suicide, was a purely selfish act. And his suicide, like any suicide, said first and foremost that he could not bear the pain of his own life. There can be nothing idealistic about the act of suicide, because idealism is predicated on the notion of a community, and suicide negates the interests of the community as surely as it negates the life of victim. I don't think Kurt Cobain's suicide symbolised anything other than his desire to be dead, which isn't a symbol at all – it's a literal fact.

I'm laying all of this out because I'm about to pivot into a suggestion that *identifying* with this self-negation has in it the seeds of idealism, and I don't want to be misunderstood. This is easier to see in a softer light. There's a streak of self-negation that runs through Bart Simpson's character, as well, manifesting itself primarily in his wishes and fantasies. An example: when Bart is expelled from school in Episode 9F18 ('Whacking Day'), he contemplates a future spent as a taster of dangerous food additives. In the ensuing fantasy sequence, Bart imagines himself drinking a soft drink called Nature's Goodness, which causes him to grow into a grotesque monster. He's excited at the prospect. Another example: in Episode 2F32 (''Round Springfield'), Bart receives 500 dollars as his share of a cash settlement in a lawsuit against the makers of Krusty-O's Cereal (the jagged metal O in his cereal box had made him sick). 'I can't believe it – five hundred bucks!' Bart raves. 'Just think what I can do with that money.' Another fantasy sequence follows: Bart is at a roulette wheel. He puts the 500 dollars on red. Black wins. Bart, back in the present, goggle-eyed: 'Coooool!' Even in his dreams, Bart wants to fail, to be deformed, to experience depravity. His only rock-star fantasy is to be a debauched English metal god playing a song called 'Me Fans Are Stupid Pigs' and hurling whisky bottles at his best friend, Milhouse.

Obviously, you have to look closely, wishfully, to find the embryonic politics buried in Bart's (or anyone else's) dreams of self-negation. But here it is: if he *wants* this kind of nothingness, then he has implicitly rejected all conventional notions of success. That's the idealistic seed. Likewise, although actually committing suicide is an act of surrender, relating to it – identifying with Cobain's desire to be done with the world, claiming to understand it – is a categorical rejection of the world as it's currently ordered, and in this there lies a desire for renewal, for some better world built from a new starting point. To project a political argument onto such a resolutely private and wholly destructive act: this is the seed.

This is the idealism of the mosh pit. A thousand sweaty bodies bouncing, thrashing, pounding into each other in a ritual pantomime of the nihilism in the music: it's an embrace of that message, a commitment to it, an acceptance of the collective will of the crowd to implode, to negate *itself* as the first step towards dismantling the whole failed society. Or at least this is how it could be, when the audiences were still small enough and their identification with the music deep enough to understand that this was not just a crowd but a like-minded community.

'Punk rock means freedom.' Kurt Cobain wrote variations on this line repeatedly in his journals. And that's what a mosh pit can feel like: joyful release, the dissolution of self into a larger whole. The intense feeling of community that comes when you stumble and the crowd parts around you to let you back up, or when the guy next to you – who'd just been trading ferocious head butts with a like-minded friend – excuses himself for stepping on your toe. The 1999 movie *Fight Club* (and the Chuck Palahniuk novel it was based on) describes a sort of exaggerated version of the mosh pit, divorced from the music, reduced to its essence: one-on-one combat between alienated, emasculated men as a form of liberation. Most of the pits I witnessed were coed, but part of *Fight Club*'s message still fits: that alienation is so widespread and intense that the first step to changing it, the one remaining option, is to connect in the most brutal physical sense, to inflict and feel pain. From this awakening, this rediscovery of self and of community, greater change can come – in *Fight Club*, it involves destroying the office towers of credit-card companies – but it begins with a ritual of self-negation.

Nirvana's most nakedly political song, 'Territorial Pissings', also opens with a negation of a sort: a savage, tuneless reading of the chorus of The Youngbloods' feel-good hippie anthem 'Let's Get Together', sung by Nirvana bassist Krist Novoselic. (Novoselic, it warrants mention, became a committed political activist after Nirvana's premature demise.) The sound of the vocal is fuzzy and distant, as if recorded onto a cheap tape long ago and long since forgotten. 'C'mon people now, smile on your brother,' Novoselic yelps. 'Everybody get to*gether*' – his voice seeming to bottom out on this syllable, exhausted by the strain of making the sentiment sound plausible – 'try to love one another right *now*.' Even before he's done, a single ominous note of feedback-drenched guitar invades. It repeats four times, waiting. The lyric ends, and a jagged wall of fuzz takes over. A double-time drum roll comes up underneath it, and then the song hurtles into blistering 4/4 punk. Cobain snarls the lyrics, building to a full-blown scream at the chorus as he dedicates himself to finding a better way and then immediately decides instead to put off the search for another time. By the end of the song, the yell has unravelled into a soul-sick howl. Finally – pushed beyond reason, rendered sublingual by his rage – Cobain only screams. It's a brutal, desperate sound, the sound of threads giving way on the frayed rope that tethers the voice to some dim sense of hope.

This is a backhanded idealism: a plea for change, and then, in the very next breath, a retreat. It mirrors the politics of Nirvana's fans, of a youth culture deeply troubled by the state of the world but trapped by a sense of powerlessness and a deep distrust of elected officials. Activist booths were almost as plentiful as body-piercing stalls at events like Lollapalooza, but this was a generation of young people who were opting out of voting at record-breaking levels. There would be no John F. Kennedy or Pierre Elliot Trudeau to restore their faith in government, and the most serious problems (climate change, global trade and poverty, overweening corporate power) seemed too vast and intractable to even be appraised, let alone fixed. Tellingly, one of the few overtly political movements launched by an alt-rock band – Pearl Jam's effort to break up Ticketmaster's monopoly on ticket sales for large-scale rock concerts in North America – ended in failure. And so the idealism turned on itself: the alt-rock legions embraced a highly personal politics.

There's abundant evidence of this myopia at Hullabalooza – the Simpsonian alt-rock festival indeed serves as a kind of abridged documentary of the generation's muddled politics. 'Generation X may be shallow, but at least they have tolerance and respect for all people,' Lisa notes as the Simpsons arrive at the festival. On cue, they pass a booth labelled BUNGEE JUMP AGAINST RACISM. A short while later, she and Bart voice their outrage in the shrill tones of political correctness when Homer attempts to appropriate Jamaican culture by donning a Rastafarian hat. Homer should have listened:

later, when he tries to blend into the crowd, a group of kids accuse him of spreading hate crimes. As punishment, they crowd surf him to the back of the throng. Cut to the heart of the audience, where Bart and Lisa stand amid a crowd of fans swaying half-heartedly in time to 'Zero' by Smashing Pumpkins, apparently too exhausted by their disillusionment to do anything more than jerk their limbs slightly with each beat. The explanation for their apathy comes later, after Homer has joined the tour. 'You know,' he tells Billy Corgan, 'my kids think you're the greatest. And thanks to your gloomy music, they've finally stopped dreaming of a future I can't possibly provide.' Adding to the audience's woes is the ubiquity of corporate control, even at this supposedly 'alternative' festival. As Lisa observes at the festival entrance, 'It's like Woodstock, only with advertisements everywhere and tons of security guards.' Before Cypress Hill can start their set, MC B-Real has to make an announcement: 'We have a lost child here. If she's not claimed within the next hour, she will become property of Blockbuster Entertainment.'

In the face of all of this – ineffectual politics, a bleak future, corporate co-optation of the one place where they feel they belong – the alt-rock kids have turned inward. Activism is reduced to denouncing the hate crimes and political incorrectness of fellow concertgoers. Freedom is subject to the whims of Blockbuster Entertainment and Ticketmaster. And as for the personal liberation of dancing, of getting lost in the music – who knows, maybe the Hullabalooza mosh pit was too chaotic, maybe security put a stop to it – but the fans do little more than oscillate minutely to the beat.

BACKHANDED IDEALISM (II): ONE ISLAND NATION UNDER A GROOVE

Meanwhile, on the other side of the Atlantic, there were markedly different beats – beats so dense they were measured by the hundreds per minute – and they had the kids dancing with euphoric abandon, in celebration of the first joyous bloom of rave culture. This new British youth culture hit not with the violence of an exploding punk bomb but with the warm embrace of a deep groove. Funny thing, though: these wildly divergent vectors would very nearly intersect by the early 1990s and then continue in parallel for the rest of the decade.

At first, the rave scene possessed a seemingly boundless, world-beating optimism. Its roots – like those of alternative rock – led directly back to the first wave of punk, but the English strain crossbred in the mid-1980s with the dance-floor beats of house music (born in Detroit and Chicago but buried deep in the cultural underground) and European techno and received an extra boost from an influx of the euphoric drug Ecstasy, brought home by vacationing English clubbers from the Spanish party island of Ibiza. These elements, mixed together in a cavernous warehouse of a club, produced a cosmic explosion. Dominic Utton, describing the vibe ten years on in the *Independent*, summarised it thusly: 'Imagine the optimism, togetherness and sheer belief in the future of the Sixties tempered with the savvy, energy and arrogance of punk.'

By the early 1990s, this new dance culture had spread throughout Europe and to cities around the world, planting the seeds for countless new subgenres of the 'acid house' music that had launched the movement. Meanwhile, 'Madchester' pop bands – particularly the Stone Roses and Happy Mondays – fused dance grooves to traditional rock & roll and conquered the British pop charts. But prodigious drug use and ridiculous legal squabbling sucked the energy out of the Madchester scene just as it was about to launch the second British invasion of America. British clubs were infiltrated by gangs looking for a piece of the rave scene's lucrative drug trade, and the optimism of the first flowering of rave soon dissipated. If there'd once been more to it, the movement became primarily about hedonistic escape, about getting off one's head, about losing oneself completely on the dance floor. Writing in the British music magazine *The Wire* in 1992, Simon Reynolds described the ''Ardkore' subgenre then sweeping the British club scene in language that could just as easily have been used to describe the mosh pits that were at the same moment becoming ubiquitous in North America. The 'Ardkore dance floor,' Reynolds wrote, 'is where the somnambulist youth of Britain snap out of the living death of the 90s to grasp at a few moments of bliss.' Note Reynolds's phrase: 'the living death of the 90s'. This is what united the euphoric dance floors of England with the grinding mosh pits of North America: a sense that the status quo was something so degraded and oppressive that it had to be escaped from as much and as often as humanly possible.

And another uniting factor: a firm belief that the best tool for escape – perhaps even for change – could be abbreviated DIY.

DIY: PUNK'S ENDURING IDEAL

In Episode 1F08 ('$pringfield (or, How I Learned to Stop Worrying and Love Legalized Gambling)'), the people of Springfield decide to legalise gambling in an effort to dig the town out of an economic slump. Soon, Mr Burns's Casino is Springfield's social focal point, and even underage Bart is having a go at the slot machines. A casino employee – the squeaky-voiced teenager, Springfield's ubiquitous service-industry drone – catches him in the act and tosses him out. Bart, defiant to the end, fires off an insult as his butt hits the street: 'By the way, your martinis suck!' The irritated casino employee replies, 'Oh, yeah? What are you going to do? Start your own casino? In your tree house? And get all your little friends to come? I'd like to see that!' And he dissolves into scoffing laughter. Cut to Bart's tree house, rechristened 'Bart's Casino,' where a tuxedoed Bart welcomes a steady flow of children into his new gambling den like a Vegas pro. Looking on is the very same squeaky-voiced casino employee. 'Well, he certainly showed me,' he admits.

And that, in a nutshell, is DIY.

The initials stands for do-it-yourself, and it's really just that simple. If the system does not work for you, if it has no place for you, then do it yourself. Start your own record label, produce your own album, organise your own tour. DIY was an inevitable by-product of punk, born of the necessity of providing an alternative to the loathsome (and hostile) corporate mainstream. And yet the by-product actually proved more durable, more adaptable, than the music itself, crossing musical genres, skipping to new media, even instigating fundamental shifts in the way entire entertainment industries functioned. It was an incendiary little acronym.

The DIY philosophy emerged soon after the first wave of punk bands shook their audiences out of the bloated torpor of 1970s arena rock and disco, but it was the American punk scene of the 1980s that proved to be the most fertile ground for DIY ventures. Independent record labels and an independent network of clubs emerged across North America to support the radically marginalised punks, eventually giving rise to an entire indie-rock subculture that played wet nurse to a scruffy young band called Nirvana (among hundreds of others). Beyond that, though, the DIY approach launched an entire parallel media universe. It led to the founding of countless handmade fanzines. It provided the first work for scores of talented artists and designers, who developed their own unique graphical styles designing the handbills that advertised punk gigs. Ditto for young photographers and journalists – and cartoonists. Among these was a young man fresh out of Evergreen State College in Olympia, Washington – a major centre of alternative culture – who got his start drawing cartoons for the college newspaper. When he moved to Los Angeles after college, he started producing his own little hand-stapled comic book, which he sold to the punks who shopped in the record store where he was working. This is how Matt Groening and his *Life in Hell* cartoon first found an audience. And since that cartoon was what brought Groening to the attention of big-shot TV producer James L. Brooks, it's no exaggeration to say that without the DIY-driven punk scene of the 1980s, there'd likely be no *Simpsons*.[8]

Groening is a telling example, in that his cartooning (like that of most indie cartoonists) had no real connection to punk beyond the fact that it was too weird and/or subversive and/or unproven for the mainstream. This was the real power of DIY: it eventually gave rise to entire cottage industries with no direct ties to the music. By the late 1980s, for example, 'zines' – independently produced, desktop-published magazines – had become a full-blown subcultural phenomenon of their own. The first of these were straightforward punk fanzines, focused on record reviews and interviews with musicians, but they soon branched out. *Far* out. Any place or person or topic was potentially zine-able, and indeed the best of them were often the most esoteric. *Beer Frame*, for example, was a brilliant journal of pop-cultural anthropology that featured in-depth explorations of the origins and purposes of truly bizarre consumer goods (for example, Kraut juice, a beverage derived from the juice used to pickle sauerkraut). Another gem was *Duplex Planet*, which was composed of interviews with the residents of the senior citizens' centre where the zine's creator worked, and which masterfully maintained a tricky balance between genuine empathy and absurdist humour. And these were just the ones that by luck or skill came to some degree of mainstream attention. Any given city's indie record or bookstore had a shelf full of local zines, documenting and augmenting the local culture.[9]

The same DIY spirit pervaded rave culture, not just in its English birthplace but anywhere it spread. Again, necessity was invention's mummy: the very structure of raves demanded DIY. Someone, after all, had to find and book and set up a venue, had to spin the tunes, had to produce the graphics for the flyers. And so every rave scene became a de facto training camp for DJs, graphic designers and small-business entrepreneurs. And the music itself – sample-heavy, self-produced, endlessly changeable – is by far the most DIY-friendly music genre in pop history.

By the early 1990s, the notion that culture was something produced far away, that it required enormous stacks of cash and elaborate infrastructure, had been replaced by the sense that all real innovation happened far away from these stifling mainstream trappings. This was punk's greatest legacy, passed on through rave and alt-rock to the entire culture – and to Bart Simpson, its foremost mass-culture avatar.

Bart's devotion to the DIY ethos is not as evident as his affinity for punk rock's spirit of creative destruction, but it's been an essential part of Bart's character throughout *The Simpsons'* run – at times allegorically, on occasion (such as in the founding of Bart's Casino) quite literally. Inside the conformist halls of Springfield Elementary, Bart is the consummate slacker: apathetic and disruptive, smart-assed and lazy. As soon as he leaves the building, though, he reveals himself to be self-motivated and ambitious, a ringleader and entrepreneur. Beaten up by a bully in Season 1, Bart organises his classmates into a militia in order to fight back. In need of money for a rare comic book in Season 2, he promptly sets up a lemonade stand and then makes beer his stock-in-trade to expand his customer base. Bart leads the rebellion against the fascist leadership of Kamp Krusty, he rallies the assault on Shelbyville to reclaim Springfield's beloved lemon tree, he becomes a faith healer preaching to his very own jam-packed tent of believers. Send Bart down to the Department of Motor Vehicles to hang out with his aunts for career day, and he'll soon figure out a way to make himself a fake ID and then use it to take his pals on a wild trip to Knoxville, Tennessee.

In a nod to the ambitiousness of Bart's extracurricular activities, the show's writers have over the years added semi-professional trappings even to his childish pranks. As he helps Lisa plot revenge on a class rival, for example, an unrelated pranking idea comes to him; he produces a handheld tape recorder, turns it on, makes a note of his idea, and then – after a sober pause – flips the recorder back on to add a few extra malevolent chuckles. On another occasion, he experiences a tortured artist's moment of self-doubt at the release ceremony for the school weather balloon – he's worried about the quality of his illicit caricature of Principal Skinner on the side of it. 'I don't think I really captured the eyes,' he frets. 'Bart,' says faithful sidekick Milhouse, 'if you have a failing, it's that you're always demanding perfection.' Another sober pause. '*If* you have a failing.' A few moments after the balloon's release, Skinner interrogates Bart about the crime – and discovers that Bart has blueprints for the caricature on his person, not to mention notarised photos of the work-in-progress and an alternate wording for the insult on the balloon. Which is to say, with considerable hyperbole, that Bart *works* at his mischief. Like many a DIY punk, he's at his most productive when he's working outside – indeed working *against* – the mainstream of society.

Much as Bart has applied the DIY ethos to summer-camp rebellions and school pranks, so too did the DIY spirit inspire revivals in places far removed from the music industry. For example: Hollywood, which had by the late 1980s sunk into a period of intense stagnation, rampant greed and creative bankruptcy. The film industry was in the kind of bloated rut that music had occupied a few years earlier, churning out little besides overpriced, over-produced, brain-dead spectacles. And then out of nowhere came the shoestring-budgeted, myth-making indies, whose tales of how they got their movies made became almost as well known as the movies themselves.

Kevin Smith's story was typically dramatic and inspiring. In 1991, only 21 years old, he drove from his New Jersey home to New York City to see a quirky pseudo-documentary called *Slackers* – Richard Linklater's self-produced stream-of-consciousness examination of the elaborately idle lives of young people in his hometown of Austin, Texas. Watching the movie was an epiphany for Smith, and before long he was maxing out credit cards and shooting after-hours at the strip mall where he worked to make *Clerks* (1994). It was an archetypal indie: ultra-low-budget (talking up its total production costs – $27,575 – even became part of its marketing appeal), gritty in appearance, somewhat clunkily acted (mostly by amateurs), but quick-witted and passionate. Similarly rough-edged films with similarly endearing creation myths abounded in the early 1990s. Robert Rodriguez, for example, made his indie debut, *El Mariachi* (1992), for only $7,000, raising the cash by volunteering for laboratory experiments. And then there was the kingpin of the indie-film movement: a former L.A. video store clerk, a brainy walking film encyclopaedia, a lisping, somewhat dorky kid who became the hippest director of his age. His name, as you may have already guessed, was Quentin Tarantino.

In some respects, Tarantino became to indie film what Kurt Cobain was to alt-rock: its poster child, its best-known purveyor, its unofficial spokes-person. Largely on the strength of two gritty, ultraviolent films about under-world thugs whose conversations were long-winded, brainy, weighted with slang and drenched in pop-cultural allusion – his 1992 debut, *Reservoir Dogs*, and the blockbuster 1994 follow-up, *Pulp Fiction* – Tarantino became a full-blown icon to the same people who were making Cobain a rock star and *The Simpsons* a religion. Which was no coincidence: Tarantino's movies, and indie film generally, mined the same terrain as alt-rock. They were edgy and brash, they felt honest and authentic, they focused on subject matter that was extreme and disquieting or else emotionally intense and thus deeply resonant to a generation awash in dysfunction. And they were as ironic and as obsessed with pop culture as *The Simpsons* was.

It was perhaps only a matter of time, then, before Tarantino showed up on *The Simpsons*. And so he did – in caricature, with his famous squeaky voice provided by Dan Castellaneta – in Episode 3G03 ('Simpsoncalifragil-isticexpiala-D'OH!-cious'), as the guest director of a particularly stylish instalment of 'Itchy & Scratchy' called 'Reservoir Cats'. Towards the end of the cartoon, Tarantino enters – as if walking onto the cartoon's set – to explain the deep meaning of the cartoon's violence in a bang-on lampoon of the real Tarantino's caffeinated rants about his work: 'What I'm trying to say in this cartoon is that violence is everywhere in our society, you know, it's like even in breakfast cereals, man.' Itchy then decapitates him with a razor. There's certainly no other young director (and very few other directors, period, the Scorsese/Coppola/Spielberg/Lucas pantheon excepted) whose aesthetic style, personality and verbal quirks would be identifiable enough to *The Simpsons'* audience to be effective in this kind of a parody.

In time, the indie-film boom would seriously reconfigure the structure of Hollywood. Miramax – the production company that backed numerous influential indies, including Tarantino's – eventually earned a degree of power and prestige in Hollywood that rivalled the major studios. The majority of those major studios, meanwhile, either bought up the most successful indies or else launched their own pseudo-indie distribution arms to compete. Many of the major record companies used the same approach to deal with the alt-rock boom. Of course, the mainstream film and music industries continue to spew significant torrents of formulaic garbage, but that garbage now exists alongside an elaborate web of DIY indie artists and companies in a sometimes-hostile, sometimes-symbiotic relationship. Little pillars of creativity and opportunity now fill the field around the monolith.

DIY's most pervasive influence, though, was on the one medium that didn't already have a monolith to topple: the Internet.

The relationship between technology and the DIY movement has always been cosy and causal. The DIY approach taken by alt-rockers and especially dance-music producers was made possible by technological advances that lowered the cost and upped the quality, availability and user-friendliness of electronic instruments, recording equipment and – more recently – professional-quality recording software such as Pro Tools. The liner notes of Nirvana's indie debut, *Bleach*, for example, include a proud mention of the total cost of the recording: $606.17. The same is true of the indie-film boom, which would've been impossible without the development of cheaper, easier-to-use cameras and editing equipment. And the advent of desktop publishing was essential not only to the birth of the zine but also to the availability, quality and inventiveness of rave flyers, punk handbills and the liner notes of self-produced cassettes and CDs. In each of these cases, though, the DIY upstarts had to compete against larger, slicker, more powerful players.

But the Internet was a vast and essentially uncharted wilderness. Anyone with a computer could contribute content quickly, easily and extremely cheaply. And that content was just as readily available to other Internet users as the slick websites of the megacorporations. The playing field was at first completely level – or if it wasn't, then it was actually tilted slightly towards the DIY early adopters, who understood the new medium's strengths and weaknesses and unique cultural quirks far better than their big-shot competitors. The rhetoric of punk and rave and indie film said that anyone could be a musician or filmmaker or artist or impresario, but there was still the problem of getting to know the right people, finding the right tools, being in an urban centre that had a punk or rave or indie-film community. With the Internet, though, literally anyone anywhere could contribute, so long as they had Internet access. If there were, at a guess, perhaps a few thousand indie punk and alternative bands making noise on albums or in clubs across North America at the peak of the music's popularity, there were *millions* of websites up and running within a few years of the Internet's launch, not to mention millions of other active participants in newsgroups and bulletin boards and chat rooms.

The Internet, which soon became an enormously important and influential communications tool, had DIY in its DNA from its very birth. On the Internet, not just content production but *distribution* – by far the most critical and elusive element in any mass-cultural enterprise – is DIY. And this helps to explain why it has managed in a few short years to have a far greater impact on other media in the cultural sphere than all previous DIY efforts combined. After their initial challenges, the indie movements in both music and film were essentially subsumed into the old-guard mainstream, with some concessions and minor changes made to reach a grudging equilibrium (namely, the pseudo-indie record labels and film studios). The Internet, though, has fundamentally altered the mainstream.

The strongest example to date is in the music industry, which continues as I write this to fight a battle it has already lost. In 1999, an 18-year-old student at Northeastern University – kid by the name of Shawn Fanning – built a slick little piece of software that allowed Internet users to trade songs with each other over the Internet. He called it Napster. And that was pretty much that. Whatever equilibrium is eventually reached in the industry, it will be dramatically different from a system in which consumers buy CDs for 20 dollars from huge megastores that carry the produce primarily (if not quite exclusively) of the world's six largest record companies. The alt-rock boom widened the parameters of the mainstream music business; Napster and its file-sharing descendants fundamentally shifted the ground on which the whole industry stands. Similarly slick little pieces of software will eventually unleash similar sorts of earthquakes on film, television and publishing. The first rumblings have already been felt in all of these industries. It's only a matter of time before the earth really starts to shake.

At the very beginning of the opening credits of every episode of *The Simpsons*, Bart is alone in his classroom at school, writing lines on the chalkboard. The lines change every episode. The ones for an episode first aired in January 2001 read NETWORK TV IS NOT DEAD. It isn't, of course. Not yet. When it does die, though, its obituary should contain the name of its killer: DIY.

NOTES & MARGINALIA

1. **A product plug:** Here, and in several other places in this book, I'm indebted to *Lipstick Traces: A Secret History of the Twentieth Century*, Greil Marcus's excellent, expansive study of punk music and nihilism in twentieth-century pop culture.

2. **Nazi supermen are *not* our superiors:** Itchy & Scratchy's creator may have made Nazi propaganda films, and Mr Burns, of course, spent the Second World War making the Germans shells that worked, dammit! – but 20th Century-Fox is no collaborator. Though Bart's parent corporation mostly accepted that it was powerless to stop the onslaught of bootlegged merchandise, it drew the line at 'Nazi Bart' T-shirts. In May 1991, Fox sued Tom Metzger of the White Aryan Resistance – an American neo-Nazi group – for infringing on its copyright by selling T-shirts sporting an image of a *seig-heil*ing Bart in a Gestapo uniform. Metzger agreed to stop peddling the shirts.

3. **Eat *whose* shorts?** Apparently, the shorts of some guy in Dayton, Ohio, the city where Nancy Cartwright – the voice of Bart Simpson – grew up. Cartwright was a trumpet player in her high-school band, which would parade from the school to the stadium every Friday night for football games, playing a simple drum march along the way. At the end of each run of the march cadence, the entire band would chant their bandleader's initials: 'D! R! F!' One night, though, for reasons lost to history, the chant was changed: 'Eat! My! Shorts!' It stuck – and stuck with Cartwright, who introduced it to Bart's lexicon, and thus to the entire world. (It should also be noted that the epithet predates Bart: it is memorably employed by Bender, the juvenile delinquent played by Judd Nelson, to tell off his sadistic principal in the beloved 1985 teen comedy *The Breakfast Club*.)

4. **Bart's crank calls:** Not counting the staff of Springfield Elementary, the most frequent target of Bart's pranks is Moe, the cantankerous proprietor of Moe's Tavern (and at best a pseudo-authority). With Moe, the prank plays out the same each time: Bart calls the bar asking for a fictitious patron, Moe calls out for I.P. Freely or Mike Rotch or Amanda Huggenkiss, and he realises he's been had as the bar erupts in laughter. The most amusing part of the prank is the series of increasingly inventive means by which Moe threatens to punish the caller if he ever discovers his identity: 'I swear I'm gonna slice your heart in half'; 'I'm gonna gut you like a fish and drink your blood'; 'I'm gonna carve my name in your back with an ice pick'; 'I'm gonna use your head for a bucket and paint my house with your brains'; 'I'm gonna shove a sausage down your throat and stick starving dogs in your butt.'

5. **Win, place or d'oh!** The horse race for which Bart picks the winner is, incidentally, a fine

example of *The Simpsons* at its dense, multilayered, self-referential best. The call of the home stretch goes like this: 'As they come out of the turn, it's Sufferin' Succotash by a neck over Yabba-Dabba-Doo. Two lengths back it's Ooh Ain't I a Stinker and That's All Folks. I Yam What I Yam can see them all, but here comes Don't Have a Cow flying on the outside, and coming down to the wire it's all Don't Have a Cow!' It's a race between cartoon-character catchphrases, with Bart's own 'Don't have a cow!' victorious over Popeye's 'I yam what I yam', Porky Pig's 'That's all folks', Bugs Bunny's 'Ooh, ain't I a stinker', Fred Flintstone's 'Yabba-dabba-doo' and Sylvester the cat's 'Sufferin' succotash.' The whole gag is over in a few short seconds – an incidental detail turned into a lightning-quick homage to the classics of American animation.

6. **Kurt Cobain, humorist?** 'I Hate Myself and I Want To Die' – a Nirvana song that appeared on *The Beavis & Butthead Experience* (1993), a tribute to the popular MTV cartoon – is probably the strongest evidence of the band's robust sense of humour in its entire discography. The title in particular is pure self-parody, Cobain having fun with his media image as the ultimate tortured soul. In case the parody of the title was too broad, the song also features a softly spoken monologue by Cobain deep in the mix of the guitar break after the second chorus. It goes like this: 'Most people don't realise that large pieces of coral, which have been painted brown and attached to the skull by common wood screws, can make a child look like a deer.' The line is lifted from 'Deep Thoughts' by Jack Handey, a recurring series of absurdist aphorisms that appeared on *Saturday Night Live* in the early 1990s.

7. **Harsh realm, dude:** For the record, here's the full lexicon of grunge as published in *The New York Times*:

Wack slacks: Old ripped jeans
Fuzz: Heavy wool sweaters
Plats: Platform shoes
Kickers: Heavy boots
Swingin' on the flippity-flop: Hanging out
Bound-and-hagged: Staying home on Friday or Saturday night
Score: Great
Harsh realm: Bummer
Cob nobbler: Loser
Dish: Desirable guy
Bloated, big bag of bloatation: Drunk
Lamestain: Uncool person
Tom-tom club: Uncool outsiders
Rock on: A happy goodbye

8. **Random nugget of Matt Groening trivia:** The record store in Los Angeles that Groening worked in – and where he first sold copies of *Life in Hell* – was called Licorice Pizza.

9. **Full disclosure:** In the fall of 1993, I co-published a zine with two friends. It was called *Stun*. It lasted for two issues. It had really, really cool covers. One had this line drawing of Greek philosophers lounging on the steps of this classical lyceum, all of them gathered around this monolith, and we cut-and-pasted a baby's head onto the top of the monolith. It was awesome. The less said about the content inside – particularly my pretentious record reviews and rants about how the '60s were like *over*, dude – the better.

CHAPTER 4

Citizen Burns

I know of nothing more despicable and pathetic than a man who devotes all the hours of the waking day to the making of money for money's sake.

John D. Rockefeller, Sr.

I'll keep it short and sweet. Family, religion, friendship: These are the three demons you must slay if you wish to succeed in business.

C. Montgomery Burns, speaking to a group of schoolchildren, Episode 4F17 ('The Old Man and the Lisa')

MONTY BURNS: ROBBER BARON REDUX

IT STARTS LIKE A TYPICAL current-affairs programme. The blow-dried news anchor is at his desk, surrounded by newsroom props. He summarises a key issue from the day's headlines: 'The power-plant strike – argle-bargle or fooforah?' A panel is introduced: an industry titan, a union kingpin, talk-show mainstay Dr Joyce Brothers (who, as she proudly declares, has brought her own microphone). There's a hard question for the union kingpin, a characteristic evasion, and then the anchor turns to the industry titan, who has requested an opening tirade. The industry titan fixes the camera with a fierce, withering glare. His eyes are beady and merciless, his teeth bared and carnivorously sharp, his desiccated, contorted figure giving him the bearing of Death Incarnate. He begins to speak, his voice pinched and pitiless, his message nakedly malicious, brutally honest, utterly unspun. 'Fifteen minutes from now,' he rages, 'I will wreak a terrible vengeance on this city.' He raises a clawlike hand, waves it menacingly, forms it into a fist that shakes with rage. 'No one will be spared!' His eyes bulge madly as he lurches towards the camera. '*No one!*' Cut to the anchorman, who chuckles reassuringly. 'A chilling vision of things to come,' he summarises pleasantly.

And so please allow me to introduce Charles Montgomery Burns, a man of wealth and taste. To friends he's known as Monty, but to you it's Mr Burns, and he is far and away Springfield's oldest, richest and most powerful citizen, the owner of the Springfield Nuclear Power Plant, a briber of federal officials and buyer of local judges, a backroom political kingmaker, a war profiteer, a Yale alumnus. A robber baron, in short, in the nineteenth-century mould. Burns is the sneering face of capitalism on *The Simpsons*. He is big business made wizened, liver-spotted flesh, the embodiment of the corporate world's black, rapacious heart. He *is* capital: ruthless, unfeeling, greedy, invincible.

If the goal of *The Simpsons'* satire is to entertain and subvert, then of course it needs big nasty authorities to fuel its subversion. It needs a machine to rage against. There are plenty of contemptible authority figures in Springfield – Mayor Quimby, Police Chief Wiggum, Principal Skinner, 'Itchy & Scratchy' media baron Roger Meyers, even (particularly in more recent seasons) a handful of ultra-slick New-Age corporate stooges – but none of them wields the vicious power that Monty Burns does. At the push of a button, Mr Burns can plunge Springfield into darkness or summon a squadron of oily-hided lawyers to annihilate his opponents. With a wave of a withered arm, he can bend the board of directors of Springfield University or the brains trust of the Republican Party to his will. He can buy his way out of a laundry list of environmental violations with the petty cash in his wallet, and then make an impulse purchase of the court's statue of Justice as an afterthought. In many ways – some figurative and some extremely literal – Mr Burns *owns* Springfield.[1]

Mr Burns is a throwback to the days when big money made no apologies and big industry, sure of its own omnipotence, never worried a whit about its public image, which makes Burns anachronistic as hell. The corporate world in the time of *The Simpsons* has become a place of rampant fake populism and co-opted radicalism and flat-out-bullshit ethicalism. In every other TV commercial, we find mammoth multinational conglomerates testifying to their down-home folksiness (one recent and egregious example is an ad for Halliburton that closes with a soldier in desert camouflage on the phone, celebrating the birth of his daughter). Other corporations spend millions of bucks a pop on ads demonstrating their deeply held countercultural bona fides (viz. Nike, assorted Pepsi-Cola products, any number of car manufacturers, ad infinitum et ad nauseam). Or they pump 0.01 per cent of their operating budgets into green technologies and a hundred times that amount into testimonials claiming they love Mother Earth more than the crunchiest of granola munchers (a tactic particularly prized by giant oil companies like Royal Dutch/Shell and BP). Against these fetid piles of testimony in favour of What Should Be, Burns runs roughshod and unrepentant over the unwashed masses of Springfield as a one-man army of What Is. He's the ogre behind the warm, friendly corporate mask, his vow to club the consumers who made him rich and feast on their bones a stark counterweight to all those corporate giants – no less callous than old Monty, no less calculating – who tell us they love us so very very much in the TV ads that run between *Simpsons* segments.

In Mr Burns's uncloaked cruelty, we're presented with *The Simpsons*' most strident critique of authority. Other authority figures on the show – cops, politicians, entertainers – might be just as unworthy of the public trust as Burns is, but it's usually because they're merely stupid or incompetent or hypocritical or greedy. Only Burns – only this figurehead of Big Business – is pure evil.

Over the years, the Simpson family has learned exactly what sort of man C. Montgomery Burns is. 'You can't marry Mr Burns,' faultlessly moral Marge tells her mother. 'He's an evil man!' On another occasion, a suddenly penniless Burns – whose stock portfolio has remained unchanged since just before the 1929 crash and still includes significant shares in Confederated Slavery Holdings – approaches virtuous Lisa to ask for help in a new recycling venture aimed at rebuilding his business empire. 'I'd never help you,' Lisa replies. 'You're the worst person in the world!' So yes: Mr Burns's cruel nature is no secret.

Not that old Monty is trying to disguise his wickedness. In fact, often as not, he positively wallows in his own crapulence. He adores the misery of others. He is reduced to fits of uncontrollable hysteria by the memory of beating a poor Irishman when he (Burns, that is) was a child. He lavishes affection on the snarling hounds who guard his grand estate, joyfully reminiscing about the time one of them – old Crippler – bagged his first hippie. ('That young man didn't think it was too . . . *groovy*,' Burns merrily recalls.) On another occasion, he watches on a security monitor in his office with mounting glee as Homer chows down on doughnuts. 'That's right,' Mr Burns purrs. 'Keep eating. Little do you know you're drawing ever closer to the poisoned donut.' He starts in on a devilish laugh, stops abruptly. 'There is a poisoned one, isn't there, Smithers?' he calls to his ever-vigilant assistant. 'Uhhh – no, sir,' Smithers replies. 'I discussed this with our lawyers. They consider it murder.' 'Damn their oily hides!' bellows Monty. And this is a man, too, whose first viewing of 'Itchy & Scratchy' brings him to tears of laughter as he revels in the cartoon's brutality. 'That was delightful!' he howls. 'Did you see that? That mouse butchered that cat like a hog! Is all TV this wonderful?'

Consider how Mr Burns's life looks to the tyrant himself. In Episode 1F16 ('Burns' Heir'), his lackey Smithers accidentally leaves a sponge sitting atop Mr Burns's top hat as he bathes his boss. The weight of it sends the frail billionaire sinking into his deep tub, where his life flashes before his eyes. He recalls his infant self firing his nanny for providing substandard milk; he remembers amusing himself no end as a young man by firing a pistol at the feet of a pauper to make him dance; and he lingers on the memory of disguising himself as Wavy Gravy (all that time he was smoking harmless tobacco) just so he could sink a Greenpeace ship. These are the highlights of his nasty life.

This is Mr Burns's essence: he's a man not just ruthless in business but utterly rotten in all facets of his life. He's disgusted by the very sight and smell of the Johnny Lunchpails and Sally Housecoats of the world, not just thinking but *knowing* he's a superior breed of human being. 'Your honour,' his lawyer states at the beginning of Monty's trial for running over Bart Simpson in his car, 'my client has instructed me to remind the court how rich and important he is, that he is *not* like other men.' Then Mr Burns rises and barks, 'I should be able to run over as many kids as I want!' And not just

Simpson kids: Mr Burns also hates fat children and simply loathes babies. (On one happy occasion when Smithers isn't around to thwart him, he indeed attempts to take candy from a baby.) He proudly made shells for the Nazis (ones that worked, *dammit*!) and had a wedding party that consisted, in its entirety, of a single German First World War veteran in a Kaiser-style spike-topped helmet. (The wedding – to Marge's widowed mother – was aborted, and Burns's essential isolation, save for the bootlicking companionship of Smithers, was restored.) 'Since the beginning of time man has yearned to destroy the sun' – so goes one of Monty Burns's malevolent aphorisms. 'From hell's heart I stab at thee!' he bellows as he launches another assault on the people of Springfield.

Perhaps even the archetype of the robber baron can't fully explain Burns's tyrannical nature; an older model – the bloodthirsty demon of medieval Christian myth, say – might be more precise. After all, Mr Burns himself once listed fear, famine and pestilence as his gifts to the people of Springfield, and his Halloween-episode depiction as a vampire required no altering of his character whatsoever.

But Mr Burns retains just enough vague traces of humanity to serve as more than a mere cipher for the writers' attacks on the rich and ruthless. There is, for example, his enduring relationship with his omnipresent executive assistant, Waylon Smithers, a deep-in-the-closet homosexual who's madly in love with his boss. Truly, romantically so: Smithers even dreams of a naked Burns flying in through his window to finally consummate their pseudo-marriage. In return, Burns heaps little but abuse on his lackey – a typical incident has Burns scalding Smithers with a cup of tea because it's brought to him too hot. But there's something about Smithers's steadfast devotion, which has only ever wavered once – that being the time Burns actually did try to destroy the sun – that humanises the old bastard just the tiniest little bit.

And there's also something faintly humanising – not to mention endlessly hilarious – in Monty Burns's exaggerated agedness. For the varying purposes of the show, Mr Burns has been a man in his early eighties and a man in his early *hundreds*. He's ultimately sort of ageless, impossibly old, a man with first-hand knowledge of 113-round boxing matches between an Eskimo fellow and 'Gentleman' Jim Corbett (whose prime fighting years were the 1890s) and of baseball games featuring Connie Mack (another star athlete of the Gilded Age). Mr Burns goes looking for 'petroleum distillate' at the gas station and peppers his speech with references to silent-film stars. Oh, man, is Mr Burns *old*. And of course there's the requisite response: *How old is he?*

It's in answering that question that *The Simpsons* writers have taken yet another long-established comedic formula and breathed into it new and vigorous life. In their hands, Burns's antiqueness has become a baroque masterpiece of one-liners and obscure references and decrepitude-driven sight gags. In one scene we find Burns, in old-timey goggles, driving a quadricycle (Henry Ford's first horseless carriage, built in 1896). On another occasion, Burns is revealed to be a devotee of phrenology, which as Smithers points out was dismissed as quackery 160 years ago.[2] And when a puppy stands on its hind legs, it reminds old Monty of Rory Calhoun, a character actor from 1930s Hollywood. His knees fill with fluid the moment he kneels, every joint in his body creaks mightily with each bend, and he loses a tug-of-war with one-year-old Maggie Simpson.

At their best, the show's how-old-*is*-he? jokes transcend their clichéd origins completely, giving rise to incomparable moments such as Mr Burns's visit to the post office in Episode 3F06 ('Mother Simpson'). 'I'd like to send this letter to the Prussian consulate in Siam,' he tells the bewildered clerk. 'Am I too late for the 4.30 autogyro?' (Prussia ceased to exist as an independent political unit in 1934, Thailand stopped calling itself Siam in 1939, and no one's sent anything anywhere by autogyro since the end of the Second World War.) A big part of the humour here is the sheer surprise at hearing such outdated terminology – *autogyro!* – but just as essential is the oblivious earnestness with which Mr Burns makes his antiquated references.

And these old-old-*old*-man gags are also a critical component of Burns's humanity. He's a man *waaay* out of his time, and this character detail is so often used to evoke sympathy in other narratives – indeed it is very often a tragic thing – that it lends a little compassion even to evil Monty. This is a point made explicit in Episode 7F18 ('Brush with Greatness'), in which Marge is commissioned to paint a flattering portrait of Mr Burns. She depicts him as a frail figure not long for this world in order to downplay his essential nastiness. 'He's bad, but he'll die,' a Springfieldianite gallery-goer observes. 'So I like it.' Exactly.

More than the withered body and senility, though, it's Mr Burns's distinctive voice that defines the character, tying together his slithering viciousness and vile sadism and tragicomic frailty into a rounded, semi-realistic whole. It's the voice that gives Burns life, and it's this life that takes him beyond archetype, producing a singular and enduring character. And how to describe that voice? It's a breathy half-whisper of doom, a tyrannical wheeze that reeks of lifelong privilege and hints at unbridled power. It sounds like John D. Rockefeller, Sr. looks – palsied, penny-pinched, omnipotent – in photos of the robber baron's robber baron as an old man. Its author is the versatile voice actor Harry Shearer (who also produces Smithers's sycophantic squawk), who has said he derived it from the voices of screen legend Lionel Barrymore and senile ex-president Ronald Reagan.[3] The Reagan influence is the most overt, the Old Gipper's soft tone and mild drawl – *Wehhhl* – mimicked in the pitch and cadence of Burns's signature line: *Ehhhk-cellent.* In Burns's voice, though, the brutality of Reagan's neoconservative Cold Warrior agenda is made manifest, the honeyed smoothness betrayed by the vague trace of menacing growl. Reagan almost never showed anger in his public pronouncements – even when he was threatening violence against godless communist regimes or throwing unionised labourers out of work – but Mr Burns does so frequently, and usually with real delight. In a representative outburst, Burns learns from his company's own market research that the public sees him as something of an ogre. 'I ought to club them and eat their bones!' he rages in response. Just as often, though, he delivers the nastiest of orders with the offhandedness of someone fully at ease with controlling the fate of others. 'Smithers, dismember the corpse and send the widow a corsage,' he quips after attacking an insubordinate university administrator with a baseball bat. The line is delivered with neither malice nor regret. Destroying adversaries is, for Burns, a routine event.

Just another day in the life of an archaic robber baron.

ROSEBUD, BOBO & THE SPRUCE MOOSE: FURTHER EVIDENCE OF MR BURNS AS AMERICAN EVERY-MOGUL

If Mr Burns were solely a beyond-the-grave revisitation of the nineteenth-century capitalist, he'd be a dwarf star in the *Simpsons* firmament, a one-note character in the same vein as, say, Disco Stu, who pops up from time to time as an excuse to parody the pop culture of the 1970s. But Burns is much more than this: he *is* capital, the decrepit embodiment of the whole economic order of the industrialised West and the primary representative of Big Business in Springfield. And so *The Simpsons'* writers have tied Burns not just to the Rockefellers and Carnegies of bygone days but to a range of business icons, transforming him into Industrialism Incarnate.

Thus, for example, we find Burns ensconced in the luxurious confines of the Springfield Heights Millionaire's Club, having lunch with Aristotle Amadopolis, the owner of the nearby Shelbyville Nuclear Power Plant and an obvious stand-in for Jackie Kennedy's second husband, the Greek shipping magnate Aristotle Onassis. On another occasion, Mr Burns sells off his plant to two German efficiency experts, which ties him to the eclipse of American manufacturing by foreign (particularly German and Japanese) firms and foreshadows the 1998 sale of Chrysler (whose head until 1992, Lee Iacocca, was one of the biggest celebrity CEOs of the 1980s) to Daimler-Benz.

There has even been a veiled suggestion that Burns's business experience might have included some time as the regime-toppling titan of some Latin American banana republic, which would place him in a fine American industrial tradition best exemplified by the ultimate banana-republican conglomerate, the United Fruit Company (which, with its partners in the CIA, more or less hand-selected the governments of many Central American countries for much of the twentieth century). Burns's banana-republican moment comes as he addresses the assembled workers of the Springfield Nuclear Power Plant from his Peronesque balcony, which apparently sends him into a reverie. 'Compadres,' he orates, 'it is imperative that we crush the freedom fighters before the start of the rainy season. And remember: a shiny new donkey for whoever brings me the head of Colonel Montoya.' He comes to at this point and switches into American rhetorical mode, but the message is clear: Burns has some Latin American blood on his hands.

Burns has also been depicted, at a full episode's length, as Springfield's very own Howard Hughes. This comes in Episode 1F08 ('$pringfield (or, How I Learned to Stop Worrying and Love Legalized Gambling)'), in which Burns opens a casino and soon becomes a reclusive, delusional hermit, wearing tissue boxes on his feet and collecting his urine in jars as he obsesses over the germs that cover Smithers's face. (Which germs, incidentally, band together at one point to chant, 'Freemasons run the country!') Burns – who in this and the rest of his dementia is very much *à la* Hughes – builds a model of a giant wooden airplane called the *Spruce Moose*, which he claims will take passengers from New York's Idyllwild Airport to the Belgian Congo in 17 minutes. This lapse into obsolete terminology is of course Burns's alone, but by equating him with twentieth-century industrialists like Hughes, the show's writers build themselves a satirical vehicle as big and sturdy as the *Spruce Moose* itself.

The most frequent and elaborate of the show's allusions has been to the greatest icon of doomed business ambition in the history of American cinema: Charles Foster Kane, the protagonist of Orson Welles' 1941 masterpiece, *Citizen Kane*. If Burns is anyone's doppelgänger, he's Kane's, a connection that the show's writers use for two purposes: to humanise Burns further (lest his cartoonish malevolence sink the show's realism), and to make a sharply satirical point about the amplified ruthlessness of big business in our time. The humanisation stems from the fact that Kane, for all his hubris, is a profoundly tragic figure, a compassionate champion of the Eddie Punchclocks of the world whose ego and ambition eventually destroy his humanity. By the end of the film, Kane has been reduced to a pitiful creature, longing on his deathbed for a beloved toy from his innocent youth (Rosebud, the most famous sled in pop-cultural history). In Episode 1F01 (allusively titled 'Rosebud'), *The Simpsons* draws an episode-long parallel between Kane and Burns, providing possibly the first illustration in the whole series (and certainly the most graphic one) of a tragic, emotionally scarred side to Burns's character. The episode opens with an homage to *Kane*'s opening sequence: Burns, in fitful sleep, recalls a blissfully innocent but materially impoverished scene of his youth, into which comes a twisted, joyless billionaire who whisks young Monty away to a life of empty luxury. Burns's beloved teddy bear, Bobo, lies abandoned in the winter snow, subbing in for Kane's sled. 'Wait!' Burns's father calls after the departing limousine, waving the bear in the air. 'You forgot your bear – a symbol of your lost youth and innocence!' Here we have the first and pretty much only time it's been suggested that Mr Burns is now or has ever been innocent in any way. Cut to present day, in the master bedroom of Burns Manor (which in this and other episodes features a wrought-iron gate crowned with an encircled 'B', a direct reference to the circle-K'd gate of Kane's Xanadu),[4] where a despondent Burns lies next to a box of NEV-R-BREAK snow globes. He hurls one and it smashes, still *à la* Kane and the snow globe that drops from his hand in the throes of death. (Kane, though, didn't have a whole crate of them.) The rest of the episode follows Burns's efforts to find and reclaim his beloved Bobo.

Numerous other episodes have used this Burns-as-Kane motif. In one, Burns runs for governor (as did Kane) and gives a speech in front of an enormous banner emblazoned with his face and surname (ditto). Burns, though, is undone not by revelations of sexual impropriety (Kane's downfall), but by the three-eyed fish his power plant's waste has created in Springfield's waterways. In another episode, Smithers organises an elaborate song-and-dance number for his boss that uses the tune and parodies the lyrics of the number that greets Kane in his office upon his newspaper's victory over its chief rival. The ode to Kane begins, 'There is a man / A certain man ...' Kane's *Daily Inquirer* cronies then sing, 'What is his name?' 'It's Charlie Kane!' the dancing girls reply. 'It's Mr Kane!' a crony pipes up, mock-indignant. Then all sing: 'He doesn't like that 'Mister' / He likes good old

Charlie Kane!' In *The Simpsons* version, the second line starts with Smithers: 'He's Mr Burns!' Burns himself replies, 'I'm Mr Burns!' Smithers: 'He's Monty Burns!' Burns, scowling, genuinely indignant: 'It's *Mr* Burns!' Then Smithers and the dancing girls sing, 'To friends he's known as Monty / But to you it's Mr Burns!' *Mr* Burns demands that his status be underscored – like those modern captains of industry who have no time for Charlie Kane's populism, who instead spend the bulk of their lives in high-security office towers, gated mansions, private island retreats and curtained-off business class (or on private jets).

The idea that the *Simpsons*-era business elite has become irredeemably greedy and amoral, that it can't sustain the tragedy of a Kane because it is so bereft of human decency that there's no way to find a state of grace within it from which to fall – this point is hammered home in the ending to the 'Rosebud' episode. Now, *Citizen Kane* itself ends in pure fallen-from-grace tragedy: Kane, who has betrayed his most deeply held principles, ruined his media empire and been abandoned by his wife and friends, dies utterly alone in his cavernous tomb of a palace, longing for his long-lost Rosebud. But Burns eventually gets *his* Rosebud back. Bobo turns up in a bag of ice at the Kwik-E-Mart and passes into the hands of Maggie Simpson, becoming her favourite toy.[5] After attempting to buy, steal and coerce the bear from little Maggie, Mr Burns finally wins it back by imploring her not to make the mistakes he made – to keep the bear, hang onto her innocence, stay pure. This rare outpouring of emotion from the old tycoon moves Maggie to give Mr Burns his Bobo back. Burns is ecstatic, momentarily overcome with renewed love for the world. But of course it doesn't last, and Bobo is quickly lost once again. There's ultimately no room in Burns's cruel life for something as sentimental as a tattered teddy bear – he has a power plant to run.

HI-D'OH, HI-D'OH: THE WORKING WORLD OF SPRINGFIELD

Above all else, Mr Burns is a boss. And vast as his fortune may be, its cornerstone remains his beloved Springfield Nuclear Power Plant. It's at the plant that we find Burns at his most casually evil, and it's there that we get the clearest picture of his relationship to the workers of the world – and of the nature of working life in Springfield.

There's no ambiguity to this relationship: Burns is a pure tyrant, abusive, penny-pinching, grossly exploitive, and his workers are a horde of faceless drones. Often as not, Burns embraces the plant's employees only through a

TV monitor, watching contentedly from his office as they march to work in a lifeless line. On those rare occasions when there's a break in the monotony – when, for example, Homer Simpson shows up one morning in a shirt accidentally dyed pink – Mr Burns is outraged. Believing that Homer must be 'some sort of free-thinking anarchist', Burns has him tossed into the New Bedlam Rest Home for the Emotionally Interesting. Mr Burns does occasionally meet his employees in person – he greets them, for example, at company picnics and the like, reading their names off cue cards supplied by Smithers – but even at these times they're nothing more than a stream of interchangeable faces to him.

Indeed, Mr Burns's utter contempt for his employees is the inspiration for a long-running series of gags. These start with the conceit that Burns does not, under any circumstances, remember who Homer Simpson is. Now, the lives of Monty Burns and Homer Simpson have of course become deeply intertwined over the years, and the increasing strain on the conceit of Burns's ignorance is itself mined for laughs. Here's one of the more elaborate examples of this phenomenon from Season 4:

> *Burns and Smithers watch on the office monitor as Homer is elected union president.*
>
> *Burns:*   Who is that firebrand, Smithers?
> *Smithers:* Uh, that's Homer Simpson, sir.
> *Burns:*   Simpson, eh? New man?
> *Smithers:* [*chuckles*] Actually, sir, he thwarted your campaign for governor, you ran over his son, he saved the plant from meltdown, his wife painted you in the nude . . .
> *Burns:*   Enh. Doesn't ring a bell.

Missing from this exchange – but present in most other 'Simpson, eh?' incidents – is a central component in the running gag: a dismissive phrase used by Smithers to identify Homer. A typical dialogue begins with Burns noticing Homer on the monitor and asking who he is. 'He's Homer Simpson, sir,' Smithers replies. 'One of your drones from Sector 7G.' With each recurrence, though, Smithers's dismissal has grown more spiteful. In early episodes, Homer is simply one of Burns's *drones* or *boobs* or *schmos* from Sector 7G. But later in the series, Homer becomes one of his *carbon blobs* or *organ banks* or *fork-and-spoon operators*. It's hard to imagine anything more categorically dismissive than these last phrases, which reduce Homer to the absolute basics of his existence: he's carbon-based, his body's functional, he eats. Combine their callousness with the mechanistic precision of 'Sector 7G', and you've reached some kind of absolute zero in the employer-worker relationship, a coldness in which all the joy of a life's labour ceases, leaving nothing but physics, science, the hard facts of force applied, energy produced, profit accrued.

The other facets of Burns's corporate governance are no more admirable than his approach to labour relations. He bends and twists safety regulation and environmental standards, and bribes every public official he's ever met. He's even been known to offer his bribes in the showy style of a TV game show. 'Now,' he tells an inspector from the Nuclear Regulatory Commission, post-meltdown, 'you can either have the washer and dryer where the lovely Smithers is standing. Or you can trade it all for what's inside this box.' On another occasion, Burns joins Smithers to dispose of the plant's radioactive waste, skipping the playground – 'All those bald children are arousing suspicion,' he notes – and instead loading it into a tree trunk in a nearby park. Another time, he and Smithers sit watching a news story on TV about the tragic decline in the duck population at a local pond. 'Smithers,' Burns asks softly, wiping away a tear, 'do you think maybe my power plant killed those ducks?' Smithers: 'There's no "maybe" about it, sir.' Burns, sniffling: 'Excellent.'

Burns, in other words, doesn't give a good goddamn. If his carbon blobs get hurt on the job at his profoundly unsafe plant, he can replace them with illegal immigrants, and if his regulatory violations produce bald children or kill wildlife, well, what of it? Burns's sense of privilege is unconditional, his contempt for everyone but himself (even Smithers, who during one meltdown is denied the second seat in the escape pod because Burns likes to put his feet up)[6] is nothing short of absolute. And in the age of Enron – a time when the heads of corporations that lose billions give themselves millions in bonuses, a time when abject failures are given multimillion-dollar golden parachutes, a time when even outright thieving corporate executives slither through the wreckage they've caused with impunity – in the face of all of this, Burns emerges as a somewhat typical example of the contemporary CEO.

And what sort of workplace does this create? Frankly, it creates the kind of workplace that employs lazy, incompetent Homer Simpson for his entire adult life, and indeed actively encourages his indifference towards his work and his lifelong devotion to slacking off. And Homer's just the most prominent of the plant's uninspired workers: in Episode 9F05 ('Marge Gets a

Job'), Monty's routine scan of the security monitors reveals a group of employees playing limbo with a pipe suspended between two drums of toxic waste. 'Jackanapes!' Burns growls. In the next monitor, he sees two workers in radiation suits playing chess. 'Lollygaggers!' he spits. Then the worst offender: a small crowd of his employees has gathered to watch a cock fight. 'Noodleheads!' fumes Burns. But at least there are signs of life in this inspection; a far bleaker picture of working life at the power plant emerges later in the same episode, when Burns pays a visit to his newest employee, Marge Simpson, whom he's fallen in love with. He presents her with a bouquet of orchids and fragrant bath oils, which he insists he lavishes on all his employees, causing Marge to wonder why morale is so low. She points to a line of employees nearby: a man slumped over on his workstation, weeping openly; a woman, her mouth agape, her face fixed in a wide-eyed stare of total despondence, slugging back shots from a whisky bottle; and a man with a twitchy right eye who is studiously polishing a rifle ('I am the Angel of Death. The time of purification is at hand,' he announces). Marge suggests having a theme day – 'Funny Hat Day' – and piping in some upbeat music. Cut to the very same employees: the first man, in a gaudy sombrero, still in tears; the woman, wearing a jaunty baseball cap adorned with large moose antlers, knocking back yet another shot from her bottle; and the man with the rifle, his head crowned with a propeller-topped beanie, hunched over his weapon and chuckling. And this triptych of despair is set to the grotesquely jaunty rhythm of Tom Jones's 'What's New, Pussycat?' giving the scene a deranged aspect that's like a hyperbolic version of the professional smiles required of corporate spokespeople and service-industry drones.

This is the image of work most often projected by *The Simpsons*, and it stands in stark contrast to many prominent myths of the digital age: that work had grown more exciting, more fulfilling, more egalitarian, that corporations had come to hate hierarchy, that grey-suited conformity was as out of date as the ducktail haircut. Some of these doubtless rang true – if, that is, you happened to be in the tiny minority working on the creative side in certain media industries and content-producing high-tech firms. The same years, though, saw the greatest redistribution of wealth in the history of capitalism throughout the corporate West – particularly in the United States, where by the late 1990s the richest 1 per cent controlled more than 40 per cent of the nation's wealth (up from 20 per cent in 1979). At the same time, job security for those on the social ladder's lower rungs all but vanished, and working-class workplaces moved by the thousands to the Third World where wages were counted in pennies per hour and labour and environmental regulations were so lax that even the Springfield power plant probably couldn't violate them.

This was the fate of labour in the 1990s, and it surely played a part in making Homer a working-class hero and Monty Burns a resonant villain. It also gave rise to the massive mainstream success of the *Dilbert* comic strip, the cult sensation of the film *Office Space*[7] and the canonisation of Douglas Coupland's novel *Generation X*, in which characters worked 'McJobs'[8] in offices made up of 'veal fattening pens' – not to mention the widespread use of non-Coupland neologisms like 'cubicle farm' and 'wage slave' to describe the post-industrial workplace. In all of these, as on *The Simpsons*, work is portrayed as mind-numbing, soul-sucking, maddeningly bureaucratic and utterly devoid of job security.

'If you don't like your job, you don't strike,' Homer Simpson tells his daughter. 'You just go in every day and do it *really* half-assed. *That's* the American way.' You pin a *Dilbert* strip to the wall of your veal fattening pen or you trade lines from *Office Space* or you surf half-heartedly from McJob to McJob. You post details about your doomed high-tech employer and its worthless stock options on Fuckedcompany.com. You work temp jobs (for a time in the 1990s, Manpower – a temporary-employment broker – was America's largest employer, until it was eclipsed by Wal-Mart). Your work might not look like the manual labour at the Springfield power plant, but you might well have felt as eager to slack off as Homer or even as despondent as that poor bastard in the gaudy sombrero. Whatever this New Economy was – *wherever* it was – it didn't touch everyone in the bountiful West, not even *most* of us. And the half-assed work carried out in Springfield served as an exaggerated allegory for life on the cubicle farm.

Work sucks just as often for Springfieldianites who toil outside the power plant. It sucks so bad, in fact, that it's given rise to two recurring characters, each embodying a modern work archetype. The first of these is the ubiquitous Pimple-Faced Kid (aka 'Puberty Boy', aka 'The Geeky Teenager'), the boy with the octave-skipping voice and enduring acne problem who fills many of Springfield's most menial jobs. He's the kid behind the counter (or over the drive-thru speaker) at the Krusty Burger, the usher at the movie theatre, the attendant at the roller coaster at Duff Gardens, the clueless counter clerk at seemingly every store and fast-food joint in Springfield. The Pimple-Faced Kid *is* Springfield's service industry, the generic representative of the millions whose place in the New Economy included a stint as a greeter at Wal-Mart or a shirt-folding expert at the Gap or a *barista* at Starbucks or a 'sandwich artist' at Subway or any of the other high-growth professions of the 1990s.[9]

When the Pimple-Faced Kid is employed elsewhere, you're likely to find the counter manned by a guy the show's online fans have dubbed 'Sarcastic Middle-Aged Man', a slouchy fellow with a whisk-broom moustache who soldiers on through a wide range of occupations – limousine driver, caricature artist, motel clerk, assistant to 1980s videogame star Donkey Kong – with a biting sarcasm that never wavers. He's the clerk at the Copy Jalopy when Lisa arrives to have her political pamphlets printed: 'Twenty-five copies in canary, 25 in goldenrod, 25 in saffron, and 25 in paella.' 'Okay,' he replies, oozing disinterest. 'One hundred yellow.' He's behind the counter again at All Creatures Great and Cheap when Lisa shows up looking for a hamster for her science project. 'I want the most intelligent hamster you've got,' she says. 'Okay,' Sarcastic Middle-Aged Man replies, randomly plucking a hamster from a cage. 'Uh, this little guy writes mysteries under the name of J.D. MacGregor.'

The interchangeability of Springfield's service-industry clerks is part of the satire: these jobs, in Springfield as in our world, can be filled by virtually anyone. The employer just needs a body, and the worker just needs the money. Their jobs don't even have the personal touch, poison-tipped as it may be, of a Monty Burns. They are simply the front-line façade of a vast corporate order.

THE SIMPSONS, INC. (I): CORPORATE MOPPETS & MARKETING MADNESS

There's a scene in Episode 8F04 ('Homer Defined') in which Mr Burns is being interviewed by Kent Brockman about an unfolding disaster at the Springfield Nuclear Power Plant. 'Mr Burns,' Brockman says, 'people are calling this a meltdown.' Burns chuckles with feigned warmth. 'Oh, "meltdown",' he replies. 'It's one of those annoying buzzwords. We prefer to call it an unrequested fission surplus.' Though a fine piece of spin-doctoring, this is entirely out of character for unapologetic Monty, whose usual attitude in such situations is enraged irritation that anyone – reporter, government official, judge, *anyone* – would dare to question his right to do whatever the hell he wants. There are few, if any, further examples of Monty playing the public-relations game;[10] it's just not him. Maybe for this reason, *The Simpsons* has long featured a rotating cast of grotesquely slick corporate mannequins who pop up when the show's satirical target is the communications apparatus of the contemporary corporation (as opposed to Burns, who usually serves as the embodiment of the truth behind the message).

In early episodes, the most prominent PR shill in Springfield is Jack Larson, president of Laramie Cigarettes. We encounter Larson, for example, in a TV commercial for the Little Miss Springfield Pageant in Episode 9F02 ('Lisa the Beauty Queen'). In the ad, a friendly family man and his daughter have just shared a heartwarming moment. Larson enters, in power suit and corporate haircut, all but leaving a trail of slime. 'This year, Laramie is sponsoring the Little Miss Springfield Pageant,' he says, with that slightly-too-polished broadcast-ready smoothness that instantly reads as phoney. 'You see, government regulations prohibit us from advertising on TV.' He inhales deeply on a cigarette, holding up a pack of Laramies for the camera. 'Ah, that sweet Carolina smoke!' He returns to the task at hand: 'But they can't prohibit us from holding a beauty pageant for little girls aged seven to nine.' On one level, this little scene brings the subtext of tobacco-company sponsorship to the foreground. On another, it's pretty ham-fisted satire, all but announcing its criticism in blinding, blinking neon. It's always this way with Jack Larson: in another episode, he responds to the theft of a truckload of Laramies by telling a reporter that another truck is on its way, and its driver has been advised to ignore all stop signs and crosswalks. Larson is entirely too obvious, too outwardly evil.[11] He's got none of the velvet-gloved smoothness and presumed innocence that characterise sophisticated modern PR.

The true face of corporate gloss appears later in *The Simpsons'* run, in the sensible-suited, eternally perky person of one Lindsey Naegle. We first meet Naegle (though she hasn't yet been named) at an animation company's boardroom table in Episode 4F12 ('The Itchy & Scratchy & Poochie Show'). Naegle's a slick corporate mouthpiece right out of the gate, explaining the new character for 'The Itchy & Scratchy Show' to the show's writers in a poised, persuasive torrent of marketing buzzwords and vacuous corporate newspeak. 'We at the network want a dog with attitude,' she tells the show's assembled production staff. 'He's edgy, he's "in your face". You've heard the expression "Let's get busy"? Well, this is a dog who gets "biz-*zay*"! Consistently and thoroughly.' Elsewhere in the episode, Naegle prattles on about outrageous paradigms and fundamental shifts in the key demographic. She's pure corporate, radiating a kind of cancerous professional sheen that envelops all it encounters, using what it needs and destroying the rest.

Like the Pimple-Faced Kid, Naegle moves freely from job to job; she's the public face not of *a* corporation but of The Corporation. (In one episode, her name even changes to Mindy, but the smart suit and MBA voice make it clear we're dealing with the same shill.) And her weightless, persuasive banter and hard-headed business sense fit any old conglomerate: a pharmaceutical giant, a toymaker, a telecommunications company. She's right at home as the PR rep for OmniTouch, a cellular phone company, stepping in to implement a win-win solution after Homer accidentally destroys priceless artifacts at the OmniTouch Traveling Exhibit (formerly the Smithsonian Traveling Exhibit). The massive humming monstrosity OmniTouch installs in Lisa's bedroom to compensate for Homer's damages, Naegle calmly explains, is not a cellular transmitter but a 'keep-in-touch tower'. By the next scene, she's got Homer referring to the antenna as a 'progress tree' and beseeching Lisa to examine her predicament from OmniTouch's point of view. In another episode, she represents Springfield's telephone company, her hands folded in a pyramid on her desk in a hollow pantomime of concerned concentration as she greets Homer and Marge. 'Now,' she tells them, 'how may I best dispense with you today?' This is how corporations talk to us: warm and friendly, vapid and shallow. Quietly duplicitous. Spun.

What truly differentiates Lindsey Naegle from an obvious hypocrite like Jack Larson or an unrepentant tyrant like Mr Burns, however, is the depth of her commitment to the corporate ethos. There are no fangs behind her superficial smile, no anger or malice or even joy underneath her polished surface. She's all business, a pure careerist, a perfect product of her workaholic time. Even at an Alcoholics Anonymous meeting, Naegle doesn't lose her executive poise. 'We all know why we're here, don't we?' she announces to her fellow addicts. 'To keep ourselves sober . . . and to network.' And when Marge asks Naegle – a phone-company rep just then – why she keeps changing jobs, she answers, 'I'm a sexual predator,' her voice wavering not at all from the one she uses to explain the need for keep-in-touch towers. This is what makes Naegle such an excellent allegory for the modern corporate age: you don't see through her, and you don't see through her because there's nothing else to see.

Even when Naegle is ostensibly not a PR flack, she can't help but shill. Case in point: Episode AABF22 ('Brother's Little Helper'), in which Naegle appears as an unnamed research scientist for the Pharm Team, a drug company that manufactures Focusyn, a cure for attention deficit disorder (ADD). Marge and Homer pay the drug company a visit after Principal Skinner threatens to expel Bart if he doesn't submit to a 'radical, untested, potentially dangerous' Focusyn programme. Naegle and a fellow scientist demonstrate the experimental drug on a cage full of rambunctious guinea pigs, which seat themselves in orderly rows in a guinea-pig classroom after being sprayed with Focusyn. 'They've become your slaves,' Homer observes. 'Yes,' Naegle enthuses with her usual PR polish, 'but it's not about slavery. It's about helping kids concentrate. This pill reduces class-clownism 44 percent!' In a business world where marketing has become the most important component of any enterprise, bringing talk of profit and customer service even to schools and hospitals and pre-emptive wars (viz. White House Chief of Staff Andrew Card in 2002 on the timing of the march to war in Iraq: 'From a marketing point of view, you don't introduce new products in August') – in this world, Lindsey Naegle is the end result: a force of pure corporate-communications gloss, a woman so immersed in the professional obfuscations of big business that she herself believes the hype.

AABF22 extends its satire of corporate gloss far beyond automatonic Naegle, however, saving its sharpest blade to hack away at a far bigger and nastier beast: the symbiotic relationship between pill-pushing pharmaceutical giants, medical and educational professionals, and a corporate working world that needs hyper-obedient workaholics like Homer needs beer. Which is to say that the episode's satirical target is practically the entire corporate-capitalist system. So it goes that in AABF22 free-willed, rebellious Bart is diagnosed at school with a trendy disease (ADD), prescribed an experimental drug, and thereby transformed into a slick, overachieving executive embryo. His first day on Focusyn finds Bart suddenly absorbed in a poetry assignment and reading *The Seven Habits of Highly Effective Pre-Teens* instead of watching Krusty the Clown after school. That night at dinner, Marge finds a note from her son: 'Thank you in advance for a world-class meal. You're an inspiration to our entire organization.' Seeing his mother's pleasure, Bart expresses his satisfaction in the style of a famous credit-card commercial. 'Cost of paper: five cents,' Bart narrates to himself. 'A mother's love: priceless.' In the coming days, he organises all the lawsuits against his father into a single class action and takes on the extracurricular chore of tutoring an underprivileged Navajo boy, during which Bart adds a decidedly corporate spin to classic nursery rhymes – teaching the kid, for example, that Humpty Dumpty fell off the wall 'because he took his eyes off the prize'.

Eventually, Bart's experiment with Focusyn drives him to paranoia, and he's taken off the drug, but not before the episode has accomplished its task. To wit: it graphically suggests that the most significant problems facing the millions of North American kids being prescribed Ritalin and anti-depressants and the rest might not be their diagnosed disorders, but rather any one or more of: (1) the increasing laxness of testing regimes for new drugs, particularly for children; (2) the over-prescription of such drugs, especially to children; (3) an education system that too quickly inflates the misbehaviour endemic to childhood into mental illness; (4) the pharmaceutical industry's relentless drive to expand its customer base; and (5) an entire hyper-corporate society that forces kids to live and learn and toe the line in a ruthless, zero-sum system designed to churn out middle-management drones. Or, to put it more bluntly, Episode AABF22 posits the notion that the point of a drug like Focusyn might not be to help children learn but to numb them into submission, to turn them into good little corporate citizens. After all, the corporate world order that feeds their hyperactivity with frenetic entertainment spectacles and sugary junk food is the same one that makes big money treating the 'disorders' this stuff then induces in them. It is cause, analyst and solution.

The Simpsons expands on this theme in Episode BABF07. ('Grift of the Magi'), in which Springfield Elementary School goes bankrupt and a private company, Kid First Industries, steps in to run the school. Suddenly, behaviour problems like Bart's are no longer in need of correction – 'humour is a sign of intelligence,' notes a Kid First 'teacher' – and classwork increasingly consists of talking about favourite toys. It turns out that Kid First has turned the entire school into a market-research division for its new Christmas toy, mining the kids for information on how to give it the broadest possible appeal. (In one of Lisa's classes, the guest speaker is 'Phil from marketing'.) The result is 'Funzo', a soft and cuddly robotic doll with lots of firepower that walks and talks and is hardwired to destroy its competition. ('You mean like Microsoft?' Bart wonders. 'Exactly,' Lisa replies.) Kid First's marketing machine cranks into overdrive to make Funzo the must-have toy of the season – 'If you don't have Funzo, you're nothin'!' goes the tagline – and soon there's a stampede at the doors of the Try-N-Save as Springfield's gullible consumers scramble to get their hands on one of the dolls. Cut to an executive hot tub, where Kid First's top executives – one Jim Hope and (but of course) the job-hopping sexual predator Lindsey Naegle – watch the debacle on a monitor, calculating that the speed with which the crowd went from muttering to stampeding equates to $370 million in sales. Jim's still a little worried about the toy's success, though, until he sees some trampling. All of which is barely parody: Cabbage Patch Kids created this kind of carnage in the early 1980s, as did the Tickle Me Elmo doll a decade later. And all of them pale in comparison to the (on occasion literally) homicidal frenzy created by the consumer demand for a certain kind of running shoe, the product of one of the greatest marketing machines of our time. I'm talking of course about Nike, leader of the brand revolution.

THE SIMPSONS, INC. (II): THE BRAND REVOLUTION

There's not much hyperbole here: Nike did indeed launch a revolution. It even declared it in just such terms, in a 1987 TV commercial that used The Beatles song 'Revolution' as its soundtrack. That ad – big-budgeted, gorgeously shot and wicked cool – was the first major action in Nike's ultimately successful campaign to convince the world of the innate value of corporate brands. In the years that followed, Nike transformed itself from specialty-shoe company to pure marketing machine – a New-Age business with few fixed assets and no manufacturing facilities (Nike has subcontracted the entirety of its shoe manufacturing to other companies) whose value resides primarily in a swoosh, a slogan and an attitude.

Few of us ever found ourselves enclosed entirely within the apparatus of modern marketing like the kids at Springfield Elementary, but anyone who's seen a few thousand ads, which is to say all of us, has experienced the brand revolution. The extraordinary power of advertising is nothing new – it was Coca-Cola's print advertising, after all, that gave the world the fat, jolly, red-and-white-suited version of Santa Claus – but the years since Nike's 1987 declaration have played host to a staggering growth in the ubiquity of marketing messages. In addition to the ads that fill our TV screens and thicken our magazines and blanket our roadsides, advertising has in recent years colonised countless new territories (the space above urinals, the labels on bananas, the ten minutes before a feature film begins). Strategically placed products and logos fill the sets of TV shows and movies (from *E.T.*'s Reese's Pieces to *Seinfeld*'s Snapple), stadiums and sporting events have become extended branding exercises (the Florida Panthers of the NHL, for example, currently play hockey at the Office Depot Center), and the line between certain star athletes and the Nike brand (viz. Michael Jordan, Tiger Woods) has been pretty much obliterated. I had occasion a few years back to interview a man whose sole job was to sell ad space *inside* videogames – to line the boards of a hockey videogame, for example, with corporate logos. And once I thought about it, I had to admit that the logos on the boards actually did enhance the gaming experience, as this guy was claiming. They were a key component in the game's verisimilitude. A videogame arena without logo-plastered boards would seem not just fake but *faked*, white-washed, intentionally inaccurate. This is how pervasive corporate marketing has become in the age of *The Simpsons*: it's an essential part of the scenery.

There's another revolution of a sort at work in Nike's 1987 branding exercise: its 'Revolution' ad marked to many observers a bold new low in corporate crassness. Here, after all, was a sacred anthem of the 1960s counterculture being used to sell overpriced sneakers. And lo, the keepers of that counterculture's sacred artifacts – the Baby Boomers – were verily and mightily pissed. Boomer-aged pundits sounded off in every other newspaper in the English-speaking world about the 'Revolution' heresy, and The Beatles themselves sued Nike, its ad agency and the record companies that were involved. (The band had lost control of the publishing rights to most of its songs a few years earlier, in a bidding war with Michael Jackson.) Eventually, Nike agreed to stop airing the ad, but that didn't stop the force the shoe company had unleashed. In the years that followed, the very idea of non-conformity became little more than a marketing strategy (see, for example, Apple Computer's 'Think Different' ads), and the recasting of 1960s rebellion as 1990s consumption eventually ceased to ruffle many feathers. By the mid-1990s, when both Canada's Bank of Montreal and the multinational accounting firm Coopers & Lybrand set their financial-services commercials to Bob Dylan's 'The Times They Are A-Changin'', it caused only feeble and ultimately impotent criticism. (The Bank of Montreal ad, in particular, was a gut-wrenchingly foul example of the new crassness: it depicted a choir of angelic children mounting a hilltop to extol the revolutionary virtues of a range of personal-banking services.) It's as if the corporate order somehow seems far too powerful – too *inevitable* – to be deterred.

Lisa Simpson runs into this problem in Episode 5F05 ('Lisa the Skeptic'), after she and her classmates discover a winged skeleton – an angel, apparently – at an archaeological dig on the site of the parking lot for a new megamall. The people of Springfield quickly embrace the angel as a sacred idol, though Lisa remains sceptical of its holiness. Then the skeleton disappears, only to reappear magically to lead the faithful to a hill next to the new mall, where it comes to rest with an etching on its stone base that reads, 'The End Will Come at Sundown'. The amassed Springfield populace waits there anxiously for the Rapture. As the sun sets, it's revealed to be an elaborate marketing stunt: 'the end of high prices' at Heavenly Hills Mall. Lisa berates the mall's developer: 'You exploited people's deepest beliefs just to anoint your cheesy wares. Well, we are outraged, aren't we?' A distracted Police Chief Wiggum responds, 'Oh. Oh, yeah, yeah . . . we're outraged, very much so. But look at all the stores! A – *a Pottery Barn!*' The townsfolk rush off eagerly into the mall, leaving Lisa alone and impotent in her disgust.

Lisa's frustration is understandable: the consumer juggernaut in the *Simpsons* era has indeed seemed unstoppable and all-encompassing, a multi-headed mutating giant impossible to escape – and almost as hard to satirise.

Still, *The Simpsons* has tried gamely to chart the sleazy scope of modern marketing. In one episode, Lindsey Naegle sits at a boardroom table helping her colleagues invent a new holiday so they can have an excuse to sell yet more 'assorted gouge-ables'. Naegle suggests they do 'something religious' – they've had previous success with 'Christmas II' – but they pass on a colleague's suggestion ('Spendover') and go instead with the secular 'Love Day'. Another time, the Simpson family gathers at the kitchen table so Homer and Marge can teach the kids about romance. 'Romance is dead,' Lisa replies flatly. 'It was acquired in a hostile takeover by Hallmark and Disney, homogenised, and sold off piece by piece.' And there's even a recurring character on the show who embodies all the self-importance and over-statement of contemporary marketing: Duffman, a hip-thrusting, slogan-spouting, muscle-bound beer company shill in a superhero costume. 'Hey, look!' Lenny enthuses as Duffman invades Moe's Tavern one evening. 'It's Duffman – the guy in a costume that creates awareness of Duff!'

All of these digs certainly ring true, but they're also quite likely to be eclipsed by crass reality. Back in the 1980s, for example, Budweiser ads created a poster and T-shirt craze not for anything as spectacular as a superhero but for a dog – a good-timing babe magnet of a bull terrier who went by the moniker 'Spuds McKenzie'.

What's more, ads are only the visible tip of a mammoth corporate iceberg, a huge force that in recent decades has usurped much of the power of traditional authorities like church and state, becoming in many ways the most important locus of power on the planet. This transformation, too, has precipitated the odd satirical swipe from *The Simpsons*. For example, there's the time Bart heads down to the local mall to get his ear pierced. He scoots past several Starbucks outlets into In 'n' Out Ear Piercing. 'I'd like to get my ear pierced,' he quite reasonably requests. 'Well, better make it quick, kiddo,' the clerk – Sarcastic Middle-Aged Man – replies. 'In five minutes this place is becoming a Starbucks.' As Bart leaves the store, it transforms into a Starbucks, as if touched by a magic latte wand, to match every other store in the mall.

There's certainly a hint of the speed and power of corporate conquest in this quick-wash changeover, in the image of row upon row of Starbucks. But only a hint. Indeed, the best illustration of the scope of the corporate world and the difficulties and contradictions built into trying to attack it from within might be the show itself: as a corporate entity, as a merchandising machine, as a collection of more or less anti-establishment individuals who nonetheless have high-paying jobs and collect corporate paycheques.

THE SIMPSONS, INC. (III): TROJAN HORSE OR COURT JESTER?

The Simpsons, unlike many a cultural enterprise, has never had to contend with the tricky notion of 'selling out'. Beloved indie bands, the directors of edgy low-budget films, writers and artists of nearly every stripe – in short, pretty much everyone who creates the rest of the pop culture near and dear to the hearts of *Simpsons* fans – all of them have at least potentially had to wrestle with the contradictions between art and commerce, and with the potential loss of authenticity that can accompany a contract or distribution deal with a multinational media corporation. Not *The Simpsons*, though, perhaps because it's never been anything but the product of just such a media giant. From its first appearance on *The Tracey Ullman Show*, *The Simpsons* has been a product of the Fox Network, itself a subsidiary of News Corporation, one of the planet's largest media conglomerates. (News Corp.'s CEO, Rupert Murdoch, is indeed one of Big Media's most prominent – and most loathed – figureheads.) What's more, the enormous popularity of *The Simpsons* was essential to the survival not just of Fox in the United States but also of News Corp.'s British satellite-TV station, Sky One, and its pan-Asian cable service. *The Simpsons* is not just the product but the cornerstone of a global corporate enterprise.

In addition, the show has always been a willing corporate shill. Matt Groening has speculated that it was the first Butterfinger ads that sold Fox on the cartoon's viability as a series, and its massively successful first season spawned a marketing and merchandising juggernaut that continues to this day. In addition to Bart pushing Butterfingers, *Simpsons* characters have been used to advertise Japan Airlines and hawk Australian pasta. They've been stuffed into kids' meals at Burger King, and their faces have been plastered on almost as much junk as Krusty the Clown's. By one estimate, licensed *Simpsons* merchandise rang up $2 *billion* in sales in the first 15 months of the show's run. At the height of the show's first wave of popularity, the American department-store chain J.C. Penney had *Simpsons* boutiques in more than a thousand of its stores, and the Sharper Image catalogue featured a Bart Simpson phone. There were *Simpsons* watches, *Simpsons* backpacks and bubble gum, *Simpsons* boxer shorts and key chains.[12] In the mass-marketplace, the show is just another brand, one in a long line of Officially-Licensed-Product franchises to be milked for millions. And then, of course, there have been the millions more in broadcast and syndication rights (an ongoing windfall for News Corp. that cleared $1 billion in 2000 and grows by millions more every year), plus yet more millions for the ads that air – at premium rates – between the segments of each new episode.

Even as it mercilessly mocks consumer culture and the corporate world, *The Simpsons* is an avid participant in both of them. So how does this resolve itself with Groening's self-professed countercultural values? Is the show a Trojan horse, invited inside the corporate gates and proudly displayed in the middle of the primetime courtyard, only to unleash a punishing barrage of satirical arrows on the authorities that brought it in? Or is it rather a court jester, invited inside the castle at the monarch's leisure and permitted to poke a little fun at his opulent wardrobe and expansive girth so long as it keeps the people happily paying tithes? Could it be both?

There's certainly a case to be made for *The Simpsons* as Trojan horse – or, to skip to another metaphor, as a rabid dog let loose in the house of its corporate owners. It has, after all, gnawed relentlessly on every hand that ever fed it, seeming often to dare its masters to cast it out or put it down. Its attacks on the Fox Network number in the dozens: everything from digs at the overall quality of the network's programming to suggestions that the network's executives are vicious criminals. The Fox-sucks gags are often quick and easy – as when the Simpson family is shown watching parodic Fox fare like *World's Funniest Tornadoes* and *When Buildings Collapse*.[13] On other occasions, though, there have been more elaborate and audacious assaults. In Episode 3G01 ('The Springfield Files'), for example, Homer encounters an alien in the Springfield woods and drags Bart along to try to document it. 'This Friday,' he tells his son, 'we're going back to the woods, and we're going to find that alien!' 'What if we don't?' asks Bart. His dad responds, 'We'll fake it and sell it to the Fox Network.' Bart starts to giggle. 'They'll buy *anything*,' he says. 'Now, son,' says Homer with exaggerated piety, 'they do a lot of quality programming, too.' A one-beat pause, and then both of them collapse into hysterical laughter.

But beyond the relatively simple task of poking fun at Fox's poorest and cheesiest programmes, *The Simpsons* has occasionally taken shots at the corporation behind this trash. When a shady character named Mr Blackheart shows up at the house to buy the elephant Bart has won in a radio contest, for instance, Lisa is immediately sceptical about the nobility of his intentions – after all, his boots and hat and even his cheques are made of ivory. 'Are you an ivory dealer?' Lisa asks him. Mr Blackheart chuckles. 'Well, little girl,' he replies, 'I've had a lot of jobs in my day: whale-hunter, seal-clubber, president of the Fox Network. And like most people, yeah, I've dealt a little ivory.' In another episode, as the Simpsons enumerate Lisa's many activist campaigns,

Homer notes that she won't let them watch Fox because the company owns chemical-weapons plants in Syria. These are random and baseless jabs at the show's corporate parent, and they blip quickly past. Still, they not only associate Fox's executives with some of the most reprehensible business activities on the planet, they also subtly suggest that building a corporate empire – *any* corporate empire – necessitates becoming involved in deeply immoral activities.

The Simpsons has also made frequent sport of self-flagellation, particularly in the lampooning of its own merchandising machine. Bart confronts Krusty the Clown about the abysmal quality of his officially licensed summer camp, for example, with this knowing line: 'How could you, Krusty? I'd never lend *my* name to an inferior product.' And a segment of the Season 3 Halloween episode – 8F02 ('Treehouse of Horror II') – parodied the show's commercial overexposure at length. In the segment, the Simpson family obtains a cursed monkey's paw and receives Bart's wish of fame and fortune. Instantly, Springfield overflows with the kind of officially licensed junk that filled real-world stores during the show's own merchandising boom: overpriced T-shirts, a *Simpsons Sing Calypso* album, even Bart's image on a giant billboard, with a word balloon coming from his mouth that reads GET A MAMMOGRAM, MAN! The show has also attacked its most famous product endorsement – Butterfinger – by name. In a Season 13 episode, the Springfield court imposes a total ban on sugar. A giant bonfire is built to burn all the sugary treats in Springfield, and some police officers attempt to throw a pile of Butterfingers onto the blaze. As they hit the fire, though, a sort of force field surrounds them, and they're thrown back, unburned. 'Not even the fire wants them,' Chief Wiggum notes ruefully.

There's an almost apologetic gesture in all of this that's somehow both subversive and resigned. The writers know the show's on a network that even by mass-market-TV standards is a shameless panderer to the lowest common denominator. They know the show was overexposed, that it made buckets of cash on cheap crap, that it shilled for a mediocre candy bar. And so they pepper their scripts with winking references to shoddy merchandise and corporate nastiness, as if to say, *Hey, what can you do? This is how popular entertainment works. It's ridiculous. We know it. You know it. Maybe we're subverting it, maybe we're not, but at least we all know the score.*

This could be the foundation for the argument that the show is more court jester than Trojan horse. Consider, for example, the case of Rupert Murdoch's own appearance on *The Simpsons*. Murdoch, like any other celebrity guest, was not allowed to tinker with the script. And so it came to pass that the Fox Network's owner made his debut as a scowling egomaniac on a TV show that had made him billions of dollars and all but created his TV empire. His appearance comes in Episode AABF08 ('Sunday, Cruddy Sunday'), in which Homer and a gang of his pals go to the Super Bowl. After a series of mishaps, they find themselves in a lush private skybox, where they feast at the trough of plenty until a helicopter lands on the skybox roof and Murdoch himself comes bursting through the door. 'I'm Rupert Murdoch, the billionaire tyrant!' he announces. 'And this is my Skybox!' Chief Wiggum challenges him to prove his identity. Murdoch mumbles a few words into a cellphone, and the Super Bowl game screeches to a halt as the players on both teams line up to spell out the words 'Hi Rupert.' Humbled, the Springfieldi-anites begin to plead their case. 'Silence!' Murdoch bellows. He magically summons three armed guards, who chase Homer and the gang out of his skybox. And so concludes Murdoch's appearance.

So what to make of his willing self-satire? Is he having a little good-natured self-deprecating fun with his own image, or has he been trapped into confessing to his corporate crimes? Is there subversion in all of this, or is it just a cartoony Friar's Roast of the unassailable elite? The answers to these questions might depend wholly on you as a viewer – your preconceptions, your politics – and that might, in the end, be the point. This is a show, after all, that counts among its fans both anticorporate crusader Ralph Nader and former Reagan speechwriter Peggy Noonan.

Maybe the point is that *The Simpsons* is most definitely subversive – more antiauthoritarian by far than almost anything else that's ever aired in primetime, rivalled on the sedition scale only by $M*A*S*H$ and the first couple of seasons of *Saturday Night Live*. But it also has to play by the rules of the primetime game. It has to remain likeable enough that it can appeal to a mass audience and thus stay on the air. It can tweak its boss's nose, but it can't tear him to shreds. *The Simpsons* may not like Murdoch's authority, or Mr Burns's or Lindsey Naegle's or anyone else's. It may indeed attempt to dismantle these authorities tweak by tweak. But the balance of power is, in the end, tipped steeply against it.

George Meyer: 'It's a guerrilla battle. I mean, the authorities have the high ground. They have all the money. They have the tradition. They have the history in their favour. So we have to just kind of take potshots and then run back up into the hills.'

Groening apparently learned this lesson the hard way when he set out in the late 1990s to create a new series for the Fox Network, a satirical sci-fi cartoon called *Futurama*. Fox executives were initially ecstatic about the prospect of a new series, but soon worried that it was too edgy and eventually bumped the show from its plum post-*Simpsons* time slot in favour of *Family Guy* – a cartoon that was nakedly derivative of *The Simpsons* itself. *Futurama* then bounced around Fox's schedule, which may be part of the reason it took some time to find its audience and its stride as a series. Groening was palpably wounded by the process. 'It has been by far the worst experience of my adult life,' he told *Mother Jones* magazine. Groening concluded from *Futurama*'s woes that *The Simpsons*, barely ten years old, was a relic from a bygone age, far too subversive to survive the contemporary corporate grind intact. 'I don't think *The Simpsons* would be allowed on air now in its undiluted form,' he explained. 'The show would be run through the deflavoriser.'

So then: much as *The Simpsons* may from certain angles look like any other mass-entertainment franchise, it *was* a Trojan horse of sorts. It snuck into primetime when the guardians of bland, safe corporate conformity had their backs turned, tucked inside the junk-TV underbelly of the desperate upstart Fox Network. Ten years later, the network – now well established – wanted only safe clowns and edgeless spoofs. Court jesters.

Imagine trying to pitch *The Simpsons* to Fox nowadays. Think of it as a scene you'd only see on the show as it is: Fox owner Rupert Murdoch, the billionaire tyrant, calls a meeting of his marketing VP, Lindsey Naegle, and his most deep-pocketed sponsor, Monty Burns, to plot out a safe corporate version of *The Simpsons*. They review the pitch for the new cartoon, an unbridled social satire starring a buffoon who works at a nuclear power plant. Burns is keen to be seen as hip in the eyes of young consumers, but doesn't like the nuke bashing. No problem, says Naegle. We'll just white-collarise the guy by 20 per cent or so. Murdoch doesn't want *any* of his advertisers to get so nervous they won't cut cheques, so why not a neutral workplace: maybe a bank? Sure, says Naegle. And shows starring stand-up comics are hot right now, so we'll find one of them to play Homer. Keep the middle-American setting, toss in a few 'wacky' friends and neighbours, lose the egghead references (we don't want to confuse anyone, after all) and, oh yeah, we've gotta add a laugh track so there's no missing the fact that this is all light-hearted fun.

Result? Your typical forgettable 1990s sitcom. *The Drew Carey Show*, most likely. And at the risk of stating the painfully obvious, I'll point out that it's unlikely you'd make it this far into a book-length examination of *The Drew Carey Show*.

CORRUPT MAYORS, CROOKED COPS, & OTHER UNINSPIRING SCENES FROM INSIDE THE LEADERSHIP VACUUM OF THE CONTEMPORARY WEST

Burns, Naegle, Murdoch. There's a notable absence of traditional figureheads thus far in my analysis of power and authority on *The Simpsons*. This is no accident. Still, you're probably starting to wonder what happened to the cops and teachers, the politicians and preachers? Oh, they're around. Springfield has its mayor ('Diamond Joe' Quimby), its chief of police (Clancy Wiggum), its elementary-school principal (Seymour Skinner), its Christian minister (Reverend Timothy Lovejoy). It's just that in Springfield – as in our world – these are second-tier authorities compared to captains of industry. In Springfield, there is no authority left uncorrupted by the relentless forces of corporate commerce, and none who is their equal in power. There is a leadership vacuum, and business has filled it.

The discounting of public institutions in Springfield results in part from the gross incompetence and/or deep corruption and/or simple indifference of the officers of those institutions. Take Mayor Quimby, Springfield's very own John F. Kennedy, complete with JFK's *er-uh* stammer and Boston drawl. In his time, Kennedy was the King of Camelot, a magnet for the best and brightest, but Quimby embodies all the unseemly shit that has tarnished the Kennedy myth (and big-time politics in general) in the decades after his death. Quimby comes from a big family prone to partying too hard and falling afoul of the law; he's a dedicated womaniser; and he's a man far more interested in his own status and power than in serving the people of Springfield.

Quimby is an extended study in lousy, hypocritical, self-serving politics. He plays to the lowest common denominator (blaming high taxes, for example, on a non-existent illegal-immigrant crisis). He uses his office for personal gain (spending two months in Aruba, for example, to determine that it's unfeasible to build a super-train link between it and Springfield). And he conspires with Springfield's other public officials to rake in the cash and cover his ass. Quimby is so crooked he'd need servants to screw on his pants (to borrow a marvellous phrase from Hunter S. Thompson's eulogy of Richard M. Nixon). His mayoral seal reads 'Corruptus in Extremis' – he can't hide his treachery even from himself.

Fresh evidence of Quimby's corrupt reign emerges every time he appears on the show, but perhaps the most telling is the reaction he gets on those extremely rare occasions when he's *not* nakedly self-serving. One of the most pointed examples occurs in an episode in which Homer becomes Quimby's bodyguard and uncovers a ludicrously shady deal: the mayor's on the take from Fat Tony's Springfield Mafia to look the other way as they sell rat's milk to the town's schoolchildren. A short time later, Homer saves Quimby's life – but only after extracting a promise that Quimby will crack down on the rat's milk fiasco. Cut to Fat Tony's social club, where the Springfield police burst in to bust up the phony-milk ring. 'Gentlemen,' Fat Tony replies calmly, 'if you would simply consult my dear friend Mayor Quimby, I am confident that this can be . . .' Quimby interrupts him: 'Not this time, Fat Tony. The mayor's office is not for sale!' Everyone in the room roars with laughter. And in the knowing mirth of all involved, there are echoes of the cynical chuckling of the modern democratic electorate and their alleged watchdogs in the media. When a political campaign is covered like a horse race, when commentators and even random citizens talk of a politician's 'performance', when indeed a near-majority of eligible voters don't cast ballots (as happened in both the United States and Canada in the 2000 elections) – the subtext of all of this is this braying laughter. As if the candidates care about anything other than getting themselves elected. As if their campaigns aren't bought and paid for by corporate donors and private-sector lobbyists, and as if they don't govern on behalf of the corporations who fill their coffers. As if it's even in the realm of possibility that a true man of the people is in the running, and as if anything's going to change. Har-de-fucking-har.

The Simpsons itself plays out this deeply ironic gag at a full episode's length when Lisa becomes a finalist in a patriotic-essay contest sponsored by Reading Digest. Early in the episode, there's a montage of kids' essays being read nationwide that serves as a catalogue of the most beloved symbols of American democracy: the Statue of Liberty and the melting pot, freedom and opportunity, an informed electorate and checks and balances. (The contestants are graded in four categories: originality, clarity, organisation, and jingoism.) Lisa wins the regional contest with her essay 'The Roots of Democracy', but when she and her family travel to Washington for the finals, Lisa stumbles on a scandal in the office of Springfield's congressman: he's taking a bribe from a developer to open up the Springfield National Forest to logging. So she quickly drafts a new essay: 'Cesspool on the Potomac'. ('This will be one nation under the dollar,' it concludes, 'with liberty and justice for none.') Word of this unfolding tragedy – 'A little girl is losing faith in democracy!' – soon reaches the office of a powerful senator. Official Washington springs into action in an instant, and within two hours Springfield's crooked congressman is nailed in a sting, Congress passes a bill to expel him from the House, and President George H.W. Bush signs it into law. After the contest, Lisa sees a headline – 'Imprisoned Congressman Becomes Born-Again Christian' – and marvels that the system appears to work after all. This sequence is of course pure irony, a broad satire of the notion that revelations of corruption would outrage a contemporary politician and especially that several branches of government would react to such news not with obfuscation and damage control but with a quick, concerted effort to eradicate the problem entirely. *As if.*

There's a far more realistic picture of contemporary politics in Episode 2F02 ('Sideshow Bob Roberts'), in which pardoned felon Sideshow Bob becomes Mayor Quimby's rival in a mayoral campaign that exposes the cynical apparatus of modern politics in all its fetid glory. The episode opens with Sideshow Bob in jail for his attempted murder of Bart in a previous episode. Birch Barlow, Springfield's very own Rush Limbaugh, turns Bob's imprisonment into a *cause célèbre*, and Barlow's loyal listeners soon rally to demand Bob's release. Mayor Quimby quickly capitulates to this mob and pardons Bob, who immediately launches a campaign to unseat Springfield's spineless mayor.

It's in the ensuing election race that the full range of dirty tricks and media schemes and old-fashioned shallow posturing endemic to contemporary politics are laid bare. Both candidates engage in the timeless political arts of mugging for photos with cute kids and shamelessly sucking up to senior citizens, but they save their vilest stuff for their campaign commercials. Quimby's ad employs a jingle to celebrate his meagre accomplishments (a tyre yard and mid-sized roller rink, a gallows and shiny Bigfoot trap), while Bob's commercial attacks Quimby for supporting the very 'revolving-door prisons' that led Bob himself to be released in the first place. Then comes the televised debate on the nakedly partisan Fox Network, which superimposes flames around Quimby's head to vilify him and permits Birch Barlow to ask ludicrously leading questions, thus producing this stellar example of the debased quality of contemporary public discourse:

Barlow: Mayor Quimby, you're well known, sir, for your lenient stance on crime. But suppose for a second that *your* house was ransacked by thugs, *your* family tied up in the basement with socks in their mouths. You try to open the door but there's too much *blood* on the knob . . .

Quimby: What is your question?

Barlow: My question is about the budget, sir.

On Election Day, we see the result of this inane campaign, as Springfield's misinformed and self-absorbed voters glibly elect Bob in a landslide. Bob's election is soon exposed as a case of massive electoral fraud, and Mayor Quimby – for once the lesser of two evils – is returned to power. The idea that the town might actually find an honest, capable mayor, however, is never entertained.

The thing about Episode 2F02, though, is that it's barely even parody – especially not when it's compared to the vacuous carnival of mudslinging and spin-doctoring that is big-time American politics. Bob's attacks on Quimby for being soft on crime, for example, are actually less underhanded and misleading than the ads from George H.W. Bush's 1988 presidential campaign that they're lampooning. And Sideshow Bob's electoral fraud has nothing on the removal of thousands of African-Americans from the voter lists in Florida – under the gubernatorial watch of the Republican candidate's brother, no less – that helped elect George W. Bush in 2000. A handful of Hollywood movies released in the 1990s (among them *Bulworth*, *Wag the Dog*, and of course the Tim Robbins mockumentary *Bob Roberts*, which 2F02 references in its title) ran into the same problem. As pointed as the satire sometimes was, it somehow fell short of the real thing. Maybe that's why the darkest satire of the modern American political process in recent years was a genuine documentary: *The War Room*, a 1993 film about Bill Clinton's first presidential run that so fully revealed the behind-the-scenes brutality of American presidential politics that it seemed impossible to exaggerate it for satirical purposes thereafter. Sideshow Bob calls his electoral fraud 'a work of Machiavellian art', but I bet Clinton's ferocious campaign manager, James Carville, could beat the green goo out of Sideshow Bob's backroom ghoul. And not even Monty Burns at his most hissingly villainous could top George W. Bush's top political operative, Karl Rove, an attack dog so rabid he terrifies former Nixon aides. Politics, we all understand, is a silly, sleazy business, so the satire's sharper – and more surprising – when *The Simpsons* depicts Washington functioning selflessly than when it shows Springfield's politicians behaving abominably. Springfield's politicians are hypocritical, calculating, flat-out larcenous? Well, join the club.

The people of Springfield are no better served by their other local authorities. Police Chief Wiggum, for example, may occasionally enforce the law – as in the aforementioned case of the rat's milk – and his chief crime is actually massive incompetence, but he's certainly no stranger to corruption. There's a single scene in Episode 1F09 ('Homer the Vigilante') that tells you pretty much all you need to know about the interconnected crookedness of

Springfield's public officials. In the episode, Homer has formed a vigilante mob to track down a cat burglar, as the local police are too bumblingly incompetent to catch him. Homer's mob succeeds, but the townsfolk are so charmed by the burglar – a suave senior citizen named Mr Molloy – that they want to let him go. It's at this point that Wiggum and his force step in. 'Gee, I really hate to spoil this little love-in,' Wiggum tells the crowd, 'but Mr Molloy broke the law. And when you break the law, you gotta go to jail.' Mayor Quimby steps out from the crowd. 'Uh, that reminds me,' he tells Wiggum, 'er, here's your monthly kickback.' Wiggum, exasperated but far from outraged: 'You just – you couldn't have picked a worse time.' This blatant display of hypocrisy and corruption ruffles not a feather among the crowd, of course.

The Springfield PD's daily routine is rife with casual corruption and gross incompetence. Springfield's cops accept free beer from Moe, watch boxing matches on Homer's stolen cable, and throw parties at the site of marijuana busts. And the people of Springfield are little better served and protected when they're actually on the case. Consider, for example, Chief Wiggum's expert police-radio description of a suspect who's fleeing the scene of a burglary: 'Put out an APB for a male suspect driving a . . . car of some sort, heading in the direction of . . . you know, that place that sells chili. Suspect is hatless. Repeat: hatless.'

You can find the same mix of indifference, incompetence and immorality at any institution in town. Springfield Elementary struggles along with out-dated textbooks,[14] an incompetent principal who commands no respect whatsoever, and teachers who uniformly radiate total apathy towards the task of shaping young minds. 'Whose calculator can tell me what seven times eight is?' instructs Mrs Krabappel in a characteristically bland lesson. And on a rare occasion in which Mrs Krabappel actually seems interested in her job – strictly to bolster the teachers' union's demand for higher salaries – it precipitates a profoundly disheartening exchange between Mrs Krabappel (Edna to her colleagues) and Principal Skinner in the middle of a cafeteria packed with kids. 'Our demands are very reasonable,' she says. 'By ignoring them, you're selling out these children's future!' Principal Skinner: 'Oh, come on, Edna. We both know these children *have* no future!' Skinner suddenly remembers where he is. He titters nervously and turns to face his students. 'Prove me wrong, kids,' he intones half-heartedly. 'Prove me wrong.'

Skinner, though, is downright buoyant compared to Springfield's most prominent religious leader, Reverend Lovejoy. Lovejoy's just fine from the pulpit – he can chastise the sinners and rattle off biblical lists of who begat whom and take ill-informed cheap shots at the evils of pop culture with the best of 'em – but he's of little other comfort to his flock. When Principal Skinner calls him seeking advice on how to deal with yet another conflict with his mother, for example, Lovejoy answers mechanically, 'Well, maybe you should read your Bible.' Skinner: 'Um, any particular passage?' Lovejoy: 'Oh, it's *all* good.' And the good reverend is openly contemptuous of his most devoted parishioner, the obsessively Christian Ned Flanders. When Ned learns that the Simpson children haven't been baptised, for instance, it sends him into a panic. He calls Reverend Lovejoy, babbling incoherently. 'Ned,' Lovejoy replies, 'have you thought about one of the other major religions? They're all pretty much the same.' And then he hangs up.

Almost without exception, Springfield's civic authorities are either power-less or undeserving of what power they have. Lovejoy and Wiggum and Quimby might be permitted their petty fiefdoms, but the real higher authority is the almighty dollar, and its high priests are not public servants or men of the cloth but captains of industry. Indeed, Springfield's corporate titans are occasionally presented with the opportunity to simply buy Springfield's public institutions outright. In one episode, the local church is destroyed in an accident, and Mr Burns quickly steps in with the cash to rebuild it. The only catch is that it be built to Burns's profit-making specifications, so the new church is plastered with ads inside and out. And as I've mentioned, when Springfield Elementary School runs into revenue woes, Kid First Enterprises is soon on the scene to privatise the school, converting it into an elaborate market-research laboratory while shrouding its diabolical plans in the can-do language of corporate efficiency. 'You know,' Kid First executive Jim Hope[15] explains to intrepid reporter Kent Brockman, 'when public schools drop the ball, it's up to the private sector to fall on that fumble and run for the end zone.'

With this sentiment, Jim Hope comes closer than any other Springfield business leader to joining the swelling chorus of corporate voices that articulated the dominant ideology of the corporate world in the 1990s. And in many cases the ideology was just as simple and binary as Hope's comment suggests, built as it was on this crude cornerstone: public sector = bad (antiquated, wasteful, socialistic, bureaucratic, unprofitable), private sector = good (modern, efficient, rational, democratic, market-driven, profitable). This ideology and the corporate elite it served never did find a definitive name – though the related phenomena of consumerism and globalisation and neo-conservatism and the New Economy all certainly contributed to it. It was instead one of its most insightful detractors, the American cultural critic Thomas Frank, who ascribed to it the most evocative catch-all term: market populism.

SHOPPERS OF THE WORLD, UNITE!

How did the 'democracy of the supermarket' triumph over electoral democracy throughout the West? What ushered in the 'Washington consensus' of the 1990s – that unprecedented agreement among business and media elites and political parties of almost every stripe throughout the developed world that free markets were the backbone of democratic society? How did the American business elite and its allies in the government and the media justify the unprecedented economic polarisation of the 1990s (the greatest such redistribution of wealth in American history)? These are the questions Thomas Frank wrestles with in his 2000 book *One Market under God: Extreme Capitalism, Market Populism, and the End of Economic Democracy*. Frank's book is a thorough examination of the varied means by which corporate masters have transformed themselves from demonic Burns-like figures into warm, fuzzy men-of-the-people like Jim Hope. How did that makeover happen? The answer, Frank writes, is market populism:

> At the center of the 'New Economy' consensus was a vision of economic democracy as extreme and as militant-sounding as anything to emanate from the CIO [a radical American labour union] in the thirties. From Deadheads to Nobel-laureate economists, from paleoconservatives to New Democrats, American leaders in the nineties came to believe that markets were a popular system, a far more democratic form of organization than (democratically elected) governments. This is the central premise of what I call 'market populism': that in addition to being mediums of exchange, markets are mediums of consent. With their mechanisms of supply and demand, poll and focus group, superstore and Internet, markets manage to express the popular will more articulately and meaningfully than do mere elections. By their very nature markets confer democratic legitimacy, markets bring down the pompous and the snooty, markets look out for the interests of the little guy, markets give us what we want.

At the time of its pre-industrial birth, the corporation was understood to be an institution that existed only by the benevolent grace of the state. Even through the industrial revolution and on into the second half of the twentieth century, capital's enormous and growing power was balanced by that of the government, the media and most ordinary citizens – all of whom understood to greater or lesser degrees that the interests of big business were at best indifferent and quite possibly diametrically opposed to their own. In the 1980s and especially the post-Cold War 1990s, however, this balance of power shifted dramatically, and the inversion of the relationship between state and corporation was complete. Not only did corporations now hold supreme power in affairs both public and private, it was believed to be *right* that they possessed that power. Corporations, not public institutions, were the guardians of the public good.

What's more – and here we move from Frank's market populism to the alleged global triumph of 'Western liberalism' that set the stage for it – there might not have been any real need for governments any more, and *politics*, at the very least, was increasingly irrelevant. This argument lay at the core of Francis Fukuyama's hugely influential essay 'The End of History?' which appeared in a 1989 issue of the journal *The National Interest* and soon became required reading in the corridors of Western power. Fukuyama's argument was simple enough: the collapse of communism represented the death of the last remaining alternative to 'Western liberalism'. The war was over. The good guys won. All that was left was to get fat and tidy the lawn.

And what happened in the 1990s to prove him wrong? The great stories of the decade were the ones about consolidating Western liberalism's victory and expanding its scope, and the engine of all of this was the free market. There's a McDonald's *where* now? Beijing? Not only can you watch CNN in Timbuktu, dude, you can send an e-mail from there to the South Pole. Then maybe use E-trade to buy some stock in a Bermuda-based dot-com run by an expat Australian Buddhist, a Taiwanese math whiz and a game-theory expert from Kazakhstan. 'For our purposes,' wrote Fukuyama, 'it matters very little what strange thoughts occur to people in Albania or Burkina Faso, for we are interested in what one could in some sense call the common ideological heritage of mankind.'

In Episode 4F17 ('The Old Man and the Lisa'), Mr Burns learns that he's bankrupt. Surrounded by mendacious yes-men and firm in his belief that his position of omnipotent privilege was unassailable, Burns hadn't noticed that his stock ticker had been on the fritz since September 1929. Likewise, Fukuyama surveyed the world's ideological landscape and saw only the placid sea of Western liberalism. The glorious view was spoiled by the rubble of Marxism and a few ancient theocratic relics on distant shores, but since these were easily tossed in history's dustbin, he decided this sunny vista was as eternal as God's ample grace.

As long as you were lucky enough not to be born in the southern hemisphere or the rougher parts of Detroit, the decade that followed Fukuyama's essay could indeed seem like a time without history. Tremendous changes were underway – corporations expanding into and branding every corner of the planet, a communications revolution shrinking that same planet even as it churned out millionaires by the bushel, new scientific breakthroughs announced every other day – but still the days seemed inconsequential. There were few signposts, and the ones that were planted seemed weirdly skewed towards weightlessness and decadence. O.J. Simpson's murder trial in Los Angeles and Princess Diana's death in Paris made for bigger landmarks than the brutal genocide in Rwanda. The tragic downfall of famous individuals from the lands of Western liberalism was far more relevant to history than the mass brutality of obscure tribes. Spectacle, not substance, ruled the public agenda. And so we in the wealthy and booming West who were living after the end of history sat back and watched the parade.

So maybe Fukuyama *was* right, but not in the way he thought he was. It's true that it no longer matters what's being said in Burkina-Faso or Albania; what matters (and what Fukuyama and the free-market triumphalists failed to recognise) is that Burkina-Faso and Albania – and Tuvalu and Timbuktu and Afghanistan – are part of a single multifaceted entity created by the global reach of Western liberalism and corporate power. They are part of the conversation, whether we (or they) like it or not, and if we're too busy shouting congratulations at each other to listen to what they're saying, they may just force their way in.

Put another way, history was storing its energy. It was building for something massive. It abhors vacuums. And then it came, flew in out of a sky so clear and blue that it was a key part of the story, a detail everyone felt compelled to note.

It was such a beautiful day. Not a cloud in the sky.

In Episode 2F11 ('Bart's Comet'), Springfield is under imminent threat of total destruction by a comet hurtling towards the earth. The town's best minds get together and decide to launch a rocket at the comet, but their rocket misses its target and plummets back to earth, destroying the only bridge out of town. Cut to the floor of the US Congress, where a bill is tabled to provide funding for the evacuation of Springfield. Just before the vote, a congressman adds a rider to the bill providing $30 million 'for the perverted arts'. The bill is defeated. Cut to news anchor Kent Brockman, who turns to his viewing audience with this summary: 'I've said it before and I'll say it again: democracy simply does not work.'

This was a sentiment that occurred to me often in the days after 11 September 2001, as I tried somehow to reconcile the horror of watching the two tallest buildings in New York collapse live on television with the extraordinarily banal responses put forward by the elected leaders of the world's democracies – especially that self-proclaimed last best hope for humanity, the United States of America.

Even before the fires had gone out in the pile of rubble that was once the World Trade Center, America's leaders had carefully surveyed the damage, considered its enormous impact on everyday life and had then risen as one in a brave chorus, imparting their sage advice to a shaken nation. The advice? Go shopping. By the tragedy's two-week anniversary, President Bush had called for 'continued participation and confidence in the American economy'. New York Mayor Rudolph Giuliani advised, 'Just spend a little money.' Vice-President Dick Cheney was urging 'a normal level of economic activity'. Senator Bob Graham explained that buying a new car was 'an act of patriotism'. The president's brother, Jeb, added going to a restaurant and taking a cruise to the list of patriotic acts. Senator John McCain, beloved for his straight-talking ways, cut succinctly through the politicking. 'We need,' he explained, 'to spend money.'

No longer living after history, we in the West, and in many other places, were instantly awake to a new and grave reality. We were horrified but res-olute, finally ready to move beyond the trivialities of reality TV and day-trading and a new pair of Nikes. But in the weeks and then months after September 11, not a single one of the great leaders of our peerless West – these lands of the free, cradles of civilisation, beacons of liberty and justice, wellsprings of unparalleled opportunity and prosperity – not a single one could articulate even a vague notion of what it was we were defending. All agreed it had to be defended, but none had a clue what would help on the home front. Except this: we were being told, in emphatic terms, that the thing we were defending and the way to defend it were one and the same; we were the great globalised Republic of Buying Stuff, and we should bravely go on buying stuff to protect our right – our most basic, most cherished right – to buy more stuff.

We will never know just how great an opportunity was lost, how much passionate momentum squandered. Here were the people of virtually the entire world rising as one, ready to sacrifice, wanting to help. Who knows how many oversights could have been corrected, inequalities eliminated, hypocrisies inverted? Who knows what glorious civilisation could have emerged from the ashes of those towers? One thing is for certain: our national leaders on that day failed us completely – particularly those of the

United States. America's primacy of place and supremacy of power in world affairs, be they economic, political, military or cultural, has never been more apparent than in the wake of September 11, when, as if in some half-witted Hollywood movie, the whole world looked to its leaders for direction. And was told to go shopping.

But then who among the world's political leaders on that day of infamy would have been capable of oratory – of leadership, of a sense of purpose – on the level of Franklin Delano Roosevelt (or Lincoln or Churchill or Gandhi, or even Trudeau or Kennedy)? Tony Blair, whose posh accent and classical oratorical skills can hardly hide the facts that his political philosophy was cribbed from Bill Clinton and his moral philosophy isn't really that much more complex than Bush's? United Nations Secretary-General Kofi Annan, whose entire job seems to consist of saying absolutely nothing of consequence in a superficially substantial manner? The answer, of course, is neither of these – and no one else. We're rudderless, completely adrift. Or, worse, the people with their hands on the rudder have ferocious, tragically misguided convictions, driving us full steam into the abyss prophesied by W.B. Yeats in 'The Second Coming':

> Things fall apart; the centre cannot hold;
> Mere anarchy is loosed upon the world,
> The blood-dimmed tide is loosed, and everywhere
> The ceremony of innocence is drowned;
> The best lack all conviction, while the worst
> Are full of passionate intensity.

The passionate intensity of the perpetrators of the September 11 attacks collides with the passionate intensity of the architects of the 'war on terror', and in the anarchic din of the collision there is no insight, no dawning awareness, no new direction pointing to a place where these collisions are no longer possible. Tragically, the one piece of oratory that truly resonated with the American public after September 11 had no wisdom in it at all. It was merely a captain's order: full speed ahead. It was a line President Bush borrowed from a regular-guy-turned-hero on one of the incinerated airplanes, a line that's closer to Nike's 'Just Do It' tagline than to anything Lincoln ever said: 'Let's roll.'

In the age of market populism, an ersatz ad slogan is apparently the most we can hope for. After all, Mr Burns is the man in charge, and he's far too busy by now with war profiteering to offer us anything more substantial.

NOTES & MARGINALIA

1. **Hollywood's pawn:** There is one notable exception to Mr Burns's supremacy, one institution that bends Burns to *its* will: the local movie theatre. In Episode 1F16 ('Burns' Heir'), Burns appears in a short pre-movie commercial to solicit auditions from the Springfield populace for the lifetime role of heir to his vast fortune. At the end of his appeal, Burns announces, 'And now our feature presentation!' This appears to be the end of it, but Burns turns his head to take in some off-camera muttering. 'Oh, very well,' he accedes, and then launches into the classic 'Let's all go the lobby' jingle as he dances jovially with a line of anthropomorphised concession-stand snacks.

2. **So what does a tremendous overbite indicate?** Phrenology – aka cranioscopy – is the 'scientific' study of the size and shape of the head as a measure of a person's intelligence and the nature and strength of his or her character. Based on the theories of an oddball Viennese physician named Franz Joseph Gall (1758–1828), phrenology came to America in the 1830s, where it was spread from town to town by itinerant, medicine-show-style lecturers, enjoying more than a decade of widespread popularity before being pretty much completely discredited. (At the peak of its vogue, some employers would demand a character reference from a local phrenologist before hiring a new employee.)

Monty Burns, for his part, expresses his tenacious dedication to this brand of junk science in Episode 3F06 ('Mother Simpson'), when he explains to the police that he recognised his old nemesis Mona Simpson – Homer's mom, who'd helped destroy his germ-warfare laboratory in the 1960s – by her phrenological traits. 'Who could forget such a monstrous visage?' Burns tells the authorities. 'She has the sloping brow and cranial bumpage of the career criminal.' When Smithers points out that phrenology is bunk, Monty replies, 'Of course you'd say that – you have the brainpan of a stagecoach tilter!'

3. **Beyond the voice:** In an interview with America's National Public Radio, *Simpsons* producer Al Jean hinted that Mr.Burns's behaviour, if not his voice, draws on numerous other sources. Among them: Fox owner Rupert Murdoch, powerful entertainment-company executive Barry Diller, the 'evil banker character' in *It's a Wonderful Life*, and 'any boss that any of us has ever had'.

4. **Xanadu Redux:** In 1F01 and several other episodes, the staggering luxury and abundance of Burns Manor and of Mr Burns's vast, vast, *vast* fortune (*vast!*) are laid out in some detail, which both echoes the lavishness of Xanadu and ultimately puts it to shame. Both castles feature massive oversized fireplaces, stores of exotic animals, elaborate classical statuary – all the usual trappings of impossible wealth – but Burns Manor boasts some accoutrements that set it on a gilded pedestal of its own. Among them:

- King Arthur's famed sword 'Excalibur'
- the only existing nude photo of Mark Twain
- a rare first draft of the US Constitution with the word 'suckers' in it
- the suit Charlie Chaplin was buried in
- a toy train that takes three hours to complete its run and sometimes reappears in the toy room covered with snow
- a 'play room' in which an elaborate theatrical play runs non-stop
- a room containing a thousand monkeys banging away at a thousand typewriters (one has thus far come up with 'It was the best of times, it was the *blurst* of times')
- a room containing the largest television in the free world
- a room called 'The Patriots' lined with portraits of Mr Burns's ancestors (including a painting of Mr Burns himself that contained the only trillion-dollar bill the US ever issued until Mr Burns gave it to Fidel Castro)

5. **Globetrotting Bobo:** After young Monty abandons Bobo, the bear is washed away down a river, where it falls into the hands of Charles Lindbergh, who carries it with him to France on his historic trans-Atlantic flight. Then Bobo passes into the possession of Adolf Hitler, who

blames the bear for the fall of the Third Reich moments before committing suicide. It turns up next in the present-day Arctic, encased in a block of ice that's harvested and bagged for sale at Springfield's Kwik-E-Mart.

6. Great moments in sycophancy: In Episode 3F14 ('Homer the Smithers'), Smithers recruits Homer Simpson to fill in for him as Mr Burns's lackey so he can take a long-overdue vacation. He enumerates the duties of his job thusly: 'answering Mr. Burns's phone, preparing his tax return, moistening his eyeballs, assisting with his chewing and swallowing, lying to Congress, and some light typing.' Conspicuously absent from this list is Smithers's most common and critical task: shameless sycophancy. Herewith, some classic examples of Smithers's incomparable skill at the fine art of ass-kissing:

- As a meltdown looms in Episode 8F04 ('Homer Defined'), the power plant's owner and his bootlick share a last moment together. 'Oh, Smithers,' Burns laments, 'I guess there's nothing left but to kiss my sorry ass goodbye.' Smithers promptly replies, 'May I, sir?'
- As Mr Burns half-heartedly unwraps his birthday presents in Episode 1F01 ('Rosebud'), Smithers presents his boss with his own elaborate gift. 'Sir,' Smithers explains, 'I've arranged for the people of Australia to join hands tonight and spell out your name with candles. There's a satellite hookup on that monitor if you'll just turn your head slightly.' Lo and behold, the monitor displays just that, but Burns declines to witness the spectacle. 'Bah – no time,' he barks.
- In the final scene of Episode 3F14, Mr Burns lies in traction at the hospital, crippled as a result of Homer's tenure as his assistant. Smithers, back at his beloved boss's side, makes it up to the old tyrant by feeding him Spanish peanuts, carefully skinning each one and placing it in Burns's mouth in an homage to the final scene of *A Clockwork Orange*.
- In Episode 4F17('The Old Man and the Lisa'), Burns goes bankrupt. But even as professional wrestler Bret 'the Hitman' Hart contemplates buying the old man's enormous mansion, Smithers keeps on bootlicking. 'Eww,' the Hitman declares. 'This place has got old-man stink!' Burns is momentarily wounded. 'Don't listen to him, sir,' Smithers retorts. 'You've got an enchanting musk.'

7. *McJob: The Movie*: The slow, steady evolution of Mike Judge's 1999 film *Office Space* from box-office bust to cult hit – or 'stealth blockbuster', as *Entertainment Weekly* put it – is a powerful symbol of the resonance of the work-eviscerating tale in the *Simpsons* era. The movie – a scathing satire of working life in a bureaucratic nightmare of a cubicle farm – barely recouped its modest $10-million budget in its theatrical release. Since then, however, *Office Space* has slow-burned its way to a place in the satirical-comedy pantheon, with sales of more than 2.5 million copies on DVD and VHS earning it a place in the Top Twenty titles in Fox Filmed Entertainment's catalogue.

The film has also accomplished a feat far more essential to the establishment of a pop institution: it has become a fount of everyday references in the culture at large. The phrase 'TPS reports' – a nasty bit of bureaucratic arcana that haunts the film's protagonists – has become shorthand for office-regulation madness, even popping up in a 2003 Super Bowl commercial for Reebok starring 'Terrible Terry Tate, Office Linebacker'. *Office Space* also immortalised the photocopier-jargon term 'PC Load Letter' as a catch-all for office-chore frustration.

Its most spectacular achievement, however, was the simultaneous invention and canonisation of the fire engine red Swingline stapler, the coveted office supply of the film's neurotic office weirdo, Milton. At the time *Office Space* was filmed, Swingline didn't manufacture its iconic stapler in red. But demand for Milton's prized possession eventually became so great that Swingline added the 'Rio Red Stapler' to its product line in April 2002.

8. McJob: the dictionary entry: In June 2003, *Merriam-Webster's Collegiate Dictionary* added the term 'McJob' to its pages, defining it as 'low-paying and dead-end work'.

9. Full disclosure: My own conscripted service-industry tour of duty came in the summer and fall of 1996, when I parlayed my freshly minted honours degree in history into a cushy just-barely-above-minimum-wage gig as a *barista* at Starbucks. To this day I can readily recall the proper 'calling order' for a Starbucks drink – it goes number of shots, size, customisations, drink type, as in 'double-tall-decaf-skim-vanilla latte' – and the preferred term for the chain's slushy drink ('Frappuccino blended beverage', never just 'Frappuccino' or, heaven forfend, 'Frapp', which might encourage the Kleenex-isation of Starbucks' hard-earned trademark). I'm still waiting to be offered stock options.

10. **Another case of Burnsian spin:** In Episode 1F02 ('Homer Goes to College'), a platoon of Nuclear Regulatory Commission inspectors arrive at the plant's entrance and ring a buzzer. Mr Burns, disturbed from his naptime, tries simply to dismiss them over the intercom, but they persist. 'This is a surprise test of worker competence,' one announces. Burns: 'There must be some mistake. We . . . uh . . . we make cookies here. Mr Burns' Old-Fashioned Good-Time Extra-Chewy . . .' He's cut off by the invading agents before he can finish.

11. **Mmmm . . . Soylent Green:** *The Simpsons* has frequently dragged to the surface the darker truths hidden beneath the smooth corporate facade. Episode 3F07 ('Marge Be Not Proud'), for example, begins with a snippet of Krusty the Clown's holiday special. '*It's a Krusty Kinda Christmas,*' an announcer intones, 'brought to you by ILG: Selling your body's chemicals after you die. And by Li'l Sweetheart Cupcakes – a subsidiary of ILG.'

12. **Can't get enough of that wonderful Duff:** In late 1995, Lion Nathan Australia, an Australian brewery, expanded *The Simpsons'* merchandising range to include Homer's favourite brew, Duff beer. The beer – packaged in a can made to resemble the one Homer wraps his chubby mitts around – filled Australian shelves for several months, selling briskly at $29.95 (Australian) per case. In May 1996, however, an Australian court ordered it removed for exploiting the show's intellectual property. The court case was by all accounts wildly entertaining, featuring screenings of numerous *Simpsons* episodes that delighted lawyers and judge alike and at least one for-the-record detailing of the meaning of Homer's trademark exclamation *D'oh!*

In a graphic illustration of the thirst for *Simpsons* merchandise, sales of the beer then moved underground: an Australian newspaper reported in 1999 that surviving cans of Duff were selling for $200 (Australian) each, with one fully intact case of the beer fetching $13,000 (US).

13. **Zing!** Probably the most vicious parody of Fox's programming came in Episode 1F13 ('Deep Space Homer'), at the expense of *The Simpsons'* own follow-up on Fox's Sunday night schedule, the crude sitcom *Married . . . with Children*. In the episode, NASA officials, disturbed by the plummeting TV ratings for their space launches, watch a survey of 'the most popular personalities on television'. After viewing a scathing parody of the sitcom *Home Improvement*, the NASA officials' TV screen fills with a cartoon version of *Married's* living-room set. Al Bundy sits sullenly on the couch next to his trampy wife. 'Al, let's have sex!' she whines. 'No, Peg,' Al retorts. The audience erupts in laughter and cheering. Then Al leans over and flushes a toilet that's conveniently installed next to the couch. Explosions of whooping and whistling from the audience. And that, in less than ten seconds, is *The Simpsons'* summation of the brand of humour being peddled by its colleague – a colleague that was frequently paired with *The Simpsons* in media analyses of the emergence of 'blue-collar' sitcoms in the early 1990s.

14. **The kids have to learn about Tek War sooner or later:** In Episode 2F19 ('The PTA Disbands'), we learn that Springfield Elementary's collection of textbooks consists primarily of books that were banned by other schools. It includes the following enlightening and informative titles: *Tek War* by William Shatner; *The Theory of Evolution* by Charles Darwin; *Sexus* by Henry Miller; *40 Years of Playboy* by Hugh Hefner; *Steal This Book* by Abbie Hoffman; *Hop on Pop* by Dr Seuss; and *The Satanic Verses* (Junior Illustrated Edition) by Salman Rushdie.

15. **Ironic casting note:** The voice of Kid First Industries executive Jim Hope is provided by Tim Robbins, who is half of the most prominent left-wing activist couple in modern Hollywood, with his wife, Susan Sarandon. Among many other progressive causes, Robbins was a vocal supporter of the 2000 presidential campaign of pioneering anticorporate crusader Ralph Nader.

CHAPTER FIVE

Lisa Lionheart

There is a time when the operation of the machine becomes so odious, makes you so sick at heart, that you can't take part; you can't even passively take part, and you've got to put your bodies upon the gears and upon the wheels, upon the levers, upon all the apparatus, and you've got to make it stop. And you've got to indicate to the people who run it, to the people who own it, that unless you're free, the machine will be prevented from working at all!

Mario Savio, speaking from the steps of Sproul Hall,
University of California at Berkeley, 2 December 1964

An open letter to the people of Springfield: Today, our town lost what remains of its fragile civility, drowned in a sea of low-fat pudding. We are a town of lowbrows, nobrows, and ignorami. We have eight malls, but no symphony. Thirty-two bars, but no alternative theater. Thirteen stores that begin with 'Le Sex.' I write this letter not to nag or whine, but to prod. We *can* better ourselves!

Lisa Simpson, Episode AABF18 ('They Saved Lisa's Brain')

AS A RULE, THERE'S NO judgement in the Simpson household more sound than that of Lisa Simpson. Though she's only eight years old, Lisa possesses an astonishing wealth of knowledge and wisdom, able with equal ease to trade palindromes with Springfield's intellectual elite or to counsel Homer on his marital problems. But in Episode 4F17 ('The Old Man and the Lisa'), Lisa reluctantly acts against her better instincts: she joins the ranks of big business.

Lisa's one and only foray into the corporate world begins with a chance meeting with Mr Burns down at the Springfield Retirement Castle. As previously noted, Burns's ridiculously outdated stock portfolio has rendered him penniless, and he finds himself committed to the retirement home after his first-ever trip to the local supermarket leaves him hopelessly confused. ('Ketchup? Catsup? Oh, I'm in way over my head,' Burns admits before being escorted out of the store.) Bored by the retirement home's routine, Burns spies Lisa – she's there hunting for recyclable materials – and becomes instantly convinced that her disruptive idealism is just what he needs to rebuild his industrial empire. Lisa knows full well that Burns is the worst man in the world, and she initially refuses. But Burns follows her to the Simpson home and begs her on bended knee to help him. 'If I did agree to help you,' says Lisa, reluctantly warming to the idea, 'you could only earn money by doing good, socially responsible things. Nothing evil.' Burns: '"Nothing evil" – that's exactly the kind of radical thinking I need!' And so she and Monty enter the recycling business together, and soon they're scouring the local beach for recyclable litter. Lisa finds a fish caught in a discarded six-pack ring, and she explains to her new partner that the rings need to be cut up to keep them from trapping fish. Burns, though, learns a different lesson – and therein lies the tragedy soon to be wrought by Lisa's corporate adventure.

A few short scenes later, Burns is back in big business, cutting the ribbon on the Li'l Lisa Recycling Plant. On the surface, the plant seems like a treehugger's dream: it's powered by used newspapers, the machinery is made from recycled cans, and the windows are constructed of old liquor bottles. For a shining moment, Lisa is content that her name and face (the latter of which is rendered in a logo several stories high on the plant's wall) have been adopted by a corporate enterprise that even she can be proud of. But then Burns shows her the real source of the plant's profits: the Burns Omni-net, a giant blanket made from six-pack rings that scours the sea floor of all life, dragging it into a machine that grinds it into Li'l Lisa-brand animal slurry – a versatile product that can be used as high-protein animal feed, insulation for low-income housing, or even 'a top-notch engine coolant'. 'And best of all,' notes Burns the pseudo-ethical industrialist, 'it's made from 100 percent recycled animals!' Lisa is of course appalled. 'I was a fool to help that horrible old man!' she exclaims. Her keen moral compass won't let her keep her $12-million share of the profits made by Burns's new empire. She's learned her lesson. She won't get fooled again. She tears up Burns's cheque so she can return, untainted, to her usual routine.

It's a busy one, Lisa's usual routine. For li'l Lisa is the social conscience of *The Simpsons*. She is the bright yellow face of the show's political activism, the pint-sized embodiment of its countercultural sympathies, the aching heart of its existential angst and the keeper of its worldly knowledge. She's the antithesis not just of Burns's rapacious corporate greed but also of Homer's bumbling id and Bart's bratty nihilism and Marge's naive family values. Insofar as *The Simpsons* has a worldview, a political slant or an ethical stance – and to some degree it has all three – it expresses them most explicitly through the words and deeds of Lisa Simpson.

It is, to be sure, quite a heavy load for a prepubescent girl in a red dress and pearls to carry, but rest assured, Lisa's more capable of meeting the challenge than any second-grader in pop-cultural history.

So let's meet this Lisa Simpson.

She's the slightly geeky academic star of Springfield Elementary School, destined to become its only graduate ever to read at an adult level. She's also the school's most gifted musician, a jazz-loving saxophone ace so bored by the usual school-band fare that she often introduces a new riff into the opening credits of the show. Lisa is a vegetarian, a committed environmentalist, a debunker of false patriotic histories, a fierce defender of scientific reason over the superstitions of the unenlightened masses. Lisa foils local electoral frauds, reveals federal corruption scandals and sings songs for striking workers. She quotes from the Talmud and paraphrases Allen Ginsberg. She reveres the founders of the American Republic and embraces the diversity of the multicultural nation it has become. She is a Zen Buddhist, a tree-sitting Dirt First activist, a Mensa member, a full-blown latter-day Renaissance Girl.

In an age when many would-be left-leaning activists – especially the young – were supposedly apathetic and apolitical, disaffected and cynical, so deeply immersed in irony they were choking on it, *The Simpsons* served up Lisa Simpson every week as a reminder that progressive ideals weren't yet dead. In Lisa there are certainly traces of the traits that paralysed the left, and the young generally, for much of the 1990s. But in her too are the seeds of the anticorporate, egalitarian ethos that would inspire a growing activist movement against overintrusive marketing, overzealous privatisation and unchecked global trade liberalisation late in the decade.

Lisa might not be many viewers' favourite Simpson[1] – she's not as mischievous as Bart and nowhere near as funny as Homer. But when her sober voice fills the quiet spaces after the laughter has died down, telling us why we find this debased world so funny in the first place, how many of us have to admit she's the one who's most like we are (or like we wish we could be)? I know I do. Insofar as we're laughing at our own folly, insofar as we're laughing to keep from weeping at the hypocrisy and injustice of our world – and this is, I'd wager, a big part of what makes us laugh at *The Simpsons* – we're on Lisa's side. We don't like her all that much, maybe – she's too strident, too idealistic, too *honest* – but we might very well think she's right.

She is, for all of this, a child. Lisa used to dig *The Happy Little Elves*, but now she's into 'Itchy & Scratchy'. Her love for Malibu Stacy has remained constant. She fights with her brother, seeks solace from her mother and yearns for the understanding of her dopey dad.

This, in brief, is Lisa Simpson. Now let's learn a few things about her at some length.

LISA SIMPSON (I): GENIUS

When we first meet Lisa in the *Tracey Ullman* shorts, there's no sign of the intellectual giant she'll become. In these first appearances, she's little more than a bratty foil to devilish Bart, her angry eyes and scowling mouth betraying no brilliance whatsoever. In the second-ever *Simpsons* short, Lisa spends practically the entire 52 seconds mindlessly pestering Bart to change the channel. But by the series's first full-length episode, we begin to see traces of the character who will become the smartest Simpson. Early in this tale of how Homer saved Christmas, Lisa's still a bit nasty – delighting, for example, in poking Bart's injured arm – but towards the end, she launches into one of the reasoned sermons that have become her stock-in-trade. 'What, Aunt Patty?' Lisa asks, overhearing one of her aunt's routine attacks on Homer's character.

'Oh, nothing dear,' says Patty. 'I was just trashing your father.'

'Well, I wish you wouldn't,' says Lisa. 'Because, aside from the fact that he has the same frailties as all human beings, he's the only father I have.

Therefore, he is my model of manhood, and my estimation of him will govern the prospects of my adult relationships. So I hope you bear in mind that any knock at him is a knock at me, and I am far too young to defend myself against such onslaughts.'

This is trademark Lisa – equal parts philosophy, psychology and homespun wisdom – and it sets the tone for her character for the many seasons to come. Hereafter, Lisa may squabble with Bart, may throw a mild tantrum when her father lets her down, may need her mother's advice and consolation, but in matters of intellect, she's no eight-year-old girl. She is, in fact, the voice of the overeducated eggheads, many of them Harvard grads and nearly all of them closet intellectuals, who write *The Simpsons*' scripts.[2]

This is a point that needs to be understood before we go any further, because it's central to understanding why Lisa has been endowed not just with abundant intellectual gifts but also with high-minded cultural interests and deep political passions. Lisa is, in many ways, the animated public face of the show's creative team, as many of the show's key behind-the-scenes people have stated for the record. Matt Groening: 'At the end of the day, I have to admit that if I have a favorite it would be Lisa. She's the only one who will escape Springfield.' Al Jean, long-time *Simpsons* staffer and executive producer since 2001: 'The character we're closest to is Lisa Simpson, a character who reads a lot and hopes for a better life.' And, perhaps most significantly, Lisa is to a considerable degree the doppelgänger of George Meyer, the master of the show's rewrite room. In a 2000 profile in *The New Yorker*, Meyer's friend David Owen wrote that Lisa 'has developed an inner life that in some ways probably comes closer to Meyer's than does that of any other character on the show'. To wit: Meyer, like Lisa, is a vegetarian and a practitioner of Eastern spirituality (yoga for Meyer, Buddhism for Lisa). Meyer also shares with Lisa a deep commitment to environmentalism (this is an L.A. resident whose car has no air conditioning because he considers it wasteful), a strong distrust of authority and a general distaste for the excesses and banalities of the modern world.

The Simpsons' writers – who, like many humorists, want the focus to be on the comedic and/or artistic merit of the jokes they make – have in general avoided bald statements of their political and cultural biases. (Groening is the exception to this rule.) But many of these biases have been broadcast anyway, through the mouth of Lisa Simpson. And this begins, in a profoundly anti-intellectual age, with her unabashed braininess. Her smarts serve as a sharp rebuke both to the widespread distaste for book-learning in contemporary culture and the alleged illiteracy of TV itself. With Lisa, the show's academically inclined writers demonstrate that TV is fully capable of providing a loving home for a character who's not just quick-witted but genuinely learned.

Lisa's genius has been evident since her infancy. In one flashback episode, we find her bleating out her first word – 'Bart' – and moments later wrapping her tiny tongue around the elaborate name 'David Hasselhoff'. As a toddler, she's quickly recognised as a gifted child by Bart's school psychologist – though only three and three-eighths, she demonstrates a mastery of basic arithmetic – and this inspires Homer and Marge to buy her first saxophone. (The music store just happens to be placing a sign in its window reading MUSICAL INSTRUMENTS: THE WAY TO ENCOURAGE A GIFTED CHILD just as Homer walks by wondering how to encourage his gifted child.) By the time Lisa is eight, there are few subjects outside her purview. Perhaps the most dramatic example of Lisa's scholarship comes in Episode 9F09 ('Homer's Triple Bypass'), when her anxiety about her father's impending triple bypass sends her to poring over medical textbooks. And it's a good thing, too, because Homer's surgeon, the bargain-basement, TV-advertised quack Dr Nick Riviera, desperately needs her help. As he prepares to make the first incision, he pauses, confused – his only memory of medical school is of trying to pick up a coed by bragging about how he can prescribe any kind of medication he wants. Fortunately, Lisa notices his hesitation and calls down from the operating room's observation lounge: 'The incision in the coronary artery must be made *below* the blockage! *Below!*' ('Thanks, little girl!' Dr Nick calls back.)

It's always like this with brainiac Lisa. When misbehaving Bart is banned from seeing *Itchy & Scratchy: The Movie*, for example, Lisa goes to her father to urge him to end this cruel and inhuman punishment. 'He has the demented melancholy of a Tennessee Williams heroine,' she notes hyper-literately. Her rejoinder to her gym teacher's suggestion that she join an extracurricular peewee sports team to improve her grade overflows with psychological insight. 'You mean those leagues where parents push their kids into vicious competition to compensate for their own failed dreams of glory?' she asks sardonically.

Lisa's use of the Springfield Public Library to transform herself into an instant expert on whatever subject obsesses the Simpsons in any given episode has even become a recurring gag. In Episode 7F08 ('Dead Putting Society') she heads to the library to figure out how to transform Bart into a master mini-golfer. After greeting the library's staff by name, she heads to the card catalogue, reading off subject headings in a staccato series of one-off jokes at the expense of both the game of golf and the unique idiom of the card catalogue itself: "'Golf" . . . "Anecdotes" . . . "Eisenhower and" . . . "fishing" . . . "humour" . . . "Japanese obsession with" . . . Ah, here it is: "Putting". An even funnier list of subject headings occurs when Lisa's desire to bond with her father sends her hunting for information about football: 'Football . . . football . . . "Homoeroticism in" . . . "Oddball Canadian rules . . ."[3] . . . "Phyllis George and" . . . ' Lisa's card-catalogue hunts serve a dual purpose, demonstrating not only her own bookish nature but also the decidedly academic bent of the show's writers themselves for making repeated jokes about the linguistic nuances of card-catalogue headings in the first place.

Even without her beloved card catalogue, Lisa can be counted on to deliver a little erudite expository dialogue at the slightest prompting. Sometimes she's got a piece of reading material at the ready, such as when the Simpsons host an exchange student from Albania in Episode 7G13 ('The Crepes of Wrath'). Quoting from a reference text, Lisa briefs her father on what to expect from little Adil when he arrives, noting that Albania's currency is called 'the lek', its flag is a two-headed eagle on a red field, and its chief export is 'furious political thought'. On other occasions, Lisa disseminates her wide-ranging knowledge off-the-cuff. When Germans buy the Springfield Nuclear Plant, for instance, Homer naturally turns to his young daughter for some background. She quickly explains that Germany is a major economic power as a result of the famous efficiency, punctuality and strong work ethic of its citizens.

There's seemingly no limit to Lisa's thirst for knowledge. Consider the time Bart becomes Mr Burns's heir, and Burns hires a troupe of actors to portray the rest of the family in a ruse intended to fool Bart into thinking they don't miss him. Later, we learn that the actors (among them Michael Caine, who plays Homer) shadowed the Simpsons for days to get their characters right. 'That midget taught me a lot about his native Estonia,' Lisa observes about her double. For Lisa, even Burns's devious plots can apparently provide rich learning opportunities.

It comes as no real surprise, then, when we learn in Episode AABF18 ('They Saved Lisa's Brain') that Lisa's high IQ qualifies her for membership in Mensa. After all, this is an eight-year-old who vocally laments a teachers' strike, worried that the blow to her education may leave her unable to gain acceptance to venerable Vassar College, let alone the Ivy League, and who later narrows her standards even further, having a full-blown nightmare about winding up at one of the Ivy League's less celebrated schools (Brown University, where Otto, the spaced-out bus driver, reportedly almost got tenure). In AABF18, Lisa comes to the attention of Springfield's Mensa chapter after she publishes a high-minded letter in the *Springfield Shopper*. She's soon revelling in the group's brainy minutiae, inventing new palindromes and dressing in Renaissance costume. Things turn serious for the Mensans, though, when Mayor Quimby abdicates and the governance of Springfield falls to their 'council of learned citizens', as per the town's bizarre charter.[4] This sets the stage for a lengthy Simpsonian critique of the 'philosopher king' concept: Plato's notion that the ideal form of government would be a consortium of the state's greatest minds. Beloved by marginalised brainiacs and sci-fi writers, this utopian scheme implies that the main problem with modern government (indeed with almost all our contemporary woes) is that the people in charge simply aren't smart enough. This is one of *The Simpsons*' numerous attacks on the self-importance of the smart and scholarly – which critiques, taken together, save Lisa from deification and the show from uncritically celebrating intellectual snobbery.

In AABF18, the piss-take of the intellectual elite comes in the form of the authoritarian mess produced by the overbearing regime of the Mensa gang. The group's project begins, of course, with idealistic dreams. 'With our superior intellects,' Lisa raves, 'we could rebuild this city on a foundation of reason and enlightenment. We could turn Springfield into a utopia!' Soon, though, flaws appear. Their blanket bans on sports ranging from cockfighting to hockey (anything, as Professor Frink notes, that requires the embarrassment of removing one's shirt) anger the town's residents. And the Comic Book Guy calls for a selective breeding programme that pleases no one but him. Soon the council is reduced to internal bickering, and the people of Springfield appear on the verge of one of their frequent riots. Until, that is, 'the world's smartest man', astrophysicist Stephen Hawking, appears, dismissing the council's utopia as a 'Fruitopia' and inspiring the dim schmucks of Springfield to reclaim their town. Which they do – by rioting, of course. Lisa is forced to flee the melee with Hawking on his propeller-equipped wheelchair. 'Oh, Dr Hawking,' she laments. 'We had such a beautiful dream. What went wrong?' Hawking, via electronic voice box: 'Don't feel bad, Lisa. Sometimes the smartest of us can be the most childish.'

The show's censure of Lisa's intellectualism pops up more subtly elsewhere in the series. When Springfield's teachers go on strike, for example, the sudden absence of praise for her brilliance reduces Lisa to sheer panic. 'Grade me . . . look at me . . . evaluate and rank me!' she rants to her mother. 'I'm good, good, good, and oh so smart! *Grade me!*' Her mother scribbles an 'A' on a piece of paper, and Lisa wanders off clutching her fix with a junkie's delirious relief. Another time, a new student joins Lisa's class – a girl a year younger than Lisa who has skipped a grade and soon proves herself Lisa's superior in academics *and* the saxophone. The shame of being second-best reduces Lisa to nightmarish visions of life as a runner-up and devious schemes to sabotage her rival's success.

These critical portrayals of Lisa – who is otherwise supernaturally brilliant and virtuous to a fault – serve several purposes. In addition to being a nifty dodge of the trap of elitism, they make Lisa more realistic. No character, after all, can aspire to realism without a few all-too-human flaws. And they also make it clear that the show's satire plays no favourites, not even with the character who most closely resembles its creators. More broadly, Lisa's flawed nature implies that reason and knowledge alone do not pave the path to human perfection. Smart people have no greater claim to virtue than rich people or victorious warlords or Moe the bartender. It was *very* smart people, after all, who invented machine guns and atomic weapons and non-biodegradable petrochemical products. If there are unforeseen and potentially disastrous repercussions to the rash acts of the ignorant, so too are there unanticipated consequences buried in works of genius.

This is a point made explicit on *The Simpsons* in the person of Professor John Frink, a lab-coated science whiz whose Jerry Lewis voice masks a massive intellect, and whose brilliant inventions frequently produce undesirable results. Possibly the most revealing case is that of the AT-5000 Autodialer – Frink's first patent – which falls into the hands of Homer Simpson in Episode 4F01 ('Lisa's Date with Density'). Homer programmes the machine to call Springfieldianites randomly and invite them to send a dollar to 'Happy Dude', with the promise of eternal happiness as their reward. Homer uses the AT-5000, in other words, to run a telemarketing scam. In due course, the AT-5000 calls Frink himself. 'Aw, would you listen to the gibberish they've got you saying – it's sad and alarming,' Frink tells his old invention. 'You were designed to alert schoolchildren about snow days and such.' In another episode, Frink steps in as Springfield Elementary's substitute kindergarten teacher during a strike, and soon demonstrates the ugliness of intellectual elitism. Frink stands before the class pushing a toy vacuum cleaner back and forth, asking the children to note the erratic oscillation of the multicoloured balls encased in a bubble on the vacuum's head. A little girl asks if she can play with it. 'No, you can't play with it,' Frink snaps indignantly. 'You won't enjoy it on as many levels as I do.'

Lisa Simpson, of course, is never this arrogant, but she is just as human. Indeed she is, in some respects, a typical eight-year-old girl.

LISA SIMPSON (II): LITTLE KID

Lisa has many interests – not just intellectual but cultural, political and spiritual – that fall far outside the range of your average American eight-year-old. *The Simpsons* trades heavily in realism, however, and one of the key tools the writers use to make their favourite prepubescent genius more plausibly prepubescent is her occasional little-kid touches. For all her intelligence, Lisa is also a girl who loves ponies and Malibu Stacy dolls and Hollywood heartthrobs named Corey. She has sleepovers during which she and her friends give Maggie grotesque makeovers and play Truth or Dare. Occasionally, the writers even put some genuinely childlike babble in her mouth. See, for example, a scene in Episode 3F08 ('Sideshow Bob's Last Gleaming') where Lisa comes scampering up to her parents and describes her current adventure – the admittedly grown-up task of foiling Sideshow Bob's plan to eradicate television from Springfield – in the stream-of-consciousness of a typical overexcited kid: 'Mom! I found Sideshow Bob's hideout and I got a secret message to the police and I had a blimp fall on me and I was in an atomic blast but I'm okay now!'

Or consider Episode 5F20 ('Lard of the Dance'), in which Alex Whitney, an overly mature hipster girl from Capital City, comes to Springfield Elementary. At first, Lisa attempts to befriend Alex, introducing her to the timeless kids' stuff that's all the rage at the school: playing with dolls and jacks, pony rides and singalongs. But Alex is a perfume-wearing, cellphone-carrying pseudo-teenager, and she soon organises the school's first dance. When Lisa learns that girls are expected to bring dates to the event, though, it's more than she can bear. 'I don't want a date!' Lisa fumes. 'And I don't want to wear perfume and cocktail dresses. Am I the only one who just wants to play hopscotch and bake cookies and watch *The McLaughlin Group*?' Notwithstanding the quick ironic nod to Lisa's own adult interests at the end of this list (*The McLaughlin Group* is possibly the most cerebral current-affairs show on American TV), her protest falls on deaf ears. The dance goes ahead as scheduled – and turns out to be an unmitigated disaster. As it happens, the kids at Springfield Elementary *are* too young for Alex's lifestyle, and so they merely stand awkwardly on opposite sides of the gym trading nervous stares. Alex is baffled, but Lisa explains the problem in her usual precocious manner: 'It's because they're kids! And so are we! Come on, Alex, we've only got nine, maybe ten years tops when we can giggle in church and chew with our mouths open and go days without bathing! We'll never have that freedom again.'

Note that Lisa is celebrating the fact of her own childhood with mature, reasoned sociological analysis. This is about as clear an example as any of the tightrope Lisa walks as a character, delicately balancing her enormous intellect with the fact of her tender age. And yet somehow it works. Even when Lisa's lecturing like a college professor or mounting yet another protest, she never becomes a full-grown adult trapped in a kid's body. In fact, she remains more childlike than your average sitcom's precocious kid, who often as not speaks in the nightclub-ready repartee of your average sitcom writer. It's an impressive feat, Lisa's balance of girlishness and grown-up genius. Why is it that Lisa can toss around psychology and philosophy and still maintain her essential kid-ness, while the wisecracking teen Bud Bundy on *Married . . . with Children* comes across like a seasoned stand-up comic, and the smart-mouthed kids on *Home Improvement* feel like a midget improv troupe? It might stem in part from the way that children – even prepubescent ones – are sexualised on many sitcoms, the way even a sitcom kid as young as Lisa might be used to deliver double entendres. Lisa, by comparison, is realistically chaste in her juvenile yearnings for famous Coreys.

But it's the delivery, too, that differentiates Lisa from her sitcom peers. Lisa's voice – though supplied by a full-grown actor – always sounds like the voice of a very bright eight-year-old, even when it's deconstructing peewee sports or psychoanalysing the unique bond between father and daughter. Lisa's voice isn't polished like Bud Bundy's, and she doesn't smirk as she waits for the laugh track like the *Home Improvement* kids. Furthermore, most sitcom kids toil in a highly constructed universe that tries in vain to make itself seem real even as it positively gleams with slick showbiz polish. Lisa, though, lives in a self-contained parallel universe that, artificial as it obviously is, allows for a greater suspension of disbelief. *No way* are those sitcom kids like the real kids they're pretending to be, the kids we all know in real life. As for Lisa, well, maybe that's what kids are like sometimes in Springfield.

It also helps that, for all her brains, Lisa is as obsessed with pop culture as any other kid of her age. She loves Krusty the Clown and 'Itchy & Scratchy' just as fervently as Bart does, and when she guffaws at the on-screen carnage, there's no analytical distance, no irony. She's a kid, and kids find cartoon violence funny. It's Lisa, not Bart, who comes up with the idea of the Simpson kids writing an episode of 'Itchy & Scratchy' themselves, and she's an equal partner in their elaborate schemes to cajole their parents into taking them to the Itchy & Scratchy Land theme park. When Lisa returns from seeing *Itchy & Scratchy: The Movie,* her enthusiasm is decidedly girlish: she's covered from head to toe in Itchy & Scratchy paraphernalia as she raves all kidlike about the greatest cinematic event of her life. 'You wouldn't believe the celebrities who did cameos! Dustin Hoffman, Michael Jackson – of course, they didn't use their real names, but you could tell it was them.' Here again we see the tricky equilibrium of Lisa's character: her clothing and demeanour and tone are pure eight-year-old, but the *object* of her passion – celebrity cameos – is at least teenaged. No matter how precocious she gets, Lisa still retains an aura of innocence.

This is, however, a delicate balance, and sometimes it spills over in the direction of maturity. Consider, for example, her relationship with her favourite doll. Malibu Stacy is Springfield's answer to Barbie: a beautiful blonde rendered in impossibly curvaceous plastic whose many accessories are the must-have toys of every little girl in town.[6] Lisa is no exception: she's as delighted as can be when Homer, flush with gambling winnings, showers her with practically every Malibu Stacy accessory there is (though the store was, alas, sold out of Malibu Stacy lunar rovers). But Lisa's play does have its intellectual touches. Her Stacy, for example, lives for a time in a shoebox done up as a modern studio apartment, complete with a workspace where she prints a feminist newsletter. And when Lisa finally obtains a coveted talking Malibu Stacy, her first moments with her new doll have her acting out a scenario in which Stacy gives a speech to the United Nations. 'A hush falls over the general assembly as Stacy approaches the podium to deliver what will no doubt be a stirring and memorable address,' Lisa narrates. She pulls the doll's cord. Stacy: 'I wish they taught shopping in school!' Lisa pulls the cord again. Stacy: 'Let's bake some cookies for the boys!' Lisa pleads with the doll: 'Come on, Stacy – I've waited my whole life to hear you speak. Don't you have anything relevant to say?' Again she pulls the cord. And Stacy delivers her most vacant line yet: 'Don't ask me – I'm just a girl.'

Then Malibu Stacy giggles coquettishly, and in that sound you can almost hear Lisa's internal equilibrium tipping. Listen to it reverberate, as if in an echo chamber – it doesn't, actually, in the episode itself, but stay with me here – listen to it reverberate, as Lisa the little girl gives way to Lisa the cultural critic and to Lisa the existential hero, driven first to despair and then to radical action by the empty platitudes of the modern world.

Driven, in short, to become Lisa Lionheart.

LISA LIONHEART (I): EXISTENTIAL ANGST & CULTURAL CRITICISM

Lisa's dissatisfaction with modern life is primarily a product of that great intangible burden of Western society in the second half of the twentieth century: existential angst. And so, appropriately enough, Lisa first and most prominently expresses her own case of the modernist blues through two of its first and most prominent pop-cultural manifestations: free-form poetry and jazz music. Lisa's been hepcatting her way through her own existential crisis since Season 1, when she arrives at the kitchen table in the opening scene of Episode 7G06 ('Moaning Lisa') too bummed out to eat her breakfast. Later that day, her status-quo music teacher, Mr Largo, cuts off her 'crazy bebop' improvisations on 'My Country 'Tis of Thee'. Lisa pleads her case. 'I'm wailing out for the homeless family living out of a car,' she tells her teacher. 'The idle farmer whose land has been taken away by uncaring bureaucrats. The West Virginia coal miner caught ...' But Mr Largo interrupts her. None of those unpleasant people, he points out, will be at the Springfield Elementary recital. And so by lunchtime Lisa has a Camus-sized case of the blues. 'Every day at noon a bell rings,' she notes flatly, 'and they herd us in here to feeding time. So we sit around like cattle, chewing our cud, dreading the inevitable.'

That evening, she explains her mood to her father: 'I'm just wondering what's the point? Would it make any difference at all if I never existed? How can we sleep at night when there's so much suffering in the world?' Homer, trying to cheer her up, offers her a horsey-back ride, but as Sartre surely could've told him, that's no consolation. What *is*, though, is her chance encounter with Bleeding Gums Murphy, a legendary saxophone player.[7] After an evening belting out a down-and-dirty blues number with Murphy and another spent watching him wail at the Jazz Hole, Lisa finds a mix of acceptance, commiseration and self-expression that gives her enough energy to soldier on with the Sisyphean task of being an eight-year-old in a cold, meaningless world.

Lisa's despair is never far from the surface, though. When Bart destroys the centrepiece she spent hours making for her family's Thanksgiving feast – 'a tribute to the trailblazing women who made our country great,' she explains – Lisa is devastated. Retreating to her room, she finds some cold comfort in her saxophone before turning to the embrace of that other great salve for the aching existential soul: Beat poetry. Lisa sets to composing 'Howl of the Unappreciated.' 'I saw the best meals of my generation destroyed by the madness of my brother,' she writes, seated at her desk beneath a shelf tellingly lined with volumes of Kerouac and Ginsberg. 'My soul carved in slices by spiky-haired demons.'

And so it goes for poor oversensitive Lisa. On her eighth birthday, faced with her own looming mortality, she takes solace in writing 'Meditations on Turning Eight' ('I had a cat named Snowball / She died, she died! / Mom said she was sleeping / She lied, she lied!'). Let down by her father before the Super Bowl, she spends the game blasting out searing riffs of heartache on her sax. After the first few seasons of the series, the fact of Lisa's angst has become so central to her character – so *given* – that it's rarely illustrated in this kind of detail. Instead, it's the understood precondition for her sharp criticisms of the status quo and the foundation of her passionate activism, and it needs no further explanation.

You can see this at work even as early as Season 2. In Episode 7F21 ('Three Men and a Comic Book'), Lisa attends a comic-book convention with her brother, picking up a few copies of *Casper the Friendly Ghost* and *Richie Rich* comics for herself. (There's that adult/kid balance again: Ginsberg-reading Lisa buys age-appropriate kiddie comics.) On the drive home from the convention, Bart speculates that Casper is in fact Richie Rich's ghost. 'Wonder how he died?' says Bart. Lisa: 'Perhaps he realised how hollow the pursuit of money really is and took his own life.' Another time, Bart stumbles on a stack of portraits of Ringo Starr in the Simpsons' attic and shows them to the family. They turn out to be the work of a young Marge. 'Hey, Mom, these paintings are good,' Lisa observes. 'While I know first-hand how fragile young talent is, I'd love to hear the particulars of how *your* gift was squashed.'

There's a particularly revealing instance of Lisa's world-weariness in Episode 2F07 ('Grampa vs. Sexual Inadequacy'), in which old Abe Simpson brews up a powerful aphrodisiac, an 1800s-style patent medicine that soon has couples all over Springfield drawing their curtains early. Springfield's kids are baffled by the sudden urge of every parent in town to go to bed before dark, but Bart and Milhouse gather the kids in Bart's tree house to hash out an explanation: it's a massive conspiracy. Bart – given of late to reading books about UFOs – thinks it's painfully clear that Springfield's adults are paving the way for an alien invasion, while Milhouse (evidently under the influence of Oliver Stone's film *JFK*) sees a massive government conspiracy. They wrestle (literally) over their disagreement until Lisa – scientifically reasonable, ultra-realistic Lisa – breaks up the fight. 'Why are you guys jumping to such ridiculous conclusions?' she remonstrates. 'Haven't you ever heard of Occam's Razor? "The simplest explanation is probably the correct one."'

'So what's the simplest explanation?' Bart asks condescendingly.

'I don't know,' Lisa replies, dripping sarcasm. 'Maybe they're all reverse vampires and they have to get home before dark.'

The rest of the kids miss the joke and erupt in a fresh panic over the imminent attack of the reverse vampires. And Lisa, exhausted, heaves a mighty sigh.

It's entirely appropriate to Lisa's time – and her place in it – that she's the most world-weary Simpson, the one with the greatest sense of what's wrong with the world, the one who vacillates between optimism and despair. For if Homer is the quintessential Baby Boomer and Bart is the punk-age nihilist, then Lisa is the embodiment of so-called Generation X: the generation so jaded that one of the few times it rose to speak in one voice was to reject its own label, the very idea of a 'generation'. While Homer lives content in the knowledge that he has inherited the world and Bart plots to destroy it entirely, Lisa can only sigh at the futility of her own convictions. Lisa's not quite a perfect representative of 1990s youth – her activism has always been too close to the surface, her optimism too resilient. But she's got certain of their characteristics in spades – the strong commitment to tolerance and the cultural relativism, in particular. And on occasion, Lisa's resolve fails her, and she lapses into overly introspective Gen-X navel-gazing, withdrawing in disgust from mainstream society and lobbing ironic quips about 'reverse vampires' and such with exhausted detachment. This is the reflexive cynicism that was misinterpreted as apathy by the Boomer-aged pundits who 'defined' the youth of the 1990s in the mainstream media. In an uncharacteristically dispassionate moment, Bart tells his father, 'Nothing you say can upset us. We're the MTV generation.' Lisa, on more familiar ground, adds, 'We feel neither highs nor lows.' Homer, amazed: 'Really? What's that like?' Lisa, in a perfect semiotic reduction of the default defensive posture of her age, merely shrugs: 'Enh.'

LIKE, YOU KNOW, WHATEVER: IRONIC CULTURE & THE SLEEK SURFACE OF MODERNITY

A world-weary sigh, an indifferent shrug: two powerful signposts marking the turf of youth culture in the 1990s. On the one hand there is the land of the sigh, signifying a young life lived under the weight of too much information, too many horrors and dark truths revealed, too much innocence lost far too soon. This is a neighbourhood filled with the long shadows of the Vietnam War and Cold War *realpolitik* and the failed dreams of the 1960s, a place populated by kids who observed their parents' nostalgic memories of sex and drugs and rock & roll through the lens of their own degraded age – a time of AIDS epidemics, crack addiction and meaningless hyper-corporate pop. On the other hand there is the shrug, the surrendering salute of a land of flatness, of impermanence, a neighbourhood of cheap façades where nothing – not marriage, not God, not even the earth itself – *nothing* can be counted on to last, a place where caring and passion are inextricably linked to betrayal and loss. 'I have seen too much / I haven't seen enough / You haven't seen it / I'll laugh until my head comes off / Women and children first.' So sings Thom Yorke on 'Idioteque', a track from the 2000 album *Kid A* by Radiohead. Seeing too much or maybe too little or maybe both, and laughing at it all, certainly, even as the ship goes down and the children run for the lifeboats – this has long been the nature of reality for the kids who came of age in the *Simpsons* era.

Let's start with the shrug, the dark laughter, the sense that there's nothing really worth giving a shit about. Or, more to the point, that it's not at all cool to give a shit about anything. This is the tyranny of cool.

The idea of cool originates with Lisa's beloved jazz musicians and the Beat-generation hipsters who brought their music – as well as their lifestyle and its preferred pose – to a mainstream audience in the 1950s. Cool, at its birth, was a direct by-product of heroin use: cool was a statement of detachment, a self-imposed distance from strong emotion of any sort that mimicked the impassive mindset of the heroin high. Through the Beats, through iconic film performances (especially those of Marlon Brando in *The Wild One* and James Dean in *Rebel Without a Cause*), and eventually through rock & roll, cool moved from the bebop fringes to the very centre of the emerging youth culture of the 1950s and 1960s. By the time The Beatles and Rolling Stones launched the British invasion, circa 1964, cool was the price of admission to the counterculture and the supreme goal of Western youth. And thus codified, it became the most resilient element of youth culture, maintaining its pride of place even as countless cultural trends came and went, surviving more or less intact to Lisa Simpson's day.

The attainment of cool is all over Lisa's radical self-transformation in Episode 3F22 ('Summer of 4 Ft. 2'). Tired of being unpopular, Lisa decides to redefine herself for the Simpsons' summer vacation at a cottage in Little Pwagmattasquarmsettport. She replaces her red dress and pearls with hip threads and sunglasses, and abandons her brainy diction and intellectual pursuits for the 'like, you know, whatever' indifference of the hip preteen. Sure enough, the makeover works, and Lisa quickly makes some cool friends. She takes them to the local library's abandoned parking lot, where there's plenty of room for skateboarding, and where she and her new pal Erin engage in some archetypically cool banter. 'I usually hang out in front,' Lisa says, explaining how she knew about the library. Erin: 'You like to hang out too?' Lisa, flatly: 'Well, it sure beats doing stuff.' Erin, with finality: 'Yeah. Stuff sucks.'

But being cool is a delicate state of grace. Once her new friends learn (from a yearbook supplied by Bart) that Lisa was until recently a yearbook editor, spelling-bee queen and bookwormish teacher's pet – that, in short, Lisa does stuff, that she *cares* – her aura of cool is gone forever. Somewhat implausibly, the episode closes with a sentimental reconciliation, as Lisa's friends accept her for who she truly is.

Real cool, however, is never this forgiving. And *The Simpsons'* writers know it, as they demonstrate in the final scene of Episode 3F21 ('Homerpalooza'), which is set against the backdrop of the most effective disseminator of cool the world has yet devised: pop music. In the episode, Homer's new career as the star of the freak show in a travelling rock festival earns him the unprecedented admiration of his son. At the start of the episode, Homer's carpool lectures about Grand Funk Railroad are a source of shame for Bart, who tells Homer he wouldn't 'par-tay' with him if he was the last dad on earth. But now that Homer's on tour with a host of hip bands, Bart peppers his father with questions for a school assignment on the person Bart admires most. Alas, Homer's freak-show act – taking cannonballs in the gut – does so much internal damage that he has to quit the tour. As he drives back from his last performance, he learns that his kids no longer think of him as cool, and moreover that he no longer even knows what cool is:

Homer:	So, I realised that being with my family is more important than being cool.
Bart:	Dad, what you just said was powerfully uncool.
Homer:	You know what the song says: 'It's hip to be square.'
Lisa:	That song is so lame.
Homer:	So lame that it's . . . cool?
Bart and Lisa:	No.
Marge:	Am I cool, kids?
Bart and Lisa:	No.
Marge:	Good. I'm glad. And that's what makes me cool: not caring. Right?
Bart and Lisa:	No.
Marge:	Well, how the hell do you be cool? I feel like we've tried everything here.

Homer: Wait, Marge. Maybe if you're truly cool, you don't need to be told
          you're cool.
Bart: Well, sure you do.
Lisa: How else would you know?

How else would you know, indeed? You need to be told.

That's the thing about cool: it's perpetual, but it's also in perpetual motion. 'Cool's eternal but it's always dated' – so sang the erudite anti-corporate punk band Fugazi circa 1993. Cool feeds on newness and originality, and it needs to be fed constantly. No wonder, then – as Thomas Frank explains at length in his 1997 book *The Conquest of Cool* – that cool has been the strongest tool in the mass-marketeer's arsenal more or less as long as cool has existed. In many ways, it is a product not of countercultural artists but of advertising copywriters and corporate-media scribes. The common image of the hippie was as much a product of the mass media as it was of anything going down at the corner of Haight and Ashbury in San Francisco, and Volkswagen's self-mocking ads for the diminutive Beetle pre-dated – and predicted – the ad parodies of the 'culture jamming' movement of the 1990s by a good three decades.

Cool – even in its most rebellious poses – has always been as much a marketing strategy as a cultural force. And this fact has only grown more undeniable as the armies of corporate marketing have grown more powerful, more ubiquitous and more stealthy. In the 1990s the relationship between sub- or countercultural cool and big-business marketing became so cosy and symbiotic that it approximated a single cohesive whole. Whether it was the dressed-down looks and fuck-it-all poses of grunge or the logoed sportswear and get-paid vibe of hip-hop or anything else that had about it a whiff of cool, fashion and style in the 1990s moved from urban street to boardroom to suburban strip mall in a process so smooth it could provide a semester's worth of case studies for Harvard Business School. Pop icons aspired to self-incorporation (see the ascending mogulhood of Sean 'Puff Daddy' Combs or the corporate machine that is the contemporary Rolling Stones), while mammoth advertising agencies talked about 'guerrilla campaigns' and sent 'street teams' into urban neighbourhoods to spray-paint corporate logos illicitly. Indeed there's a whole agency – Electric Artists of New York – that specialises in 'viral marketing', which consists primarily of having in-the-know twentysomethings hang out in Internet chat rooms talking up the hip-seeking brands represented by the agency. (Electric Artists first hit the public radar when it was given credit for being a key player in creating the online buzz that helped launch the intergalactic superstardom of Christina Aguilera. Its client list now includes the pharmaceutical giant Pfizer and the household-product conglomerate Procter & Gamble in addition to practically every record label in the free world.)

Cool is the lifeblood of consumerism, and so as consumerism has sped up and spread out, so too has cool. It is everywhere, and it is a tyranny. The default pose of cool's most slavish devotees is best represented by the stereotypical slacker who appears for a brief moment in Episode 1F21 ('Lady Bouvier's Lover') to express the cynicism of his age. The slacker's cameo is occasioned by an infomercial – starring Troy McClure, of course – hawking genuine hand-drawn 'Itchy & Scratchy' animation cels. This, McClure states, is 'your chance to own a piece of Itchy and Scratchy, the toontown twosome beloved by everyone – even cynical members of Generation X!' Cut to the slacker dude, sprawled on his couch watching the infomercial. 'Pffft, yeah,' he says sardonically, his hands rising to make ironic quotation marks. 'Groovy.'

Those ironic quotation marks are as strong a symbol as any of the way consumer-driven cool became a pose of blanket ironic detachment that permeated every corner of pop culture in the 1990s. And irony refers only to a subset of the bigger picture, that wide array of attitudes, styles, modes of discourse and expression that have emerged collectively as testament to the extraordinary sophistication of the kind of consumerism now practised by young people in the post-industrial West. Think here of logo-parodying T-shirts (ENJOY COCA-COLA becomes ENJOY COCAINE); of advertising meticulously crafted to anticipate and derail cynicism about advertising (Sprite's 'Taste is Everything' campaign comes to mind); of getting your news via late-night-TV monologues; of the so-bad-it's-good movie; of the dominant tone of the discussions in many online forums. Recall that the Spice Girls movie, *Spice World*, was knowing and self-referential and self-parodying. So are many beer commercials. All of this, taken together, is what it looks like when a culture moves from merely nibbling at its own tail to devouring it in exquisite eight-course meals. The Renaissance Man may be dead, classical education all but forgotten, but our streets teem with professional consumers of the highest calibre. We know how our products are packaged, how our media content is produced, and we will only buy those products that let us know that they know that we know.

One of the undisputed kings of this stance is the satirical online newspaper *The Onion*. Born as a student humour newspaper at the University of Wisconsin in the 1980s, *The Onion* became one of the hippest (and funniest) websites in cyberspace soon after it went online in 1996. (It has since been spun off into several bestselling books, among them *Our Dumb Century*, *Dispatches from the Tenth Circle*, and an annual almanac called *The Onion Ad Nauseam*.)

The core of *The Onion*'s readership, though, remains the million-plus Net surfers who read it online every week. And what they find at theonion.com is a note-perfect parody of your average dumbed-down newspaper. Indeed, *The Onion* is overtly modelled on the pioneer of dimwitted print news, *USA Today*, complete with lots of full-colour photos, trivialising infographics and a weekly 'talking heads' survey of the opinions of random Americans on a given issue called 'What Do You Think?' The big gag in 'What Do You Think?' is that in addition to being totally fabricated by the paper's writers – as is all of *The Onion*'s 'news' content – it uses the same six photos of the same six people every week. The names and occupations and comments change, but the same six heads reappear. And of course the opinions remain uniformly vacuous.

Beyond these *USA Today* touches, *The Onion* is a magnificently executed parody of the daily newspaper in general – indeed, of the very notion of 'news'. As with *The Simpsons*, *The Onion*'s success was predicated on the notion that the average young reader was potentially cynical about anything that was happening in the world, from presidential politics to international conflict. The paper's headlines are often perfectly rendered minimalist portraits of the biases and banalities of the daily news, whether the given topic is international affairs ('Crazed Palestinian Gunman Angered By Stereotypes', 'U.N. Factoid-Finding Mission Discovers Liberia About The Size Of Tennessee'); national news ('The JFK Jr. Tragedy: About A Year Or So Later'); scientific breakthroughs ('Marijuana Linked To Sitting Around And Getting High'); or the annals of big business ('Just Six Corporations Remain'). And then there's *The Onion*'s sublime take on local news, which documents the uneventful lives of 'area men' and 'local women' in an extended lampoon of the way newspapers churn out non-news to fill space ('Area Man Consults Internet Whenever Possible') and also manages to satirise slyly the trivialities of contemporary social life ('Area Man Hasn't Told Co-Workers About His Billy Joel Fanpage Yet,' 'Local Hipster Over-Explaining Why He Was At The Mall').

The site's deadpan news parodies have also proven remarkably adept at cataloguing the variant strains of unease and dissatisfaction floating freely through the culture. *The Onion* speaks, frequently, to the numbness at the core of modernity. 'Aging Gen-Xer Doesn't Find Bad Movies Funny Anymore.' 'Twelve Customers Gunned Down In Convenience-Store Clerk's

Imagination.' 'Klingon Speakers Now Outnumber Navajo Speakers.' 'Fast-Food Purchase Seething With Unspoken Class Conflict.' 'Everything In Entire World Now Collectible.' 'Account Manager Fondly Remembers Day In College When Everyone Hung Out On Roof.' 'U.S. Dept. Of Retro Warns: "We May Be Running Out Of Past."' 'New Crispy Snack Cracker To Ease Crushing Pain Of Modern Life.'

In the writings of the Situationists – the French activist-philosophers whose ideas were a primary force behind the Paris student uprising of 1968 – modern capitalist society is described as a world of pure spectacle, incapable of providing any real benefit or meaning to anyone outside the ruling bloc. Alongside calls to revolution, the Situationists advocated political activities that would draw people's attention to the fact of this spectacle, the absurdity of the society. This is what *The Onion* does on its best days.

Unintentionally ironic culture, though, is rarely this weighty. *The Onion*'s sustained satirical attack on the daily newspaper injects its readers with a strong dose of healthy scepticism about the media's pretensions to objective truth, but most ironic icons serve only to remind us of the sheer volume of trash churned out by mass culture and reward our cynical selves for being above such dross. Think, for example, of one of the few so-bad-it's-good movies that comes anywhere close to being a universal touchstone: Ed Wood's *Plan 9 from Outer Space* (1959), a movie whose comically clumsy acting and laughably inept special effects are so infamous that it's become a staple of many repertory cinemas. *Plan 9* is the pioneering clunker of so-bad-it's-good movies, inspiring generations of moviegoers to take up the hobby of laughing at the worst of Hollywood's increasingly frequent follies. Indeed *Plan 9* is so well known that it even inspired a big-budget homage to its director – Tim Burton's 1994 film *Ed Wood*, with Johnny Depp in the title role of American cinema's most beloved cross-dressing hack. But then consider that film's tender portrayal of Wood as a passionate, guileless man whose love of movies is so boundless that he wills himself into the director's chair and forces his films onto the screen despite his total lack of any real talent for film-making. *Ed Wood* is ultimately an homage not to sneering irony but to wide-eyed innocence. Contrast this with the contemporary films that have carried on *Plan 9*'s tradition of being watchable only as accidental comedies. Think of the fantastically ill-conceived sci-fi epic *Battlefield Earth* (2000), or of the bombastic *Independence Day* (1996), or of the many monuments to the oversized egos engendered by the modern entertainment industry (Madonna in *Swept Away*, George Lucas in *Star Wars Episode II: Attack of the Clones*, Mariah Carey in *Glitter*, Kevin Costner in *The Postman*, million-dollar-salaried screenwriter Joe Eszterhas in *Showgirls*, ad infinitum). Laugh at these, and you're participating in a kind of meta-cynicism, chuckling cynically at the professional cynicism of the corporate studios and the focus-group-derived, test-screened committee thinking that leads to the green-lighting of this crap.

Or think of your personal touchstones of ironic culture. For every *Plan 9* or *Showgirls* or widely disseminated MP3 of William Shatner butchering 'Lucy in the Sky with Diamonds', there are countless obscure nuggets of pop-cultural trash that somehow lodge themselves in this or that psyche. I could cite dozens from my own experience, but I'll stick with one of the most pointedly obscure: an early-1990s TV commercial for Benylin, an over-the-counter flu medicine. The ad was set in a medical-school classroom, with a hard-nosed professor grilling his students on the proper diagnosis of the flu. The prof asks what should be prescribed for the ailment, and one hapless sap blurts out, 'Cold medication . . . I mean *flu* medication.' He slaps at his skull, amazed at his error. As were my friends and I: there was probably a solid year of our lives during which the mere recitation of the line 'Cold medication . . . I mean *flu* medication' could reduce us to braying laughter. I mean, can you imagine the sheer stupidity – not of this one student, but of the whole damn premise of the ad? That a solemn med-school lecture would focus on an illness that every mother on the planet can diagnose? That one of the students would be so flustered by the lecture's gravitas that he'd blurt out 'cold' instead of 'flu'? That people got paid – got paid *well* – to write this shit, act in it, film it?

This has long been one of my favourite masochistic pastimes: sitting in a mind-meltingly dumb movie, calculating all the things I could have done with the tens of millions of dollars it cost to make it. Thinking that in my entire life I'd never see as much money as it cost to make, market and distribute, for example, *The Astronaut's Wife*, a 1999 sci-fi movie so bad that it couldn't hold my attention even though I saw it in Bangkok and it was the first North American-accented English I'd heard in months. In my experience, this is the ultimate by-product of ironic culture: a kind of maniacally amused frustration at the wastefulness and vacuousness and stupidity of the whole society.

And then, of course, once you've settled down a bit, you're ready once again to shrug it off.

In recent years, even when movies – arguably the dominant medium of the 1990s, particularly in terms of sheer star-making and spectacle-building might – aren't appalling, they rarely have very much to say. Mainstream movies have certainly become brilliant marketing and money-making vehicles, perfecting the art of the six-month promotional campaign and the product tie-in, ever more adept in the ways of selling themselves across demographic and geographic borders. But how many of them really affect your understanding of the world?

This is true not just of big, dumb action movies but even of some of the most resonant films of the 1990s. Films like *Reservoir Dogs* (1992), *Pulp Fiction* (1994), *Swingers* (1996), *Trainspotting* (1996) and *Being John Malkovich* (1999) may have struck deep chords and won rabid fans, but their reverberations were discernible primarily in brief trends in music, fashion and slang. In other words, in the iconography of cool. They are all indeed eminently cool films – *cool* as in detached, ironic, referential. This tone is particularly prevalent in *Reservoir Dogs* and *Pulp Fiction*, the pair of Quentin Tarantino crime movies that set the tone for hip filmmaking in the 1990s. Both feature countless references to other films, both pointedly subvert the impact of horrific violence, and both revel in the ironic juxtaposition of said violence with banal, pop-culture-obsessed dialogue. In fact, there might be no better example of ironic culture than the scene in *Reservoir Dogs* in which Michael Madsen dances whimsically to a throwaway 1970s pop confection – Stealers Wheel's 'Stuck in the Middle with You' – and then sets about hacking off a kidnapped police officer's right ear while the same bouncy tune plays on. This is the cultural tone of the age in a single vignette: backward-looking, trivia-centred, self-possessed, and offhandedly vicious. Also technically sound, gorgeously shot, clever as hell and somehow very, very hollow.

Films like *Reservoir Dogs* were not the kind of movies that changed what you thought about the world, really; instead, they changed the way you thought about *movies*. This is true of many of the other great filmmakers to emerge in recent years. In a series of films in the 1980s and 1990s – among them *Miller's Crossing* (1990), *Barton Fink* (1991), *Fargo* (1996) and *The Big Lebowski* (1998) – the Coen Brothers have masterfully reworked Hollywood's most beloved myths. Wes Anderson's brilliant fables *Bottle Rocket* (1996), *Rushmore* (1998) and *The Royal Tenenbaums* (2001) together provide valuable lessons in the construction of perfectly realised parallel universes. Even Steven Soderbergh's overtly political 2000 double bill, *Erin Brockovich* and *Traffic*, simply hammered home long-standing arguments ('large corporations are careless and cynical' and 'the War on Drugs is a misguided failure', respectively), speaking most loudly and originally on the subject of how to turn TV-movie-of-the-week fare into stylish, artful cinema.

This, then, was the state of the Hollywood art. There were good movies about making movies and bad movies about making money, but there were few films that spoke directly to their age in the tradition of *Easy Rider* or *The Graduate* or *Apocalypse Now* or *Heathers* – or even *Top Gun*, which, lest we forget, precipitated a dramatic rise in US Navy enrolment in the mid-1980s.

There was one exception, a micro-genre I'll refer to as the entropy movie. The genre hit its commercial apex with Sam Mendes's *American Beauty*, but it also includes Ang Lee's *The Ice Storm*, Robert Altman's *Short Cuts*, David Fincher's *Fight Club*, P.T. Anderson's *Boogie Nights* and *Magnolia*, several Richard Linklater films (*Slacker*, *Dazed and Confused* and especially *Suburbia*), and the collected works of Neil LaBute and Todd Solondz. These films were often but not always set in faceless suburbs; what unites them, however, is not the physical but the *psychological* setting: these are movies peopled by characters whose detachment is so complete, their numbness so totally isolating, that the moral compass that should be guiding human interaction is either broken or warped or else entirely absent. These are movies that explore Lisa Simpson's weary sigh at length, spinning it out until it is no longer (as it is with Lisa) a sign of occasional resignation but an act of total surrender. In an entropy movie, characters have to beat the shit out of each other or swap spouses at key parties to feel the most basic sense of community; they find belonging not in their homes but on the sets of porn movies; they engage in brutal emotional warfare with each other simply because they can get away with it. In these films, priorities have become so arbitrary, and thus so skewed, that the characters are like molecules firing off randomly as an elaborate system collapses into disorder. Into entropy.

What, after all, is the greatest outrage in *American Beauty* – that the protagonist lusts after his daughter's friend? That he acts on that lust? Or that he, his wife, his daughter, his neighbours – all of them – have built worlds for themselves in which they can barely remember what it means to be passionate? All, that is, except the strange, intense, self-confident Ricky with his digital video camera. It is Ricky who sets *American Beauty* apart from most entropy movies, because it is he who points the way out. *Fight Club* ends with nihilism, *Boogie Nights* with chaos, *The Ice Storm* with quiet desperation. But in Ricky's simple video of a plastic bag dancing in the wind – such a pointedly ugly and banal object, such a powerful symbol of synthetic, antiseptic, generic modernity – there is a bold, simple declaration: this is beautiful. Even this. If you look the right way, anything is. Care about this, or about anything else, but *care*. Start with that.

The numbness, though, could prove very hard to shake. This was an era, after all, characterised by unprecedented levels of prescription-drug use, of parents gobbling Prozac and Zoloft to fight off creeping depression while they fed their kids Ritalin to keep them in line. And it was a time, too, during which the most fashionable new recreational drug – Ecstasy – provided not psyche-delic visions of a better reality but a hyper-energised escape into an alternate universe free of the lethargy, confusion and social awkwardness of daily life.

Further promises of escape abounded. There were videogame worlds of increasing depth and beauty that inched ever closer to the ultimate escapist goal of virtual reality. There was the 'consensual hallucination' of cyberspace (to use William Gibson's seminal phrase), a fantastically vast parallel universe where community and truth and the self could all be reinvented at will. Other consensual hallucinations took place in a stock market full of temporary paper millionaires, in a universe of political theory where history itself was finished, in a working world where actual physical labour and the boundaries between employer and worker and between work and leisure would soon, it was said, be eliminated. And there were genetic-engineering breakthroughs right out of the pages of a sci-fi novel, amazing discoveries that offered tantalising visions of a near-future where illness, aging, physical and mental deformity, even death itself were gone forever. This was a half-realised world of flawless automation, of physical perfection, of sleek, clean surfaces. This was modernity, perfected.

And yet alongside all this (for some at least) there was a coldness, a creeping dread, a sense that certain fundamental things had been lost or destroyed. Things like the stability of family and/or a lifetime of steady work and/or a society that looked and felt like it did last week, the idea of a benevolent god at the controls, the grim but unifying certainty of a big enemy over the horizon. There was even the horrific possibility that the planet itself (or at least its thermostat) was irrevocably damaged. But what to do with such feelings, couched as they sometimes were in the terminology of irrational emotion and superstitious hunch (or at least as-yet-unproven theory)? What use was such timid apprehension in the age of market populism, the time after history's final perfect end when free markets and technological genius were a few short weeks away – a year, tops – from realising the long-promised utopia of a global liberal democracy?

But then what to do with the increasing evidence that this emerging world order had an indifference verging on contempt for any human need that couldn't be bought or sold, that couldn't be measured by polling data, that didn't in some way contribute to per-capita GDP or the balance sheet of a multinational corporation? What to do, in short, about all these hairline fissures on the sleek surface of modernity?

Well, for one thing, you could listen to Radiohead. You could listen, especially, to the band's 1997 album, *OK Computer*, which was released right around the moment that those cracks seemed too definite to deny any longer. The album opens with a sort of rebirth: the near-death experience of a car crash, with salvation courtesy of technological progress ('Airbag'). Over the 11 loosely linked tracks that follow, it's as if the accident has caused a subtle but potentially fatal case of schizophrenia, as the songs' narrators reel desperately from scenes of madness and terror to visions of escape, retribution and narcotised peace. Throughout, the marvels of the modern world that saved lives in the opening track (neon signs, intastella bursts, the airbags in fast German cars) are recast as cogs in a soulless, inescapable machine. Lightning-fast transportation only leaves us let down and hangin' around; we are haunted by buzzing fridges and detuned radios; alarms are not only incapable of ensuring safety but are themselves a clanging tyranny. Vast swaths of *OK Computer* sound like the kind of twitching, nerve-shredding blowout that must precede road rage, or a killing spree, or the nervous breakdown of a middle manager who winds up dead in a suburban garage full of carbon monoxide. Amazingly, the album – this seething mass of noisy nightmares and twisted revenge fantasies – became immensely popular. It was one of those albums that seemed to speak directly to its time, giving voice to all the fears and doubts its millions of listeners had as they flew through their lives at Internet speed.

As with Nirvana's misconstrued *Nevermind*, *OK Computer* was so awash in anguish and despair that it was easy to miss the torrid, cathartic rage at its core. The latter was lifted explicitly to the surface in the video for 'Karma Police'. The video tells a muddled tale: lead singer Thom Yorke sits in the back seat of a car that rolls slowly down a dark country road. A desperate man in corporate-issue white dress shirt and slacks – not a captain of industry, clearly, just a post-industrial working stiff – is trapped in the car's headlights, arms flailing as he runs, his doom seemingly assured. 'This is what you get,' Yorke sings, his voice barely above a whisper, but firm and self-assured. 'This is what you get when you mess with us.' The man caught in the headlights stops. The car stops and reverses, leaving a trail of leaking gas between it and the man. The man sets it alight, and the car is quickly engulfed in flames. The back seat of the car, though, is now empty. Only the driver of the car – from whose perspective we view the entire video – is consumed. The viewer is left with the certainty that righteous vengeance was carried out. But upon whose guilty soul? Who was driving the car?

There is varying evidence of the driver's identity elsewhere on *OK*

Computer. There are networking yuppies and 'kicking, squealing Gucci little piggies' on 'Paranoid Android', and madly ambitious politicians armed with riot shields and voodoo economics, cattle prods and the IMF, on 'Electioneering'. On 'Exit Music (for a Film)' there is an unnamed enemy who wields rules and wisdom and laughs a spineless laugh. Or perhaps the driver is us, all of us, 'all these weird creatures who lock up their spirits / Drill holes in themselves and live for their secrets', as aliens hovering above our planet observe on 'Subterranean Homesick Alien'.

On *OK Computer*'s follow-up, 2000's *Kid A*, these oppressive forces are all-encompassing. If *OK Computer* felt like a full-throated warning of imminent collapse, a kind of digital-age musical update of Allen Ginsberg's 'Howl', then *Kid A* sounds like a news report from the rubble. The sense of terrible inevitability that permeates the album is a kind of dark mirror of the triumphal narrative then playing out in the business sections of Western newspapers and the boardrooms of Silicon Valley venture capitalists. Arriving as it did at the end of a period of prosperous complacency, Radiohead's anguish came as a powerful rebuke, a kind of oblique dissent. A voice, finally, for the growing number of people in the West who couldn't see their salvation in the steep, vertical line graphs of the Dow and NASDAQ indexes, who found no lasting solace in Internet chat rooms.

By the time of Radiohead's 2001 album, *Amnesiac*, the voice seems to have backed off from the abyss. On *Amnesiac* there is instead – albeit sporadically – renewed strength and redoubled defiance. On 'I Might Be Wrong', there is even a mood that verges on genuine optimism:

> I might be wrong
> I might be wrong
> I could have sworn
> I saw a light coming on
>
> I used to think
> I used to think
> There is no future left at all
> I used to think
>
> Open up, begin again . . .

Suddenly, there is a light – dim though it may be, wrong though Yorke may be – at the end of the tunnel. The afterglow, perhaps, of the battle of Seattle?

Perhaps, yes, because even as Radiohead toiled in the studio throughout 1999 and early 2000 on the recording sessions that would yield both *Kid A* and *Amnesiac*, there was all of a sudden a huge and energetic protest movement chasing international trade organisations around the globe. As the world's newspapers recorded in startled headlines, the anti-globalisation movement announced its existence in dramatic fashion, with tens of thousands of protesters filling the streets of Seattle, Washington, in November 1999 to bring a World Trade Organization (WTO) meeting to a screeching halt. Stealthily organised online, and uniting disaffected groups ranging from huge old-school trade unions to single-issue environmental groups and (famously) balaclava-clad anarchists, the Seattle protest was a shock – both in its size and its intensity – after a complacent decade during which the WTO and related organisations (particularly the World Bank and the International Monetary Fund) advanced the cause of liberalising global trade in quiet, orderly near-anonymity. After Seattle, the broadening protest movement transformed a series of subsequent meetings by global capitalism's top proponents around the globe – most notably in Prague, Genoa, Quebec City and Washington – from orderly closed-door affairs into noisy street theatre.

And if this new wave of activism had decided that it needed a poster child, it could easily have looked to the one TV star who railed throughout the complacent 1990s against the very same injustices now being opposed in the streets of Seattle. That TV star, of course, was Lisa Simpson.

LISA LIONHEART (II): LISA THE ACTIVIST

So let's revisit Episode 1F12 ('Lisa vs. Malibu Stacy'). Recall the retrograde bimboisms spouted by her talking Malibu Stacy doll ('Don't ask me – I'm just a girl!') and take note of Lisa's outrage as she sits at the Simpson kitchen table, fuming and plotting. 'They *cannot* keep making dolls like this,' she growls. 'Something has to be done!' The rest of her family, well acquainted with Lisa's politics, tries to dissuade her:

Marge: Lisa, ordinarily I'd say you should stand up for what you believe in. But you've been doing that an awful lot lately.

Bart: Yeah. You made us march in that gay-rights parade [*holds up newspaper featuring photo of gay-pride parade with Bart front and centre, looking bewildered*].

Homer: And we can't watch Fox because they own those chemical-weapons plants in Syria.

But Lisa persists in her anti-Stacy crusade, first with an ineffectual visit to the company that manufactures the dolls (naturally, the company's spokes-woman dismisses Lisa's concerns with smiling corporate efficiency) and then with a visit to the doll's creator, Stacy Lovell (voiced with boozy flintiness by Kathleen Turner). Lovell immediately understands Lisa's concern – she's an ex-activist herself, who spent the early 1970s funnelling profits from sales of her doll to the Viet Cong.[8] After some prodding, she agrees to help Lisa launch a new doll, and the result is 'Lisa Lionheart', an exemplary role model for little girls who says things like 'Trust in yourself and you can achieve anything!' when you pull her string. Alas, the Malibu Stacy people remodel their doll to compete with Lisa Lionheart – they give Stacy a new hat – and only one little girl in the toy-store stampede goes for the Lisa doll.

For Lisa, though, reaching that one girl is enough. She's been an activist for long enough to know that change doesn't happen overnight. So she continues in her role as a steady voice for change in the placid sea of apolitical complacency that is Springfield, USA. And in the myriad causes Lisa has taken up over the years, in the long list of injustices she has decried and the many acts of corporate and political malfeasance she's opposed, we can see a microcosmic history of the rebirth of political activism in the 1990s. If the WTO protests in Seattle in 1999 took the world's political elite and the mainstream press by surprise, it was only because they weren't paying enough attention to Lisa Simpson.

Lisa's activist career includes considerable time spent mucking about in the quicksand of identity politics, political correctness and single-issue crusading that obsessed the political left in the West for much of the 1990s. She chastises her mother for ordering veal, and later becomes a full-fledged vegetarian. She frets about the environment and opposes the keeping of elephants as pets. After being proclaimed Little Miss Springfield, Lisa soon decides to reject her assigned agenda – working as a shill for Laramie Cigarettes – and instead devotes her reign to speaking out against the evils of society ('from dog-napping to cigarettes,' as she puts it). At Hullabalooza, Lisa sings the faint praises of her generation's idealism. 'Generation X may be shallow,' she says, 'but at least they have tolerance and respect for all people.'

This was about all you could hope for among the insular, self-limiting progressive movements of the 1990s. In the face of fast-growing and seemingly unopposable corporate control and the left's own lack of direction in the wake of the collapse of global communism, progressives fought small battles – this approach was even codified in the environmentalist mantra 'Think Globally, Act Locally' – and fell to vicious in-fighting. Though the media-driven backlash against it may have exaggerated the threat, there's no denying that political correctness reduced progressive politics to a near-catastrophic paralysis.[9] I was at university in the early 1990s – probably the most PC place on earth at the most PC time in history – and I remember it as a stiflingly oppressive movement. If you spent any time on campus in those days, you'd be forgiven for thinking that the greatest threats to human civilisation were Eurocentric reading lists and the spelling of the word 'women'. (Wider use of either 'wimmin' or 'womyn' was the first step in toppling the patriarchy.)

The really disheartening thing about political correctness, though, was its apparent love of divisiveness. While I was an undergraduate, a newly elected neoconservative government in Ontario embarked on an escalating series of ill-conceived tuition hikes and funding cuts that drastically reduced the quality of life and learning on the province's campuses. Many students opposed the cuts, but the movement against them was so fractious and certain factions of it so dogmatic that it could attract only the hardcore, identity-politicking left-wingers who were already involved in various campus crusades. And so the rest of us were left to take some grim consolation in the general mood of tolerance and to maintain our personalised commitments to environmentalism and international human rights and so on without having anything close to a unified voice.

On one notable occasion, Lisa's own alleged political correctness brings her up against a backlash. This comes in Episode 3F13 ('Lisa the Iconoclast'), when Lisa's research for a school report on Jebediah Springfield – the town's founder – leads her to discover that old Jebediah was not a noble pioneer but a nasty pirate named Hans Sprungfeld who tried to kill George Washington.[10] Her report, 'Jebediah Springfield: Super Fraud', earns her an F. 'But it's all true,' she tells her teacher, Miss Hoover. Miss Hoover replies with a categorical dismissal lifted straight from the anti-PC screeds of countless outraged right-wing pundits: 'This is nothing but dead-white-male-bashing from a PC thug. It's women like you that keep the rest of us from landing a husband.' But Lisa soldiers on with her research, even going so far as to exhume the body of Jebediah Springfield to prove her argument. And prove it she does, but when she gets a chance to tell the whole town about her discovery at Springfield's bicentennial parade, she loses her nerve. Jebediah, she tells the crowd, was just great. She later tells the local historian who'd helped her with her research that Jebediah's mythic life had brought out the best in the people of Springfield, so there was nothing to be gained by debunking it. This is an act either of impressive restraint or of hypocritical jingoism, depending on your point of view. But I'd wager the activist left would have been a far more effective counterweight to the free-market-*über-alles* crowd in the 1990s if it had had a larger dose of Lisa's pragmatism.

After all, Lisa doesn't back down when victory means not just being right but making the world a better place. In Episode 3F04 ('Treehouse of Horror VI'), for example, Lisa leads a valiant battle against one of the most insidious beasts in modern society: advertising. This takes place during a Halloween segment entitled 'Attack of the 50-Foot Eyesores', in which an ionic disturbance in the Van Allen Belt causes lightning to rain down on Springfield's giant billboards and franchise mascots, bringing them to life to rampage through the town. Naturally, the invasion sends everyone in the town into a panic – everyone, that is, except Lisa, who heads to the advertising agency that created the monsters to figure out how to stop them. 'Well, sir, advertising is a funny thing,' the ad man tells her. 'If people stop paying attention to it, pretty soon it goes away.'

'But people can't help looking at them,' Lisa replies. 'They're wrecking the town.'

'You know,' says the ad man, 'maybe a jingle would help.'

In short order, Lisa takes her anti-ad jingle public, urging Springfield-ianites, in the language of advertising itself, to simply stop looking at the rampaging mascots. It works: the mascots fall over dead as soon as they're denied the public's gaze. This is a concise summary of one of the first tactics employed by the activists who would later play lead roles in the protests against the WTO and the rest in 1999 and 2000. The approach is usually referred to as 'culture jamming', and it's as straightforward as Lisa's anti-ad jingle: you use advertising's own tools against it. 'Subvertise', in the words of one of its foremost practitioners, the Vancouver-based magazine *Adbusters*.

Culture jamming was one of the first effective methods devised for expressing opposition to the amorphous forces of corporate control in the 1990s. It was tentative and sporadic – a defaced billboard here, a logo-parodying T-shirt there – but what made it exciting was that it seemed, finally, to provide a way to speak not just to a single specific act of corporate injustice but rather directly to the entire corporate system. This is not to take anything away from the effective single-issue campaigns of the era. The pan-European protest movement against oil giant Royal Dutch/Shell in 1994 and 1995, for example, stopped an impending environmental disaster – the planned sinking of the Brent Spar oil rig in the North Sea. Similarly, a protest movement that spread through American college campuses in the mid-1990s against the working conditions in the Asian factories that made Nike shoes embarrassed the company into employing full-time inspectors to monitor wages and conditions at those factories. Nothing accomplished by the culture-jamming movement – not even the *Adbusters*-led institution of 'Buy Nothing Day' – can boast these sorts of concrete results.

The real power of culture jamming was symbolic. In the few hours that a billboard for Camel cigarettes survived in its reworked form (depicting the company's mascot receiving chemotherapy); in the ad parodies that filled the pages of *Adbusters*; in the pages of Naomi Klein's *No Logo* (a book that laid out the full scope and force of corporations and their brands and became a bestselling primer for newly minted activists) – in all of these things, the unnamed dread that had been building throughout the decade was finally given a focus, a target and a name. 'Anti-globalisation' may have seemed too limited a term to describe the wide range of grievances being voiced on the streets of Seattle, and the WTO and the World Bank remained half-understood organisations that weren't *literally* responsible for all of these injustices, but that wasn't really the point. The point was that there suddenly seemed to be a way to apprehend the murky forces that were fundamentally altering societies around the world. There was a crack on the surface of corporate power, a thin ray of light, and people jumped at it.

There's a much goofier version of what I'm talking about here at the end of Episode BABF07 ('Grift of the Magi'), in which Kid First Industries has surreptitiously turned Springfield Elementary into a marketing tool. Lisa, as always the first young Springfieldianite to grow suspicious of the machinations of a friendly corporation, soon discovers Kid First's hidden market-research office. But when she brings the local authorities to see it, it's been magically returned to its original trappings as a broom closet. Still, Lisa remains sceptical about Kid First's motives, and when she sees a TV commercial for Funzo, she's certain something's amiss. 'Bart, they lied to us!' she rants to her brother. 'Instead of giving us an education, they tricked us into designing a toy! Aren't you outraged?' Bart: 'No, but if you're gonna throw a spaz, I'll come with.' And so it's off to Kid First's headquarters (which is inexplicably guarded by *Diff'rent Strokes* star Gary Coleman), where Lisa confronts the company's top executives – Jim Hope and the omnipresent Lindsey Naegle – who confirm her suspicions about their manipulation of Springfield Elementary's students but are of course unrepentant. So Lisa tries to organise a Funzo boycott at the Try-N-Save. That fails too. She's ready to give up until the Simpsons' very own anarchist, Bart, proposes a devious plan: they'll get Homer to dress up as Santa and steal the Funzos out from under everyone's Christmas trees. The plan goes off more or less without a hitch until the Simpsons arrive at the town dump to dispose of the Funzos and are confronted by Kid First security guard Gary Coleman. 'Please, Mr Coleman,' Homer tells him, 'we can explain.' And there follows an impassioned debate:

Lisa: Your toy company is evil.

Coleman: Well, isn't it possible for an evil company to make people happy?

Lisa: Are you saying the end justifies the means?

Coleman: That's a very glib interpretation.

Bart: Hey, don't talk to my sister that way!

Lisa: No, Bart, he's right. I *did* oversimplify.

Homer: Perhaps, but let's not get bogged down in semantics. I think what Lisa *meant* to say is . . .

At this point, a narrator's voice intrudes: 'And so Gary Coleman and the Simpsons argued long into the night. And then, as day broke, the spirit of the season entered their hearts.' Lisa then tells Gary Coleman, 'Let's just agree that the commercialisation of Christmas is, at best, a mixed blessing.'

'Amen,' Coleman replies.

Thus, in silly Simpsonian fashion, is the seeming impasse between the pro- and anticorporate camps settled on a fine Christmas morn. Lisa, as the avatar of the protest movement, is willing to admit that she's overstated the crimes of Kid First, and Coleman learns to be less dogmatically committed to his employer's bottom line.

Goofy as this scene is, it'll do as an allegorical rendering of the globalisation debate. The protesters in the streets have been cast as opponents of the very idea of trade – a stance which, though it may seem reasonable to the odd black-clad 19-year-old anarchist, is ludicrous – while the three-piece-suited elites inside the trade meetings have become cackling caricatures whose alleged evils would shame Monty Burns. The real distance between their worldviews, though – as Lisa Simpson and Gary Coleman so touchingly demonstrate – is not that vast. Lisa does not want to bring the whole system down. The goal of her many protests is simply to be included in the dialogue, to restore some balance to the process, to have her priorities taken into account. They are, after all, eminently reasonable: baseline respect for human rights and the environment, corporate accountability, the punishment of the corrupt, and the enforcement in law and policy of the democratic values that are the allegedly unassailable bedrock of Western liberalism. An end, in short, to institutional hypocrisy, a closing of the gap between the long-standing promise of What Should Be and the imperfect fact of What Is.

And if accomplishing this is beyond the abilities or the will of world leaders and captains of industry and the overzealous crusaders in the more extreme wings of the protest movement, well then perhaps it has to fall to a cartoon character – and a cartoon series – to lead the way.

SIMPSONIAN LIBERALISM: THE POLITICAL SLANT OF THE SIMPSONS

The Parents Television Council (PTC) is an ultra-conservative American organisation dedicated to promoting 'positive, family-oriented television programming'. Its president is L. Brent Bozell III, who also presides over the PTC's sister organisation, the Media Research Center, whose self-proclaimed raison d'être since its founding in 1987 has been to 'neutralise' the alleged liberal bias in the American media. So it surely surprised no one down *Simpsons* way when their show made the PTC's list of the ten most liberally biased programmes on television for the 1990–1 season. *The Simpsons* – along with its comrades at the much more obscure cartoon *Captain Planet and the Planeteers* – were, Bozell explained in a press release, 'slick propaganda tools for the contemporary left's agenda, aimed at politically indoctrinating America's youth'. In particular, Bozell said, *The Simpsons* 'routinely parrots the radical environmentalists' slams against the nuclear power industry'. The show made Bozell's list again the following year. 'The police and their piglike chief,' Bozell explained this time, 'are repeatedly shown as blundering fools. The show frequently lampooned religion and religious figures.' In 1994 Bozell tagged *The Simpsons* with a 'red light', indicating that it 'frequently attack[ed] traditional values and conservative views'. Although the PTC appears to have discontinued its 'Most Biased' list – replacing it with lists of the ten best and worst shows judged by 'appropriateness for family audiences' – *The Simpsons* remains suspect in the PTC's eyes, receiving a cautionary yellow light at the group's website. '*The Simpsons* is not recommended for younger viewers,' reads the summary. 'The show ridicules entrepreneurs, religion, educators, and law enforcement officials, and has occasionally incorporated foul language into its dialogue.'

Hey, L. Brent: good call, man. These are all more or less accurate assessments of the content of *The Simpsons*. Does it have a liberal bias? Yes. What's less certain, though, is whether this indicates that the show is a propaganda tool of some dogmatic 'contemporary left'. In politics, as in all things, *The Simpsons* is a good deal too smart – and an even greater deal too firmly dedicated to mocking the hypocrisies of the left as well as the right – to be so easily pigeonholed.

Still, it's a fair question: does *The Simpsons* have an overarching political slant? Answer: definitely. So what is it? Well, it's a uniquely Simpsonian liberalism, a general fondness for the kind of progressive ideals espoused by Lisa Simpson, tempered with an abiding conviction that extreme beliefs of any stripe inevitably produce the kinds of hypocrisy and pomposity that the show is genetically predisposed to satirising.

Take for starters the show's creator, Matt Groening. Groening is in many ways a model leftie: a child of the 1960s, a graduate of a college known as a hippie mecca, a former employee of a punk record store, an underground cartoonist. But Groening has described his 1960s childhood in liberal Portland, Oregon, as something far less uniform in its progressivism than it might seem on the surface:

> The mythology about the sixties was that everybody was smoking dope and had long hair and was listening to the best rock & roll of the day, but I remember kids having to have their hair cut and conform to a dress code. But there was a college nearby, Portland State University, where they had underground films, and great rock groups came to play, and where they hated the Vietnam War, so I got to be in two worlds; I played football and also marched in anti-war parades.

The same goes for Groening's time at Evergreen State, where he was surrounded by doctrinaire lefties – and spent his time drawing scathing caricatures of them for the school newspaper. (One of Groening's cartoons, which satirised his fellow students' communes, inspired a protest petition a hundred names strong.) 'Matt was like this guy who was a kind of straight guy at a hippie college, but so militantly straight that he was hipper than the hippies,' according to his old college chum and fellow cartoonist Lynda Barry.

As it was for the youthful Groening, so for the most part it remains for *The Simpsons*. 'We are of a liberal bent,' executive producer Al Jean admitted in early 2003. But he quickly added, 'If I had to say the overriding philosophy of the show, I would say it's probably nihilism, where I tend to think that government and big business are really out to screw the little guy, and that, you know, it's more important, you know, to see what the feelings and emotions of a family are.' You can see this approach in the way the show has treated Lisa – the character Jean and many of the other writers most closely identify with.

Consider one of Lisa's most strident progressive campaigns: her decision to become a vegetarian. Lisa's vegetarianism, precipitated by a visit to a petting zoo, soon becomes not just a personal choice but a contentious subject for the whole Simpson family and for practically the entire town. At first, this broadness of scope serves to illustrate how deeply meat-eating is engrained in Western society – and, moreover, how principled dissent of any sort threatens the established order. At school, Lisa refuses to dissect her worm in biology class and demands a vegetarian option at lunch, setting off Springfield Elementary's 'Independent Thought Alarm' twice in one day. Principal Skinner scrambles to do damage control, screening an 'educational film' for Lisa's class: a hilarious specimen of corporate propaganda entitled *Meat and You: Partners in Freedom* produced by the Meat Council. (Afterwards, the good folks at the Meat Council even treat the kids to some delicious tripe.) Things are no less divisive for Lisa at home, where half of Springfield has gathered for Homer's meat-centric barbeque. Lisa offers the crowd a vegetarian option, but her gazpacho inspires only mocking laughter. And so Lisa, in an uncharacteristically insensitive moment, sabotages the barbeque. Homer, devastated, demands an apology. Lisa, overflowing with self-righteousness, says, 'I'm never ever apologising, because I was standing up for a just cause, and you were wrong, wrong, wrong!' She's just as shrill the next morning at breakfast, storming from the table after denouncing her father as a 'prehistoric carnivore'.

It's obvious, by this point, that the episode's sympathies have shifted. What at first seemed a reasoned, principled stance being unfairly resisted by a conformist society has now turned ugly: Lisa has become inconsiderate, appallingly sanctimonious, downright grotesque. The point is underscored when she learns that Apu down at the Kwik-E-Mart is also a vegetarian. Apu takes Lisa to his lush rooftop garden, where celebrity vegetarians Paul and Linda McCartney just happen to be hanging out. Safely ensconced among fellow enlightened souls, Lisa continues with her self-righteous speechifying:

Lisa:	When will all those fools learn that you can be perfectly healthy simply eating vegetables, fruits, grains and cheese?
Apu:	Oh, cheese!
Lisa:	You don't eat cheese, Apu?
Apu:	No, I don't eat any food that comes from an animal.
Lisa:	Oh – then you must think I'm a monster!
Apu:	Yes indeed I do think that. But I learned long ago, Lisa, to tolerate others rather than forcing my beliefs on them. You know, you can influence people without badgering them always.

Chastened, Lisa apologises to her father. 'I still stand by my beliefs,' she tells him, 'but I can't defend what I did.'

Taken as a whole, the episode is a prime example of Simpsonian liberalism, its shifting sympathies sketching out the boundaries of the show's loose ideology. In this instance, the writers show considerable support for the idea of vegetarianism, both as a personal choice and as a sound alternative to the factory-style cattle ranching portrayed in the Meat Council film and the morbid obesity of carnivores like Chief Wiggum, who winds up so overstuffed with burgers at Homer's barbeque that he can't even rise to fetch himself another. But as Lisa grows more rigid in her beliefs, she crosses the show's ideological line. The episode's most lasting message is that progressive voices are no less prone than conservative ones to shrill authoritarianism.

There are satirical laughs scored at the expense of Lisa's idealism in numerous other instances. In Episode 5F17 ('Lost Our Lisa') she takes the bus to the local museum, singing the praises of the beloved progressive institution of public transit as she waits: 'Clean, reliable public trans- portation. The chariot of the people. The ride of choice for the poor and very poor alike.' Even before she's finished her ode, though, Moe the bartender – who was waiting with her – grows exasperated by her monologue and hops into a cab instead, asking to be taken to the venereal-disease clinic. On the bus ride itself, the irony's piled even higher: an old woman won't let her have the seat next to her because she's using it for her change purse, the Comic Book Guy will only let her sit next to him if she answers three trivia questions, the bus passes through exotic Springfield neighbourhoods such as Crackton, and then – the final insult to Lisa's proletarian ritual – it turns out she's on the wrong bus entirely.

In another episode, Lisa cajoles Marge into taking her to Alaska to clean up after an oil spill. At Baby Seal Beach, Lisa has high hopes of saving the lives of seals and otters. It turns out, though, that the glamorous chore of cleaning the animals has been reserved for celebrity environmentalists such as Rainier Wolfcastle. Lisa and her mom are reduced to scrubbing oil off rocks. After a long day of backbreaking labour, the stereotypically hippiefied environ- mentalist in charge of the cleanup calls to them, 'Quitting time!' Then he lays out the evening's festivities: 'We're having kelp burgers, and we're going to watch a tape of Johnny Arvik – he's the Eskimo comedian.' In the blink of an eye, the Simpson women are in their car, fleeing as fast as they can. 'Faster, Mom, faster!' Lisa pleads, her commitment to saving the planet easily overcome by the horrors of the actual task.

There's probably no more pointed rebuke of Lisa's constant crusading, though, than in Episode 5F03 ('Bart Star'), when Lisa shows up to try out for Springfield's peewee football team. She arrives at the field itching for an oppressive system to rail against. 'That's right!' she calls. 'A girl want to play football. How about that?' It turns out, though, that there are four girls on the team already. Lisa is momentarily thrown, but quickly finds another axe to grind: 'Well . . . football's not really my thing. After all, what kind of civilised person would play a game with the skin of an innocent pig?' The coach informs her that the team uses synthetic balls, and one of the players – one of the *female* players – points out that a dollar from the sale of every ball goes to Amnesty International. This reduces Lisa to frustrated tears, and she flees the scene. Pity poor Lisa, but understand that the show's first priority is no-holds-barred satire.

Still, there's a definite sense that the show's lampoons of Lisa's liberal excesses are affectionate jabs at one of its own, the constructive criticism of a protégée. The tone is much sharper when the target is a genuine opponent. Consider a high-profile case study that begins with a stump speech made by President George H.W. Bush during his failed re-election campaign in 1992. So-called family values were a cornerstone of Bush's platform, and they were front and centre in a campaign-trail speech he gave to the National Religious Broadcasters' convention in Washington. 'The next value I speak of,' Bush said, 'must be forever cast in stone. I speak of decency, the moral courage to say what is right and condemn what's wrong, and we need a nation closer to the Waltons than the Simpsons' – here he was interrupted briefly by a round of applause – 'an America that rejects the incivility, the tide of incivility and the tide of intolerance.'

Bush made the speech on 27 January 1992, a Monday. The next *Simpsons* broadcast was that Thursday, 30 January. It was a rerun of Episode 7F24 ('Stark Raving Dad'), which had first aired the previous September. The January 30 broadcast, however, opened with a short new vignette, hastily assembled in three days to respond to Bush's speech. The scene begins with a shot of the Simpson living room. Homer sits on the couch with Patty and Selma. Maggie's in her high chair next to the couch. Bart and Lisa are sprawled on the carpet. All eyes are fixed on the TV, which shows President Bush in a live inset.

A couple of precedents have already been set: a rebroadcast had never before featured a new prologue, and no real-world news clip had ever appeared on the Simpsons' TV. And the writing, recording and animation of a *Simpsons* scene in less than 72 hours – even one as short as this – must have set some kind of record.

Back to the scene: 'We need a nation closer to the Waltons than the Simpsons,' Bush intones, his voice filling the Simpsons' living room. 'Hey, we're just like the Waltons,' Bart replies. 'We're praying for an end to the Depression, too.' End of prologue.

Later in that election year Groening would tell a reporter, 'I'd vote for a statue of Bob's Big Boy over Bush.' Rest assured he felt that way – most of the show's creators felt that way – long before Bush took his cheap shot at *The Simpsons*. And Simpsonian liberalism seemed, in this case, to be winning the fight. Bush's speech, with its comically nostalgic reference to the Waltons and their idealised rural life that never was, spoke directly to the retrograde forces of What Should Be. He was speaking to the whingeing Moral Majoritarians who had spent much of the previous twenty years urging a return to the Puritans' fabled Christian City on the Hill, speaking to those who would deny the passage of time and the change of the social landscape. And watching *The Simpsons* throw this nonsense back at them, watching anti-hero Bart tear their sanctimony to shreds with a single well-phrased barb, you might surmise that the What-Should-Be world was dying, that it had been eclipsed, that the knottier but also more inclusive and especially more *truthful* world of What Is, portrayed in such vivid detail each week on *The Simpsons*, could never again be hidden from view.

A decade later, the son of the show's old political foe is now president. In an episode from the 2002–3 season, Ned Flanders greets a happy turn of events with this gleeful declaration: 'I haven't felt this good since we stole the 2000 election!' He speaks on behalf of George W. Bush's fundamentalist-Christian supporters, but the subtext is that the forces of What Should Be are again ascendant.

No wonder, then, that Lisa's many crusades haven't been able to bring lasting solace to her discontented heart.

LISA LIONHEART (III): LISA THE SEEKER

As the tales of Lisa's many activist struggles have piled up over the years, it has become increasingly clear that underneath her passionate politics and her dedication to the pursuit of rational, scientific truth, there lies an anguished soul whose yearning for contentment amid the sleek corporate surfaces and glaring injustices of her world is the real engine of her rage. Much like the protagonists of entropy movies and the narrators of Radiohead songs, Lisa is hunting desperately for guidance, for meaning, for a lasting truth larger than herself. 'Self-improvement can be achieved,' she moralises at the end of an episode in which a shallow self-help guru has taken all of Springfield for a doomed spiritual ride, 'but not with a quick fix. It's a long, arduous journey of personal and spiritual discovery.' And no Simpson's journey has been more arduous than Lisa's.

The *Simpsons* era has been a particularly abusive time for souls in search of higher meaning. It's a time when traditional authorities all seem corrupt or uninspired, a time characterised by deep cynicism and cool irony, a time when faith in a greater power can't seem to compete with the cold logic of science, but also a time when faith in technology is haunted by its own dystopian demons. Everyone and their dog is in therapy or on anti-depressants or drinking too much or eating too much or shopping too much or working too much to fill the void, however temporarily. For someone like Lisa Simpson, who lives with her eyes and mind wide open, who has rejected the false idols of acquisition and consumption, who has felt the limits of existential self-absorption and rational debate, this can indeed be a time of deep, abiding despair.

The Simpsons faces this quandary head-on in Episode 5F05 ('Lisa the Skeptic'). The episode, as previously noted, centres on the discovery of the fossilised skeleton of what appears to be a winged angel in a field near a new shopping mall. The very notion of an angel, Lisa claims, is preposterous. So she takes a sample from the skeleton to the eminent scientist Stephen Jay Gould for analysis. Science can't settle the matter – Gould's test, he claims, was inconclusive – but Lisa remains disgusted by the naive faith of her fellow citizens and takes to pacing around the Simpson kitchen denouncing them as morons. Marge gently informs her that her own mother is among those 'morons' who believe in angels. Lisa is baffled:

Lisa:	You? But you're an intelligent person, Mom.
Marge:	There has to be more to life than just what we see, Lisa. Everyone needs something to believe in.
Lisa:	It's not that I don't have a spiritual side, I just find it hard to believe there's a dead angel hanging in our garage.
Marge:	[*with genuine pity*] Oh, my poor Lisa. If you can't make a leap of faith now and then, well, I feel sorry for you.
Lisa:	[*patronising*] Don't feel sorry for me, Mom. I feel sorry for you.

Undeterred, Lisa takes her scientific argument to Kent Brockman's current-affairs show *Smartline* (it's her 13th appearance). Springfield's true believers, watching the broadcast at the local church, are so incensed by Lisa's logic that they go on an anti-science rampage, pillaging the Springfield Natural History Museum, the Springfield Observatory and the Springfield Robotics Lab.[12] Lisa is soon vindicated – the angel turns out to be a crass publicity stunt – but in the episode's final scene, she is too shaken to gloat. 'I guess you were right, honey,' Marge tells her, 'but you have to admit that when the angel started to talk you were squeezing my hand pretty hard!' Lisa tries to shrug it off: 'Well it was just so loud and . . .' She softens. 'Thanks for squeezing back,' she tells her mother. Lisa has learned a valuable lesson: there is a part of life – a part of her own mind – that science can neither account for nor satisfy.

Lisa embarks on other quests to find solace for her yearning spirit – most notably, she converts to Buddhism a few seasons later – but the most reliable source of truth she finds is the one she has always believed in: her own family. It is from the other Simpsons that Lisa draws stability, meaning, content-ment. And not just from Marge: in Episode 2F15 ('Lisa's Wedding'), Lisa's unwavering love for the Simpson who frustrates her most – her father – is vividly illustrated in a flash-forward. Lisa is to marry a pompous British gentleman named Hugh Parkfield, but learns minutes before the ceremony that he has refused to wear the cartoon-pig cufflinks Homer has given him – and, what's more, that he has not even a basic respect for Lisa's family. The impending marriage collapses in a short dialogue between Lisa and Hugh:

Lisa: I can't believe I'm hearing this. I don't want to cut my family out of my life.

Hugh: Really? But, Lisa, you're better than this place. You're like a flower that grew out of a pot of dirt.

Lisa: That's a horrible thing to say!

Hugh: Well, come on – *you* complain about them more than anyone.

Lisa: Maybe, but I still love them! And I don't think you understand that.

And so Lisa walks out on Hugh. Cut back to the present day, where Lisa – whose wedding disaster was being revealed to her by a psychic at the Springfield Renaissance Faire – runs to find her family on the fairgrounds. When she spots her father, she gratefully runs into his arms, and then listens with rapt attention as Homer tells her about his adventures at the fair.

In this case it's Homer who brings her solace, but Lisa knows – all the Simpsons do – that the real pillar of the Simpson clan, its spiritual centre, is Marge.

NOTES & MORGINALIA

1. **Popularity contest:** In a 1998 Internet poll, *Simpsons* fans rated Lisa their fourth-favourite character. She received 3.7 per cent of the total votes, finishing behind Homer (who received 24.2 per cent), Bart (9.9 per cent) and Ralph Wiggum (5.1 per cent). Meanwhile, *Simpsons* fans used the poll to indulge in some of their trademark obsession with trivia, casting single votes for 74 ridiculously minor characters. Among them: basketball star Magic Johnson (who had a cameo in a Season 3 episode), Sideshow Raheem (Krusty's short-lived black-power sidekick), Chocolate-Smoking Aztec (who has a non-speaking cameo in a Troy McClure educational video), The Guy Who Calls Homer 'Bill' (a barfly at Moe's Tavern mentioned by Homer once, in passing), and the Inanimate Carbon Rod (which steals Homer's limelight after his trip to outer space).

2. **Excuse me, Professor Brainiac:** The mildly pejorative term 'egghead' is both self-applied and self-caricatured in the case of *The Simpsons'* writers. In Episode 9F16 ('The Front'), they depict themselves as slightly pompous Ivy Leaguers who write 'Itchy & Scratchy' cartoons – one of them notes that he wrote his thesis on life experience – inspiring their boss, Roger Meyers, to dismiss them as 'eggheads' with 'fancy degrees.' Then in Episode 4F12 ('The Itchy & Scratchy & Poochie Show'), the writers expand on this self-image, portraying themselves sitting around a boardroom table at Itchy & Scratchy Studios speaking in the overeducated tongues of hyper-academic theoreticians. One – reportedly a caricature of *Simpsons* writer Bill Oakley – bristles at the idea of introducing a new character to the show. 'I don't want to sound pretentious here,' he says, 'but Itchy and Scratchy comprise a dramaturgical dyad.' Then Lindsey Naegle explains that the new character will be 'the original dog from hell'. Oakley's reply: 'You mean Cerberus?'

3. **More oddball Canadian rules:** The vagaries of the Canadian Football League have come in for parody on *The Simpsons* on one other occasion. In Episode 7F23 ('When Flanders Failed'), we find Homer idly watching exciting 15th-round action of the CFL draft. 'So,' an announcer enthuses, 'the Saskatchewan Roughriders have scored only four rouges all last season.' For the record, a 'rouge' in Canadian football is a single point scored when a punt or missed field goal is kicked into the opposing team's end zone and not returned. (Incidentally, as many a hack Canadian stand-up comedian has noted, the CFL for many years had two teams with essentially the same nickname: the Saskatchewan Roughriders and the Ottawa Rough Riders.)

4. **Charter, oddball clauses in:** A NOBLE SPIRIT EMBIGGENS THE SMALLEST MAN – so reads the inscription on the base of the statue of Springfield's founder, Jebediah Springfield. And the town charter is no less nonsensical. Among its decrees:

- that Springfield's 'chief constable . . . shall receive one pig every month and two comely lasses of virtue true'
- that 'spiritous beverages are hereby prohibited in Springfield under penalty of catapult' (passed 200 years ago, repealed 199 years ago)
- that 'ducks shall wear long pants'
- that 'if foodstuff should touch the ground, said foodstuff shall be turned over to the village idiot'

Springfield's municipal law also includes a statute making it illegal to put squirrels down one's pants for the purposes of gambling.

5. **Why would they come to our concert just to boo us?** Lisa's fear of a life as an also-ran leads to a great gag at the expense of the lesser members of several prominent singer-songwriter duos of the 1970s. 'There's no shame in being second,' Lisa tells herself, and then drifts into a daydream of her future. Dissolve to a packed concert hall, where an announcer enthuses, 'And now, Avis Rent-a-Car is proud to present the second-best band in America. Will you welcome Garfunkel, Messina, Oates and Lisa, singing their number-two hit, "Born to Runner-Up".'

Lisa's bandmates are, of course, the less-celebrated halves of their respective duos: Art Garfunkel was runner-up to Paul Simon; Jim Messina was overshadowed by his partner

Kenny Loggins; and John Oates was sidekick to Daryl Hall. As for Avis, it built a long-running marketing campaign around the slogan, 'When you're number two, you try harder.'

6. Two fun facts about Malibu Stacy:

(a) The owner of the world's largest collection of Malibu Stacy dolls is Waylon Smithers, Mr Burns's ever-effete right-hand man.

(b) The two least popular Stacy dolls ever introduced were 'Achy-Breaky Stacy' and 'Live from the Improv Stacy'.

7. 'Legendary' is not the same as 'good,' apparently: In Episode 2F32 ('Round Springfield'), Bleeding Gums Murphy returns to Springfield for a repeat engagement, setting the stage for a huge blot on *The Simpsons*' otherwise outstanding musical record. Lisa bumps into Bleeding Gums at the local hospital, where he's not long for this world. Overjoyed to be reunited, the legend and the little girl jam together in his hospital room. The result is 'Jazzman', a cover of a 1974 Top Ten hit by Carole King. I can't speak for King's original, but the version played – *twice* – by Lisa and Bleeding Gums is far and away the worst song ever performed on *The Simpsons* (and I include in this assessment Homer's 'Mr Plow' rap jingle, which is at least funny). The Simpsonised 'Jazzman' is an overwrought, middle-of-the-road, lite-jazz abomination that verges on the jazz-for-people-who-don't-actually-like-jazz territory epitomised by Kenny G. It is to the Thelonious Monk tune ('"Round Midnight') referenced in the episode's title as food-court Chinese with its chicken balls and neon-red sauces is to classical Szechuan cuisine: syrupy, mildly nauseating and pretty much entirely unrelated to the style it claims to be celebrating.

8. Life imitates (toy-making) art: Stacy Lovell's melodramatic life inspires several great gags in Episode 1F12. By way of explaining her world-weariness to Lisa, for example, Stacy notes that her 30 years of living the Malibu Stacy lifestyle has taken its toll. She then lists her five ex-husbands: Ken (the Barbie doll's long-term boyfriend), Johnny (as in Johnny West, a cowboy action figure from the early 1970s), Joe (as in G.I. Joe, another famous action figure), Dr Colossus (a generic action-figure-type villain) and Steve Austin (1970s TV's *Six Million Dollar Man*).

This sets up an even better gag a moment later, when G.I. Joe himself arrives at the door of Stacy's estate in full military regalia. 'Stacy, please,' Joe says, taking her into his arms. 'I must have you back. Just come for a ride with me in my Mobile Command Unit.' Stacy: 'Joe, I told you, it's over. Now release me from your kung-fu grip.' (Both the Mobile Command Unit and the kung-fu grip were prominent features of the 1980s-era G.I. Joe action figure.)

9. A case study in the excesses of political correctness: In Episode 4F18 ('In Marge We Trust'), Ned Flanders winds up trapped in Baboon County, USA – the baboon enclosure at the Springfield Zoo. As the Simpsons look on helplessly from outside the enclosure, a gang of angry baboons closes in on poor Ned. Luckily, a zookeeper strolls by just then. 'You've got to get him out of there,' Marge implores him. 'Geez, I'd like to,' he replies, 'but if they don't kill the intruder, it's really bad for their society.' Now, *that's* cultural relativism.

10. Five fun facts about Jebediah Springfield:

- His full name is Jebediah Obediah Zachariah Jedediah Springfield.
- In 1796, after misinterpreting a passage in the Bible, Jebediah and his partner, Shelbyville Manhattan, set out from Maryland with a band of pioneers to build a new society.
- Later in 1796, the sweet moment of Springfield's founding was celebrated with the planting of a lemon tree (lemons being the sweetest fruit available at the time).
- Jebediah's founding vision was of a town where people could 'worship freely, govern justly, and grow vast fields of hemp for making rope and blankets . . . and live a life devoted to chastity, abstinence, and a flavourless mush I call rootmarm'.
- Jebediah coined Springfield's cromulent motto: 'A Noble Spirit Embiggens the Smallest Man'.

11. Robotic irony: The angry mob's rampage through the Springfield Robotics Lab in Episode 5F05 results in massive destruction – and in a brilliant one-off gag. As flames engulf the building, scientists and robots alike come streaming out the front door, fleeing the fire. As one robot exits, waving its arms in agony, it sums up the injustice of its plight. 'Why?' it hollers in its electronic voice. 'Why was I programmed to feel pain?'

CHAPTER SIX

Marge Knows Best

For wee must consider that wee shall be as a citty upon a hill. The eies of all people are uppon us. Soe that if wee shall deale falsely with our God in this worke wee haue undertaken, and soe cause him to withdrawe his present help from us, wee shall be made a story and a by-word through the world.

> John Winthrop, 'A Modell of Christian Charity', sermon delivered to the Puritan founders of Massachusetts aboard the Arbella *en route to America, 1630*

This never would have happened if Marge Simpson was here.

> Maude Flanders, surveying a riot in Springfield,
> Episode 9F20 ('Marge in Chains')

BLESSED ARE THE PEACEMAKERS

In Episode 3F09 ('Two Bad Neighbors'), former president George H.W. Bush and his wife, Barbara, move into a mansion directly across the street from the Simpson home on Evergreen Terrace. It's definitely not the start of a beautiful friendship: even before they meet, Homer resents George for stealing his thunder at the neighbourhood rummage sale. Soon, George is driven to exasperation by the exploits of unruly Bart, finally giving the boy a spanking – 'for the good of the country' – after Bart destroys his memoirs. From then on, Homer and George are at war, exchanging insults, pranks and acts of vandalism across the formerly peaceful street like armies on the Arabian desert. Days after moving in, George decides he simply can't tolerate living in Homer Simpson's world, and the Bushes head elsewhere in search of a place to pass their golden years.

Originally aired in January 1996, Episode 3F09 was the final conflict in the war between *The Simpsons* and the Bushes for the moral high ground. Four years after Bush had chastised Homer and his family for not being a sepia-toned fantasy family of hard-working, God-fearing mountain folk like the Waltons, the show exacted its full revenge. Using obnoxiousness and irreverence and messy, unvarnished truth – all those potent weapons of What Is – *The Simpsons* drove Bush and his hectoring jeremiads about What Should Be from Springfield for good. It was a messy battle: Homer got his front yard torn up, Bart got his butt smacked, Bush was made to show weakness in front of the Russians. And it was perhaps an unnecessary fight: if only these rowdy, impulsive boys had followed the example of Barbara and Marge, it might never have come to such nastiness.

Even as George and Homer wage their pointless war, Mrs Bush and Mrs Simpson sit amicably in the Simpson living room, sipping tea and noting the many similarities between their husbands. It's a lovely, genteel scene of what might have been – and, indeed, of what *had* been, back in 1990, when the first Bush–Simpson feud erupted.

It started mildly enough, with a profile of the First Lady that appeared in the 1 October 1990 issue of *People* magazine. Barbara Bush made a few offhand observations about the state of contemporary American pop culture, noting that she'd recently checked out an episode of *The Simpsons*, which at the time was the hottest new show on television. 'It was the dumbest thing I had ever seen,' she concluded, 'but it's a family thing, and I guess it's clean.' The first part of the quote – that *The Simpsons* was 'the dumbest thing' Barbara Bush had ever seen – got picked up by news outlets the world over, and word of the insult soon reached Marge Simpson herself. Rather than escalate the battle, Marge chose the route of explanation, discussion, conciliation – the path of peace. With the help of *Simpsons* executive producer James L. Brooks, Marge sent a firm but friendly letter to the First Lady – a letter that also appeared in newspapers around the world. It read in part: 'Ma'am, if we're the dumbest thing you ever saw, Washington must be a good deal different than what they teach me at the current-events group at the church. I always believed in my heart that we had a great deal in common. Each of us living our lives to serve an exceptional man. I hope there is some way out of this controversy. I thought, perhaps, it would be a good start to just speak my mind.' Polite to a fault, Marge closed her letter, 'With great respect, Marge Simpson.'

In short order, the First Lady responded with similar good cheer. 'How kind of you to write,' she greeted Marge. 'I'm glad you spoke your mind . . . I foolishly didn't know you had one. I am looking at a picture of you . . . depicted on a plastic cup . . . with your blue hair filled with pink birds peeking out all over. Evidently, you and your charming family . . . Lisa, Homer, Bart and Maggie . . . are camping out. It is a nice family scene. Clearly you are setting a good example for the rest of the country. Please forgive a loose tongue.' It was signed, 'Warmly, Barbara Bush.' And then a postscript: 'Homer looks like a handsome fella!'

It could've gotten ugly. But that's just not Marge's style. Her heart's too kind, her manner far too deferential. She is the one (and often only) firmly planted anchor in the churning maelstrom that is daily life on *The Simpsons*, the moral and psychological and spiritual centre that keeps her family and their world from spiralling off into total chaos.

Marge pacifies, she calms, she brings understanding and order and even the possibility of salvation to the Simpsonian project. If the shadow of apocalypse looms menacingly on Springfield's baby-blue horizon – and indeed this is the case, for all satire positions itself to some degree as the last remaining bastion against impending doom – then Marge points towards the way out. No portrait of Armageddon – or at least no portrait of Armageddon that hopes to be watched by tens of millions of people every week – is complete without a hope of salvation. A preacher might attract the attention of the masses with talk of hellfire and brimstone, but he'll lose his new flock if he can't promise redemption at the end. And on *The Simpsons*, redemption starts with Marge.

In *The Simpsons*' universe, there is, of course, plenty of evidence of looming apocalypse. Some of this – hypertrophied consumerism, grim nihilism, unabashed official corruption and unchecked corporate greed – we've already discussed. But there is a dark cloud that envelops all of it, a corrosive anxiety born of a world whose centre has come loose from its moorings, a crisis of moral authority that permeates all of the show's satire. As a satirical mirror of our own society, the Simpsonian world is a place where traditional roles and responsibilities are muddied or neglected or else simply absent, where isolation and alienation have bred a deeply dysfunctional hyper-individualism, where the very idea of faith is in doubt. On *The Simpsons*, as in our world, there is profound social decay.

And *The Simpsons* itself has provoked ill-advised attacks on the alleged agents of this decay. Since its first season, *The Simpsons* has been entangled in the ongoing battle over so-called family values. This misguided crusade has noticed the same social ills depicted in the show's satire, but it has attacked the symptoms instead of the disease and sometimes even prescribed the disease itself as a cure – some bogus patent-medicinal mix of old-time religion and newfangled technology. If the God of the Israelites can't banish these demons from your life, then you need a doohickey implanted in your TV set to block them out entirely. Only pure faith – or else faith in technology – can save you.

In marked contrast, there is on *The Simpsons* abundant evidence of the true agents of the West's social decay – everything from SUV-induced road rage to the isolating chill of a self-cleaning kitchen. And though there is plenty of talk about faith and God and the human spirit as well, the show yields no simple, prescriptive, cure-all morals. Instead, it offers a small spark of hope that begins with Marge. Marge is the towering-blue-haired paragon of authentic family values on *The Simpsons*; she is the symbol of the show's (barely) enduring morality. From Marge comes the Simpson family's faith in itself, and from that comes its cohesion, and from that cohesion comes the show's one unqualified conviction: that even amid the dysfunctional mess of a society that appears to be on the brink of some kind of apocalyptic endgame, there remains the unassailable fact of a family's love. There is, through it all, this spark of hope. This might back the show's writers into an overreliance on the sentimental ending as a plot device, but it is in the end the only kind of salvation that can be trusted to endure. Society may collapse completely, but the Simpson family won't. Not on Marge's watch.

MARGE SIMPSON (I): MATRIARCH

Here's a frequently recurring opening scene on *The Simpsons*: an establishing shot of the family kitchen, Homer and/or the kids and/or the dog and cat in evident need – of breakfast, of advice, of a lucky red hat or a mended pair of pants – and Marge at the counter, hard at work. There's a representative example at the start of Episode 7F09 ('Itchy & Scratchy & Marge'): Homer comes into the kitchen to find his wife busily preparing his beloved pork chops. Marge at the stove is a whirl of fluid activity, tossing in spices and flipping chops with an effortless grace, her joy and pride in the work abundantly clear.

At first glance, this appears to be the primary role that Marge plays: she is Supermom. She can do laundry, change Maggie's diapers and put together hearty lunches all at once. She whips up huge feasts for the day's other two meals – food so good her family dives in without a word, gobbles noisily, belches contentedly, the gratitude self-evident. At breakfast she might arrange the bacon and eggs into cheery happy faces. For dinner she might glaze a ham to an incandescent shine of retina-scarring brightness. Off the top of her head, Marge can recite Homer's blood type and earmuff size, Lisa's shoe and ring sizes, Bart's allergies, and a precise accounting of Maggie's baby and permanent teeth. In these moments of flawless domestic efficiency, Marge is a broad, hyperbolic parody of the rock-solid, ultra-nurturing sitcom mom. She makes Harriet Nelson look lazy and June Cleaver seem cold. She's almost freakishly maternal.

Marge's improbable perfection as a matriarch has come in for repeated self-parody on *The Simpsons*. Over the years, there have been several sequences of sped-up domestic hyperactivity, with Marge all but sprouting extra limbs in order to carry out a dozen household chores simultaneously. At the start of Episode 3F01 ('Home Sweet Homediddily-Dum-Doodily'), for example, we find Marge bouncing kinetically around the kitchen, preparing a full breakfast as well as packed lunches. She gives Maggie some Melba toast that she melba-fied herself. Lisa enters, and Marge hands her a stack of newspapers she dug out of the town dump for her daughter's history project. Bart comes in next, and in an instant Marge has detected the Dracula fangs he's wearing and pulled them out of his mouth, stopping him from ruining another school photo. Then she hands Bart and Lisa their lunches, explaining that she's used a trick to make the bread stay dry and the lettuce moist till lunchtime. 'Mom, you fuss over us *way* too much!' Lisa says as she exits. Marge happily agrees. Finally, Homer comes in. He needs Marge to shoo a spider away from his car keys, which she eagerly does. And even when he surprises her a moment later with a morning at the local spa, Marge's superheroic mothering instincts won't subside. 'I'm taking something to iron with me in the car,' she insists as Homer drags her away.

Marge is often just as ideal – in a creepy, 1950s-style, *Invasion of the Body Snatchers* sort of way – in her role as long-suffering wife. This is a woman, after all, who has been enduring Homer Simpson's bumbling and carelessness with gentle good humour since high school, when he lied to her about needing a French tutor in order to trick her into dating him.

You have to wonder whether Marge's Supermom and Dutiful Wife acts are at least part of what Peggy Noonan had in mind when she took to the pages of *Good Housekeeping* in 1997 to declare *The Simpsons* 'the best family values show on television.'[1] Noonan, after all, was a speechwriter for both Ronald Reagan and the first President Bush – a frontline sloganeer for Reaganite 'family values'. And Marge, in her Supermom moments, is the loyal, hardworking homemaker of a backward-looking anti-feminist reactionary's dreams. She seems at such times to exist only to make her husband happy and keep her children safe and healthy; her natural habitat – her *only* habitat – appears to be the kitchen; she is every inch the pillar of the stable nuclear family that was put forward during the 1980s – in numerous speeches crafted by Peggy Noonan and elsewhere – as the cornerstone of freedom, democracy and the (traditional, white, Christian) American way.

Yes, indeedy: on the surface, Marge can seem like some 1950s-vintage automaton who's been cut-and-pasted into *The Simpsons* out of a Norman Rockwell painting. *Simpsons* writers, however, never stick to formula, and so you don't have to look very deep to find the satire lurking behind Marge's dutiful façade.

One form this satire has taken is a kind of involuted hyperbole that builds from the extraordinary superficial blandness of Marge's character. The one-dimensional nature of her life – and, by extension, of the life of any woman who so slavishly devotes herself to traditional roles in our time – is cartoonishly overstated on *The Simpsons*. Marge has sexual fantasies about an aging professional golfer (Jack Nicklaus, to be exact) and repeatedly urges her children to bring potatoes to school for show and tell. ('I just think they're neat,' she explains.) When the Simpson family is set to claim a $10,000 prize in a radio contest, Marge pipes up with a ludicrously level-headed suggestion for what to buy with the money: double-ply windows. 'They look just like regular windows, but they'll save us 4 per cent on our heating bill,' she notes with what for her amounts to unbridled enthusiasm. On another occasion, when Homer laments a recent visit to a record store during which he learned he was no longer 'with it', Marge replies, 'Record stores have always seemed crazy to me, but it doesn't upset me.' And then, almost proudly: 'Music is none of my business!'[2] The subtext of all of this is unmistakable: for Marge to be such a ridiculously devoted wife and mother, she must have a private life so relentlessly dull that making her kids' lunches and stiff-upper-lipping her way through her husband's misadventures seems comparatively fulfilling.

The show's lampooning of the ideal housewife also takes more overt forms. For example, it's demonstrated – repeatedly – that Marge's sense that all's well in her tidy little world survives only through sustained delusion. There's a particularly pointed instance of this in Episode 4F01 ('Lisa's Date with Density'). Lisa has developed a crush on Nelson Muntz, Springfield Elementary's biggest bully, in the face of her own better judgement. Her romance soon turns sour, though, when Nelson betrays her. Lisa talks over her predicament with her mother, wondering how she could've been so foolish, and Marge dispenses some hard-earned wisdom: 'Well, most women will tell you that you're a fool to think you can change a man. But those women are quitters! When I first met your father, he was loud, crude and piggish. But I worked hard on him, and now he's a whole new person.' Lisa begins to protest, but Marge cuts her off with crazed forcefulness: 'He's a *whole new person*, Lisa.'

At other times, Marge reveals the Supermom ideal to be totally untenable, an impossible goal that's bound to take a brutal toll on those who pursue it. There have been subtle examples of this, relatively rare moments when we glimpse the precariousness of Marge's equilibrium and the quiet desperation lurking just under her preternaturally stable surface. In one episode, for example, Lisa and Bart are both away from the Simpson home overnight, leaving Marge to gaze blankly at late-night infomercials and finally to creep into Maggie's room looking for a child to dote on. Maggie's fast asleep, so Marge hacks out forced coughs and then simply pokes Maggie to rouse her.

For the most pointed illustration of the impossibility of the ideal that Marge represents, however, look to Episode 8F14 ('Homer Alone'), which opens with a particularly frenzied version of Marge's Supermom routine. As Homer and the kids all bark commands and complaints simultaneously, Marge screeches at them with uncharacteristic impatience to state their problems one at a time, then solves each of them with doubly uncharacteristic irritation. Marge's woes continue after breakfast: Bart and Lisa miss the school bus and then spend the whole drive to school engaged in petty bickering; Maggie takes to tossing groceries out of the cart at the supermarket; and Marge trudges all over town in a vain search for a bowling shop that will remove the bottle cap stuck in the finger hole of Homer's ball. Finally, as Maggie spills milk all over the car and the radio blares grating ads and crass disc-jockey banter, Marge loses it completely. She squeals to a halt in the middle of a busy bridge, and she doesn't budge for hours. When Homer finally talks her into giving up her protest, Marge is sent to jail for causing a traffic jam. The female officer taking her mug shot informs her that all the gals at the police station know just how she feels. Because there's so much sympathy for her plight among the town's 'chick vote', Mayor Quimby pardons her – and declares Marge Simpson Day in Springfield. As for Marge, she spends the rest of 8F14 on a solo vacation at Rancho Relaxo, putting her head back together even as her home falls into chaos in her absence. The episode's message, meanwhile, is as clear as the natural spring that feeds Rancho Relaxo's spa: the sainted housewife of 1950s sitcoms and recent neoconservative political rhetoric is pure fiction. And no amount of time spent at Troy McClure-endorsed two-star resorts is going to turn her into fact.

In light of this – and in a nod to contemporary reality – *The Simpsons*' writers have repeatedly sent Marge to work outside the home. The working world, though, has been nothing but a string of disasters for Marge. She takes a job alongside her husband at the Springfield Nuclear Power Plant, and winds up mired in a sexual-harassment suit. She joins the Springfield police force, but its rampant corruption is so offensive to her principles that she soon quits. Her only foray into entrepreneurship – a pretzel-wagon franchise – succeeds only after Homer sells her out to the Mafia. And her attempt to become a player in the real-estate game is foiled by her lack of a true salesman's killer instinct.

There are any number of ways to interpret Marge's hapless career. It might be a cautionary tale about the persistence of sexism in the modern workforce. It could be an ironic exercise, repeatedly illustrating the inability of a June Cleaver clone to adapt to the hard-nosed business world of 'the go-go '90s', as one of the members of Marge's investment club puts it. Or maybe it's evidence of a subconscious neoconservative bias on the part of *The Simpsons*' creative team, inasmuch as it sort of implies that women shouldn't be trying to find jobs. Or is it just a simple plot device? (Probably.)

Anyhoo, Marge's brief stabs at gainful employment always end the same way: she returns to her home. She becomes, once again, the pillar of her family and the wellspring of the show's morality. It's her most vital role on *The Simpsons*, and her most interesting one.

MARGE SIMPSON (II): MORALIST

Various critics have cited both unrelenting cynicism and overweening sentimentality as defining characteristics of *The Simpsons*. In the pages of the *New Statesman*, a writer summarises the overall Simpsonian vibe as 'edgy, irreverent, cynical', while a critic at the *Independent* put 'cynicism' first in a 1999 list of the hallmarks of Matt Groening's oeuvre. An article that appeared a year earlier in that very same newspaper, however, described the Simpson family as 'essentially good, sweet people', and an earlier notice – this one from 1990, just as *The Simpsons* prepared to jump the pond to British TV – pointed out that the show 'harbours a sentimental heart, the curse of all US comedy'. So: is it possible to be both cynical and sentimental? Probably. Does such a characterisation actually fit *The Simpsons*? In a word: no.

The frequent charge of cynicism arises from a fundamental misunderstanding of the nature of satire. Satire employs humour to deflate its subjects, which is often mistaken for *dismissing* those subjects – a cynical stance. But satire has far more ambitious goals: it starts from a belief that the ideas and things it mocks – usually ideas and things invested with authority – are wrong, and that exposing this fact through satire will erode their authority and precipitate change. Satire is in this sense inherently optimistic. And moreover it is inherently *moral*: it sees itself as a force for right, engaged in a crusade against what's wrong. What's often derided on *The Simpsons* as 'sentimentality' usually implies a cynicism on the part of the show that simply isn't there. If there are sentimental moments on *The Simpsons*, that is, they arise from a *genuine* connection to the audience on an emotional level, not from manipulating the audience's emotions (which is what pop critics usually mean by 'sentimental') nor from a cynical derision of sentiment itself. So the staunch moralism of Marge Simpson, even if it's sometimes used to satirically examine the values of mainstream American society, shouldn't be read as a categorical dismissal of morality itself. On the contrary: Marge is the tender heart of a deeply moral show.

Maybe it's the superficial trappings of Marge's moralism that sometimes make it tough to see her sincerity. Heaven knows she's got no shortage of the surface-level stuff. Marge is the one who browbeats the family into attending church every week, and she's the one who brings Reverend Lovejoy to the house for dinner after Homer decides he's through with organised religion. Marge is steadfast in her support of Lisa's crusade against her father's theft of cable TV, and she never hesitates to tell Bart when his mischief crosses the line into genuine sin. Even Marge's frequent worried groan – her trademark

'Hmm-mmm', the closest thing she has to a catchphrase – speaks to a maternal overprotectiveness born of fear. 'You know, Homer,' Marge tells her husband in response to the news that he's started training to become an astronaut, 'when I found out about this, I went through a wide range of emotions. First I was nervous, then anxious, then wary, then apprehensive, then . . . kind of sleepy . . . then worried, and then concerned, but now I realise that being a spaceman is something you have to do.' Her final acceptance notwithstanding, Marge's default reaction to change is to find a half-dozen different ways to fear it. And if you have watched only more recent episodes of *The Simpsons*, you might conclude that her character is a broad lampoon of moralising Middle America, a spoilsport whose self-righteous façade masks a fearful, narrow-minded hatefulness. This is the Marge we meet in a Season 10 episode, forbidding Bart to spend time with Nelson with this spiteful rationale: 'Nelson is a troubled, lonely, sad little boy. He needs to be isolated from everyone.'

There's a scene later in the same episode, though, that speaks to Marge's larger role in the moral universe of *The Simpsons*. The episode – 5F22 ('Bart the Mother') – is centred on her relationship with her son, and in its first scenes she's devastated to learn that Bart not only disobeyed her order not to play with Nelson but also shot and killed a bird with Nelson's new BB gun. A short while later, though, she finds out that the killing was an accident, and that Bart's been carefully tending what he believes to be the dead bird's eggs. They turn out, however, to be lizard eggs, and after they hatch, Marge and her kids head to a meeting of Springfield's birdwatching society to figure out what's going on. The hatched lizards, they learn, are Bolivian tree lizards – oviraptors whose mother ate the bird's eggs and replaced them with her own. Because they're a non-native species, they have to be destroyed. Bart and Marge step out of the meeting room to decide what to do. 'Everyone thinks they're monsters,' Bart tells his mother, distraught. 'But I raised them, and I love them. I know that's hard to understand.' 'Mmm – not as hard as you think,' Marge answers knowingly. After a moment's pause she whispers, 'Run for it!' and then sets about obstructing the birdwatchers so Bart and his lizards can get away.

This particular case illustrates her unique understanding of Bart – her 'special little guy', a bratty kid whose kind heart and creative potential only she sees – but it's the same for the rest of her family. Maggie feels so close to her mother that she toddles away on an epic adventure to reunite with her the first time Marge leaves her alone with Homer. Lisa knows that underneath her mom's shallow advice to smile away her existential anguish lies as deep an empathy as she'll find in her family. And Homer is of course profoundly, sometimes even pathetically aware that Marge is the only thing saving his life from total chaos.

These relationships are not strictly one-sided. If Marge puts the most overt effort into her family's stability, she receives much love in return. In Episode 3F07 ('Marge Be Not Proud'), for instance, Bart is caught shoplifting, and he's as devastated as Marge is by the chilling doubt it brings into their relationship. By episode's end, he's gone to enormous lengths to heal the rift: he buys his mother a thoughtful Christmas gift (a framed photo of himself in which, for once, he isn't making silly faces) and even feigns enthusiasm for the boring golfing videogame she's given him. Homer, meanwhile, offers Marge a life of constant surprise and excitement that, while undeniably problematic, is also in some ways enviable. Marge admits as much in Episode DABF05 ('Jaws Wired Shut'), in which Homer takes a blow to the face that requires him to have his mouth wired closed, which transforms him into a calm, attentive and deeply empathetic husband. Marge revels in the new dynamic for a short while, but soon finds herself so bored that she enters a demolition derby to try to instigate some Homeric excitement of her own. Beyond the fun and games, though, Homer shares with Marge an enduring love that's rare in this divorce-prone age. And, what's more, it remains a *passionate* love: Homer and Marge have a much more active sex life than your average G-rated sitcom couple.[3] Whatever weaknesses their marriage might have, it's far from stale.

Here we find the core of Simpsonian family values: a mutual love and respect among the Simpsons that is one of the few truly beautiful and uncorrupted things in their world. And it's not Marge alone holding back the forces of decay – faith in the family unit is a core belief that *all* the Simpsons share. In Episode 3F01 ('Home Sweet Homediddily-Dum-Doodily'), there's a poignant example of this that occurs after a series of misunderstandings leads to Marge and Homer being declared unfit parents by the Springfield Child Protection Agency. They're forced to attend staggeringly condescending parenting courses,[4] while Bart and Lisa are summarily tossed into foster care and wind up moving in with their next-door neighbours – the fundamentalist Flanderses. The Simpson kids are immediately and intensely troubled by family life at Casa de Flanders – 'everything's got a creepy, Pat Boone-ish quality to it,' Lisa observes – and their only solace is in reminiscing warmly about life with their parents. 'Remember how Mom used to microwave our underwear on cold days?' Bart recalls. Lisa, equally wistful: 'Or the way Dad used to call the radio station with fake traffic tips?' They both laugh, and then they both sigh, and then Lisa, anguished, continues, 'They're ten feet away, and we can't even talk to them. I wish I could tell them how much I miss them.' Meanwhile, in the Simpson house, Homer and Marge are recalling their kids' quirks with an identical mix of affection and sadness. The doorbell rings – Bart's signature ring, as both parents immediately recognise – and they rush to the front door to find a fake newspaper featuring the headline 'Simpson Kids Miss Mom & Dad'.

Of all the chaos and conflict that has befallen the Simpson family, nothing sends it into full-blown crisis the way a threat to its own cohesion does. And the things the Simpsons miss about each other are not clichéd, Norman Rockwell scenes, but moments true to character: they love each other because of things that are intrinsic to each of them as individuals. In the final scene in this sequence, Homer and Marge are on the porch, a loving message from their kids in their hands, their faces betraying both mild relief and, beneath that, deep distress. In the midst of a cartoon whose stock-in-trade is raucous satire, this scene somehow works. It's not at all jarring. It doesn't feel mawkish. It is genuinely touching.

On *The Simpsons*, our emotional connection to the characters is played for something other than laughs only when it truly fits. (This stands in stark contrast to many other TV shows – comedy as well as drama – where heartstrings are clumsily plucked every episode in an attempt to manufacture a stirring climax.) Because these characters are on some level believable, because we in the audience *identify* with the Simpson family, we find their trials and tribulations and tragedies affecting. We feel for them when they are wronged. We're on their side.

This is a critical distinction between *The Simpsons* and, say, *Saturday Night Live*. Both shows mock the powers-that-be and blow satirical holes through the conventional wisdom of the day. (Or, at least, this is what *The Simpsons* does and what *SNL* used to do.) On *SNL*, though, as in most sketch comedy, there is a resolutely amoral nihilism to the project. Nothing's sacred and everything's at least potentially full of shit. The sketches might be funny or thought-provoking, but they're never moving, because we can't possibly be *emotionally* involved in them. Not so with *The Simpsons*. This is a world with emotional depth to it. The characters care about each other, and more importantly *we* care about them. Notwithstanding all the nastiness of their world, the Simpsons comprise a family, and we are not indifferent to its survival.

This is a big reason why *The Simpsons* has endured for so long, and why it has such enormous appeal across a wide range of demographic and geographic boundaries: because almost everyone has a family, and everyone's family is in some ways a mess, and damn near everyone loves their family, or tries to, or wishes they could. In a time of enormous instability – of rapid social change and light-speed technological advancement, of crumbling institutions and eroded religious faith – in such a time, families (loosely defined to include tight-knit groups of friends and professional colleagues as well as close blood relatives and romantic partnerships) are for many of us the only pillars we can cling to, the closest things we have to a moral centre. This is, to be sure, a highly tenuous morality – born of imperfections and inadequacies, and under siege from all sides by a calamitous and ultimately amoral consumer culture. But it remains, despite it all, the best hope we have for clarity and stability in a radically uncertain world.

And because we can see all of this in the Simpsons' family dynamic, the show has a moral authority far beyond that of your average sitcom. The Simpsons are a *realistic* family, with deep flaws and messy lives, successes and failures. A family that nurtures and brawls. A family built on a solid foundation of love and guided by its own imperfect morality. A sitcom might moralise from time to time, but *The Simpsons* – unrefined, imperfect, realistic – has a moral authority throughout. Put another way, any given episode of any given sitcom might have *a* moral, but *The Simpsons is* moral.

As if to broadcast this distinction, *The Simpsons* has openly mocked the notion of the tidy sitcom-style moral on several occasions.[5] There's a particularly drawn-out case at the end of Episode 7F22 ('Blood Feud'). This is an episode that's tightly focused on a moral issue: the nature of altruism. Mr Burns has fallen gravely ill. He needs a blood transfusion to save his life, but he has a rare blood type. Luckily, Bart Simpson shares Burns's blood type. Initially, though, Bart refuses to donate his blood, and he remains reluctant even after Marge (of course) explains that it's the right thing to do. But Homer's botched rendering of a fable convinces Bart he'll be showered with riches if he saves Burns's life, and in short order he has donated his blood and Burns is once again 'full of pith and vinegar' (his phrase). Burns sends Bart a thankyou card, but the distinct absence of gold, diamonds and rubies enrages both Homer and Bart, who together compose an inflammatory reply and send it to the old bastard. The vicious letter in turn gets Homer fired, and all seems lost until Smithers pleads with Burns to show some compassion for his stiff from Sector 7G, whose son, after all, did save his life. Surprisingly, Burns agrees, and sets out to buy the Simpsons 'an extravagant present. A mad, unthinkable, utterly impossible present. A frabulous, grabulous, zip-zoop-zabulous present!' (Again, his phrase.) And so he buys them a giant carved-stone idol, the three-thousand-year-old head of an Olmec god named Xt'Tapalatakettle. After Burns departs, the Simpsons gather in the living room, and eat dinner off TV trays and gaze upon their Olmec idol, and they engage in a debate about the meaning of their latest adventure:

Homer:	Save a guy's life, and what do you get? Nothing! Worse than nothing! Just a big scary rock.
Bart:	Hey, man, don't bad-mouth the head.
Marge:	Homer, it's the thought that counts. The moral of the story is: A good deed is its own reward.
Bart:	Hey, we *got* a reward. The head is cool.
Marge:	Then I guess the moral is: No good deed goes unrewarded.
Homer:	Wait a minute. If I hadn't written that nasty letter, we wouldn't have gotten anything.
Marge:	Well, then I guess the moral is: The squeaky wheel gets the grease.
Lisa:	Perhaps there is no moral to this story.
Homer:	Exactly! It's just a bunch of stuff that happened.
Marge:	But it certainly was a memorable few days.
Homer:	Amen to that!
	[*all laugh*]
	[*fade to closing credits*]

It's not just the formulaic plots of sitcoms that are being mocked here; it's the very idea that the intricacies of human interaction and the ambiguities of the soul can be reduced to slogans. After years of simplistic moralising – not just on pandering sitcoms but in the pronouncements of televangelists, in the *mea culpas* of drug-addicted star athletes and greed-addicted corporate crooks, in the just-say-no approach to drug use and the unemployment-equals-laziness take on poverty favoured by politicians of the Reaganite-Thatcherite breed – after so much of this reductionism that morality itself had come to seem as irrelevant and hokey as a Hallmark card, *The Simpsons* came along to reclaim the *complexity* of human morality. On *The Simpsons*, if in few other places in mainstream culture, moral issues are not bandied about like ad jingles. Timeless ethical paradoxes will not be reconciled in twenty-two minutes or less. And indeed if a *Simpsons* character starts to spew easy answers to tricky moral questions, it means one of two things: (1) the character is soon to be mercilessly schooled in the ample grey area surrounding tricky moral questions; or (2) the character is a Flanders.

More will be said later on the colossal piousness of the Flanders family. For now, it's sufficient to note that maniacally cheerful Ned and his clan – wife, Maude, and sons, Rod and Todd – are avid adherents of the bumper-sticker school of moralism in all its cultural and social manifestations. When *The Simpsons* needs a benchmark against which to measure its moral complexity, it simply marches a Flanders or two onstage to spew some sanctimonious drivel. They are the prime audience for Ziggy comic strips and the target market (perhaps the *only* market) for unflavoured non-fat ice milk. They have state-of-the-art satellite TV with more than 230 channels locked out. As for Ned's distinctive speaking style – *okily-dokily, a dilly of a pickle, absitively posilutely* – it's a study in self-infantilisation. He worries about the effect the cartoon devil on the package of Red Hots candies may have on his son. He avoids homeowner's insurance entirely because he thinks insurance is a form of gambling. He frets to his minister about coveting his own wife. He's the head of the PTA and a prominent member of the Citizens' Committee on Moral Hygiene. Ned Flanders is, in short, a dedicated foot soldier in the Family Values Crusade.

THE FAMILY VALUES CRUSADE

In Episode 7F09 ('Itchy & Scratchy & Marge'), the Great Family Values Crusade comes to Springfield – and it's not a Flanders but a Simpson who launches it. Marge, to be exact. It starts when innocent, impressionable Maggie sees an 'Itchy & Scratchy' cartoon in which Itchy clubs Scratchy with a giant mallet. She then toddles down to the Simpson basement and does the same thing to Homer. A short while later, Marge happens to catch the same 'Itchy & Scratchy' cartoon – and several others that inspire imitative behaviour in Maggie – and she's quickly convinced that Springfield's favourite unspeakably violent cat-and-mouse team is corrupting her children. After a polite letter to the head of the cartoon studio fails to affect any change, Marge founds S.N.U.H. ('Springfieldians for Nonviolence, Understanding, and Helping') and leads a vociferous protest outside the studio gates. (Her picket sign reads: I'M PROTESTING BECAUSE ITCHY & SCRATCHY ARE INDIRECTLY RESPONSIBLE FOR MY HUSBAND BEING HIT ON THE HEAD WITH A MALLET.)[6] S.N.U.H.'s protest is an instant triumph, leading to TV appearances for Marge and a landslide of angry letters to the studio. 'The screwballs have spoken,' studio head Roger Meyers concedes, and a radically transformed 'Itchy & Scratchy' is soon introduced. The theme song – formerly 'They fight! They bite! They fight and bite and fight!' – has been changed to 'They love! They share! They share and love and share!' The first new episode finds the duo sitting quietly on a porch sipping lemonade.

Springfield's kids soon flee their darkened living rooms en masse and wander out into the sunlight of a perfect new day – precipitating a classic Simpsonian montage. Rubbing their eyes and stretching as they step tentatively outdoors, the children of Springfield, finally liberated from the tyranny of violent cartoons, soon engage in a wide variety of wholesome (and mostly antiquated) kids' pursuits. As the camera pans around town to the strains of Beethoven's Sixth Symphony, we see young Springfieldianites gaily kite-flying and rope-skipping and hoop-rolling. By the final vignette, Springfield has become the nineteenth-century Illinois of Tom Sawyer and Huck Finn, with Nelson and a chum whitewashing a fence as another kid in flapping bib overalls looks on. The Simpson household is equally trans-formed: Bart and Lisa arrive home for dinner that night with tales of fishing and birdwatching and plans to build soapbox racers, and they excuse themselves with impeccable politeness after the meal is done. The removal of violence from 'Itchy & Scratchy' cartoons, in short, has transformed Springfield into the pre-modern paradise of a family-values crusader's wildest fantasies.

But, alas, this *is* Springfield, and so the tranquillity can't last. Soon the rank-and-file of S.N.U.H. is back at Marge's door, ready to unite behind her to stop an art exhibit – the local art museum is planning to host a touring exhibition of Michelangelo's *David*. 'It's filth!' fumes Helen Lovejoy, the good reverend's wife. 'It graphically portrays parts of the human body which, practical as they may be, are evil.' Marge, though, is a fan of *David* – one of the world's finest depictions of the human form, naked or not – and so Springfield's true moral guardians march off without her. And Marge has this to say on the occasion of her next TV appearance: 'I guess one person *can* make a difference, but most of the time, they probably shouldn't.'

But this evisceration of the logic of the Family Values Crusade, thorough as it was, didn't come close to bringing the battle to an end. Indeed, the crusade's mindset, rhetoric and tactics had so fully permeated mainstream American society that sporadic attacks against *The Simpsons* seemed to come from everywhere: from hand-wringing teachers, from the spokespeople for the alleged moral majority, from the White House of George H.W. Bush, even from the offices of the very corporation that aired the show. In addition to the usual evangelical-Christian subjects, other faiths have proven themselves to be just as easily offended by Simpsonian values over the years. In the mid-1990s, for example, the California-based Federation of Hindu

Associations bristled at the depiction of the Hindu god Ganesha in several episodes,[7] though it withdrew its objection once a Fox Network executive explained that the show poked fun at all faiths, not just Hinduism.

Less easily placated was America's Catholic League for Religious and Civil Rights, which publicly decried the portrayal of its faith on *The Simpsons* several times in 1998 and 1999. The first episode to raise the ire of the Catholic League was AABF03 ('Lisa Gets an "A"'), an episode that examines the ethical dilemma of the noble lie. The Catholic League apparently never got past the opening scene, in which Reverend Lovejoy's markedly uninspired sermon drones on longer than usual. As the Simpsons, starved after the overlong service, hurry home for sustenance, Bart pipes up from the back seat, 'Mom, can we go Catholic so we can get Communion wafers and booze?' Marge testily replies, 'No, no one's going Catholic. Three children is enough, thank you.' This brief and relatively gentle dig at the church's dogmatic rejection of contraception prompted a vehement protest from the Catholic League, which in turn led to a letter of explanation from Fox's head of standards and practices. A few months later, though, the Catholic League was back up in arms over another gag: a spoof of overwrought Super Bowl commercials that pops up on the Simpsons' TV set as Marge and Lisa watch the big game. With a look and soundtrack lifted from a 1980s ZZ Top video, the ad depicts scantily clad women suggestively servicing a car at a roadside gas station. A close-up of one lovely lady's cleavage reveals that she's wearing a glittering cross, and then a voice-over lasciviously intones, 'The Catholic Church – we've made some . . . *changes*.' The sequence mainly mocks not religious but commercial mores – namely, the gauze-thin connections between the subject matter of Super Bowl ads and the products they're promoting. Still, the Catholic League's membership deluged Fox with angry letters, and so Fox snipped the word 'Catholic' from reruns of the episode – an unprecedented capitulation by *The Simpsons* to a myopic complaint from a special interest group.

On several other occasions, secular public guardians have proven as hypersensitive as religious authorities to the minutiae of *The Simpsons*. In one of the most bizarre instances, Episode 8F16 ('Bart the Lover') raised the hackles of suicide-prevention organisations across the United States when it first aired in 1992. The problem, explained assorted spokespeople in the muckraking press reports that stirred up this argle-bargle, was the educational film that opens the episode, a spectacularly over-the-top scare flick called *The World Without Zinc* that gets shown to Bart's class in lieu of actual learning. In the film, a teenager named Jimmy is trapped in a nightmare world in which zinc doesn't exist. Without zinc, his car's battery is dead, so he's late for his date with Betty. But he can't call to tell her he's late: in this ghastly alternate reality, there's no zinc to make telephones. So distraught is poor Jimmy that he puts a gun to his head and pulls the trigger – but there's no zinc for the firing pin. Jimmy is saved, and awakens from his nightmare blubberingly thankful to be living in a world with zinc.

Of course you've surely spotted the potentially catastrophic problem with this sequence: 'imitative behaviour'. Like Maggie with her mallet, impressionable young children might watch Jimmy's adventure and decide to try firing a gun at *their own* heads. (Many experts doubtless believe that cartoons that contain broad parodies of educational films that in turn contain depictions of failed suicide attempts are a key factor in teen suicide.) What if kids out there saw Jimmy's zincless world, mistook it for their own, and went around firing guns at their heads willy-nilly in the fatally mistaken belief that those guns wouldn't fire? I'm kidding about this last bit, of course, but, amazingly enough, I'm *not* kidding about the rest of it. 'There's no references that it's not OK,' one suicide-prevention worker told the *Los Angeles Daily News*. 'That's what worries me. They may understand it's a cartoon, but they don't understand it's not an appropriate choice. It's laughed off. It desensitises children and adults to a suicidal person's behavior or gesture.' (Indeed Matt Groening *did* laugh it off, in the very same article: 'Does this encourage teen suicide? If anything, it possibly cheers up suicidal teens by giving them something to laugh at.') At any rate, the zinc-film tempest subsided in time, without any of the letters of apology or re-editing required by the Catholic-Super-Bowl-ad fiasco.

What's truly amazing about this zinc-film thing, though, is that it might not even be the most ridiculous attempt in *Simpsons* history to take offence to the show's content. The world champ in this endeavour might be the Fox Network itself. Like any decent TV network, Fox has censors who audit the scripts of its many quality programmes – *World's Deadliest Police Chases, Temptation Island, Models, Inc.*, all of it – to ensure that the network doesn't broadcast anything that contravenes federal regulations or violates its own lofty standards. Over the years, these censors have on occasion sent notes to *The Simpsons*' creators asking them to change or remove certain potentially offensive details, and over the years *The Simpsons*' creators have disputed these changes (almost always successfully). And so it came to pass, circa 1993, that Fox's censors anticipated a problem with a line that had been enshrined in the annals of pop history almost thirty years earlier for causing a 'scandal' that was considered comically overwrought even then. To wit: in 1966, in an offhand remark to a British newspaper reporter, The Beatles' John Lennon said of his band, 'We're more popular than Jesus now.' In Britain and practically everywhere else the remark was shrugged off as a bit of nonchalant overstatement from a smart-mouthed young man. In the United States, however – particularly in the Bible Belt – the comment resulted in blanket bans of Beatles music, record burnings, even a torching of an effigy of Lennon tied to a cross by the Ku Klux Klan. Fast forward 27 years to Episode 9F21 ('Homer's Barbershop Quartet'), in which Homer reminisces to his kids about his short stint as a major pop star in the mid-1980s as the front man of a barbershop quartet called the Be Sharps. In awe of their father's decidedly Beatles-esque rise in the music world, Bart and Lisa wonder aloud how he and his band could have fallen from such heights. 'What'd you do?' Bart asks Homer. 'Screw up like The Beatles and say you were bigger than Jesus?' Homer promptly replies, 'All the time! That was the title of our second album.' And as proof he holds up a copy of the Be Sharps' 1985 smash *Bigger Than Jesus* (complete with a cover photo that's a Simpsonian copy of The Beatles' *Abbey Road*).

To the untrained eye, this might look like a clever reference to the aforementioned Bible-Belt foofaraw and a sly nod to acknowledge that what was once so offensive was by 1985 little more than a catchy title. But to Fox's censors, whose senses were no doubt precision-tuned to the delicate sensibilities of 1993 – the peak of the family-values era – this scene was a potential mindbomb in need of defusing. 'We understand that Bart's dialogue about Homer's group saying that they're bigger than Jesus directly relates to the uproar over John Lennon's statement,' the censors wrote to *The Simpsons*' producers. 'We would like you to include some put-down of such a claim in a direct reference to the John Lennon-Beatles fiasco, since many viewers may be angered by such a sacrilegious suggestion; something like "you weren't as crazy as John Lennon were you?" or "look what happened to the Beatles" instead of just a knowing look between Bart and Lisa would help take the onus off Homer's statements in the album title *Bigger Than Jesus*.'

Could it have been that Bart's original line was simply 'What'd you do? Say you were bigger than Jesus?' Was the 'screw up like the Beatles' qualifier inserted at the behest of Fox's censors? The historical record's unclear. But it remains, regardless, a ridiculously paranoid analysis of the show's audience and of the mood of that moment. It would appear that Fox's censors feared that a general audience in the early 1990s was as hypersensitive to sacrilege as the KKK of the 1960s.

Then again, maybe I'm being too hard on Fox's censors. Maybe that kind of care was necessary at the height of the Family Values Crusade.[8] It is, at any rate, a vivid illustration of the degree to which the culture's scales were tilted in favour of the easily offended. This is the common thread running between the overt family-values organisations, the suicide-prevention groups and Fox's censors: a sense that modern society was so close to crisis that the slightest nudge could push it over the edge, and moreover that pop culture was a primary perpetrator of this kind of nudging. This was a belief held most fervently and vociferously by religious conservatives in the United States, but its skewed logic influenced the rhetoric and actions of a far broader range of people and groups, permeating practically the whole of Western society during the 1990s. You could see this logic operating on the left side of the political spectrum as progressive groups across North America and around the globe sifted through the culture as obsessively as their counterparts on the religious right in search of evidence of racism or misogyny or any other prejudicial hate crime to take hysterical offence to.

Consider hip-hop superstar Eminem, whose intentionally inflammatory lyrics never failed to raise the hackles of a wide range of left-wing organisations, politicians and pundits. Never mind that Eminem, as aware as the makers of Bart Simpson dolls of the marketing value of being America's baddest bad boy, was all but begging to be labelled offensive, and never mind that his tales of thuggish white-trash life were usually meant as satire or cartoonish exaggeration or stream-of-consciousness fantasising (or all three). The self-righteous spokespeople of the humourless, hyper-PC left took his bait every time, fighting a protracted campaign to establish the rapper as the ultimate poster child for contemporary bigotry. And in the process they implicitly argued (in unintentional lockstep with their enemies in the Christian right) that pop culture was not a mirror of society but rather its engine. That – in this case – the root cause of homophobia and misogyny and youth violence and all manner of other social ills was to be found not in systemic social inequalities or divisive public policy but in ephemeral pop confections such as hip-hop lyrics.

The ideology of the Family Values Crusade also extended beyond the borders of the United States. It was transplanted to Canada practically in its entirety by the Reform Party (in time transmogrified into the present-day Conservative Party) to formulate its conservative, crypto-religious social-policy platform. It popped up in Australia in the guise of a 1997 press release from John Howard's Conservative government announcing the country's inaugural National Family Day. And there it was, too, in the 1996 election campaign in Britain, as John Major and Tony Blair both made rhetorical claims to speak on behalf of the nation's true 'family values'.

All of that said, the crusade had its greatest strength and influence in the United States. The defence of family values was, of course, a pillar of George H.W. Bush's 1992 re-election campaign, during which he took cheap shots at *The Simpsons* while his running mate Dan Quayle demonised the protagonist of the sitcom *Murphy Brown* for being unashamed of her single motherhood. And it was there again in the 1996 campaign of Republican presidential candidate Bob Dole, a central theme of which was the moral bankruptcy of Hollywood. And again in the 2000 election, which Republican House Majority Leader Tom DeLay characterised as a 'battle for souls'.

Meanwhile, a wide range of public-interest groups with names like Focus on the Family and the National Institute on Media and the Family served as constant and rabid watchdogs of public morality, ready at a moment's notice to produce a list of the ten videogames most noxious to America's youth or transcribe the filthiest of gangsta-rap lyrics for submission as Exhibit A in the case for the entertainment industry's moral bankruptcy. Their work has been impressively wide-ranging. In 1993, for example, under pressure from the American Family Association, the multinational consumer-goods giant Unilever pulled its advertising from the NBC police drama *NYPD Blue* because the show dared to give a millisecond of screen time to David Caruso's bare ass. In 1997 the Southern Baptist Convention pushed its 15 million members to boycott the Walt Disney Company because it offered health benefits to the partners of its homosexual employees and hosted theme nights for homosexual visitors at its amusement parks. By 2003 there were at least three dozen websites specialising in movie reviews from a family-values perspective. (One of the most prominent of these, Screenit.com, breaks down its analysis of each film into such categories as 'Profanity', 'Disrespectful/Bad Attitude', 'Imitative Behaviour' and 'Music (Inappropriate)'.)[9]

Hysterical as such critiques often were, they were predicated on increasingly evident truths. Social decay *did* seem dangerously widespread; there *was* an alarming absence of moral authority; all was manifestly not right. These were indeed the same troubling truths that fed *The Simpsons*' angry satire. 'You know what I blame this on the breakdown of? Society,' Moe the bartender tells Homer at one point, the fact of rampant decay so self-evident – so *assumed* – that it's implicit even in the grammatical construction of his sentence. The tricky part, though – the divisive question – was *how* society had broken down. What had caused the decay? Who or what was responsible?

Many family-values crusaders, of course, singled out *The Simpsons* or *NYPD Blue* or Eminem. They talked about the corrosive effects of violent videogames and Hollywood movies. Or they pointed more generally to the social liberalism that came into vogue in the 1960s and had been a dominant social force ever since, all that sex and drugs and rock & roll that had led the great democratic project astray.

It's extraordinary how wilful such self-deception can be. Newt Gingrich could divorce his wife while she lay dying of cancer and then set himself up in Congress a few years later as a zealous defender of traditional family values. William Bennett could lead America's War on Drugs even as he was nursing a multimillion-dollar gambling habit. *The Simpsons* could be cited as a corrupter of youth even as class sizes in North American schools ballooned and budgets cratered and damn near every other kid was being fed one kind of pill or another to help them cope or keep them in line. And all those false agents of decay were trucked out to try to explain why two of these kids walked into their high school in an affluent suburb of Denver one fine spring day in 1999 with a small arsenal of firearms and started shooting.

The facts of the tragedy at Columbine High School in Littleton, Colorado, are stark and horrific. On 20 April 1999, two students named Eric Harris and Dylan Klebold murdered 12 of their fellow classmates and one teacher before taking their own lives. The pair had more ambitious plans involving dozens of homemade bombs that they'd planted all over the school. They both came from affluent families that looked at least as stable as the average family. They listened to music, watched movies, played videogames. Both had been convicted of theft in the recent past; both had been required to attend anger management courses. Harris was taking an antidepressant at the time of the massacre; Klebold's medical records have never been made public.

In light of the limited clues provided by these facts; in light of the tendency to demand a definitive answer to the question *Why?* even when none exists; in light of a decade of rhetoric about the negative influence of pop culture on young people's behaviour – in light of all this, the mainstream media and the world's moral watchdogs soon focused on certain details about Harris and Klebold. They wore black trench coats, were indeed members of something called 'the Trenchcoat Mafia', had maybe modelled themselves after the gun-toting, trench-coated heroes of the film *The Matrix*. They were fans of goth music and its attendant subculture, and in particular of the shock-rock artist Marilyn Manson. They played videogames avidly, especially 'first-person shooter' games like *Doom*. (It's a safe bet, given their age and media-consumption habits, that they had also watched a few episodes of *The Simpsons* in their day.) Watching *The Matrix*, listening to Manson and playing first-person shooters put Harris and Klebold in a category with literally millions of other American teenagers who hadn't committed mass murders, but never mind. Don't give much thought, either, to the fact of Harris's use of an antidepressant called Luvox that was part of a class of drugs (selective serotonin reuptake inhibitors) that would in early 2004 be linked to suicides and 'suicide-related events' among youths in North America and Britain. Equally irrelevant, apparently, were the lax gun-control laws that had permitted Klebold and Harris to assemble their murder weapons so effortlessly. The constant bullying at school, the profound feelings of alienation, the possibility of heads muddied by straight-up insanity or hearts blackened by unfathomable evil – none of these apparently had as much potential for explaining (or explaining *away*) the horrific actions of these kids as their pop-cultural consumption habits did.

If cultural habits had that much influence, though, then why was so little attention paid to reports that Klebold and Harris had spent the final morning of their young lives bowling? If a Marilyn Manson record from last week or a game of *Doom* played last year could incite such violence, what about a game played that very day? This, of course, was the satirical question posed by Michael Moore in his film *Bowling for Columbine*, a 2002 documentary about the massacre and the fear-mongering, violence-obsessed culture its perpetrators were raised in. Moore's point was not to suggest that bowling incited the shootings, but rather to illustrate the ridiculously illogical lengths to which the discussion of Columbine had gone to avoid asking difficult questions. To Moore, Columbine was a powerful symbol of a society's self-delusion.

There are moments in *Bowling for Columbine* when Moore might be guilty of the oversimplification he loathes in the rhetoric of the family-values crusaders and pro-gun zealots. In these moments, Moore seems to suggest that the evidence he submits – of America's long history of vigilante violence, of the sizeable intercontinental-ballistic-missile-manufacturing industry in Littleton, Colorado, of the hysterical fear that flows through the entire culture – could be aggregated together into a complete answer to the question of why Klebold and Harris did what they did. To reiterate: there isn't a complete answer, unless it's a definitive summary of all of moral philosophy from the Old Testament to the teachings of the current Dalai Lama, which is well beyond the scope of Moore's movie and of this book.

Still, I bring up the tragic case of Columbine to demonstrate (as Moore did) the inherent absurdity of the Family Values Crusade's critique of pop culture. The crusaders see the evidence of social decay – they see a pop culture, that is, that clearly reflects the chaos and confusion of the society itself – and they call it the cause. Maybe it's that they're so invested in defending the society as they think it should be that they can't see it as it is: a 'quick-fix, one-hour-photo, instant-oatmeal society', as Lisa Simpson once put it, where comfort and convenience mask the true agents of decay. And Lisa ought to know. *The Simpsons*, after all, provides an impressively sharp-focused picture of that society – and of the sources of its rot.

TRUE AGENTS OF DECAY: ROAD RAGE, LONELY OLD CRANKS, SEVEN KINDS OF FROZEN BROCCOLI

In Episode AABF10 ('Marge Simpson in: "Screaming Yellow Honkers"'), something very strange – in fact, something practically unprecedented – happens in Springfield: Marge Simpson turns into a bad citizen. Every time she leaves the house, she becomes impatient, combative, verbally abusive. She hurls insults at her fellow Springfieldianites and barks impatiently at the chief of police. It all turns out to be the fault of the Simpson family's new automobile, a gargantuan sport-utility vehicle called the Canyonero: 'a squirrel-squishin', deer-smackin' drivin' machine' that's '12 yards long and two lanes wide, 65 tons of American pride' as its jingle explains.[10] Behind the wheel of her Canyonero, Marge – upstanding, moral-to-a-fault Marge, vocal advocate of civic pride, sobriety and self-denial – becomes a menace to society. In short order, her reckless driving gets her tossed into a seminar for people with road rage, but even then Marge can't control herself in the driver's seat. On the ride home from the seminar, she literally rolls over the compact cars of two fellow attendees, and then ploughs into the front gate of the local jail. In the end, though, Marge does find a productive use for her Canyonero: she flips it into the path of a charging rhinoceros, saving her husband and children from certain death. Thankfully, the manoeuvre also destroys the Canyonero, freeing Marge to return to her virtuous ways.

Marge's tragic story, alas, is not exceptional. Sales of SUVs grew by about 341 per cent between 1990 and 1999, and road rage, which barely existed in 1990, was a widespread phenomenon by the time Marge set out on the expressways of Springfield in her Canyonero. SUVs and road rage – separately or in tandem – were in fact the most prominent new trends in automotive transportation in the Simpsonian age. And they were, especially in tandem, a stark emblem of the age's social decay.

Here, for example, is a nasty story that struck such deep chords among northern Californians that media coverage of the incident eclipsed reporting on the February 2000 federal election primary in the state. The story: on 11 February 2000, a station wagon and a black SUV were involved in a fender bender near the airport in San Jose. In the customary fashion, the drivers of both vehicles pulled over, ostensibly to exchange insurance information. The driver of the SUV, a man in his twenties, approached the window of the station wagon. The station wagon's driver, a woman in her late thirties, rolled down her window. Her small white dog, Leo, jumped in her lap to see what was happening. The man reached in the window, snatched the dog and threw it into passing traffic, where it was run over and killed. The man returned to his SUV and drove off.

By the time Leo's murder became a regional *cause célèbre*, this type of incident had already been given a name – road rage – and analysed at length. It had spread to Canada and the UK. It had been the subject of a full episode of *The Simpsons*. It had even spawned spinoffs: air rage, office rage, school rage. It had, in short, been incorporated into the fabric of Western society. It was disparaged, to be sure: it was ugly, antisocial, even in many cases criminal. But by assigning it a name and a pathology, society also *accepted* it. Such rages were apparently the cost of living in the free and prosperous West at the dawn of the twenty-first century.

The voluminous news articles and op-eds and psychologists' analyses on the subject of road rage pointed to the usual suspects in cases of abhorrent behaviour in the 1990s: general stress and anxiety, the rapidly accelerating pace of life, traffic congestion, violent images in the media. I found not one report, however, that suggested that the active encouragement of fanatical individualism – its uncontested position, by the 1990s if not earlier, at the very pinnacle of the hierarchy of Western values and civil rights – might be partially to blame.

None that is, save for *New York Times* reporter Keith Bradsher's 2002 book *High and Mighty*, an exhaustive study of the rise of the SUV. Paraphrasing from SUV manufacturers' own market research, Bradsher compiled this profile of the typical SUV owner:

> They tend to be people who are insecure and vain. They are frequently nervous about their marriages and uncomfortable about parenthood. They often lack confidence in their driving skills. Above all, they are apt to be self-centered and self-absorbed, with little interest in their neighbors and communities. They are more restless, more sybaritic, and less social than most Americans are. They tend to like fine restaurants a lot more than off-road driving, seldom go

to church and have limited interest in doing volunteer work to help others.

They sound, that is, like prime candidates for road rage. And they sound, moreover, like people with a deeply warped sense of the breadth of their rights and the narrowness of their responsibilities as citizens. This is what extreme individualism looks like.

Now, there is nothing inherently bad – and much that is good – about the individualist ethos and its vehement advocacy of personal liberty and civil rights. Societies built upon an individualistic social contract (where the primary political relationship is between the state and the individual, as opposed, for example, to the state and some larger collective unit like a workers' committee or hereditary kinship) tend to be freer, more socially mobile and more egalitarian. The health of such societies, though, is predicated on the idea that the state's protection of the rights of the individual is part of a contract wherein the individual accepts certain civic responsibilities: voting, paying taxes and obeying the state's laws, in particular, along with things like jury duty, military service, sweeping the sidewalk in front of one's house (Germany), treating tourists shabbily (France) and so on. The sickness of many Western democracies in the present consumerist phase lies in our growing abdication of civic responsibility. The driving ideological force behind the consumerist ethos is the argument that the individual's primary role in democracy is not *citizen* but *consumer*. It's all about buying. You have the right to buy almost anything, and in exercising this right you make your primary (if not sole) contribution to public life: you strengthen the economy. Buy junk food, buy an SUV, buy Enron stock – this is how you exercise your civic duties. And this consumer activity – built on individual need, fed by individual desire, aimed at individual acquisition, measured by individual success – is inherently individualistic. This was the relentless argument made by deregulating governments, corporate free-marketeers and sloganeering advertising copy-writers throughout the 1990s.

And I can think of no more powerful symbol of how, taken too far, this argument poisons a society than this image: a man hurtles down a divided highway in an oversized, overpriced, greenhouse-gas-emitting SUV he has no intention of ever driving in the off-road environment it was ostensibly built for. A man alone, putting pedal to floor in an air-conditioned behemoth built for seven plus a kayak. A man in what is (more or less) a car, that enduring symbol of the unbridled freedom of the American individual. This man, so certain of his absolute freedom in that SUV, of his SUV's sovereignty over that piece of road; this man, overworked and stressed out and seething with rage; this man, responding to a routine, minor traffic accident as an act of war, responding with a warning shot fired over his enemy's bow, responding by throwing an adversary's little white dog into oncoming traffic. And driving off down the American highway, unrepentant.

This hyper-individualism creeps into the social cracks rent by faster and more frequent travel, by suburbs built for the needs of cars instead of people, by a culture increasingly focused on watching spectacles instead of participating meaningfully in less extravagant events. Here the asocial violence of road rage finds its source in self-absorbed, atomised isolation. Here *Bowling for Columbine* dovetails with Robert Putnam's *Bowling Alone: The Collapse and Revival of American Community*, a 2000 study that charted the decline in social engagement in the West. Putnam's title and central analogy are drawn from these two concomitant trends: between 1980 and 1993, the total number of bowlers in the US increased by 10 per cent, while participation in bowling leagues declined by 40 per cent over the same period. ('Lest this be thought a wholly trivial example,' Putnam added, 'I should note that nearly 80 million Americans went bowling at least once during 1993, *nearly a third more than voted in the 1994 congressional elections* [Putnam's italics] and roughly the same number as claim to attend church regularly.') The example is American, but social fragmentation is a phenomenon that crosses borders. Fewer and fewer citizens in the Western democracies are voting and volunteering and joining civic organisations, clubs and fraternal lodges.

The fact of this steep decline in the quality and quantity of civic life is what makes the Simpsons' hometown of Springfield an anachronism. The Simpson family lives an otherwise realistic middle-class life in a stereotypical suburban home, but the town that surrounds it is not a cookie-cutter suburb or a bedroom community or a gutted, decomposing rural burg. Springfield, on the contrary, is a thriving small town right out of the 1950s (and even in some respects out of the 1920s). Its small businesses – from Moe's Tavern to King Toots Music Store to Apu's Kwik-E-Mart – are locally owned and reasonably prosperous. An insanely diverse local industrial base manufactures seemingly everything your average Springfieldianite needs, from staples like sugar and steel and grease through consumer goods such as crackers and fake vomit all the way up to cultural products like 'Itchy & Scratchy' cartoons. Town meetings are frequent and ridiculously well attended. Civic organisations, from citizens' committees to vigilante gangs to angry mobs, spring up constantly and attract members instantly.

As if to compensate for this inaccuracy, the show's creators have from time to time littered Springfield with smatterings of urban decay or exurban sprawl. Much of the town's shopping, for example, occurs at a bland suburban-style mall. The squid-gutting industry that once dominated the town harbour has been replaced with a tacky promenade lined with upscale chain boutiques. Episode 1F08 ('$pringfield (or How I Learned To Stop Worrying and Love Legalized Gambling)') opens by making a stark comparison between the booming Springfield of bygone days and the blighted mess of today in a pitch-perfect parody of a 1940s newsreel entitled *Springfield: City on the Grow.* In the newsreel, we see bucolic scenes of the town's bustling galosh factory and gleaming new aqua-car manufacturing plant; its local celebrity, Professor Rubbermouth; even a can-do-spirited little dog tugging a wagon with a sign on it that reads I'M PULLING FOR SPRINGFIELD. As the newsreel ends, we see a young Abraham Simpson walking out of a theatre with his pal Jasper onto a Norman Rockwell main street that's literally paved with gold. The scene dissolves into a shot of the same streetscape in present day, with wrinkly old Abe and Jasper walking through an urban nightmare of destitution, filth and crime. This is still more compensation: we've seen downtown Springfield in many other episodes, and it's never been so decrepit.

The most overt manifestation of Simpsonian social fragmentation, though, lies not in the antiquated setting but in its elderly characters – Abe Simpson in particular. It is in Abe that we find the gaping hole in the façade of Simpsonian values: notwithstanding Marge's keen moral compass and the family's often admirable cohesion, its oldest member has been essentially discarded. In this detail there is a kind of concentrated realism, as if Abe's isolation is intended to represent the entire society's atomisation. The setting, the liveliness of the town's civic life – these are ironies looking for a stark reality to be juxtaposed with. And they find it in lonely Abe, the Simpson family's neglected Grampa.

There's no missing Abe's isolation: it is intense, nearly absolute. It is in fact a running gag, a kind of situational catchphrase for Abe's character, and it has been demonstrated in the most unambiguous terms. In Episode 9F08 ('Lisa's First Word'), for example, a flashback to the unforgettable spring of 1983 reveals a rare warm moment between Abe and his son when Homer asks the old man for $15,000 to buy a home for his growing family. (Marge is newly pregnant with Lisa.) Abe agrees to sell his beloved old dump so he can give Homer the money. 'Dad,' says Homer tenderly, his voice cracking with emotion. 'First you gave me life. Now you've given me a home for my family. I'd be honoured if you came to live with us.' Abe eagerly accepts the offer. Cut to present day. Bart: 'So how long before you shipped Grampa off to the old-folks' home?' Homer, gleefully: 'About three weeks.' And then the whole family laughs.

This is Abe's place in the Simpson household: mostly out of sight and entirely out of mind. Even on those rare occasions – the third Sunday of every month, for example – when the rest of the Simpsons condescend to spending time with Abe, they do so with a grim sense of duty and no real enthusiasm. No one pays much attention to his long, rambling, semi-fictional reminiscences, no one's much interested in his advice, and most of the time the other Simpsons are actively irritated at his presence. 'Dad, I love you,' Homer tells him during one strained visit, 'but you're a weird, sore-headed old crank, and nobody likes you'. Another time, Abe begs to be included in Homer's new hobby – leading a vigilante mob – only to be patronisingly dismissed like an overeager toddler. 'Aw, Dad,' Homer tells him, 'you've done a lot of great things, but you're a very old man now, and old people are useless.' And then Homer tickles his father playfully as he chants, 'Yes they are! Yes they are!'

The show's portrayal of Abe's daily life at the Springfield Retirement Castle is even more brutally bleak. The place is dreary and lifeless, with a sign out front that reads THANK YOU FOR NOT DISCUSSING THE OUTSIDE WORLD. On Thanksgiving, the home's orderly reads out the names of residents whose relatives have sent word that they wish they could visit. There are other brief moments of middling excitement when it's time for the daily dose of medication or the weekly broadcast of *Matlock*. But Abe's home is otherwise nothing more than an antechamber to the great beyond, full of tired, lonely people waiting to die. After a disheartening flip through his mail – one of the few potential joys at the Retirement Castle – Abe observes to no one in particular, 'This junk was hardly worth getting up for. Maybe if I go back to bed for a few days some good mail will build up.' And then he returns to his sad solitude.

It should be noted, in the midst of all this gloom, that Abe Simpson is a very *funny* character. His stream-of-consciousness ramblings,[11] his decrepitude, his tendency to fall asleep at a moment's notice, even his loneliness – all of these are played for laughs on *The Simpsons*. It is, to be sure, a very dark laughter. In Episode 2F18 ('Two Dozen and One Greyhounds'), for example, the Simpsons adopt a female mate for their dog, resulting in an oversized litter of 25 puppies. That's far more than they can handle, and so there's a family meeting to discuss the possibility of giving the little miracles away. Typically, Lisa is outraged. 'Is that what we do in this family?' she fumes. 'When someone becomes an inconvenience, we just get rid of them?' Cut to the Springfield Retirement Castle, where Abe sits in his room, looking forlorn. He lifts the phone. 'Hello?' he calls hopefully. 'Is anybody there?' And then, with a heavy heart, he hangs up.

This is about as black as the satire gets on *The Simpsons*. But there is laughter to be mined from Abe's desperate cry into the phone – first at the incongruity between Lisa's impassioned defence of the puppies and her family's total indifference towards Grampa, then at the surprising honesty of it. We see our own hypocrisy, the staggering indifference we as a society have towards our elders, and we laugh. There's a shock in this laughter, a sense of stunned recognition, an amazement that *The Simpsons* is willing to stare this directly – this *pointedly* – at the ugliest part of our society.

And make no mistake: it is the ugliest part of Western society. As a demonstration of the West's social fragmentation and its self-absorption, as a symbol of the gnawing decay that betrays the grandiosity of its idealistic rhetoric, there are few things to match the West's treatment of its elderly. Travel to India, for example, and you'll find there a degree of baffled disgust at the Western institution of the retirement home that at least matches the West's distaste for arranged marriage. You'll likely find similar sentiments in any society where industrial development and technological advancement have not yet eroded the primacy of family. And with good cause – for there *is* a barbarity in this routine neglect of old people that is, in its quietly tragic way, just as devolutionary as road rage. There's an indefensible abdication of responsibility here, an implicit argument that not only do we as citizens owe nothing to the institutions that gave us our comfortable and prosperous lives, but that we as individuals owe no debt to the *people* that gave us life. This is individualism so smug in its triumph that it's become pure egotism, and such egotism has an enormously destructive impact on the tensile strength of the social fabric. Which is to say: a society in which familial bonds have been surrendered so completely to convenience is a society in deep crisis.

It's not just old folks, either. If there's a potentially fatal social epidemic running rampant through the world's richest nations, it's an epidemic of loneliness. If Abe is much more isolated than the rest of the Simpsons, he's really not that much more alone than a large and growing number of people in the world on the other side of the TV screen. People are not just bowling alone but are living the majority of their lives solo, engaging in quasi-permanent partnerships as easily discarded as the wisdom and companionship of their elders, skipping through 'affinity groups' that change with the seasons (or, at least, with their own evolving interests), passing up on child rearing because the task seems insurmountably difficult without the support network of a real family. And from this lonely existence emerges the telling sociological data: the consistently high rates of divorce and skyrocketing rates of depression, the steady uptick in the number of hours spent staring at a TV screen and/or computer monitor each day. There are studies, too, that have found that a growing number of people – possibly as many as 40 million, mostly women, in the U.S. alone – are habitually overspending when they go shopping. And doing so, often, as 'retail therapy' – to ease stress, anxiety, depression, general unhappiness. To feel fulfilled.

In Episode 3F23 ('You Only Move Twice'), Marge Simpson learns all too well the fallacy of materialism's promise of contentment. For Marge, though, the lesson comes not from a shopping spree but from the acquisition of a fabulous new home in a posh company town called Cypress Creek, where Homer has landed a cushy new management position. Cypress Creek is the epitome of turn-of-the-millennium prosperity, a place of high-tech employment and corporate 'fun runs', pricey sports-memorabilia shops, a half-dozen hammock stores and ridiculously abundant Starbucksian coffee outlets. The new Simpson home is a sparklingly modern and wondrously automated McMansion three times the size of their old digs, tricked out with every gadget and creature comfort a career homemaker could possibly dream of. Initially awed by the place, Marge soon feels oppressed by it: between the automatic vacuum, the self-cleaning oven and the self-watering garden, she's finished her daily housework well before lunch, and so she mirthlessly takes to slugging back a glass of wine each day to pass the time. Within a few days she and the Simpson kids are hounding Homer to take them back to messy, inefficient, down-market Springfield. So Homer goes to his boss – the ever-ebullient Hank Scorpio – to explain the situation. Scorpio asks what's bothering his family. 'Nothing big,' Homer replies. 'It's just a lot of little things.' Scorpio: 'Well, you can't argue with the little things. It's the little things that make up life.' And so the Simpsons leave this apparent paradise for the 'happy little rut' (to quote Marge) of their old lives in Springfield.

With all due respect to Homer's assessment, it isn't a lot of little things that grinds his family down so much as one big one. In Episode 3F23, the Simpsons have tumbled headlong into a flawless consumerist fantasy – and found it completely unsatisfying. Much like those millions of women caught in the endless cycle of retail therapy, Marge learns that the moment of ecstatic satisfaction that comes from having her every need met and her every desire instantly gratified soon crashes hard into numb soulsickness.

She walks into a vision lifted wholesale from a magazine advertisement – the Perfect American Home – and finds only greater need. Underneath the broad parody of the high-tech workplace, this is the satire that gives the episode its real sting: there's nothing less fulfilling than the ideal hawked by modern consumer culture, not even the Simpsons' craptacular existence. The West's virulent strain of hyper-consumerism can't possibly deliver lasting fulfilment, because lasting fulfilment would be the death of consumer society. Its lifeblood is unfulfilled desire. Not for nothing is 'new' the most commonly used word in all marketing. The shopaholics in retail therapy – and the rest of us – are always one revolutionary new product from satori, one purchase away from heaven.

And as it is with utter contentment, so it is with many of democratic society's other great promises and sacred values in the consumer age. The citizen is actually a shareholder, and voting happens on the stock market. The public agenda can be read in TV ratings and box-office grosses, and public discourse happens at the checkout counter, in consumer surveys, in focus-group reports. And as for freedom – the West's vaunted freedom – it exists primarily in the exercise of consumer choice. If your shopping options are seemingly limitless, you might then understand yourself to be perfectly free.

I can remember the emptiness of this promise hitting me hard as I walked the aisles of a supermarket in Poughkeepsie, New York, in the summer of 1997. It had been a few years since I'd last been in the United States, and in typical Canadian fashion I was keenly attuned to the many minute differences that separated my native land from the one laid out so ostentatiously before me. There I was, staring into a frozen-food cooler and marvelling at the subtle but significant gap between life in my hinterland colony of America's consumer empire and this, its triumphal homeland. It wasn't just that the cooler I was staring into contained seven different brands of frozen broccoli, although that was the first thing that struck me. In a Canadian supermarket, you might get two brands of frozen broccoli – three at the most – but *seven* was well beyond my ken. What, after all, can be done to frozen broccoli to distinguish it in seven separate and unique ways? This illusion of infinite choice creates an aura of satisfaction – even of luxury – and that in turn carries the promise of freedom.

But pull the lens back a bit to take in the surroundings. Poughkeepsie – a small burg a couple of hours north of New York City – was by 1997 several years into a severe economic depression. Poughkeepsie was essentially a company town, living and dying at the whim of IBM, and it had been crippled by massive layoffs in the early 1990s as the company fanatically pursued greater efficiency. (It was the same story throughout the region; indeed if all of upstate New York were treated as a separate state, it would've ranked last in America in job creation from 1990 to 1998.) Surrounding me in this supermarket, then, were the victims of IBM's renewed profitability. Fittingly enough, it was in that supermarket that I saw government food stamps for the first time. The store's aisles were messy, its floors dirty. Indeed, all of Poughkeepsie – aside from the extraordinarily posh campus of Vassar College, which I was visiting[12] – felt dishevelled and dangerously tense. Shoppers were barking commands at each other, brushing gruffly past each other, paying for their purchases with food stamps. Yet in the cooler there were seven kinds of frozen broccoli, seven brightly packaged, distinctly logoed varieties of the exact same thing.

To shop in a decaying supermarket in destitute Poughkeepsie; to select from seven kinds of frozen broccoli, two dozen varieties of bread, a hundred kinds of soda; to pay using food stamps, drive home, lock the door, peer out the barred window. To hope that the next trip to the supermarket or the mall provides a new job, a brighter day, a better life. To shop in America – to shop anywhere in the consumerist West – is not just an economic activity. It is also a secular prayer – for happiness, for fulfilment, for an end to this constant need – that will never truly be answered.

'Don't worry, kids,' Marge tells Bart and Lisa as they watch live footage of their father's seemingly doomed space mission. 'I'm sure your father's all right.'

'What are you basing that on, Mom?' Lisa wonders.

'Who wants ginger snaps?' Marge replies with crazed cheeriness. Saying a consumer prayer, that is.

THE FIRST CHURCH OF SPRINGFIELD: FAITH & RELIGION ON THE SIMPSONS

Here's another somewhat anachronistic thing about the Simpsons: the practice of a traditional faith remains a central part of day-to-day life, and the local church – the First Church of Springfield, a house of apparently non-denominational Christian worship – is a pillar of the community. The Simpson family attends services at the church every Sunday, as do most of the people they know in Springfield; all of the Simpsons turn to the church in times of trouble; and on several occasions of particularly intense spiritual crisis, the church's leader – the endlessly sermonising Reverend Lovejoy – comes by the house in person to offer guidance and solace. At a time when church attendance is plummeting in the West – even in the still-devout

United States, where more than nine in ten citizens claim to believe in a higher power but less than half attend religious services regularly – the prominence of the First Church of Springfield is an anomaly. 'God, Christianity and Christians are more a part of the Simpsons' daily lives than any other primetime network series, at least shows not devoted to religion' – so decreed Mark I. Pinsky, whose 2001 book, *The Gospel According to The Simpsons*, catalogued the show's close connection to the West's dominant faith.

That said, the Simpsons are by no means Bible-thumpers. Though religious, they are not particularly pious. Even Marge – the only Simpson who views going to church as anything other than a chore – is much more interested in the family-bonding and community-building aspects of religion than she is in scripture. Her daughter Lisa's brief but intense obsession with sin and damnation in Episode 7F13 ('Homer vs. Lisa and the 8th Commandment'), for example, leads to a confrontation at the grocery store after Marge pilfers two grapes in the produce section. 'Don't you remember the eighth commandment?' an indignant Lisa chastises her. 'Oh, of course,' Marge replies. 'It's "thou shalt not, um, not covet, um, graven images" . . . something about covet . . .' Lisa supplies the accurate scriptural citation hellfire-and-brimstonily: '*Thou shalt not steal!*' Later in the episode, as Lisa sits in the front yard boycotting the family's stolen cable and worrying after the fate of her father's soul, Marge consoles her with an appeal not to the Almighty but to the family. 'When you love somebody,' Marge tells her daughter, 'you have to have faith that in the end, they will do the right thing.'

Even when Marge becomes the First Church of Springfield's most active volunteer, she does so out of a desire to strengthen the community, not to spread the Good Word. 'Sermons about "constancy" and "prudissitude" are all very well and good,' she tells Reverend Lovejoy in Episode 4F18 ('In Marge We Trust'), 'but the church could be doing so much more to reach out to people.' So Marge soon becomes the church's 'Listen Lady,' fielding phone calls from troubled parishioners and dispensing friendly advice instead of passages from the Bible. For Marge, religion's importance is institutional – it's a social force that creates belonging and togetherness and a bulwark of community spirit. Faith, meanwhile, is primarily a private matter.

Here Marge's – and the Simpsons' – spiritual life is much more in keeping with off-screen reality. On *The Simpsons*, church is a hollow ritual and/or a pillar of community, but *faith* is practised at home, privately. Relationships with God are individual, idiosyncratic, informal. There are bedtime prayers and yearning appeals to a higher power in desperate moments. There is a general sense of right and wrong in the Simpson household that is as much a product of Marge's belief in the sanctity of the family and Lisa's deeply held humanistic ethics as it is of any particular gospel. The spiritual life of the Simpsons is, indeed, mostly divorced from church and Sunday school – much like that of a growing number of Westerners who profess a faith while shunning organised religion.

As an omnipresent reminder of why a reasonably moral, somewhat spiritual family might not be keen on dogmatic adherence to scripture in these times, we need only look next door, where the Simpsons' neighbours, the Flanderses, serve as a constant reminder of the ugliness of organised religion's most significant trend in recent years: the rise of fundamentalism.

There can be little doubt about the depth – and the rigidity – of the Christian faith of Ned Flanders and his family. In early episodes, the Flanderses were only mildly religious folks – Ned even indulged in an occasional beer or game of pool back then – and their primary role was to be so cloyingly perfect as to annoy and shame the Simpsons. By a few seasons into *The Simpsons*' run, however, the Flanders family had become an extended satirical study in American evangelical Christianity. Their life is an endless cycle of prayer, Bible study, Gospel-themed games, Christian television and the occasional attempt to baptise the Simpson children, all of it conducted with a delusional, exaggerated happiness that would shame a game-show host. At dinner, Ned's family gives thanks to God not just for the meat but for the middlemen who jacked up the price and the humane but determined boys down at the slaughterhouse. Ned and his kids explode into excited cheers at the prospect of the arrival of Judgement Day. One of the kids, Todd, even imposes a ban on the relentlessly Christian cartoon *Davey & Goliath* because he decides the idea of a talking dog is blasphemous. And Ned himself is so worried about offending God in some tiny way that he regularly exhausts the patience of God's putative spokesman, Reverend Lovejoy. As a friendly children's game is launched – at a church picnic, no less – Ned wonders aloud whether playing sports on a Sunday will anger the Lord. 'Oh, just play the damn game, Ned!' the reverend snaps.

In Ned's unbearable piousness we find *The Simpsons*' sharpest critique of organised religion. The show's implicit argument seems to be that humourless obsessives like Ned – a man Homer has called 'Charlie Church' and 'Churchy LaFemme' in two of his many anti-Flanders rants – have hijacked religious institutions, removing them from the centre of society, where all might potentially find a home, to a place where only those who know their bridal feasts of Beth Chedruharazzeb from their wells of

Zohassadar can seek solace. In fact, this is the very explanation Reverend Lovejoy gives to Marge for his own cynical indifference to his flock when she becomes his parish's Listen Lady. After recounting a series of Ned's invasive, panicked phone calls (in one cutaway, we see Lovejoy's vacation in Paris interrupted by a call from Ned, worried he's just swallowed a toothpick), the reverend tells Marge, 'Finally, I just stopped caring. Luckily, by then it was the eighties, and no one noticed.'

The Simpsons' writers have lost patience with the Flanders brand of fundamentalist Christianity in recent years, their somewhat playful ribbing turning into palpable disgust. In a Season 10 episode, for example, we learn that baby-faced Ned is in fact 60 years old. At first, Ned credits clean living and relentless resistance of all the major urges for his youthful vigour, but then he realises he's wasted his 'whole dang-diddly life' and is reduced to taking tips from Homer on how to make the most of his days. More vicious is a parody of the sickly-sweet Christian claymation cartoon *Davey & Goliath* that appears in Season 12. In the episode, Ned Flanders happily permits his kids to watch the cartoon, which here goes by the stage-winking title *Gravey & Jobriath*, and which follows the moralistic adventures of a wide-eyed boy (Gravey) and his drawling canine sidekick, Jobriath. In this instalment, Gravey is making a pipe bomb 'for to blow up Planned Parenthood' (a pro-choice organisation). Jobriath isn't sure about the plan, though, and Gravey, disgusted at his lack of faith, stuffs the pipe bomb in his dog's mouth and blows the pooch to smithereens. Cut to the Flanders living room, where budding pro-life activists Rod and Todd Flanders cheer righteously. As satire, this is about as subtle as that pipe-bomb explosion, but it does illustrate the distance between Simpsonian morality and fundamentalist moralising.

On occasion, there have been other blanket dismissals of Christianity on *The Simpsons* – usually a bit more subdued if no less categorical. In Episode 1F18 ('Sweet Seymour Skinner's Baadasssss Song'), for example, Principal Skinner gets fired and Ned Flanders becomes the interim principal of Springfield Elementary. When Superintendent Chalmers arrives to see how the new arrangement is working out, he hears Ned thanking the Lord for a beautiful day. 'That sounded like a prayer,' Chalmers exclaims, growing quickly furious. 'A prayer. A prayer in a public school! God has no place within these walls, just like facts have no place in organised religion.' On another occasion, Bart asks his father what religion he is and receives this offhand reply: 'You know, the one with all the well-meaning rules that don't work out in real life. Uh . . . Christianity.'

Notwithstanding these periodic lapses into anti-religious spite, faith is usually treated with sincerity and uncommon respect on the frequent occasions when it comes up on *The Simpsons*. *Organised* religion – like all authoritarian institutions – is a target for snarky asides on the show, but topics such as the nature of belief, the uses of ritualistic worship and the meaning of existence are approached seriously and discussed in depth. Bart's glib decision to sell his soul to his buddy Milhouse for five bucks, for example, sets up an episode-length examination of the soul's sanctity. And when Bart breaks down into prayer in the final scene of that episode, tearfully begging his maker for his soul's return, there's not an ironic note to be found. There's even a bit of relativistic theology tossed in at the very end – by Lisa, of course, who has generously bought Bart's soul back for him. 'You know, Bart,' she opines, 'some philosophers believe that nobody is born with a soul – that you have to earn one through suffering and thought and prayer, like you did last night.'

In the Flanders home, spirituality often appears to be fragile and otherworldly – couched in antiquated language, in need of constant protection from the rough-and-tumble of everyday life – but in the Simpson household and elsewhere in town, faith is flexible, responsive, debatable, *alive*. By far the most conspicuous example of this is Episode 9F01 ('Homer the Heretic'), in which Homer stays home from church one Sunday, has himself a grand old time, and promptly becomes a church of one, setting out on his own personal relationship with God. Faith in its many forms permeates every scene of 9F01, from Krusty the Clown's door-to-door canvassing on behalf of the Brotherhood of Jewish Clowns to Homer's condescending attempt to feed Ganesha a peanut down at the Kwik-E-Mart to Homer's dreaming dialogues with God on the nature of worship.

What's most remarkable about 9F01, though – as with the role of faith on *The Simpsons* in general – is not what it has to say specifically about Christian rituals but simply that it's a half-hour of primetime TV dedicated to vigorously, irreverently, humorously depicting the religious beliefs and practices of contemporary America. Contemporary pop culture usually treats faith with some mix of dismissiveness, consumerism, sentimentality and abstention. On *The Simpsons*, though, faith is a simple fact of everyday life. *The Simpsons* doesn't evangelise on behalf of any particular faith; rather, it rescues faith from the clutches of the Ned Flanderses of the world and serves as a counterweight to the discounting of the soul that's so prevalent among Flanders's secular detractors. The prevalence of faith on *The Simpsons* might, that is, be an attempt by the show to re-establish a middle ground between the blindly fundamentalist and the militantly faithless.

Consider Episode DABF02 ('She of Little Faith'), in which Lisa Simpson converts to Buddhism. Now, Lisa is not only the most philosophically minded of the Simpsons but also the one whose thinking most closely resembles that of the show's creators. In previous episodes we've seen her wrestle weightily with the wages of sin, wax theological about the nature of the soul, and finally emerge – in Episode 5F05 ('Lisa the Skeptic'), which predates DABF02 by about four years – as a pessimistic atheist whose only faith is in clear-eyed scientific reason.

In DABF02, though, Lisa suddenly exhibits a renewed enthusiasm for her inherited Christian faith – spurred, it would appear, by an attempt by crass corporate interests to colonise the First Church of Springfield. The church has been destroyed (the victim of Homer's ill-fated experiment with model rocketry), and Mr Burns and his newly hired brand manager Lindsey Naegle have agreed to donate the money to rebuild it – provided they can do so on their terms. Reverend Lovejoy reluctantly agrees, and the First Church of Springfield is soon reborn as a profit-turning, ad-drenched eyesore, a 'faith-based emporium teeming with impulse-buy items' (to quote Naegle). There's a big neon Jesus waving to parishioners out front, billboards inside advertising Buzz Cola and the Kwik-E-Mart and a half-dozen other businesses, padded seating, even a sports-stadium-style Jumbotron TV with a 'Godcam' that broadcasts candid shots of the faithful. 'Money changed!' a hawker calls from his booth as the Simpsons enter their renovated church. 'Get your money changed right here in the temple!' When Reverend Lovejoy takes to the pulpit, he opens with a quick pitch for Crazy Larry's electronics store and then solemnly intones: 'And now to deliver a special sermon on the sanctity of deliciousness: The Noid!' And lo and behold, out comes The Noid himself – a crimson-costumed cartoon villain who shilled for Domino's Pizza in a series of TV commercials in the 1980s – to address Springfield's faithful.

This is the final straw for Lisa, who promptly storms out of the church in search of a new faith. There follows some soul-searching: Lisa reads Paul Reiser's book *Religionhood*, thumbs through the *Zagat's Guide to World Religion*, wanders Springfield's mean streets, passing Bed, Bath & Baha'i and the Church of the Latter-Day Druids on her journey. And then she stumbles upon the Springfield Buddhist Temple. Inside she finds Richard Gere ('the world's most famous Buddhist,' as Homer's apparently Buddhist co-worker Lenny notes breathlessly) and in no time our Lisa is a mantra-chanting, bodhi-tree-planting follower of the Buddha's eightfold path. Her conversion ruffles many feathers – her mother and the First Church of Springfield's congregation fear for the fate of her soul, while Lisa herself lapses into combative self-righteousness – but soon enough (with some further spiritual guidance from Richard Gere) Lisa learns to co-exist with her Christian family and friends. And thus, by the end of DABF02, Lisa's long-troubled soul seems finally to have found peace.

It'd be way off the mark, though, to think of this episode as a half-hour commercial for Buddhism. Though much of its satire is directed at the disturbing cosiness of contemporary Christianity's relationship with corporate-sponsored materialism, it also lampoons Buddhism's Hollywood-sponsored trendiness. Of particular note: Lenny knows infinitely more about Richard Gere than he does about the Dalai Lama, and fellow Buddhist Carl interrupts his own meditation to ask Gere a trivia question about the film *An Officer and a Gentleman.* Even Lisa learns most of what she knows about her faith from Gere – a man who is almost as much a product of consumer culture as The Noid is.

It makes you wonder: Would it be that much less fulfilling, really, to worship at the altar of some bit of pop-cultural ephemera? If a movie actor is the public face of Buddhism in the West, why *not* a fast-food mascot to sell Christianity? Or why not just put your faith in pop itself?

THE FIRST CHURCH OF THE SIMPSONS

In Episode 5F23 ('The Joy of Sect'), the Simpson family, and most of the population of Springfield along with it, abandon Christianity to join a bizarre quasi-religious cult called the Movementarians. Wedged on the spiritual spectrum somewhere between the Church of Scientology and the alien-obsessed Raelians – with a dash or two of the cults of the Reverend Sun Myung Moon and Bhagwan Shree Rajneesh thrown in for added colour – the Movementarian faith requires its adherents to devote their entire lives, all their money and everything they own to helping the Leader (the cult's unseen godhead) build a spacecraft, which the Leader will then use to transport his people to a perfect existence on the distant planet of Blisstonia (well known for its high levels of bliss). Practical, traditional Marge is the only Simpson unswayed by the Movementarians' brainwashing techniques, and she soon joins forces with Springfield's remaining non-Movementarians – Reverend Lovejoy, Groundskeeper Willie and the Flanderses – to pry her beloved family loose from the Leader's hypnotic clutches. Bart and Lisa are reconverted to the Simpsonian way of life by the promise of space-age hover bikes, while a single drop of sweet, sweet beer is all it takes to remind Homer of the many joys of his old life outside the cult.[13] And thus, as usual, the last scene finds the Simpsons back to normal and gathered in front of the TV set in their living room. 'It's wonderful to think for ourselves again,' Lisa declares. 'You said it, sister!' Bart adds. The very next moment, a voiceover announces: 'You are watching Fox.' All the Simpsons gaze at the screen with the thousand-yard stares of the brainwashed. 'We are watching Fox,' they chant. As 5F23 ends, there is little doubt as to the identity of the true high-growth quasi-religious cult of our time.

It's not just TV – although with one study estimating that the average American TV is on for seven hours and forty minutes each day, TV's certainly a primary pulpit for many of this cult's major deities. But beyond the chattering household cyclops, there are a host of other demigods and churches in the pantheon. There are movies and videogames, musicians and authors, sports teams and fashion designers. This is the great and good Cult of Pop, a fast-growing, constantly mutating ersatz religion that has filled the gaping hole in the West's social fabric where organised religion used to be.

I wonder if this assertion even needs elaboration in an age when the day-to-day lives of celebrities fill the daily papers, when entire TV channels are established to document the exploits of individual professional sports teams, when thousands of people can boast some degree of fluency in Klingon and one of the world's most famous prophets is a shrivelled green muppet from a long time ago and a galaxy far, far away who proselytises on behalf of the Force. Further evidence of pop's quasi-religious status is at any rate not hard to find. Go, for example, to Père Lachaise Cemetery in Paris and wander past the graves of former presidents and revolutionary heroes, past the final resting places of Balzac and Chopin and Oscar Wilde, until you find the headstone of the cemetery's most revered resident: Jim Morrison, the lead singer of the Doors. Or catch a worldwide broadcast of the Super Bowl or soccer's World Cup or the Academy Awards ceremony – secular high holidays one and all. Then there are the scores of lesser sub-cults and regional deities – hockey in Canada and rugby in New Zealand, *Coronation Street* in the UK and Bollywood musicals in India, the vast pantheons of *Star Trek* and *The Lord of the Rings* – each of these smaller in number of adherents but no less devoutly worshipped. Here on my bookshelf is *The Day John Met Paul*, a meticulously researched, 180-page study of pop music's genesis according to one of that cult's most devout sects. (The book is an exhaustive account of everything that happened in Liverpool, England, on the day John Lennon first met Paul McCartney.)

The British pop zealots in Nick Hornby's 1995 novel *High Fidelity* (or their American equivalents in Stephen Frears', 2000 film adaptation) agree at one point that knowing someone's favourite pop touchstones – covering 'all the music/film/TV/book bases' – is the essential first step in a successful romance. 'There was an important and essential truth contained in the idea,' Hornby's narrator explains, 'and the truth was that these things matter, and it's no good pretending that any relationship has a future if your record collections disagree violently, or if your favourite films wouldn't even speak to each other if they met at a party.' Which is to say that almost anywhere in the West, pop affiliations could be as great a sociocultural divide as religion once was. If the faiths of (say) Jews and Christians once created an almost insuperable gap between individuals, so now might those of punk rockers and fans of show tunes. And if, in the end, Hornby's narrator realises that pop isn't – isn't *quite* – the final arbiter of compatibility, the fact that he plays with the notion for as long as he does is a powerful testament to the pseudo-spirituality of pop in our time.

On the surface, this fervent worship of pop might seem absurd. And certainly it's easy to scoff at the passion of the obsessive fan, at the piles of money wasted on random bits of pop memorabilia, at the deep emotion invested in a TV broadcast or a plastic disc or a scrawled signature, at the seemingly limitless appetite for arcana on such superficially trivial subjects. But to dismiss the Cult of Pop as a balm for overgrown children or a fantasy world for reality-averse nuts is to greatly underestimate the importance of faith in human life and to ignore the increasing dearth of places – icons, institutions, people, *anything* – to put that faith in. Religious institutions are out of touch, national institutions untrustworthy, the very existence of the intangible world of the soul and spirit under attack from the rapidly advancing forces of scientific progress. And yet no number of cloned sheep or papal decrees transplanted from the seventeenth century seem capable of quelling our desire to believe.

I WANT TO BELIEVE. This, tellingly, was the slogan emblazoned on a poster that hung on the office wall of FBI agent Fox Mulder, the alien-obsessed hero of *The X-Files*, a Fox Network TV show that for a time in the 1990s rivalled *The Simpsons* in its ability to tap into the *Zeitgeist*. *The X-Files* was a veritable catalogue of popular fears and desires. Its plots focused on paranormal activity and unexplained phenomena and especially alien abduction, but the truly compelling thing about *The X-Files* was an elaborate narrative arc that ran through the series: a dark, labyrinthine, paranoid tale about a vast conspiracy to hide the truth about human contact with aliens from a terrified world. At its most ambitious, *The X-Files* seemed to be shooting for some grand unified conspiracy theory, a single whopper of a parable that would explain everything from crop circles to cancer to global warming. The truth, the show's opening credits famously proclaimed, was out there, and a rogue FBI agent (Mulder) and his sceptical partner, Scully (significantly, a scientist by training), would one day find it and bring it to light. This was Mulder's creed, which he laid out in no uncertain terms during a visit to Springfield.

That visit came in Episode 3G01 ('The Springfield Files'), in which *The Simpsons* gave a firm nod to the cultural resonance of *The X-Files* by bringing its alien-hunting duo to Springfield with voice-acting guest spots by David Duchovny and Gillian Anderson. In the episode, Homer has a close encounter with an ethereal, glowing humanoid in a local field, prompting Mulder and Scully to travel to Springfield to see if the creature might be further evidence of alien life. The agents find nothing, but as they prepare to leave, Mulder pauses to lay out his unshakeable faith. 'Somewhere out there,' he lectures, 'something is watching us. There are alien forces acting in ways we can't perceive. Are we alone in the universe? Impossible. When you consider the wonders that exist all around us . . .' We skip ahead to the same scene much later that evening, as Mulder continues to enumerate the evidence for his beliefs. '. . . voodoo priests of Haiti, the Tibetan numerologists of Appalachia, the unsolved mysteries of . . . *Unsolved Mysteries*. The truth is out there.'

In the end, Homer's alien turns out to be Mr Burns, hepped up on painkillers and shrouded in a 'healthy green glow' courtesy of a lifetime spent working in a nuclear plant. Mulder and Scully's cases rarely turn out to be this easily explained, however, and their quest to unearth the vast conspiracy continued unabated. *The X-Files*, after all, was simply TV's answer to a far broader desire for something to believe in. Recent polls, for example, have found that as many as half of all Americans believe in the existence of UFOs. More earthbound conspiracists, meanwhile, have turned the mystery surrounding the assassination of John F. Kennedy into a global cottage industry and speculated about the nature of an elaborate plot by the House of Windsor to murder Princess Diana. Hillary Clinton talked of a 'vast right-wing conspiracy' to slander her husband. In some circles, George W. Bush's membership in Yale University's no-longer-so-secret society, the Order of Skull and Bones, has become a telling footnote in his improbable rise to the presidency. And Homer Simpson became the spiritual figurehead of the Stonecutters, a vast, ancient brotherhood who keep the electric car out of the marketplace (among many other exploits).[14]

What was particularly notable about all of this paranoid theorising was that in the 1990s it was no longer the delusional domain of a few lonely, marginalised freaks. Instead, it became the fixation of a huge and growing subculture, an increasingly popular hobby and a full-blown mainstream trend. Conspiracy theories became as much a part of mass culture as *The Simpsons* was. And they did so because they provided sustenance to a faith-starved society. Together, all these varied and proliferating theories formed a single creed, a paranoid, backhanded faith built on the firm belief that nothing can be trusted and that nothing is worthy of faith.

But believing in a conspiracy theory is itself an act of faith, a creed right out of a Puritan sermon about a city on a hill. In all conspiracy theories, there is a fall from grace, a revelation of the true way to heavenly glory, an act of purification, and then salvation. Similarly redemptive faiths are buried in all pop cults, from rock & roll (the best hope for salvation in the 1960s) to *Star Trek* (in which the Prime Directive – a cultural-relativist take on the do-unto-others doctrine – clarifies all ethical dilemmas and secures intergalactic peace).

John Lennon's more-popular-than-Jesus quip was, it turns out, actually prophesy: pop *is* a religion, and one of the fastest-growing religions of our time at that.

And if this can be said about pop in general, it can most certainly be said about one of the Cult of Pop's most prominent sects: *The Simpsons*. The show might indeed be most significant not for what it has to say about religion but for its what it's accomplished *as a religion*. Like many a beloved pop icon, the show has fostered community among its fans, a social role often filled by religious institutions in previous generations. Look no further than *The Simpsons'* vibrant, tight-knit online fan base for evidence of the show's most prominent – though surely not its only – community-building effort. And recall, too, that *Simpsons* fans trade lines from the show as a signifier of mutual devotion, as a way to indicate shared values and a similar worldview. And then there are the legions of *Simpsons* fans who use the show as shorthand to summarise an issue or illustrate a point. This, too, is a role formerly provided by a religion, by its sacred texts and learned scholars. When, in autumn 2000, Toronto city councillor Olivia Chow was looking for a clear and potentially universal analogy to explain to her fellow legislators and to the city's populace the misguidedness and immorality of a proposed new waste-management plan, she used a clip from an episode of *The Simpsons*.[15] In a fragmented and secularised culture, it was *The Simpsons*, not a religious text (or a folk tale or a Shakespeare play), that was deemed capable of speaking most clearly and directly to the ethical quandaries of its time.

Or in another, more subjective way: I can't think of any other single institution in *my* recent experience that's given me as much moral guidance, as many useful allegories for making sense of the world, nor – truly – as much plain old solace as *The Simpsons* has. The show is an excellent yardstick for measuring right and wrong, and it is pop culture's most versatile tool for deciphering the daily news. Rarely a day goes by where I don't find some incident in my life or in the world at large that's best explained with a *Simpsons* reference. A well-placed *Simpsons* reference can even seem to *correct* the situation, defuse the bomb, bring righteous order to an ugly world. Beyond this, though, the show is a constant and reliable companion. On days where my life – or the news – has turned to shit, I can count on *The Simpsons* to provide me with a solid twenty-two minutes of truth, of righteous anger, of hypocrisies deflated and injustices revealed, of belly laughter and joy. It is food for my soul. Seriously. I think many *Simpsons* fans would agree. And that, as far as I'm concerned, makes it a kind of religion.

Don't get me wrong, though: *The Simpsons*, like any pop institution, has certain undeniable limits as a spiritual force. For starters, there is its transience – it's a one-time-only spectacle fed to us via an inherently disposable medium. It's a TV show, and TV hates permanence, abhors deeper meaning, longs to make everything it touches temporary and superficial and insignificant. Dense writing, a heavy-rotation syndication schedule, enhanced DVD versions and online discussion forums can only partially compensate for these inescapable facts.

But it's not really the spectacle that handicaps *The Simpsons* as an ersatz religion. No, the real problem is the show's ownership. It is ultimately a corporate entity, controlled by a notoriously inconsiderate parent corporation and separated from its devotees by a cold barrier of copyright laws and syndication rights.[16] If, say, the Catholic Church is no less inflexible and bureaucratic than the Fox Network, it still knows the value of its symbols and the meaning of its scripture. You will not show up at church one Sunday to find a credit-card company's slogan tucked into one of Christ's sermons, nor a page removed from the Gospel of John to make room for an ad for a local car dealership. But in *The Simpsons*' case, well – here comes Homer during the 2004 Super Bowl broadcast, shilling for MasterCard. And there's one of the finest gags in Episode 1F13 ('Deep Space Homer') – in which Buzz Aldrin, the second man on the moon, introduces himself to Homer and Barney by jovially declaring, 'Second comes right after first', to weighted silence – hacked off in syndication so that my local Fox affiliate can tell me about the new financing deals down at the Ford dealership.

There might be no better example of the limits of the Simpsonian faith than the tale of one of Fox's only attempts to embrace the show's cult directly. This was the 'Simpsons Global Fanfest', a three-day convention the network hosted to celebrate *The Simpsons*' tenth anniversary. It happened in Los Angeles in late 2000. By all reports other than Fox's own, it was a travesty. A sacrilege, if you will. The musical guests on the opening night were Sheila E. and Apollonia, two second-rate refugees from the 1980s dance-pop scene. The next day, one of the main events was 'Bart's Extreme Extravaganza', a skateboarding competition right out of a *Simpsons* parody. (All that was missing was Poochie the in-your-face cartoon dog doing a third-rate rap.) The grand finale featured giant foam-costumed characters, lousy comedic master-of-ceremonies work by the host of *Temptation Island*, and a tedious press conference. In the end, only a read-through of an episode of *The Simpsons* by almost the entire cast saved the event from abject crapitude. The Fanfest managed, as Bart once put it, to both suck and blow. This is what happens when a corporation controls your chosen faith: you arrive in Mecca to find that the hajj has been replaced by a Koran-salesmen's conference. You show up in Dharamsala to see the Dalai Lama, and all you can find are souvenir photos of Richard Gere. Your faith can be messed with, badly edited, despoiled.

This is not just a Simpsons thing, nor even just a TV-network thing. Just look at what happened to one of the most exciting, invigorating socio-cultural movements of the Simpsons age: hip-hop. From its birth in the 1970s until the early 1990s, hip-hop was the vanguard force of a dramatic transformation in urban African-American life. Hip-hop was not just one of the most important innovations that pop music had seen in a generation but a whole culture, encompassing new styles of dance and dress and speech and a new form of visual art (graffiti). It promised to reclaim the primacy of black artists in pop music. It was, moreover, an embryonic political movement. When Chuck D of Public Enemy declared rap music 'black America's CNN' in the late 1980s, there seemed to be considerable truth to the claim, and enormous potential in the cause.

Within a few short years, though, hip-hop – at least in its mainstream incarnation – would be horribly disfigured and all but entirely disconnected from its uplifting, block-partying roots. The world's multinational entertainment conglomerates co-opted its sound and pose, fed on its credibility, discouraged its constructive traits and celebrated its worst impulses. Hip-hop artists were reduced to ultraviolent cartoon characters spinning musical horror flicks for white suburbanites, while the culture was stripped down to its most saleable elements and put to work as a marketing vehicle for sportswear and running shoes (and, in time, for seemingly everything). Rap soon looked more like white America's Home Shopping Network than black America's CNN. Hip-hop had been processed into a corporate sub-genre, a brand identity, a tidy package of cool.

Of course, there were some nurturing, self-supporting hip-hop communities that continued to survive in isolated pockets, much as *Simpsons* fans continue to find subversive meaning in the show despite the corporate interference of Fox. When Bart turns up in a Season 5 episode with a megaphone called the Rapmaster 2000 – a cheesy toy that sets his amplified voice to generic, tinny hip-hop beats – it's a sharp jab at the commodification of hip-hop, but the impact of the blow is tempered a bit by the underlying fact that Fox would happily sell its viewers Rapmaster 2000s by the crate if it reckoned there was an extra buck to be made.

In the end, there's a bittersweet quality to being a disciple of *The Simpsons*. The show does a magnificent job of showing us what's wrong with our society, but because it is a TV show, and because it is a satire, it can't really follow through. It can't, on its own, build what's right.

THE NECESSITY OF SENTIMENTAL ENDINGS IN A CRUEL SATIRICAL WORLD

There is a trap embedded in the art of satire: if you practise it with ruthless skill, you may destroy everything. The whole gaudy stage set of modern society may wind up in splinters at your feet, leaving your audience with nothing to hold onto. Think here of the final scene of Stanley Kubrick's *Dr. Strangelove*, in which Slim Pickens' delirious earthward plunge astride an atomic bomb seals the planet's doom. Or think of any number of Monty Python routines, in which the very notion of meaning is so efficiently lampooned that only pure absurdity remains. Or think of any number of episodes of *The Simpsons*, round about five minutes from the end, before the blow has been cushioned by a calming, curative and often sentimental ending.

It is easy to resent the show for these endings. Not only are they sometimes mawkish, but often they can seem like cop-outs, improbable reversals of the implications of the show's own satire. In Episode 1F20 ('Secrets of a Successful Marriage'), for example, Homer gets kicked out of the house after betraying Marge's trust by revealing her most intimate secrets to his night-school class. Lisa explains to her father that Marge will take him back only if there's something he can offer her that no one else can. The best Homer can come up with is this: he offers Marge 'complete and utter dependence'. 'Homer, that's not a good thing,' she notes. Seconds later, though, she concedes that he sure does know how to make a gal feel needed, and with this glib concession, everything's back to normal for the Simpsons.

There's a similar implausibility to the final scene of Episode 2F05 ('Lisa on Ice'), in which Bart and Lisa – fierce opponents on competing peewee hockey teams – simultaneously recall fond memories of each other, quit the game, and skate arm in arm around the rink as the fans fall to rioting. An episode-length satire of the hyper-competitiveness of organised kids' sports ultimately lays not just the blame but the *consequences* solely at the feet of the pushy parents in the stands, as if kids – even Simpson kids – are simply too pure to be fully corrupted by the proceedings.

But let's not be too hard on the Simpsonian sentimental ending, because just as often an episode will hit a final note that rings true. For example, Episode 9F14 ('Duffless'), which follows Homer's titanic struggle to give up his beloved Duff beer for a month at the behest of his worried wife. Thirty days of marital bliss ensue, but the moment Homer's oath is fulfilled, he's headed out the door to Moe's Tavern. 'Send the kids to the neighbours, I'm coming back loaded,' he tells Marge. Once he gets to Moe's, though, he sees the dank pit and its lifeless barflies with newly sober eyes, and he turns tail back home to go on a bicycle ride with his wife. And so when 9F14 closes with Homer and Marge riding in tandem into the sunset, tenderly singing a duet of 'Raindrops Keep Falling on My Head', there's a genuine sweetness to the scene. It's cute, to be sure, but it also feels *honest* – after all, people who are truly in love share embarrassingly cute moments together all the time.

The Simpsonian sentimental ending, though, is also practical. Other kinds of art might be able to risk angering or alienating the mainstream – in some disciplines, indeed, it seems to be required – but TV shows have to hold the attention of millions of viewers in order to survive. That is why few long-running TV shows other than *The Simpsons* have made scathing satire their stock-in-trade. To compensate for the series's fierce satirical content, *The Simpsons*' writers toss in these soothing moments and cutesy final scenes to provide a hopeful note or two. The cohesion of the Simpson family – against considerable odds – is one such compensatory device. The sentimental ending is another. In both cases, the goal is the same: to give the audience something to love alongside the many hypocrisies to loathe, to find a sliver of optimism amidst the decay.

Overwrought as *The Simpsons*' sentimental moments can be, they are almost always sincere. They're sometimes used to parody the *structure* of a syrupy sitcom, but this doesn't diminish their emotional weight. You can see this dynamic at work in the final scenes of Episode 3F06 ('Mother Simpson'), in which Homer's mother suddenly resurfaces after 27 years in the underground as a hippie outlaw. The episode establishes some emotional import well before the final act – Homer is ecstatic to finally have his beloved mother back in his life, and she dispels his long-standing fear that she left him because he was a horrible son. Several clichéd dramatic conventions pile up as the episode builds towards its climax: FBI agents ply stereotypically folksy eyewitnesses for details about the fugitive Mother Simpson's whereabouts; Homer and his mom get tipped off about the impending arrival of the feds by an anonymous last-minute phone call; the investigation peaks with an overblown raid straight out of a cheesy action movie. Despite all of this, Mother Simpson's departure is genuinely poignant. She and Homer race to the outskirts of Springfield to meet up with a hippie in an electric van who will take her back into hiding. She bids her son a tearful farewell, then whacks her head on the van's roof as she climbs in and barks out a motherly 'D'oh!' that confirms the bond between mother and son. Homer watches her drive off, and then he takes a seat on the hood of his car and stares contemplatively into the distance as night falls and the closing credits roll. In this quiet ending, we see both the contentment Homer has found in his mother's love and his heartbreak at having her torn away from him. And *we* are heartbroken for Homer. We want him to be happy. We want to believe – even if only in Homer, this blustering buffoon of a cartoon character – and we want to belong.

And if our society has come apart to the point where it can't give us any of this in the ways that it used to, then we *will* look elsewhere. To a cartoon, even.

NOTES & MARGINALIA

1. **The Reaganite Simpsons:** In case you let your subscription to *Good Housekeeping* lapse, Peggy Noonan's praise of *The Simpsons*' 'family values' focuses on the strength of Marge and Homer's marriage and the honest depiction of its many faults (evidence that it is 'the realest show on television'); on the non-judgementally 'liberal portrait' of the Bible-thumping Flanderses; on the offhanded multiculturalism of Springfield; and on the fact that both she and her son find it funny. 'Thank you,' Noonan writes, addressing the show's creators, 'for a family that sticks together through thick and thin in a good and imperfect place called America.'

2. **The funny one:** Full-grown Marge may want nothing to do with pop music, but teenaged

Marge was in fact an obsessive music fan: her schoolgirl crush was on Ringo Starr, the least significant Beatle. Marge even painted a portrait of Ringo and sent it to him in England. In Episode 7F18 ('Brush with Greatness'), Ringo finally opens the package more than twenty years after it was sent, and immediately composes this reply: 'Dear Marge: Thanks for the fab painting of yours truly. I hung it on me wall. You're quite an artist. In answer to your question – yes, we do have hamburgers and fries in England. But we call French fries "chips". Love, Ringo. P.S. Forgive the lateness of my reply.'

3. **Marge Simpson, sex symbol:** The April 2004 issue of the American edition of *Maxim* magazine is a 'Special Collector's Edition' boasting two separate covers, each featuring a different scantily clad pop icon. The two icons: Paris Hilton and Marge Simpson. Marge is depicted on all fours in the middle of her kitchen, her hair fetchingly dishevelled as she scrubs the floor, gazing out at *Maxim*'s lascivious readers with sleepy bedroom eyes from under the headline 'D'oh-Eyed Beauty'. This depiction – in a spot that has become one of the primary repositories of certified babeness in Western culture – amounts to incontrovertible evidence of Marge's sexuality. It should also be noted, with all due respect to Garth in *Wayne's World*, that the *Maxim*-ised Marge looks much sexier than Bugs Bunny ever did when he dressed up as a female bunny.

4. **Now *That's* Condescending!:** Herewith, two of the practical lessons taught to Marge and Homer at their 'Family Skills' class:

- 'If you leave milk out, it can go sour. Put it in the refrigerator or, failing that, a cool wet sack.'
- 'Put your garbage in a garbage can, people. I can't stress that enough. Don't just throw it out the window.'

5. **No 'very special' episodes:** Blatantly denying the existence of a simple moral is something of a recurring gag on *The Simpsons*. Two stellar examples:

- In Episode 7F21 ('Three Men and a Comic Book'), Bart, Milhouse and Martin combine their savings to buy the coveted premiere issue of *Radioactive Man*, only to destroy it in a ferocious battle over who gets control of the sacred comic book. As the boys consider the causes of their ruin, Bart points out, 'We worked so hard, and now it's all gone. We ended up with nothing because the three of us can't share.' Milhouse promptly inquires, 'What's your point?' Bart, dismissively: 'Nothing. Just kind of ticks me off.'
- In Episode 1F02 ('Homer Goes to College'), Homer finally passes his remedial class in nuclear physics at Springfield University by getting his new computer-geek friends to digitally change his grade. Back in the Simpson living room, Homer ponders the deeper meaning of the adventure. 'Look,' he announces, 'the important thing is that we all learned a lesson. These guys learned the richness and variety of the world outside college.' 'No, we didn't,' one of the geeks pipes up. Homer: 'Oh. Then I learned the real value of college is to study and work hard.' Lisa: 'No you didn't. You only passed your course by cheating, which you always taught us was wrong.' Homer considers. 'Hmm . . . true.' Marge then takes over, insisting that Homer must take the course again without cheating. And so concludes the Simpsons' hunt for a moral in Episode 1F02.

6. **Freeze frame fun:** The protest scenes in Episode 7F09 are overflowing with assorted Springfieldianites wielding protest signs, setting the stage for a handful of freeze-frame gags. Among the signs visible during S.N.U.H.'s picketing of Itchy & Scratchy Studios are: DEATH ISN'T FUNNY ANYMORE; DESTROY ALL VIOLENT PEOPLE; SAVE THE CARTOON ANIMALS (this one held aloft by Ned Flanders); and BRING BACK 'WAGON TRAIN' (hoisted by Moe the bartender, an apparently diehard fan of 1950s TV Westerns).

7. **Simpsonian Puja:** The Hindu elephant god Ganesha – 'Lord of the Hosts', Remover of Obstacles, god of wisdom and intelligence, and guiding light in the spiritual life of Kwik-E-Mart proprietor Apu Nahasapeemapetilon – has been a recurring guest in multiple guises on *The Simpsons*. Among his most auspicious appearances:

- In Episode 9F01 ('Homer the Heretic'), Homer heads down to the Kwik-E-Mart one Sunday morning after deciding that he will worship the Christian God in his own style. He notes that Apu's not foolish enough to be stuck in church either, prompting Apu to point out his shrine to the multi-armed elephant deity in the employee lounge. Homer approaches it with an offering. 'Hey, Ganesha, want a peanut?' he says. 'Please do not offer my god a peanut,' Apu replies indignantly.

- In Episode 3F20 ('Much Apu About Nothing'), Springfield is gripped by anti-immigration fever after Mayor Quimby uses immigrants as a scapegoat for skyrocketing local taxes. Apu's Kwik-E-Mart is soon mobbed with protestors, and when Marge and her kids finally claw through the crowd to get into the store, they find Apu feeding his Ganesha statue a bottle of Yoo-hoo and praying that the Remover of Obstacles will get rid of the protestors.

- In Episode 5F04 ('The Two Mrs. Nahasapeemapetilons'), Apu reluctantly agrees to an arranged marriage with his parents' chosen bride, an Indian woman named Manjula. Homer, believing Apu wants his wedding broken up, storms the ceremony in a crude Ganesha costume. 'I am the god Ganesh!' Homer orates deifically. 'This wedding angers me. It will break up or all will die.' The Hindus at the wedding are, of course, mortified. One guest turns to Homer and announces in Hindi, 'You are not Ganesh – Ganesh is graceful.' He then chases the false idol around the yard, eventually running Homer up a tree. 'Ganesh has been subdued,' Apu's mother announces. 'Resume the ceremony!'

8. **Bible-Belt saltines:** In Episode 4F04 ('A Milhouse Divided'), *The Simpsons* makes a game attempt to parody the heightened sensitivities of the family-values crusaders. In the episode, Milhouse's bickering parents decide to get a divorce. His father, Kirk Van Houten, is soon called to his boss's office at Southern Cracker (tagline: 'The Dryyyyyy Cracker'), the cracker factory where he was heretofore a superstar. Kirk learns to his shock and dismay that he's being fired because he's no longer married. 'Kirk,' his boss explains dryyyyyy-ly, 'crackers are a family food. Happy families. Maybe single people eat crackers – we don't know. Frankly, we don't want to know. It's a market we can do without.'

9. **What would Jesus watch?:** Screenit.com's tireless efforts to ensure that no offensive cinematic behaviour escapes its notice have given rise to a remarkably thorough approach to cataloguing vice and a vigorous brand of subtextual analysis that sometimes verges on the gnostic. Some samples:

- from the 'Profanity' notes for *Pulp Fiction*: 'At least 260 "f" words (40 used with "mother" – with another written on a wallet – and 4 used sexually), 80 "s" words, 2 slang terms for male genitals (the "d" word), 1 slang term for female genitals (the "p" word), 44 asses (4 used with 'hole'), 7 damns, 5 hells, 1 S.O.B., and 24 uses of "G-damn," 3 of "Jesus Christ," and 1 each of "God" and "Jesus" used as exclamations.'

- from the 'Sex/Nudity' notes for *My Big Fat Greek Wedding*: 'We see a classic statue that shows bare breasts.'

- from the 'Sex/Nudity' notes for *Dude, Where's My Car?*: 'Several voluptuous alien women show up, stating that they'll give Chester and Jesse erotic pleasure in exchange for the Continuum Transfunctioner. The leader then takes Jesse's long Popsicle, inserts the entire thing into her mouth/throat, and then pulls out the empty stick (in a deep throat move). This excites these guys and the woman again repeats her offer of pleasure in exchange for the device. Chester then tells Jesse, "For the love of God, they're offering us oral pleasure."'

- from the 'Our Word to Parents' overview for *The Lord of the Rings: The Fellowship of the Ring*: 'Various characters also smoke pipes, but we're never quite sure of the content of what they're smoking (whether it's tobacco, some sort of narcotic or something else).'

10. **A country-fried truck endorsed by a clown:** Marge Simpson is not the first Springfieldianite to be corrupted by the Canyonero. The gargantuan SUV first appears in Episode 5F10 ('The Last Temptation of Krust'), dangled in front of Krusty the Clown in an attempt to convince him to abandon his newfound integrity as a straight-talking stand-up comedian. Krusty initially resists the offer from two slick corporate executives to make a bundle by endorsing the Canyonero, but then he takes one for a test spin. 'I'm tellin' ya,' Krusty explains to his disappointed fans, 'the Canyonero is the Cadillac of automobiles.' His stand-up career is killed by his sellout, and 5F10 closes with a brilliant parody of an SUV ad depicting Krusty driving the Canyonero through a rugged desertscape as the gruff Marlboro-Mannish voice of Hank Williams Jr. sings the Canyonero theme song, accompanied by gritty

country guitar and whip cracks. The first verse: 'Can you name the car with four-wheel drive / Smells like a steak and seats thirty-five? / Canyonero! / Canyonero!' And it goes on like that.

11. **Stories that don't go anywhere:** In addition to Abe Simpson's meandering story of Depression-era deprivation in Episode 9F15 (see Chapter 1), here are two other fine specimens of Abe's unique brand of rambling semi-fiction:

- In Episode 1F12 ('Lisa vs. Malibu Stacy'), Abe's decision to give away his inheritance before he dies sets him to reminiscing. He gives his family a box of mint-condition 1918 Liberty Head silver dollars, and off he goes: 'You see, back in those days, rich men would ride around in zeppelins dropping coins on people, and one day I seen J.D. Rockefeller flying by. So I run out of the house with a big washtub and . . .' There's a brief interruption, and then the tale continues, detailing how turkeys used to be called 'walking birds', football used to be called 'baseball' and the beloved Thanksgiving dishes of his youth included 'Injun eyes' and 'yams stuffed with gunpowder'.

- In Episode 3F19 ('Raging Abe Simpson and His Grumbling Grandson in "The Curse of the Flying Hellfish"'), Abe pays a visit to Springfield Elementary for Grandparents' Day to regale Bart's class with stories. 'My story begins in 19-dickety-two,' Abe lectures. 'We had to say "dickety" 'cause the Kaiser had stolen our word "twenty". I chased that rascal to get it back, but gave up after dickety-six miles.' This tale goes on to explain how Abe invented the 'terlet' ('I spent three years on that terlet!') and how he turned dogs and cats against each other.

12. **Vassar bashing:** During my stay at Vassar College (I was there for its Bacchanalian Founders' Day party), I was informed that several *Simpsons* writers were Vassar grads. I've never been able to determine which writers they were (though I did discover that Ian Maxtone-Graham is the son of a Vassar grad). But the show's occasional references to the school stand as persuasive circumstantial evidence:

- In Episode 7G04 ('There's No Disgrace Like Home'), Homer spends his kids' college fund on family therapy. As he hands the cash to Dr Marvin Monroe's receptionist, Lisa observes, 'There go my young-girl dreams of Vassar.'

- In Episode 2F19 ('The PTA Disbands'), the staff of Springfield Elementary School goes on strike, and Lisa is soon lamenting the quality of her substitute teacher – Abe Simpson's senile pal, Jasper. 'There's no way I'll get into an Ivy League school now,' she whines. 'At this rate, I probably won't even get into Vassar.' Homer is instantly outraged. 'I've had just about enough of your Vassar-bashing, young lady!' he bellows.

13. **Simpsonian deprogramming techniques revealed:** In Episode 5F23, Groundskeeper Willie is revealed to be the local expert in deprogramming cult members. Quoting his reasonable rates – $50 for a kidnapping, $100 for a deprogramming and $500 for a murder – Willie offers his services to Marge. Bart and Lisa are easily broken of their love of the Leader through bribery, but Willie's attempt to deconstruct the Movementarians' logic in order to free Homer from their clutches is less successful. 'The Leader knows all and sees all,' Homer explains. 'Oh,' Willie replies, 'well, that *is* impressive.' A few quick exchanges about Movementarian philosophy later, Willie himself is an avid follower of the Leader.

Perhaps the Simpsons should have gone with Conformco Brain Deprogrammers, whom they hired in Episode 1F16 ('Burns' Heir') to loose Bart from the clutches of Mr Burns. The celebrated career of Conformco's expert deprogrammer includes deprogramming Jane Fonda and getting Paul McCartney out of Wings. ('You idiot!' Homer berates the deprogrammer. 'He was the most talented one!') And so of course he has no trouble with Bart, whom he sequesters at a motor inn and bombards with a lecture about how he loves Homer and Marge, not Mr Burns. The technique works, except that the deprogrammer accidentally kidnapped not Bart but Hans Moleman, Springfield's favourite shrivelled blind man, who now believes he's a Simpson. In the end, Bart turns on Mr Burns of his own accord, and Homer keeps Hans around for the simple joy of kissing his wrinkled head. 'It's like kissing a peanut!' Homer enthusiastically observes.

14. **They do:** In Episode 2F09 ('Homer the Great'), the rituals and exploits of the Stonecutters take centre stage when Homer joins the secret order and turns out to be its 'Chosen One' – the

leader whose coming had long been prophesied. At one Stonecutter meeting, a feast of ribs is preceded by the singing of the order's celebratory theme song – a *Simpsons* musical classic that catalogues the Stonecutters' many behind-the-scenes activities. Among their accomplishments: controlling the British crown, keeping the metric system down, leaving Atlantis off the maps, keeping the Martians under wraps, holding back the electric car, making Steve Guttenberg a star, robbing cave fish of their sight and rigging every Oscar night. The Stonecutters also appear to be allied with the nefarious Egg Council.

15. **Life imitates cartoon art:** Toronto City Hall, 10 October 2000. The city council is mired in a marathon debate about Toronto's garbage problem. The landfill currently in use must be closed by 2002, and there is a proposal to 'solve' the impending crisis by trucking Toronto's waste to an abandoned mine in Kirkland Lake, 600 kilometres north of the city. With the whole of the council and a packed public gallery looking on, Councillor Olivia Chow shows an excerpt from Episode 5F09 ('Trash of the Titans'), in which Homer is elected Springfield's sanitation commissioner. He promptly spends his entire annual budget in the first month. To raise new funds, he turns an abandoned mine on the outskirts of the town into a giant garbage dump, accepting trash from cities across the country. In short order, Springfield is overrun with garbage – it spills out of sewers, erupts out of the ground, pours out of fire hydrants. Eventually, the entire town is moved 'five miles down the road' to 'solve' the problem.

16. **Community spirit with a Fox attitude:** In 1995, just as *The Simpsons*' fan base was beginning to congregate in force on the Internet, Fox introduced itself to the most devoted fans of its most popular programme in a manner worthy of Mr Burns. To wit: the network's lawyers – *damn their oily hides!* – sent stern 'cease and desist' letters to the proprietors of various *Simpsons* fansites, ordering them to remove copyrighted images and audio and video clips from their online shrines. 'It's not our intention to shut down bona fide fan websites,' an anonymous Fox spokesperson told the Associated Press. 'It is our intention to insist that all websites meet guidelines that protect the creative integrity of the programmes they represent.' The fansite proprietors reluctantly complied.

CHAPTER SEVEN

The Simpsons in Cyberspace

We are in great haste to construct a magnetic telegraph from Maine to Texas; but Maine and Texas, it may be, have nothing important to communicate.

Henry David Thoreau, Walden

Last night's 'Itchy & Scratchy' was, without a doubt, the *worst* episode ever. Rest assured that I was on the Internet within minutes, registering my disgust throughout the world.

Comic Book Guy, Episode 4F12 ('The Itchy & Scratchy & Poochie Show')

THE DIGITAL DECADE (BRIEFLY)

FROM A NEWSPAPER ARTICLE DATED 2 February 1996: 'The Net appears to be the harbinger of a new, virtual feudalism, its online villages uniting not around a petty king but around a petty subject – a TV show, a celebrity, any number of narrowly defined worldviews . . . The Internet is not devoid of merit. Many Web sites offer up-to-the-minute news, many others are quite entertaining, and e-mail is a cheap and effective form of communication. It is not, however, the kind of community I want to live in . . . I don't need to *interact* with my reading material. Call me a fossil, call me a Philistine, but I like just reading it.'

Who, exactly, was the reactionary grump who scribbled this rant? The answer is yours truly, about two years before I became an intern at a 'digital culture' magazine. It appeared in my alma mater's campus newspaper under the headline 'Uneasy Virtual Future'. I thought of myself as young and idealistic in those days – which is to say that I was ignorant and self-righteous – and there was more than enough hype built up around this Internet thing by that point that I wasn't buying any of it. I'd started messing around on my own computer – a Commodore 64 – when I was like nine years old. Once I spent two days home from school sick typing in the code for a *Donkey Kong* knock-off called *Jumpman*. I'd processed some words since then, spread some sheets, sent an e-mail or two. So the hell what? Getting all worked up about it was like building a religious cult around a toaster. It was a frickin' tool, folks. Get over it.

I was wrong, of course. So very wrong.

The Internet first appeared on *The Simpsons* under similarly derisive circumstances. Now, computers in general had been a frequent but marginal presence in Springfield since the show's inception. (In a Season 1 episode, for example, Homer attempts to buy a mammoth recreational vehicle at Cowboy Bob's RV Round-Up, and Cowboy Bob uses his office computer to run a credit check on Homer, which soon sets off sirens and flashing lights.) The first full-on appearance of the Internet, though, didn't come until an episode in Season 5, which originally aired in October 1993. Homer goes to Springfield University for remedial job training, soon becoming a would-be Bluto Blutarsky on a campus decidedly lacking in Animal Houses. Instead, three classic nerds – poor of fashion sense and complexion, pocket-protectored and bespectacled, given to quoting Monty Python routines – become Homer's partners in hijinks. His ill-conceived pranks get the geeky trio expelled, and Homer eagerly takes them into his home. 'They're geniuses,' he explains to Marge, 'and they'll solve all our problems. They'll elevate us to the status of kings on earth.' In the very next scene, Marge attempts to make a phone call, but she can't because the receiver is awash in 'crazy noises'. The nerds, installed at a row of computer terminals in the Simpson living room, respond with contempt. 'Those "crazy noises" are computer signals,' says one sarcastically. Another explains the gravity of their work: 'Some guys at MIT are sending us reasons why Captain Picard is better than Captain Kirk.' 'Hah!' exclaims the third. 'They're outta their minds!' All three dissolve into the chirruping laughter of the smug, self-involved geek. Within days, Bart, Lisa and even Marge want these geeks out of their house. King-makers? Not bloody likely. In 1993 – or even, for certain slow-learning campus journalists, as late as 1996 – cyberspace looked like little more than a playpen for *Star Trek* nuts. The Internet was a souped-up ham radio, the high-tech gadget du jour for asocial weirdos.

It's understandable, then, that someone penning a *Simpsons* script in 1993 didn't realise the Net would soon become the driving force for entire episodes of the show. As countless breathless media reports would soon note, the Internet was to conquer Western society in the 1990s with a speed and force unparalleled by any other new technology in recorded history. In 1995, there were about 16 million Internet users worldwide; in 1999, there were 200 million. Today, there are more than 600 million. The Internet was the single most important new development the world saw in the 1990s – not just technologically but socially, culturally, politically, economically. It inspired idealists and utopians – young and old, geek and hipster, from the affluent West to the developing world and back again – to dream of a radically, magnificently transformed world just around the corner, free at long last from famine and inequality and oppression. One giddy early adopter – the erstwhile Grateful Dead lyricist John Perry Barlow – insisted that the Internet was not just the most revolutionary communication tool since Gutenberg's printing press but 'the most transforming technological event since the capture of fire'. It gave birth to new subcultures of its own and nurtured many others. It fuelled one of the most feverish investment bubbles in history, gave rise to dozens of entirely new sectors of business activity and radically transformed the nature of work in many others. A lexicon was born online, icons and touchstones and trends minted there. Cities, regions, even entire nations were reconfigured to join the digital age. The Internet wove itself into the very fabric of society, becoming in less than a decade as much a part of daily life for millions of people as the TV set or the microwave oven. No wonder evangelists like Barlow were so excited.

This steep explosive arc from margin to mainstream is in abundant evidence in *The Simpsons*. Indeed no other pop institution tracked the medium's rise as vividly, and few if any other cultural enterprises can claim as massive a presence on the Internet itself nor as close and symbiotic a relationship with its own online community. *The Simpsons* would have soldiered on without the Internet, and the Internet surely would have erupted without *The Simpsons*, but the decade's most important cultural institution and its most disruptive technological force certainly fed eagerly off each other.

WIRED SPRINGFIELD: THE INTERWEB ON *THE SIMPSONS*

For the first eight years or so of the show's run, the Interweb – uh, Internet[1] – is a peripheral phenomenon on *The Simpsons*. It's a source of minor details and side gags that enforce the parallels between Springfield and our own world, heightening the show's satirical verisimilitude. Homer's pal Lenny, for example, shows up for their regular poker game with a deck of pornographic 'Girls of the Internet' cards. ('I'd go online with them any day!' Homer enthuses.) At the start of another episode, Bart scrawls 'My butt does not deserve a website' on the Springfield Elementary School chalkboard. And in 1995, a Season 6 flashback to the time of Maggie's birth a year or so earlier features a scene-setting introduction by Homer containing the obligatory list of pop-cultural touchstones: 'It was a tumultuous time for our nation. The clear-beverage craze gave us all a reason to live. The information superhighway showed the average person what some nerd thinks about *Star Trek*. And the domestication of the dog continued unabated.'

On occasion, though, even in these earlier seasons, the Internet came in for closer examination, and the town already had a resident geek: the Comic Book Guy, the blubbery, trivia-spouting loser who presides over all things dorky and obsessive from behind the counter at the Android's Dungeon.[2] Although the Comic Book Guy's day job primarily involves peddling offline treasures – the prized first issue of the *Radioactive Man* comic, an animation cel of Snagglepuss, a rare photo of Sean Connery signed by Roger Moore – he's a natural fit for the role of Internet obsessive. He's shamelessly obese, seen on one occasion pushing a full wheelbarrow-load of tacos down the sidewalk (adequate sustenance for a *Dr Who* marathon); he's humourlessly enthralled by pop-cultural minutiae, truest to himself when he's brandishing a list of technical errors he's found with the 'so-called silent propulsion system' employed by the submarine in the film *The Hunt for Red October*; he's a sarcastic, repulsive, middle-aged virgin. He is, in short, a waddling embodiment of the stereotypical Internet user constructed by the mainstream media in the years before everyone and their grandma went online.

Naturally, then, the Comic Book Guy is the one who introduces surfing the Internet to Springfield. In Episode 2F17 ('Radioactive Man'), Bart and Milhouse have come to the Android's Dungeon in search of more *Radioactive Man* comics for their collections. The Comic Book Guy informs them – smug as ever – that a *Radioactive Man* movie is in the works. 'Who's going to play Radioactive Man?' Bart asks breathlessly. 'I will tell you in exactly seven minutes,' the Comic Book Guy retorts, logging onto his favourite newsgroup: alt.nerd.obsessive.[3] 'NEED KNOW STAR RM PIC,' he types (in the requisite shorthand of the infant Internet, when messages had to be kept as brief as possible to travel smoothly along ancient copper wires). The message bounces around cyberspace, from a geek in a Happy Little Elves T-shirt to another in Spock ears to Prince (as in the pop musician, an avid early netizen) to a guy hiding under the boardroom table at the Hollywood studio where the casting of Radioactive Man is being discussed. The part goes to Rainier Wolfcastle, the Ahnold-accented action hero, but that's not important here. What's important is that, with this quick snapshot, the Internet has fully arrived in Springfield.

The general population of Springfield soon joins the Comic Book Guy in cyberspace. In Season 9, Reverend Lovejoy consults a Hindu website for instructions on performing Apu's wedding ceremony. Marge's sisters, Patty and Selma, looking to find Marge a new husband, help her send an e-mail to her high-school flame, Artie Ziff. Even Fat Tony and his associates in the Springfield Mafia go online, setting up their website at crime.org. By Season 10, when Episode AABF20 ('30 Minutes Over Tokyo') begins with the opening of the Java Server – Springfield's first cybercafé – the Internet has moved well beyond the dorky confines of the Android's Dungeon. Sure, it's brainy Lisa who suggests the Simpsons pay the café a visit, but Bart's just as eager, and he entices his father to come along with the promise of 'a website that shows monkeys doing it'. When they arrive at the Java Server, they find Groundskeeper Willie checking out the Up-Kilt Camera website and Lenny surfing chat rooms for dates. The Internet is now as much a part of Springfield's landscape as Kent Brockman's newscasts and the indefatigable local tyre fire. The occasional well-targeted dig still occurs – when Milhouse suggests that Springfield's kids go online to expose their parents' hypocrisy, for example, Bart replies, 'No, we have to reach people whose opinions actually matter' – but the Internet itself has become as much a part of the show's mediascape as Homer's beloved TV set.

It's been noted by some critics that one of the most curious aspects of *The Simpsons'* vaunted realism is the simple fact that the Simpsons, like practically everyone in the Western world but *unlike* the characters who populate the vast majority of TVland, spend enormous amounts of time watching television. Archie Bunker watched a lot of TV, and the *Cheers* gang sometimes gathered around the bar's TV to gawk at sports. And other shows have sometimes used the TV as an expository-dialogue machine. But to watch most TV shows (particularly family sitcoms) is to visit a fantasy world in which TV itself barely exists. Think of all those sassy teens and tots, all those exhausted working parents, all of them perpetually gathered in their living rooms and somehow abstaining from the one activity that dominates the majority of North American living rooms. *The Simpsons'* latter-day contemporaries are a bit more true to life: the presidential staff members on *The West Wing* keep one eye on CNN, the male friends on *Friends* keep both eyes glued to the bouncing chests of *Baywatch*, and the potty-mouthed kids on the avowedly *Simpsons*-influenced *South Park* learn new expletives from their beloved 'Terence and Philip Show'. But *The Simpsons* remains the show that has most fully integrated America's number one leisure activity into its *mise en scène*.

The show has been similarly pioneering when it comes to the Internet. Your average sitcom might include an occasional glib one-liner about e-mail, but only *The Simpsons* has added the Net to the daily lives of its characters. And it has accomplished this feat in lockstep with the advent and growth of the medium itself – a kind of mirror-imaging that's a key reason why the show appears so much more realistic than most sitcoms. Because the real live people on other sitcoms don't watch TV or surf the Net, these cartoon characters who do come across as more plausible, more real. Homer starts an ill-conceived Internet company from his living room? Sure. Why not? Much more representative of our world, of our time, than someone in a blandly 'typical' living room devoid of a computer or even a TV set who appears not to have even heard of this Internet thing at all.

In Season 9, Homer does start an ill-conceived dot-com – in Episode CABF02 ('The Computer Wore Menace Shoes'). Then in Season 12, he becomes 'Mr X', the proprietor of a website specialising in scandalous rumours. Later the same season, Bart creates *Angry Dad*, a simplistic and poorly animated cartoon that briefly becomes an online hit at BetterThanTV.com. This is the end point of the arc that began with a couple of horn-rimmed geeks at Springfield U., passed through the Comic Book Guy's alt.nerd.obsessive newsgroup and Springfield's new cybercafé, and then bled into total saturation with episodes like these, in which the Internet has become the engine of the episode's plot. And it's the same steep curve as that of the medium itself: one day an oddball subcultural phenomenon, the next an established fact on the periphery of daily life, and then the next a central force.

But the show's increasingly elaborate Internet-centred plot lines weren't the most telling way in which it adapted to the new medium. A far more direct means by which *The Simpsons* embraced the Internet was in a recurring phenomenon that the show's online fans dubbed 'Freeze Frame Fun', which began as a sort of natural by-product of the intense comedic density of the show itself. Every episode of *The Simpsons* is so packed with gags and pop-culture references and background details that a single viewing is never enough to take it all in. Presumably, this density emerged from its creators' desire to construct a complete universe, much as period movies make sure to get the costumes and set decoration just right. Rather than making sure the candlesticks and linens are appropriate to a film's historical setting, though, *The Simpsons*' writers took to burying gags in the show's incidental details. Thus, in a Season 1 episode in which Reverend Lovejoy lectures the Springfield faithful on the evils of gambling, the sign in front of the church lists that week's activities:

BINGO – TUESDAY NIGHT

MONTE CARLO NIGHT – WEDNESDAY

RENO RETREAT – SATURDAY

Gags like these were frequently so elaborate – or blipped across the screen so briefly – that the only way to catch them in their entirety was to tape the show and then pause your VCR when they appeared. Hence Freeze Frame Fun.

There was a tremendous presumption buried in the writers' inclusion of these sorts of gags in the early seasons of the show's run. They assumed that *The Simpsons* had (or would come to have) a fan base obsessive enough to bother ferreting them all out. 'The scripts are . . . much more dense than any you find on TV,' writer-producer David Mirkin told a reporter in 1993. 'They're packed with twice as many jokes as other sitcoms. I mean, it will take us hours just to come up with a freeze-frame joke designed for the one guy out there who wants to stop his VCR and look at it.' Freeze Frame Fun was a product of the writers' obsessive dedication to their craft – a point of pride and a bit of a lark. *Maybe* someone will bother to look – *one guy* – and if so, then what a fun little reward he'll find.

Back in 1993 – a year before the founding of alt.tv.simpsons, the first Internet newsgroup for *Simpsons* fans – 'one guy' was probably a reasonable expectation for the average audience of a freeze-frame gag. But it was, it turned out, an idea tailor-made for the newborn Internet, which fast became the primary vehicle for *Simpsons* fandom and almost as quickly made clear that the Freeze Frame Fun of the first few seasons was, if anything, a serious *under*estimation of the obsessiveness of the show's fans.

There was way more than one guy out there in cyberspace – there were soon millions – and many of them were *Simpsons* nuts, and they were watching each episode *very* closely.

VIRTUAL SPRINGFIELD: THE SIMPSONS ON THE INTERWEB

In Episode 2F06 ('Homer: Badman'), the Simpsons' babysitter accuses Homer of sexually harassing her. (She sat on his prized gummi *Venus de Milo* while being driven home, and he was merely extracting the sweet candy from her pants.) The tabloid-TV show *Rock Bottom* fuels the politically correct crusade against Homer, heavily editing an interview with him to make him appear to be a lecherous animal. It turns out, though, that Groundskeeper Willie videotaped Homer's altercation with the babysitter, and his tape exonerates Homer of the crime. On the next episode of *Rock Bottom*, the show's sleazoid host, Godfrey Jones, apologises for his baseless allegations in the syrupy *mea culpa* tones of the chastened journalistic crusader. 'In our mad pursuit of the scoop,' Jones confesses, 'we members of the press sometimes . . . make mistakes. *Rock Bottom* would like to make the following corrections.' The Simpson family looks on from home as a fast-scrolling blur of text zooms up the TV screen. That blur is the most elaborate example of Freeze Frame Fun in the show's history. And it also attests to three critical aspects of *The Simpsons*' relationship with its fans: first, that the show's writers know full well by this point (in Season 6) that no gag they make is too elaborate, no reference too obscure, that their fans won't dig up the details in full; second, that they (the writers) are familiar with the online institution of Freeze Frame Fun; and third – and most significant – that they are willing to address their hard core audience directly.

And so the faithful multitudes who froze their videotapes on the *Rock Bottom* corrections list and advanced them frame by frame were treated to a hysterically funny list 34 items long.[4] Among them: 'Styrofoam is not made from kittens'; 'Bullets do not bounce off of fat guys'; 'The Beatles haven't reunited to enter kick boxing competitions.' This was no hastily assembled filler. It was *crafted*. Several items on the list even nodded to the ridiculously obsessive relationship between fan and writer to which it was a testament: 'If you are reading this, you have no life'; 'The people who are writing this have no life'; 'Our viewers are not pathetic sexless food tubes.'

Also: 'The nerds on the internet are not geeks.' Or, to paraphrase: *Howdy hi, alt.tv.simpsons members!*

It goes practically without saying that the alt.tv.simpsons cognoscenti caught the *Rock Bottom* corrections list. Caught it, catalogued it, placed it on their list of Freeze Frame Fun items in the episode capsule for 2F06. And this goes without saying because by this point in *Simpsons* history, the alt.tv.simpsons gang caught essentially *everything*. Born, like any other newsgroup on the fledgling Internet, as a place for netizens to post information and engage in debate about their shared interests, alt.tv.simpsons soon became a kind of uniquely single-minded salon for the advancement of *Simpsons* studies. In addition to its members' highly opinionated reviews of each episode (registered throughout the world within minutes of each episode's airing), the forums and threads at alt.tv.simpsons also became an online museum of Simpsonalia, producing 'capsules' of each episode that eventually found a permanent home at the newsgroup's companion website, The Simpsons Archive (http://www.snpp.com), which was and remains among the most thorough and thoughtful pop-cultural monuments on the web. The Archive contains exhaustive files on the show's characters and setting; lengthy bibliographies of articles about the show and interviews with its creators; comprehensive guides to *Simpsons* merchandise, the show's myriad references, and the layout of the Simpson home; in short, almost anything you could possibly want to know about *The Simpsons*.[5]

The Archive's most essential files, though, are its capsules of each episode. Arising initially from trivia-laden threads at alt.tv.simpsons, these capsules eventually adopted a standard form: a detailed plot synopsis and fragmentary script, including a record of the chalkboard and couch gags in the title sequence; a list of the episode's references to other media (especially film) and a separate list of all other references (to current events and historical figures, for example); a list of animation and continuity errors; a selection of the most trenchant and/or cutting reviews of the episode that were posted to alt.tv.simpsons; and of course Freeze Frame Fun. The Archive (and alt.tv.simpsons) even has a kind of politburo, a small coterie of hard core contributors whose reviews feature prominently in many capsules and who curate the Archive's contents to ensure accuracy. Is a given scene's camera angle, for example, a genuine reference to Hitchcock, or is it just a coincidence?

This kind of obsessiveness, this extraordinary myopia – this eventually became the Internet's stock-in-trade. But alt.tv.simpsons and The Simpsons Archive were among its first practitioners and remain among its most dedicated. And they exist merely as the central node of a vast web of online fandom – there are dozens of websites dedicated to every major *Simpsons* character, a handful for each of the minor characters, the odd site dedicated to a single one-off character. (I seem to recall that there was a Disco Stu fan site up and running after his first appearance, which consisted of two lines of dialogue.) There are sites that obsess over the geography of *The Simpsons* world, sites that catalogue its references to Canada or Broadway musicals or Stanley Kubrick. There are French and Brazilian and Thai sites. And if there are now far fewer sites than there were at the peak of the show's online popularity (circa 1998, coinciding with the first major mainstream wave of Internet adoption and comprising a far more dedicated fanaticism than the Bart-mania phenomenon of 1990), well, there are still an awful lot.

The Simpsons has rewarded this commitment like no other pop culture institution. Since around the time of *Rock Bottom*'s corrections list, the show has engaged in a legitimate (if sporadic) dialogue with its diehard fans. Words from the Archive's reviews emerge from characters' mouths. In one notable instance, Bart talks more or less directly to the most rabid and temperamental fans. It's a genuine relationship.

If you read carefully through the capsules at The Simpsons Archive, you'll soon stumble on scholarship befitting an associate professor and an attention to detail worthy of an archaeologist. Consider Episode 8F02 ('Treehouse of Horror II'), whose capsule begins with this editor's note: 'I belong to the old school of English orthography, so I spell Hallowe'en with an apostrophe.' In Episode 1F17 ('Lisa's Rival'), Lisa is asked by her new friend's father (a professor) to come up with an anagram of the name of the Hollywood actor Jeremy Irons that forms a description of him. Lisa can only come up with 'Jeremy's Iron'. (The professor then offers Lisa a ball that perhaps she'd like to bounce.) In the episode capsule, the alt.tv.simpsons crowd comes up with seven, including 'Jerry is omen,' 'Mr enjoys ire' and 'is on my jeer'. Not the most inspired anagrams, admittedly, but don't miss the point: they took the time to produce *seven*.

The dedicated contributors to alt.tv.simpsons are equally diligent on those occasions when *The Simpsons*' writers themselves appear onscreen, most notably in the two episodes in which we're taken behind the scenes to see the making of 'Itchy & Scratchy': 9F16 ('The Front') and 4F12 ('The Itchy & Scratchy & Poochie Show'). In both of these, the offices of the company that produces 'Itchy & Scratchy' are populated by animated versions of *The Simpsons*' writers, and sleuthful Archivists have hunted down their real-life identities in both cases. Jon Vitti, for example, one of the show's most prolific writers, is the 'Itchy' writer in 9F16 who gets fired and then has 'Itchy' studio boss Roger Meyer's desktop nameplate bounced off his forehead.

At times like these, there appears to be a certain warm camaraderie between the writers and the diehards, like the kind of not-quite-friendship you see in regional music scenes where the fans and the performers are nodding acquaintances. It's perhaps only natural that the alt.tv.simpsons crowd has taken a proprietary interest in the show's staff. After all, they're among the only members of the show's audience who could pick out Jon Vitti or Matt Groening – or even voice actor Dan Castellaneta – in a police lineup. 'Cartoons have writers?' an amazed Bart asks in Episode 9F16, as *The Simpsons*' writing team acknowledges its own obscurity.

In recognition of the passion of their only real groupies, the show's creators have directly addressed two of the recurring debates at alt.tv.simpsons – topics known in a.t.s.-speak as 'Is Smithers Gay?' and 'Where is Springfield?' In Episode 3F31 ('The Simpsons 138th Episode Spectacular'), actor Troy McClure, who is hosting a self-referencing showcase of clips, deleted scenes and counterfeit *Simpsons* history, reads a letter from a fan that takes on the question of Smithers's sexuality. 'Ambassador Henry Mwabwetumba of the Ivory Coast writes, "What is the real deal with Mr Burns' assistant Smithers? You know what I'm talking about."' McClure laughs knowingly, and a series of clips rolls documenting Smithers's overt lust for Mr Burns, including a fantasy sequence in which Smithers imagines his boss emerging naked from a birthday cake and a clip of his computer's welcome screen, which consists of a pixelated Mr Burns saying, 'Hello, Smithers. You're quite good at turning me on.' Cut back to McClure: 'As you can see, the real deal with Waylon Smithers is that he's Mr Burns' assistant. He's in his early forties, is unmarried, and currently resides in Springfield. Thanks for writing!' Of course, the Smithers debate is barely a debate at all – he's gayer than Liberace's picnic basket – but some alt.tv.simpsons wags have kept it going by arguing that he's not actually homosexual but merely 'Burns-sexual' – attracted only to his boss.

The exact location of Springfield has provided fodder for more nudge-nudging fun on the show, even though it's a quandary answered just as easily as the question of Smithers's sexuality: Springfield is of course Anywhere, USA, a movable feast that suddenly finds itself by the ocean or near a mountain range as the exigencies of the plot dictate. Still, *The Simpsons* has mined the debate for a series of gags that toy with the notion that Springfield has an exact real-world location. In one instance, Lisa is about to point out Springfield on a map of the US when Bart walks in, his head blocking the view. Another time, a Hollywood producer interested in filming a movie in Springfield clicks on his intercom and tells his secretary, 'Get me two plane tickets to the state that Springfield is in.' Here, as the writers gently mock the quixotic interests of their fans, is the fan–writer relationship at its most collegial.

If only it were always such a sunny thing. Alas, the show's most rabid fans have frequently turned on the show's creators. In part, the volatility of the show's diehards is a natural by-product of their degree of devotion to the show. Love turns to hate far more quickly than indifference turns to either, and a scorned lover is far more dangerous than a snubbed acquaintance. And *The Simpsons* was a show so widely loved, so universally lauded, so much the pinnacle cultural institution of its fans' lives, that a backlash was inevitable. As well, the show's writers *are* satirists, and a fan base so passionate and erratic that some of its members had taken to regularly lamenting the show's overall decline by only its fourth or fifth season – this was a scenario ripe for satire.

As early as 1994 Matt Groening acknowledged that he and some of the show's other creators 'lurked' from time to time at alt.tv.simpsons. And he, for one, found the myopic harangues he sometimes found there more than a little frustrating: 'Sometimes I feel like knocking their electronic noggins together.' *Simpsons* writer Ian Maxtone-Graham was even more dismissive in a 1998 profile in Britain's *Independent* that was widely disseminated among the show's hardcore fans and earned Maxtone-Graham their lifelong enmity. In the article, he professed to hate TV, admitting he'd barely seen a single episode of *The Simpsons* before he was hired as one of its writers. Then he launched into a snarky attack on 'the beetle-browed people on the internet', dismissing their criticism of a particular episode of the show with a shrug. 'Go figure! That's why they're on the internet and we're writing the show.'

Maxtone-Graham's not-so-witty rejoinder might seem a little petty, but his frustration with the show's online fans is certainly not unfounded. By Season 5 – among the two or three best in the series's history, boasting more than a dozen flat-out-brilliant episodes – a nasty phrase had become an established part of the alt.tv.simpsons critic's standard repertoire. 'I think we can end the debate over the worst episode ever after watching "Homer Loves Flanders",' wrote one disgruntled viewer of Episode 1F14. 'This one just stunk.' The very next episode (1F15) invited a similar review from another online fan: '"Bart Gets an Elephant" was the WORST Simpsons episode I have ever seen, hands down.' There it was: *Worst. Episode. Ever.*

By Season 6, the denizens of alt.tv.simpsons had grown even more vicious. 'Grrrr!' goes one review of Episode 2F05 ('Lisa on Ice'). 'Who was responsible for last night's monstrosity? He should be forced to apologise on the air, and then be fired from the show, sterilised, and sent to live like an animal in the sewers below Los Angeles for the rest of his life.' There's something either laughable or creepy (or both) about this review, particularly when you bear in mind that the reviewer was talking about his *favourite* TV series. It's so over-the-top you can almost hear the Comic Book Guy's clipped, snarky voice as you read it. And so you would – or words to this effect, anyway – as part of the most direct and contentious counterattack *The Simpsons* ever unleashed on its fans: Episode 4F12 ('The Itchy & Scratchy & Poochie Show').

The premise of Episode 4F12 is this: the ratings for 'Itchy & Scratchy' have dropped off precipitously, and the show's producers – after consulting a focus group made up of Lisa, Bart and a handful of other young Springfieldianites – decide to add a new character in an attempt to revitalise the cartoon. They decide on Poochie, a proactive, in-your-face dog, with the intent of introducing a totally outrageous paradigm to the show (to paraphrase Lindsey Naegle, the buzzword-spouting corporate executive who explains the new character to the show's writers). In these early scenes, the creative team behind 'Itchy & Scratchy' – stand-ins for *The Simpsons'* staff – is itself the target of vicious satire: the writers are pretentious and lazy, and the executives are bereft of original ideas and beholden to shallow lifestyle trends.[6]

The sequence that raised the hackles of the alt.tv.simpsons gang, though, portrays the reaction of hardcore 'Itchy & Scratchy' fans to the new character. As a callous marketing campaign stirs up Poochie-mania in the days leading up to his debut, the Android's Dungeon plays host to an autograph session for June Bellamy (voice actor for Itchy and Scratchy) and Homer (who has won the coveted role of Poochie). The crowd is a sea of nerds. One, sporting a GENIUS AT WORK T-shirt, asks a long, involved question about the inconsistencies in the musical notes produced in a scene where Itchy plays Scratchy's ribcage like a xylophone. 'I hope somebody got fired for that blunder,' the nerd finishes. Another asks an obscure technical question about the show's CD-ROM video game. Homer, presumably speaking on behalf of the show's exasperated writers, tells them both off. 'Let me ask *you* a question,' he admonishes the guy spouting xylophone trivia. 'Why would a man whose shirt says "Genius at Work" spend all of his time watching a children's cartoon show?' The geek is of course silenced.

As it turns out, 'The Itchy & Scratchy & Poochie Show' is an unmitigated disaster – the first episode is a plotless mess. ('When are they going to get to the fireworks factory?' Milhouse whines as he watches, before breaking into tears.) Poochie himself is a grotesque caricature of every ill-conceived 'hip' character ever introduced to a TV show or commercial to try to speak to the kids and jump-start the ratings. He breaks into a godawful rap at one point, and rides a dirt bike up a half-pipe to slam-dunk a basketball a few scenes later. And the viewers hate it – none more so than the Comic Book Guy, who fills his store the next day with rhetoric lifted practically verbatim from alt.tv.simpsons postings. 'Last night's "Itchy & Scratchy" was, without a doubt, the *worst* episode ever,' his rant begins. Bart, a less fickle fan, replies, 'Hey, I know it wasn't great, but what right do you have to complain?' Comic Book Guy's smugness is unshaken: 'As a loyal viewer, I feel they owe me.' Bart launches into a pointed retort: 'What? They've given you thousands of hours of entertainment for free! What could they possibly owe you? If anything, *you* owe *them*!' Comic Book Guy, after a pause free of reflection: 'Worst episode ever.'

The regular contributors to alt.tv.simpsons were on the Internet within minutes of the ending of 4F12, of course, registering their disgust throughout the world. Or, in many cases, their pleasure: several of the postings that eventually made it into the episode's capsule took the lampooning with good humour, and some seemed genuinely tickled to be satirised by their beloved *Simpsons*. But there was also a long dissection of the episode from an alt.tv.simpsons 'veteran', a former keeper of the newsgroup's FAQ who had lost faith in the show the previous season. This veteran's attack, sprawling across some sixteen paragraphs, acknowledged some of the group's shortcomings, but these flashes of level-headedness were severely undercut by the scornful tone that soon seeped in: the show's 'Imperial Writers', led by 'Darth (I'm sorry, David) S. Cohen' (4F12's author), were merely trying to 'flame-bait die-hard fans'; Bart's rebuke of the Comic Book Guy must have come from the mind of 'Emperor Oakley' (*Simpsons* writer Bill Oakley); and none of them respected the characters they wrote for nor the institution whose legacy they were perpetuating. In short, this attempt at explaining the disillusionment of the show's hardcore fans couldn't escape the overheated rhetoric so common to the newsgroup in general.

In this respect, the fractured dialogue between *The Simpsons* staff and alt.tv.simpsons is an apt metaphor for the Internet itself (at least in its infancy). In its first decade of widespread use, the Internet has given rise to a unique culture with a particular kind of discourse (or more accurately a closely related cluster of kinds), often reeking of knee-jerk sarcasm and exaggerated venom. The Internet is uniquely suited to cataloguing minute detail, to creating vast archives, to assembling reams of information far too bulky and variable in quality to make it into the heavily edited content of other media. It gives average folks unprecedented access to information, especially stuff that was heretofore too obscure or too specialised, or was sequestered behind closed doors for the use only of certain elites. But the sheer quantity of information on any given subject – not to mention the overwhelming confusion that comes from trying to address the Internet's near-limitless scope – has tended to encourage netizens to dive perhaps a bit too deeply into certain passions, at the expense of their sense of perspective. Out of this rises the overwrought critical language of alt.tv.simpsons, and of the show's presumably wounded writers.

The Internet has opened new worlds of communication – but it has also created whole new breeds of *mis*communication. As often as not, these miscommunications arise from the *tone* of Internet discourse (and from the difficulty of accurately conveying tone online in the first place). Users are anonymous and more or less free from responsibility for their comments; messages are sent instantaneously (before overstatements can be qualified or overheated digs deleted); conversations tend to occur within communities where common interests and attitudes are assumed, but those conversations can be viewed by any random passerby. All of this makes the Internet a uniquely receptive medium for shrillness, sarcasm and hyperbole. You see it not just at alt.tv.simpsons but in political discussion forums, in the postings of online columnists, in the blunt language of pop-up porn ads. Cultural critic Thomas Frank has described this 'wise-ass tone' (perhaps a little too wise-assedly) as 'the internet's greatest gift to civilisation'. And it's not just the tone of postings to alt.tv.simpsons; it's the tone of *The Simpsons* itself. In fact, it might well be that the alt.tv.simpsons newsgroup (one of the most heavily trafficked in the early 1990s) and the enormously popular show that spawned it played a significant role in shaping this style of discourse for the entire medium.

There is, for example, a website I post to from time to time called MetaFilter, which has about 17,000 members. The site's ostensible purpose is to provide a catalogue of links to interesting and obscure Web phenomena, but the real meat of it is the sometimes lengthy debates between community members, in which a highly specific and oft-mutating slang has evolved. Two of the most prominent bits of slang are lifted directly from *The Simpsons*. When a participant vastly overstates the degree of oppression or social control expected to arise from the topic in question, or when the discussion is the product of a link to a news story detailing some new brand of authoritarianism, a contributor will reply, 'I, for one, welcome our new [fill-in-the-blank] overlords', a statement lifted from Kent Brockman's hysterical on-air reaction to the ants he sees floating past the camera on Homer's space mission ('I, for one, welcome our new insect overlords'). If a contributor has made a banal or ignorant comment or tried to steer a debate in a strange new direction, someone will post a quick bit of screenplay-style stage direction enclosed in asterisks, such as *tumbleweed blows by* or *coyote howls in the distance*. While these may be established devices for indicating isolation, I'm quite certain that they've made it to MetaFilter directly from their recurring appearances on *The Simpsons*, where they're used to imply not literal but metaphorical solitude. The tumbleweed-blows-by bit occurs, for example, when Homer tries to out-quip a brainy film critic ('Camus can do, but Sartre is smartre') with the line, 'Scooby-Doo can doo-doo, but Jimmy Carter is smarter.' Everyone in the Simpson living room pauses. Dead silence. A tumbleweed blows through.

These references pop up with such frequency on MetaFilter, I'd wager, because *The Simpsons* is the closest thing to a universal cultural touchstone that the site's members – younger and older, North American and European, urban/suburban/exurban/rural, hardcore techie and casual Internet user – that all of these people have in common. Only *The Simpsons* can presume universality of recognition, respect, and especially resonance. And as it is at MetaFilter, so it is in many other places in cyberspace: if you're looking for a cultural reference with the widest possible meaning in *any* online communication, you probably can't beat *The Simpsons*.

From this comes my hunch that *The Simpsons*, more than any other cultural force, helped create the snarky one-upmanship that dominates many Internet debates. Which makes even more sense when you consider that the first non-academic users of the new medium were drawn primarily from the demographic most dedicated to *The Simpsons*. Which is to say: young people.

THE YOUTH SHALL INHERIT THE INTERNET

In Episode CABF06 ('Skinner's Sense of Snow'), a ferocious blizzard traps the children of Springfield in the elementary school. Homer and Marge watch a news update on the storm at home. 'This is terrible!' Marge frets. 'How will the kids get home?'

'I dunno,' Homer responds casually. 'Internet?'

This comment would have appeared almost rational at the height of the Internet's first tidal wave of hype, alluding as it does to two of the age's most widely held myths: that the Internet was so revolutionary a technology it could solve virtually any problem humanity currently faced; and that kids in particular could use the Internet in ways no one who reached adulthood before around 1980 could possibly understand.

There might well be some kernel of truth to this, but the real secret is simply that those who have grown up using computers are not afraid of them. Because of this relative comfort, young folks were given greater control of the Internet than any other medium going, and because of *this*, the culture of the Internet developed a certain youthfulness. This points towards one of the fatal miscues of the overwhelming majority of the doomed dot-coms: their belief that because people were doing certain things online, they wanted to do *everything* online. It wasn't, that is, that young people wanted their whole culture delivered to them online; it was that there were certain kinds of culture they could find only on the Internet. And this was partially because the rest of the culture was so thoroughly dominated by a hyper-corporate, top-down approach that many young people felt completely alienated from it. It had very little to do with them.

If you were under the age of 30 at the time of the Internet's first boom, you'd spent your entire life as a cultural nonentity, a footnote to the all-consuming Baby Boom. You were worthy of interest only insofar as you could be categorised by the Boomers for marketing purposes (*you're part of Generation X, kid, now buy this bag of Doritos Extreme*) or used as a repository for Boomer nostalgia (witness, for example, the popularity of Oliver Stone's 1991 film *The Doors* among Gen-Xers). You were told practically every day of your childhood and/or young-adulthood that social change had ended with Woodstock, that the corpse of politics had been found years ago in a burgled room at the Watergate Hotel, that pop culture's final significant achievement was Led Zeppelin's fourth album.

But the Internet – which these putative Gen-Xers had packed full of the stuff they *could* relate to – was seemingly all theirs. This was what initially made the Net so appealing: it wasn't on CBS or Global or the BBC. It wasn't brought to us by Pepsi or Ford. It wasn't controlled by the regulatory arm of any particular government. And it was emphatically *not* better when the Boomers wore their hair long. You could make it your own.

It's difficult to talk about the 'culture' of a place as vast and diverse as the Internet. What common culture exists, after all, between a Christian discussion forum, a stock-trading tool and a fetish-porn gallery? But what if we edit out online extensions of well-established offline phenomena, all that pornography and day trading and old-time religion, not to mention the corporate websites and gambling dens and Grand Funk Railroad fansites? What does that leave us with? Well, it leaves us with stuff like *Angry Dad*, for starters.

Angry Dad is Bart Simpson's first venture into online content production, a simplistic cartoon he creates after being inspired by a professional animator's lecture at his school in Episode DABF13 ('I Am Furious Yellow'). Bart draws the first issue of *Angry Dad* freehand and self-publishes it in 'dead tree' format – as a comic book, that is – which draws the attention of a youthful dot-com entrepreneur, who wants to take it online. 'Wow!' Bart marvels. '*Angry Dad* – an Internet cartoon! I'll be in cyberspace next to the Nabisco cookie website!' Animated in the crude, blocky style typical of first-generation online cartoons (and bearing a passing resemblance to the first *Simpsons* shorts), *Angry Dad* is soon a big hit at BetterThanTV.com, becoming the Internet's number-one non-pornographic site, which makes it ten-trillionth overall.

The premise of the cartoon is ridiculously simple: Bart spies on Homer until his father bumbles himself into a rage. Then Bart transforms the incident into an episode of *Angry Dad*. ('I'm a rage-aholic,' Homer tearfully admits after seeing the cartoon. 'I just can't live without rage-ahol!') *Angry Dad*'s appeal lies solely in its extreme graphic content – upon seeing a newspaper headline that reads, 'You suck, Angry Dad,' for example, Angry Dad's head inflates like a balloon until his eyes pop out of their sockets and explode. This is apparently BetterThanTV.com's stock-in-trade – the site's previous blockbuster was a cartoon called *Bin Laden in a Blender*, whose title tells you everything there is to know about it. Complex, nuanced dramas these ain't. Which makes them pretty accurate specimens of the first fruits of digital pop culture.

Recall, if you will, some of the most ubiquitous cultural touchstones of the Internet's first wave. There was that enigmatic 'Dancing Baby' that eventually made it onto the TV series *Ally McBeal*. There was the even more enigmatic home page of some Turkish guy named Mahir, who captured the cyberspace spotlight with his goofily endearing mix of pidgin English and sincere yearning: 'I KISS YOU!!!!!' There was 'HampsterDance', a site featuring line after line of cartoon hamsters 'animated' with vague spinning and bobbing motions that make *Angry Dad* look like *Fantasia*, who bopped along to a helium-voiced, speed-addled candy-pop tune. And of course there was probably the most pervasive of Internet fads: the meteoric rise to interstellar fame of the catchphrase 'All Your Base Are Belong To Us', a line from the English translation of an old Japanese videogame called *Zero Wing*, which demonstrated a command of the Net's lingua franca that made Mahir look like Shakespeare.[7] All of these are pointedly silly things. Novelties, really. This is a significant means by which the strange new culture of the Internet first entered the mass consciousness.

And it's no anomaly: a façade of mere novelty is quite often the way in which imposing new technologies and paradigm-shifting cultural forces endear themselves to the masses. What is the 'Dancing Baby' but a digital update of the Lumière Brothers' seminal silent film of a train speeding towards its audience, a marvel for the simple fact that it was moving so fluidly, so realistically? Look closely at the 'All Your Base' or 'HampsterDance' clips, and you'll find the same nonsensical, hypnotic charm that propelled Little Richard's 'Tutti Frutti' and Manfred Mann's 'Doo Wah Diddy' to the top of the pop charts in rock & roll's early years. Yes, 'All Your Base' barely made sense. No, scratch that: it emphatically *didn't* make sense. That was the point: it was a code. And it was new, and strange, and it had no precedent. It was enticing as all hell, especially if you were young and bored and suffocating on your parents' culture and desperate – just desperate – for something original.

A-wop-bop-a-loo-bop, a-lop-bam-boo.

What you say? All your base are belong to us.

You could see the Internet's promise – its youthful, transformative energy – in all kinds of stuff that didn't make it to the level of fame that the cutesy shit did. There were homemade cartoons and video games, fan fiction and amateur political commentary, digital art galleries and digitised movies by aspiring artists of every stripe. If you spent any time online, you'd eventually stumble on some curious DIY project that awoke you to the enormous potential of the medium – its ability not only to let you produce and exhibit your work (whatever it was, whatever level of skill you had) but also to exhibit it to potentially *the whole world*. To communicate in ways you'd never dreamed, to people you'd never met. In 1998, for example, the Internet buzzed for a time with talk of a short film by some random dude named Kevin Rubio. This was *Troops*, a note-perfect parody of the Fox Network's reality-TV series *Cops* set in the fantasy world of *Star Wars*, in which Stormtroopers shake down a gang of Jawas for theft and respond to a domestic-disturbance call at Uncle Owen and Aunt Beru's farm. The thing had the production values of an ambitious student filmmaker's weekend project, but it (briefly) catapulted this Rubio guy to international fame. Or perhaps you heard the story about this nasty little cartoon called *The Spirit of Christmas* in which a gang of potty-mouthed tots watch Jesus and Santa Claus duke it out for control of the holiday. It was a $2,000-budgeted video greeting that some Hollywood exec commissioned as his 1995 Christmas card. But then the cartoon got traded hand to hand and made its way online and became an instant cult classic. By 1997, the thing had spun out into the hottest new series on television – *South Park* – and the show's wise-assed creators, Trey Parker and Matt Stone, stared out from the pages of magazines, all slouchy-clothed and bad-haired and shit-eating-grinned, poster children for the notion that obsessive dorks could become the very embodiment of hip superstardom.

Or maybe it hit you less tangibly, less rationally. One of my first serious surfing expeditions – this was in 1996 – took me through Yahoo!'s 'Weird' listings to something called oo. That was the site's title, and it sat at the top of the main page in stark black lettering – 'oo' – with five columns of enigmatic links laid out below it: 'The Pain', 'The Promise', 'The Inventory', 'The Mission', and so on. Click on one of these, and you'd bounce to a white page with some kind of – not an explanation exactly – but some kind of revelation. 'The Heat' – *click* – 'BURNS LIKE THE SUN'. 'The Mutation' – *click* – 'oOo.' 'The Monster' – *click* – 'oo is for cookie. That's good enough for me.' Click on 'The Pain', and you'd see a whole page filled with lines of text like this: 'OWOWOWOW'. I spent a good half hour clicking around. There was no explanation anywhere. It was like wandering through the mind of a strange, sporadically funny, potentially psychopathic mind.[8] What's more, it conveyed the *feeling* of rattling around such a mind with a precision and ease that'd be the envy of many a thriller novel or serial-killer movie or Pink Floyd song. It was only a few columns of text, a handful of phrases. But it felt powerful somehow. It said that the world was a stranger place than you normally understood it to be, and that the secret would get out – we could no longer hide from our weird, diverse, messed-up selves – and that it would happen *here*. Online. Change is gonna come. Or, as the ambiguous but slightly menacing tagline at a website called Disinformation put it, 'It's coming down fast.'

What was coming down at Disinformation? It might be everything. The site itself is a multifaceted clearing house of uncommon knowledge: conspiracy theories, paranormal phenomena, drug culture, metaphysics, radical politics.[9] If the Marquis de Sade and Emma Goldman had got hitched and hosted a weekly salon, it might've looked a bit like Disinfo. And it was but one of a metastasising multitude of sites giving voice and home(page) to every odd notion and queer obsession in the known universe. Recall Bart's enticement to get Homer to take him to Springfield's cybercafé: the promise of a video clip of monkeys doing it. So what, then, was coming down fast? Barriers. Illusions. Taboos. Old orders and ancient prejudices. The early Internet was the manifestation of a kind of cultural chaos theory, destroying the idea of 'normal' – *any* idea of normal – in the same way that science had been finding itself increasingly unable to confirm the existence of an ordered, predictable universe.

Consider one of the Internet's most widespread new social conventions: the forwarding of an e-mail with a subject line such as 'Check THIS out!' to vast numbers of one's friends and colleagues with relative impunity. Now consider the usual content of such an e-mail. The dirty jokes and silly lists are nothing new, but the Web links are another story entirely. Click on one of those, and there is really no limit to what might be revealed. A new study on the dangers of drinking too much milk. A snippet of erotic *Little Mermaid* fan fiction. An entire site dedicated to the fine art of stuffing kittens into bottles. An op-ed piece from a British newspaper. Anything. It's not that this kind of human diversity didn't exist before the birth of the Internet; it's that it was never this accessible, nor this *acceptable*. Does everyone who receives this kind of e-mail approve of everything they receive? Of course not. But many of them, I'd argue, are much more amenable than ever before to the idea that their world is a very weird and extraordinarily diverse place.

Greil Marcus, writing in *Lipstick Traces:* 'The goal of every secret society is to take over the world.' The Internet in its early days was one vast, growing, multivalent secret society. A parallel universe, almost – a phenomenon far wider in scope, anyway, than the insular punk scenes and esoteric philosophical movements Marcus was talking about. And so naturally it encouraged its members to dream of taking over the world.

THE GEEKS SHALL INHERIT THE EARTH (I): THE UTOPIANS

In the opening scene of Episode CABF02 ('The Computer Wore Menace Shoes'), Homer arrives for work at the power plant to find it closed for fumigation. An e-mail notice had been sent to all plant employees, but Homer – who doesn't own a computer – didn't receive it. So it's off to Honest John's Computers to buy an overpriced PC, and before long Homer's happily surfing the Web. He sings along with 'Dancing Jesus', even builds his own home page. But his site, a gaudy thing stuffed with stolen copyrighted material, attracts no one, and so Homer, hungry for attention, christens himself 'Mr X' and begins an online trade in local gossip. Soon, Homer has become Springfield's answer to Matt Drudge, revealing Mayor Quimby's corruption, Apu's sale of week-old donuts as 'bagels' and Mr Burns's sale of uranium to terrorists – to the adoration of a grateful local populace. Homer even wins a Pulitzer Prize. He has to reveal his identity to claim the prize, however, and after that, the town's gossips will no longer tell secrets in his presence. Bereft of new scoops, his site stagnates: traffic drops so low that there's a digital tumbleweed bouncing across the screen. So Homer, in the best blameless fashion of the responsibility-challenged Internet news business, takes to making up news items. It's outlandish stuff: news of a race of strange humanoids living under the city of Denver, the revelation that Spanish and Italian are the same language, a damning assertion that flu shots are a mind-control device. In short order, Homer's kidnapped and whisked away to 'The Island', a tropical prison for people who know too much. It turns out Homer has stumbled onto a diabolical plot: flu shots *are* a mind-control tool, given just before Christmas 'to drive people into a frenzy of shopping'.

'Of course,' Homer replies to the mysterious man who reveals the plot. 'It's so simple.' He pauses, considering. 'Wait. No, it's not. It's needlessly complicated.' No matter: Homer's knowledge of the conspiracy dooms him and the rest of the Simpsons to spending the rest of their lives sequestered on The Island.

It's quite a wild digital ride for Homer in Episode CABF02: from ogling animated novelties to uncovering the most elaborate and sinister conspiracy the world has ever known in a few short weeks as a netizen. Like many of the Internet's pioneers, Homer discovers with dizzying quickness that cyberspace is fertile soil for ambitious dreams, a place that might even incite revolutions. After his website's first big revelation of the mayor's corruption brings City Hall to its knees, Homer boasts, 'I did it! I've changed the world! Now I know exactly how God feels!' Just like that, Homer is a convert to the digital revolution – a full-blown techno-utopian.

Now, to be fair, it took the real-world techno-utopians a good deal longer than a couple of weeks to begin imagining themselves the nucleus of a brave new world. This dream was born around 1985, with the founding of the Whole Earth 'Lectronic Link – the WELL – as an online community for readers of *Whole Earth Review*, a journal that was itself a spinoff of the hippie encyclopedia *The Whole Earth Catalog.* The co-founders were the improbably named Larry Brilliant (epidemiologist, techie, editor of the *Review*) and the incomparable Stewart Brand, who'd be the most stereo-typical hippie this side of Wavy Gravy if it weren't for his long-standing belief in the liberating potential of digital technology and his comparative practicality.

Brand's hippie credentials are impeccable: founder of *The Whole Earth Catalog,* which derived its name from a sandwich board Brand used to carry as he paraded past the gates of Columbia University in 1966. ('Why haven't we seen a photograph of the whole earth yet?' Brand's board demanded, imploring America's space programme to reveal its secrets.) Founder of the 'America Needs Indians' campaign (circa mid-1960s). Prominent member of Ken Kesey's Merry Pranksters (also circa mid-1960s; Brand was the guy driving the pickup truck in the opening scene of Tom Wolfe's *The Electric Kool-Aid Acid Test*). Lead organiser of the Trips Festival, the last and biggest event in the Pranksters' mercurial movement, at which the Grateful Dead were more or less born.

Atypically, Brand has techno-utopian roots that run as deep as his countercultural ones. He was a frequent visitor to Stanford University's pioneering computer centre from the early 1960s onward and a major influence in the 1970s on the thinking at the Xerox Palo Alto Research Center, a groundbreaking techie think-tank. He was also the progenitor of the techno-utopian rallying cry: 'Information wants to be free.' Brand, circa 1994: 'Communes failed, dope failed, politics failed. The main thing that survived and thrived was the computer . . . The computer nerds were the ones who came closest to carrying out the countercultural agenda.'

Brand, believing the revolution in values and community promised by the social revolution of the 1960s could finally find a permanent home online, begat the WELL. And the WELL in turn more or less begat techno-utopianism. Throughout the late 1980s and early 1990s, the WELL was *the* place to rub elbows with the Internet's pioneering dreamers. Apple founder Steve Wozniak contributed money to get the WELL running. Grateful Dead-lyricist-turned-techie John Perry Barlow met Mitchell Kapor – the libertarian founder of the software giant Lotus – at the WELL, and together they launched the Electronic Frontier Foundation to map out and protect the civil rights of cyberspace. And it was also a regular hangout for one of Brand's protégés, Kevin Kelly, who would co-found *Wired* magazine in 1993 and thence bring the idealistic fantasies of the WELL to a mass audience.

Wired was where many of us first met the idealised digitised future. Its articles promised eye-poppingly innovative gadgetry and/or the imminent arrival of artificial intelligence and/or the birth of super-intelligent robots and/or a whole digital planet of self-actualising work and boundless abundance and lasting peace. *Wired* – its colour palette a Day-Glo riot, its ads and content seamlessly linked by revolutionary graphic design, its editorial pages filled with (for example) a recurring mini-catalogue of the Internet's latest lexical inventions (a feature dubbed 'Jargon Watch') – came across more like a user's guide to the near-future than a lifestyle magazine. In a 1998 article in *Upside*, a competing techie journal, Michael S. Malone summed up the kind of prophesies found in the pages of *Wired* and the threads at the WELL – which he dubbed 'techno-absolutist' – thus:

> [The digital revolution] will undoubtedly change every human institution, tear down almost all our political models, annihilate the traditional nation state and transform money, commerce, art, literature, entertainment, sports and even organized religion. The digital revolution will have an irrevocable impact on the neighborhood, the family, the self.

Such grand pronouncements were commonplace by the mid-1990s – 'our fin de siècle mantra', wrote Malone – repeated in AT&T's Orwellian 'You Will' ads and on the pages of Bill Gates's bestselling book, *The Road Ahead* (which, by *Harper's Magazine*'s count, employed the phrase 'You will' an average of once every five pages). If you didn't quite yet understand *how* things would change – indeed even if you didn't yet understand how to use an online search engine – never you mind, because the great wave of change would just come along and bodysurf you into a comfortable lounge chair on the warm sun-kissed beach of techno-paradise anyway.

If all this sounded a little too pat, a little too neverlandish, a little too – you know – *hippie*, well, that's because it *was* a little too hippie. Brand was a hippie, and so was Barlow, and the WELL owed a sizable chunk of its early membership to its use as a meeting place for Grateful Dead fans between tours. And so perhaps it shouldn't be much of a surprise that the prognostications and communal models of the techno-utopians displayed many of the same strengths and weaknesses as the protest movements of the 1960s. On the plus side, there was the sheer world-beating audacity of it, the sense that enough beautiful people with enough good intentions and a little genius and inspiration could remake the entire planet. It was an energetic and evangelical and intoxicating mix that could certainly feel like freedom. And, once again, it had youth on its side: this was not just a bunch of greybearded love-in veterans, but a bunch of those *plus* all manner of whip-smart, ultra-hip youngsters whose reference points were Nirvana and *The Simpsons* and videogames. This was The Sixties 2.0. It had science and even a little cynicism on its side this time. But like '60s radicalism, the digital dream suffered from solipsism and self-importance, and – most troublingly – a seemingly wilfully naive understanding of the blunt, powerful hammer represented by multimillion-dollar-sized piles of capital.

There's a throwaway gag in Episode 3F06 ('Mother Simpson') that hints at the troubled, intertwined relationship between 1960s radicalism and the corporate consumerism of the 1980s. Homer's mother has resurfaced after 27 years finally to tell her family the tale of her life as a hippie saboteur on the run from the law. 'But how did you survive?' Lisa asks her. 'Oh, I had help from my friends in the underground,' Mother Simpson explains. 'Jerry Rubin gave me a job marketing his line of health shakes, I proofread Bobby Seale's cookbook, and I ran credit checks at Tom Hayden's Porsche dealership.' It's a plausible résumé: former Black Panther Bobby Seale did indeed author a cookbook – 1988's *Barbeque'n with Bobby*, which included an introduction entitled 'A Barbeque Bill of Rights' – and yippie Jerry Rubin was the marketing genius behind a nutritional beverage called Wow that hit store shelves in the early 1990s. I don't think Tom Hayden ever owned a Porsche dealership, but he certainly did become a California state senator, a far more mainstream politician than the young radical who authored 1962's 'Port Huron Statement'. Mother Simpson's 'underground' had been almost totally integrated into the over-ground of big-time consumerism. 'The Times They Are A-Changin'' was a marketing slogan for Bank of Montreal and the Coopers & Lybrand accounting firm; Ben & Jerry's ice cream (founded by real hippies) was no less a capitalist enterprise than Fruitopia juices (staffed by Coca-Cola executives). The underground was a memory and the counterculture a marketing strategy.

And yet somehow the myth persisted. Somehow – like Mother Simpson resurfacing out of thin air after 27 years of presumed corpsehood – the first digital evangelists resurrected the revolutionary spirit of the '60s counterculture. They believed they could somehow keep the Internet free and equal, that it would be a people's space, resolutely public and safe from the profit motive that drove the ultra-privatised, hyper-consumer West where it was born. More dangerously, they believed the Internet was such an absolute good that it could, by the simple fact of its libertarian, egalitarian nature, bring a prosperous peace to the long-standing clash between communal liberty and private capital. That it could not only conquer the world but redeem capitalism's soul.

THE GEEKS SHALL INHERIT THE EARTH (II): THE FREE-MARKET LIBERTINES

Eventually, the story of a few crazy, obsessive kids spinning their favourite hobby into a free-wheeling, world-beating company with a multimillion-dollar IPO would become an archetype, and then a cliché, and finally – after the bubble burst – a cautionary tale. In 1995 and 1996, though, it was a single thing, a brand-new bauble to stare at in wonder. It was simply marvellous. Just plain fun. Yahoo!

I mean, *dig* these guys: David Filo was the monk, the one who slept under his desk and kept driving his sputtering 1980 Datsun even after Yahoo!'s IPO in April 1996 made him a millionaire. Chih-Yuan 'Jerry' Yang was the flamboyant one, the go-getter. He had the big house in Los Altos and the card that said his corporate title was 'Chief Yahoo!' You just knew he'd be able to sell the *whole world* on this thing.

And the blazing seat-of-your-pants gall of it all, you know? What were these kids, 20? Were they even old enough to drink yet? Actually, Filo was 29 and Yang 27 at the time of the IPO, but never mind. Never mind at all, because this was *it*, man, this was the whole damn stake-your-claim, grab-the-brass-ring, go-West-young-man American Dream here. This was the wagon train to the New Frontier, and happy days are here again! And there was such great *detail*, too, so many Horatio Alger touches. Stories about the rise of Yahoo! inevitably revelled in the suburban-kid mediocrity of it. Yang and Filo had been Stanford computer geeks working out of a trailer, surrounded by piles of fast-food containers. Later, when they got a real office, there were toys and computer games as well. Late-night coding sessions, vats of caffeinated drinks, a foosball table, pizza boxes covering the floor like tiles. And they were millionaires!

How'd they do it? That was the best part: they were slackers-made-good. They liked playing around on their computers, but it was hard to keep track of where everything was as this World Wide Web thing kept growing, so they decided to try to organise it somehow. Turned out that was *exactly* what everyone needed as soon as they went online, because this Web was just ridiculously vast, impossibly complex. It was a universe.

And it became just as inviting a dreamscape for visions of capitalist utopia as it had been for the communal fantasies of Stewart Brand and his band of dreamers. The vast piles of venture capital and stacks of half-baked business plans churned up by the Internet gold rush don't need too much further elaboration or analysis here – it was, after all, an exceedingly well-documented gold rush, churning out business tomes and how-to guides and futurist manifestos just as readily as it did dot-com IPOs. It's perhaps sufficient for our purposes merely to note that '*burn*' became an acceptable term for describing what the neophyte companies of the dot-com boom did to the money thrown at them (i.e. they *burned* through it). And to note that the free market had, by the late 1990s, almost completely supplanted the digital commons embodied by sites like the WELL as the primary locus of the revolution. What the explosive growth of Yahoo! and its first-generation dot-com brethren did was transform the Internet – not just rhetorically but also in many manifest and lasting ways – from small-s socialist utopia to capital-C Capitalist enterprise. Trace the evolution of the pop-up advertisement from irritating side effect of visiting porn websites to ubiquitous fact of Internet life, found everywhere from Amazon.com to the digital version of *The New York Times*, and you'll see a dramatic illustration of how an idealistic, tech-obsessed, community-minded subculture got almost completely commodified.

Wired itself quickly transformed from newsstand mouthpiece for the WELL-ian social revolution to front-rank standard bearer in the new dot-com army, prophesying the coming of a bountiful paradise to be ushered in by the 25-year 'long boom' it claimed the Internet had set in motion. As the tremors of that boom shook the world to attention, *Wired* soon found itself fighting for shelf space with a bevy of breathless dot-com journals, magazines like *Fast Company* and *Business 2.0* and *Red Herring*. All of them eagerly embraced the boom's emerging dogma: a free-market libertarianism predicated on the belief that Moore's Law (a computer-age maxim that states that computer-processing power doubles every year) and the digitisation of Adam Smith's invisible hand had destroyed the business cycle (possibly for good). Faster and faster computer chips and lightning-quick fibre optic networks were creating hyper-efficient businesses and hyper-informed knowledge workers, and those same networks were dissolving regulations and destroying borders, and this was all combining to rewrite the very laws of global capitalism. And, moreover, this period of rapid change was inevitable and practically effortless and categorically good for one and all.

Several of these magazines – *Wired* especially – provided a forum for one of the boom's most vocal and most optimistic prophets, George Gilder. Among his prognostications were that the telecom company Global Crossing would 'change the world economy' (it went bankrupt before it could) and that the Internet would soon bring about the complete demise of both television and non-digital mail (both still pending). Meanwhile, the *Gilder Technology Report* – a newsletter stuffed with high-tech news and stock picks that attracted 65,000 subscribers at $295 per annum – was so integral to the stock-market bubble that it created a phenomenon known as 'the Gilder effect', wherein his recommendation alone would drive up a given stock's price.

The geeks who built the Internet were soon joined at the boardroom tables by an army of stylish, lingo-spouting hipsters who cashed in on the fact that few of the middle-aged, business-suited relics of the 'old economy' who doled out the money had a firm grasp of what this new medium was all about. In 1998, for example, a small cabal of European fashionistas managed to scare up some $135 million in venture capital on little more than a vague idea (retailing high-end clothing for urban hipsters like themselves online) and their own Eurotrash charm. This was the short-lived Boo.com, one of the dot-com bubble's most spectacular supernovas, a website that stayed online a mere seven months and managed to sell barely a single frock, serving mostly as a (poor) justification for the extraordinary rate at which the cool kids at Boo.com were burning through their gold-rush pile.[10] This was one testament to the overheated hype of the dot-com bubble, which soon made the pronouncements of Brand and Barlow and the rest seem downright cautious. Here's another: a coterie of Hollywood titans – among them Steven Spielberg, Jeffrey Katzenberg and David Geffen of DreamWorks and Ron Howard and Brian Grazer of Imagine Entertainment, as well as Microsoft co-founder Paul Allen – put their entertainment empires together in 1999 to build POP.com, conceived as a high-profile online portal for short films. (Steve Martin and Eddie Murphy, among others, were slated to appear in POP.com shorts.) Katzenberg claimed it would become 'MTV on the Internet'. After burning through a sizeable (though not quite Boo-sized) stack of money – at least $7 million in less than a year – POP.com never launched at all.

It was perhaps inevitable that a bubble this big and boisterous would eventually attract Homer Simpson. And so it does, in Episode 5F11 ('Das Bus'), when he accidentally receives a piece of his neighbour's mail labelled 'Flancrest Enterprises' and learns that stupid, sexy Ned Flanders and his wife are 'making some good scratch' selling religious trinkets over the Internet. Homer, never one to pass up a get-rich-quick scheme (nor a chance to outdo Ned), is soon working his way to dot-com riches. 'What exactly is it your company does again?' Marge asks him. 'This industry moves so fast it's really hard to tell,' Homer explains, in the detail-deficient conversational style native to the would-be digital mogul. 'That's why I need a name that's cutting-edge, like CutCo, EdgeCom, InterSlice . . .' Homer eventually settles on Marge's suggestion – 'CompuGlobalHyperMegaNet' – and floods cyberspace with pop-up ads that proclaim him 'the Internet King'. Soon, the Comic Book Guy sees Homer's ad and comes to the Simpson house looking for a way to speed up his access to online porn. Homer's reply to the Comic Book Guy's elaborate request is a pretty accurate summary of the subtext of every pitch a dot-com entrepreneur ever made to a venture capitalist:

Comic Book Guy: I'm interested in upgrading my 28.8-kilobaud Internet connection to a 1.5-megabit fibre optic T1 line. Will you be able to provide an IP router that's compatible with my token-ring Ethernet LAN configuration?

Homer: [*stares blankly for a long moment*] Can I have some money now?

Homer hits the big time, of course: his next visitor is none other than Bill Gates himself, who makes a pitch for CompuGlobalHyperMegaNet. 'Your Internet ad was brought to my attention,' Gates tells Homer. 'But I can't figure out what, if anything, CompuGlobalHyperMegaNet does. So rather than risk competing with you, I've decided simply to buy you out.' Gates's lackeys then trash the Simpson living room, after which Gates – displaying more shrewdness than many a dot-com-gobbling CEO – leaves without writing a cheque. And so ends Homer's short stint as the proprietor of an Internet start-up.

The dot-com bubble's signature mix of pseudo-revolutionary self-importance and wonky business sense comes in for further lampooning in Episode DABF13 ('I Am Furious Yellow'). The founder of BetterThanTV.com – the start-up company that brings Bart's cartoon to the Web – is a buzzword-spouting twentysomething who likens producing crude cartoons to giving birth. His office is a playground for overgrown teens, and his company quickly goes belly up after distributing its stock – Bart receives 52 million shares – from a toilet-paper roll. There's a metaphorical precision to this last detail: it captures both the dot-com frenzy's boundless optimism and the certainty of its coming collapse, because surely such a toilet-paper tiger can't be long for this world. There's considerable hubris, too, in handing out stock in such an unproven company, and hubris was as central to the Internet bubble as fibre-optic cable and office foosball tables.

To take the rhetoric of the dot-com libertines at face value, to buy into the notion that the business cycle had been banished to the dustbin of history – this was most revolutionary in the way it redefined risk. Some Yahoos got filthy rich, but many more lost it all. During the dot-com revolution, it was all too common to wind up with some pretty massive wads of worthless toilet-paper stock in your hands.

'What's 52 million times zero?' Bart beseeches BetterThanTV.com's founder. 'And don't tell me it's zero!' In his voice, you can hear the disillusioned anguish of the true believer.

THE GEEKS SHALL INHERIT THE EARTH (III): THE INTERNATIONALE

Even as late as July 2000, *Wired* felt confident enough in the boom's endurance to run a long feature entitled 'Venture Capitals', which surveyed more than 40 of the world's biggest high-tech hubs. This was how it went in the boom years: every college town or exurb with a half-dozen technology companies imagined itself to be Silicon Fill-in-the-Blank, and every local chamber of commerce dreamed that its local nondescript strip-mall breakfast joint would soon play host to $100-million deals, just like the ones made over scrambled eggs at Buck's Restaurant in Silicon Valley. And so a few lofts in Manhattan became Silicon Alley, and Cambridge, England, became Silicon Fen, and a stretch of road between Glasgow and Edinburgh became Silicon Glen. Ireland was Silicon Bog, and Bangalore, India, was Silicon Plateau. Austin, Texas, couldn't decide if it was Silicon Hills or Silicon Ranch or Silicon Corral, while the Okanagan Valley in British Columbia – formerly famous as a producer of fruit and wine and as a retirement destination – rechristened itself Silicon Vineyard. The list of emerging high-tech hot spots went on and on, from Hong Kong ('Cyberport') to Taiwan ('Silicon Island') to Hyderabad, India ('Cyberabad'), to Israel ('Silicon Wadi') to un-nicknamed hubs in the Czech Republic and southern Germany and Sâo Paulo, Brazil. Dot-com dreams, like the Internet itself, were surprisingly communicable, and they crossed borders with extraordinary ease.

If you were geographically or psychologically close to the boom's Silicon Valley epicentre – if, that is, you were in the First World – it wasn't hard to see holes in the logic, to hear the echoes emanating from the hollow core of the rhetoric. In Toronto, for example (a middleweight tech hub that never found a suitable nickname), there was, by around 1998, a lavish dot-com launch party every other week as block after block of old textile warehouses in the city's west end got retrofitted with fibre-optic cable and expensive desk chairs to provide workspace for the city's digital revolutionaries. At the same time, though, there was an almost palpable air of impermanence to it all. Working as we did for a tech-obsessed magazine – *Shift*, the now-defunct journal of 'digital culture' – my colleagues and I were often invited to Toronto's dot-com launches, and it became decadent sport to see who could eat the most sushi and drink the most martinis – and, much trickier, to see who could figure out what the company throwing the party actually did. The parties, the fashionable loft-style offices, the beer fridges and foosball tables – all of it was getting out of hand, becoming ridiculous. It felt late-Roman. The only question was *when* the bubble would burst, and whether any of us would make a million in the stock market before it did. And even as we were speculating about speculating, we tossed around that famous quote from the 1920s about knowing it was time to get out of the market when you heard the shoeshine boys trading stock tips. Sub in 'magazine intern' for 'shoeshine boy', and that was the vibe in 1998 and 1999.

Far away from the overheated marketing hype and the free-flowing venture capital of Silicon Valley, however, the dot-com boom could seem almost innocent in its profound faith in itself. In fact, there was sometimes an exaggerated purity to the way the rhetoric of the boom was interpreted in its farthest-flung outposts. The promise seemed simply enormous – *Here is The Future, one size fits all, take one while supplies last* – and there seemed to be no great price to pay. It could truly seem, from such a distance, that it was simply a matter of doing it.

That, at any rate, was how it looked from St John's, the sleepy capital city of Antigua, in early 1999. At that time, Antigua – one of the smallest islands in the Caribbean, 15 kilometres across and 19 kilometres top to bottom, with a total population of 64,000 – was a few years into its reign as the world capital of Internet gambling, and the mood was giddily optimistic among the local officials and foreign entrepreneurs involved in the business. Gambling was the second online industry to begin generating real profits for dot-com entrepreneurs (porn, of course, was the first), and the size of those profits was doubling or tripling every quarter. There seemed no natural limit to the industry's growth. And Antigua, because it was the first sovereign nation on the planet to make it legal to operate an online casino within its borders, was fast becoming the Las Vegas of Internet gambling. Deep-pocketed, get-rich-quick entrepreneurs from the wealthy West – Canada, the US and Britain, especially – relocated part or all of their gambling businesses to Antigua so they could operate their sites without fear of prosecution. (In much of the world, the legality of online gambling was and remains hazy; only the United States has pursued legal action against the industry's practitioners with any real zeal.)

If you were in Boston or Ottawa or Hong Kong, the dot-com boom was, for all its evangelical hype, just one business trend among many, one sea change in a new world order that was transforming daily life on a dozen fronts. But in Antigua, the only other gig in town was the tourist trade, and most of that was tucked away in all-inclusive resorts outside the capital. When online gambling came to town, it was singular and massive and *new* – a stiff wind that hammered the tiny island with earth-shaking force and seemed to foretell the coming of a great hurricane that could blow the country clear into the front ranks of the fabled New Economy.

These were the early days of a gold rush, and St John's was the boomtown. As of 2001 about 80 per cent of the world's gambling websites were hosted on Antigua. And with every online casino paying an annual fee of US$100,000 for its gambling licence, Antigua's government was swimming in dot-com riches. The Internet gambling industry's epicentre quickly shifted elsewhere, however – to places with cheaper licences and even fewer legal hassles – and Antigua went bust almost as quickly as it had boomed. A scant two years later, Internet gambling employed less than half as many Antiguans as it had at its peak as the island's share of the global online-gambling market shrank to less than 2 per cent.

The short-lived boomtown of St John's is dwarfed by Cyberjaya – the grandest monument on the planet to the colossal ambition of the Internet's early days. Cyberjaya: 'Where High Tech & Paradise Meet'. Cyberjaya: 'The Model Intelligent City in the Making'. Cyberjaya: a whole freaking *city* built from scratch in the late 1990s amid the vast palm plantations south of Kuala Lumpur, Malaysia. *Two* cities, actually: Cyberjaya the dot-com paradise and Putrajaya the 'smart capital', plus the Petronas Twin Towers (the highest buildings in the world at the time of their completion) in downtown Kuala Lumpur to the north and possibly the world's most modern airport to the south, all of it forming a swath of land 15 kilometres wide and 50 kilometres long. This is the 'Multimedia Super Corridor' (MSC), the brainchild of Malaysia's recently retired authoritarian prime minister, Dr Mahathir bin Mohamad (Dr M for short). Dr M hatched the MSC plan in the mid-1990s after a two-month working holiday spent querying the world's best high-tech minds on how to transform his country from emerging-nation tiger to first-class citizen of the information age, and he stuck to his grandiose vision even after Malaysia's economy nearly imploded in 1997.

I visited the MSC in late 1999 – the slogans cited above came from my room key and mouse pad at the Cyberview Lodge Resort & Spa – and I simply don't have the room here to relate in full the surreal splendour I found there. From a certain angle, it resembled a half-completed stage set for

Futurama, Matt Groening's cartoon vision of life in the year 3000. Cyberjaya itself was strewn with hyper-modern office pods and the blue-roofed buildings of a fully equipped multimedia university and a dozen half-finished roads leading nowhere, all of them separated by tracts of palm forest and glades of freshly turned earth. Putrajaya had a big old neo-classical capital building and neat orderly rows of pink townhouses and a mammoth pink mosque already peopled by handfuls of prostrate faithful. There was a Web address prominently displayed on the sign in front of the national mosque in the heart of downtown Kuala Lumpur. There were regional headquarters and research-and-development shops for a long list of major high-tech players (Microsoft and Motorola and NTT and Nokia and Sun Microsystems and on and on). There were Malaysian-run start-ups by the handful. And – maybe this says it best – there was a resort hotel in Cyberjaya called Cyberview Lodge, and Cyberview Lodge was not far from Cyber Heights Villas and Cyber Gardens. And – yes, especially this – when you checked into Cyberview Lodge, the desk clerk handed you a 'smart card' (still quite a novelty in 1999), and when you got to your room and walked in and popped the smart card into the 'E-Switch' slot just inside the door, the lights came up just right and the a/c started blowing and the computer on your desk came to life and played a short AV orientation thing for you. Never mind the V, but check out the A:

Create a vibrant vision of the future city. *Place* it – in a verdant location of natural beauty. *Harness* it – with leading-edge IT and multimedia networks, infrastructure and world-class companies. *Protect* it – with eco-friendly resources and strategies. *Cherish* it – with nature sanctuaries, cultural parks and tropical gardens. And we have. *Cyberjaya*: Malaysia's first model cybercity in the Multimedia . . . Super . . . Corridor. A futuristic intelligent city, born of the people's vision and collective will. To *reach out* to next-generation technology in the information age and make it their own. To deliver world-class infrastructure and knowledge facilities linking industry and research. To extend a global invitation to celebrate a creative, energising [*unintelligible*] in a global community of creative enterprise, industry, recreation and choice lifestyles of the future. In a cybercity called *Cyberjaya* – the city of tomorrow, created and developed today. *Cyberjaya!*

This was the voice-over for your virtual tour of Cyberjaya, and that voice – slightly Australian in accent and slightly Orwellian in general vibe – managed in about a minute to give a succinct and characteristically muddled summation of the rhetoric that had filled the pages of *Wired* for the previous five years.

The MSC was indeed downright Simpsonian: an entire country whose somewhat impulsive leader, swayed by the overblown speechifying of a fast-talking salesman from out of town, commits it to an overblown public-works project, a technological marvel of extraordinary magnitude and highly debatable utility. It actually bears some similarities to the plot of Episode 9F10 ('Marge vs. the Monorail'), in which the shameless huckster Lyle Lanley convinces the people of Springfield to dump a municipal windfall into building a monorail. Lanley's well on his way to Tahiti with a suitcase full of Springfield government money before the people of Springfield learn they've been had, watching helplessly as their poorly constructed and utterly unnecessary monorail careens out of control along its track. Disaster is narrowly averted in the end: the monorail's quick-witted conductor, Homer Simpson, fashions an anchor and hooks it to the giant sign of a local donut shop. ('Donuts', Homer marvels. 'Is there anything they *can't* do?') 'And that', Marge informs us in a voice-over as we pan back from the salvaged train, 'was the only folly the people of Springfield ever embarked upon. Except for the Popsicle-stick skyscraper' – we see it in the foreground, swaying precariously – 'and the 50-foot magnifying glass'. As the camera continues to pan back, the magnifying glass comes into view next to the skyscraper, concentrating the sun's rays on it and causing it to burst into flame. 'And that escalator to nowhere.' We see the escalator towering even higher than the magnifying glass. The episode closes with random Springfieldianites tumbling over the escalator's edge to their certain deaths. Clearly, there is much to fear about colossal public-works projects.

And so you can almost imagine Dr M skipping town with a sack full of cash as hapless Malaysians hurtle towards empty palm plantations along the new rapid transit line or one of Cyberjaya's half-empty expressways, trains and cars all crashing in a great pileup as the road ends in a pit of red earth where the high-tech worker's paradise is supposed to be. The planned Cyber Tower teeters in the distance, Popsicle-stick-like. The 'celebrity' guest at the opening of the new Cyberjaya Café is Gallagher. In all seriousness, the computer network at Cyberview Lodge was down for my entire first night there – I was offline in Cyberjaya. It sure looked, from some angles, like the MSC was simply an enormous monument to Malaysia's folly.

Except that it isn't. Contrary to the prevailing wisdom of the age – the market-populist doctrine that says the information economy abhors regulation and top-down solutions and government intervention of any kind

– the MSC is working. As of September 2003, the MSC had attracted 900 foreign and domestic firms, almost double its target of 500. The Malaysian economy, which Western experts had insisted back around 1999 would be destroyed by such lunacies as the MSC and the pegging of the Malaysian currency to the US dollar, grew by 4.2 per cent in 2002, outpacing both Singapore and Hong Kong. In a lengthy comparative study of the MSC and Manhattan's faded Silicon Alley in the February 2003 issue of the journal *Urban Studies*, sociologist Michael Indergaard concluded, 'While Silicon Alley was a temporary base for circulating capital, the MSC effort is creating an enduring foundation for digital industry.'

So then: Antigua subscribed to the digital-age axiom that information wanted to be free, transforming itself into a haven for the voluminous wagers of online gamblers, and its dot-com dreams quickly faded. Information was free, all right – free to leave whenever it wanted. Malaysia came at the whole thing ass-backwards: it believed the hype a little too whole-heartedly, and then it stuffed its digital fantasia with all the tools the boom itself had allegedly rendered obsolete (government-subsidised infrastructure, geographical continuity, central planning), and it wound up with something enduring. The lesson, maybe, is that even if the Internet's first wave spawned delusions of unattainable grandeur, and even if it churned out New Economy dogma that was as weightless as cyberspace – even despite all of this, there *was* a huge and powerful new force at work in the world. It just couldn't be predicted.

The awesome power of the digital age could indeed bring about revolutions in the unlikeliest places.

DOT-COM DREAM, ECOLOGICAL NIGHTMARE: THE CASE OF TUVALU

The stock analogy used to explain chaos theory is 'the butterfly effect'. The flap of a butterfly's wings in Brazil, so the saying goes, can cause a tornado in Texas. Which is to say that complex systems may obey certain general rules, but their behaviour is highly susceptible to unpredictable changes by countless minute phenomena. It was just such a tiny and ridiculously random event occurring far, far away that brought the Internet to Tuvalu.

Until the mid-1990s, Tuvalu was one of the few spots on earth that remained entirely outside the global village. Tuvalu is a chain of nine coral atolls in the middle of the Pacific Ocean, about 1,000 kilometres north of Fiji. The atolls, with a total land area of 26 square kilometres, are scattered across more than 900,000 square kilometres of the Pacific. For Tuvalu's 11,000 inhabitants, subsistence fishing remains the main occupation. Check the old reliable *CIA World Factbook 2002*, and here's a sampling of what you'll find:

Agriculture – products: coconuts; fish
Telephones – main lines in use: 1,000
Telephones – mobile cellular: 0
Television broadcast stations: 0
Railways: 0 km
Highways: total: 19.5 km

Life on Tuvalu, in short, chugged along more or less pre-industrially through most of the twentieth century. Sure, it was part of the British Empire until 1978 – as an undeveloped outpost that mostly helped to ensure the veracity of the famous saying that the sun never set on Britannia – and the American military built an airstrip on one of the atolls during the Second World War, and a few hundred adventurous tourists turned up on boats out of Fiji every year. For the most part, though, Tuvalu had nothing to do with the great leaps in technology that created the global village.

But at some point in the early 1990s, as the Internet began moving from academic obscurity to the global mainstream, it fell to one of the medium's founding fathers, Jon Postel of the University of Southern California, to assign 'top level domains' (TLDs) – the letters after the last dot in a Web address. In addition to the general-use TLDs (.com, .net, .edu, etc.), Postel gave a TLD to every country in the world. Thus was Tuvalu assigned the 'country code' TLD of .tv. It was an obvious choice: an abbreviation. It probably took Postel but a moment to make the assignment. He surely wasn't thinking about how those two letters are recognised the world over as a short form for 'television'. Nor that a few years later Internet domain names would become a hot commodity as companies and institutions around the world scrambled to scoop up every word and phrase and abbreviation they thought might resonate with a global online audience. No, the butterfly merely flapped its wings once, quickly, and Tuvalu's fate was changed forever.

It wasn't until around 1995 or so that an enterprising Canadian by the name of Jason Chapnick realised the full import of Tuvalu's chance assignment. He got in touch with the Tuvaluan government, which it turned out had already entertained an offer of $5,000 for control of its TLD. Luckily, a Tuvaluan member of parliament – one Koloa Talake – had a passing familiarity with this Internet phenomenon, and he reckoned that dot-tv was worth far more than five grand. So the Tuvaluans responded with a bold counteroffer: the kingly sum of $10,000. The first suitor balked. Then Chapnick came along and showed the Tuvaluans riches far beyond their wildest dreams. By 1998 Chapnick's Internet start-up, The .tv Corporation, had sealed up the rights to Tuvalu's fortuitous domain name for $50 million over ten years, including $21 million up front. The Tuvaluan government's annual operating budget was less than $15 million. This was like winning the lottery. 'This dot-tv,' said Tuvalu's prime minister, 'it just came out of Heaven!'

And did the Tuvaluans – like the poor Pacific islanders who once fell under Homer Simpson's spell – wind up corrupted by their winnings? Did the sudden influx of Western riches ruin their tropical paradise? Emphatically not. In short order, the Tuvaluan government set about spending its windfall on all sorts of good things: the country got its first paved road, free health care and education were offered to all Tuvaluans, and the tiny country finally had enough extra cash to pay its dues and become an active, voting member of both the British Commonwealth and the United Nations. As Talake put it, 'The world's recognition of Tuvalu as an independent country has been made possible by the relationship with dot-tv.'

It would all make for the sunniest success story of the Internet age, a script right out of a Disney movie, if not for a few other butterflies – millions of them, really – beating their wings elsewhere. There might even be one in your garage right now: one of the millions of vehicles and power plants and factories around the world that produce greenhouse gases, which are almost certainly altering the planet's climate, which in turn is most likely causing the sea level of the planet's oceans to rise. All of which might well cause low-lying Tuvalu to disappear into the sea before the twenty-first century is through. Anecdotally, there is already evidence of Tuvalu's perilous existence: a cyclone of unprecedented strength completely inundated the Tuvaluan atoll of Tepuka Savilivili in 1997, erasing 50 hectares from Tuvalu's minuscule land mass. The country also saw record tidal swells in 2001. Ask a climatologist, and she'll explain to you that there's no way to completely understand climate change until we completely understand the behaviour of glaciers – we don't yet – and so there's no way of saying for sure what will happen to Tuvalu. (Ask a mathematician, and he'll tell you that *no* system can possibly be completely understood, its behaviour never totally predictable.) But it is at the very least a possibility that the dot-tv domain name will outlive Tuvalu itself. And it's this possibility that spurred the Tuvaluan government to immediately use its dot-tv money to pay its UN dues – for the purpose of pleading for action on climate change on the world stage before Tuvalu ceases to exist.

This is Tuvalu's unique paradox: just as a wondrous information-age technology has given it a voice, the impact of many other technologies threatens to destroy it. If you'd dreamed up Tuvalu's situation as the central symbol in a novel about the revolutionary changes of the 1990s, no one would've bought it: it's far too perfect, too self-contained. Here is the global village reaching out to absorb one of the last remaining unglobalised nooks and crannies of the planet. Here, too, the potent unpredictability central to chaos theory: the random assignment of a domain name, the cumulative action of a billion gasoline engines. Here is the Internet inspiring a genuine revolution, literally reordering a nation. And here, finally, is the canary in the coal mine of the modern world, a dying bird clinging desperately to its perch to tell us that the whole project might be doomed. It's the kind of symbol Jesse Grass would totally dig.

Jesse, for his part, turns up in Episode CABF01 ('Lisa the Treehugger'). He's the dreamy, dreadlocked teenager who leads Dirt First, a radical environmental group whose activist exploits – and hunky leader – inspire Lisa Simpson to take up residence in the branches of Springfield's oldest redwood tree to save it from the chainsaws of a wealthy Texan developer. The giant redwood is soon toppled anyway – by a bolt of lightning that strikes it while Lisa's taking a break from her vigil. All of Springfield is immediately convinced that she died in her crusade, and photogenic Jesse soon pops up on the TV news to celebrate Lisa's sacrifice and exploit her symbolic power. 'In death,' Jesse declares, 'she will do more for our cause than she ever could have done in life.'

Notwithstanding his obnoxious opportunism, Jesse's sense of urgency is almost reasonable. He's hungry for a metaphor equal in scale to the scope of our planet's environmental crisis. He'd probably argue – and I will, anyway – that Tuvalu might do more to combat climate change if the Pacific, swelled by melted ice and agitated by extreme new weather patterns, rose up tomorrow to sink it for good. Might that be enough to make it clear that environmental catastrophe is a real and huge and growing threat to our survival? Because if it is even in the realm of possibility that an entire nation could disappear into the sea as a result of manmade climate change – if this is even *remotely* possible – then we're obliged to rethink our way of living. Sustainability is not a buzzword invented to sell investors on a new high-tech scheme, and it's not a marketing strategy. It's a necessary condition for humanity's continued existence, the change we have to make if we want to survive as a species.

The Internet – a potent metaphor itself – has recently demonstrated that we're capable of this. We *can* change. A lot. In a hurry. We just did.

NOTES & MARGINALIA

1. **Just log up on your computrix:** In an episode from Season 13 – DABF06 ('The Bart Wants What It Wants') – the Simpson family attends an open house at Springfield's toniest private school, where Marge stumbles on a snack booth run by celebrity chef Wolfgang Puck. He offers a customer a Rice Krispie square – 'wasabi-infused, with a portobello glaze' – prompting Marge to note, 'I make mine with M&Ms.' Puck replies, 'With M&Ms? Now that's what I call fusion! I could sell them on the interweb!'

Though the term 'interweb' had probably floated around in cyberspace for some time, it entered widespread usage after Puck used it on *The Simpsons* in February 2002, becoming a shorthand way of indicating that someone's knowledge of digital technology is a little weak. Or, as interweb hot link UrbanDictionary.com puts it: 'interweb: A sarcastic term for the internet. Often used in the context of parody regarding an inexperience [sic], unskilled, or incoherent user.'

2. **Best. Improvised voice-acting. Ever.** The Comic Book Guy's trademark vocal style – a clipped, nasal sneer – is as critical to his personification of digital-age geekiness as his bloated figure. This voice is the creation of Hank Azaria, who was presented with a script in which the Comic Book Guy had a couple of funny lines and improvised the voice to deliver them on the spot.

3. **Freeze frame fun:** The brief flash of the Comic Book Guy's computer screen reveals that the other newsgroups to which he subscribes are:

   alt.binaries.pictures.erotica
   rec.arts.startrek.fandom
   rec.org.mensa
   rec.games.corewar
   alt.comics.radioactiveman

This bang-on accurate list of early-adopter obsessions (pornography, *Star Trek* trivia, international associations of geniuses, niche videogames for computer programmers, and superheroes, respectively) clearly indicates that someone filling in incidental details down *Simpsons* way had a *very* intimate knowledge of cyberspace.

4. **The complete list of *Rock Bottom*'s corrections:** 'Peoples' Choice Award' is America's greatest honour; Styrofoam is not made from kittens; The U.F.O. was a paper plate; The nerds on the Internet are not geeks; The word 'cheese' is not funny in and of itself; The older Flanders boy is Todd, not Rod; Lyndon Johnson did not provide the voice of Yosemite Sam; If you are reading this you have no life; Roy Rogers was not buried inside his horse; The other U.F.O. was an upside down salad spinner; Our universities aren't 'hotbeds' of anything; Mr Dershowitz did not literally have four eyes; Our viewers are not pathetic, sexless food tubes; Audrey Hepburn never weighed 400 pounds; The 'Cheers' gang is not a real gang; Salt water does not chase the 'thirsties' away; Licking an electrical outlet does not turn you into a Mighty Morphin Power Ranger; Cats do not eventually turn into dogs; Bullets do not bounce off of fat guys; Recycling does not deplete the ozone; Everything is 10 per cent fruit juice; The flesh eating virus does not hide in ice cream; Janet Reno is evil; V8 juice is not ⅛ gasoline; Ted Koppel is a robot; Women aren't from Venus and men aren't from Mars; Fleiss does floss; Quayle is familiar with common bathroom procedures; Bart is bad to the bone; Godfrey Jones's wife is cheating on him; The Beatles haven't reunited to enter kick boxing competitions; The 'Bug' on your TV screen can see into your home; Everyone on TV is better than you; The people who are writing this have no life.

5. I should mention here that this book could not have been written without The Simpsons Archive. Let me take the opportunity now to thank the Archive's many contributors for their unknowing assistance with my research, though I know it's a virtual certainty they'll find my analysis inaccurate, incomplete and/or generally beneath contempt. (Perhaps even the worst. Book. Ever.)

6. **Youth-marketing newspeak:** As Poochie evolves from laboured concept to cloyingly hip cartoon character, various 'Itchy & Scratchy' executives suggest changes, employing the latest in pseudo-technical marketing lingo. Observing a rough sketch of Poochie, Lindsey Naegle suggests that the show's animators 'rasta-fy him by 10 per cent or so'. Krusty the Clown, meanwhile, wants to see 'a schmeer of surfer'. And when it comes time for voice actor auditions, studio mogul Roger Meyers dismisses Homer after his first attempt at Poochie's voice with this harangue: 'You've got no attitude, you're barely outrageous, and I don't know what you're in, but it's not *my* face.'

7. **Total market saturation:** 'All Your Base Are Belong To Us' was an Internet fad so widespread it even made it onto the comics page of mass-circulation newspapers. In the 12 March 2001, instalment of the comic strip *FoxTrot*, an adolescent boy barks the phrase repeatedly as he marches past his confused parents. This is extraordinary when you consider that *FoxTrot* shares real estate with a gaggle of 1950s teenagers (*Archie*), a typical 1950s couple (*Blondie*), a World War II buck private (*Beetle Bailey*), and a twentieth-century English souse (*Andy Capp*, Homer Simpson's favourite wife-beating drunk). *FoxTrot*'s 'All Your Base' reference might indeed have been the first reference ever made on many papers' comics pages to *anything* unique to the society and culture of the 1990s.

8. **Happy surfing:** As of this writing, oo is still up and running online. Take a peek at http://www.alcyone.com/oo/.

9. **The Anti-Disney:** By 2003, Disinformation had metastasised into a miniature media empire, with 200,000 copies sold of its coffee-table dissent encyclopaedias – *You Are Being Lied To* and *Everything You Know Is Wrong* – and a TV series on Britain's Channel 4, in addition to the website itself.

10. **A few snapshots of Boo.com's staggering burn rate:** Four-hundred-plus employees at its peak; $42 million spent on advertising; more than $1 million spent on an 'interactive magazine' that published a single digital issue; $200,000 *per month* on travel expenses; $150 Spoon watches as launch presents for staffers. The official company cocktail, for the record, was vodka and grapefruit juice.

CHAPTER EIGHT

The Ugly
Springfieldianite

We wish to learn all the curious, outlandish ways of all the different countries, so that we can 'show off' and astonish people when we get home. We wish to excite the envy of our untraveled friends with our strange foreign fashions which we can't shake off. All our passengers are paying strict attention to this thing, with the end in view which I have mentioned. The gentle reader will never, never know what a consummate ass he can become, until he goes abroad.

Mark Twain, The Innocents Abroad

Always remember that you're representing our country. I guess what I'm saying is, don't mess up France the way you messed up your room.

Homer Simpson, parting advice to Bart upon his first trip abroad,
Episode 7G13 ('The Crepes of Wrath')

THE SUN NEVER SETS ON THE SIMPSONIAN EMPIRE

THERE ARE MANY DIFFERENT FACES to American hegemony. There's a consumer face: a lurid visage adorned with the logos of Coca-Cola and Marlboro and Nike that's given rise to the famous (and contestable) maxim that no war has ever been fought between two nations with McDonald's franchises on their soil.[1] There's a military face: sometimes a shadowy silhouette sketched high in the sky by the contrails of B-52s, other times a vivid, close-up portrait of nervous faces watching over the dusty streets of Arab cities. There's a big-business face drawn by connecting the dots between Microsoft's regional offices, the low-wage factories of Gap's subcontractors, and ExxonMobil's oil drills. There are rock & roll faces and IMF faces, evangelical Christian faces and the faces of emigrants back home for visits. And in more than 70 countries around the world, there is one of the most beloved of all of these faces – a bright yellow face. The face of *The Simpsons*.

In addition to the 10 or 15 million Americans who see it on the Fox Network, each new episode of *The Simpsons* will eventually be watched by more than 60 million viewers worldwide. Not counting your Super Bowls and Academy Awards broadcasts and the like, *The Simpsons* probably has the largest international audience of any American TV show. (The online magazine *Salon* has asserted that it surpasses even *Baywatch* in this regard.) Far more impressive than the size of the show's global audience, though, is its fervour. In many of the 70-plus countries where *The Simpsons* airs, it isn't just watched but *adored*. It's a ratings titan in the rest of the English-speaking world, a cult hit in most of Europe and Latin America, and a noteworthy phenomenon everywhere else. *Simpsons* characters are used to sell lemon soda in Japan, and the show inspires academic essays in Mexico. The show's vast array of Internet fansites is a digital United Nations, with significant representation from Russia and Israel and Japan in addition to large contingents from Western Europe and North America. The proprietor of the web's most significant shrine, The Simpsons Archive, is Scandinavian. *The Simpsons* is a truly global phenomenon.

All foreign markets are not equally enamoured of Homer and his brood, of course. The show's heartland outside the United States is undoubtedly the rest of the English-speaking world, where *The Simpsons* is, if anything, *more* deeply worshipped than it is at home. *Simpsons* broadcasts account for nearly one-fifth of all viewers on the Sky One satellite channel in Britain, even as it has also become a hit in reruns for BBC2 and Channel 4. When the show's cast announced that they'd be appearing at the 2000 Edinburgh Festival to give a live reading of a script, it provoked 'something close to mass hysteria' – so said the *Guardian* – as tickets sold out in less than an hour. In Canada, Global TV not only broadcasts new episodes of the show each week but also throws a couple of repeats into what seems like every spare timeslot in its schedule, while the CBC chips in with one rerun every weeknight. Australians, meanwhile, have made *The Simpsons* one of the country's highest-rated comedy programmes.

The show has proven to be a slightly harder sell in translation. In Germany, for example, *The Simpsons* was initially dismissed as kids' stuff before finding the audience that has since made it the top-rated American show in the country among young men and the heavily discussed focal point of a vibrant German-language online community. Mainstream Czech viewers, meanwhile, were turned off by the crude animation and racy writing, but once the show was repackaged as an 'extreme' series – an agent not of America's mass market but rather its counterculture – it became a favourite of students and intellectuals. In Japan, there was all kinds of cultural friction when *The Simpsons* first debuted (on a pay channel called Wowow): the characters' four fingers were read as a sign of decidedly unhip low-class status, for example, and Bart's brattiness was seen as anything but charming. Once the show's marketing put the spotlight on overachieving Lisa, however, Japan found a Simpson it could love. In general, *The Simpsons* has become a major cultural presence in most of Western Europe and quite a bit of Latin America (particularly Mexico, Argentina and Brazil); in the rest of the world, it has attracted small but influential audiences of cool kids and intellectuals.

Beyond the factoids of its international success, though, there's the more curious question of why *The Simpsons* has captured so many of the world's hearts and minds. The rule of thumb in mass entertainment is that shameless pandering to the lowest common denominator is the easiest way to go global – Hollywood's chief cinematic export, for example, is the blowed-up-real-good action flick, and *Baywatch* has long been the pacesetter in small-screen globe-trotting. Comedy is a legendarily poor traveller, particularly when it comes to social satire, with its reliance on hard-to-translate stuff like context and colloquial language and wordplay. (*The Simpsons'* closest sitcom cousin, *Seinfeld*, for example, has been nowhere near as big a hit internationally.) How, then, did *The Simpsons* conquer the world? How did this densely written, whip-smart, culturally precise, hyper-colloquial cartoon become a global phenomenon?

The answer starts with the show's universality. Some details, of course, are far from universal: plot lines involving home snowplough businesses or bowling leagues, characters like the ambulance-chasing lawyer or the misanthropic bartender, guest appearances by Gary Coleman and Bret 'The Hitman' Hart. But *The Simpsons* does boast a number of bedrock elements that translate easily to the rest of the West and (to some extent) to the rest of the world: physical humour, sight gags and exaggerated emotion make sense to audiences everywhere, regardless of their mother tongue. Kids who have never seen a skateboard can still get a laugh out of Homer's extended tumbles into Springfield Gorge, and foreign viewers who've never heard of *Tom & Jerry* can still comprehend the mayhem of 'Itchy & Scratchy.' (They might be appalled by it, but they still *comprehend* it.)

The show's use of archetypal – and stereotypical – characters and settings also helps it cross borders. If the bratty boy doesn't resonate, then surely the doting mom will. Or if, as in Japan, the bratty boy actively repels the audience, then the brainy girl will serve as a suitably sympathetic character to relate to. The fact remains, though, that *The Simpsons* is just as much Homer's show in Timbuktu as it is in Toledo, Ohio. And Homer crosses borders with ease: stripped of his American Everyman touches – the Duff, the donuts, the bowling ball and rock & roll – he's a big fat clown, a bumbling doofus, an all-but-universal dimwit. *Simpsons* viewers far from America's shores who are living in circumstances unimaginable to your average American slob can still get a kick out of Homer's head trauma and frequent electrocutions, and the whole world knows exactly what he means when he yells *D'oh!*

Homer's most universal gesture, however, might be the angry strangulation of his son. And at any rate his most universal *role* is certainly that of dad, husband, head of household. The real key to the show's ability to connect with audiences from Scandinavia to South America is the Simpson family itself. By focusing on a single family, no matter how American in its incidental details, *The Simpsons* speaks to potentially the entire planet. And it's this focus on family that leads the show to be not just watched but *adopted* by viewers in many of the foreign markets it airs in. 'The Simpsons are not just cartoon characters; they're real people living the kind of lives we all can identify with,' decreed London's *Daily Mail*, throwing aside its usual distrust of anything foreign to claim Homer and his family in the name of the queen. Another British tabloid, the *Daily Express*, went even further. 'The Simpsons,' it claimed, 'are now as much a part of this culture as roast beef and poor sporting achievement.' *Mmmm . . . roast beef*, Homer eagerly agrees, and then he heads off to Winnipeg, Manitoba, where folks are so eager to make their strong identification with the Simpson patriarch official that they have happily made him an honorary citizen.

None of this is incidental, nor inevitable, nor commonplace. Canadians have been delighting in the comedy of Monty Python for years, but no attempt has ever been made to bestow citizenship on Michael Palin for his work on 'The Lumberjack Song'. It is practically inconceivable that anywhere other than New York will ever try to lay claim to the self-absorbed neurotics of *Seinfeld*. With *The Simpsons*, though, there is such a strong connection, such a sense of shared worldview, that its international fans want to make it their own. The desire for connection – for direct identification with the show – is a feature of its audience the world over. And so international and/or foreign-language *Simpsons* fansites are abundant, and a catalogue of every reference the show has ever made to the site's home country is a common feature.

This, too, is a near-universal trait among *Simpsons* fans: a deep appreciation for those rare occasions when the show has consummated the relationship with a direct reference.[2] When Sky One asked *Simpsons* fans in Britain in 2000 to vote on their favourite episode of all time, they chose Episode 2F15 ('Lisa's Wedding'), which just happens to feature the most prominent English character in the show's history: a pompous prat named Hugh who nearly weds Lisa in a flash-forward to her college days. In both Canada and Australia, meanwhile, the media treated *The Simpsons*' on-screen visits like headline news. There's an implicit subservience in the way the show's international audiences pore over the details of these brief glimpses of themselves in the Simpsonian mirror, a gratefulness that's almost colonial. Even when a Canadian newspaper is detailing the many ways *The Simpsons* got Canada wrong or an Australian letter to the editor expresses contempt for the reckless way the show wields national stereotypes, there's a built-in deference. Notwithstanding the nitpicking, viewers out in the distant hinterland of the empire are thankful that the show has noticed them at all.

Consider one of the show's most prominent recurring international references – Apu Nahasapeemapetilon, the jovial Indian immigrant who runs Springfield's Kwik-E-Mart. For *Simpsons* fans of Indian heritage who reside in the show's Western heartland, Apu is a mixed blessing. On the one hand, he is a broad stereotype with a cartoonishly thick accent who works a low-wage job and proudly overcharges his customers and sells them rotten hot dogs – reinforcing any number of prejudices about South Asians. On the other hand, Apu is a bona fide pioneer: he was the *only* recurring South Asian character on a major American sitcom when he first took his place behind the Kwik-E-Mart's till in the early 1990s. And he remains the most prominent South Asian on primetime TV, an iconic part of one of America's most important cultural institutions – strong evidence that South Asians have become a significant segment of the social fabric of the West. 'Is Apu a truly harmful stereotype, or a caricature to be laughed at?' asked *India Abroad*, a magazine covering the Indian diaspora, in a 2001 profile of Hank Azaria. The profile's author ultimately couldn't say for sure, but Apu was such a prominent icon for the magazine's readership that it didn't really matter. For better and/or for worse, Apu was the cartoon face of Indians in America. He'd have to do.

Viewers in the colonies must generally resign themselves to a similar fate. They may see one of their kind from time to time in the streets of the cartoon metropolis, but he'll be made to parade about in stereotypically traditional dress like an Iroquois warrior brought to perform for the royal court. And maybe an emissary or two – or a whole family of emissaries – will be dispatched from Springfield to acknowledge the tribute flowing in from the far corners of the empire, but they will see only what they want to see when they arrive on those distant shores.

THE UGLY SPRINGFIELDIANITE (I): SOUND BITE-SIZED WORLD

Travel has been an occasional feature of Simpsonian life since Bart spent a semester in France on a student exchange back in Season 1, but the Simpson family's first trip abroad en masse didn't happen until Episode 2F13 ('Bart vs. Australia') in Season 6. The trip isn't quite a holiday: the US State Department brings the Simpsons to Australia so Bart can apologise for tricking a naive Australian lad into accepting a 900 dollar collect phone call.[3] Bart's prank, it turns out, has come on the heels of America's abandonment of Australia's kitschy pop culture after a brief late-1980s love affair that made fleeting stars of Crocodile Dundee, Yahoo Serious and Jacko, an Aussie-rules football star dressed as an Energizer battery. 'Americo-Australian relations are at an all-time low,' explains the State Department's Evan Conover (slimily voiced by Phil Hartman as a kind of political-hack twin of Troy McClure).

So it's off to Australia for the Simpsons – or, more precisely, to a Simpsonian version of Australia, rife with stereotypes and overflowing with inaccuracies. The Australia that the Simpsons visit is a land populated by ignorant, simple-minded yokels, where the pubs serve only Foster's beer, kicking wrongdoers with a giant boot is a national institution, koalas and kangaroos abound even in the cities, and there's a major national monument to dirt. The inaccuracy of this Australia is quite pointed: the country's government, for example, meets in a building labelled 'Parliament Haus der Austria' (the missing -al- has been added belatedly), and when an angry Aussie mob gives chase to Bart and Homer, it includes a good chunk of the cast of the Australian sci-fi movie *The Road Warrior*. 'It may as well be called *The Simpsons Go to Mars* – that's how much it has to do with reality,' Matt Groening explained to an Australian reporter. 'We're playing with all sorts of silly stereotypes.' Groening added that he'd considered doing some research on Australia for the episode, but his creative team talked him out of it. 'We decided that if it had any resemblance to reality, then the stuff we got wrong would stick out even more, so we just went with the idea of getting everything wrong.'

This is not a portrait of the country in the style of Springfield's semi-realistic America-in-microcosm, then, so much as a satirical sketch of the Australia that resides in America's popular consciousness. This is a place of roughly drawn caricatures and hazily recalled details, where fictitious pop icons coexist with regular folks and genuine regional linguistic nuances smack up against wholly invented ones. ('These bloody things are every-where,' says an Aussie store owner, shooing bullfrogs out the door. 'They're in the lift, in the lorry, in the bond wizard, and all over the malonga gilderchuck.') This is, in short, a portrait of Australia in sound bites. 'Australia was originally founded as a settlement for British convicts,' Marge reads off the plaque at the base of a statue, setting up a gag in which passersby lurch with criminal intent towards Lisa's camera – and condensing the tone of most *Simpsons* travels into a single factoid.

Long-distance travel is a recurring plot device on *The Simpsons*, and each foreign destination has been rendered in just such a broad-strokes collage of postcard images, crude caricatures and dusty clichés. Simpsonian Japan is a quick-cut kaleidoscope of seizure-inducing children's television, automated talking toilets, sumo wrestling matches, Shinto shrines and Hello Kitty factories. The Simpsons go to Africa, and there they find Masai villagers drinking cow's blood, spear-toting jungle tribesmen, giant carnivorous flowers, and enough exotic animals to fill a half-dozen *National Geographic* documentaries. In India, it's overcrowded trains, mendicants with shaved heads, and a rail-thin sage with a flowing beard seated cross-legged on a mountain top. In Toronto, the Simpsons find the CN Tower, curling and conformist graffiti. 'It's so clean and bland,' Marge announces, greeting Canada's largest city with its most shopworn stereotype. 'I'm home!'

And in a very real way she is, because the Toronto she visits – like the

Simpsonian Africa and Australia and Japan and the rest – bears a much closer resemblance to the imagination of middle Americans like herself than to the actual place it's pretending to be. In fact, the Simpsonian versions of these places are even one degree further removed, because they represent what the show's L.A.-based, Ivy League-educated writers believe to be the commonly held stereotypes of unsophisticated middle Americans. Thus even when the Simpsons go to New York, they wind up in a foreign wonderland reduced to a handful of famous landmarks: Chinatown, Broadway musicals, gruff locals spewing profanities, a wealthy dowager right off the cover of a 1920s issue of *The New Yorker*.

This travel through the mid-American looking glass is indeed something of a Simpsonian institution in its own right. 'The Simpsons are going to [some faraway place]!' a Simpson announces, and off they go. And what they find, invariably, is a caricature, a broadly parodic Elsewhere in which certain foreground details are uncannily accurate, a few others represent insightful exaggerations, and the rest are deeply flawed. 'Whenever the Simpsons go to another country, we always get it wrong and get into trouble,' Matt Groening admitted in a 2003 interview. Or – in another, more accurate way – whenever the Simpsons go to another country, we always get a revealing glimpse of how America sees the rest of the world. When the action takes place in Springfield, *The Simpsons* usually exhibits a social realism that's at times almost preternatural; but as soon as Homer and company get on a plane, an atypical sloppiness soon pervades. For all its many humanist trappings, for all the universal themes it deals with, *The Simpsons* becomes most chauvinistically American when it leaves the United States.

Just ask the good people of Rio de Janeiro, who hosted a visit from the Simpson family in a Season 13 episode – DABF10 ('Blame It on Lisa') – and soon became entangled in one of the most acrimonious international incidents the show's skewed diplomacy ever inspired. The Simpsons' trip begins with the best intentions, inspired by Lisa's sponsorship of an orphan boy from Rio's slums. When the boy goes missing, they decide to travel to Brazil to track him down. With uncharacteristic diligence, Bart spends the long flight to Rio listening to a series of Spanish-language instruction tapes called *Español Para Dummies*. Finally, he yanks off his headphones and announces, 'Get ready, Brazil – I now speak fluent Spanish!' Marge: 'Well done, Bart! But in Brazil, they speak Portuguese.' Bart launches into a diatribe in polished, lightning-quick *español* – something about wasting all that time studying for nothing. Then, on Homer's orders, he sets about forgetting everything he's learned. He whacks himself on the head with the in-flight phone – not once, not twice, but thrice – and proudly proclaims, 'All gone!' Just then, and with ominous portent, the cabin fills with the voice of the Brazilian captain. 'This is your captain speaking,' he announces in a cartoon-thick Spanish accent. 'The temperature in Rio de Janeiro is hot, hot, hot! – with a one hundred per cent chance of *passion*!' *The Simpsons'* best intentions have vanished as quickly as Bart's language training: as the inaccurately accented, cliché-spouting pilot makes abundantly clear, Episode DABF10 will display the usual Simpsonian insensitivity to foreign cultures from here on out.

As the Simpsons' adventure unfolds, the show's portrait of Brazil abounds with crude generalisations and stereotypical details, some pertaining to Rio, some to Brazil, still others to Latin America and/or the Third World generally. The Simpsons travel from the airport to their hotel by conga line, and the hotel's staff kicks room keys around like soccer balls. ('They sure love soccer here,' Bart announces, in case you missed the gag.) The TV in their room, meanwhile, broadcasts a semi-pornographic children's show, and practically every other Brazilian man they encounter is lascivious and avowedly bisexual. The streets teem with monkeys and rats. Prepubescent pickpockets prey upon Lisa and Marge, while the driver of an unlicensed taxi (its door conveniently labelled 'Unlicensed Taxi') kidnaps Homer. Simpsonian Rio is a sort of all-purpose, catch-all Latin American Everyslum, a generic tropical metropolis with just enough distinctive postcard details in the background – Copacabana Beach, the statue of Christ the Redeemer on Corcovado, the gaudy parade of Carnival – to counterweight the undifferentiated-Third-World-poverty stuff that drives the plot. From a certain angle, the show's caricature of Rio could seem crass, condescending, almost racist. Downright offensive. This, alas, was the angle from which many of Brazil's public officials apparently saw it.

The episode first hit the North American airwaves on 31 March 2002. Within days, the outrage of the people of Brazil at the crudeness of their Simpsonian likeness was international news. Never mind that the episode had not yet been broadcast in Brazil – word had reached Rio from Brazilian expats in the United States that one of America's most beloved TV shows had portrayed their fair city as a filthy, chaotic, crime-infested hellhole. Brazilian president Fernando Henrique Cardoso protested that this was 'a distorted vision of Brazilian reality'. Sérgio Cavalcanti, a spokesperson for Riotur – Rio's now-beleaguered tourism board – was more precise about the nature of the insult. 'What really hurt,' he told Reuters, 'was the idea of the monkeys, the image that Rio de Janeiro was a jungle . . . It's a completely unreal image of the city.' What also really hurt, he added, was that Riotur had just spent millions promoting the city internationally in an attempt to repair the damage caused by an outbreak of dengue fever in Rio a few years earlier. Might this savaging at the hands of *The Simpsons* have ruined all their hard work? Riotur was considering legal action.

The Simpsons' producers hastily drafted a decidedly Simpsonian apology. 'We apologize to the lovely city and people of Rio de Janeiro,' it went. 'And if that doesn't settle the issue, Homer Simpson offers to take on the president of Brazil on Fox's *Celebrity Boxing*.' The fooforah practically ended there, and Rio, one presumes, survived the mailed satirical fist of *The Simpsons* to fight and dance and breed enormous rat colonies another day.

Here's the thing: by the show's standards, DABF10 wasn't even a particularly insensitive portrait of the vast *terra incognita* that lurks outside the town limits of good old Springfield, USA. On the one hand, yes, the conga is a Caribbean style of dance, and Rio has posh promenades as well as slums, and there's not actually a kids' show called *Teleboobies* on Brazilian TV. On the other hand, one of Brazil's most popular kids' shows *was* hosted by former *Playboy* centrefold Xuxa. And while there might not be swarms of monkeys and hordes of rats in Rio, there *are* plenty of both nonetheless. And, most of all, this was *The Simpsons*, so Rio should have been proud of its induction into that prestigious global clique of places the show has treated to reductionist satirical portraits. Or, if not quite proud, Rio might at least have been unperturbed. It was, after all, nothing personal. This is just how the rest of the world looks from Springfield.

The oversimplistic portrayal of the rest of the world on *The Simpsons* can be understood to some extent as a satirical device – as a broad comment on the insular nature of American society. And this satire penetrates to the streets of Springfield itself, where absurdly broad stereotypes coexist with the town's more realistic details. This is a town, after all, whose Irish inhabitants are essentially leprechauns and whose Italian restaurant is run by a fellow named Luigi who is, if anything, a *broader* stereotype than Chef Boyardee. There's a local Latino celebrity, usually referred to as Bumblebee Man, who stars in 'unpredictable Mexican sitcoms' in which he stumbles around screaming *Aye-yi-yi*, and who wears his bumblebee costume off-screen as well as on.[4] Springfield's Mafiosi are right out of a B-movie, its occasional French visitors are invariably suave, sophisticated playboys, and its dentist uses a thick tome called *The Big Book of British Smiles* to intimidate children into brushing their teeth more diligently. *The Simpsons* trades widely and gleefully in the most inane of American prejudices, employing them with wide-eyed and mocking amazement. 'It's so beautiful!' Marge raves as she and Homer walk down Springfield's tacky Squidport promenade, taking in the pseudo-exotic sight of upmarket chain stores and restaurants. 'This is what I imagine Paris must be like.' This, the show's writers seem to be saying, is how little your average American knows about the rest of the world.

To be fair, there's undoubtedly plenty of fun to be had playing around ironically with stereotypes like this. Consider one of *The Simpsons'* most frequently appearing foreigners, Groundskeeper Willie, who is about as unrestrained as a parody can get. His flaming red eyebrows and beard are bushier than a Scottish heath, and his accent's thicker still, with *rrr*s that roll for hours. The parody is so over-the-top, in fact, that Willie's nationality becomes incidental: he's much more cartoon than Scot. And his most famous sobriquet – *cheese-eating surrender monkeys* – has nothing to do with Scotland and everything to do with American prejudice. It was, to be sure, a memorable line: Willie, recruited to teach French class down at Springfield Elementary, announcing to a room full of seven-year-olds, '*Bonjourrrrrrr*, you cheese-eating surrender monkeys.' As I noted earlier, the phrase – a three-word summary of the average red-blooded, patriotic American's contempt for France – made it to the front pages of newspapers and on the nightly news as the US prepared for war in Iraq in 2002, often employed unironically and without attribution by jingoistic right-wing commentators. This was surely the apex of *The Simpsons'* parody of American narrow-mindedness: a one-liner so flawlessly attuned to the sentiments of America's bigots that it actually found itself wholeheartedly embraced by them. Or was it instead the nadir? Had the show become so adept at parodying American prejudice that it had become a source of it?

This hints at the deeper metaphorical level on which *The Simpsons'* voyages work: as specimens of the same self-centredness they attempt to satirise. There's an arrogance to *The Simpsons'* use of foreign lands as fodder for cheap laughs that's symptomatic, in its way, of the egotism that pervades America's sense of itself and guides its behaviour on the world stage. Several of the show's travel episodes are conspicuously weak – the backdrops a little too glibly drawn, the satire of American arrogance far too dull to excuse the way they run roughshod over entire societies. When the Simpsons go to Toronto, for example, the closest thing to a clever dig is a brief glimpse of a hall whose sign reads 'Dodgers of Foreign Wars', making note of one of Canada's historical roles in American foreign affairs. Otherwise, the visit is little more than an excuse for outdated generalisations – about Canadian reserve, about the cleanliness and blandness of what is quite possibly the world's most multicultural city – and half-hearted jabs at ridiculously easy targets (who couldn't poke fun at curling?). Tear Canadian pieties to shreds or reduce the country to a collection of goofy clichés, certainly, but at least put it to some good use. Make it a satirical tool or a metaphorical device – or at least make it funny.

It's the same story with the Simpsons' trip to Africa, which turns an entire continent into a zoo so Homer and his family can have themselves a wacky adventure. And it builds to a convoluted climax in which the Simpsons arrive at a chimpanzee researcher's compound only to learn that she's turned her chimps into diamond-mining slaves, and the poachers who've been chasing them all episode turn out to be Greenpeace activists in disguise. The point of this satirical exercise is so muddied by the end that you're left with the sense that all of Africa's been reduced to caricature just so Homer can have a stage to clown upon.

The Simpsons' habit of casually trashing foreign cultures for increasingly meagre comedic returns hits perhaps its lowest ebb in Episode BABF11 ('Missionary: Impossible'). The episode's premise is that Homer flees Springfield to the South Pacific to become a Christian missionary in order to avoid fulfilling a monetary pledge he made to PBS. He winds up on the tiny island of Microatia, a non-specific tropical paradise spoiled only by a few years of evangelical Christianity and an epidemic of Polynesian stereotypes. The Microatians, as befits a catch-all race of Everyprimitives, have silly names like Ak and Qtoktok and consume exotic foods (ox testicles, which Homer seems to enjoy more than the Microatians). But what really distinguishes the Microatians is their simple, suggestible minds and their childlike wonder at the wisdom of the West. They are, it turns out, a missionary's dream: all Homer needs to do is fall to the ground chanting, 'Oh God! Oh God!,' and the assembled populace of Microatia falls to the ground with him.

Maybe – to be generous – the episode is an attempt to satirise the way the West has forced itself upon the developing world. Upon learning that there's not much happening on the island, Homer tries to add some razzle-dazzle by setting up a casino, which rapidly turns the Microatians into drunken, violent gambling addicts who gorge on bowls of macaroni salad between bouts of compulsive card-playing. The intrusion of Western consumer culture destroys this once-proud society, see? And when Homer tries to fix the mess with yet more Western corruption – a church – the church's bell sets off some kind of earthquake, and lava flows and . . . well, by about this time, not even the show's writers could think of what to do. Suddenly, former

Golden Girl Betty White intervenes – she'd been hosting the PBS telethon earlier in the episode – to reveal that this has all been a broadcast of a TV show detailing another of Homer's wacky adventures. Cut to credits. And save for a couple of fun gags that involved Homer licking hallucinogen-excreting toads, BABF11 has for no good reason made an utter travesty of the South Pacific, missionary work, the inherently corrupting influence (it would seem) of casinos on indigenous peoples the world over and Betty White.

This, then, is the legacy of the ugly Springfieldianite: send Homer abroad, and the show will wind up reinforcing the rest of the world's worst suspicions about America's callous disregard for anyone or anything other than itself. Homer sees the world as a collection of easily understood and manipulated symbols that are valuable only inasmuch as they are useful to Homer, to the show, to America. Exotic locales and regional customs are interchangeable and ultimately meaningless – what matters is how America sees these places and how its 'national interests' are best served by them. This has been a tragic and enduring flaw in American foreign policy since at least the end of the Second World War, from the days of the domino theory to the current 'Clash of Civilizations'. In the best of *The Simpsons*' travels, the show's portrayal of the ugly Springfieldianite overtly satirises this bias in the American character; just as often, though, the show itself is guilty of the same self-centredness it tries to lampoon.

Not that *The Simpsons* hasn't taken occasional satirical digs at American self-absorption. Consider the only other appearance of the poor, gullible Microtians. It's a cameo in Episode 8F12 ('Lisa the Greek'), a momentary flash of colour to enliven the pre-game show of a Super Bowl broadcast. 'Today, we're going to be seen by people in 150 countries all over the world!' the sportscaster on Homer's TV screen marvels, and then there appears on the screen a group of traditionally garbed South Pacific islanders seated on a log in front of a TV set. They are sucking back beers, munching on pizza slices, chomping on potato chips. The message is clear: America's most beloved spectacles are so universal in their appeal that the whole world is fascinated by them.

And this points to another deeply engrained American bias: a firm conviction that everyone, everywhere, would choose to be an American if they were offered the opportunity. Just ask the immigrant clerk with the thick accent down at the Kwik-E-Mart – he'll tell you all about it.

THE WORLD OF APU

Is Apu Nahasapeemapetilon proud to be an American? Or – more to the point – should America be proud of Apu Nahasapeema-whatever (as Aunt Selma once called him)? There's no simple answer to this question. Even Apu himself doesn't seem entirely sure.

What is certain, though, is that his story starts, like many an immigrant's tale, with alienation, indifference, even bigotry. When we first find Apu toiling behind the counter of Springfield's Kwik-E-Mart, he is as much a hollow stereotype as the gullible primitives of Microatia – an anonymous Indian with a funny voice. His ethnicity was surely chosen for no better reason than the fact that a great many convenience store clerks in America these days are South Asian. Who would Bart hand his money to when he bought squishees at the local convenience store in Season 1? A South Asian. They could just as easily – and as accurately – have made him Korean. Maybe they decided that an Indian accent was more humorous, or at least that Hank Azaria's Indian accent was.

There was little more to Apu than this silly accent for the first few seasons of *The Simpsons*. Even in Episode 7G12 ('Krusty Gets Busted'), a Season 1 instalment in which an armed robbery at the Kwik-E-Mart is a pivotal event, Apu does little more than his over-polite-Indian schtick. 'Hello, steady customer!' he greets Homer. 'How are you this evening, sir!' During the robbery, he responds to the assailant's demands thusly: 'Yes, yes, I know the procedure for armed robbery. I do work in a convenience store, you know.' When the burglary's done, that's practically the last we see of Apu until the next time a Simpson needs a salty snack.

Apu's job at first is merely to be a stock character: a convenience-store clerk who knows convenience-store things like how to behave during an armed robbery and how to overcharge for groceries. Even when he finds himself invited to the Simpson home for the big boxing match or bumping into Lisa and Marge outside an adult-education class, his role remains narrowly defined: he shows up with 'an assortment of jerky', or explains that he's taking a screenwriting class so he can write an epic screenplay entitled *Hands Off My Jerky, Turkey*. (The word 'jerky', you see, sounds kind of funny in an Indian accent.[5]) Apu tends his shrine full of totems to some strange and exotic religion, and when someone exits his store, he erupts in his very own cutesy catchphrase. 'Thank you, come again!' he chirps over-jovially, adding just a little wacky-immigrant colour to early episodes of *The Simpsons*.

In Episode 9F01 ('Homer the Heretic'), Springfield's volunteer fire department – which includes Apu, Ned Flanders and Krusty the Clown – races to the Simpson house just in time to save Homer from a blazing fire. Once they resuscitate him, Homer's convinced that the fire was the punishment of a vengeful God for skipping church. 'Homer,' says Ned Flanders, 'God didn't set your house on fire.'

'No,' Reverend Lovejoy pipes in, 'but he *was* working in the hearts of your friends and neighbours when they came to your aid, be they Christian' – pointing to Ned – 'Jew' – pointing to Krusty – 'or . . . miscellaneous' – pointing to Apu.

'Hindu!' Apu replies indignantly. 'There are 700 million of us.'

'Oh, that's super,' Reverend Lovejoy replies, his condescension so thick you could caulk a shower with it.

With this exchange, though, the satirical target shifts from Apu's beliefs and customs to Lovejoy's smarmy ignorance. Sure enough, Apu soon becomes a much more prominent and respected member of the Springfield community. In Episode 1F10 ('Homer and Apu'), Apu becomes the *main* character: the plot revolves around him losing his job at the Kwik-E-Mart and moving in with the Simpsons until he can get his life back on track and atone for poisoning Homer with a rotten hot dog. There's even a brief but informed exchange on Hindu theology. 'I am selling only the concept of karmic realignment,' Apu tells Homer when he shows up on the Simpsons' front stoop to work off his spiritual debt. 'You can't sell that!' Homer retorts. 'Karma can only be portioned out by the cosmos.' Apu has become a much more nuanced character with real emotional depth, and the show's take on Indian culture has grown considerably more sensitive and knowing. In a scene that was ultimately cut from the episode – later to reappear in Episode 3F31 ('The Simpsons 138th Episode Spectacular') as an outtake[6] – Apu introduces the Simpsons to Bollywood cinema. There's still a trace of astonished gawking in the Simpsonised Hindi film, but it also overflows with accurate detail – syrupy love songs, gaudy costumes, over-the-top melodrama.

In later episodes Apu expands upon his status as an important and fully rounded supporting player. There's an episode centred on his arranged marriage, for example, that has a bit of fun with Indian wedding customs without slipping into judgemental mockery, and another in which his marriage strains under the weight of his 18-hour workdays. Apu's job at the Kwik-E-Mart, his Indian heritage, his Hindu faith – these have now become *details* of his character, not defining traits. It might seem, then, that Apu has achieved the ultimate goal of the immigrant: he has been fully integrated into his adopted society. What the whole world wants – or so it's alleged – Apu's got. He's an American. Indeed in Episode 3F20 ('Much Apu About Nothing'), we watch him go through the ritual of becoming a full-fledged citizen. The funny thing about 3F20, though, is that it's far from a ringing endorsement of the American Dream. Now that Apu's a fully developed character, the writers can no longer ignore the ambiguities of his outsider existence in Springfield. His arrival at the immigrant's ultimate goal of citizenship leaves the question of the righteousness of that goal – and of America – an open question.

Here's what happens: in Episode 3F20, Mayor Quimby arbitrarily lays the blame for Springfield's high tax rates on illegal immigrants. This leads in short order to a referendum on a proposed bylaw to deport all immigrants from Springfield – Proposition 24 – and to widespread anti-immigrant hysteria. Apu, who has overstayed his student visa by many years, gets caught up in the madness, and he's soon forced to take his fate into his own hands: he obtains a forged birth certificate and other citizenship documentation from the Springfield Mafia, and takes to wearing sports paraphernalia and speaking in a broad middle-American drawl to try to avoid deportation. Homer soon stops by for a snack, interrupting Apu's game attempt at small talk about baseball – the 'Nye Mets' are his favourite 'squadron' – to ask what happened to his Ganesha statue. Apu's ruse falls apart, and he rushes back to his stockroom in shameful tears to retrieve his beloved Ganesha idol:

> *Apu:* Who am I kidding? I am no citizen! This passport is a cheap forgery! A cheap, two-thousand-dollar forgery. [*tears up passport*] I have brought shame to my parents, to my homeland, and to myself.
>
> *Homer:* Don't forget Ganesha.
>
> *Apu:* I cannot deny my roots, and I cannot keep up this charade. I only did it because I love this land – where I have the freedom to say and to think and to *charge* whatever I want! I want to stay, but as the real me – not as some yahoo from Green Bay.

Apu can't maintain the façade. He doesn't want to become an American badly enough to surrender everything to the task. Or, more precisely, Apu simply doesn't want to be an American at all if losing himself – his faith, his heritage, his *soul* – is part of the process.

Homer is quickly swayed to Apu's point of view on Proposition 24, and soon the entire Simpson clan goes to work trying to find a way to keep him in Springfield. Selma balks at a marriage of convenience, though, and all seems lost until Lisa figures out that there's an amnesty on the books for illegal immigrants who have been in the country for as long as Apu has. In short order, Apu passes his citizenship test, and the threat of deportation is gone forever. It's a good thing too, because Proposition 24 passes in a landslide, and soon unwelcome foreigners – Groundskeeper Willie, in particular – find themselves loaded onto boats bound for their homelands.

In Episode 3F20, *The Simpsons* attempts to purge the memory of its early-season stereotyping of Apu, putting its sharpest satirical weapons to the task of dissecting the contradictions between the lofty ideals enshrined at the base of the Statue of Liberty and the everyday realities of contemporary America. On the day of the referendum on Proposition 24, Chief Wiggum explains to his fellow officers, 'First we'll be rounding up your tired, then your poor, then your huddled masses yearning to breathe free.' There are deep-seated ambiguities in America's relationship with outsiders – so deep, indeed, that they've pervaded *The Simpsons'* own portrayal of foreigners – and in 3F20, the show examines them at length. Choosing to be an American is not quite the same thing as surrendering to American superiority on all fronts. Not every American immigrant wants to take a relaxed attitude towards work and watch baseball, much as not all the Pacific Islanders who watch the Super Bowl wish they could live in America. And the same goes for many of the world's Coke-drinkers and McDonald's-eaters and *Simpsons* fans.

There's a friendly tyranny embedded in the American assumption that the world yearns to be American. Removing democratically elected left-wing leaders from Latin American nations, holding off the advances of Communist insurgencies in Southeast Asia, liberating oil-rich Arab monarchies, decapitating brutal Arab dictatorships – America undertakes these international missions (or at least justifies them to its citizens) with the assumption that it knows what's best for these places and with the unwavering faith that they will quickly become happy little mini-Americas once the opportunity presents itself. And it has been America's enduring frustration to find that the world outside its borders refuses to fully embrace its way of life.

It can be dangerous to reduce an argument this expansive to a single anecdote, but every so often there's one sufficiently apt to carry the load. I stumbled on one on a bus ride from southern Portugal to the grand Spanish city of Seville in the spring of 2002. Sitting near me on the bus were two young American men who were comparing instances of alleged anti-Americanism they'd recently experienced. I fell into conversation with them, and we took to trading impressions and sharing travel advice. One of the

Americans, it turned out, was not a tourist but a student – he'd been living in the north of Portugal for a few months, studying Portuguese at a university there. He'd found the experience quite frustrating, he said, particularly because of the Old World formality of his Portuguese classmates. He told a story to explain: he'd been living in a dormitory with two other students, both Portuguese, and they'd encountered the usual frictions roommates do: differences in lifestyle, minor squabbles over dirty dishes, that sort of thing. What really drove this American guy nuts, though, was that it was like pulling teeth to get his roommates to talk about their disputes. All he wanted to do, he explained, was confront the problem right away, talk it out, settle it and move on. But he had to browbeat his roommates into opening up the slightest bit, push and cajole them to talk it through – and even then little seemed to be accomplished. They were just too formal, too closed. Why, he wondered, did his Portuguese roommates refuse to adopt what was so obviously a superior way of addressing frictions and grievances? His intentions were wholly admirable, his approach democratic and honest, his goal quite possibly beneficial to all involved. And there was no way to explain to him that his frustration was a result of his faults, not theirs. It hadn't occurred to him that his Portuguese roommates might have their own problem-solving methods, that they might have their own *values* – polite formality with acquaintances, a preference for an imperfect status quo over confrontation – and that they might hold these values just as deeply as he maintained his own preference for open dialogue and efficient resolution. Worst of all, it didn't seem to occur to him that he was a *guest* in a foreign country, that the Portuguese approach, even if flawed, inherently carried more weight than his own in the dormitory of a Portuguese university. The home-field advantage of Portuguese culture was simply not on his radar. He'd been born and raised in the greatest society on earth, the place where Old World injustices had been corrected and Old World problems solved. It was practically his birthright – and his nature – to impose his will upon this Portuguese dorm.

Few Americans seem capable of understanding that their conversations with the world are mostly one-sided, that America usually chooses the rules of the game and the parameters of the debate. And that people the world over tend to resist a solution – even the right one – when it is forced upon them. Most Americans know that they're citizens of the most powerful nation on earth, and yet few seem capable of seeing the way that power factors into their country's relationship with the rest of the world. America, no matter how powerful it gets, just can't see its own hegemony.

If you are not American, you know where you stand with America. You are outside, looking in. And even when what you see is a vision of your own wildest dreams – and it frequently is – you know that it is not yours, and you know that you do not meet it as an equal. Such is the case even with *The Simpsons*: as a foreign viewer, your love of the show will always remain somewhat unrequited. The stories it tells, even the ones about you, will always be American stories.

This is not, however, the only plane on which this relationship functions. For foreign viewers much more than for Americans, one of the strongest attractions of *The Simpsons* is the sharpness of its critique of America itself. It is that rare pop institution that seems to suggest that the wisest minds in the imperial court are as disenchanted with American hegemony as anyone. *The Simpsons* seems, in short, to be telling the whole world that the emperor's buck naked.

THE UGLY SPRINGFIELDIANITE (II): THE SIMPSONIAN PALACE COUP

'We've always had this image of big, strong Americans: Superman, Bruce Willis, the Terminator, the mighty hero. From the television programmes, we never really understood very well what happened in Vietnam. I think there are some people who think the gringos won.' The commentator here is Ernesto Vanegas, a professor of international economics at the National Autonomous University in Mexico City and author of a collection of Spanish-language essays about *The Simpsons*. In Mexico, as Vanegas explained in a 1998 *Salon* feature, the United States is seen as a veritable paradise, a place that fuels the dreams of Mexican children. The problem, though, is that the dream has always been overidealised, unattainable, a fantasy. Even for many of the Mexicans who relocate to the US, the everyday reality of low-wage labour and omnipresent fear of deportation is far removed from the glossy righteousness of Hollywood movies. It isn't just action heroes, either – the father figures in American pop culture have generally been benevolent, all-knowing, flawless. Taken as a whole, American pop broadcasts an image of impossible perfection to the Mexican people, a relentless and inescapable assertion of American superiority.

The antidote, in Vanegas's view, is Homer Simpson – a fat, flawed anti-hero whose lifestyle is eminently attainable. 'In *The Simpsons*,' Vanegas has said, 'we're not asked to identify ourselves with American nationalism and patriotism, but rather with life's weaknesses, its human side.'

'For the first time,' he concluded, 'gringos are universal.'

To Vanegas, *The Simpsons* redeems the American way of life by putting it within reach. Much as Homer is beloved in the US itself in part because he validates a slothful, slovenly lifestyle, so too does he comfort the rest of the world with the notion that Americans, for all their wealth and power and action-hero bluster, are just as dimwitted and incompetent as anyone. They don't have all the answers, and they haven't achieved perfection. The United States of America is not Paradise – not by a long shot, if Springfield is any indication.

But this is not the whole story. To be sure, viewers around the world seek out ways to identify with *The Simpsons*: everything from the familiar dynamics of family life at *casa de Simpson* to the occasional appearances of Mexican comedians, Indian convenience store clerks, Canadian cityscapes. At the same time, though, there is a pent-up resentment among the world's consumers of American pop culture, born of too many encounters with patriotic superheroes and too many lectures from infallible father figures. This is the anger of those living under a hegemonic order that is not their own. And a part of what they love about *The Simpsons* – a *big* part, maybe the biggest – is that it gives voice to this anger. The show can look, at times, like a pirate broadcast from inside the palace gates, the work of double agents whose sympathies might well lie as much with those caught under America's thumb as with the people in charge. In the realm of mainstream, mass-market American pop disseminated worldwide, *The Simpsons* is – by a *wide* margin – American society's most strident critic.

Self-criticism is as intrinsic to *The Simpsons* as Homer's tremendous gut. There have been certain moments, though, when *The Simpsons* has seemed to speak directly to the frustrations of its international viewers, attacking the arrogance, self-satisfaction and sense of entitlement endemic to America's conduct in foreign affairs with particular viciousness. These moments often occur when the Simpson family's insular existence collides with a foreign culture. In Episode 7G13 ('The Crepes of Wrath'), for example, a headstrong Albanian boy named Adil comes to live with the Simpsons as part of the student exchange that sees Bart sent to France.[7] At an assembly on Adil's first day at Springfield Elementary, Principal Skinner introduces him with a sort of shorthand overview of American xenophobia. 'You might find his accent peculiar,' Principal Skinner warns. 'Certain aspects of his culture may seem absurd, perhaps even offensive. But I urge you all to give little Adil the benefit of the doubt. This way, and only in this way, do we hope to better understand our backward neighbours throughout the world.' Later, Adil – a proud distributor of Albania's alleged chief export, 'furious political thought' – proves just as prejudiced against the US as the people of Springfield are against him. 'How can you defend a country where 5 per cent of the people control 95 per cent of the wealth?' Adil asks Lisa. 'I'm defending a country where people can think and act and worship any way they want,' Lisa retorts. A nasty fight ensues until Homer arrives on the scene as the voice of reason. 'Please, please, kids – stop fighting,' he instructs. 'Maybe Lisa's right about America being the land of opportunity, and maybe Adil's got a point about the machinery of capitalism being oiled with the blood of the workers.' We sort of expect this kind of dogmatic anti-American rhetoric from a European intellectual (even a prepubescent one), and Lisa's defence of America's civil liberties is a stock response. What's remarkable, though, is that the show – a popular, primetime American TV show broadcast around the world – is giving equal time to both sides of this debate. 7G13 was a Season 1 episode, the first real indication that the geography of *The Simpsons* stretched beyond Springfield's town limits; you could almost sense the world's ears prick up as they heard Adil's rhetorical attack. Okay, so the kid's the villain in this episode. (He turns out to be gathering information on how to build a nuclear power plant for the Albanian government.) Still, he got equal time, and Sylvester Stallone never showed up to terminate his speechifying with extreme prejudice or anything.

Adil's by-the-numbers Marxist critique is nothing, though, compared to the savage caricatures of the ugly Springfieldianite that have turned up on other occasions. When the Simpsons travel to Australia, for example, Bart has only one question for American ambassador Avril Ward: 'Do the toilets go backwards here?' 'No,' the ambassador promptly replies. 'To combat homesickness, we've installed a device that makes them swirl the correct, American way.' He indicates a huge, unwieldy apparatus next to the embassy's toilet. He gives it a demonstration flush, and the apparatus chugs noisily to life, bringing the toilet's water to a stop in mid-flush and reversing the direction of its swirl. Homer, staring at the spinning water with tearful awe, is moved to song: 'Sweet land of liberty, of thee I sing ...' He begins to weep, too overcome with pride to carry on. And anyone who's ever seen an American tourist demand 'real' coffee in an Italian café or suffered through a devastating regimen of IMF austerity measures to bring their national economy in line with the current thinking in Washington has a new symbol for American self-righteousness: the jingoistic toilet.

This line of criticism is reduced to its very essence in a minor detail that pops up during the Simpson family's visit to Brazil. As Homer and Bart walk onto Copacabana Beach, a nearby lifeguard blows his whistle. 'Excuse me – Americans!' he calls. Homer gasps. 'How did you know?' he asks, turning to face the camera. Cut to a tight shot of his T-shirt, which is emblazoned with a caricature of Uncle Sam, his mouth open voraciously wide, the whole earth in his clutches. A huge bite has already been chomped out of it, and Uncle Sam is lifting the globe again towards his gaping maw. TRY AND STOP US, reads the caption underneath.

You want a fiercely critical assessment of America's disposition towards the rest of the world? Well, you don't have to rely on Albanian ideologues anymore – Homer Simpson's T-shirt can do the job just fine. You want an honest, self-effacing reconsideration of American pre-eminence? Just ask Homer about health care in the United States. 'Don't worry, Marge,' he tells his wife as he prepares for coronary bypass surgery. 'America's health-care system is second only to Japan, Canada, Sweden, Great Britain – well, all of Europe. But you can thank your lucky stars we don't live in Paraguay!'[8]

Or let's say you're Canadian, and you've been conditioned since birth to expect the American pop culture you constantly consume to be totally oblivious to your existence (or else, on very rare occasions, aware of it in an exceedingly condescending, *Sgt. Preston of the Yukon* sort of way). And then all of sudden there's an episode of *The Simpsons* in which a Vietnamese immigrant child waxes poetic on the singular promise of the American Dream, and his speech goes like this: 'When my family arrived in this country four months ago, we spoke no English and had no money in our pockets. Today, we own a nationwide chain of wheel-balancing centres. Where else but in America, or possibly Canada, could our family find such opportunity?' And a few seasons later, there's Bart Simpson greeting a boatload of would-be immigrants – from the crown of the Statue of Liberty, no less – by hollering, 'Beat it! Country's full!' An officer aboard the ship immediately turns to the huddled masses on the deck. 'Okay, people, you heard the lady,' he announces. 'Back into the hold. We'll try Canada.' If you're Canadian, you know America very well – and you also know that your home is at least as dedicated to freedom and democracy, at least as enamoured of justice, at least as welcoming to immigrants. But to have an American TV show agree with you? Repeatedly? Ay, carumba!

In Canada – as in many of the countries where *The Simpsons* has become a beloved institution – there's a passion for self-critical American pop that far exceeds the domestic demand for the stuff. There are few corners of the globe where you'll encounter a shortage of fierce critics of the US, but to find an authentic American one is a rare and cherished thing. This is why *The Simpsons* seems to have an even higher profile in places like Canada and the United Kingdom than it does at home.

The British case provides an especially vivid illustration. Britain's considerable enthusiasm for all things Simpsonian is well documented. Beyond the examples I've already mentioned, there have been annual in-depth analyses of the show in every major British newspaper and raves from the prime minister and the archbishops of Canterbury and Wales. There was BBC2's 'Simpsons Night' in 2000 – more than three hours of classic episodes, interviews and analysis to coincide with the show's tenth anniversary. There was a 2003 poll in which Homer Simpson beat out even John Cleese's beloved misanthrope Basil Fawlty for the title of greatest TV character of all time. (The poll was commissioned by Channel 4, which had paid nearly £1 million per episode to steal the rebroadcast rights to the show from BBC2.) And in 2002, when the *Financial Times* quoted Matt Groening's half-joking suggestion that the series might soon be finished, a Fleet Street wag observed: 'Even a hint, a whisper, of their demise saw the free world descend into panic.'

Right then. So what is it about *The Simpsons* that makes the British love it so? The answer lies in Britain's long-standing affinity for authentic American rebels – it was English art students, after all, who rescued American blues music from near-oblivion in the early 1960s. And the answer can be seen even more clearly by considering Britain's unmatched enthusiasm for Bill Hicks, an edgy American stand-up comedian who became a cult sensation in the UK right around the same time *The Simpsons* first did.

Appropriately enough, Bill Hicks came to the attention of the British public by way of Canada. He was spotted by executives from the UK's Channel 4 at the Just for Laughs comedy festival in Montreal in the summer of 1991, where his dark, angry stand-up routine was one of the festival's most compelling acts. What was particularly astonishing about Hicks's act – and particularly exciting to a non-American audience – was his strident stance against the recent Gulf War. 'First of all, this needs to be said: There never was a war . . . a war is when two armies are fighting' – so began Hicks's antiwar rant, which portrayed the liberation of Kuwait as little more than a masturbatory exercise for techno-fetishists. This was incendiary stuff, particularly coming as it did in the midst of a bout of exceptionally boisterous God-bless-America jingoism and docile conformity. (As I recall, even David Letterman's Saddam-mocking Top Ten lists bore the disclaimer 'Approved by US Department of Defence Censors' or some such.) In short order, Hicks's Just for Laughs routine was a hit comedy special on Channel 4, and Hicks himself had relocated to England to launch two sold-out stand-up tours, write a regular column for *NME*, and begin work on a TV series. And then, as if dutifully playing out the expected ending for someone of his mercurial-underground-icon status, Hicks was gone – a victim of cancer at the age of 32.

The enormous discrepancy between the enthusiastic embrace of Hicks in Britain and his obscurity in the United States provides an explicit snapshot of the contrasting cultural attitudes in America and its close pop cousins. Not only did Hicks never hit the big time in the country of his birth, he never even became a cult hero. Aside from the unique honour of being the only stand-up comedian ever to have his routine entirely edited out of *Late Show with David Letterman*,[9] Hicks quickly faded back into obscurity in the United States after his death. In the UK, however, Hicks remains an alternative-culture martyr, meticulously dissected and rapturously eulogised in Britain's pop press as if he were the second coming of Elvis, thanked in the liner notes of Radiohead albums, namechecked by rave junkies in the film *Human Traffic*. And in February 2004, he even became the subject of a motion in British Parliament, when MP Stephen Pound rose to ask that the House of Commons take note of the tenth anniversary of Hicks's death, recall 'his assertion that his words would be a bullet in the heart of consumerism, capitalism and the American Dream', and mourn 'the passing of one of the few people who may be mentioned as being worthy of inclusion with Lenny Bruce in any list of unflinching and painfully honest political philosophers'. In this short statement, we find a succinct summation of what Britain – and much of the world – values in an American dissident. Small wonder, then, that the very same dissent-hungry 1990s audience that adopted Hicks as a hero in the UK also took a particular shine to *The Simpsons* – the most biting American satire the world had seen in years.

Here's one more thing worth noting about Bill Hicks: the anti-hero status he achieved in Britain was highly contingent on the fact that he was an American. The same holds true for *The Simpsons*, not just in Britain but worldwide. There's a cluster of semi-linked qualities that the American dissident is assumed to possess more or less innately: heightened authenticity, enhanced symbolic weight, the intimate first-hand knowledge only a defector can boast. The world craves critics of American hegemony, but to some extent it really trusts only *American* critics. There's a conflicted, paradoxical, pseudo-colonial dynamic at work here, and you can perhaps see it most clearly from the distant vantage point of Southeast Asia, through the lens of one of the most distinctive *Simpsons* websites in cyberspace: The Simpsons in Thailand.

There is a sharp paradox governing The Simpsons in Thailand (let's call it SiT for short) that captures the contradictions of the world's relationship with *The Simpsons* – and with America. For the most part, SiT is a typical fansite, dense with Thai broadcast information, notes on the vagaries of the show's Thai subtitles, and an exhaustive list of its sporadic references to Thailand.[10] It is, in short, a *fan's* site – a carefully assembled labour of love. At the same time, though, half of SiT's homepage is given over to chronicling the tragic tale of 'Melted Bart'.

Now, Melted Bart is an iconic piece of debris from a fire that devastated Kader Industrial, a toy factory in an export-processing zone on the outskirts of Bangkok, in May 1993. More than 180 Thai factory workers were killed and almost 500 more injured in the blaze, many of them young women. Labour activists, fighting in vain for compensation for the fire's victims, for an explanation of the fire's cause, and for changes in industrial working conditions in Thailand, chose Bart Simpson dolls – one of the cheap consumer items the factory was producing at the time of the fire – as a central symbol of the Kader disaster. Melted and distorted, disfigured but still instantly recognisable as the world's favourite ten-year-old American brat, Melted Bart is the first image you see at SiT. You can almost imagine that the sags and stretches in poor Melted Bart's face come from all the symbolic weight he's carrying. Think about it: here's a beloved cartoon character, a symbol of American rebellion and an iconic member of the cast of one of America's most self-critical TV shows; here's the cheap disposable produce of a Thai export-processing zone, a piece of consumer debris from a factory jointly owned by Thai and Hong Kong industrialists; here's a doll from a factory that churns out inexpensive toys for Europe and North America. Here's an image on the World Wide Web – the electronic commons of the global village – an image of an icon of the global consumer culture, a synthetic doll produced by Thai labour for absentee Chinese owners in an industrial centre set up for the expressed purpose of global trade.

Here is Melted Bart: globalisation's perfect poster child.

THE WORLD OF MELTED BART

In Episode 1F08 ('$pringfield (or, How I Learned to Stop Worrying and Love Legalized Gambling)'), Marge Simpson develops a nasty gambling addiction, leading her to neglect her home, her husband and even her children so she can keep feeding coins into the slot machines down at Mr Burns's Casino. When a tearful Lisa laments that her horrible costume for the geography pageant, half-assedly assembled by her father, has turned her into a monster, Homer quickly corrects her. 'The only monster here,' he announces, 'is the gambling monster that has enslaved your mother. I call him Gamblor, and it's time to snatch your mother from his neon claws!'

In the 1990s globalisation was a lot like Gamblor: a big multi-headed beast that stalked every corner of the world, ill-defined but undeniably disruptive, sometimes amorphous and ethereal, other times as tangible as the family TV set or the local airport, and frequently quite absurd. The overheated hype about the monster – both pro and con – could make it seem about as legitimate as a sales pitch extolling Duff's ability to fill your Q-Zone with pure beer goodness, about as coherent as a black-clad anarchist's rhetoric and about as lasting as a speculative bubble on Wall Street. But behind the neon-clawed calamity was an emerging, coalescing truth about the dramatically altered state of affairs in the global village. This new world order was hard to pin down – it was changing too quickly and encompassed too much – but it was undeniable. 'Globalisation' was a shorthand way of describing this world of instantaneous electronic communications that circled the globe in the blink of an eye and of cheap international airline tickets that could take you around the world almost as fast. It referred to fast-growing and rapidly accelerating international trade that paid even less attention to borders than globe-trotting tourists did, to production chains that snaked through a dozen far-flung nations, and to movies and music and irreverent cartoons that dominated the mediascape of dozens more. Globalisation was the reordering of global geopolitics ushered in by the fall of the Soviet Union and the global reach of American hegemony, by the re-emergence of China and the unprecedented unity of Europe. Globalisation was, as I mentioned, a melted Bart Simpson doll in the ruins of a toy factory in a Thai export-processing zone owned by Hong Kong investors with an eye on markets in Europe and America.

And globalisation is the explanation for The Simpsons in Thailand – not just the fact of the website's existence, but also its paradoxical efforts both to celebrate an American pop institution and document the abuses committed in its name. If the two things seem to be interconnected, that's because *any* two scraps of global culture might be. If it seems hypocritical to love Bart Simpson and loathe the system that delivers him to your TV set or your local store, well, such is the ubiquity of globalisation. Unless you're living in a shack in the Montana woods or a hut in the hills of northern Thailand, you're in it with both feet. You breathe, and the toxins of global industry's pollution invade your lungs. The tomatoes you eat are from California, the bananas are from Chile, the cooking oil's Italian and the pot you cook with was made in China. Your shirt was styled in Europe, sewn in Indonesia and branded in the USA. And all of it came in on a ship that's owned by a Norwegian company and registered in Liberia, and when there's nothing left of that ship but buckets of rust, it'll be salvaged for scrap on a beach in India by people who've never heard of globalisation.

There is a profound sense of dislocation that accompanies all of this movement and change, a sort of sociocultural equivalent of jet lag that is also global in scope. You can find it, most certainly, in the wide aisles of the gargantuan big-box stores of Western suburbia. MONSTROMART – WHERE SHOPPING IS A BAFFLING ORDEAL, reads the sign at Springfield's biggest big-box, where Marge prices a 12-pound carton of nutmeg. But the same dislocation is present in the farmer's fields of India, where local varieties of fruits and grains are being replaced with seeds engineered on the other side of the world to yield unprecedented amounts of produce only once and never reproduce themselves. It is in the stalls of the hawkers along Bangkok's Khao San Road, who have taken to selling ersatz African statuary as well as Thai handicrafts to the backpacker crowd; in the industrial towns of eastern Germany, where unemployed Aussies have found as much solace in nostalgia for the hard certainties of the collapsed dictatorship as in the chaotic realities of warp-speed capitalism; and in the streets of Seattle, Prague, Genoa, Quebec City, where a hundred different kinds of dislocation turned to rage.

Until globalised terror stole the spotlight, much energy was spent and much ink spilled trying to explain why thousands of people in the most prosperous societies the world had ever seen would attempt to derail the processes that kept the cash flowing and the shelves filled with 12-pound boxes of nutmeg. There were sober analyses of the policies and practices of the World Bank, the WTO, the IMF – as if these were the *actual* source of the dislocation and not just its agents, its symptoms, its most tangible symbol. There were sneering offhand dismissals of these enemies of progress, these petulant children afraid of change, these flat-earth Luddites and brainwashed Marxist revivalists. To my mind, though, the most empathetic and insightful thing written about the anti-globalisation movement was American journalist David Samuels's 'Notes from Underground', a report on the most radical of the protesters – the notorious Black Bloc anarchists of Eugene, Oregon – that appeared in *Harper's Magazine* a few months after they and dozens of other 'affinity groups' had shut down a meeting of the WTO in Seattle in November 1999. Here's Samuels on the stream of lurid images of rioting that filled the world's media in its aftermath:

What the pictures from Seattle captured was an anger whose true sources had less to do with Nike's treatment of its labour force or other objectionable practices than with a broader, more unreasoning sense of being trapped in a net. My favourite picture from Seattle showed a group of kids perched on top of the entrance to NikeTown, using hammers and chisels to pry off the brushed-steel letters that spelled 'Nike.' At least one of the kids was wearing a pair of Nike sneakers. The picture was powerful because it so accurately captured an emotion shared by many people in their twenties and thirties, raised on advertisements whose carefully screened and focus-grouped vocabularies and images have insinuated themselves into the weave of the generational unconscious almost since birth.

You can't help wanting Nike sneakers. At the same time, the desire to smash the windows of NikeTown makes sense, too. Not because Nike sneakers are bad, or because they are manufactured in Third World countries by slave-wage labour, but on the more general principle that someone should be held responsible for the feelings of absence and compulsion that overwhelm us all at some point or another in our lives and that are not our fault, or even the fault of our parents, but are rather the products of the addictive vacuum that that has manifested itself through the combined karmic energies of millions of cathode-ray tubes and digital cables.

The mass protests of 1999 and 2000 in Europe and North America, the portion of The Simpsons in Thailand website given over to a toy factory disaster, the ardent viewership of *The Simpsons*' sharp satire in more than 70 countries around the world – all of this stands in opposition to the same entity, this same shape-shifting beast we've named globalisation.

This opposition is not really anti-American, though there have been many post-9/11 attempts to characterise it as such. And this is because the target of this opposition – and of *The Simpsons*' satire – is not strictly American. America is its birthplace, its spiritual home and its leading proponent, but the locus of this power is not an American empire but a hegemonic order led by the United States that crosses many borders. It's an order that includes the Chinese owners of Thai toy factories, the Australian media baron who owns the Fox Network, the Spanish government that lent troops to America's invasion of Iraq against the will of the majority of the Spanish people. This is an opposition to global authority – whichever creed or nation it ostensibly represents – and it finds its most prominent pop-cultural voice in the stridently antiauthoritarian *Simpsons*.

In Episode AABF20 ('30 Minutes over Tokyo'), Homer Simpson and his kids head down to the Java Server, Springfield's new Internet café, to introduce themselves to globalisation. In no time, Homer's surfing the Internet like a pro: betting on jai alai matches in the Cayman Islands, buying shares in News Corp. and ultimately losing his family's entire savings to bad investments and outright thievery. The newly impoverished Simpsons attend a self-help seminar – the 'Chuck Garabedian Mega-Savings Seminar' – to learn how to make the most of their meagre income. A few short scenes later, we find the Simpsons at the Springfield International Airport. Following one of Garabedian's money-saving tips, they're waiting for a last-minute cancellation so they can jet off to some faraway land on the dirt-cheap. Garabedian says the key is not caring where you go, but the Simpsons clearly have their preferences: each of them is dressed in the national costume of the destination they're hoping for. Marge, dreaming of Hawaii, is decked out in a floral dress and a lei. Beret-wearing Lisa is pulling for France, while Bart is sporting vampire fangs in anticipation of a trip to Transylvania. And Homer, him been in Babylon too long, mon – he's got not just the dreads and Rasta cap but the *accent* of Jamaica, his preferred destination. In any event, none of them gets what they want – the next cancellation turns out to be a flight to Japan. Homer is initially reluctant, but the prospect of the Flanderses getting the flight changes his mind right quick. 'The Simpsons are goin' to Japan!' Lisa gleefully announces, and off they go to the other side of the world.[11]

As they sit in the departure lounge waiting for a cheap flight somewhere – *anywhere* – far away, the Simpsons are the very personification of the unparalleled freedoms that globalisation has created. By the 1990s there was almost nowhere left on the planet that was beyond the reach of your local airport (and/or your local Internet café). If everything was changing and much seemed to be getting lost in the flux, there were also spectacular new vistas on the globalised horizon. Not only could you communicate instantly with new friends on the other side of the world – on the Internet, as the early-nineties saying went, you could chat about *Star Trek* with someone from Japan – but you could also zoom there to meet them in person.

Travel was both the literal and metaphorical embodiment of globalisation and one of the strongest portents of the digital age's enormous promise. So it was only natural that all those dislocated twenty- and thirtysomethings would throw on their Nikes and hightail it to the departure gate. Hence the phenomenon of 'summit hopping': opponents of global trade turned their protests into a moveable feast of activism, skipping rapidly from G8 summits in Genoa to free-trade meetings in Quebec to international social-justice conferences in Brazil. The ease of mobility ushered in by globalisation became an essential tool in opposing it – which didn't mean that the protesters were hypocrites, but only that opponents of the IMF and the WTO and the rest were not for the most part trying to stop all progress dead in its tracks (as the smuggest of their critics have alleged). The protesters saw at least as much potential in international interconnectedness as the CEOs cutting billion-dollar deals did.

Travel has moved rapidly from the realm of luxury to something verging on a birthright for citizens of the globalised West. In 1939 about one million people partook of international travel. In 1997, 500 million crossed national borders for the purposes of holiday-making alone. Throw in the countless thousands travelling for business purposes, thousands more on work or study visas, and you have human mobility on a staggeringly unprecedented scale. Here's one striking pair of comparative stats among many: about a hundred thousand Christian soldiers embarked upon the First Crusade in the eleventh century, while the hard-partying Spanish island of Ibiza – birthplace and spiritual home of rave culture – hosted an estimated 1.5 million visitors during the summer of 2001 alone.

Here was the vanguard of a new global culture: a fast-growing army of backpackers and teachers of English as a second language, of business consultants and international-development workers and IT entrepreneurs, of ravers and techno-pagans and utopians. Wielding backpacks and/or laptops and/or glowsticks, they fanned out across the globe, building grand new trading posts like the export-processing zone that gave birth to Melted Bart, laying fibre-optic cable to bring *Simpsons* fansites to all the world's peoples, and founding or expanding colonies of leisure to feed the spiritual and recreational needs of the freethinking residents of the global village.

Like much about globalisation, though, the vanguard of global culture had its paradoxes. In particular, it was as a group both stridently internationalist and a semi-accidental agent of Western hegemony. Talk to a backpacker trekking in the shadow of Annapurna or a tech-company executive on the eightieth floor of the Petronas Twin Towers in Kuala Lumpur, and both would agree that borders of ethnicity and nation were growing deservedly irrelevant, that a single culture of Net-surfing, *Simpsons*-watching, world-travelling global villagers – a wonderful new social order that nurtured heretofore unimaginable levels of both interconnectedness and diversity – had just been born. At the same time, though, the people with the leisure time to spend a couple months hiking in Nepal or the capital to establish a regional R&D office in Malaysia were something less than a portrait of the United Nations in miniature. About 80 per cent of all the world's travel, for example, was being done by the citizens of only 20 countries. When the glossy jet-set magazine *Wallpaper** declared Iceland the hot new party destination, it was speaking exclusively to a Western audience. The rave-music subgenre of Goa Trance may have been born on the powder-soft beaches of India's west coast, but the DJs who invented it and the record labels that profited from it were almost exclusively European. If the World Bank and the IMF and the rest were dark, malevolent agents of Western domination, then to some extent the one-world evangelicals on the backpacker trail were pushing the same hegemony with a shiny, happy smiley face.

Travel to Melted Bart's birthplace – magnificent Thailand, whose well-earned reputation for hospitality is enshrined in a tourism slogan that dubs it 'The Land of Smiles' – and you can see all of this firsthand, for Thailand has seen practically every one of globalisation's paradoxical smiles in recent years. Back in the early 1990s Thailand was an 'Asian Tiger' – one of a handful of emerging nations whose turbo-driven economies were held up to the world as a sterling example of the benefits of liberalised, free-market-oriented globalisation. Fast-forward to 1997, and Thailand had become one of the most spectacular casualties of money-market speculation of all time, as nervous investors abandoned its currency (the baht), setting off an economic crisis that defanged all the Tigers and nearly plunged the whole of East Asia into a depression. Next up for the smiling Thais was a painful package of reforms from one of globalisation's most misguided minions, the IMF – which almost certainly delayed Thailand's recovery and provided one of a number of case studies of the deep flaws in the free-market orthodoxy of globalisation.

And through it all, the bright-eyed youths of the global village continued to arrive at Bangkok International in droves, bound for the country's blissful beaches in the south or the blissed-out opium dens along its trekking routes in the north. If there was a single travel destination that embodied the new global culture of the *Lonely Planet*-reading, diversity-embracing, rave-going traveller, it was Thailand. The Land of Smiles was grinning warmly at about seven million visitors per year by 2000, and more than a third of those were young people. Khao San Road – Bangkok's increasingly grotesque warren of guest houses, moneychangers, Internet cafés, travel agencies and souvenir stalls – is possibly the most teeming backpacker ghetto in the world (the Thamel district of Kathmandu gives it a run for its money), and it is most certainly the most renowned. Bangkok's Patpong Road, meanwhile, has been transformed from a seedy red-light district into something of a sex-tourism theme park. (There's a McDonald's at one end of it. No shit.)

It was certainly no accident that Alex Garland's novel *The Beach* – a dark satire of backpacker culture – was set in Thailand. And no random detail, either, that before heading off in search of a fabled paradise, its protagonist, Richard, delights in the delicious treat of banana pancakes at a grimy café on Khao San Road. There is indeed a kind of perfection in that detail, for banana pancakes are a powerful symbol of the global culture of backpacker travel. Though extremely rare in – if not completely foreign to – the cuisines of the backpackers' various countries of origin, banana pancakes are possibly the single most ubiquitous menu item in Westerner-oriented restaurants across Asia. They are, then, a perfect distillation of the produce of globalisation's disjointed interactions: a thing created by one culture to try to conform to the tastes of the other that results in some hybrid that's got very little to do with either of them. And it's a safe bet that the finest banana pancakes in all the world are served up on Khao San Road – a place that has more to say about the mixed blessings of globalisation than a thousand World Bank conferences.

The Beach's Richard, like many of the millions who pass through Khao San, is soon headed south, obsessed with finding a mythic island paradise that he's learned about through the deranged ramblings of his neighbour at a Khao San guest house. In due course, he finds his paradise: a backpacker's dream of an island with a flawless beach, verdant green fields of marijuana and a photogenic, multi-ethnic tribe of romantics and idealists right out of a Benetton ad. And – oh yes – not a Thai in sight.

Richard's quest takes him through Ko Pha-Ngan, a gorgeous island in southern Thailand that is a real-world, mass-market analogue to the exclusive little colony he eventually finds. For more than ten years, thousands of backpackers have descended on Ko Pha-Ngan for its now-legendary Full Moon Party – a huge monthly rave held outdoors on the island's pristine beach. At the peak of the tourist season, Ko Pha-Ngan's Full Moon Parties have been known to attract as many as 50,000 revellers. And though there are a few Thais in sight at these parties, most of them are working – transporting, hawking, dealing, cleaning up. One or two Thais might spin some tunes alongside the imported star DJs. For the most part, though, the Full Moon Party is a special kind of celebration: a grand ball in honour of globalised culture's inclusive ideals with attendance by *very* exclusive invite only. The price of admission: wealth, leisure time, a passport from one of the handful of nations who have so far been invited to participate in globalisation without restrictions.

All this notwithstanding, the Full Moon Party remains an *idealistic* ball. A quest, in fact: for unity, escape, transcendence. A brief hallucinatory vision of a kind of utopia: flawed, conflicted, temporary, hedonistic, ultimately doomed. A desperate utopia.

DESPERATE UTOPIAS

In Episode 3F23 ('You Only Move Twice'), executives from a high-tech firm called Globex Corporation approach Homer Simpson about taking a cushy management position with their firm. In an effort to seal the deal, the executives provide him with a promotional video entitled *Cypress Creek: A Tale of One City*. The video provides a guided tour of the model company town Globex has constructed for its employees. It opens on a scene of abject urban squalor: a filthy city street lined with boarded-up buildings, the towers of a nuclear plant belching black smoke into the air in the distance. Pan out to reveal a clean-cut yuppie couple taking in the scene with evident disgust. 'Look at this place,' says the woman. 'Somebody oughta build a town that works,' the man adds. Just then, a voice-over intervenes. 'Somebody did,' it says firmly. In a series of dissolves, the decrepit cityscape is magically transformed: a dilapidated five-and-dime store becomes a gleaming coffee bar, an abandoned hardware store turns into a coffee house, an overflowing dumpster transforms into a coffee cart, and a dishevelled panhandler becomes a mailbox. 'It's called Cypress Creek,' the voice-over explains. 'A planned community for the workers of the Globex Corporation.' Pause. 'Cypress Creek: Where dreams come true.' A second voice-over voice hastily adds, 'Your dreams may vary from those of Globex Corporation, its subsidiaries and shareholders.'[12] But the Simpsons take no heed of this warning, and in short order they've settled into a big new house and a cushy new life in Cypress Creek. The dream quickly sours, however, and within a few days the Simpsons flee the model town for the familiar imperfections of Springfield.

In 3F23, then, the Simpsons come face to face with an entire town built in the service of an ideal, and they find that this utopian dream can hold back the tide of reality for only a few days.

Here's a factoid: for three days in August 1998, Lemonwheel – the concert/festival/universe that marked the end of the summer tour of the jam-rock band Phish – was the second-largest city in the state of Maine.

Now, the name Thomas More gave to his ideal society – Utopia – was an intentional pun. It meant both 'good place' and 'no place'. Though the term utopia has long since lost its ambiguity, Lemonwheel – and a great many other festivals and events and parties in the past decade – seemed implicitly to understand (and embody) the double meaning.

Lemonwheel was an extraordinary event, a mass gathering of about 65,000 people from wildly diverse subcultural tribes (among them aging hippies, neo-hippies, bikers, computer geeks, skate punks, frat boys, rave kids and at least one Jewish klezmer band) on an abandoned air force base a full day's drive from any major urban centre. Besides the ostensible main attraction of the event – the music of Phish, delivered in seven sets over two days – the festival included dozens of enormous art installations, a Zen rock garden and a vast temporary city of tents and vans and Winnebagos that sprawled between the base's two runways. When Phish wasn't on stage, the tent city became Lemonwheel's focal point, playing host to countless impromptu raves and mini-concerts, drum circles and keg parties, skateboard parks and street-theatre exhibitions, as well as a commercial district of temporary food and merchandise stalls that ran the length of both runways. It was a self-contained world, with its own values and rules, its own customs and language (including a staggering array of slang terms for marijuana, from usual suspects like 'weed' to more esoteric coinages such as 'dank nugs' and 'kind buds'). Unmarked black helicopters (almost certainly from the United States' ever-vigilant Drug Enforcement Agency) circled the site throughout the daylight hours, but Lemonwheel was otherwise entirely self-governing. It was a utopia. It was a good place, and it was also no place: the band, its fans and the state troopers at the gate all understood that it would be gone after three days, that it would be dismantled, that everyone involved would return to whatever world they actually lived in.

I describe Lemonwheel in some detail because it was the grandest one of these utopian experiments I personally attended, but the same structural and temporal limitations governed nearly all of the most exciting cultural events of the 1990s. The Burning Man festival occurred but once a year, for a specified time period, in a distant patch of the Nevada desert, and its core rule was that it leave no trace of itself behind. Berlin's Love Parade was also a once-a-year extravaganza. Rave scenes, which sprung up in nearly every urban centre in the Western world at some point in the last decade, were limited almost exclusively to weekend parties in constantly changing locations. Online communities rarely even attempted to leave the no-place of cyberspace. The decade's most important political movement – anti-globalisation – was unable to sustain itself outside the parameters of concise events organised by its opponents (not to mention its chronic difficulty in maintaining any kind of consensus for the duration of those brief summits).

Nonetheless, all these events provided potent doses (even overdoses) of essential human needs – political involvement, spiritual fulfilment, social freedom, the transcendent joy of communal unity – that couldn't be found in adequate measure in day-to-day society.

These were desperate utopias.

They were ideal societies in microcosm, parallel micro-universes, and by most reports any given one of them could feel at certain exquisite moments – as the shamanistic dancing hit its peak, as the great idol was set alight, as word reached the barricaded streets that the leaders of the free world had called off their meeting – like the first eruption of a force that would reshape the entire world.

I remember a moment at Lemonwheel during one of the evening sets, just after full dark. The band began to play an expansive and joyous tune, and a few fans near the stage tossed glowsticks into the air. The few became a handful, and then dozens and then hundreds, and soon the sky in front of the stage was filled with a glittering cascade of phosphorescent green that rose and fell and shimmered and danced in time to the music. Though I later heard that this had happened before at Phish concerts, I felt I was witnessing a moment of spontaneous communal *art* drawn in looping glowstick trails against the New England sky. You felt it first somewhere below your stomach, a sense of joyous uplift that rose and rose all the way through you until you were floating, humming, throbbing in perfect harmony with the crowd. In that moment, I had no doubt that the music and the dancing light and the sheer yearning energy of the crowd could conquer the world and make it new. Such was the power of a visit to a desperate utopia.

The enlightened tried on occasion to make such a moment last. The Full Moon Parties in southern Thailand were an attempt at this; the globe-trotting rave circuit, which skipped from London to Ibiza to Goa to Ko Pha-Ngan and back around again, was a more ambitious project. So, in its way, was the summit-hopping circuit of 1999 and 2000. People from (seemingly) every corner of the globe, with the (apparent) freedom to go anywhere the vibe was right or the cause righteous, imagined that the swirling maelstrom kicked up by their frenetic travels might transform the world as easily as collapsing five-and-dimes became Cypress Creek coffee bars.

Yet the party would inevitably end. Too many people would show up for the group's uniquely transcendent cohesion to be maintained, or the realities of career and family and adult life would begin to pull too strongly in the direction of home, or the authorities would decide to crack down on drug use on the beach or freedom of speech in the streets. There might be a devolution into something verging on pure hedonism: too many drugs, a nihilistic orgy of mud-flinging, the trashing of a NikeTown. And then everyone would return to the real world, re-emerge into the daylight, go home. And realise that a party couldn't change the world on its own. Not *this* one, anyway.

At Lemonwheel, it was the porta-potties that burst my utopian bubble. Driving through the wreckage of the tent city that final day – piles of garbage, half-collapsed tents, sprawled spent bodies in sleeping bags – I passed a row of porta-potties that had all been filled to overflowing. The ground around the toilet stalls was a soup of mud, shit and toilet paper. This wouldn't be a functional utopia until someone figured out what to do with the waste.

Still, Lemonwheel had several lessons to teach about the shape the global culture might take if the ravers and activists were given a voice alongside the WTO and the Fox Network. Lemonwheel wasn't anti-capitalist: there was entrepreneurial commerce all up and down the runways – T-shirt stalls, burrito vendors, dealers on skateboards holding illicit wares beneath their chins as they rolled by. The longest line I encountered all weekend was at the parallel universe's only direct link to the other world – a cash machine. The *either/or* construct of the debate (pro- or anti-globalisation, say) was a false dichotomy. The folks at Lemonwheel, at raves, even in the streets of Seattle as they filled with tear gas, were making an argument for *and also*. The prosperous, global-trading society we've built, *and also* the inclusiveness and spiritual uplift of the party. Economic opportunity for as many of the world's people as possible, *and also* guarantees of workers' rights and environmental protections. Art *and* commerce. Wealth *and* beauty. A new utopian ideal to strive for, even if it couldn't be reached. A recognition of What Is *and* What Should Be.

Here's one more enduring image from Lemonwheel, this one from the vantage point of the media platform in the middle of a sea of Phish fans as the band launched into the first song of the first set on the first day. There was a roar from the crowd, a sudden burst of movement, the explosive release and undulating energy of 65,000 people set in motion all at once. As the crowd shimmied and swayed, the sun glinted off an object in the distance, an idol held aloft about halfway between the platform and the stage. A golden bust, staring out over the sea of revellers – *worshippers?* – with wide eyes. Homer Simpson. Yes. The godhead of this global village was Homer Simpson.

Who was I to argue?

NOTES & MARGINALIA

1. **McPax Americana:** 'The Golden Arches Theory of Conflict Prevention' is the invention of *New York Times* columnist Thomas L. Friedman. In December 1996 Friedman asserted that 'no two countries that both have a McDonald's have ever fought a war against each other'. Friedman later expanded the assertion into the 'Golden Arches Theory' in his 2000 book *The Lexus and the Olive Tree*. Friedman's theory is not an unqualified truth but rather somewhat dependent on how you define 'war'. Case in point: South Asia. In 1996 India became a McDonald's country, and Pakistan got its first Golden Arches in 1998. In the spring of 1999 the Pakistani army took up positions in the Himalayan mountain passes high above the town of Kargil, on the Indian side of the ceasefire line in Kashmir. There followed a short, bloody fight for control of the Kargil heights, with Pakistan eventually retreating. In South Asia, this battle is usually referred to as 'the Kargil Conflict' or 'the Kargil War', and it was certainly a war in spirit.

2. **In your face, Medicine Hat!** In the opening scene of Episode AABF07 ('Wild Barts Can't Be Broken'), the Simpson family attends a Springfield Isotopes baseball game. Even before the game begins, Homer starts deriding the 'stupid Isotopes' for breaking his heart in a previous season. 'But you've got to support the team, Dad,' Bart protests. 'They're already threatening to move to Moose Jaw!' Hearing that name spoken in Bart's voice, I discovered a civic pride I never knew I had for the place where I was born: Moose Jaw, Saskatchewan, a quiet prairie town of 35,000 that's probably best known for its oddly evocative name. (I suspect the inherent comedic value of the name was indeed the reason it was chosen by the show's writers for this random reference.) Though my family moved from Moose Jaw when I was only three years old, I couldn't help but feel somehow validated by the town's surprise appearance on the Simpsonian map. Such is the unique allure of having your own life referenced on *The Simpsons*.

3. **Fun with urban legends:** Bart makes his collect call to Australia to test Lisa's assertion that something called 'the Coriolis effect' causes toilets to drain counter-clockwise in the northern hemisphere and clockwise in the southern hemisphere. Bart makes several failed attempts to call other southern hemisphere locales – the toilet is frozen in Antarctica, the president of some South American banana republic mistakes Bart's question for a coded message that the rebels will soon be taking the capital, Adolf Hitler can't get to his car phone in time. Finally, he calls Australia, where he gets a straight answer: the toilets there, a boy named Tobias confirms, drain clockwise. This might be true, but it's got nothing to do with the Coriolis effect – more accurately known as the Coriolis force.

For once, Lisa Simpson doesn't know what she's talking about. The Coriolis force is a legitimate phenomenon caused by the rotation of the earth, but it has no discernible effect on toilet drainage. The Coriolis force works mainly on large-scale phenomena such as air masses, which will twist counter-clockwise in the northern hemisphere and clockwise in the south, owing to the fact that their speed relative to the earth increases as they move away from the equator. A widely disseminated urban legend has it that this influences the direction in which water spins when you flush a toilet, but it's each individual toilet – its fixtures, its position, its levelness, etc. – that determines the direction of water drainage.

This is but one of many times that *The Simpsons* has trafficked in urban legends. In Episode 2F06 ('Homer Badman'), for example, Homer eludes a mob by shaking up a can of Buzz Cola, pouring in some Pop Rox candy, and then tossing the can grenade-style at his pursuers, at which point it explodes action-movie-style. This is an allusion to another famous urban legend – also false – that alleges that the kid who played Mikey in the Life cereal commercials was killed by a lethal mix of soda and Pop Rocks candy, which had caused his stomach to explode. Elsewhere in *The Simpsons*' run, references have been made to alligators living in the sewers, from yet another false urban legend claiming that a thriving colony of alligators resides in New York City's sewer system.

4. **The real Bumblebee Man unmasked:** Absurd as he is, Springfield's Bumblebee Man – the mostly anonymous star of a string of slapstick comedies on Channel Ocho – is not a purely Simpsonian creation. He's actually a close cousin of 'El Chapul'n Colorado' ('The Red Cricket'), a bumbling anti-superhero decked out in red-and-yellow tights and bobbing antennae who was created by the legendary comedian Roberto Gómez Bolaños for Mexican TV. Bolaños also starred as a goofy homeless child who lived in a barrel in the TV series *El Chavo del Ocho* ('The Kid from Eight'), which is likely the provenance of the Simpsonian Channel Ocho. (Channel Ocho's call letters, KMEX, have also appeared on *The Simpsons* on a couple of occasions.) Though the Bumblebee Man's bowling shirt reads 'Pedro' in Episode 3F10 ('Team Homer'), many *Simpsons* fans refer to him as 'Chesperito', Bolaños's stage name. *Muchas gracias, amigos, por todas las memorias. Y super-gracias a Goya!*

5. **Best. Rant. Ever.** In Episode 1F18 ('Sweet Seymour Skinner's Baadasssss Song'), Apu shows us something else that sounds funny in an Indian accent: a frothing-at-the-mouth rant. Its target is Principal Skinner, who has recently lost his job. When Bart and Milhouse bump into him in line at the Kwik-E-Mart, he explains that he's embarked on a new career: 'I finally have time to do what I've always wanted: write the great American novel. Mine is about a futuristic amusement park where dinosaurs are brought to life through advanced cloning techniques. I call it *Billy and the Cloneasaurus.*' Apu, instantly more indignant than we've ever seen him, launches into a tirade: 'Oh, you have *got* to be kidding, sir. First you think of an idea that has already been done. Then you give it a title that nobody could possibly like. Didn't you think this through . . .' As time passes in a series of quick cuts, Apu enumerates myriad other problems with Skinner's idea. By the end of the rant, Apu is apoplectic with indignation. He barks out a final dismissal – 'What were you thinking?!?' – and then quickly composes himself. 'I mean, thank you, come again,' he concludes cheerfully.

6. ***The Simpsons*' cutting-room floor:** The Hindi film Apu shows *The Simpsons* – it made every Indian critic's Top 400 list, but for Homer it's mostly about the funny clothes – is only one of more than half a dozen outtakes cut from previous episodes that appear in Episode 3F31 ('*The Simpsons* 138th Episode Spectacular'). Two more gems from the cutting-room floor:

• Footage of the monstrous robotic Richard Simmons that Monty Burns releases to chase Homer from his front porch in Episode 1F16 ('Burns' Heir'). After Homer flees, the robot runs amok, maniacally shake-shake-shaking its aerobicising ass. Even a blast from Smithers's shotgun can't stop it – it merely reconstitutes itself like the robot in *Terminator 2*. Eventually, its ass explodes, and the horror is finally over.

• Footage of Homer as a colossally incompetent blackjack dealer at Burns's Casino, cut from Episode 1F08 ('$pringfield (or, How I Learned to Stop Worrying and Love Legalized Gambling)'). In the outtake, Homer deals cards to James Bond. 'Joker?' says Bond in a thick Scottish burr. 'You're supposed to take those out of the deck.' Homer deals him another card. 'What's this card? 'Rules for Draw and Stud Poker'?' This mix-up allows the diabolical Blofeld to get the drop on Bond, who is summarily dragged from the casino by the villain's henchmen.

7. **The ugly Frenchman:** Episode 7G13 marks the first and most extensive bout of French-bashing in *Simpsons* history, as Bart travels to France on a student exchange only to be put to work as a slave labourer in the vineyard of two boorish French chauvinists. Although these two vintners are perfect embodiments of the stereotypical Frenchman so loathed in the United States, their lineage betrays a remarkable knowledge of French pop culture on the part of *The Simpsons*' creative team. To wit: these two Frenchmen – César and Ugolin – are drawn from *Manon des Sources*, a 1952 film written and directed by Marcel Pagnol, a pioneer of French cinema. (Pagnol later turned his screenplay into a novel, which was subsequently turned into a much more famous film in 1986.) Part of the cast of *Manon des Sources* are César and Ugolin, two ill-mannered, narrow-minded French peasants who are typical of the bigoted rural Frenchmen of yesteryear.

In a later *Simpsons* episode–8F12 ('Lisa the Greek') – César and Ugolin reappear in a brief vignette in which they're shown watching the Super Bowl. '*Stupide!*' one of them exclaims, and they change the channel to a Jerry Lewis film. '*Formidable!*' the other declares, in keeping with a popular American factoid involving France's love affair with Jerry Lewis that's frequently used to illustrate the inexplicable tastes of the French.

8. **South America, oddball nations in:** The apparently abysmal quality of health care in Paraguay comes in for passing insult on *The Simpsons* on one other occasion, in Episode 9F02 ('Lisa the Beauty Queen'). When Lisa enters the 'Little Miss Springfield' pageant, the favourite to win the event is Amber Dempsey. Adorable Amber's most endearing feature is a set of improbably long and lush eyelashes – her 'big guns', as one contestant calls them. When she first flashes her lashes, a fellow contestant dryly remarks, 'Eyelash implants.' Lisa, awestruck, announces, 'I thought those were illegal.' Her fellow contestant replies, 'Not in Paraguay.'

Paraguay's cognate cousin, Uruguay, receives some equal time in Episode 2F13 ('Bart vs. Australia'), as Homer inspects the Simpson family globe to discover, to his amazement, that there is in fact a nation called 'Australia'. Homer gives the globe a playful spin, then starts to chuckle. 'Look at this country!' he giggles, pointing at Uruguay. 'U-R-gay.' More laughter. To the enormous pride, no doubt, of millions of *Simpsons* fans in Montevideo.

9. **Stupid censor tricks:** On 1 October 1993, Bill Hicks taped a short stand-up routine for CBS's *Late Show with David Letterman*. Counting his appearances on Letterman's previous NBC show, it was to be Hicks's twelfth guest spot. But CBS's department of standards and practices balked at so much of Hicks's routine that the show's producers were forced to pull the entire appearance from the broadcast. According to Hicks, the notes he was given by CBS indicated that the network was unable to tolerate jokes in his routine involving children's books about lesbian mothers, the hypocrisy of 'pro-lifers', the strangeness of the Easter Bunny myth and the possibility that crosses might not be the first thing Jesus wants to see when he arrives for the Second Coming.

10. **Siamese *Simpsons*:** Over the years, *The Simpsons* has made a half-dozen or so references to Thailand, beginning with Mr Burns's attempt to send a letter to the Prussian consulate in Siam by autogyro in Season 7. Two of the most prominent subsequent Thai references illustrate the twin poles of Simpsonian internationalism. There's a brief glimpse of the ugly Springfieldianite in Episode BABF08 ('The Mansion Family'), in which Homer has some fun making long-distance phone calls while house-sitting Mr Burns's mansion. One such call is placed to Thailand. 'Hello? Thailand? How's everything on your end? . . . Uh huh. That's some language you've got there.' Homer starts to chuckle. 'And you talk like that 24/7, huh?' End transmission.

In Episode CABF01 ('Lisa the Tree Hugger'), we get a more nuanced view of Thai culture when a Thai character is introduced to Springfield: the nameless owner of a new restaurant called You Thai Now. Though the restaurant owner talks in a cartoonishly clipped 'Oriental' accent – 'You need job? I have job for you,' he tells Bart – he's also clearly an honourable and hard-working entrepreneur who dreams of sending his daughters to 'small liberal-arts college'. Apu began with considerably less.

11. **Big in Japan:** *The Simpsons*' trip to Japan in Episode AABF20 has as much to say about Japanese stereotypes of America as it does about America's impressions of Japan. Shortly after arrival in Tokyo, the Simpsons head to Americatown, a restaurant recommended by their hotel's high-tech toilet that specialises in ersatz American food. 'I'd like to see the Japanese take on the club sandwich,' Marge enthuses. 'I bet it's smaller and more efficient.' At Americatown, each table is shaped like an American state, and the waiter is a fine specimen of multileveled Simpsonian satire: speaking in an American stereotype of Japanese English, he spews anti-American epithets that are a mix of Japanese prejudices and American stereotypes of Japanese prejudices. 'Howdy, gangstas!' he greets the Simpsons. 'I'm average American Joe Salaryman waiter.' Lisa has a question: 'Don't you serve anything that's even remotely Japanese?' The waiter's reply: 'Don't ask me. I don't know anything! I'm product of American education system. I also build poor-quality cars and inferior-style electronics.'

Japan also serves as the departure point for some of the finest, funniest foreign-culture riffs in *The Simpsons*' run: the Mr Sparkle subplot in Episode 4F18 ('In Marge We Trust'). It all starts when Homer and the kids find a box of Japanese dish detergent on a visit to the town dump. The brand name is 'Mr Sparkle', and the brand logo appears to be a likeness of

Homer's head. Homer takes the box to Akira, the waiter down at the Happy Sumo sushi restaurant, where he learns that Mr Sparkle identifies himself as a magnet for foodstuffs and boasts that he will banish dirt to the land of wind and ghosts – but nothing about why Mr Sparkle looks like him. So Homer calls the detergent company in Japan, where the factory's only English-speaking employee talks a mile a minute in Japanese-flavoured English (he answers the phone, 'Hello, chief, let's talk, why not?') and eventually agrees to send Homer something that will 'answer question, hundred per cent!' A few weeks later, a videotape arrives at the Simpson home: a promotional video for Mr Sparkle. Lisa pops the tape in the VCR, and what appears on the Simpsons' TV screen is a broad parody of frenetic Japanese TV commercials that ranks among the funniest sequences of non sequitur visual gags in the show's history and can't possibly be adequately described in words. The disembodied head of Mr Sparkle soars from scene to scene, issuing pronouncements in Japanese; the subtitle of one of these reads, 'I am disrespectful to dirt. Can you see that I am serious?' At one point, Mr Sparkle zooms past a two-headed cow being interviewed by a Japanese journalist regarding its plans for the summer vacation. It goes on like this, and we eventually learn that the Mr Sparkle logo is a combination of the fish logo of the Matsumura Fishworks and the light-bulb logo of the Tamaribuchi Heavy Manufacturing Concern that just happens to look exactly like Homer's head. 'There's your answer, fishbulb,' Bart announces. And so ends the riff.

12. Around the corner from Coffee Boulevard: Though Cypress Creek's promotional video promises an endless abundance of coffee shops, the town's most absurd feature might be its Hammock District, which we learn about when Homer asks his boss, Hank Scorpio, where he should go to find business hammocks for his overworked underlings. A short discussion ensues:

Scorpio:	Hammocks? My goodness, what an idea. Why didn't I think of that? Hammocks! Homer, there's four places. There's the Hammock Hut – that's on Third.
Homer:	Uh-huh.
Scorpio:	There's Hammocks-R-Us–that's on Third too. You got Put Your Butt There.
Homer:	Mm-Hmm.
Scorpio:	That's on Third. Swing Low, Sweet Chariot . . . Matter of fact, they're all in the same complex. It's the Hammock Complex on Third.
Homer:	Oh, the Hammock District.
Scorpio:	That's right.

Scorpio pauses for a moment to threaten the free world with destruction, then points out that there's also Mary Ann's Hammocks, and the great thing about that place may or may not be that Mary Ann gets in the hammock with you. Cypress Creek is, at any rate, well equipped to handle all your business-hammock needs.

CHAPTER NINE

The Simpsons Go Hollywood

The way to become famous fast is to throw a brick at someone who is famous.

Walter Winchell

I believe that famous people have a debt to everyone. If
celebrities didn't want people pawing through their garbage
and saying they're gay, they shouldn't have tried to express
themselves creatively.

*Homer Simpson, Episode 5F19 ('When You Dish upon a
Star')*

THE PRIME MINISTER AND THE EROTIC CAKE

IMAGINE THE SCENE AT 10 Downing Street, London. It was 11 April 2003, two days after the fall of Baghdad. The media was filled with stories of the ongoing war, of gun battles in Kirkuk and Tikrit, of an anxious Britain torn in two over the presence of its soldiers on Iraqi soil. Prime Minister Tony Blair's own government was no less divided. Blair had lost a cabinet minister over his decision to go to war. Even as statues of Saddam Hussein were toppling into the Baghdad streets, there was talk in Britain of pyrrhic victories and encroaching quagmires. Rumours and allegations and angry words were raining in on Downing Street from all sides. Yet in the midst of this maelstrom, Blair made time to welcome a VIP from Britain's closest ally, the United States. In April 2003, in the middle of a war, Tony Blair spoke with Homer Simpson and his family.

In another, more accurate way, Tony Blair took the time on that tense April day to record a guest appearance for a Season 15 episode of *The Simpsons*. In the episode, the Simpson family travels to England to find Grampa's wartime girlfriend, and Blair is there at Heathrow Airport to greet them as they come out of the gate:

Blair:	Hello. Welcome to the United Kingdom.
Lisa:	Prime Minister Tony Blair!
Bart:	Why are you greeting lowlifes like us at the airport?
Blair:	Because I want to encourage all the world to come see the beauty of twenty-first-century Britain.
Homer:	[*decked out in tropical shirt and shorts*] Would an *American dollar* encourage you to leave us alone?
Blair:	[*snatches dollar and pockets it*] No. But thank you.
Marge:	Tony – I mean, Mr Prime Minister – what should we see first?
Blair:	There's so much to see here. Parliament, Stratford-on-Avon, the White Cliffs of Dover. Oh, and you Americans love castles – there's a huge one in Edinburgh, the city where I was born.
Homer:	The place I was born is now a gator farm.
Blair:	Smashing.
Lisa:	Maybe you could give us a personal tour of your country.
Blair:	I'd love to, but I'm late for an appointment. I'm greeting a lovely Dutch couple at Gate 23. [*straps on jet pack and flies off, calling:*] Cheerio!
Homer:	Wow! I can't believe we met Mr Bean!

With this short meeting, Tony Blair became the first head of state to appear as himself on *The Simpsons*, beating out an illustrious list of world leaders – Bill Clinton, George H.W. Bush, Mikhail Gorbachev, Fidel Castro, Richard Nixon and John F. Kennedy among them – who have visited Springfield only in caricature, their voices provided by *Simpsons* cast members. Many had been asked to do their own voices, including George W. Bush (who flatly declined the offer) and his 2000 election opponent, former vice-president Al Gore. Gore turned down a guest spot on *The Simpsons* when he was merely Clinton's VP, but he reconsidered during the 2000 election campaign. His aides approached the show's producers of their own volition to plead for a guest spot – presumably to inject their candidate with a much-needed jolt of self-deprecating cool. 'As far as I was concerned,' *Simpsons* producer Mike Scully later told London's *Times*, 'he'd had his chance.' Gore was turned down.

Tony Blair, though, knew better than to pass up such a golden opportunity. A self-professed '*Simpsons* addict' who watches the show regularly with his kids, Blair was well aware that his guest spot on *The Simpsons* meant, as *The Economist* noted, that he was being inducted into 'the grandest of American halls of fame'. Blair offered a similar (if more personal) explanation to *Simpsons* producer Al Jean on the question of why he agreed to become a cartoon character. 'I just want to do one thing that will impress my kids,' said Blair. This, for a real-world celebrity, is the promise contained in a visit to Springfield: *The Simpsons* confers status and authenticity upon its guests, and sends a clear message to the show's predominantly youthful fans that these guests are their kinda guys. Even for a leader of the free world, it's an unparalleled opportunity to impress the kids.

Homer Simpson – perhaps more resigned than Blair to the notion that he'll never really impress his kids – has deigned only once to submit to the equivalent torture of a visit to our world, in 'Homer',[3] the third chapter of the show's Season 7 Halloween special (Episode 3F04, 'Treehouse of Horror VI'). Trying to find a hiding place to ride out a visit from his hated sisters-in-law, Homer stumbles upon a dimensional portal behind the living-room bookcase, steps through it and finds himself in an interzone of green grids, bouncing geometric shapes and flying equations in which he's been transformed into lumpy 3-D.

For the show, if not for Homer, this step into 3-D animation was an event as unique and significant as Tony Blair's appearance. The animation of the segment, which the pioneering computer graphics (CG) animation firm Pacific Data Images took three and a half months to produce, was the first ever use of CG in primetime. It also marked the only segment in the show's history produced by CG and the only time *Simpsons* characters ever appeared as fully rounded three-dimensional beings. In short, a lot went into bringing Homer to our earth.

As far as Homer's concerned, though, those CG eggheads can cram it with walnuts. The shock of his protruding stomach and ass as he gets his first look at his 3-D self is bad enough, but then a bouncing cone goes and lodges itself in his newly bulgy butt. Homer extracts it and tosses it away, and when it hits the gridded surface of the dimension, it begins to carve out a fast-deepening chasm. Bart is sent into the dimension to save Homer, but the grid collapses too quickly. (Bart, back in the Simpsons living room, explains: 'We hit a little snag when the universe sort of collapsed on itself. But Dad seemed cautiously optimistic.') Cut to a back alley – a real, live American back alley – into which 3-D Homer, screaming, plummets from the sky, landing with a crash in a dumpster. He climbs out, takes his first glimpse of our planet and passes judgement: 'Ewww . . . this is the worst place yet.' He walks out onto a dingy city street – Ventura Boulevard in Los Angeles. As startled Angelenos scoot out of his path and shoot him odd looks, Homer walks on down the street, taking tiny, uneasy steps and whimpering with each one. He recoils with each new horror he encounters, his arms curling up against his chest protectively. He's terrified. He wants out. He spots an inviting store, reads the sign: 'Ooh, erotic cakes!' In he goes, escaping from the unspeakable horror of an L.A. street. And so ends his adventure in real-life America.

He never makes it to Hollywood.

The symbolism here is almost certainly unintentional. Still, even though Homer's in the L.A. area, he makes no effort to reach the celebrity factory. From then on – as before – the rich and famous can come to *The Simpsons*, or they too can cram it with walnuts. As with Homer, so with the show: *The Simpsons* does not court celebrity. If celebrities want to, they can make their way onto *The Simpsons*. And when they get there, they will abide by the show's physics, its rules, its logic. The show is bigger than any single one of them, whether they be British prime ministers or A-list movie stars or world-renowned scientists. This is the bedrock of *The Simpsons*' relationship with celebrity and of its critique of same. And this is the lesson of this little two-part fable about Tony Blair's wartime summit with Homer and Homer's brief foray into the universe Blair inhabits: Tony can take a break from the war to entertain the Simpson family, but *The Simpsons* as a show will not abandon its own agenda to honour Tony's real-world status. Or anyone else's.

THE VIEW FROM PLANET HOLLYWOOD

It's not that *The Simpsons* dismisses celebrity out of hand. Quite the contrary: celebrities have been a part of *The Simpsons* universe from the earliest episodes. They appear sometimes as themselves, sometimes as characters unique to Springfield. And there are also a handful of celebrities born and bred in the show's world, homegrown entertainers with massive followings and even bigger egos. Celebrities are often central to the plots of the episodes in which they appear, and it's very possible that the other characters on the show will treat them with the quasi-religious hero worship typical of the cult of celebrity in contemporary Western society. What's more – as Blair's appearance attests – becoming a guest star on *The Simpsons* has in recent years supplanted the guest-hosting gig on *Saturday Night Live* as the coolest TV appearance available to the modern celebrity.

The difference, however, is in how the show treats these celebrities. The people of Springfield may or may not bow in reverent deference to a given celebrity, but said celebrity will at any rate be used as the show, not the celebrity's publicist, sees fit. Celebrities have been required, for as long as the show has existed, to surrender control of their appearance – what they say, how they're animated, how they're portrayed – to the show's producers. If they appear as themselves, they'll almost certainly be mocked mercilessly, and if they appear as someone else, it'll be a supporting role – the Simpsons themselves are always the stars. A Beatle-sized legend like Paul McCartney might have only a few lines in the third act, while a character actor like James Woods becomes central to the plot of the episode he appears in. Fringe-dwelling art-rock band Sonic Youth spends considerable time on tour with Homer in their *Simpsons* appearance, while intergalactic pop stars U2 serve primarily as background detail in a couple of scenes. Second-tier *Saturday Night Live* alumnae (Phil Hartman and Jon Lovitz) and B-list movie actors (particularly Albert Brooks and Joe Mantegna) have created beloved characters; meanwhile, the characters contributed by some of the most celebrated Hollywood stars of our time (including Meryl Streep, Dustin Hoffman, Kirk Douglas and Elizabeth Taylor, to name only a handful of the most prominent) have been comparatively forgettable. On *The Simpsons*, in other words, the usually immutable laws of celebrity – that the biggest stars get the biggest and best parts, that leading men and ladies are infallible and heroic in any and all endeavours, that the world in general treats top-tier celebrities like a separate and superior species – do not apply.

I'm guessing I don't need to elaborate too much on the pervasiveness of the cult of celebrity in the West, nor the fact that it was, as the UK's *New Statesman* put it, 'the growth industry of the '90s'. But quickly: *Entertainment Tonight*, a daily news programme about celebrity culture, has been on the air for twenty years, and it is merely the highest-rated of the half-dozen daily celebrity-news broadcasts on North American TV. There is an entire magazine – *In Style* – dedicated to showing us what kinds of things celebrities own. Britain's three most prominent glossy weekly celebrity-news magazines – *Hello!, OK!* and *Now* – together sell more than 1.3 million copies each week. You, me – practically all of us – carry with us storehouses of knowledge about the lives of celebrities, stuff we maybe can't remember the source of and likely as not didn't seek out, but there it is anyway. For example, off the top of my head: Brad Pitt has a deep passion for architecture and design. Demi Moore and Bruce Willis had three children together, and those children were given the unique names Rumer, Scout and Tallulah Belle.[1] (Before he became an actor, incidentally, Willis was a bartender at a New York tavern frequented by showbiz heavyweights.) Nicolas Cage owns a Lamborghini that used to belong to the shah of Iran. Sandra Bullock is allergic to horses. And I need only to turn on my TV or surf over to the Internet Movie Database or pick up today's newspaper to add a fresh load of trivia to the pile.

Even when the celebrity in question is actually talented and truly accomplished, and even when the worship of this celebrity is intelligent and artful – even then, there is something perversely exaggerated about the modern relationship with celebrity. Here, for example, is an excerpt from Mike Sager's erudite profile of the gifted actor Robert De Niro in the August 1997 issue of *Esquire* magazine:

> Celebrities give us faith that there's something more to life than mere existence, something more than work, family, grind. They give us faith that a kind of heaven exists right here on earth and that some of us might actually attain it. They may not be holy, but neither are they ghosts. Push a button and there they are – playing celebrity softball, attending a star-studded opening, pulling a gun on a perp, taking a gratuitous bubble bath with a costar, dropping the soap. Because we can't know God, in other words, we need Robert De Niro.

Sager's not exaggerating, as far as I can tell. He's reporting. After all, which holy scripture is more instantly familiar to you, and more resonant: Psalm 23 or Travis Bickle in front of the mirror asking, 'You talkin' to me?' And how many of us would cite Ezekiel 25:17 as the only passage of the Bible we know by heart, by virtue of the fact that it's the one that Samuel L. Jackson so bad-assedly intones in *Pulp Fiction*?

This, then, is the landscape against which *The Simpsons'* treatment of its guest stars distinguishes itself. Ours is a world in which celebrity has come to refer to a separate Olympian peak upon which the deities from all walks of life – sports, politics, business and crime as well as entertainment – meet and interact and give meaning to the lives of the rest of us, the great uncelebrated masses. Celebrity is no longer a state attained through unique achievement but a kind of person, a tribe to whose ranks we all presumably dream of being elected. If not quite everybody will be famous for fifteen minutes, everyone at least wants to be, because to be famous – to become a celebrity – is now the presumed goal of all human endeavours. Against this backdrop, *The Simpsons* performs a tricky, paradoxical feat: it mocks and deflates individual celebrities and relentlessly attacks the cult of celebrity itself, even while it serves as a significant participant in that cult, a central vehicle for bestowing special honour upon chosen celebrities.

This is a conflicted and contradictory relationship. And you can see its paradoxes at work in the unique celebrity enjoyed by the members of the show's own creative team.

NO STARS, ONLY TALENT

Episode BABF19 of *The Simpsons* ('Behind the Laughter') is an extended parody of the overwrought VH1 documentary series *Behind the Music*, complete with candid interviews with the show's 'stars' (Homer, Bart, et al.), melodramatic recountings of drug abuse and backstage squabbling, and a chronicle of the Simpsons' fast-lane off-screen lives. 'I want to set the record straight,' Homer says in one interview clip, in the deliberate cadence of a repentant Hollywood star. 'I thought . . . the cop . . . was a prostitute.' We're left to imagine the scandal that occasioned this *mea culpa*, the headlines splattered across the covers of tabloids, the daily coverage of the trial on Court TV, the redemptive tell-all interviews with Larry King and/or Barbara Walters.[2] The entirety of BABF19 is an exercise in sustained irony: although the show's characters may be among the most recognised icons of our time, no one's ever caught a glimpse of them knocking back martinis at the Viper Room or chatting up their new projects with Jay Leno. Successful as the show is, its stars – not just the cartoon characters themselves but its flesh-and-blood creators – are not part of the cult of celebrity. Not one of the actors who produce some of the world's most recognised and beloved voices is a household name, and none of the show's principal producers and writers has ever been mobbed at a movie premiere.

The incongruity is startling: in a recent British poll, 74 per cent of respondents properly identified a picture of Homer Simpson; I'm sure (though there was no comparable poll) that fewer than *one* per cent could identify a picture of Dan Castellaneta. The same goes for the middle-aged women – Nancy Cartwright and Yeardley Smith – who provide the voices of the Simpson children.[3] The show's two most prolific voice actors, Hank Azaria and Harry Shearer, might be recognised on the street for their live-action work – Azaria, for example, was the Latino house boy in *The Bird Cage*, and Shearer played mutton-chopped bassist Derek Smalls in *This Is Spinal Tap* – but few celebrity worshippers would connect them to the busloads of minor characters they've breathed life into on *The Simpsons*.

This state of affairs is partially deliberate. Until fairly recently, the show's actors have avoided public appearances in which they use their famous voices. 'I think it destroys the illusion,' Julie Kavner once said. 'People feel these are real people.' In other words, the audience has come to think of the *Simpsons* characters themselves as the actors in the show, an effect that would be ruined if Kavner and her co-stars were famous figures in their own right. When we watch Marge, our vision isn't clouded by a competing image of Julie Kavner. We just see Marge. It's a powerful effect, akin to the way soap-opera fans think of actors on those series as indistinguishable from their characters (and have been known to chastise the actors in public for their characters' behaviour). In the case of *The Simpsons*, this phenomenon enhances the immersive aspect of the show. Your average mega-hit sitcom's viewer brings to the tube a wealth of information about the cast that can get in the way of suspended disbelief – we see *Cheers*' Sam Malone, for example, and are maybe reminded of Ted Danson's scandalous blackface routine at his former flame Whoopi Goldberg's Friar's Club roast, rather than just seeing a retired baseball player named Sam who owns a Boston bar. When we watch *The Simpsons*, though, there's no gossip-column white noise. That man there on the screen is Homer Simpson. He is *only* Homer Simpson. He casts no real-world shadow.

The show's fans, however, are not above hero worship: rare live read-throughs of *Simpsons* scripts by the show's cast were the undisputed highlights of both the 2000 Edinburgh International Festival and the 2002 Just for Laughs comedy festival in Montreal. And the cast's appearance on the popular PBS series *Inside the Actors Studio* in 2003 generated far more interest than any of the series's regular guests (a who's who of Hollywood) ever has. But the excitement around these events is the inverse of the hysteria around a movie star's public appearance. The thrill for us is not in finally seeing in the flesh someone we've seen so often on-screen, but in seeing real flesh-and-blood people – and strangers at that – speak in such instantly recognisable voices. If you have occasion to meet a Hollywood star, what you'll probably notice is a giddy sense of surreality, a feeling that *you* can't possibly be in the physical presence of someone so famous.[4] But when you see *The Simpsons'* voice actors speaking in character – in person or onscreen – what amazes you is that *they* are these characters. How can this real, live person be Mr Burns? How can this one guy – Harry Shearer, that is – be both Burns *and* Smithers (and Principal Skinner and Kent Brockman and Ned Flanders)? It's like a magic trick.

The Simpsons' celebrated writing staff has been similarly wary of the spotlight. They've given interviews only occasionally, and profiles are rarer still. Indeed the show's most prolific writer, John Swartzwelder, is reputed to be a recluse. And with good cause: near as I can tell, there are no existing profiles or photos of Swartzwelder – nor even a single quote – in the public domain. And even the most visible of the show's creators, Matt Groening, is far from a famous face, despite the dozens of in-depth interviews and profiles he's submitted to – many more than any other *Simpsons* creator. Groening's not even a famous *name*: in almost every one of these articles, the author feels obliged to clarify the pronunciation of his last name. (It rhymes with 'raining' and 'complaining'.)

The anonymity of the show's creators has had a single powerful effect: the focus of the media and (most of) the fans has remained on the show itself. Admittedly, there have been occasional eruptions of low-intensity media attention on backstage tiffs (co-creators Groening and Sam Simon once quarrelled in the press about the show's evolution) and on contractual tangles (Maggie Roswell, the voice of Maude Flanders, once held out for a higher salary and found herself out of a job; this may or may not have been the motivation for killing off her character in Season 11). For the most part, though, *The Simpsons* creative team has managed to achieve the goal of many a reluctantly famous artist: it has kept the attention of its fans and critics almost solely on the work.

And in that work lies a second device – this one built-in – that distances the show from the celebrity world. Which is this: cartoon characters *cannot* become off-screen celebrities. It's an impossibility. (Among other things, it would be a terrible strain on the animators' wrists to try to conduct live public appearances.) This fact is, of course, the wellspring of the deep irony of Episode BABF19. There is no 'behind-the-laughter' drama to be documented.[5]

Even better, the (reasonably) good judgement of the show's producers and the labour-intensive exigencies of animation have meant that even though the Simpsons have endorsed the odd product – Butterfinger chocolate bars, most notably – they haven't been media-blitzed into serious overexposure. We will not get sick of seeing them hawking crap on every other TV channel, nor of reading about their on-again, off-again romances with J.Lo or their painful struggles with alcoholism. We'll never know anything about their lavish estates in the Hollywood Hills. When we see *The Simpsons*, it's where we want to see them: on TV, on their show, amusing the hell out of us.

And it is only there, on the show, that we'll see them cavorting with Hollywood's A-list.

SELF-PORTRAITS IN YELLOW

The first celebrity sighting on *The Simpsons* sets the tone for the dozens to follow. It's a single line of dialogue. Blink and you miss it. Season 2, Episode 7F05 ('Dancin' Homer'): Homer, who has found a new vocation as 'Dancin' Homer', a baby-elephant-walking baseball-team mascot, lands a job as the understudy to the king of mascots, the Capital City Goofball. As the Simpsons drive into the metropolis, pointing out Capital City's many sights – the Cross-Town Bridge, the Penny Loafer restaurant, street crime – their slack-jawed touristing is set to a Sinatra-esque soundtrack. 'It's the kind of place that makes a bum feel like a king,' an unseen singer croons. 'And it makes a king feel like some nutty, cuckoo super-king.' Suddenly, there he is out the window – the singer himself. 'Look!' Marge exclaims, 'It's Tony Bennett!' A tuxedoed Bennett, complete with requisite Simpsonian yellow skin and overbite, replies, 'Hey, good to see you.' And then he returns to his ode to his home sweet swingin' home. And just like that, the first appearance of a real-world celebrity as himself on *The Simpsons* is over.

Many of the celebrity guest spots on *The Simpsons* would continue in this vein over the next few seasons: brief appearances, often without fanfare, to add just a little colour. Talk-show host Larry King narrates a books-on-tape version of the Bible – only his voice is used. Deep-voiced soul singer Barry White appears on the podium at the launch of Whacking Day – introduced by Mayor 'Diamond Joe' Quimby as 'Larry' White – and later sings one of his tunes ('Can't Get Enough of Your Love, Babe') to lure Springfield's snakes to safety. James Brown is an honoured guest at the town's inaugural 'Do What You Feel' Festival, energising the crowd with a rendition of his signature song, 'I Got You (I Feel Good)', until the sloppily constructed bandstand behind him collapses. (This occasions the Godfather of Soul's only line of dialogue, delivered in an hilariously over-the-top version of his patented soul-brother staccato: 'Hey, wait a minute! Hold on here! This bandstand wasn't double-bolted!') There's a pointedly mundane quality to these *Simpsons* guest spots, a kind of implicit 'So what?' directed at the celebrities. Certainly it's well worth mining James Brown's singular voice and long-standing reputation for reckless living for a line of ironic dialogue, but neither characters nor plot point giddily at the Godfather, or anyone else, to indicate the enormity of their fame.

There are two particularly celebrity-packed episodes – one each from Seasons 3 and 4 – that illustrate the show's deft use of the rich and famous for its own purposes, and its adroitness in avoiding enslavement at the hands of same. The first of these is Episode 8F13 ('Homer at the Bat'), in which Mr Burns stacks his company softball team with nine of professional baseball's biggest superstars: Wade Boggs, Darryl Strawberry, Jose Canseco, Roger Clemens, Don Mattingly, Ozzie Smith, Mike Scioscia, Steve Sax and Ken Griffey Jr. (All of the players supplied their own voices for the episode.)[6] Homer and his co-workers are duly impressed, though Homer, who had until then been the softball team's star, is disappointed that Darryl Strawberry will be taking his position in the starting lineup. But the episode never becomes a vehicle for celebrating this impressive gathering of baseball talent. Quite the contrary: the famous ballplayers are slaves to the show's various needs. Some serve as straight men for a non-stop string of gags that lampoon the players themselves: Strawberry, as well known for his bad behaviour and lengthy criminal record as for his bat, is portrayed as an ass-kissing coach's dream, and the notorious glory-hog Jose Canseco is an overeager good Samaritan. Others are props in absurdist gags: Ken Griffey Jr falls victim to gigantism, his head swelling up to the size of a beach ball after he drinks Mr Burns's nerve tonic; Ozzie Smith tumbles into another dimension at Springfield's 'Mystery Spot' tourist trap; Steve Sax finds the honest work at the power plant a welcome relief from the pressures of big-time baseball. And only Strawberry actually plays in the climactic softball game, in an explicit defiance of expectations that has become a recurring device in *Simpsons* celebrity appearances.

Episode 9F19 ('Krusty Gets Kancelled') marks an even more impressive balancing act between star power and the show's integrity. When Gabbo the wise-cracking ventriloquist's dummy pushes Krusty the Clown off the air,[7] Springfield's favourite clown is reduced to begging on the street until Bart and Lisa come along to plan his comeback special. The TV special's guest list – and thus the episode's roster of guest voices – would turn a talk show's booker enviously green: Hugh Hefner, Bette Midler, Elizabeth Taylor, Luke Perry, all four members of the Red Hot Chili Peppers and Johnny Carson (the only guest spot he's made on a TV series and one of his few public appearances anywhere since he retired from *The Tonight Show*). When it first aired in 1992, this episode was easily the most star-studded in the show's history, a sort of coming-out party for this new celebrity institution.

And yet despite Hef and Johnny and the rest, 9F19 keeps its focus on the show's cast. *Krusty's Komeback Special* is first and foremost about Krusty. Midler comes out to serenade Krusty with 'Wind Beneath My Wings' (a reference to her performance of 'One for My Baby' on Johnny Carson's gala finale), but Krusty soon joins in and upstages her with his gravelly, tuneless harmonising. Luke Perry, as previously noted, is employed as a prop in an elaborate sight gag. Carson – the King of Late Night himself – is reduced to vaudevillian-sideshow antics, coming onstage to juggle a 1987 Buick Skylark while singing opera and telling nary a joke. In the end, it seems only natural that superstar Krusty would have such superstar friends, only fitting that the post-broadcast party at Moe's Tavern would culminate with Bart's toast to the evening's biggest star: Krusty. 'To Krusty,' Bart announces, 'the greatest entertainer in the world.' Beat. 'Except for that guy.' Cut to Johnny Carson, balancing a bench on his head upon which sit Grampa Simpson and his pal Jasper, who play chess as Carson tap dances and plays 'Good Night, Ladies' on the accordion. And then Carson segues into *The Simpsons* theme.

This relentless schticking is merely a mild jab at Carson's unwavering professionalism, but it hints at the savage satire of celebrity employed in other episodes. In many cases, *The Simpsons* goes much further, standing as primetime TV's foremost practitioner of an art that's best summarised by the excellent English phrase 'taking the piss'.

Look no further than another Season 4 episode – 9F10 ('Marge vs. the Monorail') – for a prime example of Simpsonian celebrity piss-taking. The grand marshal for the monorail's inaugural run is the target of the piss-take: Leonard Nimoy, better known as Spock on the original *Star Trek*. 'I'd say this vessel could do at least warp five,' says Nimoy, all Spock-like, to appreciative laughter from the gathered crowd. Mayor Quimby, confused as usual about the identity of his guest of honour, replies, 'And let me say, "May the force be with you!"'

'Do you even know who I am?' an irritated Nimoy responds.

'I think I do,' says Quimby. 'Aren't you one of the Little Rascals?'

When Nimoy climbs aboard the monorail, the abuse (which, given that he does his own voice in the episode, is actually a kind of self-abuse) gets nastier. In the train's luxurious lounge, Nimoy tries to regale a passenger with a drawn-out anecdote about how the special effect of the automatic doors on the starship *Enterprise* was created. But Nimoy's neighbour is utterly unregaled, and replies with annoyed, sarcastic half-interest. Later, Nimoy sits contentedly in a passenger seat, gazing out the window at an impending solar eclipse. In the sombre, mythopoetic tones he used as host of the 1970s documentary series *In Search Of*, Nimoy announces, 'A solar eclipse. The cosmic ballet continues.' The man sitting next to him looks desperately around the train. 'Does *anybody* want to switch seats?' he pleads. In Springfield, at least on this day, it's the celebrities who intrude annoyingly, while the average Joes fight desperately to escape the conversation. And they're right: Nimoy's banter is banal, his anecdotes boring, his overwrought observations irritating as hell. No one, frankly, should be paying much attention to this guy.

This point is made more emphatically in Episode 8F11 ('Radio Bart'), as Krusty the Clown works to organise a charity recording for Timmy, a little boy stuck in a well in Springfield whose plight has become a *cause célèbre*. (In actuality, 'Timmy' is Bart, who has dropped a radio down the well and is using a toy microphone to play the part of the trapped boy.) Krusty's musical tribute – 'We're Sending Our Love Down the Well', a ridiculously schmaltzy hymn in the 'We Are the World' vein – attracts a star-studded roster of contributors, including Sting (voicing himself). And of course Channel 6's Kent Brockman is on the scene, pressing Krusty to tell the tale of how he got Sting involved. 'I called my good friend Sting,' Krusty explains. 'He said, "Krusty, when do you need me?" I said, "Thursday." He said, "I'm busy Thursday." I said, "What about Friday?" He said, "Friday's worse than Thursday." Then *he* said, "How about Saturday?" I said, "Fine." True story!'

Skull-boringly dull as Krusty's 'anecdote' is, it's really only a slight exaggeration of the kind of prosaic patter that fills the screen on entertainment-news shows and fills out the celebrity profiles in glossy magazines. Think, for example, of how many times you've read in some detail about what stars are eating, how they hold their forks, how they interact with waiters – because of course the average 'profile' has been written by a journalist whose sole firsthand knowledge of the profile's subject is a single shared lunch. Or try to imagine the monument to sustained emptiness that is a given star's full round of publicity for a new blockbuster. Imagine it packaged together – the morning talk-show interviews, the newspaper Q&As, the late-night talk-show interviews, the bantering behind-the-scenes features for *Access Hollywood*, the 'in-depth' chats with writers from *Vanity Fair* and *Maxim* – imagine all of this in a single reel, a unified, relentless assault of banalities, cute anecdotes and well-crafted sound bites. It'd play like an anthropomorphic version of Andy Warhol's *Empire* (an experimental film consisting of a single eight-hour shot of the Empire State Building). And it'd make Krusty's scheduling conversation seem like a non-stop thrill ride.

The self-important, self-absorbed banality of the rich and famous is of course hardly breaking news, but *The Simpsons* often uses its celebrity guests to satirise the entire celebrity apparatus – and, more broadly, the entire culture for providing celebrities with the foundation for their self-importance in the first place. Consider one of the show's oddest guest spots: the appearance of Ernest Borgnine in Episode 1F06 ('Boy-Scoutz N the Hood'). In 1F06, Bart joins the Scout-like Junior Campers, and Borgnine is brought in as a fatherless boy's 'special celebrity dad' for the troop's father-son camping trip. The gag is sort of conceptual, playing off the conceit that a celebrity – *any* celebrity – would make a fatherless kid happy, and thus suggesting that seemingly any problem the world faces can be solved by the mere magical presence of a celebrity or two. Jane Fonda goes to Hanoi, Sean Penn to Baghdad, John and Yoko lie in bed in a Montreal bedroom and Sheryl Crow shows up at the American Music Awards in a T-shirt that reads WAR IS NOT THE ANSWER – and with these simple acts, world peace becomes a reality. Right? *The Simpsons*' selection of Borgnine for the job added an extra layer of ironic detail to the episode's critique, because it turned out that he agreed to the guest spot despite his total ignorance of the show. 'He's a good actor, and he read his lines just fine,' said Hank Azaria, 'but he had no idea what the show was, no idea what we were doing.' The symmetry's stunning: the celebrity machine, churning on under its own power, delivers *The Simpsons* a random celebrity to play the part of a randomly chosen celebrity.

It's a safe bet, though, that most *Simpsons* guest stars know exactly what they're doing. And the fact that they play along indicates either that they don't take themselves too seriously or else that they know the publicity value of *appearing* not to take themselves too seriously in this deeply ironic age. 'I thought they used me very cleverly,' Leonard Nimoy said of his lambasting on *The Simpsons*. 'I think they're very hip, very bright people.' And the show's celebrity guests seem to understand that the sharpest satirical barbs are not aimed at them specifically but rather at the whole celebrity circus. Hence (I've got to assume) the willingness of Kim Basinger, Alec Baldwin and Ron Howard to stand in for all of Hollywood in the series's most intensive attack on celebrity: Episode 5F19 ('When You Dish upon a Star').

In the episode's opening sequence, Homer accidentally falls through the skylight of a palatial estate while paragliding, landing in the bed of Baldwin and Basinger. In fact, Homer lands right *on top of* Baldwin, and thinks at first that he's squished Alec's brother, Billy; he'd have been happy with either of them. Star-struck, he insists on becoming the famous couple's personal assistant. Soon, their pal Ron Howard comes by for a visit, and Homer refers to him variously as Potsie (a supporting character on the sitcom *Happy Days*, which starred Howard) and Horshack (a character on another 1970s sitcom, *Welcome Back, Kotter*, which Howard wasn't in). Basinger is shown obsessively polishing her Oscar; Baldwin the bad-script magnet suggests (to the weighted silence of his fellow celebrities) that they'd forgive each other *if* any of them ever made a bad movie; Howard pitches hokily melodramatic film ideas to a producer.

The episode is indeed a veritable catalogue of the consumer fads, linguistic quirks and lifestyle pretensions of the modern celebrity. Homer is dispatched to the Kwik-E-Mart with a grocery list overflowing with 'weird and fruity items', in Homer's parlance: four kinds of mushrooms (portobello, porcini, chanterelle and shiitake), tofu, wheatgrass juice, jellied zinc, 600-dollar sunglasses, extra-wide bumper stickers for a humvee. (It's grim testimony to the marketing power of celebrity culture that the majority of these are now available at your average suburban shopping mall.) In short order, Homer himself goes Hollywood, his pants pockets overflowing with cellphones, PETA brochures and back issues of *Variety* as he talks up his own movie script, a 'project' that Ron Howard might well be 'attached to' (he's at least 'expressed an interest').

Homer's standing in, as usual, for the citizens of the celebrity-obsessed West in general, any and all of whom would surely leap just as quickly as Homer does at the chance to hobnob with the stars. After all, you no longer need to know Jack Warner personally to be a Hollywood 'insider': the mainstream media speaks of opening-weekend grosses and star vehicles and green-lighted projects, as if all the world's accountants and computer programmers and Wal-Mart greeters were a phone call away from a three-picture deal with Miramax. (*You getting points on the merchandising?* asks the kid who delivers your pizza. *No*, you answer, *but I'm getting 52 per cent of the foreign-market gross.*) Just flip through the pages of *Entertainment Weekly* –

which shares grocery-checkout-line space with ultra-mainstream titles like *People* and *Better Homes and Gardens* – for a taste of faux-insider Hollywood. You'll find detailed handicappings of the box-office potential of the season's new releases and overviews of the career arcs of stars discussed with a casting director's critical eye, offering us the opportunity not just to revel in the lavish lives of the stars but to pretend to be part of the fray.

When Homer is cast out of Eden – booted from the Baldwin-Basinger summer home for revealing their presence to the denizens of Moe's Tavern, which precipitates a stampede of stargazers to the estate – he's devastated. 'I'm sorry I blew your secret,' Homer tells his celebrity pals before being tossed. 'But you don't know what it's like to be a nobody! I just wanted to bask in your reflected glory. *Reflected glory!*' As he leaves, the mob at the gate perks up for a minute, but soon realises Homer isn't 'somebody', he's just 'nobody'. Back at home, Homer can't help but notice that his dinnertime Manwich isn't on focaccia and it's lacking in fennel, his wife couldn't open a movie if her life depended on it, and his kids will never be John and Joan Cusack.

Homer's fall from grace is a kind of exaggerated high-relief version of the dissatisfaction bred by the rise of celebrity culture and its faux-insider adjuncts. Why would anyone want to live a quiet, anonymous, glamourless life when the riches and fame and excitement of Hollywood are so tantalisingly close? Who *wouldn't* want to be inside? And indeed it's a common enough desire – simply to be famous – that it has given birth to an entire genre of TV entertainment – reality TV, which simply couldn't exist if it didn't have deep reserves of nobodies who desperately want to be somebody to draw its 'stars' from. If the genre's pioneers – *Survivor* and *Who Wants To Be a Millionaire?* – were ostensibly contests predicated on the notion of winning money, subsequent reality-TV shows have offered nothing more than a shot at celebrity. Destroy your relationship on *Temptation Island* or reveal your venal soul on *Big Brother* or sing your heart out on *American* or *Canadian* or (Britain's) *Pop Idol*, and you too could be famous.

And with fame comes an even greater promise: that your life will no longer be ordinary. That you will live, finally, in the transcendent world of Hollywood. There's an old-time diner I used to pass by at least once a week on the streetcar, a place down in the industrial wastes of Toronto's east-end rail lands called the Canary Restaurant that was my own local monolith to this promise. The Canary, you see, is a favourite of film crews, and with good cause: it's a magnificent place to behold from the street, its funky neon sign – a bright-yellow canary on a perch – jutting out into the intersection, the restaurant's name rendered in lovely art-deco, another sign (hand-painted) reading STEAKS & CHOPS. The building's all red-brick nostalgic goodness, the second storey wrapped in wrought-iron railings. It's *the* place to shoot a vintage-diner scene – as long as you zoom in tight on it, use it only for an 'EXT. Vintage Diner' shot, because the Canary stands alone in a decaying wasteland of railway overpasses, vacant lots and chain-link. I once made the mistake of going there for lunch, and found the inside sadly devoid of the chrome and vinyl-seated booths and tabletop jukeboxes usually associated with vintage diners. (You can find those across town at the Lakeview Lunch – a frequent location for 'INT. Vintage Diner' shoots, the necessary companion to the Canary's 'EXT. Vintage Diner'.) Instead, the Canary's all cheap Formica and ratty stacking chairs, and the food's merely bland.

The disappointment I felt having lunch at the Canary is – as I come around to the point of this reminiscence – the same kind felt by Homer after being exiled from the celebrity estate, by avid readers of *Entertainment Weekly* who'll never actually have a financial stake in the box-office grosses the magazine so obsessively records. When the mob gathers at the Baldwin-Basinger home's gates, one of Springfield's citizens holds aloft a sign reading YOU COMPLETE US. Sadly, it's only slight hyperbole. Even those of us who don't spend tremendous amounts of time studying the lifestyles of the rich and famous can still feel strangely dissatisfied with some part of our lives – our waistline or our bank balance or our local diner – because of the all-pervasive ideal versions relentlessly blasted out at us from the celebrity world.

In the end, the target of Episode 5F19's piss-take, and of a significant portion of *The Simpsons'* critique of celebrity, is this culture of illusions. And it has emerged as much from the audience's desire to immerse itself in Hollywood's fantasies as from a given celebrity's fondness for focaccia. As much fun as it is to take the piss out of unctuous Spock, if you will, it'd be dishonest not to lay some blame at the costumed feet of the Trekkies as well. The relationship is a codependent one.

It's a relationship, too, that's somewhat unique to film and television. To be sure, the culture of celebrity extends, for example, to the world of pop music, and there's as much hero worship at a rock concert as there is at a film opening. But the audience's relationship to music is ultimately less yearning, more personal – the music is often a vehicle for the listener's own hopes and dreams, not a factory for constructing impossibly ideal ones. This might begin to explain why there's so much less fanfare – and less ridicule – when the household names appearing on *The Simpsons* are not movie stars but musicians. The previously cited examples of James Brown and Barry White are typical: musicians are often used simply as grandiose background detail.[8] In Episode 5F09 ('Trash of the Titans'), for example, the Irish band U2 – one of the most prominent pop bands of the last twenty years – doesn't appear until the second act, and its Springfield concert is there mostly as a platform for Homer to campaign for garbage commissioner. (Later, the band serves as famous window dressing at Moe's.) When Phish pops up in a Season 13 episode, it's a similar story. Homer, suffering from an eye injury, has been given a prescription for medical marijuana, so the appearance of the famously pot-friendly Phish at a local benefit concert serves as an obvious punchline. This sets up an obligatory ironic gag about the band's stoner audience: Phish stops their Springfield concert to demand to see a prescription from a pot-smoking fan, who turns out to be withered old Hans Moleman in a psychedelic T-shirt. But this is merely a brief prelude to the real purpose of Phish's appearance: to provide a colourful stage-set for Homer to stonedly stumble across, as he urges the crowd to vote against a proposed ban on his medicine.

This backgrounding effect persists even in episodes where rock & roll takes centre stage. Consider one of the most music-saturated Golden Age episodes: 3F21 ('Homerpalooza'), in which Homer becomes a sideshow freak in the Hullabalooza rock festival. Even there, the music is a backdrop for the jokes: a snippet of Smashing Pumpkins' 'Zero' is used as the soundtrack for a gag about the bummed-out teenagers swaying along to it, Peter Frampton's 'Do You Feel Like I Do' plays to introduce a joke about his cheesy props, and the London Symphony Orchestra arrives backstage as a set-up for a gag about the conditions under which Cypress Hill may have ordered them to come to the concert (possibly while high, that is).[9]

The music is similarly downplayed in Episode DABF22 ('How I Spent My Strummer Vacation'), whose guest-voice list reads like an induction-ceremony programme for the Rock and Roll Hall of Fame: Mick Jagger and Keith Richards of the Rolling Stones, Elvis Costello, Tom Petty, Lenny Kravitz and Brian Setzer. The episode's premise is that Homer goes to Rock & Roll Fantasy Camp, where this roster of greats teaches him and the rest of the class of *Simpsons* regulars how to look, dress and act like rock stars in a series of gags about rock's most shopworn clichés. There's very little *playing* like a rock star, though – conspicuously little music at all – which feels intentional. The *trappings* of the rock lifestyle are good for a gag or two, but perhaps rock itself did attain perfection in 1975 (as Homer once argued), and so what'd be the point of an elaborate parody of something that's been coasting for so long? One of the other rockin'-est *Simpsons* episodes – 8F21 ('The Otto

Show') – stars Spinal Tap, which is itself an elaborate (not to mention brilliant) satire of rock & roll. *The Simpsons'* rock fantasy camp, with its light parodies of Elvis Costello's elaborately crafted persona and Jagger's stable of clichéd rock star poses, simply makes a wee bit more hay with whatever wasn't burned to ash and dust in *This Is Spinal Tap* – which isn't much.

It's worth noting that *Simpsons* creator Matt Groening is a huge music fan and an avid record collector. Might it be reverence that keeps the show from savaging the rock gods who make guest appearances? Actually, more likely the opposite: it's already been done. By Matt Groening, who wrote piss-taking music reviews for an L.A. alternative newspaper right up until the debut of *The Simpsons*. Here he is on his career as a rock critic, from a 2002 interview in *Rolling Stone*: 'I had a weekly column making fun of rock & roll. I used to review bands based on their publicity photo. Oh, God, I was such an asshole. I learned that nobody was buying the records that I was reviewing, so I started making up bands and records. I knew that I didn't want to do it for the rest of my life, so I just did it until I got fired.' Elsewhere in the interview, Groening professes a love for 'oddball music', stuff that's 'more challenging rhythmically than 99 percent of rock & roll'.

This hints at a plausible explanation for the show's repeated underselling of the music of its guests: it's a reflection not just of Groening's boredom with repetitive rock but of the decreasing authority of rock & roll in general. *The Simpsons* saves its heavy artillery for society's mightiest symbols, and rock simply doesn't qualify anymore. Pop music in the *Simpsons* age is irredeemably fragmented, a handful of semi-connected shards, each of them too small to stand on its own as a symbol of cultural authority nor even as a universal language for the show's audience. (Some might dig Phish, others the Stones, others an underground DJ or hip-hop hero or punk band.) In the 1950s and 1960s, rock & roll was the primary voice of youth, and any cultural icon that hoped to talk to or about youth culture simply had to have a significant connection to it. No longer: pop music is the *soundtrack* for youth, but it's also the soundtrack for middle-aged nostalgia and car commercials. Note that it's Homer, not Bart, who goes to Rock & Roll Fantasy Camp. Mocking rock, perhaps, would be like taking the piss out of the weather.

Consider how *The Simpsons* has treated the biggest pop group of all time: The Beatles. Paul, George and Ringo have each appeared separately on the show, and not one of them has played or sung a single note. Ringo appears as the object of Marge's long-ago schoolgirl crush, and then in present day as an eccentric millionaire wiling away his days in a lavish mansion, trying to reply to the stacks of Beatles-era fan mail strewn about the place. George Harrison pops up in an episode in which Homer's mid-1980s barbershop quartet, the Be Sharps, enjoy Beatles-esque success, and Homer leaves no doubt as to where rock icons from twenty years in the past figure in his – and our – cultural priorities. 'Hello, Homer, I'm George Harrison,' says the Quiet One to Homer at a Grammy Awards after-party. 'Oh my God, oh my God!' Homer replies breathlessly. 'Where did you get that brownie?' And when Paul McCartney and his wife, Linda, run into Lisa on the rooftop garden of the Kwik-E-Mart, Lisa's amazed reply is even more telling: 'Wow! Paul McCartney! I read about you in history class.'[10] In *The Simpsons*' universe, The Beatles are merely a few more famous faces. They are not inherently hipper or more beloved or more relevant than a former president or an aging actor. They're just another familiar detail used to add realism to the show's depiction of our culture.

If *The Simpsons* systematically downplays its pop-musician guests, it exaggerates the fame of another category of real-world visitors: intellectuals and practitioners of the classical arts. A handful of scientists, poets and abstract artists have been given prominent roles on *The Simpsons* – even, in some cases, the full star treatment. As I've already noted, the renowned astrophysicist Stephen Hawking shows up to critique the failed utopia constructed by Lisa and her fellow members of Mensa's Springfield chapter, then discusses Homer's intriguing theory of a donut-shaped universe down at Moe's. The scientist and author Stephen Jay Gould was a key figure in another episode. And the painter Jasper Johns – celebrated for his iconic paintings of everyday objects – pops up repeatedly in an episode where Homer becomes an 'outsider' artist; Johns is depicted as an incorrigible kleptomaniac. Each of these highbrow guests is treated with at least as much reverence as the numerous entertainers who've appeared on the show. A talk show would surely bring out a Johnny Carson ahead of a Jasper Johns (if it booked Johns at all). On *The Simpsons*, though, they're equals.

The most elaborate example of this star treatment for academic icons comes in Episode DABF15 ('Little Girl in the Big Ten'), whose 'celebrity' guest is the former US poet laureate Robert Pinsky. In the episode, Lisa pretends to be a college student so she can hang out with her intellectual peers, and winds up attending a poetry reading at a coffee house. The reader is Pinsky, whose oration of his poem 'Impossible to Tell (My Two Joke Elegy)' runs at least as long as any given rock star's performance on *The Simpsons*. The poem includes the lines '"*Bash*" / He named himself, "Banana Tree,"' and during the reading a group of pumped-up frat-boy types strip off their shirts to reveal letters on their chests that spell out BASH. 'Bash!' they whoop. 'Banana Tree!' one adds, pumping his fist. In Springfield on this night, the poet is a sports hero.[11]

The irony here is flowing about waist-deep: your average college jock wouldn't know Pinsky from the janitor who cleans his dorm, and even serious literature students wouldn't take their rapture as far as chest-painting. But the scene's irony has multiple layers. Part of it, yes, stems from the fact that *no one* behaves this way at poetry readings. More subtly, though, the audience's fist-pumping hero worship of Pinsky lays bare the absurdity of identifying so zealously with *anything*. If it's silly to get so wound up about banana trees, why is it acceptable to do the same for sports teams and pop stars? What's truly absurd is that we *expect* celebrities to be treated with such reverence and ecstasy. By shrugging its shoulders at the presence of superstars in Springfield and whooping it up over poets and scientists, *The Simpsons* has articulated a sporadic long-form critique of this founding principle of the cult of celebrity.

And in Episode AABF08 ('Sunday, Cruddy Sunday'), the show's writers let us know this is all fully intentional. The episode details a troubled trip to the Super Bowl undertaken by Homer and a gang of Springfield regulars, and features guest appearances by retired NFL stars Rosey Grier, Dan Marino and John Elway, famed football play-by-play men John Madden and Pat Summerall, media baron (and Fox Network owner) Rupert Murdoch, and Dolly Parton (whose claims to fame presumably need no elaboration). It originally aired immediately after the Super Bowl, as a heavily hyped coda to one of America's most over-the-top entertainment spectacles. With this much anticipation and expectation, you could almost forgive the show's writers if they broke with tradition and let their guests milk their high-profile appearances for some serious self-aggrandisement. But they emphatically do not. The celebrity who gets the best lines in the episode is the deceased Vincent Price (impersonated by occasional *Simpsons* voice actor Karl Wiedergott), who camps it up in an automated phone message explaining why the feet are missing in the 'Vincent Price's Egg Magic' kit that Lisa and Marge use to pass the time while the boys are at the Super Bowl. The other big names are put to work in the usual fashion: as props in the adventures of Springfield's permanent residents. In the final scene, John Madden and Pat Summerall do a sort of post-game wrap-up that underscores the incongruity of it all. 'Did it strike you as odd,' Summerall asks, 'that in a Super Bowl show with Dolly Parton we didn't see any football or singing?' Madden: 'I hadn't thought about it, Pat. But in retrospect, it was kind of a rip-off! What a way to treat the loyal fans who've put up with so much nonsense from this franchise!' The bus pulls up just then, and the door opens to reveal Vincent Price in the driver's seat. 'All aboard, boys!' he calls. 'I've been waiting for you.' Madden again: 'Now I'll tell you, that doesn't make a lick of sense!' And it doesn't, actually – unless the point is (and it is) to pointedly illustrate that the presence of a famous name or seven is no reason to change your daily routine. Celebrities aren't more important than Homer, and they're not more important than the deceased Vincent Price.

The moral of the story – a story the show has been telling since Tony Bennett was spotted out the window of an average American family's car – is that they're not more important than you, either.

INSIDE THE CELEBRITY VOICE ACTOR'S STUDIO

If you're a big star – or even a little one – and you'd rather not risk being mocked and underutilised by appearing as yourself on *The Simpsons*, there is always the option of becoming a full-fledged Springfieldianite. Meryl Streep played Reverend Lovejoy's sociopathic daughter, Jessica. Glenn Close gave voice to Homer's mother. Dustin Hoffman appeared under a pseudonym to play Mr Bergstrom, Lisa's beloved substitute teacher. The list goes on: Kirk Douglas as Chester J. Lampwick (the forgotten creator of 'Itchy & Scratchy' and an inveterate Depression-style bum); Donald Sutherland as Hollis Hurlbut (curator of the Springfield Historical Society); Michelle Pfeiffer as Homer's co-worker (and almost-lover) Mindy Simmons. There's a surprising general rule to these guest-starring roles: the bigger the star, the less memorable the character. There's no apparent design to this trend, unless the qualities that make someone a great onscreen actor somehow translate poorly to voice-acting. Meryl Streep, for example, is rarely anything less than riveting on the big screen. As Jessica, though, she's merely competent.

Admittedly, there are some bona fide classics on the list of one-off characters with the voices of screen legends. Take Kathleen Turner's turn as Stacy Lovell, creator of the Barbie-esque Malibu Stacy doll. Her performance stands out in part because it never becomes simply a showcase for her sultry purring. Instead, Turner mixes in some boozy disaffection and pathos, and so the faded, debauched woman we see on the screen *is* Stacy Lovell, fallen titan of the doll-making world, not a Simpsonised Kathleen Turner. The same goes for Michelle Pfeiffer's Mindy, a crude, gluttonous slacker (a female Homer, in other words, save that she's a gorgeous redhead). Pfeiffer's famous voice intrudes not at all on the character.

On one notable occasion, the show even tried its hand at celebrity stunt-casting. Hollywood legend Elizabeth Taylor was cast to utter Maggie's first word in the final scene of Episode 9F08 ('Maggie's First Word'). Although it was an extraordinarily small part – Maggie coos the word 'Daddy' to an empty room – the size of the star suited the job, inasmuch as it ostensibly marked the first time Maggie spoke on the show (and in her life).[12] And tiny as the role was, it managed to provide an object lesson in the unique difficulties associated with using actors unfamiliar with voice work. The story goes that Taylor had trouble getting into character – her first readings were too sultry. In the end, it would be 25 takes before she got Maggie's first word just right.

The most memorable celebrity-voiced *Simpsons* characters have been created by lesser lights in the celebrity firmament. Many of these have been wonderful one-offs. For example, Mandy Patinkin voiced Hugh, the stuffy English snob who becomes engaged to college-aged Lisa. Another classic: Lawrence Tierney's crusty department-store detective, Don Brodka, who catches Bart in the act of shoplifting a video game from the Try-N-Save. And then there's the inspired casting choice of country-music legend Johnny Cash as the voice of Homer's coyote spirit guide (aka 'Space Coyote') in Episode 3F24 ('El Viaje Misterioso de Nuestro Jomer'). Who better than Johnny Cash, with his gravelly baritone, to give the proper heft to a line like 'Clarity is the path to inner peace' – and then to provide the self-deflating counterweight when he starts gnawing on Homer's pant leg moments later? 'Sorry. I *am* a coyote,' says Cash's Space Coyote, retaining just the right amount of righteousness.

In a few notable cases, *The Simpsons'* frequent use of guest stars has even uncovered a major voice-acting talent. Two of the most prolific of these are *Saturday Night Live* alumnus Jon Lovitz and multitalented actor-comedian-writer-director Albert Brooks, both of whom have appeared on the show repeatedly, each adding a handful of great characters to the show's pantheon.

Lovitz, for his part, specialises in pretentious dorks. He's done Marge's high-school flame, Artie Ziff, a self-important brainiac who gropes the future Mrs Simpson on prom night and then offers her this rationale for keeping it a secret: 'I am so respected, it would damage the *town* to hear it.' Lovitz also played Professor Lombardo (a night-school painting teacher who sees genius in everything from Marge's portraits of Ringo Starr to the janitor's work on the school railing) and Llewellyn Sinclair, the tortured artiste who directs Marge's acting debut in *Oh! Streetcar!* And Lovitz appeared as the portly and pretentious film critic Jay Sherman, who boasts a fine eye for artful cinema, a booming belch and a tummy even more ferocious than Homer's.[13]

As for Albert Brooks, his first appearance – in the second episode of Season 1 – as Cowboy Bob, the fast-talking proprietor of Cowboy Bob's RV Roundup, was a fine send-up of the smooth salesman archetype. A few episodes later – in 7G11 ('Life on the Fast Lane') – Brooks contributed possibly the finest guest-starring performance of the first two seasons as Jacques, the consummate playboy who teaches Marge to bowl and nearly persuades her to commit adultery. Brooks's delivery – mildly French-accented and halting and overweeningly passionate – milked humour from nearly every line. (Nowhere more so than in Jacques's heated description of the institution of brunch to Marge: 'It's not quite breakfast, it's not quite lunch, but it comes with a slice of cantaloupe at the end. You don't get completely what you would at breakfast, but you get *a good meal!*')

Brooks really hit his stride in Season 5, when he gave sappy, superficial life to Brad Goodman, Springfield's briefly beloved self-help guru. Brooks went for a subtle, slow-burn lampoon rather than broad caricature: his Goodman doesn't ooze insincerity, he just lightly dribbles it. (As the minor celebrity Martha Quinn exits the stage of his infomercial, for example, Goodman turns to the camera. 'She's one of my favourites,' he says, just slightly overearnest. 'I loved her in the thing I saw her in.') At his Springfield seminar, he holds up Bart Simpson as the embodiment of the inner child he wants his clients to embrace. But Bart trips up Goodman's speechifying by using a false name – Rudiger. 'If we can all be more like little Rudiger . . .' Goodman enthuses. 'His name is Bart,' Marge interjects. 'His name's not important!' Goodman barks, then rapidly reins himself in and continues expounding pop-psychologically. For a moment, his voice hints at self-important rage before returning to polished professional empathy – in the process telling us far more about Goodman's brand of bullshit than a cartoony explosion of anger would have. Through a dozen little touches like these, Brooks created a timeless *Simpsons* character.

His real masterwork, though, is Hank Scorpio, CEO of the Globex Corporation. Scorpio steals the episode, a rare instance of a Simpson – in this case Homer – being upstaged. Brooks brings hilarious satirical seamlessness to Scorpio's paradoxical nature, his voice moving effortlessly from the we're-all-pals folksiness of the modern executive ('At Globex, we don't believe in walls') to the psychopathic posturing of a James Bond villain bent on world domination (which turns out to be his true goal). By the end of the episode, when Homer tells Scorpio he's decided to resign and return to Springfield to please his family, these two sides have totally merged. 'Well, you can't argue with the little things,' Scorpio tells Homer, his voice bubbling over with compassion. 'It's the little things that make up life.' Scorpio tosses a grenade for emphasis – his giant supervillain's lair of an office is under full-scale military invasion even as he and Homer chat. 'Homer,' he adds, still empathetic, 'on your way out, if you wanna kill somebody, it would help me a lot.' On the basis of his delivery of this line alone, Brooks's place in *Simpsons* history is secure.

As good as Brooks is, though, he's only the runner-up. For he and all other *Simpsons* guest stars must necessarily bow down before their undisputed lord and master: the late, great Phil Hartman. Hartman's *Simpsons* work was so virtuoso and the characters he created so fully woven into the fabric of Springfield life that the term 'guest star' seems like a misnomer. Hartman was a frequent cast member since the very first season, a contributor of two major recurring characters, but he never completely integrated into the full-time cast. (In part, perhaps, because he kept busy playing supporting roles in sitcoms – particularly *NewsRadio* – and movies.) Over the years, Hartman produced nearly a dozen variations of his twin trademarks – the smarmy hustler and the overwrought voice of authority – on *The Simpsons*. He played the voice of God in an early episode and appeared elsewhere as both Moses and Charlton Heston playing Moses. He was a slimy cable guy ('Your door wasn't locked in any serious way'), a football commentator named Smooth Jimmy Apollo ('the man who's right 52 percent of the time') and a self-important 'bigger brother' for Bart. And of course Hartman portrayed that ultimate fast-talking huckster Lyle Lanley, the crook who uses a catchy song-and-dance number to con Springfield into buying a decrepit monorail.

But these – even the wonderfully amoral Lanley – are mere footnotes to Hartman's crowning glory, a twin gem consisting of his two magnificently drawn recurring characters: the ubiquitous C-list actor Troy McClure and Lionel Hutz, hapless attorney-at-law. Taken together, Hutz and McClure represent the most significant contribution to the show outside its permanent cast; indeed the show's Golden Age is hard to imagine without them. Hartman's voice was a tool seemingly forged for the sole purpose of expressing self-serving bombast, brain-dead posturing and cloying showbiz smarm. And it was funny the way a habanero pepper is hot: deeply, insistently, to its core.

Take Hutz: he's an ambulance-chasing lawyer, the proprietor of a shopping-mall practice called I Can't Believe It's a Law Firm, and a recovering alcoholic. Hutz learns his courtroom techniques by watching the odd episode of *Matlock* with the sound off in a bar and lures clients with infomercial-esque enticements: a smoking-monkey doll, a pen that looks just like a cigar ('Isn't that something?'), an exquisite faux-pearl necklace (a 99-dollar value, that). Hutz is a perfect showcase for Hartman's voice, a character defined by a toxically funny mix of salesman's bluster, lawyerly pomposity and a vacillation between naive self-confidence and utter hopelessness that is Hutz's (and Hartman's) alone.

It's hard to select a single representative example from the long list of classic moments in Hutz's career as a talentless law-talking guy, but I'll go with one that most fully combines the hopeless, the self-confident and the blustery. It's from Episode 9F05 ('Marge Gets a Job'), in which the Simpsons retain Hutz's services for a legal suit against Mr Burns for firing Marge because she wouldn't date him. 'Mrs Simpson,' Hutz booms, 'your sexual harassment case is just what I need to rebuild my shattered career. Care to join me in a belt of Scotch?' He proffers the bottle, waving it across his desk at Homer and Marge, shameless and utterly oblivious of its possible connection to his shattered practice. 'But it's 9.30 in the morning!' Marge answers. 'Yeah, but I haven't slept in days,' answers Hutz, and starts chugging. It's the delivery on this last line in particular – unrepentantly smooth, with the slightest hipster drawl on *daayyys*, as if he's just a little proud of it – that nails the gag. Hutz could have been mere parody, but in Hartman's care he became something a good deal more grand, the protagonist in a slapstick tragedy called *Death of a Legal Salesman*.

And then there's actor Troy McClure, undisputed world champ of showbiz insincerity, a creature born to introduce tacky infomercials, shoddy educational films and formulaic Hollywood movies. The smarmy Hollywood type – like the shyster lawyer – has been done to death, but Hartman's version breathed new life into it with each appearance. McClure has became the apotheosis of the stereotype, a gut-achingly funny reinterpretation whose trademark introduction – 'Hi! I'm Troy McClure! You may remember me from such films as . . .' – has become a shorthand way to describe any grossly artificial media figure.

Hartman's career ended prematurely when he was murdered by his deranged wife in May 1998. 'He was a master,' Matt Groening told *Entertainment Weekly* amid the media frenzy that accompanied his made-for-the-tabloids death. 'I took him for granted because he nailed the joke every time.' Elsewhere, Groening and other *Simpsons* producers noted that Hartman's death left a gaping hole in the show's cast that could never be filled. (No one was foolish enough to even try to replace him as the voice of Hutz and McClure.) Bafflingly, though, precious few of the media retrospectives of Hartman's career highlighted his work on *The Simpsons. The New York Times* mentioned it in a single sentence alongside his impression of Bill Clinton on *Saturday Night Live* and his role in the instantly forgotten Arnold Schwarzenegger movie *Jingle All the Way. The Dallas Morning News* lumped it in with his work in TV commercials. *Time* magazine's Hartman appreciation made no mention of *The Simpsons* at all (though it did find space to note that Hartman was to appear in the upcoming film *Small Soldiers*). Only *Newsday* hinted at the importance of his *Simpsons* appearances. 'His most lasting legacy,' the paper noted, 'may be in the prolific voice-over work Hartman did for animated films and television cartoons.' Even here, though, *The Simpsons* is downplayed, listed alongside *The Brave Little Toaster* and *Animaniacs* as but one of many voice-acting gigs that will last because they 'tend to be repeated even more than live-action programmes'.

Understand: Hartman's work on the show *is* his legacy. This is not just because *The Simpsons* is the most important and lasting of the shows on which Hartman appeared but because his voice-acting was the pinnacle achievement of his career. He is the exception to the rule that says major stars use *The Simpsons* as a tool for credibility-enhancing self-deprecation. *The Simpsons* didn't deprecate Hartman, but rather allowed him to elevate his acting to levels he never reached elsewhere. And to be a major contributor to *The Simpsons* is to make a permanent mark in the annals of pop culture. You will *not* remember him from such films as *Jingle All the Way* and *Small Soldiers*. You'll remember him as Lionel Hutz and Lyle Lanley and especially Troy McClure. And that is more than enough.

LOCAL HEROES

For the most part, the hell that simply must be Troy McClure's private life is merely hinted at. There's inherent desperation, for example, in his willingness to host the infomercial series 'I Can't Believe They Invented It!' and star in crass educational films like *Meat and You: Partners in Freedom*. Only one episode – 3F15 ('A Fish Called Selma') – gives us a sustained look at McClure's off-screen life, and in so doing it elevates McClure to a rarefied world inhabited by a select few Springfieldianite celebrities, foremost among them kiddie-television king Krusty the Clown, lunkheaded action-movie hero Rainier Wolfcastle and news anchor Kent Brockman. In Episode 3F15 McClure becomes a full-fledged member of Springfield's homegrown celebrity culture, a Hollywood in microcosm that over the years has been the show's most effective vehicle for satirising the real-world cult of celebrity.

The show's usual digs at real-life celebrity culture, no matter how sharp, are undermined by the simple fact that the celebrities themselves are expanding their own cults by appearing on *The Simpsons*, which has also enhanced the whole celebrity religion by creating such a hip, trusted, resonant institution for famous people to appear on. Nimoy may look like a bit of a buffoon on *The Simpsons* and Ernest Borgnine may be completely lost, but both of them have entered a higher plane of celebrity by appearing on the show. Does the Simpsonised Bob Hope look like a self-serving spotlight junkie as he hangs from the landing gear of a flying helicopter, asking to be set down at a boat show mere moments after escaping a riot at his Fort Springfield performance? Yes – but he seems far cooler than he's been since at least the Korean War.

Springfield's own celebrities, however, have no off-screen personas to bolster. Their Simpsonian likenesses are the only measure of their characters. Thus does Troy McClure emerge, in Episode 3F15, as a creature of pure, unrelenting egocentricity. He uses his dimmed star power to entice Selma into a date so she'll give him preferential treatment at the Department of Motor Vehicles. He's bored and mechanical until the paparazzi arrive, at which point he comes alive and kisses Selma on the cheek, hungry for the positive PR of being seen in public with a woman (even one as grotesque as Selma) to offset his widely rumoured penchant for engaging in strange sexual practices with sea creatures. In short order, he and Selma are an item, and a married couple soon after that, all so McClure can regain his Hollywood stardom. (He's soon fielding offers to star in a buddy comedy with 'sick freaks' Rob Lowe and Hugh Grant – both of whom had their real-life careers derailed by sexual indiscretions – and to play the sidekick in a major action flick.)

Throughout, McClure displays an unwavering self-absorption so complete it's almost artful. 'That's too funny!' he tells Selma, his braying, ready-for-the-soundstage diction accompanied by stage laughter. 'I can't remember when I've heard a funnier anecdote!' More smug, forced laughter. Then: 'All right, now you tell one.' Troy's 'on' in domestic moments, too, referring to practically everything as 'fantastic', including Selma's iguana, Jub-Jub, who he also claims (in a paraphrase of a credit-card commercial) is 'everywhere you want to be'. Even when Selma learns their marriage is a sham, McClure's commitment to the cult of celebrity is unshaken, and he persuades her that the celebrity life – going to the best parties, meeting famous people, just plain being a celebrity – makes it all worthwhile. 'Sure, you'll be a sham wife, but you'll be the envy of every other sham wife in town!' he reassures her. In the end, Selma can't live with the hollowness of it. She won't bring a child into their loveless marriage, even though her sham husband needs a child to land a big part. But McClure remains undeterred. First he suggests they adopt 'some kid who wants in on the deal', then he pops up on *Entertainment Tonight* as a 'newly divorced comeback kid' hawking his next project.

There it is, celebrity life: empty, emotionally manipulative, rabidly careerist. So ugly that not even cruel, cynical, love-starved Selma can stand it. The suggestion is that you would have to be as hopelessly deranged as Troy McClure to live in such a world. The show is not alone in portraying the lifestyles of the rich and famous this way: a string of movies throughout the 1990s engaged in just such self-flagellation. Robert Altman's dark satire *The Player* examined the moral connections between cold-blooded murder and the daily routine of a Hollywood producer. The jet-black *Swimming with Sharks* made this equivalency explicit, depicting a young wannabe player who tortures his producer boss and kills his girlfriend to get ahead in film production. Indeed the Hollywood-is-morally-and-emotionally-bankrupt theme has inspired something verging on a subgenre, with films like *Hurlyburly, State and Main, Living in Oblivion* and even period pieces (*L.A. Confidential, Barton Fink*) and the occasional lighthearted comedy (*Bowfinger*) all vying to present the most vicious portrayal possible of the star-making machine.

Watch many a Hollywood movie, read any old celebrity profile, view any of a number of episodes of *The Simpsons*, and you'll find the same argument: fame isn't all it's cracked up to be, and achieving and maintaining celebrity requires inhuman ruthlessness. This is no kind of goal to shoot for, kids. And yet, kind of like *The Simpsons'* simultaneous critiquing and elevating of celebrity, the message is received but doesn't stick. We laugh at McClure's venality, and still we worship the famous and yearn for some fame of our own. The cults of celebrity grow. And Krusty the Clown – burned-out, addiction-riddled, pacemaker-scarred Krusty, the biggest celebrity in Springfield – shows us many of the reasons why.

First off, there's no doubt about Krusty's place in the celebrity pantheon: he's the wizened veteran, the total pro, a kind of no-bullshit old-Hollywood yin to McClure's smooth-talking-flake yang. Evidence of Krusty's old-time professionalism is abundant: he's a stereotypical Jewish entertainer who keeps his faith hidden, a mensch's mensch who shows up at a beauty pageant thinking it's a Republican fundraiser, then bounds onstage the very next instant (his tie still undone) to hit his cue in the pageant's song-and-dance number. Here's a particularly telling example of the clown's status as consummate pro: Lisa is in a recording studio to tape the dialogue for the feminist talking doll she's helped create when Krusty comes barging in, a stack of cue cards in his hands. 'All right, you Poindexters,' he tells the sound technicians, 'let's get this right!' Then he's off at warp speed: 'One: Hey, hey, kids, I'm talking Krusty! Two: Hey, hey, here comes Slideshow Mel – again – Sideshow Mel. Sideshow Mel. Three' – he laughs his patented hyuh-yuh-yukking laugh, and then – 'Budda-bing, budda-boom, I'm done.' As he turns to leave, he tells Lisa, 'Learn from a professional, kid.'

More than this, though, Krusty is a monument to the promise of celebrity. He attends gala movie openings and awards shows, jets off to Wimbledon, organises benefit recordings, bets big on the ponies. He lives in a fabulous mansion, owns a private plane (the *I'm-on-a-Rolla Gay*) and once co-owned a racehorse (named 'Krudler') with Bette Midler. His high-rolling lifestyle sometimes reaches ridiculous heights: in one sequence, he lights his cigarettes with first a one-hundred-dollar bill, then an ultra-rare *Superman* comic, then a pearl necklace. (Never mind how he got the pearls to light, there, Poindexter.) As his aides follow him from dressing room to limo, he barks orders for yet more frivolous glamour: 'Put five thousand bucks on the Lakers . . . Hire Kenny G to play for me . . . My house is dirty – buy me a clean one.'

Krusty lives the celebrity life we all dream of, a life that's much like being a great big spoiled kid who finally has the unlimited resources every kid always wanted. Which is to say that Krusty lives the life we see on *Entertainment Tonight* and on the red carpets of awards shows and in the meticulously constructed 'in-depth profiles' that fill the pages of *In Style* and *Vanity Fair*. And so even if another set of media outlets – supermarket tabloids, post-rehab TV interviews, gossipy tell-all books – show us the high price of these posh lives (and even if Krusty's pacemaker scar and omnipresent cigarette and occasional binge-induced blackouts do the same on *The Simpsons*), we live with both sets of facts simultaneously. We want the former and reject the latter, and maybe we assume that if *we* had the former we wouldn't need the latter – who knows? – but at any rate we embrace this dual consciousness.

Episode 3F12 ('Bart the Fink') offers a pointed answer to the question of why such a manifestly miserable world of phonies and cheats would be so enticing to so many. In the episode, Krusty's ludicrously lavish lifestyle has finally got the better of him: he's caught in a tax dodge by the IRS. There's no jail time – 'This is America,' an IRS officer tells him, 'we don't send our celebrities to jail' – but even garnished wages and foreclosed property are more than Krusty can handle, so he fakes his own death. The ever-vigilant Simpson children, however, discover him working under an assumed name at Springfield's harbour. Bart and Lisa beg him to return to showbiz, but to no avail: Krusty has realised he doesn't need stacks of cash to be happy, he doesn't care if he disappoints his fans, he can survive without an entourage of phonies. Finally, though, they find his remaining soft spot. 'What about the great feeling that you get from knowing you're better than regular people?' Lisa taunts him. Bart: 'What about being an illiterate clown who's still more respected than all the scientists, doctors and educators in the country put together?' That's all it takes for Krusty to return to his celebrity life. *This* is what he can't live without: the status. And it's not really the money or the babes or the stuff for the rest of us, either. These things have their appeal, don't get me wrong, but if they alone were the hook, then there'd be far more people clamouring to get into the porn business. No, what's really alluring about the cult of celebrity is the idea that it can provide status, power, legitimacy, fulfilment. That being famous will, as the Springfieldianite's sign outside the Baldwin-Basinger estate said, complete us. This belief is what makes it a *cult*, a secular religion.

We can see the same echoes of this holy celebrity allure – the hope of deliverance to the promised land – in other Springfield stars. It's all over the place, for example, in Episode DABF06 ('The Bart Wants What It Wants'), which gives us a long look at the glamorous life of Rainier Wolfcastle. Wolfcastle's actually more like our world's celebrities than Krusty – a near-perfect mirror image of Arnold Schwarzenegger. And in DABF06, we learn he's living the same kind of enviable Hollywood lifestyle right in Springfield: he's got the big gated estate, the pretty daughter in private school, courtside seats at the basketball game, even a huge honking SUV – a Hummer, just like Arnie's – that's so powerful it can drive right *over* his estate's gates. In the episode, Bart starts dating Wolfcastle's daughter, Greta, offering both him and his father a chance to peek into the life of a star and find it far superior to their own. 'Everything in your house is *sooo* cool,' Bart tells Greta as he surveys her room, which is decorated with the props from Wolfcastle's movie *The Incredible Shrinking McBain*. Then they sprawl on Greta's super-sized bed and watch 'Itchy & Scratchy' on DVD on a giant flat-screen TV. Meanwhile, Wolfcastle accompanies Homer to good ole Moe's Tavern, which of course causes the pub's regulars to lose their star-struck minds. They surround Wolfcastle, peppering him with questions about the exotic minutiae of his life. 'Is it true that if I kill you I become you?' Moe asks in all seriousness. Wolfcastle, much too elite to waste his time conversing with commoners, brings in his authorised look-alike (Chuck, who lives in his trunk) to gratify his fans. And even that is enough: the illusion of quality time with a celebrity beats the humdrum lives of the hopelessly uncelebrated.

Even among Springfield's less prominent celebrities there remain vague traces of the sense of a life lived in a magically flawless world. In Channel 6 anchorman Kent Brockman's pompous demeanour and self-aggrandising work, we see hints of a life lived importantly, of underlings ordered about and public figures mingled with. (We see the same in our own broadcast journalists.) In Mayor Quimby's repeated dalliances with dizzy, curvaceous blondes and his cavorting with his Kennedy-esque brood, we see a modern aristocratic life, an enviable sense of entitlement, a life lived beyond the rules that govern the rest of us. And indeed even Springfield's very own oddball celebrity – Bumblebee Man – occasionally displays some of the trappings of fame: guest appearances on *Springfield Squares* and *Dawson's Creek,* hob-nobbing at a TV-industry function with the likes of Krusty, simply being on TV in the first place. There's enough there, in short – much as there is with your C-list celebs in the real world, all those Kato Kaelins and Mr Ts and Joan Riverses – to suggest that even such a laughable personage lives a more remarkable life than yours or mine.

This, in the end, is how celebrity hooks us every time. As idiotic as a famous person might be made to appear, there's still an intangible quality to the whole thing that's somehow enviable. I mean, for starters, who wouldn't want to be immortalised in an episode of *The Simpsons*?

NOTES & MARGINALIA

1. **Because 'Demi' is *so* 1993:** 'Rumer' and 'Scout' are among the 26 children of Cletus the slack-jawed yokel and his wife, Brandine. These kids are roll-called onto the front porch to sample Marge's pretzels in Episode 4F08 ('The Twisted World of Marge Simpson'), which originally aired in early 1997. Many of the remaining brood sport names that are either celebrity-derived (e.g. Cody and Cassidy, the names of Kathie Lee Gifford's famous-by-association kids) or generally trendy (e.g. Jordan, Kaitlin, Kendall) or simply goofy (e.g. Q-Bert).
2. **Freeze frame fun:** The endless abundance of celebrity scandal is spun into an excellent freeze-frame gag in Episode 2F15 ('Lisa's Wedding'). The episode features a flash-forward to 2010 – the time of Lisa's engagement to Hugh the English upper-class twit. Homer drags his daughter's fiancé to Moe's Tavern, where a TV set is tuned to the news on CNNBCBS (a division of ABC). 'And tonight,' Kent Brockman announces, 'the following celebrities have been arrested.' A list scrolls rapidly by: The Baldwin Brothers Gang, Dr Brad Pitt, John-John-John Kennedy, George Burns, Infamous Amos, Grandson of Sam, The Artist Formerly Known as [the symbol adopted by the Artist Formerly Known as Prince], Tim Allen, Jr., Senator and Mrs Dracula, The Artist Formerly Known as Buddy Hackett, Madonnabots:

Series K, Sideshow Ralph Wiggum, Martha Hitler, Johnny Neutrino.

3. **Are too, Bart:** The stark dissimilarity between the actress Nancy Cartwright and the smart-mouthed ten-year-old boy whose voice she provides has been mined for a gag or two. In the credits of a Season 2 episode, for example, Bart's chalkboard lines read, 'I am not a 32-year-old woman.'

4. **Full disclosure:** I spent the summer of 1996 working at the Starbucks next door to the Four Seasons Hotel in Toronto, which is the preferred accommodation in the city for the majority of celebrities. I thus became quite intimate with the phenomenon of a passing encounter with a Hollywood icon, as I served lattes and such that summer to Rob Lowe, Martin Sheen, Dennis Miller, Sarah McLachlan, the guy who plays Paul on *The Young and the Restless*, and three of the four original members of KISS, among others.

5. *Simpsons* **shocker!** Among the behind-the-scenes scandals and gaffes detailed in Episode BABF19 are these:

• Homer develops a painkiller addiction after sustaining injuries filming the scene in which he jumps Springfield Gorge on a skateboard ('Fame was like a drug,' he explains, 'but what was even more like a drug were the drugs').

• Marge squanders the family fortune on an ill-conceived line of birth-control products ('When people reach for their diaphragm, they don't want to see my picture!' Marge admits).

• Bart gets into a scuffle with Hawaiian Airlines flight attendants on the way home from judging a Miss Hawaiian Tropic contest.

• The whole Simpson clan gets into an onstage brawl at the Iowa State Fair.

• Lisa publishes a tell-all memoir entitled *Where Are My Residuals?*

6. *Old* **Man Burns Redux:** Pity poor old Monty Burns – emphasis, as usual, on *old* – who in 'Homer at the Bat' can't get the stars he really wants because they're all dead. Burns's softball dream team includes Honus Wagner (shortstop, Pittsburgh Pirates, 1900–17), Mordecai 'Three-Finger' Brown (pitcher, Chicago Cubs, 1904–12), and a right fielder who's been six feet under for 130 years. Disappointed but undaunted, Burns dispatches Smithers to scour the professional leagues – American, National and Negro (final season: 1952) – for more lively ringers.

7. **Simpsonian Soviet realism:** Before the newcomer Gabbo causes Krusty's cancellation, he poaches the beloved clown's main attraction: 'The Itchy & Scratchy Show.' This sets up a stellar *Simpsons* one-off gag, as Krusty is forced to resort to broadcasting a cut-rate cartoon: 'Eastern Europe's favourite cat-and-mouse team, 'Worker & Parasite'!' The cubistically rendered cat and mouse bob past backdrops of abstract art and bread lines, babbling to each other in a series of guttural bleeps and blips to a tinny soundtrack that seems lifted from a grim 1930s movie about the Stalinist purges. The closing credits read: 'Endut! Hoch Hech!' Cut to Krusty, cigarette dangling derisively from his mouth: 'What the hell was that?'

8. **The Ramones steal the show:** With very little lead-up or fanfare, The Ramones appear in Episode 1F01 ('Rosebud') to deliver the best musical performance by a guest star in *Simpsons* history. The gig: Mr Burns's birthday party. Burns is already in horrible spirits when the legendary punk band takes the stage, introduced by Smithers in the style of The Beatles' legendary *Ed Sullivan* debut ('Here are several fine young men who I'm sure are gonna go far'). 'Ah,' Burns enthuses, 'these minstrels will soothe my jangled nerves.' Not quite: after announcing that the gig sucks, The Ramones count off one-two-three-four and deliver a wicked-quick and wicked-fun punk version of 'Happy Birthday'. Then, as the curtain falls, a band member addresses Burns directly: 'Go to hell, you old bastard!' Burns, disgusted, turns to Smithers. 'Have the Rolling Stones killed!' he orders. Smithers starts to correct him. Burns cuts him off: 'Do as I say!' No doubt Mick Jagger slept fitfully that night.

9. **Hullabalooza rocks:** The London Symphony Orchestra joins Cypress Hill for a few short bars of a symphonised version of 'Insane in the Brain', which turns out surprisingly funky. Sonic Youth later contributes a closing-credits take on *The Simpsons* – syncopated, punkified and awash in guitar feedback – that is, for my money, the coolest version of the show's theme to date. My choice for runner-up: Yo La Tengo's psychedelic take on the *Simpsons* theme in Episode AABF02 ('Do'h-in' in the Wind').

10. **Musical bait 'n' switch:** Later in Lisa's meeting with the McCartneys, Paul asks her if she'd like to hear a song. 'Wow! That would be great!' Lisa replies. 'Okay!' says the Cute One. 'Take it, Apu!' And so Apu does, belting out a mangled version of 'Sgt. Pepper's Lonely Hearts Club Band', accompanying himself on a bongo as Paul and Linda bop along contentedly. It's as good a monument as any to *The Simpsons*' stubborn refusal to let its celebrity guests steal the spotlight.

11. **Everybody loves poets laureate:** Robert Pinsky's generous treatment in his *Simpsons* guest appearance may well have been the product of a mutual admiration society formed between Pinsky and the show's writers. In 1998, while he was poet laureate of the United States, Pinsky penned a short love letter to *The Simpsons* in *The New York Times Magazine*. Entitled 'My Favourite Show', Pinsky's article described the show as 'brilliantly written for masterful voice actors' and argued that it 'penetrates to the nature of television itself'. Three years later, *The Simpsons* returned the favour with its poet-as-rock-star treatment of Pinsky.

12. **Maggie's other lines:** Maggie has spoken on four other occasions – twice in dream sequences and twice in Halloween episodes:

- Dream Sequence No. 1: In Episode 7F07 ('Bart vs. Thanksgiving'), Bart imagines returning home to a hostile family after ruining Thanksgiving. In his fantasy, Maggie removes her pacifier and growls, 'It's your fault I can't talk!'

- Dream Sequence No. 2: In Episode 8F08 ('Flaming Moe's'), Homer wanders in a daze through a waking dream in which everyone he encounters – including Maggie – repeats the word 'Moe' over and over.

- Halloween Episode No. 1: In one segment of Episode 2F03 ('Treehouse of Horror V'), Homer's toaster becomes a time machine that transports him to strange parallel universes. In one of them, he returns from the basement to find Maggie at the top of the stairs. She pops her omnipresent pacifier out of her mouth and speaks. 'This is indeed a disturbing universe,' she says, her voice rendered in the deep, ominous baritone of another A-list guest star: James Earl Jones.

- Halloween Episode No. 2: In Episode AABF01 ('Treehouse of Horror IX'), one segment centres on the revelation that Maggie is the daughter of the tentacled, perpetually drooling alien Kang as part of a cross-fertilisation experiment. The whole gang – the Simpson family, the now-tentacled Maggie and the aliens (proud dad Kang and his buddy Kodos) – take their weird love triangle to *The Jerry Springer Show*, where chaos and destruction ensue. Afterwards, the Simpsons trick the aliens into leaving Maggie with them. 'Come on, Maggie,' says Homer. 'Let's go home.' 'Very well,' Maggie answers in Kang's voice. 'I'll drive!' She laughs menacingly, and over the closing credits she mutters, 'I need blood.' The voice work this time is by a regular *Simpsons* cast member: Harry Shearer, long-time voice of Kang.

13. *The Critic*'s critic: Jon Lovitz's movie critic, Jay Sherman, was the title character in the closest thing *The Simpsons* has had to a spin-off: *The Critic*, a cartoon produced by former (and future) *Simpsons* staffers Al Jean and Mike Reiss. *The Critic* debuted on ABC in January 1994 and ran for half a season before being cancelled. The following year, *Simpsons* executive producer James L. Brooks moved the show to Fox, relaunching it in the coveted time slot immediately after *The Simpsons* in March 1995 with much fanfare – and a shameless plug from the Simpsons themselves in Episode 2F31 ('A Star is Burns'), in which Sherman comes to Springfield to judge the town's inaugural film festival. As Sherman arrives in Springfield, we find Bart watching TV. 'Coming up next,' a voice-over announces, '*The Flintstones* meet *The Jetsons*.' 'Uh-oh,' says Bart. 'I smell another cheap cartoon crossover.' On cue, Homer walks in with Sherman in tow. 'Hey, man,' Bart greets him. 'I really love your show. I think *all* kids should watch it!' He turns away in shame. 'Eww, I suddenly feel so dirty,' he mutters.

Despite the self-parodic sugar-coating, this cheap cartoon crossover provoked unprecedented rage from Matt Groening, who had his name removed from the episode's credits in protest. He explained his anger in a press release: 'For more than six months, I tried to convince Jim Brooks and everyone connected with the show not to do such a cynical thing, which would surely be perceived by the fans as nothing more than a pathetic attempt to do nothing more than advertise *The Critic* at the expense of the integrity of *The Simpsons*.'

Brooks, for his part, told a reporter that Groening's concerns had led to changes in the *Simpsons* tie-in episode (such as Bart's declaration of his dirtiness, perhaps?). Groening, Brooks added, 'is a gifted, adorable, cuddly ingrate. But his behavior right now is rotten. And it's not pretty when a rich man acts like this.'

In the end, *The Critic* failed to click with *Simpsons* fans. It was moved from its plum time slot after only five episodes and cancelled for good in May 1995.

CHAPTER TEN

The Simpsons Through The Looking Glass

What strikes me is the fact that in our society, art has become something which is only related to objects, and not to individuals, or to life.

Michel Foucault

Oh, Marge, cartoons don't have any deep meaning. They're just stupid drawings that give you a cheap laugh.
  Homer Simpson, Episode 8F01 ('Mr. Lisa Goes to Washington')

AS BART SIMPSON ONCE PUT it, 'The ironing is delicious.'

'The word is "irony",' Lisa promptly replied, but that's not important. What's important is that in Episode 3F08 ('Sideshow Bob's Last Gleaming'), Bart's arch-nemesis, Sideshow Bob, tries to eradicate television from the Springfield landscape. The first of many layers of ironing – uh, irony – in 3F08 is that Bob, TV's would-be destroyer, takes up this task only after his fellow prisoners at Springfield Minimum Security Prison are set to laughing so uproariously by *The Krusty the Clown Show* – the show that made Bob famous – that shockwaves from the laughter destroy the miniature model of Westminster Abbey Bob had been building inside a bottle. As he decries the braying of the infernal TV, one of his fellow prisoners points out, 'You used to be on this show.' 'Don't remind me,' Bob fumes. 'My foolish capering destroyed more young minds than syphilis and pinball combined. Oh, how I loathe that box. An omnidirectional sludge pump, droning and burping . . .' Another prisoner, looking suspiciously like Rupert Murdoch, takes offence, but it deters Bob not one bit. The first chance he gets, he escapes from his prison work detail – as it happens, at Springfield's air force base during the annual air show. He steals a ten-megaton nuclear weapon and commandeers the big-screen TV next to the grandstand to inform the crowd of his fiendishly altruistic scheme: 'I've stolen a nuclear weapon. If you do not rid this city of television within two hours, I will detonate it.' The screen clicks off. A one-beat pause, and it clicks back on. 'By the way,' he adds, 'I'm aware of the irony of appearing on TV in order to decry it. So don't bother pointing that out.'

Okily-dokily, Bob. But what about the irony of being the former star of a TV show that is itself buried within a TV cartoon, and appearing on a TV screen in an episode of that cartoon in order to decry TV? Can you decode the many layers of irony that intersect at Escher-like angles in *that* situation? Bob?

Bob's far too busy to reply, actually: he spends the rest of the episode cramming in yet more irony. It falls to Bart and Lisa to foil his plan, of course, because Simpsonian formula dictates that they always muck up his criminal plots. Naturally, there's a dramatic final chase scene – which, extra-ironically, occurs at extra-slow speed because Bob's flying the Wright brothers' plane. And of course the chase ends in a calamitous crash and Bob's arrest and the gathering of practically the whole cast, the way criminal plots always end on TV. 'How ironic,' a manacled Bob notes. 'My crusade against television has come to an end so formulaic it could have spewed from the PowerBook of the laziest Hollywood hack.' Just then, Abe Simpson pulls up on a motorcycle and announces, 'Hey, everybody! I'm gonna haul ass to Lollapalooza!' – an echo of a line Bob had overheard earlier on a horrible, formulaic sitcom, which had added fuel to his rage at the omnidirectional sludge pump in the first place.

This episode of *The Simpsons*, then, ends with a broad parody of Hollywood formula to underscore the futility of a character's efforts to destroy TV on a TV show, and then adds a coda in which another character acts out the same formulaic ending that had appeared on a TV set on this TV show as a paramount example of TV formula. If this is starting to give you a headache, that's perfectly understandable.

The Simpsons, it's clear, has much to say about a wide range of topics, but its most detailed social commentary is about itself: about the show's own conventions, the standard tropes and formulas of TV shows generally, the way the entertainment and news industries function, the machinations of the mass media, the nature of TV as a medium and the society it has created in its all-pervasive image. Simpsonian satire is a mirror held up to society, and that mirror is frequently set opposite a TV screen – itself a kind of cultural mirror. The two mirrors double and redouble each other, creating an image of infinity – a media vortex. A glimpse, that is, of the parallel universe that is modern media culture and a potent metaphor for the trap media culture creates. *The Simpsons* gives us an accurate reflection of the mass media – a mediascape in Springfieldianite miniature – and in that reflection there is virtually no meaning at all. All of it is spectacle, and most of it is monumentally dumb, and to be trapped in this hall of mirrors is to become immersed in a deeply distorted version of reality.

In the eighteenth century, the utilitarian philosopher Jeremy Bentham drew up plans for the Panopticon, a vast prison complex carefully constructed so that a single observer – a lone guard – could watch any prisoner anywhere in the complex while remaining unseen at all times. A prisoner in the Panopticon would know he could be seen by his jailer anywhere at any time, but he would never know for certain when he was being watched. 'Hence,' in Michel Foucault's summation of Bentham's invention,

> the major effect of the Panopticon: to induce in the inmate a state of conscious and permanent visibility that assures the automatic functioning of power. So to arrange things that the surveillance is permanent in its effects, even if it is discontinuous in its action; that the perfection of power should tend to render

its actual exercise unnecessary; that this architectural apparatus should be a machine for creating and sustaining a power relation independent of the person who exercises it; in short, that the inmates should be caught up in a power situation of which they are themselves the bearers.

Let's graft this concept of the Panopticon onto Aldous Huxley's vision of our *Brave New World*. Think of Huxley's soma not as a drug that's ingested but as an all-pervasive narcotic force called the mass media, and you begin to wonder if the Panopticon functions not by allowing our captors to watch us but by allowing us to constantly watch ourselves. Or, more precisely, to watch some idealised version of ourselves that has become more compelling to us than our own lives. As Huxley would have it, the greatest threat to freedom in our time is not the authoritarian Big Brother prophesied by George Orwell in *1984* but our own lust for leisure and distraction. In the foreword to his 1985 book, *Amusing Ourselves to Death: Public Discourse in the Age of Show Business*, media theorist Neil Postman wrote:

> What Orwell feared were those who would ban books. What Huxley feared was that there would be no reason to ban a book, for there would be no one who wanted to read one. Orwell feared those who would deprive us of information. Huxley feared those who would give us so much that we would be reduced to passivity and egoism. Orwell feared that the truth would be concealed from us. Huxley feared the truth would be drowned in a sea of irrelevance. Orwell feared we would become a captive culture. Huxley feared we would become a trivial culture, preoccupied with some equivalent of the feelies, the orgy porgy, and the centrifugal bumblepuppy.

Postman took stock of Western society's enormous entertainment apparatus and reckoned that Huxley might have been the more prescient of the two writers.

It's more or less the same story in Springfield, although you're not likely to find eggheads like Postman and Foucault to guide you through it – not even down at the Springfield Knowledgeum. Check out the Knowledgeum's welcome kiosk, though, and you will find someone up there on the big-screen TV who knows more than most about the vast trivialising wastelands of the contemporary mass media. 'Welcome to the Springfield Knowledgeum,' the honey-voiced actor intones. 'I'm Troy McClure! You may remember me from such automated information kiosks as Welcome to Springfield Airport and Where's Nordstrom?'

You may remember him, actually, from a lot of things.

THE SPRINGFIELD MEDIASCAPE (I): A VAST, VAST, VAST WASTELAND (VAST)

If Springfield didn't have as broad a mediascape as it does – if it didn't have Krusty the Clown and 'Itchy & Scratchy,' if it didn't boast McBain movies and *MacGyver*, if there was no Channel 6 Action News with Kent Brockman and no *Springfield Shopper* on the doorstep every morning – even if none of this existed, you might still be able extrapolate everything you need to know about the nature of the mass media from the extraordinary acting career of Troy McClure. Every time he appeared on a TV screen in Springfield – which was often, until Phil Hartman's death robbed him of his voice – McClure invariably introduced another trio of titles to his résumé: two clunkers he suggested you might remember him from, and then whatever craptacular spectacle he was currently appearing in. The titles alone testify to the existence of a showbiz Hydra that can boast nary a single brain. You might remember McClure from such movies as *Today We Kill, Tomorrow We Die* and *Gladys, The Groovy Mule*. You might remember him from such TV series as *Buck Henderson, Union Buster* and *Troy & Company's Summertime Smile Factory*, or from such cartoons as *Christmas Ape* and *Christmas Ape Goes to Summer Camp*. You might remember him from such Fox Network specials as *Alien Nose Jobs* and *Five Fabulous Weeks of The Chevy Chase Show*, or from such *Simpsons* episodes as 'The Simpsons 138th Episode Spectacular' (Episode 3F31) and 'The Simpsons Spin-off Showcase' (Episode 4F20).[1]

The last three of these credits refer to actual shows – to Fox's disastrous, dead-on-arrival talk show starring Chevy Chase, which lasted all of six weeks in autumn 1993, and to two episodes of *The Simpsons* hosted by McClure. With McClure's work – as with much of *The Simpsons'* satirical mediascape – the line between parody and documentary is so thin it might as well be invisible. It's hard to imagine that *Summertime Smile Factory* is any worse than *The Chevy Chase Show*, and McClure's smarmy persona needn't be altered one bit in order to move from hosting *Carnival of the Stars* on Homer Simpson's TV to hosting a retrospective episode of *The Simpsons* on ours. McClure serves the show's verisimilitude as well as its satire.

Consider his memorable appearance in Episode 8F12 ('Lisa the Greek'), in which he pops up during the Super Bowl pre-game show as Homer looks on from the Simpson living room. McClure and sportscaster Brent Gunsilman engage in some highly scripted pretend banter:

Brent: We've got ourselves a special guest: actor Troy McClure, whose new sitcom is premiering tonight. Coincidentally enough, right

> after the game!
>
> Troy: Thanks, Brent. My new show is called *Handle with Care.* I play Jack
>   Handle, a retired cop who shares an apartment with a retired
>   criminal. We're the original odd couple!
>
> Brent: What made you want to do a situation comedy?
>
> Troy: Well, I fell in love with the script, Brent. And my recent trouble
>   with the IRS sealed the deal!

Now, almost everything in this exchange could easily be true. On the title-as-bad-pun-on-protagonist's-name spectrum, *Handle with Care* falls somewhere between the 1980s TV drama *Magnum, P.I.* and the 1991 B-movie *Eve of Destruction* (about a sexy female cyborg named Eve implanted with a nuclear bomb). The only satirical nod is McClure's lapse into over-honesty at the end. McClure pops up plugging some dimwitted, overhyped post-game dreck, and it only makes the Simpsonian Super Bowl seem more authentic. It gives us a shock not of absurdity but of recognition.

The same dynamic governs McClure's myriad other appearances on *The Simpsons*, whether it's another instalment of the cornball infomercial *I Can't Believe They Invented It!* or a low-budget educational film being shown to the kids at Springfield Elementary. To be sure, McClure's consistently abysmal oeuvre has provided the show with many splendid satirical moments. The Meat Council-produced, McClure-hosted educational film *Meat and You: Partners in Freedom*, for example, is a brilliant lampoon of industry-sponsored teaching aides. And it also manages – in a few quick scenes – to take well-aimed satirical jabs at: (1) the sloppy work ethic of the fading movie idol (McClure erroneously refers to his youthful co-star as 'Bobby' and tousels his hair to the point of the boy's discomfort); (2) the sly means by which propagandists frame the terms of a debate ('I have a crazy friend who says it's wrong to eat meat – is he crazy?' asks little Bobby – er, Jimmy); and (3) the sporadic and garbled relationship that exists between big business, the media and the scientific community ('Just ask this scientician,' McClure intones by way of explaining the scientific inevitability of meat consumption, then a cutaway to a guy in a lab coat who blurts, 'Uhhh . . .,' then back to McClure).

McClure's real value, though, is his ubiquity. It's not just an infomercial or cheesy sitcom; it's infomercial *and* cheesy sitcom – and TV-movie-of-the-week and feature film and educational film and telethon and information kiosk. And McClure's only the most visible tip of the great mindless iceberg of Springfield's entertainment-industrial complex. Much as the cartoon format has allowed *The Simpsons* the liberty of dozens of settings per episode and intercontinental travel on the slightest whim, it also provides a literally bottomless well of possibilities for media parody. An episode might open with a snippet of *Star Trek XII: So Very Tired* or a brawny, brainless action movie. Bart's adventures as an errand boy for the Springfield Mafia are transformed by the end of the episode into an exploitive TV-movie-of-the-week called *Blood on the Blackboard: The Bart Simpson Story*, starring a bad-assed Neil Patrick Harris of *Doogie Howser, M.D.* fame as Bart and Joe Mantegna as Fat Tony the Mob boss.[2] Homer wanders into a scene from *Cheers*, complete with the lovable drunk Norm brandishing a broken bottle at the boyish bartender Woody as he snarls, 'Just give me a beer, you brain-dead hick!' Homer's father, Abe, watches a TV commercial for Buzz Cola in which Springfield's favourite soft drink turns old people young (*à la* several early-1990s Pepsi ads), and then he acts out the truth behind the hype. 'The bubbles are burning my tongue!' Abe bellows after one sip of the fizzy stuff. On *The Simpsons*, there's an entire second plane of existence, a mediascape as fully rendered and exquisitely detailed as the regular landscape.

Compare this aspect of *The Simpsons* to one of the few contemporary TV comedies that was truly in its league: *Seinfeld*. Like *The Simpsons*, *Seinfeld* trafficked heavily in astute observation and social commentary; unlike *The Simpsons*, *Seinfeld* rarely transcended its own myopic universe to fix its keen eye on the world outside New York's Upper West Side. Limited by live-action realities of budget and logistics, *Seinfeld* could only allude to the mediascape that surrounded its cynical New Yorkers on all sides. The *Seinfeld* gang habitually attended movies, for example, but we rarely learned anything more than their titles and perhaps a tagline: *Prognosis: Negative, Chunnel, Brown-Eyed Girl, Rochelle, Rochelle* ('A young girl's strange, erotic journey from Milan to Minsk'). Parodic movie titles were, on the other hand, merely our introduction to Troy McClure – the teaser before the short children's film about human sexuality or the detailed guide to our stay at Rancho Relaxo. *The Simpsons* could bring its mediascape all the way into the foreground, and then go anywhere it wanted with it.

Fortunately, its creators have always been fully aware of how rare this gift is, and have used it to its full potential, cramming the show with spectacles and diversions. Sometimes, they simply provide background clutter – such is the case with the titles on the marquee at the Springfield Googolplex, the names of videogames in the background at Bart's favourite arcade, the few seconds of TV that Homer's watching before a given episode's plot intervenes. There might be a videogame called *Larry the Looter* or – better –

Time Waster. At the movie theatre, Homer might be keen to see *Look Who's Oinking,* or Faye Dunaway and Pauly Shore might be together at last in *Honk If You're Horny!* 'Finally,' a voice-over intones as Bart idly watches TV, 'the great taste of Worcestershire Sauce – in a soft drink!' We hear a random consumer saying, 'Ahhh – steaky!' and then Homer comes in and switches the channel to *School of Hard Knockers,* an *Animal House* knock-off starring Corey Masterson. The Simpson family's media environment is as lush as our own.

The constant parade of mindless showbiz tidbits also offers *The Simpsons'* writers endless opportunities for a riff or three on the idiocy of modern entertainment spectacles. In Episode 7F03 ('Bart Gets an F'), for example, Homer and Bart watch a movie called *Gorilla the Conqueror* – part of 'Big Gorilla Week' on some third-rate cable-TV channel. Over the years, a wide range of simian-themed amusements have rounded out this caricature of Hollywood's penchant for recycling: *Gorilla Squadron, Gorilla Island VI, Apes-A-Poppin', Sing Monkey Sing, Hail to the Chimp, Editor-in-Chimp, MTC: Monkey Trauma Center,* even the Monkey Olympics live on Fox. Bart's love of violent videogames has inspired a similar riff, with Springfield's arcades and consoles and department-store shelves abounding in titles like *Bonestorm, Disemboweler IV, Escape from Death Row, Touch of Death, Robert Goulet Destroyer* and *A Streetcar Named Death.*

The Simpsonian video game industry also illustrates how the multiple and frequently crisscrossing vectors of the show's media satire collide. There's one memorable incidental gag, for example, in which we find Martin, the overachieving alpha geek from Bart's class, engrossed in a game of *My Dinner with Andre* at the Playland Arcade. There are two crude, blocky characters on the screen, sitting motionless on opposite sides of a table. One speaks: 'Thirsting for a way to name the unnameable, to express the inexpressible?' Martin, totally fascinated, gives a mild push on his joystick, saying, 'Tell me more!' Bart, meanwhile, is blowing away his opponents in *Panamanian Strongman.* When one of them finally gets the drop on him and his bullet-lacerated body falls to the ground, an electronic George H.W. Bush trots onscreen and announces, 'Winners don't use drugs!' In a couple of passing details, *The Simpsons'* writers have used video games as a vehicle for ironic and/or parodic references to existentialist art-house cinema and the hypocritical relationship between the US government and Manuel Noriega's Panama, all the while maintaining the integrity of the surface parody of the crude graphics and themes of 1980s-vintage arcade games.

There's a similar depth and variety to the satirical uses of another seeming one-note parody: the acting career of Rainier Wolfcastle. Wolfcastle initially appears on *The Simpsons* in the guise of McBain, the eponymous hero of a string of superlatively stoopid action movies. The first of these, which appears at the start of a Season 2 episode, is a broad spoof, but later snippets of the McBain franchise usually include some marvellous unexpected details. We might, for example, find McBain flying a fighter jet with UNICEF markings against his 'Commie Nazi' foes. But the real McBain-inspired fun comes when he ventures Schwarzenegger-like into other genres. In one episode, for example, McBain becomes the star of his own late-night talk show, *Up Late with McBain*, a few seconds of which quickly reveal that he is homophobic, crypto-fascistic and painfully unfunny. In another episode, he tries his hand at stand-up comedy in *McBain: Let's Get Silly* – setting up a great one-off gag about the decadence of the film industry as Wolfcastle tells a film reviewer, 'The film is just me in front of a brick wall for an hour and a half. It cost $80 million.'[3]

The Springfield mediascape adds layers of realistic detail to *The Simpsons* and lays at the writers' feet an extensive arsenal of satirical weapons for attacking the moronic mass media from almost any angle. And its flexibility has allowed the show to thrash away repeatedly at certain minor targets that must seem particularly loathsome to the show's writers. Let's take a quick look at these before we get to some of the more ambitious stuff in the show's media critique.

THE SPRINGFIELD MEDIASCAPE (II): PET PEEVES

Several times in *The Simpsons'* run, the show has taken easy – if well-aimed – shots at *Mad* magazine, the once-venerable humour magazine that hasn't been relevant since the early 1970s. A couple of the show's digs even take note of this best-before date. For instance, Bart reads the title of a *Mad* feature – 'The Lighter Side of Hippies' – and giggles darkly. 'They don't care whose toes they step on!' he observes. Another time, Bart and Milhouse flip through a 'Special Edition' of *Mad* down at the Android's Dungeon. 'Boy!' Milhouse enthuses. 'They're really sockin' it to that Spiro Agnew guy again – he must work there or something.'

Similarly, it sometimes seems like the majority of the show's writers are obsessed with kicking around long-dead carcasses, or came to the show direct from the overworked crew of a Broadway spectacle, inasmuch as the show has on numerous occasions beaten the ever-loving shit out of the musical (in both its theatrical and cinematic forms). Barely an episode goes by without one Springfieldianite or other breaking into song, and often as not the whole town joins in for a big ole piss-taking song-and-dance number. When Bart and Milhouse get all hepped up on an all-syrup squishee, they go crazy Broadway-style with a big production number about their hometown. Apu, meanwhile, tries to sing away his blues over losing his job at the Kwik-E-Mart, and the whole Simpson family joins in to help him. Elsewhere, Lyle Lanley sells Springfield on the monorail with a song, and the proprietress of the Maison Derrière (Springfield's burlesque house) saves her establishment from destruction using a persuasively catchy tune with a chorus that boasts, 'We put the "spring" in Springfield!' There have also been a few digs at the Disney-style animated musical, including episode-length parodies of *101 Dalmatians* and *Mary Poppins*.

But if the writers hate musicals so much, why are *Simpsons* characters so prone to bursting into song? As Homer Simpson laments upon discovering that the Clint Eastwood–Lee Marvin film *Paint Your Wagon* is a musical, 'Oh, why did they have to ruin a perfectly serviceable wagon story with all that fruity singing?' The answer begins with the episode in which Homer poses that query: 5F24 ('All Singing, All Dancing'), which is given over to recounting the show's many fine musical moments from past seasons. When songs spring up one at a time, you might notice a clever line or two, or the way that they serve the same kind of plot-advancing, energy-generating purposes they do in *Singin' in the Rain* or *Cats*. But piled together in 5F24, they amount to a sort of Simpsonian side project: *Springfield: The Musical*. And – here's the real crux of it – it's a very impressive side project at that.

That's the thing about the show's song-and-dance numbers: even though they're excellent piss-takes, they often cross the line from kitschy parody of a near-dead art form into a sort of skilled ironic revival of same. Musically, they're merely solid, but their lyrics are usually wildly inventive. For example, the centrepiece of the *101 Dalmatians* lampoon – Episode 2F18 ('Two Dozen and One Greyhounds') – is an ode to the great white hunter called 'See My Vest', sung by Mr Burns to the tune of 'Be My Guest' (the signature song from Disney's *Beauty and the Beast*). The first verse goes: 'See my vest, see my vest / Made from real gorilla chest / Feel this sweater, there's no better / Than authentic Irish setter/ See this hat, 'twas my cat / My evening wear, vampire bat / These white slippers are albino / African endangered rhino.' It goes on like this – brilliantly, gleefully, hilariously. Lyle Lanley's 'Monorail Song', meanwhile, includes call-and-response verses consisting of the townsfolk's questions and Lanley's slick replies. 'Is there a chance the track could bend?' Apu calls. 'Not on your life, my Hindu friend!' Lanley responds. Thus do the songs on *The Simpsons* justify their own existence. In the process of poking some fun at the musical's conventions – at the clunky way characters break into song and the goofy germaneness of the lyrics, for example – the song-and-dance numbers have inspired some of the show's most exuberant comic moments.

This is particularly true of the recurrent and remarkably thorough satirical eviscerations of the big-budget Broadway musical on *The Simpsons*. Much as the worst subjects often inspire the finest critical writing (movie critics, for example, are often at their wittiest when they're trashing a movie[4]), *The Simpsons'* spoofs of Broadway have repeatedly inspired moments of genius. Mark 'Luke Skywalker' Hamill's performance of a number called 'Luke, Be a Jedi Tonight' (to the tune of 'Luck Be a Lady') in a godawful, bowdlerised dinner-theatre production of *Guys and Dolls*? A triumph! A sci-fi musical called *Stop the Planet of the Apes, I Want to Get Off!*, with Troy McClure performing 'Dr Zaius' (to the tune of Falco's cheeseball 1980s chart-topper 'Rock Me Amadeus') and a big song-and-dance finale that begins 'I hate every ape I see / From chimpan-A to chimpanzee'? A tour de force! And finally there's *Oh! Streetcar!* in Episode 8F18 ('A Streetcar Named Marge'). 'New OR-lee-ans!' goes the chorus of the curtain-raising song, inventing a new pronunciation for that storied city. 'Home of pirates, drunks, and whores! / New OR-lee-ans! / Tacky, overpriced souvenir stores!' A few scenes later, we find Apu playing Steve – the 'humble newsie' – and singing about the unwanted advances of Blanche – the 'bewitching floozie'. Later still, there's Blanche herself flying through the air on a wire as lasers and smoke fill the stage. And in the last scene comes the masterstroke: 'The Kindness of Strangers', an upbeat, full-cast production number that turns Blanche's grim statement of existential yearning – 'I have always depended on the kindness of strangers' – into a rousing, greeting-card-ready chorus. 'A stranger's just a friend you haven't met!' the cast of *Oh! Streetcar!* sings en masse. And the satirical annihilation of Andrew Lloyd Webber's oeuvre is by this point sort of incidental.

The Simpsons' frequent assaults on the blaring banality of North American commercial radio might seem to be another case of absurdly excessive satirical force. Who, after all, would make a case *for* the generically 'wacky' banter of the North American FM-radio disc jockey so mercilessly lampooned at Springfield's own KBBL Radio by the team of Bill and Marty? Even in a media industry that includes a worn-out Krusty the Clown and a sitcom entitled *Ethnic Mismatch Comedy #644!*, Bill and Marty are the undisputed kings of bottom-feeding comedy. They rely on novelty hits, crank calls and canned sound effects (arooga horns and slide whistles and even flushing toilets) to get their laughs. Their idea of topical political satire is a gag about how Bill Clinton launched a website whose address is www-dot-(wolf-whistle sound effect)-dot-(boinging-spring sound effect). The closest they get to real sting is when they sneeringly dismiss Bart in Episode 1F11 ('Bart Gets Famous') because people are no longer tickled by the catchphrase he employs on *The Krusty the Clown Show*. 'Boy, did *that* get old fast!' Bill brays. 'Whoa! You know, if you want to last in this business, you've gotta stay fresh!' And then come the unmistakeable sounds of a slide whistle and a clown's bleating horn – both of them trademarks of the vaudeville era.

We're presented with the *reductio ad absurdum* of Bill and Marty's brand of humour in Episode 1F15 ('Bart Gets an Elephant'), in which this undynamic duo become victims of their own laboured schtick. As part of their 'lucky phone call' contest, they promise on the air to give away either $10,000 or 'something styooooopid' – a gag prize of an African elephant. When Bart wins the contest and demands the elephant, however, Bill and Marty are stuck: there is no elephant. Bart's frustrated desire for a pachyderm soon becomes a *cause célèbre* in Springfield, and Bill and Marty find themselves called before their boss, who threatens to replace them with an automated music-selection system called the DJ 3000. 'It has three distinct varieties of inane chatter,' says the boss. She presses a button on the contraption, and it begins to speak in an electronic monotone. 'Those clowns in congress did it again,' drones the DJ 3000. 'What a bunch of clowns.' Bill chuckles heartily. 'How does it keep up with the news like that?' he marvels.

Bill and Marty are the Simpsonian embodiment of white noise. They are allegedly based on an nationally syndicated American radio programme called *The Don and Mike Show*, but that's not important; what's important is that Bill and Marty are *everywhere*. There's not a car in North America without a radio, and not an urban radio market in North America without a station that builds its broadcast day around a duo or trio or quartet of mediocre comedians labouring their way through a few hours of forced wackiness during rush hour every day.

This is not the best or most famous or even the loudest or crudest stuff on the radio. That last title would go to radio host Howard Stern, who himself has come in for the odd parody or two on *The Simpsons*. In one episode, for example, Bart reveals himself to be a fan of a Stern-like show called *Jerry Rude and the Bathroom Bunch*. American radio fixtures like the right-wing blowhard Rush Limbaugh (viz. Birch Barlow, his Simpsonian alter ego) and Paul Harvey, the master of middle-of-the-road folksiness (who appears in Springfield as himself) have also taken a few blows. These radio mainstays, though, have their own unique styles with their own unique merits and faults. Stern may be a talentless vulgarian or a gifted iconoclast (I lean a bit towards the latter); Limbaugh may be a simplistic, bigoted propagandist or an insightful political commentator (I lean a lot towards the former); but there's no way you're going to mistake either of them for ordinary. And no chance you'll find either of them fading into the background and merging with the drone of rush-hour traffic. But Bill and Marty are merely two more humming voices in the ubiquitous buzz, spiking sound waves in a white noise that's grown too clamorous to truly ignore in recent years.

You can almost imagine a *Simpsons* writer crawling along some L.A. freeway during morning rush hour, struggling to get to work. Stuck, yes, in *rush hour*: the ultimate expression of white noise as a cultural institution, a daily ritual of growling engines and bleating horns and slow dull grinding sameness. A *Simpsons* writer, listening to two fully grown, well-paid men on the radio trade fart noises and arooga-horn honks. Many drive-time DJ teams have even taken in recent years to sampling *The Simpsons* itself in lieu of actually producing something of their own to fill the dead air. So you can imagine this soul-sickening scene, and you can imagine this writer just fucking snapping – storming into the office and writing the scene in Episode 8F14 ('Homer Alone') in which a 'Bill and Marty Classic Crank Call' of staggering crassness pushes Marge right over the edge. In service of their idiotic show, Bill and Marty call a random Springfieldianite and inform him his wife has just died. The man is devastated; he breaks down into tears. Bill and Marty explode into sneering laughter. Something snaps in Marge's mind as she listens. She brings her car to an abrupt halt in the middle of Springfield Memorial Bridge. She can't take it any more.

Whatever actually inspired the show's savaging of wacky DJs, they are portrayed on *The Simpsons* as a particularly ugly smear upon the modern mediascape. They are symbols of a particularly corrosive brand of banality disseminated by the mass media. A comedic black hole, if you will, that leaves white noise in its wake.

And for more on the deadly black hole that's slowly devouring Springfield's soul, let's go to Kent Brockman in the Channel 6 News copter, live on the scene.

THE SPRINGFIELD MEDIASCAPE (III): THE GLIB HYSTERIA OF THE NEWS OF THE DAY

In Springfield, as in our world, radio is a minor player in the media game. Sure, there's news on the radio, in the local paper, from the gaping mouth of the town crier during Springfield's bicentennial celebration. But when Springfieldianites really need to know what's happening in their world, they turn to Channel 6 and its anchorman, Kent Brockman. Indeed if the institution of the News has a single iconic face on *The Simpsons*, it's Brockman's chisel-chinned, blow-dried visage.

When a plot needs quick filling out or a back story needs quick filling in, Brockman's your man. He's on the scene – lowered by helicopter wearing a helmet-mounted camera, no less – when Marge has her breakdown on the Springfield Memorial Bridge. He can be counted on for live updates on Homer's trip to space or his vigilante hunt for the town cat burglar or his life-saving rescue efforts as the driver of Mr Plow's flagship truck. Brockman grills Marge about her crusade against cartoon violence and chats up Lisa about her crusades against everything else. If there's breaking news in Springfield, it's on the Channel 6 newscasts that Brockman anchors; if there are heavy issues to be discussed, the debate is mediated by Brockman on *Smartline*; if there are light-hearted lifestyle trends to be documented, Brockman's there with *Eye on Springfield*. He is CNN, *Meet the Press* and *Entertainment Tonight* in one slick package.

There's no such thing as total objectivity in journalism, however, and Brockman's got his biases as surely as Fox News has theirs. As with much of the mainstream media, Brockman's biases aren't overtly political. As the anchor for a corporate news broadcast, he's merely a staunch defender of the status quo by trade. He's neither liberal nor conservative, but in Brockman's journalism, we see some of the modern news media's ugliest biases.

The first of these is an unrelenting glibness, usually disguised as cool, professional detachment. In Episode 9F07 ('Mr. Plow'), for example, Springfield is struggling through a vicious blizzard, and Kent Brockman's Channel 6 News team is of course on the scene. Brockman goes live to his trusty traffic reporter, Arnie Pie,[5] who's hovering in a helicopter near Springfield's forbidding Widow's Peak. Shouting over the howl of the wind and snow, Arnie dutifully files his report: 'Everything's snowed in! All I can see is white!' Brockman grows quickly impatient: 'Arnie, please – the ski conditions.' Cut to Arnie, now upside-down and clearly in danger: 'Mayday! Mayday! I think I'm flying into a mountain! Tell my wife I love . . .' The visual abruptly cuts off, replaced by static. Back in the studio, Brockman erupts in a standard-issue, isn't-our-weather-guy-wacky chuckle. 'That's great, Arnie,' he says cheerfully. This is the news media's requisite glibness in a nutshell. The show must go on, and Brockman must remain an unflappable anchorman. Pie's apparent death, like that of a murder victim in a local story or of a massacre in the international news, is ultimately less important than the structural integrity of the news broadcast itself.

Such an attitude can, of course, lead to some dramatic distortions of the true import of the day's various events. Humanity's gravest threat, for example, can suddenly appear to come from the razor-sharp teeth of a shark or the fangs of a pit bull, while the slow and often unspectacular process by which we are poisoning our environment can seem less troubling than the next day's weather. The minute details in the murder trial of a former football star can come to seem far more earth-shaking than the slaughter of nearly a million people in a little-known nation in central Africa. The news media's professionally mandated 'objective' style leaves few opportunities to indicate which of these stories is trivial and which is important, nor any time to explain the difference in scope between the stabbing down the street and the rivers choked with blood in Rwanda. This is as true of other media as it is of TV. In Springfield, for example, the *Springfield Shopper* is no less slavish than Channel 6 in its dedication to maintaining a blasé tone. When Mr Burns unveils his plan to block out the sun in Episode 2F16 ('Who Shot Mr. Burns? (Part One)'), the *Shopper* announces the news with the banner headline 'Burns Plans Sunshine Halt'. Further down the page, there's a teaser: 'Special Section: Your Guide to Perpetual Darkness'.

Further distorting our worldview is the arbitrary way in which the media prioritises its content, emphasising local minutiae over distant cataclysm, and dramatic and salacious details over mundane ones, no matter how salient they may be. On one occasion in Springfield, Brockman struggles with the pronunciation of the name of Malaysia's capital in a tale of carnage spectacular enough to make the Channel 6 News. 'Tragic news tonight,' he reads. 'One hundred and twenty dead in a tidal wave in Kuala Lala-pure . . . Kuala Lum-per . . .' He hunches over his desk, and with a stroke of a pen changes the location of the killer tidal wave to France. The facts, as Brockman well knows, are ultimately irrelevant to his audience; it's the sexy details – *tidal wave, 120 dead* – that make the story newsworthy. Kuala Lumpur, Timbuktu, gay Paree – it's all *elsewhere*, far far away from the Channel 6 News studio.

At the same time, though, Brockman is free to snatch up some seemingly meaningless story on a whim and build it into great tragedy. In Episode 1F15 ('Bart Gets an Elephant'), for example, Brockman's at the forefront of the media ranks in inflating the story of KBBL's failure to deliver an elephant to Bart Simpson into a local scandal. 'Isn't that what we're all asking in our own lives: "Where's my elephant?"' Brockman editorialises, his voice oozing righteous indignation. 'I know that's what *I've* been asking.' Another time, his eyewitness reporting on a riot after a Spinal Tap concert at the Springfield Coliseum provides fodder for that night's 'My Two Cents' opinion piece. 'Of course,' Brockman sombrely intones, 'it would be wrong to suggest this sort of mayhem began with rock & roll. After all, there were riots at the premiere of Mozart's *The Magic Flute*. So what's the answer? Ban all music? In this reporter's opinion, the answer, sadly, is yes.'

Brockman excels at this kind of amplification. In Episode 8F04 ('Homer Defined'), an impending meltdown at the nuclear plant leads Channel 6 to interrupt its broadcast of *Search for the Sun* (Marge's favourite soap opera) for a special bulletin: 'Meltdown Crisis: The First Couple of Minutes'. Here we see Brockman in full twenty-four-hour-news-cycle mode, conducting an ineffectual interview with Mr Burns and not even trying to challenge Burns's characterisation of the disaster as 'an unrequested fission surplus'. Then Brockman fills the pre-meltdown news void with useless chatter, speculating wildly on what kind of society Springfieldianites can expect after the nuclear catastrophe and consulting Professor John Frink to determine just how devastating the damage might be.[6]

A few seasons later, Brockman has apparently learned a few lessons about sensationalism, as his broadcast is transformed in Episode 2F05 ('Lisa on Ice') into Channel 6 Action News. Heavy emphasis on 'Action': Brockman literally vaults onto the set, landing at his desk panting, and then delivers the news in a breathless harangue. 'Our top stories tonight,' he rants. 'A tremendous *explosion* – in the price of lumber. President Reagan *dyes* – his hair. Plus Garry Trudeau and his new musical comedy revue. But first, let's check the death count from the killer storm bearing down on us like a shotgun full of snow.' Cut to Brockman's weather guy, standing in front of a billboard-sized death-count counter – currently stuck at zero. 'It is ready to shoot right up,' the weather guy notes optimistically. Brockman, still aghast, curses the killer storm. 'Damn you, snow!' he bellows, shaking his fist at the sky.

The amazing thing about Brockman's brand of hysteria is the way it coexists so cosily with his glibness. In Action News mode, Brockman's all overblown frenzy; when he chuckles at Arnie Pie's helicopter crash, he's purely glib. Often as not, though, he manages to be both at once. In Episode 7F09 ('Itchy & Scratchy & Marge'), for example, he introduces an instalment of *Smartline* about the controversy surrounding the upcoming visit of

Michelangelo's *David* to Springfield thusly: 'Is it a masterpiece, or just some guy with his pants down?' In Brockman's estimation, this is balance: every story has two sides, both extreme, both equally plausible, with the reasonable centre occupied by the media itself. On this edition of *Smartline*, though, Marge Simpson won't play her assigned role as shrill censor, and so there's not enough *Sturm und Drang* to fill the show. Brockman wraps up early, telling his audience, 'Join us tomorrow, when our topic will be "Religion: Which is the one true faith?"'

The most blatant example of this glib hysteria on *The Simpsons* comes, fittingly enough, when Brockman is at his most unhinged. I'm speaking of perhaps his finest hour as a journalist: his live broadcast of Homer's space mission in Episode 1F13 ('Deep Space Homer'). Brockman goes live to a camera inside the space capsule just in time to mistake an ant passing by the camera's lens for one of a 'master race of giant space ants' who are hell-bent on conquering the earth. He delivers this delusional fantasy in a bang-on parody of the seasoned pro's smooth, measured tones. 'The ants will soon be here,' he concludes. With a professional flourish, he then switches his gaze to another camera. In a chipper, boosterish tone of the sort usually used to wish the local high school good luck at the band competition, he opines, 'And I, for one, welcome our new insect overlords. I'd like to remind them that, as a trusted TV personality, I can be helpful in rounding up others to toil in their underground sugar caves.' A graphic appears over his shoulder of a giant ant brandishing a whip menacingly over a prostrate human. Even in the face of imminent giant-space-ant conquest and/or the total mental breakdown of the anchorman, the show will go on, and a technician will be ready with just the right graphic.

Now, if even this is a bit too unvarnished for you, never fear: the news is just a TV show, one TV show among many, and it'll be over soon. In 1F13, Brockman regains his composure a few scenes later, reluctantly reaffirms his allegiance to the United States and its human president, tears down his HAIL ANTS banner, and then concludes, 'Oh, yes – by the way, the spacecraft is still in extreme danger, may not make it back, attempting risky re-entry, blah blah blah blah blah blah.' He shuffles his papers with finality, then smoothly signs off: 'We'll see you after the movie.'

THE SPRINGFIELD MEDIASCAPE (IV): THE SHOWS INSIDE THE SHOW

Homer and Bart are most certainly in that segment of the audience eager to get to the movie. Bart's idea of news is reality-TV schlock like *America's Most*

Armed and Dangerous, and Homer only sits through *Smartline* when the remote control's out of reach. For them, the mass media's all about entertainment, and there's almost nothing on TV too craptastically crappy to offend their low standards. As Episode 3G02 ('Lisa's Sax') opens, Bart's watching the WB – a fledgling American TV network so awful it has managed to make Fox seem discerning. His father eagerly joins him just as a glitzy new movie is about to begin. 'It's the TV movie of the year!' a fervent voice-over declares. '*The Krusty the Clown Story: Booze, Drugs, Guns, Lies, Blackmail, and Laughter!* Starring Fyvush Finkel as Krusty the Clown!' 'All right!' Bart exclaims. 'They're going to show his disastrous marriage to Mia Farrow!' Sure enough, we soon see 'Krusty' surrounded by a gaggle of adopted East Asian children, explaining to them that he and Mia are divorcing. Bart and Homer apparently don't notice that Krusty the Clown has become Woody Allen. It's a fine bit of multi-level Simpsonian satire: a big Jewish comedian from Homer and Bart's universe is portrayed in a TV movie by a marginal actor from ours who's exactly the kind of marginal actor who'd appear in a TV movie, and what's more he plays Krusty's behind-the-scenes life as a thinly veiled copy of the life of a big Jewish star from the real world. The most salient point here is that Krusty has yet again become a window through which to examine the history of mass communications.

The Krusty the Clown Show is put to many interesting uses by *The Simpsons'* creators, but we rarely see much of the current *Krusty the Clown Show* – it's usually just a snippet here or there, on screen just long enough to reiterate that it's a bottom-feeding variety show that'll happily play host to crank calls, dirty limericks, cigar-smoking monkeys and overused sight gags of the pie-in-the-face variety. We're likely only to catch a quick glance of Krusty as he introduces an 'Itchy & Scratchy' short, abuses Sideshow Mel or shills for an amusement park. Much of the real present-day action involves Krusty's debauched off-screen life, his endorsements of third-rate products or services, his tax problems, that sort of thing.

Those few occasions when we see vintage clips tend to be longer and more revealing; indeed we see almost as much of this 'Klassic Krusty' stuff as we do of the present-day show. In Episode 9F13 ('I Love Lisa'), for instance, all of Springfield is abuzz with talk of Krusty's 29th Anniversary Special, and in commercials interspersed throughout the first two acts, we're shown great moments in *Krusty the Clown Show* history: there's Sideshow Mel 'wacked out on wowee sauce', and the unfortunate segment in which Krusty learns why a simian guest is called a 'urine monkey'. In both of these, vintage *Krusty* far more closely resembles *The Tonight Show* with Johnny Carson than a kids' variety show. After all, cavorting with unruly zoo animals was a frequent Carson schtick, as was joking about the quantity of booze in sidekick Ed McMahon's mug. Later, there are clips of Krusty in 1963 dumping snow on the poet Robert Frost ('Hey, Frosty! Want some snow, man?' Krusty bellows gleefully) and of a 'Kroon Along with Krusty' from 1973 in which the clown does a caterwauling rendition of the Doors' 'Break on Through (to the Other Side)' against a pinwheeling psychedelic backdrop. *The Krusty the Clown Show* is a kind of meta-talk show, a chameleon that can reveal distant echoes of Johnny Carson, Dick Cavett, even the 1950s *Tonight Show* host Steve Allen.

If you dig deep enough into Krusty's past, you'll find traces of seemingly every major event and trend in pop history. Over the course of one memorable summer, for example, a series of 'Klassic Krusty' broadcasts includes a dry discussion of America's 1961 labour crisis with AFL-CIO chairman George Meany and 'another long raga by Ravi Shankar' ('Shankar'; 'Shankar – groovy, man') from the late 1960s. The consistent topicality of 'Klassic Krusty' is taken to ridiculous extremes in Episode 1F16 ('Burns' Heir'), in which Krusty ducks out on his show to earn big bucks delivering a pizza to Burns Manor, thinking no one will notice the difference if he just runs a repeat. His cover is blown, however, when his juggling act in the old episode is interrupted by an assistant handing him a news bulletin. 'Children, remain calm,' Krusty announces gravely. 'The Falkland Islands have just been invaded.' He immediately pulls down a map of the disputed islands to explain the news to his juvenile audience. Around 1982, it would seem, Krusty was a bit of a news junkie.

What Krusty's doing, in these dusty old segments, is bestowing a history upon a show that's otherwise set in the eternal now. There's plenty of fun in seeing Krusty decked out in love beads and hippie hair in the Shankar clip or talking collective bargaining with a 1960s-era labour leader with requisite grey suit and nerd glasses, but this level of historical detail serves another purpose: it helps transform the Simpsonian mediascape from a scattershot collage of current media tropes to a panoramic portrait of the mass media's evolution. Just consider the metaphorical value of the development arc traced by Krusty's show: from serious debates about labour relations and esteemed poets reading their work through great music and breaking news to pie throwing and product plugs. In this arc, you can read TV's own growth: its early flirtations with serving as a tool of the public good; its central role in creating the global village of pop; its eventual surrender to its true nature as an omnidirectional sludge pump and a pawn of mass marketing.

While Krusty's dealing with the macro-level stuff – the great sweep of pop history – 'Itchy & Scratchy' serves as a vehicle for the micro-level history of American animation.[7] And, more specifically, as a parodic homage to the life and work of Walt Disney. An instalment of Kent Brockman's *Eye on Springfield* in Episode 9F03 ('Itchy & Scratchy: The Movie'), which coincides with the release of a big-budget feature film starring the beloved cat-and-mouse team, leaves no doubt as to the cartoon's Disneyesque origins. In the segment, there are clips from the first two 'Itchy & Scratchy' cartoons. The first, 'That Happy Cat', is only somewhat Disney-like in its depiction of a gloved, whistling, blank-eyed Scratchy. The second, 'Steamboat Itchy', explicitly sends up the early Disney short 'Steamboat Willie', with Itchy the mouse sporting Mickey-like ears as he pilots his boat down a river. It's only when Scratchy appears and Itchy takes a Tommy gun to the cat's kneecaps that the 'Itchy & Scratchy' short detours from the Disney original.

The parody is made even more overt when the Simpsons visit a Disneylandish Itchy & Scratchy theme park in Episode 2F01 ('Itchy & Scratchy Land'). Bart and Lisa head for the park's movie theatre, which airs a short documentary on the history of the cartoon. Thus are we introduced to Walt Disney's alter ego: 'Itchy & Scratchy' creator Roger Meyers Sr. 'Roger Meyers Sr, the gentle genius behind Itchy and Scratchy, loved and cared about almost all the peoples of the world,' the film's narrator intones. 'And he, in turn, was beloved by the world, except in 1938, when he was criticised for his controversial cartoon *Nazi Supermen Are Our Superiors*.' Here, in a none-too-subtle allusion to long-standing allegations that Walt Disney was a Nazi sympathiser until the start of the Second World War, the merger of Disney and the Itchy & Scratchy franchise is complete.

Next up in the theme park's documentary is a clip from *Scratchtasia* – a brutally violent homage to Disney's *Fantasia* – and the screening concludes with a scene from *Pinitchyo*. And it's abundantly clear, as Bart and Lisa exit the theme park's theatre, that the Itchy & Scratchy franchise is not just a bloody parody of children's cartoons but the Simpsonian stand-in for a huge multinational entertainment conglomerate – *any* multinational entertainment conglomerate.

It *is* Disney. Or, when the satirical need arises, Fox.

TV TO VIEWERS: 'KILL YOUR TELEVISION' (REPRISE)

Note the slightly clumsy transitional phrase at the end of that last section. Note, too, the creeping self-awareness in this transition. Just now, I mean. And so understand that one of the primary uses of 'Itchy & Scratchy' – and

Krusty – is to reveal the *process* of producing cartoons, variety shows and televised entertainment generally. And, in so doing, to pull back the curtain on the crassness of corporate TV production and to indulge in a feast of involuted, self-referential humour. For now, let's look at the first of these functions.

There have been, over the years, two great self-immolations on *The Simpsons*. These are Episode 9F16 ('The Front') and Episode 4F12 ('The Itchy & Scratchy & Poochie Show'). In both episodes, the writers and producers of the 'Itchy & Scratchy' cartoons are depicted as doppelgängers of the staff of *The Simpsons*. Both also portray the production of a hit cartoon as a nasty business that takes place in a toxic soup of overinflated egos, corporate myopia, creative sloth and general malaise. And both episodes conclude with vicious jabs at the basic idiocy of TV.

In 9F16, Bart and Lisa decide they can write 'Itchy & Scratchy' cartoons better than the current writers. So they write one, and it *is* better, and eventually even Roger Meyers Jr agrees – after he's led to believe it was written by Grampa Simpson and not two children. In short order, Meyers fires his existing staff (a herd of dorky Harvard grads modelled closely on *The Simpsons* own staff) and Bart and Lisa become the sole authors of 'Itchy & Scratchy', using their grandfather as a front. One of Bart and Lisa's 'Itchy & Scratchy' cartoons receives a Cartoon Awards Show nomination for Best Writing in a Cartoon Series.[8] It wins, and in old Abe's acceptance speech, he makes it abundantly clear he's no cartoon writer. 'That was the first time I ever saw "Itchy & Scratchy," and I didn't like it one bit,' he announces, referring to the clip just shown in the auditorium. 'It was disgusting and violent. I think all you people are despicable! For shame!' The entire audience pelts him with produce, except for two writers, stand-ins for *Simpsons* producers Al Jean and Mike Reiss, who take Abe's critique to heart. 'He's right!' says Reiss. 'We've been wasting our lives!' 'The hell with cartoons,' adds Jean with sudden vigour. 'I'm gonna do what I always dreamed of! I'm gonna write that sitcom about the sassy robot!'

Episode 4F12 is an even harsher satire of the working world of big-time TV production, telling the tale of how an edgy, in-your-face, rapping cartoon dog named Poochie came to be briefly added to the cast of 'Itchy & Scratchy'. Once again the cartoon's production team is a mirror image of *The Simpsons'* team, and once again the entire enterprise of producing a hit cartoon is portrayed as nasty, brutish and essentially meaningless. About the only thing with any real dignity to it is Homer's attempt, during a taping of the voice-overs for the new cartoon, to convince the producers and the audience to give his character – Poochie, that is – a fair chance. 'I know there's a lot of people who don't like me and wish I would go away,' Homer pleads on Poochie's behalf, his voice crackling with sincerity. 'I think we got off on the wrong foot. I know I can come off a little proactive, and for that I'm sorry. But if everyone could find a place in their hearts for the little dog that nobody wanted, I know we can make them laugh, and cry, until we grow old together.' It's a stirring speech, and it brings stunned silence and then sincere applause to the 'Itchy & Scratchy & Poochie' taping. When the next episode of the show airs, however, Poochie has been written out of the show anyway, and with contemptuous clumsiness. Speaking in a voice that is obviously that of Roger Meyers, Poochie declares, 'I have to go now. My planet needs me.' Then the actual animation cel on which Poochie is drawn is lifted out of the frame, leaving the rest of the scene intact as Poochie lurches skyward. Cut to a title card, seemingly hand-scrawled a few minutes before airtime: 'Note: Poochie died on the way back to his home planet.' The end.

Episode 4F12, like 9F16 before it, is a veritable feast of self-loathing. 'In America,' Matt Groening once said, 'television is interrupted every seven minutes by a barrage of commercials. The overall message is that nothing matters. In fact, the more urgent the material, the more its urgency is diluted. There is no escaping that. It would be like a fish protesting against the aquarium water. You're in it, and you have to swim in it.' And yet here are two episodes vociferously objecting to the aquarium water.

Indeed the sum total of *The Simpsons*' critique is that the mass media is a horrible, mindless trap. Troy McClure infomercials and McBain movies, Kent Brockman's editorial rants, show tunes and talk radio, TV clowns and gory cartoons – all of it, including *The Simpsons* itself, combines into a great hypnotic kaleidoscope in which nothing is permanent and anything of any real value is instantly drained of meaning and then crushed into pretty shards to feed new colour to the machine. And what's more, we're all hooked so hard on TV's Huxleyan soma that even the wisest among us – even *Simpsons* writers – can't kick the habit. Free them from their addiction, and they'll just wind up writing a sitcom about a sassy robot – or another cartoon series like *Futurama* or *The Critic* or a couple of episodes of *Just Shoot Me* or *The Drew Carey Show*.

It's worth noting that *The Simpsons*' writers have invariably portrayed themselves as overeducated, hyper-literate eggheads. These are guys who talk on the show about how they wrote their theses on 'life experience' and about how Itchy and Scratchy 'comprise a dramaturgical dyad'. These are genuine intellectuals who know at least as much about the way the mass media functions as any professor of media theory. They and the so-called Ivy League Mafia who have increasingly staffed Hollywood's wittiest shows – not just *The Simpsons* but *King of the Hill*, *Seinfeld*, *The Larry Sanders Show* and dozens of lesser lights – amount to a gathering of America's (and Canada's) best and brightest. Here's Harvard alumnus Jay Itzkowitz, talking to *Los Angeles* magazine in 1998, when he was a senior vice-president at Fox, about the intellectual elite that populates Hollywood's rewrite rooms: 'My great fear for this country is: Who's going into productive industries? What I see happening is almost everyone I know who is really smart saying, "Oh, I can make a lot of money sitting around doing something frivolous? Great, I'll do that." If the choice is between going into a core U.S. industry like steel or writing for something like *The Simpsons*, the decision is a no-brainer. It makes me worry a little bit for America.'

Here, then, is the seed of the show's self-loathing: a gnawing sense that brains of this calibre might be put to better use on something other than the weekly adventures of a yellow-skinned cartoon family. In Episode 4F12, during a public appearance at which Poochie is introduced to hard-core fans of 'Itchy & Scratchy', Homer Simpson tears into a geek who asks him a ridiculously arcane trivia question about the show. 'Let me ask *you* a question,' Homer lectures. 'Why would a man whose shirt says 'Genius at Work' spend all of his time watching a children's cartoon show?' Though this dig is directed at the audience, it's ultimately an act of self-loathing, since it's surely as contemptible to spend all your time *producing* a cartoon show, even one that tries to sabotage the medium as often as *The Simpsons* does.

It begs the question: Can Sideshow Bob's ironic paradox be resolved? Can you effectively use TV to decry TV, even perhaps to destroy some of its power?

IN DEFIANCE OF PARODY

On the evening of 8 March 2002 – just another TV-saturated Friday evening in the free world – Barbara Walters fixed her gaze on the living rooms of America and announced: 'So you write a show about a lazy, fat, bald, stupid middle-aged man and what happens? You become incredibly rich and famous and your show becomes a television sensation here and around the world. And it's just a cartoon. That's the story of *The Simpsons*, the sitcom that's been called both the best programme on television today and the worst.' In the report that followed – a *20/20* feature on the enduring success of *The Simpsons* – the show's creators tried to explain the import of their work in ten-second sound bites. Matt Groening talked about how *The Simpsons* came about, James L. Brooks noted the show's unwavering commitment to realism, George Meyer pointed out that the show addressed serious subjects like homosexuality that few other TV shows dared to touch. 'Is there a purpose to *The Simpsons*?' the *20/20* reporter asked Meyer. 'If there is,' he replied, 'it's to get people to re-examine their world, and specifically the authority figures in their world.' The segment closed with 'interviews' with Homer and Bart Simpson themselves – short clips, done in the same sound-bitten style as the interviews with Meyer and Groening – followed by some lightweight banter between Walters and her fellow journalists. The show then went to a commercial break with a teaser. 'When *20/20* continues . . .' an announcer earnestly intoned, introducing a brief clip of reporter John Stossel, his voice thick with incredulous indignation, saying, 'They run out of bars and grab little people who don't want to be thrown and throw them?' Up next, it turned out, was a crusading investigative piece on the barroom sport of dwarf tossing.

It would be hard to imagine a Simpsonian parody more broad and piercing than this: from George Meyer's earnest insistence that his show tries to recalibrate its viewers' relationship with authority to a muckraking story about dwarf tossing, all in a couple of quick TV cuts and stern voice-overs.

Such is the daunting challenge facing the contemporary media satirist: Can this shit even be parodied? Could Kent Brockman ever be more unjustifiably indignant than John Stossel? Could *Smartline*'s segment intros be any more glib than *20/20*'s? I mean, for chrissake: dwarf tossing? *Eye on Springfield*'s coverage of the historic meeting between Springfield's oldest man and Springfield's fattest man is a study in journalistic integrity by comparison.

The entire Simpsonian mediascape can indeed seem as much a faux documentary as a hyperbolic satire. There are real movies from the last decade – movies that cost millions of dollars to make, movies that starred Jason Alexander of *Seinfeld* and Matt LeBlanc of *Friends*, movies that are now available at your local Blockbuster, movies like *Dunston Checks In* and *Ed* – that could be seamlessly tacked on to the end of the list of monkey-themed flicks so beloved by Springfield's masses. Here are some more titles: *Dial M for Murderousness, Leper in the Backfield, Brotherhood of Murder, Under the Hula Moon, The Greatest Story Ever Hula'd, Calling All Quakers, How to Make an American Quilt, Heaven's Prisoners, Give My Remains to Broadway, The Adventures of Pluto Nash*. Try to guess which ones starred Troy McClure and which ones starred a Baldwin brother.[9]

Or take a look at some of the Simpson family's favourite action-packed TV dramas. We frequently find Homer and company watching a show 'about a policeman who solves crimes in his spare time'. This series's protagonist is a rogue cop named McGonigle, who's got Clint Eastwood's voice and the tough-as-nails take-charge attitude of Dirty Harry on a bad day, and who exhibits the wit and subtlety of – well, of one of the lesser Baldwins. 'You're off the case, McGonigle,' the police chief intones in one stellar instalment. 'You're off *your* case, chief,' McGonigle spits back. But on other occasions, we find the Simpson clan joining Patty and Selma to watch their beloved *MacGyver*, an actual TV drama about a former secret agent who uses everyday household items to foil assorted crimes that aired on ABC from 1985 to 1992. On one occasion, Selma is watching her favourite show with her betrothed, Sideshow Bob, and we listen along with them to a snippet of *MacGyver* dialogue. First, a Spanish-accented voice: 'Thank you, *Señor* MacGyver. You've saved our village.' MacGyver, nonchalant: 'Don't thank me. Thank the earth's gravitational pull.' For all I know, these lines could have been lifted directly from an episode of the show. You've got to assume, in fact, that *MacGyver*'s inclusion on the show was a kind of surrender to its extraordinary, parody-proof stupidity.

But the show's efforts to exaggerate the silliness of TV drama amount to an evening stroll with the stars of *Police Cops* (another of the Simpson family's favourite programmes[10]) compared to the level of overstatement required to satirise the contemporary news media. Oh, what media circuses we've seen since the early 1990s, as a steady stream of bizarre criminal cases has fed the twenty-four-hour news cycle with new content as surely as the networks have unveiled new primetime shows each autumn. By early 1994, a handful of scandalous stories were wrestling for top billing in a kind of millennial-news-media equivalent of a cockfight. There were the deadlocked trials of two Cuban-American teens – the criminally vapid Lyle and Eric Menendez – who had killed their parents to get their hands on the family fortune. There was a violent rivalry between two champion female figure skaters – Tonya Harding and Nancy Kerrigan – that featured pornographic wedding-night videos and back-alley kneecappings. And there was the lurid trial of a woman named Lorena Bobbitt, who'd been driven so mad with rage by her husband's abuse that one day she just up and cut off his penis. (There must be a god of tabloid journalism – I call him 'Sleazus' – and his existence was proven by the Bobbitt story.) Early 1994 was, in short, a great time to be a tabloid journalist in America.

Still, *The Simpsons* gamely tried to find a definitive satirical statement to encompass this grand, grotesque spectacle. In Episode 2F06 ('Homer Badman'), which details the sexual-harassment case brought against Homer Simpson by his babysitter, it nearly did. The young woman's accusations attract the attention of *Rock Bottom* – Springfield's answer to the scandal-addicted current-affairs shows like *Hard Copy* and *Inside Edition* that helped make the Menendezes and Bobbitts household names – and soon every channel on TV is filled with talk of the scandal. On one talk show, a woman who's never met Homer weeps at the trauma he's caused her; on another, the topic is 'mothers and runaway daughters reunited by their hatred of Homer Simpson'. There's even a TV movie – on Fox, no less – called *Homer S.: Portrait of an Ass-Grabber.* (In an inspired bit of casting, it stars Dennis Franz of *NYPD Blue* as Homer.)

But the grand prize for callous exploitation of Homer's story goes – of course – to Kent Brockman, who leads the media charge to the Simpsons' front door and never leaves. 'This is Hour 57 of our live, round-the-clock coverage outside the Simpson estate' – so begins one of Brockman's broadcasts. 'Remember, by the way, to tune in at 8:00 for highlights of today's vigil, including when the garbage man came and when Marge Simpson put the cat out – possibly because it was harassed, we don't know.' A professional pause, and then Brockman continues: 'Of course, there's no way to see into the Simpson home without some kind of infrared heat-sensitive camera.' He stops. Beat. 'So let's turn it on.' There follows a quick survey of the Simpson home via infrared camera, during which Brockman mistakes the turkey in the oven for Homer, who he then speculates is 'literally stewing in his own juices'.

All in all, 2F06 is an impressive bonfire of the tabloid-news vanities. And it would've been tough, during the winter and spring of 1994 when this episode was conceived, to imagine a spectacle more absurd than, say, *Ben*, a Simpsonian talk show hosted by an enraged bear wearing a microphone-equipped helmet. But then one fine day in June 1994, damn near every TV station in the Western world interrupted its regularly scheduled programming to broadcast live footage of the Los Angeles Police Department's slow-speed pursuit of a white Ford Bronco down a southern-California freeway, and tabloid TV soon reached a dizzying new peak of hype and sleaze.

Oh me, oh my (as Steamboat Itchy would say): there was truly no room left for satire in a media-circus tent as overgrown, overheated, overhyped and overweighted as the one that was erected to service the murder trial of former football star O.J. Simpson. Gentle Ben might have been the equal of Bobbitt-level media insanity, but even a deranged bear on a rampage couldn't possibly take down the whole absurd army involved in the O.J. affair. Tear Kato Kaelin's vacant surfer-boy lifestyle to shreds, and here come Daryl Gates and his LAPD to destroy the bear because of the colour of its fur. Rip off Alan Dershowitz's head, and Johnnie Cochrane's will pop right up to replace it. 'If the glove don't fit, you must acquit,' blurts Cochrane – and this criminal-code-according-to-Mother-Goose thing easily outweighs Homer stewing in his own juices on the satirical scale. And then the glove *doesn't* fit, as it turns out . . . and the jury decides it doesn't buy the science of the DNA evidence . . . and O.J. walks . . . and vows – sweet Jebus – *vows* to dedicate his life to finding 'the real killers'. The only way to render the O.J. circus as satire would be to tell the story straight. I mean, who could you get to do justice to the role of Kato Kaelin besides Kato himself? Not even Troy McClure in blackface could deliver a more self-serving performance than Johnnie Cochrane did for Court TV's live satellite feed. A documentary about the O.J. Simpson trial – *there's* your satire.

So where does that leave *The Simpsons*? Where does satire go when the culture broadcasts its own absurdity live on cable TV, twenty-four hours a day, seven days a week? There's only one direction left to go: inward.

JOURNEY TO THE CENTRE OF THE SIMPSONS: SELF-AWARENESS, SELF-REFERENCE, SELF-PARODY & THE PERFECTION OF THE POSTMODERN AESTHETIC

I've said it before and I'll say it again: Ay, carumba!

Wait. No. That's Bart's line.

I've said it before and I'll say it again: *The Simpsons* is not a pretty picture of a soup can; it is, rather, a cheap copy of a picture of a soup can. All that self-aware, self-referencing irony that makes up postmodern culture's signature pose comes as naturally to *The Simpsons* as winking at the camera or having Homer bellow 'Yabba-dabba-doo!' Some shows have to manufacture their ironic references, but irony is built right into *The Simpsons*, because everything about *The Simpsons* is derivative. Its structure is pure sitcom formula. Its setting is a pastiche of nostalgic 1950s sitcoms and cartoons, with a Norman Rockwell *Life* magazine cover or two tossed in for good measure. And its characters – *all* its characters – are walking, talking, four-fingered composites of pop icons past and present. It's not just Homer's Archie Bunker lunkheadedness or Marge's blue-haired June Cleaver act, either. There's a good dose of Dennis the Menace, a little Eddie Haskell and a dollop of Johnny Rotten in Bart. Mr Burns is Lionel Barrymore, Ronald Reagan, Barry Diller and Rupert Murdoch, among others. Moe the bartender's signature gravelly squawk was lifted from a young Al Pacino; Lou the African-American cop is based on Sylvester Stallone; Police Chief Wiggum's got a bit of American broadcast journalist David Brinkley and a lot of actor Edward G. Robinson in him; and Professor Frink is of course a full-blown homage to comedian Jerry Lewis, as Hank Azaria, the versatile *Simpsons* voice actor who does the talking for Moe, Lou, Wiggum and Frink, among many others, admitted in a 1994 interview.

Not only does *The Simpsons*' abiding love of self-reference and self-parody add a layer or three to the show's density, but *The Simpsons* has raised this style of referential humour to a sophisticated comedic art form. No need for the show to borrow archly from pop to deconstruct (or redefine) 'high' art, because pop is built right into *The Simpsons*: it is, after all, an animated cartoon, one of the few genuine pop-art forms. The show flat-out obliterates the highbrow/lowbrow distinctions that turn so much of postmodern art into pseudo-academic posturing. When Lisa memorably observes of one plot twist, 'It's like something out of Dickens – or *Melrose Place*,' there's none of that cutesy-clever dig-how-I'm-slumming bullshit you find in some art-gallery installations or deconstructionist short stories; it's just plain true. *The Simpsons* needn't labour over its 'intertextuality' nor bash up against the structural limits of its form. Instead, it merely skips deliriously from genre to genre and medium to medium. Pick an episode at random, and you might find surrealistic cartooning alongside social-realist documentary, or meta-textual media criticism buried in cinematic homage, or pop-music parody serving as a narrative device. And, finally, if pop art's supposed to be at least partially about applying industrial techniques to artistic expression, then take a trip to South Korea to watch a team of hundreds drawing animation cels by the thousands to bring *The Simpsons* to life.

Or, better yet, simply watch *The Simpsons*. Yet another advantage it has over much of postmodern art is that it has engaged millions, not dozens. So simply watch. And wait for the metatextual gags to start flying.

There's a bit of ironic winking in the show's debut Christmas special, but Simpsonian postmodernism really takes off in Episode 7G07 ('The Telltale Head'), a Season 1 episode, which opens with a rush of action as Homer and Bart attempt to outrun an angry mob. The mob, it turns out, wants Bart's head because he took Jebediah Springfield's – that is, Bart decapitated a statue of the town's revered founder as a prank. The mob finally catches up with the Simpson men in the town square. 'Murderous mob,' Bart orates, 'I beg you to spare our lives, at least until you've heard the story of how we ended up with the head of our beloved town founder.' We're being presented with a standard story structure: we've entered the story at the end, and our hero will now jump back to the beginning and tell the tale up to this point. 'How long will this story take?' a Springfieldianite demands. 'Uh,' stammers Bart. He pauses. (And in the dark shadows behind him, can we see ghost traces of the anxious visages of Warhol and Magritte and Roy Lichtenstein, John Barth and Donald Barthelme, maybe even Foucault and Derrida? Well, no. But anyway.) Anyway, Bart answers: 'About 23 minutes and five seconds.' Which is, of course, the average length of a *Simpsons* episode, minus commercial breaks. And the show's awareness of itself as a show is a standard Simpsonian trope from here on out.

What this means, first of all, is more gags like this one in 7G07, more quick quips that wink at the form. On one occasion, Homer finds himself sharing a jail cell with a man who blows bluesily on a harmonica. 'What are you in for?' Homer asks him. 'Atmosphere,' the man promptly replies. As the years pass, these deconstructionist one-offs grow more pointed. In Episode 1F14 ('Homer Loves Flanders'), for example, Bart's driven to exasperation by his father's newfound friendship with the geeky Flanderses. 'Don't worry, Bart,' Lisa counsels him sagely. 'It seems like every week something odd happens to the Simpsons. My advice is to ride it out, make the occasional smart-alec quip, and by next week we'll be back to where we started from, ready for another wacky adventure.' Bart replies with his most famous smart-alec quip: 'Ay, carumba!' 'That's the spirit!' Lisa tells him.

And we in the audience have just witnessed the dialogue-induced equivalent of the collapse of the stage set around these characters. We can see the particle-board façades, the scaffolding, the boom mikes and lights. This is a TV show, dig? It's *constructed*.

I can't speak for my retelling of it, but on *The Simpsons* this stuff isn't as irritating as it can sometimes be, and this is in part because the characters themselves are rarely aware – at lease not overtly – of the constructedness of their world. Even as Lisa notes the way her life seems to conform to sitcom formula in the preceding example, her world remains real *to her*. The hyper-self-awareness usually belongs to the writers, not the Simpsons themselves. There's a scene at the start of Episode 2F33 ('Another Simpsons Clip Show'), for example, in which Lisa explains to Bart that the episode of 'Itchy & Scratchy' they're watching is actually a mishmash of clips from old episodes. Sure enough, a short while later it becomes clear that this episode of *The Simpsons* is a collection of clips from past episodes. It becomes clear only to us in the audience, though, not to Bart and Lisa.

There are exceptions to this rule, but they're few in number and usefully employed (at least until recent seasons). In Episode 3F04 ('Treehouse of Horror VI'), one of the Halloween-themed segments is about a plague of giant advertising mascots rampaging through downtown Springfield. At segment's end, Kent Brockman rants, 'Even as I speak, the scourge of advertising could be heading toward *your* town! Lock your doors, bar your windows, because the next advertisement you see could destroy your house and eat your family!' Homer abruptly steps between us and the cartoon TV screen and stares directly into the camera's eye. 'We'll be right back,' he announces smarmily, and *The Simpsons* cuts to commercial.

Or consider the Season 6 finale, Episode 2F16 ('Who Shot Mr. Burns? Part One') – one of the most heavily hyped, intentionally formulaic episodes in the show's history, the first of a two-part mystery. It ends in a cliff-hanger, with the whole town gathered around Mr Burns's prostrate body, wondering about the assailant's identity. 'I don't think we'll ever know who did this,' says Marge. 'Everyone in town's a suspect.' Dr Hibbert emerges from the crowd to deliver one of his trademark jolly chuckles. 'Well, I couldn't possibly solve this mystery,' he declares. He pauses, turns dramatically to us in the audience. 'Can *you*?' he says, pointing a finger at the camera. There's a one-beat pause, and then the camera pans back to reveal that Hibbert is really pointing at Police Chief Wiggum, who sputters out a reply: 'Yeah, I'll give it a shot. I mean, you know, it's my job, right?' It turns out Dr Hibbert was never aware of the audience; only the show's writers were. *The Simpsons* rarely simply states its self-awareness; it toys with it, riffs on it, turns it into a unique species of joke.

In a similar vein, *The Simpsons* is profoundly aware of itself *as a cartoon*, but the people of Springfield remain blissfully ignorant of this fact – an irony that has been regularly and gleefully milked for yuks. In Episode 1F06 ('Boy-Scoutz N the Hood'), the Simpson kids watch 'Itchy & Scratchy,' and Bart – a newly keen Junior Camper – points out some inaccuracies in Itchy's knot-tying skills. 'Oh, Bart,' Lisa replies, 'cartoons don't have to be 100-percent realistic.' On cue, Homer walks past the window behind her, even as he's also clearly visible sitting on the family couch. In the episode in which the Simpsons travel to Australia, Bart and Homer attempt to escape from an enraged mob of Australian officials by seeking refuge in the pouches of two kangaroos, only to find themselves waist-deep in kangaroo ooze. 'Ewww!' says Bart. 'It's not like in cartoons.' Homer agrees: 'Yeah – there's a lot more mucus.' There's a multi-tiered, multipurpose irony employed here: on the one hand, it draws our attention to the fact that *The Simpsons* is a cartoon and plays with the form's love of anthropomorphic animals (in this case the well-established cartoon motif of kangaroo-pouches-as-giant-pockets). At the same time, though, the mucus Homer and Bart find in these pouches testifies to the show's realism and the *absence* of self-awareness on the part of the Simpsons themselves. As far as they're concerned, their world is real, and in that 'real' world kangaroo pouches are anatomically correct.

The show's giddiest postmodern fun, however, is inspired by its awareness of itself as *The Simpsons* – as a mammoth mega-hit cultural institution. 'If cartoons were meant for adults, they'd put them on in primetime,' Lisa observes in one of the first adult-oriented primetime cartoons in decades. Another time, Homer becomes a semi-famous baseball mascot whose likeness winds up on T-shirts. 'A Simpson on a T-shirt – I never thought I'd see the day,' Marge marvels – this in an episode that first aired at a time when *Simpsons* T-shirts were selling at the rate of literally millions per week. This ironic celebration of the show's own celebrity reaches its apex in the opening sequence of Episode 8F20 ('Black Widower'), which finds the Simpson family gathered around the TV watching a show about anthropomorphic dinosaurs – a parody of the *Simpsons* knock-off *Dinosaurs,* a family sitcom starring cartoony dinosaur puppets that aired on ABC from 1991 to 1994. 'Would you turn off that rock-and-rock music?' says the father dinosaur, sounding distinctly like *Simpsons* forefather Fred Flintstone. 'Hey, don't have a stegosaurus, man!' says the boy dinosaur, sounding even more distinctly like Bart Simpson. 'These talking dinosaurs are more real than most *real* families on TV,' Lisa notes approvingly, repeating the praise of *The Simpsons'* own critics. Just then, on the Simpsons' TV screen, the baby dinosaur takes to bashing the father with a frying pan. 'D'oh!' blurts the dad. 'It's like they saw our lives and put it right up on screen!' Bart exclaims.

When you watch the opening sequence of 8F20, you are watching a cartoon family watch a TV show that is a parody of a TV show that is a rip-off of the TV show you're watching, and the rip-off being watched by the cartoon family parodies the actual show you're watching while the show you're watching parodies its own critics. Don't worry: not even I can follow that last sentence, and I just wrote it. The point is this: if the opening sequence of 8F20 got any more involuted, it would implode and suck all of pop culture into the rip in the fabric of space-time it created. Which is not too shabby an achievement for an incidental opening scene, *n'est-ce pas*? M. Derrida, I'm looking in your direction when I say that.

The Simpsons also indulges – practically every episode – in self-reference seemingly for its own sake. Not for nothing is there a permanent category in the capsule summaries of the show at The Simpsons Archive entitled

'Previous episode references', because there are at least a couple in every new instalment of *The Simpsons*. Maybe it's Moe yet again hosting some absurdly illegal activity in his tavern's storeroom,[11] or maybe it's Homer announcing the pursuit of yet another of his lifelong dreams, or maybe Smithers makes a yet-more-overt allusion to his white-hot lust for Mr Burns. There's even a recurring motif in which a veritable warehouse of past-episode references is crammed into a single scene. When the Simpson family's neighbourhood has a rummage sale in Episode 3F09 ('Two Bad Neighbors'), for instance, the Simpsons' table overflows with artifacts from old episodes: the giant Olmec head Mr Burns once gave the Simpsons as a gift; a copy of *Bigger Than Jesus*, the hit second album by Homer's barbershop quartet the Be Sharps; boxes of memorabilia from Bart's short-lived fame as the catchphrase king on *The Krusty the Clown Show*; and a half-dozen other totems of episodes past.

Sometimes such gags serve not just to note a past episode but to satirise the show's own conventions. Episode AABF06 ('Viva Ned Flanders') begins with the demolition of Mr Burns's Casino, a Springfield institution erected five seasons earlier. As the Simpson family looks on, Marge observes, 'Remember how excited we were when this place opened? Then a week later we just forgot about it.' Lisa quickly adds, 'I'm surprised they bothered to move it when they moved the town' – this in reference to the improbable conclusion of Episode 5F09 ('Trash of the Titans') in which Springfield's garbage problem is solved by moving the entire town five miles down the road. 'Oh, I can explain that,' Homer pipes up. 'You see . . .' But of course Homer's explanation is drowned out by the roaring of the explosion as the casino is demolished. Now, pointing out the show's indifference to continuity is no great achievement in itself, but here it's taken several steps beyond mere academic observation of the fact. This is a kind of self-parody that ultimately mocks both the show and those who would try to limit it to something as mundane as episode-to-episode continuity.

When it's at its best, metahumour of this sort is a uniquely Simpsonian thing, a feast of oxymorons: uproariously funny media theory; hilarious post-structuralist philosophy; whimsical deconstructionism. In Episode 3F10 ('Team Homer'), Homer and a few mates form a bowling team, and one fine evening they find themselves playing against a team called the Stereotypes. As Homer's teammate Mr Burns rolls a final gutter ball, sealing the Stereotypes' victory, each member of the winning team celebrates the victory in his own signature style. 'Mamma mia!' exclaims Luigi, the proprietor of Springfield's Italian restaurant. 'Hoot, man!' trills Groundskeeper Willie in his thick Scottish brogue. 'Yeehaw!' bellows Cletus, the slack-jawed yokel.

'*Arr*, me mateys!' comes Captain McCallister's sea-salty cry of victory. A one-beat pause, then cut to Homer's teammate, Apu, the Indian convenience-store proprietor. 'Whoa!' he marvels in his broad Indian accent. 'They begged me to join their team. *Begged* me!' Wearing bowling shirts labelled 'Stereotypes', *The Simpsons*' most stereotypical stock characters respond in their most stereotypical manner, at which point Apu, the show's most prominent stereotypical character, notes that he was asked to join the Stereotypes but decided he didn't quite fit. This is a self-awareness so acute it's like watching your favourite cartoon through an MRI machine in a hall of mirrors. (Which, come to think of it, would make for a pretty nifty piece of postmodern installation art.)

The Stereotypes-in-the-round sequence in 3F10, though, is nothing compared to the show's full-length exercises in hyper-postmodernity. There's Episode 1F11 ('Bart Gets Famous'), for example, in which Bart Simpson – a cartoon character who rocketed to global fame on the strength of catchphrases like 'Ay, carumba!' and 'Don't have a cow, man!' – rockets to Springfield-wide fame by uttering the catchphrase 'I didn't do it!' on *The Krusty the Clown Show*. Bart even records a cheesy rap tune to capitalise on his fame, as per the real-life hit single 'Do the Bartman'. And his sudden prominence leads to an invitation to appear on a Simpsonised *Late Night with Conan O'Brien*, thus setting up a scene in which the show's most famous character is interviewed by its most famous writer, Conan O'Brien, who was hired away from *The Simpsons* by NBC to take over *Late Night* after David Letterman left for CBS in 1993. And – but of course – there's yet another inward turn added to this involution during Bart's *Late Night* appearance, when Conan instructs a character he once scripted lines for to stop trying to talk about current affairs and just recite his catchphrase. Bart does so, and Conan replies, 'Great material.' He oughta know, right?

The Simpsons has stumbled on occasion when piling the self-references this thick, particularly in later seasons. In one such instance, we find Lisa at the kitchen table reading a newspaper called *The Daily Set-up* – which, of course, contains the key detail that sets up the next scene. Another time, Homer surprises his pals down at Moe's Tavern with his sudden commitment to being a good Samaritan. 'That's the kind of guy I am this week,' he boasts. Moments like these are the metahumour equivalent of an elbow to the ribs. It's cloying. It cloys. (Wait. Can 'cloy' be used as an intransitive verb? I should look that up. [Beat.] *OED* says yes. See how cloying this can get?)

What's particularly egregious, though, is when the smug posturing is done by the characters themselves. In one Season 14 episode, for example, Bart replies to a surprising turn of events thusly: 'If I may dust off an old chestnut: "Ay, carumba!"' Bart breaks character here, mucking with the show's realism and just generally bringing the proceedings to a halt. And it inspires a single reaction from its audience – annoyance – and a single irritated reply: *So what?*

So what, indeed? In the sudden stasis produced by such moments, you can find yourself wondering what the point is. And not just of cute postmodern self-reference, but of all allusion. The nods to past episodes, to lousy TV shows on other networks, to bad action movies, to talk shows that have been off the air for decades, even to classics of Western cinema or English literature – what does it do for *The Simpsons* in the final analysis? In short, what's referential humour *for*, anyway?

There are all sorts of partial answers to this question, many of which I've already discussed. For one thing, referential humour provides an enormously broad scope for *The Simpsons*' satire, allowing it to comment on anything from the poetry of Robert Frost to the movies of Arnold Schwarzenegger. As well, there is a bond created in the happy surprise of recognition that accompanies an allusion to a reference common to both writer and viewer. Referential humour creates common ground between *The Simpsons* and its audience. It also enhances the show's realism: we recognise a reference, and we thus equate the Simpsonian world with our own. This is the same reason, admittedly, that so many hack comedians talk about the quality of airline food and the differences between men and women. But the tool is put to higher uses on *The Simpsons*. The show is a ultimately a social satire – a skewed document of its time. And so to accurately represent our involuted, self-absorbed world, it has taken its own humour to ridiculously involuted, self-absorbed extremes.

In the moment that Bart asks us for permission to dust off an old chestnut, he acknowledges that he has joined the rest of us at the end of the line. He has come, as we have, to a place where postmodernism atomises and shared languages mutate into incomprehensible dialects. A place where art speaks only to and about itself and the only common culture is a culture of perfect solipsism. We are, every one of us, the centre of the universe, and we are all being watched, watching ourselves, watching each other – right now, always, forever. Welcome to the Panopticon, Bart.

INSIDE THE PANOPTICON

For my money, one of the most breathtaking moments in popular cinema in the last decade came about a third of the way through *The Truman Show*, Peter Weir's 1998 film about a man whose entire life since the moment of his birth has been the subject of a hit reality-TV show. The movie's – and the reality-TV show's – protagonist is a preternaturally naive and happy young man named Truman Burbank (played by Jim Carrey). Everything Truman knows – his house, his friends, his town, his *life* – is an elaborately constructed stage set, every inch of it constantly visible to closed-circuit cameras and wired for sound. In a ridiculously literal way, Truman lives inside the Panopticon. Except he doesn't know it. He awakens each morning to a quiet life, a cheerful blonde wife, a big beautiful house complete with a white picket fence. He lives in a flawless little slice of small-town nostalgia called Seahaven.[12] Except for a nagging feeling that there's more to the world than this cosy life – a feeling that manifests itself in an obsession with a short-lived high-school crush and with the South Pacific island of Fiji, where he believes she now lives – Truman is content with his caged existence.

In the film's opening sequence, however, evidence of the fragility of Truman's Panopticon literally falls from the sky: a stage light used to simulate a star in the idyllic night sky of Truman's world comes crashing to the ground in the middle of the street in front of his house. Soon, other cracks appear, technical glitches and security breaches that threaten to unmask the elaborate TV-production apparatus that surrounds Truman at all times. A rainstorm falls on him as he sits on the beach pondering his lost love, soaking only the square metre of sand where he's sitting for a good ten seconds before expanding to a more plausible size; downtown, Truman bumps into a homeless man who eerily resembles his long-lost father, and who has to be blatantly forced onto a departing bus by passersby to keep Truman from speaking to him.

Truman's family and friends quickly explain away these strange occurrences, so it's only when his car radio begins to broadcast the voices of the show's producers tracking his movements as he drives to work one fine morning that he really begins to confront the truth about his world. Truman has no idea yet about the cameras, the stage set, the production suite two hundred storeys above him; he simply opens his mind, just for a moment, to the idea that everything he knows is a lie, that everything he sees is a carefully orchestrated fiction.

As Truman arrives downtown, his radio returns to normal. He parks his car and walks slowly across the town square, curious and confused. He arrives at the building where he works, enters the revolving door. Walks in a circle inside the door – once, twice – and then steps back out into the daylight. He crosses the town square again, seeing it as if for the first time. He sits at an outdoor café, suspicious now of every glance and casual conversation. A man across the square holds Truman's gaze just a bit too long, then rushes guiltily off. You can see the idea coalescing in Truman's mind, echoing the words his high-school crush told him on the beach moments before she was hustled out of his life forever: 'It's fake. It's all for you.'

In a daze, he wanders into the street. A bus screeches to a halt inches away from him. Truman stares into the bus's window for a long moment. He embraces the idea completely: *It's all for you.* He lifts a raised palm to the bus, lifts the other hand to an approaching car. Traffic in both directions stops. From high above, we see Truman, his arms outstretched, the world as he knows it brought to a halt at his command. In this moment, he embraces the Panopticon, and it embraces him. Watcher and watched see each other for the first time. It's a moment of complete solipsism, one of the most purely solipsistic moments in the history of cinema.

Though many of the reviews of the film dwelled on its critique of mass media, *The Truman Show* actually spoke most eloquently to the nature of existence. Truman's predicament embodies one of the great fears of our time – *it's fake* – and in his life, our most widely held paranoid delusion – *it's all for you* – is made real. Truman's literal Panopticon is our virtual prison made manifest. But we're enclosed by more than just media spectacles; our imprisonment is not the sole product of too much reality TV. This stuff forms one wall of our postmodern Panopticon, to be sure, but there are many others: the triumph of individualism in politics, the conquest of the spiritual realm by scientific reason (and the resulting rise of apocalyptic, anti-scientific religious beliefs), the atomisation of society by a technology-driven consumer culture. We shop, vote, ponder, pray (if we still pray) – we *live* – as individuals, increasingly certain that only our own perception is a legitimate arbiter of what is real and true. If truth flows only from individual perception, why not everything else? Wouldn't it be comforting, actually, if that were the case? Isn't it *enviable*, the certainty that enters Truman's life when he stops traffic that morning? This is why it's such a powerful scene: not because it's terrifying but because it's sort of inspirational. You can find the limits of your cage – as Truman does in the final scene of the film – push against them, find an opening. And then just leave. You can escape the Panopticon.

'Seahaven is the way the world should be,' says its creator, the self-important TV producer Christof. When Truman turns his back on it, opens the door in the wall at the edge of the stage set, waves goodbye and departs, he chooses the world as it is.

For us, alas, it's not as simple. Our Panopticon is ephemeral. Its walls can't be so easily grasped. It is everywhere and nowhere. It has two dimensions: macro and micro, mass culture and subculture.

On the macro level, there is a mass culture that strives to include everyone, and in so doing speaks directly for no one. This is the culture of mass-media spectacle, of big dumb action movies and glib mainstream journalism and lowest-common-denominator FM radio – all those frequent targets of *The Simpsons'* satire. This is not just a media phenomenon: nearly every aspect of our society – science, politics, commerce, the arts – exists on one level as a vast and impersonal monster, present in all of our lives but truly connected to none of them. Think here of the limitless geopolitical boundaries of non-state terrorism, the universal scope and infinite complexity of climate change, the bland ubiquity of suburban chain stores and fast-food joints that sit at the end of intercontinental supply chains peddling the products of globally branded corporations.

At the same time, there is a relentless proliferation of subcultures and subdivisions. Formerly mass phenomena – mathematics and biology as well as pop music and painting – are now loose collections of highly specialised microgenres and microdisciplines that grow less and less likely even to speak to each other, let alone to the world at large.

This is the postmodern Panopticon: on one side, the alienation of a big dumb machine; on the other, the isolation of tiny, cosy cocoons. Both are reflected in the referential humour of *The Simpsons*. The show satirises both the vacuousness of mass culture and the growing breadth of our ironic distance from it. *The Simpsons'* writers assume they can take for granted our familiarity with McBain's gross stupidity, our alienation from Kent Brockman's false earnestness. At the same time, the show's wilfully esoteric allusions and self-referential contortions testify to the atomisation of the culture. There is a solipsism to *The Simpsons* because it is a realistic portrait of a solipsistic culture. And when it finds itself coming through labyrinthine referential twists to a dead end – when it stops there and dusts off an old chestnut – it has joined us, yes, at the end of many things.

Where, after all, can the arts go after abstract expressionism and the pranks of the Dadaists and their descendants? Where does the front line of fiction go after the convoluted metafictions of the postmodernists? It becomes mostly about itself: a sometimes clever but ultimately meaningless commentary on the nature of art. Art about art, that is. Same goes for politics in the West, which is increasingly a competition not between disparate ideals but between competing political strategies. The news media generates content – punditry, commentary, speculation – not because there's news to report but because there's media space to be filled. Our economies must continue to grow not because they need to reach a goal but because growth is the goal. And looming above it all are the whispers of melting glaciers and the roars of ferocious storms, making the argument that even if we escape the Panopticon we might find that there's no world left to inhabit. That this might be endgame.

Where to go, then, in the face of this?

David Foster Wallace concludes his landmark essay 'E Unibus Pluram: Television and U.S. Fiction' with a suggestion about the new direction American prose might take, a modest proposal that might be best under-stood as a desperate plea for the new direction the whole culture must take:

> The next real literary 'rebels' in this country might well emerge as some weird bunch of *anti*-rebels, born oglers who dare somehow to back away from ironic watching, who have the childish gall actually to endorse and instantiate single-entendre principles. Who treat of plain old untrendy human troubles . . . with reverence and conviction. Who eschew self-consciousness and hip fatigue. These anti-rebels would be outdated, of course, before they even started. Dead on the page. Too sincere. Clearly repressed. Backward, quaint, naïve, anachronistic. Maybe that'll be the point. Maybe that's why they'll be the next real rebels. Real rebels, as far as I can see, risk disapproval. The old postmodern insurgents risked the gasp and squeal: shock, disgust, outrage, censorship, accusations of socialism, anarchism, nihilism. Today's risks are different. The new rebels might be artists willing to risk the yawn, the rolled eyes, the cool smile, the nudged ribs, the parody of gifted ironists, the 'Oh how *banal*.' To risk accusations of sentimentality, melodrama. Of overcredulity. Of softness. Of willing-ness to be suckered by a world of lurkers and starers who fear gaze and ridicule above imprisonment without law. Who knows. Today's most engaged fiction does seem like some kind of line's end's end. I guess that means we all get to draw our own conclusions. Have to.

The Simpsons, too, is a line's end's end. It has shown us What Is, and it has exposed the many hypocrisies of What Should Be. It has leaned back with detached cool and turned ironic observation into a giddy postmodern art. But has it really made a difference? Will something more come of it?

What happens after we turn off the TV?

NOTES & MARGINALIA

1. **Troy McClure's Greatest Hits:** Some of Troy McClure's finest acting work comes not in any of those 'Movies for a Rained-Out Ballgame' that Homer winds up watching, but rather in the various educational and instructional videos McClure has appeared in over the years. And even better than the videos we get to see are the ones that he suggests we might remember him from, at least if the titles are any indication:

• In Episode 9F05 ('Marge Gets a Job'), we join Homer in watching a do-it-yourself video called *The Half-Assed Guide to Foundation Repair*, in which McClure takes us through complex home-improvement work at a jovial sprint. Previous instructional videos he thinks we might remember him from: *Mothballing Your Battleship* and *Dig Your Own Grave and Save!*

• In Episode 9F14 ('Duffless'), we see excerpts from *60 Minutes of Car-Crash Victims*, a driver's-ed film made up of documentary footage of car crashes, featuring stellar narration by McClure: 'Here's an appealing fellow – in fact, they're a-peeling him off the sidewalk!' Previous driver's-ed films he believes we might remember him from: *Alice's Adventures Through the Windshield Glass* and *The Decapitation of Larry Leadfoot*.

• In Episode 1F05 ('Bart's Inner Child'), McClure hosts a video called *Adjusting Your Self-O-Stat* that outlines the self-help psychobabble philosophies of Brad Goodman. Goodman, McClure claims, helped him with his drinking problem. 'Sweet liquor eases the pain!' McClure purrs as he downs a can of fortified wine in the video's introduction. Previous self-help videos we might remember him from: *Smoke Yourself Thin* and *Get Confident, Stupid!*

2. **Self-conscious hyper-irony alert!** Not only does actor Joe Mantegna play Fat Tony in *Blood on the Blackboard: The Bart Simpson Story*, he also provides Fat Tony's trademark Mafioso rasp in this and all other episodes of *The Simpsons* in which the character appears.

3. **Teutonic 'humour':** Herewith, two classic examples of Rainier Wolfcastle's ill-advised attempts at crossing over into comedy:

• In Episode 9F22 ('Cape Feare'), there appears a brief excerpt from *Up Late with McBain*. After being introduced, Wolfcastle launches into a gag about the flamboyant fashion sense of his band leader, Skoey. 'That is some outfit, Skoey,' Wolfcastle quips. 'It makes you look like a homosexual.' The audience responds with a chorus of boos. 'Oh, maybe you all are homosexuals!' Wolfcastle scolds. That's the joke.

• In Episode 2F31 ('A Star is Burns'), a clip from *McBain: Let's Get Silly* demonstrates Wolfcastle's unique approach to stand-up comedy. 'Did you ever notice how men always leave the toilet seat up?' he jokes. He pauses. Silence. 'That's the joke,' he adds. Then he's off with the next bit: an impression of Woody Allen. 'I'm a neurotic nerd who likes to sleep with little girls,' Wolfcastle says in his own Austrian-accented voice. 'Hey, that really sucked!' an audience member heckles. Wolfcastle produces a grenade, pulls the pin, and hurls it. Kaboom! End clip.

4. **Catty movie critics rule!** Every so often, a film comes along that's so relentlessly awful it becomes a kind of muse for exasperated film reviewers. The 2003 film *Dr. Seuss' The Cat in the Hat* was just such a film. Highlights from a thick stack of critical savagings:

• 'A vulgar, uninspired lump of poisoned eye candy' – *The New York Times*

• 'Like being run over by a garbage truck that backs up and dumps its load on top of you' – *Slate Magazine*

• 'Scarily close to the most unendurable Hollywood creation of the last dozen years . . . [starring] a free-associating Mike Myers done up as a kind of Dr. Moreau bastard spawn of Bert Lahr's Cowardly Lion and Charles Nelson Reilly' – *Village Voice*

• 'If you're hankering for a movie about an awkward yet lovable "outsider" type who wanders into a pastel mock-up of Middle America and cajoles the straights to get saucy, you're in luck. It's called *Edward Scissorhands*, and it's been available on video for years. Renting it will absolve you of having to endure *Dr. Seuss' The Cat in the Hat*, which is, in essence, *Edward* with a queasy mean streak, no concept of pacing apart from "faster," and such a remarkable rift between its charming source material and its heinous cinematic realisation that the producers may as well have skipped the hassle of licensing rights and simply called the mess *Mike Myers: Asshole in Fur*' – *Dallas Observer*

5. Two things worth noting about Arnie Pie:

(a) He hates puns: Arnie Pie's crack helicopter-aided reporting has long been a vital part of Channel 6 News, and it has invariably been called 'Arnie in the Sky' – thus distinguishing Arnie as one of the only opponents of the groaner pun in contemporary journalism.

(b) In one episode, he loses his freaking mind: The episode is CABF16 ('Children of a Lesser Clod'), and the incident occurs as Arnie reports from his helicopter on Homer Simpson's theft of a police paddy wagon. Midway through his report, Arnie suddenly announces, 'I'm going to try to nail the driver with one of my shoes!' Brockman attempts to keep him focused on the task at hand: 'Arnie, please – leave this to the police.' Arnie, agitated: 'I'm sick of being the reporter. I want to make the news!' Brockman, scolding: 'Arnie, this is not the time . . .' Arnie, in a deranged howl: 'You're not the time, Kent! You're not the time!'

6. **Best. Baseless Supposition. Ever.** In Episode 1F09 ('Homer the Vigilante'), the perpetrator of a string of cat burglaries in Springfield cajoles the whole town into embarking upon a madcap hunt for his stolen millions (in an homage to the 1963 film *It's a Mad, Mad, Mad, Mad World*). As the crazed search expands, Kent Brockman is there with reasoned analysis from a learned expert. 'Hordes of people seem to be evacuating the town for some unknown reason,' Brockman reports. 'Professor,' he continues, turning to the tweedy type seated next to him, 'without knowing precisely what the danger is, would you say it's time for our viewers to crack each other's heads open and feast on the goo inside?' The professor, with casual authority: 'Hmm – yes I would, Kent.'

7. **Vanity projects:** On three noteworthy occasions, 'The Itchy & Scratchy Show' has embraced the cinematic world beyond animation by enlisting celebrated Hollywood auteurs to serve as guest directors. The guest-directed episodes:

• A gritty, black-and-white cartoon directed by Oliver Stone in the style of *JFK*. Stone's 'Itchy & Scratchy' re-imagines the assassination of Lee Harvey Oswald as a melodramatic cat-and-mouse game, with Scratchy playing Oswald to Itchy's ruthless, gun-toting Jack Ruby. The conspiracy-minded subtext – Oswald as perennial victim and helpless patsy, Ruby as tool of the bloodthirsty military-industrial complex – is trademark Stone.

• 'Reservoir Cats', directed by Quentin Tarantino. Tarantino goes for self-homage in his episode of 'Itchy & Scratchy', recreating the scene from *Reservoir Dogs* in which Michael Madsen tortures a police officer to the 1970s AM-radio hit 'Stuck in the Middle with You'. Itchy, of course, fills Madsen's shoes, adding extra glee – if slightly less menace – to the role. Tarantino himself walks onto the cartoon's 'set' to explain the subtext, only to be decapitated by Itchy, an act that hyper-ironically brings an end to the violence between Itchy and Scratchy. The cartoon ends with the former antagonists dancing together rapturously to surf-guitar music.

• 'Circus of the Scars', directed by Steven Soderbergh. A straightforward feast of violent mayhem set against a Barnum backdrop, Soderbergh's cartoon opens with Scratchy falling from a trapeze through a safety net made of piano wire, which dices him into dozens of tidy cubes that are eagerly gobbled up by an elephant. As catholic as Soderbergh's take on the cat-and-mouse genre appears, the actors' DVD commentary attests to his perfectionism. Appearing in a small pop-up box in the bottom right of the screen, Scratchy the cat recalls: 'We shot this at four in the morning, and the crew was getting a little cranky.' Itchy the mouse then squeezes into the frame and adds, 'You can never get enough takes for Steven Soderbergh.' Scratchy is about to add another tidbit of Soderbergh trivia, but Itchy produces a pair of giant garden shears and snips off his head, splattering the screen-in-screen with blood.

8. **Action figure man was robbed!** Although there was little doubt that the Simpson kids' 'Itchy & Scratchy' episode – 'Little Barbershop of Horrors' – would win the award for Best Writing in a Cartoon Series, it did face some stiff competition. The nominees were:

• *Strondar, Master of Akom* ('The Wedding Episode'): a muscle-bound He-Man knockoff stands nervously fidgeting with his bowtie in the award-show clip.

• *Action Figure Man* ('The How to Buy Action Figure Man Episode'): A child stands before a display of Action Figure Man dolls at the local toy store. 'Please, Mommy, I want it!' he cries. His irritated mother gives in. A ten-seconds-or-less summary of the near-total conquest of cartoons by the forces of mass merchandising.

• *Ren and Stimpy* ('Season Premiere'): A black screen with text reading 'Clip Not Done Yet'. A snarky dig at one of *The Simpsons'* few real peers, which was plagued by production delays.

9. **Baldwin-or-McClure answer key:** *Dial M for Murderousness* – Troy McClure; *Leper in the Backfield* – Troy McClure; *Brotherhood of Murder* – William Baldwin; *Under the Hula Moon* – Stephen Baldwin; *The Greatest Story Ever Hula'd* – Troy McClure; *Calling All Quakers* – Troy McClure (co-starring Dolores Montenegro); *How to Make an American Quilt* – Adam Baldwin (co-starring Winona Ryder); *Heaven's Prisoners* – Alec Baldwin; *Give My Remains to Broadway* – Troy McClure; *The Adventures of Pluto Nash* – Alec Baldwin (in an uncredited cameo, but *Pluto Nash* was so awful that it starred all the Baldwins in spirit).

10. **Now *that's* high concept:** In Episode AABF09 ('Homer to the Max'), all of Springfield falls in love with a slick new TV drama, a buddy-cop series called *Police Cops*. Homer Simpson is initially a huge fan, too, because the show's catchphrase-spouting hero happens to be named Homer Simpson. His love turns to confusion, however, when his namesake becomes a bumbling loser in the second episode, so Homer heads down to the studio to demand an explanation for the retooling. Cut to the boardroom of By the Numbers Productions, where 13 vacuous TV producers have gathered to explain the show's elaborate conceptual meanderings:

Vacuous Producer No. 1:	The thirteen of us began with a singular vision – *Titanic* meets *Frasier*.
Vacuous Producer No. 2:	But then we found out that ABC had a similar project in development with Annie Potts and Jeremy Piven.
Homer:	Who's Jeremy Piven?
Vacuous Producer No. 3:	We don't know.
Vacuous Producer No. 4:	But it scared the hell out of us, so we slapped together a cop show instead.
Homer:	*Police Cops.*
Vacuous Producer No. 5:	Uh, no – actually, it was called *Badge Patrol*.
Vacuous Producer No. 1:	But the network idiots didn't want a show about high-tech badges that shoot laser beams!
Vacuous Producer No. 2:	So we asked ourselves, 'Who's behind the beams?'
Vacuous Producer No. 3:	Police . . .
Vacuous Producer No. 4:	. . . Cops . . .
Vacuous Producer No. 5:	[*brings hands together dramatically*] *Police Cops.*

11. **Moe's Den of Iniquity:** Over the years, Moe's Tavern has been used for a remarkable range of esoteric criminal activities, most (but not all) run out of his storeroom. Among them:

• some sort of panda-smuggling ring
• some sort of killer-whale-smuggling ring
• a loan-sharking business in which those with no collateral have their legs broken in advance

- a professional-football gambling ring
- a Simpson-family's-old-vibrating-washer-and-dryer-racing gambling ring
- a high-stakes Russian roulette gambling ring, run in conjunction with a gang of Southeast Asian toughs, like the one depicted in the film *The Deer Hunter*; on at least one occasion, Moe's Russian roulette game pits the wills of Principal Skinner and Krusty the Clown against each other

12. **Truth Is more utopian than fiction:** *The Truman Show* was filmed not on a Hollywood stage set but in the real-life city of Seaside, Florida, a planned community that was built from scratch in the early 1980s as a showcase for the urban-planning philosophy that became known as 'New Urbanism'.

CHAPTER ELEVEN

Planet Simpson

Are You a Consumer or a Participant?
Situationist graffiti, Paris, 1968

Where's my burrito? Where's my burrito?
Slogan chanted by Homer Simpson,
Springfield Nuclear Power Plant strike,
1988

DISTRESS SIGNALS

IN EPISODE 1F09 ('HOMER THE Vigilante'), Springfield falls victim to a rash of burglaries, leading Homer to organise a vigilante mob to guard the town and try to track down the perpetrator of the crimes. During one booze-fuelled patrol, Homer's mob comes upon Jimbo Jones – the punk kid in the black, skull-logoed T-shirt and toque who is Springfield Elementary's alpha bully – as he's spray-painting the words CARPE DIEM on a wall. 'You're that drunken posse!' Jimbo exclaims with atypical admiration. 'Wow! Can I join yuh?' In no time, he's swinging a sack of doorknobs with Homer's crew. Fast-forward a few scenes: the mob has been outsmarted once again by Springfield's cat burglar, and Homer steps out onto his front porch to greet a mob of angry citizens. Jimbo emerges from the crowd and empties his sack of doorknobs at Homer's feet. 'You let me down, man,' he announces. 'Now I don't believe in nothing no more. I'm going to law school!' Homer erupts in a melodramatic 'Noooooooo!' but it's too late to save Jimbo. The best we can hope for him now is that he doesn't take too much of our lunch money once he's become a *professional* bully.

This is what happened all too often to the idealists of the *Simpsons* age: they threw down their sacks of doorknobs at the feet of their heroes. Drowning in cheesy corporate crap and syrupy boomer nostalgia, they turned so cynical they almost choked on it. They turned on *themselves*. They imploded. 'Are you being sarcastic, dude?' says one jaded fan at the Hullabalooza music festival. 'I don't even know anymore,' his friend replies.

And so there were few unified responses to the hollow prosperity of the 1990s, no tightly woven web of icons and events and symbols that could be condensed into the kind of tidy montage that tends to pop up, for example, in films about the boomer counterculture. Many – perhaps most – merely joined the party. They got jobs at dot-coms (or in 'bricks-and-mortar' businesses), collected stock options, bought houses in the suburbs, shopped in gargantuan 'big box' stores, drank Starbucks coffee religiously. There were also widespread tendencies to either (a) to disappear entirely into a cosy, sequestered corner of the culture, attempting to build a whole society out of whatever happened to be lying around there (viz. conspiracy theorists, Trekkies and other Trekkie-like subcultures, hackers, Phish-heads, attendees of drum-and-bass and *only* drum-and-bass parties, proprietors of Internet fansites, etc.); or (b) to watch the whole parade from a comfortable ironic distance. People who didn't bowl wore bowling shirts with names sewn on the chest that weren't their names. Kitsch became a robust cottage industry, propping up everything from the sky-high ratings of soap operas like *Melrose Place* and *Beverly Hills, 90210* to the cult-hit status of films like *Showgirls* and *Battlefield Earth* to the ironic comebacks of oddball celebrities like Mr T and Gary Coleman. '20 Percent of Area Man's Income Spent Ironically,' read a revealing headline at the satirical online newspaper *The Onion*; the article detailed the consumer habits of a twentysomething hipster whose prized possessions included a *Knight Rider* lunch box and a rare Italian poster advertising the laughably lousy movie *The Adventures of Pluto Nash*. In Richard Linklater's seminal 1991 pseudo-documentary, *Slacker*, there is a character who is attempting to find a buyer for Madonna's pap smear, which nails several salient features of pop cynicism – backhanded celebrity worship, wilful obscurity, playful half-serious co-optation of the culture of mass marketing, and making a buck regardless – all in one precise anecdote.

Oh, but don't even say the word 'slacker'. Nobody was actually a slacker, nor a member of 'Generation X'. The prevailing rock music of the day wasn't really called 'grunge', and grunge sucked anyway now that corporate record labels were involved. The predominantly electronic music that was played at clubs and raves wasn't a genre of music, either, and if you had to label it, you needed to understand that it wasn't *one* genre but dozens, hundreds, and the surest way to create a new subgenre was to give a name to an old one. This knee-jerk cynicism and hip, offhand rejection was much worse – much more poisonous – than the carnival of kitsch.

In the midst of all of this, satire alone could be safely, unequivocally embraced, because it acknowledged the sanctity of nothing at all. And so satire has triumphed. *The Simpsons* is the age's greatest pop institution, and it has begotten a whole subgenre of satirical TV. As I've mentioned, *The Onion* is one of the Internet's most beloved websites. The satirist Michael Moore frequently tops the bestseller lists with his books and breaks box-office records with his documentaries. *The Daily Show with Jon Stewart*, meanwhile, is a nightly satirical newscast that is surely more trusted by *Simpsons* fans than anything on CNN. As voter turnout among young people has plummeted to all-time lows throughout most of the democratic West, politicians have taken to hiring humorists to make their speeches more accessible. There was at one point an ironic and self-referential TV commercial for Parkay margarine, of all things – this among countless other ironic and self-referential TV ads.[1]

The most strident pop-cultural manifestation of this pose, though, was another TV show: *Seinfeld*. It was 'a show about nothing'. No sincerity, no emotion, no meaning. Just nothing, nothingness, the void. In fact, one excellent *Seinfeld* sequence involves the main characters – ostensibly best friends – becoming emotionally involved in each other's lives for the first and only time in the show's run. If *The Simpsons* was to some extent a weekly portrait of the world as a pile of bullshit, *Seinfeld* was a once-a-week argument in favour of the bleak existential notion that even bullshit was bullshit. When the heavily hyped final episode of *Seinfeld* appeared, it hammered home the essential absurdity of existence in an extended homage to Camus's *The Outsider*. *Seinfeld* was a total renunciation of moral authority, and it seemed to lay to rest the confident optimism that had been the engine of the American Dream.

Satire was America's most exciting pop-cultural export in the 1990s, so it's worth recalling how sharply this contrasts with the prime pop exports of previous ages. Consider, in particular, rock & roll, which in the 1950s and 1960s was a powerful and boisterous declaration of American supremacy. Rock & roll was a sound so full of youthful energy, sexuality and joy that it could legitimately claim to be the theme music of utopia. When the free world looked to America for inspiration – and it often did – it was greeted with a gleeful burst of pure unadulterated hope in 4/4 time. America's moral authority in the postwar world was assured at least as much by Elvis Presley as by the Marshall Plan. By the 1990s, though, many of America's pop broadcasts were distress signals of one sort or another: there were the ultra-violent cartoons of hip-hop and indie film, alternative rock's soul-sick howls of rage and – perhaps worst of all – mass-market spectacles so homogenous and glossy they felt like they'd been rubber-stamped for export by some Department of Capitalist Realism (see, for example, the shopping-as-freedom subtext of *Pretty Woman*, the triumphalism of *Independence Day* or the glossy kiddie porn of Britney Spears videos). Indeed the corporate logo of Rick Rubin's American Recordings (which, among other things, resuscitated the career of Johnny Cash, the troubadour of the American outlaw hero, after he'd been cast aside by corporate Nashville) is an inverted American flag. A distress signal. To some degree, so is *The Simpsons*. From a certain angle, it can indeed be read as an unencouraging diagnosis from an observant doctor, or even an autopsy of the American Dream.

Ultimately, though, there is more hope than this in *The Simpsons*, and this is a major reason why it's been so completely embraced by a global audience in the millions. Satire comes from deep anger, and it is at its best when it is ruthless in its assessment of the subject's ills, but its final message is that the sickness, once satirically diagnosed, can possibly be cured.

THE REBIRTH OF SINCERITY

Okay. Look: whatever hope there is in *The Simpsons*, it isn't enough on its own. I'm speaking just for myself here. It *wasn't* enough. Circa 1997, my abiding cynicism was about the only thing I trusted. I sneered, therefore I was. I'd find myself – just for instance – thinking of a particular line from *Pump Up the Volume*. (For the uninitiated, this was a 1990 Christian Slater movie about a teenager who operates a pirate radio station out of his parents' basement that gives comfort and hope to the freaks at a bleak, conformist high school.) 'Everything decent's been done,' Slater's character sermonises during one of his broadcasts. 'All the great themes have been used up, turned into theme parks. So I don't really find it cheerful to be living in a totally exhausted decade where there is nothing to look forward to and no one to look up to.' I'd think of this line, and it'd ring true, and then I'd chastise myself for getting all earnest and reflective over a goddamn Christian Slater movie that had a totally cornball ending, even if it had its moments. But at least the Slater character pauses after this little sermon and then half-sarcastically declares, 'That was deep.' Did it redeem my cynicism that the cinematic moment I found so meaningful was cynical and self-mocking? I'd fret over that kind of crap. Anyway, one drab Thursday – 29 February 1997 – I reluctantly agreed to go to a rock concert. I hadn't heard of the band, and plain old rock & roll seemed more or less played out, and – well, I could always find lots of reasons *not* to do things back then – but I was invited, so I went. The show was at the Horseshoe Tavern, a venerable live-music venue in downtown Toronto. The band was called Wilco, and they were touring in support of their breakthrough album, *Being There*. And that night Wilco restored my faith in rock & roll.

There was one moment in particular, midway through the show, that has stayed with me ever since like a talisman. The band was playing 'Misunderstood', the opening track on *Being There*. Jeff Tweedy, Wilco's lead singer and main songwriter, has said that the album was the product of his own crisis of faith in rock & roll – a failed attempt to prove to himself that it ultimately didn't matter. For Tweedy, it *did* matter, and *Being There* was the proof. 'Misunderstood' is the short version of all of this, an epic tale of frustration and lost faith told in a series of lyrical vignettes that unfold like grainy black-and-white photos. Over a quietly strummed acoustic guitar, a misunderstood kid returns to his old neighbourhood. He wonders whether he should go to a party there that night, whether he still loves rock & roll, whether the fortune inside his head will ever pay off. As groaning feedback and slapping drums invade, the kid sits listening to a hard-rockin' album in the middle of the night, studying the cover art, wondering if the guitarist he's listening to will ever escape the shadows of rock's golden age that haunt him. On that night at the Horseshoe, 'Misunderstood' seemed to last for hours, building to an endless, roaring crescendo, as Tweedy – on behalf of all of these characters, and of himself, and of every musician and fan – screamed himself hoarse. 'I'd like to thank you all / For nothing / I'd like to thank you all for nothing at all / I'd like to thank you all for nothing, nothing / *Nothing, nothing* / NOTHING, NOTHING, NOTHING . . .'; Tweedy had his back to the audience, facing his band, all of them – all of us – rising and falling as one with each ferocious *NOTHING*, the tension building with each one until all at once there was a final chord, a final scream – *NOTHING AT ALL* – and then Tweedy spun to face the crowd. He was dripping sweat, exhausted, ecstatic and grinning. His eyes dancing out over the crowd. Guitar sort of swinging from his shoulders, the echo of its final scronking chord still banging around the joint. A single delirious look, a joyous look, a *sincere* look. The look of a man who has discovered rock & roll for the first time, invented it just then. He has cast aside a lifetime of deities and demons – thanked them all for nothing at all – and he now turns to face the crowd to reclaim the void from cynicism and absurdity, to teach us all how to see it not as a black hole but as a blank canvas.

That night, Wilco became for me a little oasis of sincerity. I'm sure many *Simpsons* fans found their own – something other than the show itself, something that didn't need to predicate its sincerity on withering criticism. Maybe it was music of another sort, maybe the endorphin rush of a rave or a ten-kilometre run. Volunteer work for a local charity, growing a garden, joining a book club, publishing a zine. Some personal passion, anyway, that could be embraced completely, without qualifications and without irony. Something pure. Something you might have hoped would become an emblem of the whole culture, the way, for example, you'd play the new Wilco album for friends, sure it would blow them away and confident that in a parallel universe every other song on it was a number-one hit. But aware, too, that you didn't live in that universe, and that this excellent music would likely remain sequestered in its little shrine. And then maybe you'd get a happy surprise – maybe your little oasis would face the howling storm of the mainstream head on, and you'd find your faith redoubled as it survived on little more than the strength of its own integrity.

That, anyway, is what happened with Wilco in 2001 and 2002. It started when the band delivered its new album, *Yankee Hotel Foxtrot* – a brilliant, somewhat experimental record about love and loss and faith – to the executives at its record label, Reprise Records. Now, Reprise had been Wilco's label since its first album, had watched it build a small but loyal following, had been nothing but supportive. But there had been big changes at Reprise's parent company – Time Warner – since Wilco last released an album, and they soon reverberated down the corporate ladder. The previous year, Time Warner had joined forces with AOL in the largest merger of media conglomerates the world had ever seen, and the new entity, AOL Time Warner, was hard hit by the bursting of the Internet bubble and thrown into internal chaos by the clash of the two companies' dissimilar corporate cultures. At the moment Wilco happened to deliver its new album, the prevailing wisdom was that a certain level of projected sales was necessary to warrant AOL Time Warner expending its enormous marketing might on an artist, and the prognosis for *Yankee Hotel Foxtrot* wasn't promising enough. Wilco was asked to change the album, clean it up, make it more accessible. The band declined. In short order, Wilco was cut loose – and then signed, soon after, with Nonesuch Records, another arm of AOL Time Warner. A somewhat marginal, uncompromising rock & roll band had stared down the largest media conglomerate on the planet, had found itself hard against its enormous grinding gears, had held its ground and lived to tell the tale. And even to triumph: *Yankee Hotel Foxtrot* was released in the spring of 2002 to widespread critical worship and the band's usual solid sales.

It was a victory of the band's artistic vision over the market-research abstractions and corporate priorities of a media titan. The perseverance of What Is in the face of a powerful assault from the forces of What Should Be. A rare and wonderful thing, especially in an age in which What Should Be was again ascendant.

WHAT IS & WHAT SHOULD BE (REPRISE)

In Episode EABF09 ('Mr. Spritz Goes to Washington'), which first aired in March 2003, Krusty the Clown runs for Congress as a Republican. Like many American families in this uncertain post-9/11 era, the Simpson family turns to Fox News for biased and jingoistic information on the election: in this case, interviews with Krusty and his Democratic opponent. 'Welcome to Fox News', the cable-news network's anchor intones. 'Your voice for evil.' As the ludicrously one-sided interviews progress – the anchor refers to Krusty as 'Congressman' and the hapless Democrat as 'comrade' – a news crawl snakes along the bottom of the Simpsons' TV screen. One item reads, 'Do

Democrats Cause Cancer? Find Out At Foxnews.Com'; another declares, 'Oil Slicks Found To Keep Seals Young, Supple'; still another argues, 'Brad Pitt + Albert Einstein = Dick Cheney'. All in all, it was a fine little parody of Fox News' unique approach to journalism.

A few months after this episode first broadcast, Matt Groening turned up on National Public Radio for a friendly interview. Talk turned to his show's fondness for pushing boundaries, and the interviewer asked what the show had done lately that fitted that description. Groening: 'One of the great things we did last year was we parodied the Fox News Channel and we did the crawl along the bottom of the screen. And Fox fought against it and said that they would sue, they would sue the show. And we called their bluff because we didn't think Rupert Murdoch would pay for Fox to sue itself, so we got away with it. But now Fox has a new rule that we can't do those little fake news crawls on the bottom of the screen in a cartoon because it "might confuse the viewers into thinking it's real news".' By the next day, media outlets around the world were reporting that Fox had considered suing its own show – a claim that was promptly denied by Fox executives. In due course, *The Simpsons* itself felt obliged to issue a statement. As quoted in *The Washington Post*, it read, 'Matt was being satirical and certainly there was never any issue between the show and Fox News. We regret any confusion.' *Variety*'s report on the fooforah added, 'Insiders say Groening was clearly being satirical during the interview.'

I can't speak for these 'insiders' but I heard the interview, and I wouldn't describe Groening's tone as 'satirical'. Bemused? Yes. Delighting in the absurdity of the situation? Also yes. Anyway, he retracted it, so officially it didn't happen, and perhaps we'll never know what Fox did or didn't do in response to *The Simpsons*' pointed parody of their news channel. What this anecdote makes abundantly clear, though, is that the advocates of What Should Be are once again preaching at top volume in the free world. And this time it looks like even *The Simpsons* had to back off from its defence of What Is.

The first years of this new century are beginning to feel quite a lot – quite terrifyingly a lot – like one of those historical eras in which enormous decisions that will reverberate for many decades to come are being made, and the What Should Be camp seems to be calling the shots. The deranged Wahhabists who destroyed the World Trade Center advocate with blunt brutality on behalf of a nineteenth-century interpretation of a seventh-century vision of What Should Be. The Bush administration, meanwhile, overflows with true believers in other competing ideas of What Should Be, including several followers of a literal interpretation of the Bible (the Attorney General and the President himself among them), several more who believe in the 'Noble Lie' statecraft of a deceased University of Chicago professor who based his theories on a gnostic interpretation of ancient Greek philosophy, and others who see the current crises through a distorted Cold Warrior's lens. Tony Blair, a strident Anglican, is a devotee of What Should Be, and so are Sharon and Arafat and KGB nostalgist Vladimir Putin. Saddam Hussein was so psychopathically dedicated to his own twisted vision of What Should Be that he actually built a model of it in Baghdad. The world over, our leaders talk of new eras and different priorities and changed circumstances, and then they push on in favour of the same old What-Should-Be geopolitics. They believe that democracy will spread through the Middle East in a benevolent inversion of the domino effect that never did send Southeast Asia tumbling, that evil is a finite thing that can be hunted down and executed, and that terror is not a tactic but an ersatz nation-state.

As defence against all of this, the satirical barbs of a clever cartoon seem less than adequate. *The Simpsons*, like all TV shows, is delimited by the shallow commercialism of its corporate parent and the intrinsic meaningless of its medium. Has it really mattered? Does it still? What difference, in the end, can *any* TV show really make?

THE MEDIUM IS THE MESSAGE (OR IS IT?)

In Episode 9F21 ('Homer's Barbershop Quartet'), the Simpsons attend a swap meet, where Bart stumbles upon an album by Homer's old group, the Be Sharps. 'Dad, when did you record an album?' Bart asks his dad.

'I'm surprised you don't remember, son,' Homer replies. 'It was only eight years ago.'

'Dad,' Bart answers, 'thanks to television, I can't remember what happened eight minutes ago.' The whole family starts to laugh. 'No, really,' Bart exclaims. 'I can't! It's a serious problem!' More laughter from the Simpsons, and in time Bart joins in, and after a good chuckle he says, 'What are we all laughing about?' And no one remembers, and nuts to you if you're looking for a meaning in any of this. Right?

This has long been the prevailing wisdom about TV's importance, beginning with Marshall McLuhan's famous aphorism about the medium being the message. Regarding the tube's debased content, McLuhan reckoned Shakespeare had summed it up best in *Romeo and Juliet*: 'But soft, what light through yonder window breaks? . . . She speaks, yet she says nothing.' There are few who would dispute McLuhan – or the Bard – on the basic thrust of this assertion. Even Matt Groening himself has claimed, echoing McLuhan, that TV's ultimate message is this: 'Nothing matters.'

So how does this resolve itself with Groening's more frequent claims that *his* TV show aims to 'entertain and subvert'? The entertainment part's no problem, but how can subversion happen in a vacuum?

In the introduction to the 1986 essay collection, *Watching Television*, sociologist Todd Gitlin wrote:

> For the most part, television lets us see only close up: shows us only what the nation already presumes, focuses on what the culture already knows – or more precisely, enables us to gaze upon something the appointed seers think we need or want to know. Television may do private service as a time killer or a baby-sitter; but for the society as a whole, it is the principal circulator of the cultural mainstream.

Here is where Groening's promised subversion comes in, and where *The Simpsons* might well become something more than another outpost in a vast wasteland. For if *The Simpsons* is a reflection of the cultural mainstream, then it suggests that its audience – a significant slice of mainstream Western society – is deeply dissatisfied with the status quo. It suggests indeed that there is a large segment of Western society whose priorities and values contrast as starkly with the 'mainstream' as *The Simpsons* does with *The Cosby Show* or the nightly news. A parallel universe of sorts, defined and even shaped to a significant degree by *The Simpsons*. Planet Simpson, if you will. And its existence goes a long way towards rebutting the argument that nothing on TV matters.

WELCOME TO PLANET SIMPSON

Though most of its citizens reside in the English-speaking nations of the world, Planet Simpson is not entirely a geographic phenomenon. And although its core constituency is under the age of 40, it is not strictly a demographic phenomenon either. Planet Simpson is a state of mind, a loose realm of shared consciousness. It is a place populated by folks who watch *The Simpsons* every week or even twice a day, who maintain *Simpsons* fan sites, who never lose at the *Simpsons* trivia board game, who used to watch it every chance they got, even if these days they don't watch it as much as they used to. It's a place where the show's characters are a kind of makeshift pantheon and their adventures are parables, a place whose citizens carry scenes from the show in their heads as a critical framework for understanding their society. It's a place where conversations consisting almost exclusively of *Simpsons* dialogue can go on for hours at a time, and where there aren't many arguments that can't be summarised with a quote from the show. I don't know how many people live on Planet Simpson, but I know I've met a great many people who do, and I know there are a lot more of us – probably millions more.

Anyhoo, I know that *my* worldview can be accurately represented by connecting Simpsonian dots.

I know Homer-sized desires, born of my own privileged upbringing in one of the globe's richest enclaves and enhanced by a relentless assault of TV ads and branding exercises that has made the jingles of fast-food franchises and the climate-controlled corridors of shopping malls at least as familiar to me as the twittering of birds and the warmth of a summer rain. And I know Homer's panicky fear, a *Wauggghhh!* of terror that confronts me every time I bag up my garbage or step outside into a eerily balmy Canadian spring, every time I turn on the TV to see the fires of another explosion or hear another blast of Manichaean rhetoric. And I too have quietly murmured an escapist *Woo-hoo!* as I changed the channel to the latest reality-TV hit or a rerun of my favourite cartoon.

I know Bart's rage. I spent most of my early twenties furious with almost everything, including myself. I have yelled at my TV and my morning newspaper. I have silently wished terrible harm on the drivers of Hummers and Lincoln Navigators, and I kind of wish I had the wherewithal, as Bart would, to deface their bumpers with clever graffiti.[2] My opinion of almost every single leader elected since I reached voting age – federal, provincial and municipal – is pretty close to Bart's estimation of Principal Skinner.

I've never had to work for Mr Burns, thankfully, but I see his predatory visage everywhere – in the corporate logos that encrust suburban boulevards, in the windows of office towers, in news footage of the carefully preserved oil ministry building in postwar Baghdad. Most of my first-hand experience of cold, unfeeling bureaucracy has come from corporations, not government agencies. I've found it far more dehumanising to navigate through an automated customer-service menu on the phone than to visit a passport office, and I learned about the Kafkaesque absurdity of arbitrary rules and hypocritical power working as a drone in the service industry. The faces behind much of this – the same ones responsible for changing my climate and copyrighting my culture – often look like Lindsey Naegle, but their logic is all Burns. It wouldn't surprise me all that much if I picked up the paper one morning to learn that one of them had blocked out the sun (or at least privatised it).

Like Lisa, I've tried to fight back. I've marched against wrong-headed budget cuts and against the American conquest of Iraq. I've signed petitions. I've been saying for years that I'd become politically active if I ever stumbled on a politician who talked intelligently about the things I cared most deeply about, and so just last year I joined a political party to help elect the first leadership candidate I'd ever heard speak inspirationally on the subject of sustainability.[3] I try to patronise small businesses, and I recycle diligently. Alas, I find myself despairing that this will amount to nothing far more often than Lisa does.

I cling, as Marge does, to family and close friends, and to a hazy theology that I hope comes clear one day. I worship as well at the altars of an assortment of pop icons, and some of them are surely as callous as Krusty the Clown or as venal as Troy McClure.

Above all else, I am a citizen of Planet Simpson. *The Simpsons* debuted just as I was awakening to the shape of the world and the scope of its problems. Right around the time I'd begun to suspect that my society was a very large and powerful machine moving steadily in the wrong direction, *The Simpsons* entered its Golden Age to vividly chart the movements of the beast and the chinks in its armour. I believe, nowadays, that extreme solutions are hardly ever necessary and no mob is much smarter than any other. I'd like to think a better world is possible, but I know that achieving it can only begin from an honest accounting of What Is. What Should Be is, as Lenny Bruce told us, a dirty lie.

If I have a worldview – a philosophy, a political persuasion – then I'd call it Simpsonian. And I think that's as good a place as any to start.

THE OBLIGATORY SENTIMENTAL ENDING

In Episode 3F03 ('Lisa the Vegetarian'), Homer and his daughter squabble over her newfound activism. In the episode's final scene, though, they set aside their differences and reconcile. 'I still stand by my beliefs,' Lisa tells her father. 'But I can't defend what I did. I'm sorry I messed up your barbeque.'

'I understand, honey,' Homer replies. 'I used to believe in things when I was a kid.'

And then Lisa hops on her father's back, and they walk off together into the sunset, giggling.

Cut to credits.

NOTES & MARGINALIA

1. **Hippest. Margarine Tub. Ever.** If memory serves, the self-referential Parkay commercial ran sometime in the mid-1990s. I can't remember the lead-up, but the ad ended with a shot of a tub of Parkay margarine, which since the 1970s had been opening its lid to mutter the word 'butter' until the star of the commercial acknowledged that it did in fact taste like butter, at which point the Parkay tub would sassily reply, 'Parkay!' In this mid-1990s incarnation, however, the shot of the famous margarine tub was accompanied by a pregnant pause, after which the tub muttered, 'Uh, you know.'

2. **Ask them how:** In 2000 a pair of culture-jamming activists in San Francisco named Robert Lind and Charles Dines launched a clever campaign to peacefully (if not quite legally) confront the menace of SUVs, a guerrilla sport they've dubbed 'Big Game SUV Hunting'. Lind and Hines have pioneered the practice of surreptitiously attaching bumper stickers to the largest SUVs. The stickers read: I'M CHANGING THE CLIMATE! ASK ME HOW! Free sticker templates and how-to guides are available at their virtual headquarters (changingtheclimate.com).

3. **Full disclosure:** The candidate in question was Jack Layton, who won the leadership of Canada's federal New Democratic Party in autumn 2002.